The Graphic
Design Reader

BLOOMSBURY VISUAL ARTS
Bloomsbury Publishing Plc
50 Bedford Square, London, WC1B 3DP, UK
1385 Broadway, New York, NY 10018, USA

BLOOMSBURY, BLOOMSBURY VISUAL ARTS and the Diana logo are trademarks of
Bloomsbury Publishing Plc

First published in Great Britain 2019

A catalogue record for this book is available from the British Library.

A catalogue record for this book is available from the Library of Congress.

ISBN: HB: 978-1-4725-3620-4
        PB: 978-1-4725-2647-2

Typeset by RefineCatch Limited, Bungay, Suffolk
Printed and bound in India

To find out more about our authors and books visit www.bloomsbury.com
and sign up for our newsletters.

Contents

List of figures

Acknowledgments

Substantial projects such as *The Graphic Design Reader* are not produced in isolation; rather, they rely on the contributions of many key individuals who have supported the process and ensure its publication. We want to thank, first and foremost, the authors, publishers, and Estates who gave permission for reprinting works that we identified as significant, and to our commissioned authors whose new works are set to inform future discourse in the field.

We would like to acknowledge the key role that our Eastern Michigan University (EMU) student assistants have played: Laura Adams provided a firm foundation for realizing our editorial direction, and her successor, Jasmine Winzeler, has brilliantly taken us to the completion of the project. Our gratitude also goes to the Provost's Office and the School of Art & Design at EMU for the financial support from two Research Support Awards.

This project has always had students at the center. Masters and Research Degree students at the Royal College of Art are to be acknowledged. Their discussions about the future of graphic design became the focus of PhD seminars whose students offered invaluable insights that, in part, informed our thinking for the book's Epilogue. We would especially like to highlight MA Visual Communication students who participated in our project to design the cover of the book: Abbie Vickress' cover design skillfully represents our concern for design practice and editorial processes.

As we headed toward final production, we are grateful to our critical readers: Michael Schoenfeldt, Ryan Molloy, and Roger Sabin, who helped us fine-tune the final manuscript. We are also grateful for the help of Bloomsbury's editorial assistants Abbie Sharman and her successor, Claire Constable, both of whom were quick to respond to queries.

We also thank our former Senior Commissioning Editor, Simon Cowell, who recognized the educational value for publishing books on graphic design, and his successor Rebecca Barden, who has supported this project practically from start to finish. It was Rebecca's unfaltering encouragement and support that brought the project to fruition.

Finally, we would like to thank those of you who have consistently cheered us on, consoled us when we were at wits' end, and faithfully listened to us curse the challenges, and celebrate the successes, of this substantial and rewarding undertaking.

This book is dedicated to graphic design students everywhere.

also one of the founding members of DensityDesign, a research lab in Milan specializing in the visual representation of complex phenomena. In 2013 he moved to NYC and has been a consultant and lead designer for various startups, working on digital products and user centric experiences from the pitch phase to full design and launch. Among others, Michele's work has been honored at SIGGRAPH 2009, Expo Milano 2015, and it has been in exhibitions and publications such as *Information Graphics* (Taschen), *Data Flow 2* (Gestalten), *Leonardo, Domus*, and *Wired* magazine. In 2011 he was an international visitor at Stanford University.

Sibylle Hagmann started her career in Switzerland after earning a BFA from the Basel School of Design in 1989. She explored her passion for type design and typography while completing her MFA at the California Institute of the Arts. Over the years she developed award-winning typeface families such as Cholla and Odile. Cholla was originally commissioned by Art Center College of Design in 1999 and released by the type foundry Emigre in the same year. The typeface family Odile, published in 2006, was awarded the Swiss Federal Design Award. Her work has been featured in numerous publications and recognized by the Type Directors Club of New York and Japan, among many others. Her typeface collections are available from Kontour.com, a type foundry launched in 2012. Sibylle Hagmann is a Professor of Graphic Design at the University of Houston School of Art.

Peter Hall is a design writer and educator, and graphic design course leader at Central St Martins, University of the Arts London. Before moving to London in December 2015, he was program director of Design at Griffith University Queensland College of Art in Australia where he was awarded a PhD for research into visualization and mapping as a design process. His previous appointments include: senior lecturer in design at the University of Texas at Austin, lecturer at Yale School of Art, and Senior Editor at the University of Minnesota Design Institute, where he co-edited with Jan Abrams the book, *Else/Where: Mapping—New Cartographies of Networks and Territories*. He has written widely about design in its various forms for publications including *Metropolis*, *ID Magazine*, and *The Guardian*. He wrote and co-edited the books *Tibor Kalman: Perverse Optimist*, and *Sagmeister: Made You Look*. He is a board member and founder of DesignInquiry, a non-profit experimental educational organization based in Maine, USA.

Margo Halverson's love of words together with the narrative power of the photographic image led her to the world of typography and graphic design. She received her BFA and MFA in photography from Arizona State University, where after graduation she studied graphic design with Rob Roy Kelly. She taught photography and graphic design at ASU prior to moving to Portland, Maine, where she has been a Professor of Graphic Design at Maine College of Art since 1991. Margo is co-founder of DesignInquiry with Melle Hammer and Peter Hall, a non-profit, non-traditional design organization (designinquiry.net). Together with Charles Melcher she is owner and creative director of the Portland design studio Alice Design Communication (alicedesign.com). She grew up in North Dakota, and after moving to the east by way of Arizona, she still misses living in grids.

Sylvia Harris (1953–2011) was a remarkable advocate of good design for real people—a Citizen Designer. She always lived her passions, so it is fitting that she named what was to be the last iteration of her professional practice (then Sylvia Harris LLC) Citizen Research & Design, which she envisioned as a research and planning firm designed to help public sector organizations better communicate with the people they serve. Her mantra was "Design for the Common Good." She studied under Philip B. Meggs at Virginia Commonwealth University where she received her BFA and then under Chris Pullman in the master's program at Yale University where she later became a faculty member. Harris was known as a generous, passionate, and intelligent woman, which she passed on to her students at the School of Visual Arts, Cooper Union, and Purchase College. While at Yale in 1980, she co-founded the firm Two Twelve Associates, which was involved in Citibank's first ATM design and the Central Park Zoo's display and signage remodel. Harris also served on the AIGA national Board.

Dick Hebdige is a cultural critic who has published widely on contemporary social movements, art, design and media, popular music, and the politics of insubordination. His publications include three books *Subculture: The Meaning of Style*, *Cut 'n' Mix: Culture, Identity and Caribbean Music*, and *Hiding in the Light: On Images and Things*. He has taught extensively in art schools and universities in the UK and the USA, and is currently a Professor of Art and Film and Media Studies at the University of California, Santa Barbara.

Paul H. Hefting (1933-2018) studied art history, and then worked in the 1960s as a lecturer at the Technical College. Between 1966 and 1981, he was a curator at the Museum Kroller-Müller and did his doctoral work on the painter G. H. Breitner. Hefting was Editor of the magazine *Museumjournaal* from 1981 to 1994, and worked at the Corporate Staff Art and Design designing and producing publications for the Dutch government's postal office, Posterijen, Telegrafie en Telefonie (PTT).

Jessica Helfand is an award-winning graphic designer, educator, artist, and writer. A founding editor of *Design Observer*, she has written for *Aperture, Eye, The New Republic*, and the *Los Angeles Times*, and is the author of numerous books on visual and cultural criticism, including *Paul Rand: American Modernist* (1998), *Screen: Essays on Graphic Design, New Media, and Visual Culture* (2001), *Reinventing the Wheel* (2002), and *Scrapbooks: An American History* (2008) and *Design: The Invention of Desire* (2016). Her next book, a visual history of the face, will be published in 2019 by MIT Press. Helfand, who has lectured all over the world, received her BA and MFA from Yale University where she has taught since 1996. A 2010 Resident in Design at the American Academy in Rome, and a 2011 laureate of the Art Director's Hall of Fame, Jessica Helfand won the AIGA medal, the profession's highest honor, in 2013.

Steven Heller is the co-chair and co-founder of the MFA Design: Designer As Author + Entrepreneur programs at the School of Visual Arts, NYC. He was a senior art director of *The New York Times* and is author, co-author, and editor of over 180 books on the history and practice of graphic design, illustration, and satiric art. He is a 2011 recipient of the Smithsonian National Design Award for Design Mind and a 2013 honorary PhD in Fine Arts by The College for Creative Studies in Detroit.

Nanette Hoogslag, as doctoral researcher, lecturer, and internationally acclaimed illustrator and designer for more than twenty years, she has explored the changing nature of illustration, visual communication, and publishing through research, in teaching, and in practice. With a critical and exploratory focus on digital technology, and with a deep understanding of media traditions, Nanette has created commissioned illustration projects for clients worldwide, worked on design projects, and initiated and curated public and educational projects; she has also given lectures and published papers. Nanette has a degree in Graphic Design from the Gerrit Rietveld Academie, Amsterdam, and an MA Illustration from the Royal College of Art in London, where she also got her PhD in conjunction with the University of Sussex. At present she is Course Leader for Illustration and Animation at the Anglia Ruskin University in Cambridge. Nanette is living and practicing in Brighton, UK.

Karrie Jacobs is a professional observer of the manmade landscape. She currently writes for *Architect Magazine* and *Curbed.com* and is a faculty member at the School of Visual Arts' MA program in Design Research where she teaches students how to understand and interpret the design they see all around them. She was the founding editor-in-chief of *Dwell* and the founding executive editor of Benetton's *Colors*. She is the author of *The Perfect $100,000 House* (Viking, 2006) and co-author of *Angry Graphics* (Gibbs Smith, 1992). She was a long time contributor to *Travel + Leisure*, *Metropolis*, *The New York Times*, and other publications. Her essays and articles have been published in many books including, most recently, *How Posters Work* (Cooper Hewitt, 2015) and *Design for People* (Metropolis Books, 2015).

Michael Jon Jensen has worked at the interface between digital technologies and scholarly/academic publishing since the late 1980s, and now consults in the field. For nearly 15 years, Jensen helped guide the digital strategies of the National Academies Press and the National Academies. From 2007–2012, he served as Director of Strategic Web Communications for the Office of Communications of the National Academies and National Academies Press. Prior to this appointment, he served as Director of Web Communications for the National Academies (2002–2007), and Director of Publishing Technologies (1998–2007) at the National Academies Press, publisher for the National Academy of Sciences, the National Academy of Engineering, the Institute of Medicine, and the National Research Council (www.nap.edu). In 2001, Jensen received the National Academies' "President's Award," its highest staff honor. Previously, he was Electronic Publisher at the Johns Hopkins University Press, and Electronic Media Manager at the University of Nebraska Press. See michaeljonjensen.com for more information.

Tibor Kalman (1949–1999) was an influential Hungarian-American graphic designer who worked mainly in the 1980s and 1990s. He studied journalism at NYU, and then worked for Barnes and Noble as the director of their in-house design firm. Kalman founded the design company M&Co. with Carol Bokuniewicz and Liz Trovato, and is best known for his work for *Interview* and Benneton *Colors* magazines. Kalman became the editor-in-chief of *Colors*, which typically presented controversial topics and cover designs.

Jeffery Keedy, a.ka. Mr. Keedy, is an educator, designer, type designer, and writer, who has been teaching in the Graphic Design Program at California Institute of the Arts since 1985. He has been recognized for his design work for institutional and commercial clients in branding, packaging, and publication design. His design work has been published in *Typography Sketchbooks, New Ornamental Type: Decorative Lettering in the Digital Age, The Handy Book of Artistic Printing, Boxed and Labelled: New Approaches to Packaging Design, New Design: Los Angeles, LACE: Living the Archive,* and in the textbooks *Graphic Design in Context* and *Graphic! Design History.* His essays have been published in *Eye, I.D., Emigre, Critique, Idea, Adbusters, Looking Closer One, Two,* and *Four,* and *The Education of a Graphic Designer.* His work has most recently been exhibited at MoMA, SFMoMA, CAM Raleigh, and The Biennial of Graphic Design, Brno, Czech Republic. His typeface Keedy Sans was added to MoMA's permanent Architecture and Design Collection in 2011.

Hilary Kenna is a designer and lecturer on the Visual Communication Design degree at IADT (www. iadt.ie) Dublin, Ireland, which was selected as one of Europe's top 25 graphic design programs by *Domus,* Spring 2013. Hilary's research into user experience, user interface design, and data visualization for information discovery was commercialized via the development of an online visual search and discovery product for libraries and academic research called SeeSearch. Hilary previously consulted as Head of Design and UX at INM where she re-designed www.independent.ie, Ireland's largest online newspaper and other apps including The Windmill Lane Sessions. She designed the multiple award-winning iPad App The Waste Land for publishers Faber & Faber and Touch Press UK, which was the subject of her TedX talk, Screen Typography—Words Made Usable. Hilary completed her PhD on Design Principles for Screen . . . Usable. Typography at the London College of Communication (LCC), University of the Arts (UAL).

Yasmin Khan is an LA-based educator and graphic designer. The things she is currently most excited about are: being part of the Graphic Design faculty at Otis College of Art and Design, where she teaches in the MFA and BFA programs, and her current partnership, the Workshop Project, a pedagogical practice. At the Workshop Project, she investigates teaching and curriculum design as a form of graphic design practice. Her background information goes something like this: Education: BA in Fine Art, UCLA; BFA, Art Center College of Design and MFA, CalArts in Graphic Design. Professional practice: former partner at Counterspace, a studio focused on design for cultural clients. Some clients: MOCA, *Arthur* magazine, CalArts, The Orange County Museum of Art, REDCAT, Doug Aitken. Some lectures: TYPO San Francisco; *HOW* Design Conference; AIGA Spaces of Learning; AIGA Schools of Thoughts; Ecole des Beaux Arts, Rennes; University of Missouri, St. Louis; Art Center College of Design.

Francisco Laranjo is a graphic designer based in Porto (Portugal). His writings have been published in *Design Observer, Eye, Creative Review, Grafik,* among others. He has been a visiting and guest lecturer at the Sandberg Instituut Amsterdam (NL), CalArts (US), Royal College of Art, Central Saint Martins (UK), Zürich University of the Arts (Switzerland), and he has been a a speaker at the University of Applied Arts Vienna (Austria), University of South Australia (AUS), University of Lisbon (Portugal), among others. Francisco has a PhD in graphic design methods and criticism from the University of the Arts London and an MA in Visual Communication from the Royal College of Art. He is co-director of the Shared Institute, a research center for design and radical pedagogy and he is editor of the design criticism journal *Modes of Criticism.* (www. modesofcriticism.org).

Ellen Lupton is Senior Curator of Contemporary Design at Cooper Hewitt, Smithsonian Design Museum in New York City. Her exhibition *How Posters Work,* opened in May, 2015. Recent projects include *Beautiful Users* and *Graphic Design—Now in Production*. Lupton also serves as director of the Graphic Design MFA Program at MICA (Maryland Institute College of Art) in Baltimore, where she has authored numerous books on design processes, including *Thinking with Type*, *Graphic Design Thinking*, and *Graphic Design: The New Basics*. Recent books include *Type on Screen* (2014). She received her BFA from The Cooper Union in 1985.

Victor Margolin is Professor Emeritus of Design History at the University of Illinois, Chicago. He is a founding editor and now co-editor of the academic design journal *Design Issues*. Professor Margolin has published widely on diverse design topics and lectured at conferences, universities, and art schools in many parts of the world. Books that he has written, edited, or co-edited include *Propaganda: The Art of Persuasion, WW II, The Struggle for Utopia: Rodchenko, Lissitzky, Moholy-Nagy, 1917–1936, Design Discourse, Discovering Design, The Idea of Design, The Designed World; Images, Objects, Environments, The Politics of the Artificial: Essays on Design and Design Studies,* and *Culture is Everywhere: The Museum of Corn-temporary Art*. He is currently completing the third volume of a World History of Design (Bloomsbury). The first two volumes were published in April 2015.

Luca Masud is an information designer specializing in the field of data-information visualization and visual storytelling. He currently works as Associate Creative Director in the Data Science and Visualization team at R/GA NY, where he leads the designs of award-winning data-driven products and platforms. He graduated cum laude in Communication Design (MSc) at the Politecnico di Milano, and is one of the founding members of DensityDesign, a research lab focused on the visual representation of complex social, organizational, and urban phenomena, and he practiced as a designer/researcher for four years before joining R/GA. His research background provides him with a reflexive approach towards visualization and a deep knowledge of the current state-of-art of the visualization domain. His experience in visualization research, isn't limited to analytical data visualization, it is also centered on storytelling and sense-making, always focusing on innovation and working in an interdisciplinary environment.

Katherine McCoy co-chaired Cranbrook Academy of Art's Design Department for 24 years, and was a Senior Lecturer at Illinois Institute of Technology's Institute of Design in Chicago and a Distinguished Visiting Professor at the Royal College of Art in London. Katherine is a Medalist of the American Institute of Graphic Arts, an elected member of the Alliance Graphique Internationale, and she holds an Honorary Doctorate from Kansas City Art Institute. She consults in communications design for cultural and environmental clients, including the US Forest Service and the Denver Art Museum. She writes on design criticism and history, coproduced the television documentary "Future Wave: Japan Design," and chaired the first Living Surfaces Conference on interactive communications design. With her husband Michael, she received the Smithsonian National Design Museum's first Design Mind Award and the Chrysler Award for Innovation in Design. Since 1997, they have hosted the High Ground Design Conversation, an annual gathering of design thinkers.

J. Abbott Miller has evolved a design practice that embraces the role of editor, writer, and curator in many of his exhibition and publications. He has used design as a way of exploring and interpreting art, architecture, public space, performance, fashion, and design. Before joining the New York office of Pentagram as a partner in 1999, he founded Design/Writing/Research, a multidisciplinary studio that pioneered the concept of the "designer as author." As editor and designer of *2wice*, he has created a dramatic body of work devoted to performance and visual art. Miller has also created identities, exhibitions, books, and websites for a wide range of cultural and commercial clients. He is the author of several books on design, including a monograph *Abbott Miller: Design and Content*. His work is included in the permanent collections of the Cooper-Hewitt National Design Museum, the Art Institute of Chicago, and San Francisco Museum of Modern Art.

Debbie Millman is CMO of Sterling Brands, the founder and host of *Design Matters*, (the world's first podcast about design), the Editorial & Creative Director of *Print* magazine, Chair of the world's first graduate program in branding at the School of Visual Arts in New York City, and the author of six books.

Ryan Molloy is an artist, educator, and inter-disciplinary designer. Prior to teaching at Eastern Michigan University, he was a visiting lecturer at the University of Texas at Austin's Design Division where he also received his MFA in Design. Molloy has a BArch and he has worked as both an architect and a graphic designer. His creative work has been exhibited nationally and internationally and has received several awards including the Art Directors Club Young Guns award. In 2012 Ryan Molloy and Leslie Atzmon received a National Endowment for the Arts (NEA) Art Works grant for the Open Book Workshop, held at the Jean Noble Parsons Center, and the book *The Open Book Project*.

William Morris (1834–1896) was an author, designer, publisher, and socialist public speaker, who was a founder of the Arts and Crafts movement. Morris collaborated with others to design high-quality wallpaper, tapestries, and furniture for Morris, Marshall, Faulkner & Co., which ultimately became Morris & Co. Morris felt that mass-produced books were very badly designed and produced. After attending a lecture on printing in 1888 by Emery Walker he founded the Kelmscott Press, at which he championed book design based on the Arts and Crafts aesthetic and the design and craftsmanship of early printed books.

Sean O'Toole is a writer and editor living in Cape Town, South Africa. He has written extensively about art, photography, and design for various magazines and newspapers, including *Artforum*, *BBC Focus on Africa*, *Eye*, *ID*, *Foam*, *frieze*, *Mail & Guardian* and *Sunday Times* (SA). He is a founding editor of *Cityscapes*, a magazine for urban enquiry published by the African Centre for Cities at the University of Cape Town, and a past editor of the quarterly magazine *Art South Africa*. He has contributed essays to numerous monographs, including *In Boksburg* by David Goldblatt (Steidl, 2015) and *Ponte City* by Mikhael Subotzky and Patrick Waterhouse (Steidl, 2014). He has published one work of fiction, *The Marquis of Mooikloof and Other Stories* (2006), which included a story awarded the 2006 HSBC/SA PEN Literary Award.

Rosy Penston has an MA from the RCA in Visual Communication (2013).

Sharon Helmer Poggenpohl has taught in notable design programs: The Hong Kong Polytechnic University, the Institute of Design at the Illinois Institute of Technology in Chicago, and the Rhode Island School of Design. Her focus over a long career has been post-graduate design education, both master and PhD, as well as design research. Taking a human-centered position with regard to design, she teaches to help students humanize technology, to learn to work creatively and collaboratively with each other, and to prepare them to contribute to building a body of design knowledge. For twenty-six years, she edited and published the international scholarly journal *Visible Language*. She co-edited with Keiichi Sato *Design Integrations, Research and Collaboration* (Intellect Books, 2009). She just published a book titled *Design Theory To Go* (Ligature Press, 2018).

Mario Porpora is a designer currently working at the Density Design lab (http://www.densitydesign. org/). at the Politecnico di Milano. He co-designed the board game Escape From The Aliens In Outer Space. Mario also works as a freelance designer and artist.

Rick Poynor is a writer, lecturer and curator, specializing in design and visual culture. He is Professor of Design and Visual Culture at the University of Reading. He was founding editor of *Eye*, where he writes the long-running Critique column, and co-founder of *Design Observer*. He was a columnist for *Print* and his articles have appeared in *Blueprint*, *Icon*, *Creative Review*, *Frieze*, *Metropolis*, and many other publications. Poynor's books include *Typographica* (2001), *No More Rules: Graphic Design and Postmodernism* (2003), and *Jan van Toorn: Critical Practice* (2008). He has published three essay collections: *Design Without Boundaries* (1998), *Obey the Giant* (2001), and *Designing Pornotopia* (2006). In 2004, he curated *Communicate: Independent British Graphic Design since the Sixties* for the Barbican Art Gallery, London. His exhibition *Uncanny: Surrealism and Graphic Design* was shown at the Moravian Gallery, Brno in 2010 and the Kunsthal, Rotterdam in 2011. His latest book is *National Theatre Posters: A Design History* (2017).

Jan-Henning Raff is Professor at the Faculty of Design at Hochschule für Medien, Kommunikation und Wirtschaft—University of Applied Sciences (HMKW) in Berlin, Germany, where he teaches social and interaction design. He received a diploma in Communication Design at Kunsthochschule Berlin Weißensee. He has worked as a freelancer, as a research assistant at Technische Universität Dresden, heading the Department of Media Design at the Media Center, and at Webducation, an important Austrian e-learning provider. His PhD (Technische Universität Dresden) on design aspects in students' self-regulated learning activities shows how design is used and how it structures practices. Thus, his practice, teaching, and research focuses on the use aspects of design.

Paul Rand (1914–1996) is best known for his posters and corporate identity work, including logo designs for IBM, UPS and ABC. He attended the Pratt Institute (1929–1932), the Parsons School of Design (1932–1933), and the Art Students League (1933–1934). He helped establish a version of Swiss Modernist graphic design in the US. From 1956 to 1969, and beginning again in 1974, Rand taught design at Yale University, and was inducted into the New York Art Directors Club Hall of Fame in 1972.

Mohor Ray is a designer, alumnus of the National Institute of Design (India), and the co-founder of India-based brand & communication design practice, Codesign. With interests in design, extending from contextual practice to the emergence of a new Indian design consciousness, she balances professional practice in brand design with writing and independent projects. Mohor is the editor of *Dekho*—an award-winning anthology of inspirational conversations with designers in India, probing their stories for cues to the development of design in India and highlighting approaches that are unique to designing for India. She was a founding member of Unbox—one of India's first interdisciplinary festivals—and has most recently co-founded Rising, an independent knowledge platform to explore the potential of visual communication design for change, with a focus on India.

Casey Reas is a Professor at the University of California, Los Angeles. His software, prints, and installations have been featured in over one hundred solo and group exhibitions at museums and galleries in the United States, Europe, and Asia. He holds a Master's degree from the Massachusetts Institute of Technology in Media Arts and Sciences as well as a Bachelor's degree from the College of Design, Architecture, Art, and Planning at the University of Cincinnati. With Ben Fry, Reas initiated Processing in 2001. Processing is an open source programming language and environment for the visual arts.

Donato Ricci is researcher at Sciences Po medialab, where he uses experimental design methods in Human and Social Sciences. He developed the design aspects of Bruno Latour's *AIME* project. With Latour, he co-curated the *Reset Modernity!* exhibition at ZKM Karlsruhe and at Shanghai Himalayas Museum. He is Assistant Professor of Knowledge and Representation at Universidade de Aveiro and part of the Experimental Programme in Political Arts (SPEAP) at Sciences Po.

Steve Rigley leads the Graphic Design pathway within the Communication Design Department at the Glasgow School of Art in Scotland. His practice-based research interests include the mapping of practice and the exploration of print as a form of narrative, working with found material across digital print, letterpress, relief printing, and digital textiles. He has published on themes of cross-cultural design and pedagogy and as visiting lecturer he has taught at leading schools in India, China, and the USA.

Michael Rock is a founding partner and creative director of multi-disciplinary design studio 2x4 Inc. New York, and Director of the Graphic Architecture Project at the Columbia University Graduate School of Architecture. From 1984–91 he was Associate Professor of Graphic Design at the Rhode Island School of Design and since 1991 he has been a member of the design faculty at the Yale School of Art where he currently holds the rank of Professor (Adjunct). His writing on design has appeared in publications worldwide. *Multiple Signatures*, a collection of projects, interviews, and essays, was published by Rizzoli International in 2013. Rock holds an AB in Literature from Union College and a MFA from the Rhode Island School of Design. He is the recipient of the 1999/2000 Rome Prize in Design from the American Academy in Rome and currently serves on the board of the Academy.

Design Responsibility (Second Edition). Véronique is a regular contributor to *The Design Observer*, a website dedicated to design issues. She lives in France, where she teaches in various art schools, conducts workshops on design criticism as a creative tool, and acts as a branding consultant for a number of corporate clients.

Stéphanie Vilayphiou and Alexandre Leray are graphic designers interested in the relationship between digital tools, graphic design practices, and free culture. After graduating from the Piet Zwart Institute (Rotterdam, 2009), they settled in Brussels and joined Open Source Publishing, a collective active at the intersection of graphic design, free software, and education. Besides teaching and working on commissioned and self-initiated design projects, they co-created Relearn, a summer school that aims at challenging the traditional vertical structure of education, taking free software as a model and central object.

Karin von Ompteda is an Assistant Professor of Graphic Design at OCAD University in Canada. Her background is in both science and design, having undertaken an MSc Biology (University of Toronto), BDes Graphic Design (OCAD University), and currently completing a PhD Visual Communication (Royal College of Art). Karin's doctoral research is focused on integrating scientific and design approaches to typeface legibility, with a particular interest in low-vision readers. Working with data plays a central role in her research, practice, and teaching, and she has been running cross-disciplinary "data manifestation" workshops since 2010 with students, professionals, and the public. Her work has been presented internationally through conferences (TYPO London, ATypI), exhibitions (Brno Biennial, BIO Biennial), publications (Laurence King, RotoVision), and press (BBC's The Forum, China Daily). Projects have been funded through research councils in both Canada and the United Kingdom, and clients have included Brody Associates and BBC R&D.

John A. Walker (b. 1938, Lincolnshire) is a painter, art critic, and an art and design historian. Before he retired from teaching in 1999, he was a Reader at Middlesex University, London. He is the author of many articles and books on different aspects of visual culture. His main contribution to design historiography was the volume *Design History and the History of Design* (Pluto Press, 1989).

Beatrice Warde Beatrice Warde (1900–1969) was an American typographer, writer, and scholar who lived in the UK. She became interested in calligraphy and letterforms while studying at Barnard College, Columbia. Warde was an Assistant Librarian with the American Type Founders Company, where she researched typefaces and the history of printing. In 1925 Warde moved to Europe, working for *The Fleuron*, which was edited by Stanley Morison. Using the pseudonym "Paul Beaujon," she wrote an article which traced type that was mistakenly attributed to Garamond to Jean Jannon of Sedan. In 1927 she became editor of The *Monotype Recorder* in London. A strong believer in classical typography, Warde wrote and designed the famous Monotype broadsheet "This is a Printing Office" using Eric Gill's Perpetua typeface. Her anthology *The Crystal Goblet: Sixteen Essays on Typography* (1955) describes typography as a "clearly polished window" through which ideas are communicated.

Jack Williamson is an Art and Design Historian (PhD, University of Ghent). He created the program in Design Studies at the University of Michigan where he taught design history, criticism, writing, persuasion, interpretive environments, and research, a program for which he received the AIGA National Design Curriculum Award. He also taught design management in the MBA program at the UM School of Business, and was a Visiting Professor at the Korea University of Technology, and the University of Technology in Sydney. He was also, for 29 years, Executive Director of Design Michigan, the State of Michigan's statewide design information and technical assistance program headquartered at Cranbrook Academy of Art. He has written articles appearing in *Design Issues*, *Visible Language*, *Form-Work*, and the *Design Management Journal*, and has authored or edited nine books on design for community, business, cultural, and educational revitalization. He is currently writing a book on the Ghent Altarpiece by Renaissance artist-designer Jan van Eyck and its vision of an incipient modernism that amalgamates spirituality and science, thus representing the road not taken by modernism in the West.

Dietmar R. Winkler was born in Germany and educated in design at Kunstschule Alsterdamm in Hamburg. He was a Professor of Design at the School of Art and Design at the University of Illinois at Urbana-Champaign. Previously he held an endowed chair, the Hall Chair at the Kansas City Art Institute in Missouri, where he directed the Center for Form, Image and Text. For approximately twenty years, Winkler was a faculty member of the Visual Design Department in the Cognitive Science Program of the Psychology Department at the University of Massachusetts Dartmouth. He is a member of the editorial board of *Visible Language*. He writes on design education issues and his articles have appeared in publications of AIGA, ICOGRADA, and *Visible Language*. Since 1960, Winkler has been combining professional design practice with teaching of design and communication subjects. His interdisciplinary interests are expanding traditional visual literacy to include user-based design in behavioral, social, and cultural contexts. His design work has garnered awards and has been exhibited and published by the Art Directors Clubs of Boston, New York, and St. Louis, the Type Directors Club of New York, and the American Institute of Graphic Arts.

Martha Witte is a freelance writer and collaborator who has spent time in design firms, museums, and corporations. She is a past board member of the American Institute of Graphic Arts/Philadelphia chapter.

Wendy Siuyi Wong is a Full Professor in the Department of Design at the York University, Toronto, Canada. She has established an international reputation as an expert in Chinese graphic design history and Chinese comic art history. She is the author of *Hong Kong Comics: A History of Manhua*, published by Princeton Architectural Press, four books for Chinese readers, and numerous articles in academic and trade journals. Dr. Wong was a visiting scholar at Harvard University from 1999 to 2000 and the 2000 Lubalin Curatorial Fellow at the Cooper Union School of Art, New York, USA. In 2009 and 2010, she was a visiting research fellow at the Department of Design History, Royal College of Art, and she served as a scholar-in-residence at the Kyoto International Manga Museum. She is a contributor to the *Bloomsbury Encyclopedia of Design*, and acts as a regional editor of the Greater China region for the *Encyclopedia of Asian Design*.

Michael Worthington teaches in the Graphic Design Program at the California Institute of the Arts, and was the program co-director from 1998 through 2005 and from 2008 through 2015. Worthington is the founding partner of Counterspace, a Los Angeles-based graphic design studio specializing in editorial and identity work for cultural clients. He received a BA (Hons) from Central Saint Martins School of Art and an MFA in Graphic Design from CalArts. He lives and works in Los Angeles.

The Graphic Design Reader:
An Introduction

Teal Triggs and Leslie Atzmon

Reading *The Reader*

Graphic Design is always reinventing itself. Contemporary graphic design employs new methods and engages historical and theoretical frameworks that help move design beyond erstwhile "aesthetic-led design decision making" (Walker 2017: 1). How graphic designers operate has shifted significantly since 1922 when American designer William Addison Dwiggins first coined the term "graphic design." Before Dwiggins, much early twentieth-century graphic design was referred to as "commercial art," and these practices were narrowly focused on finished print artifacts.[1] These designers employed a finite set of processes and practices. Contemporary graphic design, on the other hand, is a wide-ranging and inclusive enterprise. Today, complex political, social, and cultural issues, along with data-driven techno-logical landscapes, yield so-called "wicked problems"—social or political predicaments that are very difficult to resolve—for which designers aspire to generate solutions.[2]

Contemporary graphic design also features other expanded practices, such as hybrid digital and analogue work, and critical methods that suggest novel theoretical directions. New kinds of interdisciplinary and transdisciplinary practices synthesize design processes and products with methods and approaches from other fields to produce blended outcomes. These contemporary practices don't necessarily yield final finished artifacts. Instead they often generate flexible solutions that may or may not include artifacts. At the same time, traditional graphic design practice—which typically focuses on final artifacts as its end-product—remains an essential part of the field, and it typically plays a role in these other ways of working.

This *Reader* presents an anthology of writings and visual essays that reflect the fact that graphic design repeatedly adjusts to new media, new platforms, and new contexts. Yet what has remained central to graphic design are the ways that graphic designers employ methods for understanding audi-ences and addressing client problems through critical assessment, and particularly by thinking through making. Our intent in this anthology is to shed light on the ways that graphic designers have integrated these core practices with new comprehensive approaches in contemporary graphic design. We do so to set up the three important premises of this anthology: that graphic design practice is central to issues and ideas in graphic design, that the work we present here can be understood through the lens of contemporary graphic design, and that the expansive character of contemporary practices in graphic design frequently extends to its history, theory, and criticism. To help support these premises, we juxtaposed contributions that offer disparate points of view about practice. We contrasted pieces that come from different time periods and places, and whose content builds upon one other. We sought work that reminds us that graphic design practice and graphic design history, theory, and criticism are integral to one another. The texts in *The Reader* also demonstrate that graphic design does not operate in isolation, and that many of the propositions and practices we consider here actually come to graphic design from other design fields and non-design disciplines. Finally, *The Graphic Design Reader* does not subscribe to one single, authoritative definition of graphic design. We prefer instead a contingent interpretation of the field that contemplates the multifarious relationships among images, texts, media, and content, and users' experiences of these components. It is this dynamic combination of external and internal forces that inform and shape the landscape of contemporary graphic design.

Reading the Introduction

Before we present key themes, we would like to explain how we have structured this anthology. Substantial and capacious, *The Graphic Design Reader* is divided into seven themed Parts that are framed by seven introductions. Each Part has multiple Sections. The book concludes with an Epilogue, which explores issues in contemporary graphic design criticism and practice, and which introduces premises for thinking about the future of the field.

In *The Reader*, the contributions drawn from graphic design history, theory, and criticism are mostly separate from those about practice and education. Contemporary graphic design practice, however, is an important lens through which we interpret our historical, theoretical, and critical selections, as well as our education- and practice-based contributions. Design processes, artifacts, and the views of those who use design, are fundamental to the historical, theoretical, and critical discourses about graphic design. In each of the Part Introductions in this book, therefore, we consider how the thematic content of each Part—for example, "Education and the profession" or "Political and social change"—relates to issues and ideas in contemporary graphic design practice. Graphic design practice is the optic that we bring to bear throughout the themed Parts.

The co-editors for *The Reader* are graphic design practitioners, educators, historians, and critics. We use multiple perspectives to frame the work that we've selected for this anthology. As historians, we see history as both iterative and foundational for contemporary practice. History is a non-linear "living" subject: it is not merely a succession of ideas and facts from the past. Historical phenomena recur in new configurations; they are also fodder for critical reflection through the lens of contemporary design issues. As design critics and practitioners, we champion points of view that both understand criticism and theory through practice and comprehend practice through criticism and theory. We also share a strong commitment to design education. Our teaching experience helps us see that *The Reader* should be more than just a medium for information. As educators, we chose instead to present the content of this anthology as a conceptual framework that underlies ideas about and debates in contemporary graphic design.

We begin with this introductory essay, which is itself divided into five parts in which we discuss the objectives for the project and present ways for readers to navigate the book (see Figure 0.0 below). In Part one of this Introduction, we consider the place of *The Reader* in our cultural and historical moment.

with programmers, printers, sound designers, video designers, and so forth. As this collection goes to press, there is also exciting interdisciplinary work—that involves a genuine synthesis of approaches—happening between graphic design and the natural or social sciences. Designer and educator Phil Jones, for example, uses cognitive linguistics to decode book formats to understand spatial relations and emergent meanings (Jones 2017). Contemporary transdisciplinary practices such as biodesign, in which biology and design coalesce in a solution, challenge the boundaries between natural and artificial artifacts. In graphic designer Ori Elisar's biodesign project *Living Language* (2016), for example, letterforms made from bacteria morph from ancient to modern Hebrew letters as the bacteria grow. The work of *Alliance Graphique Internationale (*AGI*)* member Oded Ezer also merges science and design. Ezer explores unknown futures through his typographic design fiction projects, including *Biotypography* (2005–2006), which is his speculation on the formation of hybrid typographic creatures. An emerging discourse of critical design, biodesign has not yet been explored in depth by design scholars.

The contemporary design strategies and processes discussed above demonstrate how designers, stakeholders, artifacts, and environments are entangled in iterative processes and networked operations. MoMA's senior design curator Paola Antonelli uses the term "knotty objects" to describe artifacts that are not easily disentangled from the disciplines, stakeholders, and environments that contributed to their production (Oxman 2016). Networked ways of working, and the knotty objects they include, characterize much contemporary graphic design. Joanna Choukeir's 2018 essay for this anthology, "Social design: the context of post-conflict Lebanon," for instance, presents her project to disrupt barriers to social integration in Lebanon. She uses seven phases of research based on the UK Design Council's Double Diamond model: (a) *discover*, (b) *delve*, (c) *define*, (d) *develop*, (e) *deliver*, (f) *determine impact* and (g) *diverge*. To aid this process, Choukeir designed and distributed a design tool: a printed *Explorations* cultural probes kit (See Figure 7.17 in Chapter 7.2.1). Traditional graphic design practices—which typically produce artifacts like this cultural probes kit as their end products—frequently operate as essential components of networks, and in this way, they become knotty objects.

Design history, theory, and criticism are likewise entangled with practice. The essays in *The Graphic Design Reader* offer historical, theoretical, and critical exemplars for the ways that today's designers envision politics, practice social design, structure information, experiment with typography, use physical and digital media, and approach craft-based and DIY processes. In "England: The Working Party on Typographic Teaching", for example, Michael Twyman discusses a 1969 British study that presages contemporary social design. Twyman writes about the "reward of seeing a design problem satisfactorily solved for the benefit of others." And in his contribution to *The Reader*, Jack Williamson considers how design reflects changing cultural situations over time. He argues that, from the Middle Ages through Postmodernism, different ways of using the grid represent evolving world views. Williamson's ideas about grids and cultural themes point to contemporary media critic Lev Manovich's observation that those who write their own software code have spawned a "new modernism of . . . vector nets [and] pixel-thin grids and arrows" (Manovich 2002a).

Typographer Richard Eckersley's designs for philosopher Avital Ronell's 1989 *The Telephone Book* —which investigates the function of the telephone in philosophical terms—suggest connections between radical typography of the time and contemporary radical typography. In this anthology, Michael Jon Jensen presents Eckersley's designs in "About the Making of *The Telephone Book*." In response to

Ronell's textual content, Eckersley designed typographic "rivers" representing cut-off phone conversations, and "typographic representations of circuits" using hair-line rules emerging from black box shapes. Some of these 1980s typographic experiments may not seem radical by today's standards. Jensen's descriptions of Eckersley's remarkable creative making and thinking processes, though, resonate with experimental thinking in contemporary design, demonstrating that historical developments can be directly relevant to current practices.

At the same time, *The Reader* also acknowledges a set of historical developments that indicate that graphic design may be moving from a field to a discipline of study, a process that we consider in Part three of this Introduction. In summary, *The Reader* presents issues from contemporary practice and from history, theory, and criticism that together provoke debate in the field. Our approach is to provide a foundation for sparking new discussions about what an emerging expanded graphic design discourse might be. In this process, and in the spirit of reflective practice, we also reconsider the role of the editor and the intended function of this anthology.

Part two: reading the process

Editing as critical curating

The term "anthology" often evokes the classic "textbook" notion of a volume with discrete sections devoted to themes or periods of time, and a mode that does not necessarily involve new research. Instead, we see this anthology as a curatorial project. Design researcher Joanna Bletcher writes in "Prototyping the exhibition: a practice-led investigation into the framing and communication of design as a process of innovation," that thought-provoking curating in design should reveal the "complexity of design activity: the intellectual and material processes driving innovation" (Bletcher 2016: 15). Taking a cue from Bletcher, and applying this to graphic design, our anthology employs critical thinking both about graphic artifacts, and about the processes behind artifacts. We seek ways to reveal how complex design activity can be. Our strategy, then, is to see what an anthology of graphic design might "reveal" if it focuses on creative and critical graphic design activity. Taken holistically, *The Reader* can be understood as a curatorial statement that encourages readers to build narratives about how graphic design comes together in various canons rather than presenting information that stands as a single authorial and historical canon.

In *Issues in Curating and Contemporary Performance*, editors Judith Rugg and Michèle Sedgwick introduce the idea of "curating as a form of critical intervention" (2007: 7). They highlight contributor Liz Wells's proposition that critical curating happens through "careful definition[s] of the field, rigorous contextualization of the work, and consideration of the 'theater' in which the work is presented" (Wells 2007: 31). These three main propositions inform our methodology. We embrace Wells's sense of the term "critical curating," and begin with defining graphic design as a field in Part three of this Introduction. In this discussion, we consider what a series of name changes for our field over several centuries suggests about graphic design. We argue for keeping the moniker "graphic design." We address Wells's second proposition, contextualization, in the seven themed Parts of the book. In these Introductions we discuss what conceptual work our essay selections do for the theme of each Part of this book, as well as how some of our selections relate to or build upon each other.

Finally, we consider the curatorial "theater" in which the work is presented. We see our "theater" as an amalgam of the content of *The Reader*, the relationships this content forges with contemporary graphic design, and the audience expectations for this anthology. A vital part of curating this project, then, is the way that we organize this book. As mentioned, our anthology offers newly commissioned work alongside already published pieces. By doing so, *The Reader* incorporates contemporary ideas and approaches with an existing body of graphic design literature.

Contextualizing the content

The relationships among image, typography, and textual content are a significant part of practice. Visual essays are fundamental to the content of this book because they elevate practice. Ryan Molloy's visual essay, "'Iced Up' and 'Platinum Plus': The Development of Hip-Hop Typographic Ornaments," for example, considers the way personal status earned through excess pervades hip-hop culture and artifacts. Molloy, though, gives as much consideration to his design process as he does to his cultural analysis: "Like a hip-hop DJ, I integrate these older forms with my newly designed bling-bling ornaments . . . in celebration of hip-hop culture's penchant for discontinuity" (Molloy as quoted in Atzmon 2017). He describes how he manipulates Art Nouveau and Art Deco forms so that they express aspects of hip-hop culture. We include visual essays like Molloy's because we believe that designed pieces that address issues in the field have as much to offer our readers as written contributions do. They are a platform for communicating about graphic design *through* graphic design (Frayling 1994; Triggs 2017).

As part of our content, we also purposely juxtapose selected essays so that they are in dialogue with each other. For example, we include the 1993 essay "Cult of the Ugly" by Steven Heller, which argues that '90s experimental design used ugliness to trigger shock value. "Cult of the Ugly" sparked a heated debate in the field. We therefore follow "Cult of the Ugly" with "An Interview with Edward Fella," by Michael Dooley (1994), as a contemporaneous response to the Heller essay, and the 2007 article "An Unbearable Lightness?" by Steven Rigley as a more recent response to the ideas in Heller's piece. To show how ideas from different times and places can propel one another, we frequently intermingle selections from 1970s, 1980s, and 1990s with contemporary essays, and juxtapose pieces from Western and non-Western contributors.

To help lay bare the complexity of design activity, we include critical Introductions before each Part of this book that position the essays in this anthology in the context of new ideas in graphic design. Another aspect of our content, discussed earlier in this Introduction, involves incorporating the essays in this anthology with contemporary approaches to graphic design, such as social inclusion, critical practice, transdisciplinary work, and hybrid work as the lens through which we curated this book. As we note in the beginning of this Introduction, the expansive character of contemporary practices colors our interpretation of previous issues and ideas in graphic design.

Just as we were completing this book, the crucial topic of decolonizing design emerged at the Design Research Society (DRS) annual conference (Brighton, UK, 2016).[7] The way in which design impacts peoples' lives was reflected in a members' statement written to the DRS: "The struggle against the colonisation of knowledge, i.e. the colonial conditions that inform knowledge production and validation, is not only part of our work, but part of our lives" (Abdulla, Canli, Keshavarz, Martins and Oliveria 2016).

Decolonization—in which, according to design anthropologist Dori Tunstall, "design is implicated in the politics of the nation relating to colonization in a direct way"—is critical to the breadth and depth of graphic design discourse. "When you begin to ask . . . what it means as a designer to be a culture maker," Tunstall explains, "you ask harder questions about what kind of culture you're creating." (Andersen 2017). We are acutely aware that graphic design is not exclusively an Anglo-American construct, and that today it has far-reaching global implications. We were keen to include new voices, but also to take note of those in graphic design who are working across cultural and country-specific boundaries. We acknowledge, though, that we've barely scratched the surface of these issues in this anthology.

The shape that this anthology takes, then, is clearly also about acknowledging and explaining what work is left out in the selection process. Although it was difficult, we decided to limit *The Reader* to certain themes. To do so, we had to omit many thought-provoking topics that are of value in graphic design. We decided that image-making illustration (except for Nannette Hoogslag's essay), and TV/film motion graphics were for the most part beyond the scope of this volume. Imagery and illustrations support the content of most of our written essays, though. We've included images, where feasible, from the original source materials. Graphic design emerged out of visual communication, and we were keen to include selected visual references to provide a context for the written work. At the same time, *The Reader* features a broad range of themes, which also makes it a challenge to delve very deeply into any one topic. Its breadth of topics and specific themes are both strengths and shortcomings of this volume. Our intention for this anthology, then, is to curate in a critical way—to offer information, stimulate discussion, and pose questions. We believe that prompting readers to think about many aspects of graphic design is the best way to encourage innovative thinking, making, and critiquing.

Part three: reading graphic design

Defining a name

Setting design practice as the optic through which we curate *The Reader* leads to two provocative questions: What is graphic design? And how might the history, theory, criticism, and practice of graphic design constitute a distinctive field of study?

Design critic Richard Buchanan argues that, for centuries, hierarchical ideas about the value of *thinking* over *making* positioned design as an inferior undertaking. According to Buchanan, until recently, "theory was highly prized in the universities, practice was tolerated, and production or making—the creation of . . . 'artificial things'—was generally ignored as a subject of learning" (Buchanan 2001: 5). Graphic design is no exception. For most of history, much of what we call graphic design today was done by tradespeople or craftspeople, and it did not have a specific name. Under-confidence in our community of practice is insinuated, in part, by a series of name changes for our field: "graphic arts" in the seventeenth century, "commercial arts" and "graphic design" in the twentieth century, "visual communication"[8] in the 1960s, and "communication design" in the 2000s.

Revised nomenclature, of course, also reflects the evolutionary changes in the field. The term "communication design" was coined in the 1990s to reflect a new broad remit for processes and media in contemporary practice. "Communication design" foreshadows the ways that contemporary graphic design has blurred the boundaries between design and other disciplines (e.g. business, science and medicine, and social sciences). Although the term "communication design" reflects a reach beyond the traditional "subareas" of the design of posters, books, typography, etc., we feel that the term "graphic design" makes the most sense for this anthology for two reasons. First, we take a long view of the field. Although contemporary graphic design is central to this anthology, the physical and print-media foundations for the field are key to understanding our past, present, and future. As we have already argued, what we bring forward from our print-media history inevitably suffuses what we do today and what we will do in the future.

Second, we understand how important nomenclature is to how we define our field. But debate about what is in a name can also reflect under-confidence in our community of practice as discussed above. Focusing on what we call ourselves can then distract us from other consequential issues. In "The importance of the Dutch football club Ajax and Total Football (totaalvoetbal) to the sport of graphic design," Elliott Earls argues that we should use the term "graphic design" for "the sake of simplicity." And Professor of Typography at the University of Reading, Sue Walker, observes that "for many" the terms "communication design" and "graphic design" are synonymous. (Walker 2017: 2). Although we understand that debates about what we call ourselves can be useful, in this anthology we have decided that using "graphic design" allows us to focus on other significant topics.

New monikers for the field also suggest our desire to define what we do as graphic designers. AIGA, The Professional Association for Design, defines graphic design as "the art and practice of planning and projecting ideas and experience with visual and textual content."[9] Sue Walker, on the other hand, argues in *The Design Journal*, for an expanded definition: "graphic design, and certainly graphic design research, is about more . . . than the work produced by a 'graphic designer', a form of professional practice with the reality of variable quality."[10] The British design critic Rick Poynor similarly asserts that "professional identity, with all its institutionalized concerns and assumptions, can become a cage that restricts the occupant's view of what else might be possible outside" (Poynor 2008). Walker and Poynor both argue here that there is more to graphic design than just professional practice, narrowly construed. Rather than eschewing practice when considering a definition of graphic design, though, in this anthology we spotlight the ways that various aspects of practice are central to graphic design discourse.

Until very recently, graphic design practice has been given short shrift as a critical graphic design methodology. One reason, as Buchanan suggests above, is because practice has been undervalued.[11] Practice-based research methods that are used across the design disciplines position making as a critical process in graphic design. Form-making can bring up critical issues that other kinds of research may miss. Some critics are likewise beginning to write about making as a critical process.[12] The 2017 Research Through Design conference investigated "thinking through making" traditions, and selected papers are published in a special issue of *Design Issues* (Vol 33, No 3, Summer 2017). Articulating how knowledge can be produced through prototyping, for example, is a worthwhile strategy (Binder and Brandt 2017). "Research *through* practice" (Frayling 1993/4; Archer 1995) is another.

Research on ways that mainstream graphic designers can access critical discourse through practice, and other thinking-through-making strategies and tools, is still in a nascent stage. As in other design professions, such as architecture or industrial design, graphic designers in commercial design practices still typically focus on client's needs, timelines, and budgets. There are increasing numbers, however, of graphic design studios whose practices embrace exploratory and interdisciplinary approaches (normally with cultural institution clients), or designers who have integrated co-design or participatory processes directly into their making processes across design disciplines (UsCreates, IDEO, thinkpublic). There are also some graphic designers who bring their experience in commercial practice to research-focused design methods. In "From Paratexts to Primary Texts: Shifting from a Commercial to a Research-Focused Design Practice" for example, Zoe Sadokierski argues that "By conducting scholarly research, practicing designers can expand design discourse by offering insights into practice-led ways of researching" (Sadokierski 2017: 175). Graphic design has been defined by the inherent tensions between professional practice and scholarly research about the field. In their introduction to *Graphic Design History: A Critical Guide*, Joanna Drucker and Emily McVarish argue that "At issue is not just a history of designs but a history of ideas and assumptions about forms of communication" (Drucker and McVarish 2008: xxii). The productive relationships between various critical practices and commercial practices necessarily inform the definition of graphic design.

Defining a field

Our discussion about defining graphic design leads to our second question: is graphic design a field or a discipline. In his closing remarks at the conference entitled "New Views 2: Conversations and Dialogues in Graphic Design" held in 2008, Richard Buchanan observed that graphic design remains a "field" rather than a fully-fledged discipline (Poynor 2008: 76). Buchanan suggests that design's uneasiness about becoming a bona fide academic discipline may be reflected in the uncertainty about our name and our identity. In her essay "Critical of What?", Ramia Mazé proposes that we should "raise questions about what graphic designers can do that others cannot," to reveal the "particular knowledge that makes [graphic design] a discipline or a profession" (Mazé 2009: 393). This sentiment is echoed in Victor Margolin's reprinted essay "Narrative Problems of Graphic Design History," featured in Part 1 of this book, in which he calls for graphic design to show "how the various activities that fall within the construct of graphic design practice are differentiated".

In 1988, graphic design theorist Jorge Frascara wrote that graphic design "has evolved into a sophisticated practice in a piecemeal fashion, with scattered efforts aimed at the development of subareas, such as posters or books, but without either the critical apparatus in literature or the discussion present in architecture" (Frascara 1988: 18). Writing about interaction design, Forlizzi *et al.*, observe that a process of "maturation" that can define a field is realized by "theoretical contributions of design research" and design practice. Critical and theoretical discourse in graphic design is progressing (Forlizzi *et al.* 2009: 2889). Helen Armstrong's anthology *Graphic Design Theory: Readings from the Field* (2009), for example, provides an historical overview and includes authors who contribute new perspectives. In *The Reader* we build on this kind of work by choosing contributors who interrogate complex ideas in rhetoric and semiotics (e.g. Scheuermann and Triggs), along with those who address critical form-making framed by theories of deconstruction (e.g. Lupton and Miller), and those who investigate critical practice (e.g. Bush, Poynor, and Rock) in graphic design. The consistent articulation of these methods, theories, and processes, along with emerging critical positions in graphic design, helps to inform and shape the field of study.

3. See an extended discussion about defining anthologies and their roles in design education by Grace Lees-Maffei and Daniel Huppatz (2017) "A Gathering of Flowers: On Design Anthologies," *The Design Journal,* 20 (4): 477–91.

4. We give special credit here to Steven Heller and his collaborators' successful volumes, the *Looking Closer* Series (1992–2006).

5. Creativity at Work is an international consortium of creativity and innovation experts, design thinkers, and arts-based learning practitioners currently based in Vancouver, Canada. For further details see: http://www.creativityatwork.com/ (accessed August 24, 2017).

6. See Peter N. Miller (2015), "Is 'Design Thinking' the New Liberal Arts?", *Chronicle of Higher Education,* March 26. Available online: http://www.chronicle.com/article/Is-Design-Thinking-the-New/228779 (accessed August 5, 2017).

7. Anne Bush and Stuart McKee provided reflections on these issues at the AIGA conference "Geo/graphics" (2014), which they developed as subsequent selected papers in the journal *Iridescent.* The Design Research Society proceedings (2016) offered early insights into decolonizing design as proposed by some of its members from the PhD in Design community. AIGA *Eye on Design* featured work of designers exploring cultural identity through design including Johnson Witehira's Maori typeface from New Zealand; Nadine Chahine on drawing Monotype's Latin and Arabic typefaces; and Hardworking Goodlooking on self-publishing as a "decolonizing" act in the Philippines.

8. A number of author-designers have provided interpretations of these and similar terms (e.g., Drentell and Helfand 2010; Meggs 1983). Jorge Frascara, provides a useful definition of visual communication design as "seen as an activity, is the action of conceiving, programming, projecting, and realizing visual communications that are usually produced through industrial means and are aimed at broadcasting specific messages to specific sectors of the public." Frascara, J. (2004) *Communication Design: Principles, Methods, and Practice,* New York: Allworth Press, 2.

9. For a fuller definition of the term, see the proposed rationale in Cezzar, J. (2015), "What Is Graphic Design?" *AIGA,* August 15, www.aiga.org/guide-whatisgraphicdesign (accessed August 24, 2017).

10. See also the state of UK graphic design research as introduced by S. Walker (2017) "Research in Graphic Design," *The Design Journal,* 20 (5): 549–59.

11. Undervaluing practice has been less of an issue in other design fields, such as fashion design or industrial design, where vigorous critical discourse commonly emerges from practice.

12. Refreshingly, some of these same issues are being taken up by Master in Design students and interrogated in relationship to graphic design. See for example, Marie-Noëlle Hébert (2014), "Re-envisioning Graphic Design as a Dialogic Practice: An Investigation into the Constructive Potential of Disruption within Aesthetic Practices," MA Thesis, York University, Toronto, Canada, 23.

Part 1

History of graphic design and graphic design history

Part 1: Introduction

Historical contexts—including the ways designers interpret and produce design at various times and within specific cultures—provide a framework for understanding and practicing contemporary design. The essays in Part 1 contribute to research in the history of our field. They are also part of an ecology of objects, ideas, and practices that together shape contemporary design. Past design practices and discourses can also be understood as a narrative trajectory upon which contemporary practices and discourses build. Several essays included in this Part aim to present a range of ideas about, and to draw attention to, one sort of narrative trajectory: the notion of a "canon" of graphic design history. In her 1991 essay, Martha Scotford defines the term "canon" as a "basis for judgment; a standard; a criterion; an authoritative list." The traditional canon has been a singular one that celebrates individuals or "movements"—more an authoritative list than a basis for judgment. Over the last decades, the canon for graphic design has become a contested space that promotes diverse graphic design canons, as demonstrated by the essays in this Part. Collectively, these essays set the stage for the pieces that follow in this *Reader*, and they signal potential directions for prospective graphic design canons.

In the title "History of graphic design and graphic design history," the phrase "History of graphic design" refers specifically to the history of the profession, while "graphic design history" refers to historical work about graphic design. The essays are divided into three Sections: "Industry and the birth of graphic design (19th century to 1980)," "Graphic design canon(s) (1980s to present)," and "Isms and graphic design." The objective is to offer a fluid structure to the work selected for this *Reader* without enforcing a strict chronology. Nineteenth-century articles, for example, are positioned alongside contemporary essays about nineteenth- and twentieth-century graphic design; recent critiques of modernist canons of graphic design adjoin essays that are a substantive part of modernist canons. The intention is to feature both primary scholarship and recent critical work on historical material and the history of the profession.

The first Section, "Industry and the birth of graphic design (19th century to 1980)," features seminal essays about graphic design as an industry. William Addison Dwiggins, in his 1922 essay "New kind of printing calls for new design," encourages high standards in both the printing trade and commercial art (Dwiggins soon thereafter coined the term "graphic design" to replace the term "commercial art"). He addresses changes in design and technology at the time, and recommends that practitioners blend common sense with "artistic taste" to produce high-quality, professional work. Nineteenth-century type and book designer William Morris likewise calls for high standards for paper, typography, and book design in his 1895 "Aims in founding the Kelmscott Press." He recounts how medieval techniques led to well-crafted books at a time when the quality of book design and production was typically very poor. Both designers set high standards for practice and production when graphic design was beginning to be professionalized. Design historian Gerry Beegan's recent essay, "*The Studio*: photomechanical reproduction and the changing status of design" (2007), also considers the birth of graphic design as a profession. He argues that the radical 1890s monthly art and design magazine *The Studio* (London, 1893–1964), which used new halftone techniques, leveled the hierarchical structure of fine art over design and the decorative arts, and elevated the status of graphic design as a profession. These essays relate to the current resurgence in craft processes, but they also play up the importance of new technologies, high standards, and inventive experimentation to graphic design.

In the next essay, "Narrative problems of graphic design history" (1994), Victor Margolin argues for a narrative that is focused on the development of the profession beginning in the late nineteenth and early twentieth centuries. He questions a long-view narrative of graphic design history that begins with cave paintings, and suggests that focusing on the short-term history of graphic design allows historians to probe more deeply into the way that graphic design has evolved. Margolin encourages the in-depth exploration of our field that can uncover fertile associations between previous and contemporary ideas and practices. The Bauhaus, which falls within the historical timeframe that Margolin champions, for example, had a tremendous influence on graphic design pedagogy throughout the twentieth century, and into the twenty-first century. In "Elementary school" (2000), Abbott Miller discusses the theoretical and historical underpinnings of Bauhaus pedagogical methodologies. He points out that design historians focus on geometric form, the grid, and rationalist typography in Bauhaus design, without considering the theoretical principles that informed Bauhaus pedagogy and design. He contends that, because of this oversight, "▲ ■ ● became a static formal vocabulary" instead of a socio-cultural visual language. In the last essay of this Section, Michael Golec (2004) likewise stresses the importance of critical and theoretical principles. In his review of *Graphic Design History* by Steven Heller and Georgette Ballance (and *Texts on Type: Critical Writings on Typography* by Steven Heller and Philip B. Meggs), Golec writes that Heller and Ballance's goal is the idea that the socio-cultural value of graphic design as a profession depends on the "the graphic designer's knowing capacity for innovation." Golec takes the editors to task for contradicting this thesis, specifically in the interview with designer Lou Danziger. Danziger claims instead that "the idiosyncratic personality" is the most important factor in the history of the profession. The previous essays argue that designing should be an inventive process steeped in socio-cultural considerations, and that design artifacts are therefore socio-cultural entities. The authors caution that designers can easily lose sight of design's socio-cultural functions. Contemporary reflective practice responds to this concern, advocating for ongoing analysis and reconsideration of design methodologies and outcomes.

The next Section, "Graphic design canon(s) (1980s to present)," points to the present by including issues related to the notion of a canon or canons in graphic design and graphic design history. The Section begins with "Cult of the ugly" (1993) by Steven Heller, which lambasted experimental design by graduate students at Cranbrook Academy of Art and other institutions in the early 1990s. Heller argues that this work is irrelevant to professional work and is ugly merely for the shock value of being ugly. He describes a piece done by design office Segura, for instance, as a "veritable primer of cultish extremes . . . compelling for its ingenuity yet undermined by its superficiality." "Cult of the ugly" generated intense dialogue among designers and led to a series of passionate responses, including the next two essays reprinted in this Section: "An Interview with Edward Fella" (1994) by Michael Dooley and, "An unbearable lightness?" by Steve Rigley (2007). In his interview, Ed Fella respectfully pushes back against Heller's ideas, explaining that "I don't like to use terms like 'good,' 'bad,' 'beautiful,' 'ugly,' because they continually take on different meanings . . . [beauty is] in the culture of the beholder." Rigley considers the arguments in "Cult of the ugly" from a contemporary point of view, in which he ponders the ways that the so-called ugly Cranbrook work could be part of a canon of graphic design. He describes the changing landscape of ideas about beauty over several centuries, including periods in which beauty is either elevated as illuminating or devalued as superficial. He concludes by arguing that today design courses should include discussions of aesthetics along with other critical theory.

Returning to canons for design, Martha Scotford asks, "Is there a canon of graphic design history?" (1991). Calling for a balanced picture of graphic design history, she creates a chart listing the number of works reproduced, countries of birth, and gender for all designers that are included in the top five graphic design history books in the early 1990s. Scotford concludes that there was indeed a canon of graphic design history at the time, and she remarks that the majority of designers who make up the twentieth-century canon were Western, white, and male. Scotford suggests that a cultural historical focus will instead produce a balanced and realistic graphic design history. Tibor Kalman, Abbott Miller, and Karrie Jacobs take on issues of the canon and historical appropriation in the 1991 essay "Good history bad history." The authors first discuss how many graphic design history publications feature "eye candy," presenting work that is disassociated from its historical context. The authors show how this sort of history leads to graphic design in which style is a "veneer rather than an expression of content." They argue that graphic design is steeped in its historical and cultural contexts. Understanding the contexts that undergird both historical and contemporary design helps us decipher how design functions in the world.

Rick Poynor also considers visual content in "Out of the studio: graphic design history and Visual Studies" (2011). He points out that in the discipline of Visual Studies, visual meaning is "created and contested," and suggests that graphic design history would benefit from moving from its focus on design studio work to become part of Visual Studies. Consideration of visual meaning fits well with graphic design historical criticism, so Poynor is puzzled that discussions of graphic design are almost completely missing from Visual Studies work. Despite this oversight, Poynor argues, repositioning graphic design history within Visual Studies would allow it to develop as a discipline separate from design studio. Here Poynor shows the connections between graphic design and other relevant fields.

The final set of essays, which are found in the Section "Isms and graphic design," address the origins and ramifications of Traditionalist, Modernist, Postmodernist, and contemporary graphic design and design theory. In "The grid: history, use, and meaning" (1986), Jack Williamson traces changes in the grid's "constructive elements" from the Middle Ages to the Postmodern era. Williamson contends that, with few conspicuous visual changes, the grid represents changing world views. He describes how the grid evolves from a "threshold between physical and super physical worlds" in the Middle Ages, to a "representation of the surface of the physical world and the rational cognition which beholds it" from the Renaissance until Postmodernism. He then shows how Postmodernist grids represent a "threshold to the submaterial world and irrationality." Jeremy Aynsley similarly discusses how changing design and political climates shaped the content of a popular publication in "*Gebrauchsgraphik* as an early graphic design journal, 1924–1938" (1992). He addresses how the magazine's editorial policy and format—which included both traditional and Modernist graphic design from Europe and the United States—was one model for international graphic design magazines that persists until today.

Ways to theorize graphic design are considered in the next two essays by designer and educator Jeffery Keedy. "Zombie Modernism" (1995) investigates the lingering hegemony of Modernist design after Postmodernism, revealing "the [conservative] political imperative" that drove "modernism-at-all-cost" in design. Keedy is perplexed by the fact that, in the mid-1990s, Modernism hadn't yet dissipated the way that cultural practices normally do. In "Global style: Modernist typography after Postmodernism" (2013), Keedy critiques a contemporary design style sometimes used for cultural institutions that he describes as the Modernist "good old International Style . . . upgraded to a bigger and better (or at least easier) Global Style." Global style, he argues, borrows its sense of time from video; it resembles a single animation frame on a 2-D page. Keedy is again perplexed that so many designers would fix on a certain style without any criticism or self-reflection. Cultural theorist Dick Hebdige likewise laments that his 1980s students preferred the music, culture, and fashion magazine *The Face* to the social, cultural and political photography magazine *Ten.8*. Attempting to sort out the reasons for this preference in his essay, "The bottom line on Planet One: squaring up to *The Face*," he compares the magazines to two planets. Hebdige describes planet one, represented by *Ten.8*, as "a globe, a sphere of substance and depth" (Hebdige as quoted in Spencer 2008: 191), while he depicts planet two, representing *The Face*, as purely surface with no depth beyond "the single image, the isolated statement . . . the individual 'trend'." Hebdige points out that the latter approach to culture—which was also being embraced in cultural studies at the time—is merely a jumble of codes and texts that closely resembles "lifestyle consumerism." The final essay of the Section, "A brave new world: understanding Deconstruction" by Chuck Byrne and Martha Witte, considers how the literary theory called Deconstruction was employed in some typographic design of the 1980s and 1990s. Deconstruction breaks down ideas, words, or values into "parts" to "decode" them. These parts, in turn, reveal "assumptions or convictions" about the political, artistic, or philosophical elements of the original ideas, words, or values. Although some graphic designers at the time felt that literary theory was remote, Byrne and Witte point out that the essence of designing with typography involves determining the "characteristics and arrangement of type relative to the interpretation . . . of the text . . . to enhance communication."

The essays in this Part consider historical and theoretical aspects of both making and thinking in graphic design. They present a host of possible canons, all of which add substance to critical narratives of both the history of graphic design and graphic design history. Historical and theoretical insights, and the canons they make manifest, can have significant implications for ideas about, and work produced in, contemporary graphic design.

Section 1.1

Industry and the birth of graphic design (nineteenth century to 1980)

Chapter 1.1.1

New kind of printing calls for new design

W.A. Dwiggins

Old Standards of Excellence
Suddenly Superseded
Because of the Complex of
New Processes in the
Industry—Still the
Opportunity, However, for
Blending Commonsense with
Artistic Taste

Enthusiasts of a sentimental turn of mind, inspired by a verbal formula—The Printing Art—and misled by a false interpretation of the same, have worked great confusion with the boundary that divides art from printing. The subtle intoxication of the third word of the phrase induces them to materialize vague near-aesthetic halos upon the heads of various people who undertake to print.

How printed matter looks makes no conscious difference to anybody except to the designer and the connoisseur of printing. When placards are put up at the corner garage announcing the current price of gasoline they do not need to be fine art. They do their work just as they are. All the main purposes of printing can be served without calling upon the help of art. The manufacturer with something to sell has ideas about the good looks of his printing, but his ideas are peculiar unto himself, and do not usually claim any relationship with art. He may be under the illusion that his printing is art. We are not. But as a charitable act let us add him to the printing designer noted above to complete the roster of those who care how printed matter looks. Oftentimes printing seems to tell its story just as well without art.

Artists stamp the history of printing

Make a record of these two facts—printing is not an art, and art is not essential to printing—and against them as a background let us project the following surprising conclusions. The history of printing is largely a history of individual artists. The names that stand foremost in the biography of the craft are the names of men conspicuous for a fine taste for design. Out of all the mass of printing that must have been done since the invention the only noteworthy relics are those few books and documents that were made by men of artistic mind. Printed paper has been collected and cherished for three hundred years, not because it was printing but because it was printed art.

Artists have tampered with printing and diverted it to their own ends ever since Gutenberg devised movable types. All through the course of the industry they have brought their faculties to bear upon the problem of turning printing into fine art. They have tampered with it in such a thoroughgoing fashion that—so far as the old work is concerned—the practical reasons for doing printing have been lost sight of, and printed paper is noteworthy chiefly because artists did meddle with it.

It will be perceived at once by the most complex that here are two groups of facts that do not fit together at all. There is more to this matter than appears at first blush. It would seem that there are several distinct classes of things to be examined under the title "printing." There are, verily.

Let us get down to cases and pick the industry apart. We want to find out what art has to do with printing—not historic printing but printing here and now. There are plain lines of cleavage in the modern industry. Working on these we are able to pry the business apart into three rough classes—plain printing; printing as a fine art; and a third large intermediate class of printing more or less modified by artistic taste. Town reports and handbills, telephone directories and school catalogs stand in the first class. The second might be represented by books printed for the Grolier Club by Bruce Rogers. The third class of printing is so wide and so varied that you will have trouble choosing examples to represent it.

Plain variety and fine art

Printing of the first class—the plain variety—is the backbone of the industry. This class outbulks the others by an overwhelming tonnage. It performs an imposing and valuable work and performs it in a thoroughly workmanlike manner. The technical excellence of the product of the "plain" printing plant is all that anyone could ask. The class of printing proves the truth of the deduction of the third paragraph. It gets no help from art and does not need it. It is outside the domain of art.

Printing as a fine art is not—as one might rashly assume from a review of the industry—a matter of history only. The thing is still happening. The man of taste—whom our sentimentalist would extinguish by calling him a "printer-artist"—is still to be discovered in the craft. Scattered all through the industry are men of fine artistic taste pursuing printing as an art. And it is to be noted that they do it, in many instances, on an entirely practical basis, and find little handicap, indeed, in their adherence to distinguished traditions. They produce printing that is fine art because they want to—because—one is constrained to say—they are artists.

But the consideration of printing as fine art is not quite the purpose of this note. Printing on that plane is, by its very nature, removed into the province of a critic of the fine arts, and cannot be examined on an equal footing with the product of the industry at large. What contact the industry at large has with art is the question on which we are engaged. We have narrowed our examination down to the third group of printing. We may look for that contact there.

This last group has certain noteworthy characteristics. For one thing it is not made to be sold, it is made to be given away—with a very canny purpose behind the gift. Then, it is a new thing—as new as advertising. It is thoroughly democratic—everybody takes a hand in making it. It goes everywhere and is read by everyone. It probably plays a larger part in forming the quasi-social state that we call civilization than all the books and newspapers and periodicals together. Its function is to prepare the ground for selling something, or to sell something directly itself. By hook or by crook, by loud noise or subtle argument, it might fulfill its mission of getting something sold.

It is really a kind of super-printing. Its requirements have forced the industry to expand itself, to include new and strange functions—critical study of clients' markets—preparation of "literature," descriptive, educational, argumentative—sales always in view at the end. One of the functions that the press has been forced to include is performed by a section known as the art department or art service.

The art department produces something. It is what is called "art work." The expression "art work" is advertising agents' slang. "Art work" might be defined as drawings, decorations, etc., made to complicate the advertiser's message. It seems that in some advertising a plain straightforward statement of the facts will not serve. Little indiscretions must be committed. Little naïve slips and false starts need to be contrived, to catch the victim's eye. Or he must have his back rubbed and his foibles exploited before he can be coaxed into just the right position for the deadfall to get him. One infers that it is the function of the art service to provide these inducements, indirections and subterfuges.

The ingenues of the art services work most skillfully at making pictures and ornamental designs. Their products rank sufficiently high as drawings and designs. But the application of their work slips up in some peculiar way. The big carnival on Main Street needs their help to be a complete affair but their art is off up a side alley doing clever tricks.

In view of the excellent work done by some of the art departments of printing plants the foregoing comment may seem to be pitched too strong. But these people hold a key position in the whole question of art and printing and the public taste, and what they do or misdo is of great moment to the artist. You can almost say that the future of printed graphic art rests in their hands. Illustration used to be spoken of as "the people's art" but advertising "art work" has supplanted it in popular esteem. Estimate how many more people know about Coles Phillips than know about Raleigh or George Wright. If all the talk about the importance of art to the industries of a nation is anything but buncombe it is of the highest importance that the advertising draughtsmen be made conscious of their influence and of their opportunity. Art will not occur in the industries until our fellow citizens learn to know the real thing when they see it. Advertising artists are now their only teachers. Advertising design is the only form of graphic design that gets home to everybody.

The implication is that the advertising artists fail to set the proper tone. The conduct of an art as an adjunct to business is always difficult. These artists, however sound as artists they may be in themselves, are under a pressure from outside that is almost bound to make them unfit as exponents of sound standards. It is unlucky that the job of setting styles for printing should be in their hands, because they are bound by the conditions of their service to set styles on a level lower than the best.

Advertising artists can do better

But they can better their performance. They have the chance to work ably within the limitations of their handicap. They can bring some pressure to bear at least upon making salesprinting a clearer and more precise medium for the merchant's message. They need to relearn the rules of their game. Let them give ear to the words of the prophet and mend their ways. They have a moral code set down for the department of the just typographer made perfect:

Cultivate simplicity. Have simple styles of letters and simple arrangements.

In the matter of layout forget art at the start and use horse-sense. The printing-designer's whole duty is to make a clear presentation of the message—to give it every advantage of arrangement—to get the important statements forward and the minor parts placed so that they will not be overlooked. This calls for an exercise of common sense and a faculty for analysis rather than for art.

Have pictures consistent with the printing process. Printers' ink and paper are a convention for light and shade and color. Stay inside the convention.

Be niggardly with decorations, borders and such accessories. Do not pile up ornament like flowers at a funeral. Scheme the white spaces—paper is indeed a "part of the picture." Manipulate the spaces of blank paper around and among the printed surfaces to make a pleasing pattern of areas.

Get acquainted with the shapes of the type letters themselves. They are the units out of which the structure is made—unassembled bricks and beams. Pick good ones and stick to them.

It is easy to formulate rules. It is not so easy to apply them. As a matter of fact, the new kind of printing calls for a new kind of design. The revolution in technical practice is complete. Very little is left of the old methods. The standards of good printing as they stood from the beginning of the craft are suddenly superseded. There is thrust into the printer's hand a complex of new processes—halftone engraving, machine composition, quadricolor, offset, fast running photogravure. The original conception of sound printing design as it stood until the age of the machines has very little bearing on these new processes. The impression of ink upon paper is an entirely new and different thing.

In one generation of printers the continuity of tradition has "faulted." Can we design this new printing with our minds trained in the standards that guided Aldus, or Bodoni, or DeVinne? Must all these things that we looked upon as good go overboard? How much of the old standard of quality can carry across the gap, and how can it be related to the new state of things? Typesetting by hand is about to become as obsolete as spinning thread by hand. Machine composition is a settled fact. How is it to be made good in the old sense? Or is the old sense to be discarded?

Of course all these questions will be answered. The right way will be worked out and a new standard evolved. The point to be stressed is that the new standard must not be a mechanical standard merely, it must also be an aesthetic standard. Artists must take a part in thinking it out—not the art services only, but artists—artists in terms of Holbein and Tory.

Hints for artists in modern printing

There are hints in the new printing that the artist can profit by. Its material suggests a slighter and sketchier style than we at present affect—things that look like here today and gone tomorrow. Such things can still be good design and good art. The butterfly is justly admired for its good looks but is admittedly scheduled for only a brief stay. Our way of using decorative drawings that appear to have consumed months in their preparation is somehow inconsistent with the fact that the things they decorate are meant to last only for an hour. The enduring volumes of the ancients are the wrong source of inspiration for decorative styles that are to serve a purpose so ephemeral.

The French have caught the spirit of this kind of design. The leakage of their styles over into our picture making will serve us a good turn if we are able to perceive what they are about. The drawing of accessories for the new kind of printing and the layout of the printing itself need to be done at a higher rate of vibration than we are accustomed to. Some few have caught the pitch. The art director of *Vogue* and *Vanity Fair* schemes pages that are consistent with the demands of the new craft.

The problem is stimulating through the very condition of its novelty. New lines have to be run and new charts made. For the time being all fences are down and all rules off. So at least it would seem. But in spite of the completeness of the mechanical revolution, the law of art still runs. Sound design is still sound design, even though it be in novel material. The underlying purpose of printing has not changed, neither has the fundamental problem for the artist. An orderly and graceful disposition of parts continues to be desirable and printed pages are still intended to be read. On these terms the designer will attempt to do for the new printing what he undertook to do for the old. His success will still depend upon a suitable blending of common sense with artistic taste.

Chapter 1.1.2

Note by William Morris on his "Aims in founding the Kelmscott Press"

William Morris

I BEGAN printing books with the hope of producing some which would have a definite claim to beauty, while at the same time they should be easy to read and should not dazzle the eye, or trouble the intellect of the reader by eccentricity of form in the letters. I have always been a great admirer of the calligraphy of the Middle Ages, & of the earlier printing which took its place. As to the fifteenth-century books, I had noticed that they were always beautiful by force of the mere typography, even without the added ornament, with which many of them are so lavishly supplied. And it was the essence of my undertaking to produce books which it would be a pleasure to look upon as pieces of printing and arrangement of type. Looking at my adventure from this point of view then, I found I had to consider chiefly the following things: the paper, the form of the type, the relative spacing of the letters, the words, and the lines; and lastly the position of the printed matter on the page.

It was a matter of course that I should consider it necessary that the paper should be hand-made, both for the sake of durability and appearance. It would be a very false economy to stint in the quality of the paper as to price: so I had only to think about the kind of hand-made paper. On this head I came to two conclusions: 1st, that the paper must be wholly of linen (most hand-made papers are of cotton today), and must be quite 'hard,' i.e., thoroughly well sized; and 2nd, that, though it must be 'laid' and not 'wove' (i.e., made on a mould made of obvious wires), the lines caused by the wires of the mould must not be too strong, so as to give a ribbed appearance. I found that on these points I was at one with the practice of the papermakers of the fifteenth century; so I took as my model a Bolognese paper of about 1473. My friend Mr. Batchelor, of Little Chart, Kent, carried out my views very satisfactorily, & produced from the first the excellent paper which I still use.

Next as to type. By instinct rather than by conscious thinking it over, I began by getting myself a fount of Roman type. And here what I wanted was letter pure in form; severe, without needless excrescences; solid, without the thickening and thinning of the line, which is the essential fault of the ordinary modern type, and which makes it difficult to read; and not compressed laterally, as all later type has grown to be owing to commercial exigencies. There was only one source from which to take examples of this perfected Roman type, to wit, the works of the great Venetian printers of the fifteenth century, of whom Nicholas Jenson produced the completest & most Roman characters from 1470 to 1476. This type I studied with much care, getting it photographed to a big scale, & drawing it over many times before I began designing my own letter; so that though I think I mastered the essence of it, I did not copy it servilely; in fact, my Roman type, especially in the lower case, tends rather more to the Gothic than does Jenson's.

After a while I felt that I must have a Gothic as well as a Roman fount; and herein the task I set myself was to redeem the Gothic character from the charge of unreadableness which is commonly brought against it. And I felt that this charge could not be reasonably brought against the types of the first two decades of printing: that Schoeffer at Mainz, Mentelin at Strasburg, and Gunther Zainer at Augsburg, avoided the spiky ends and undue compression which lay some of the later type open to the above charge. Only the earlier printers (naturally following therein the practice of their predecessors the scribes) were very liberal of contractions, and used an excess of 'tied' letters, which, by the way, are very useful to the compositor. So I entirely eschewed contractions, except for the '&,' and had very few tied letters, in fact none but the absolutely necessary ones. Keeping my end steadily in view, I designed a black-letter type which I think I may claim to be as readable as a Roman one, and to say the truth I prefer it to the Roman. This type is of the size called Great Primer (the Roman type is of 'English' size); but later on I was driven by the necessities of the Chaucer (a double-columned book) to get a smaller Gothic type of Pica size.

The punches for all these types, I may mention, were cut for me with great intelligence and skill by Mr. E. P. Prince, and render my designs most satisfactorily.

Now as to the spacing: First, the 'face' of the letter should be as nearly conterminous with the 'body' as possible, so as to avoid undue whites between the letters. Next, the lateral spaces between the words should be (a) no more than is necessary to distinguish clearly the division into words, and (b) should be as nearly equal as possible. Modern printers, even the best, pay very little heed to these two essentials of seemly composition, and the inferior ones run riot in licentious spacing, thereby producing, inter alia, those ugly rivers of lines running about the page which are such a blemish to decent printing. Third, the whites between the lines should not be excessive; the modern practice of 'leading' should be used as little as possible, and never without some definite reason, such as marking some special piece of printing. The only leading I have allowed myself is in some cases a 'thin' lead between the lines of my Gothic pica type: in the Chaucer and the double-columned books I have used a 'hair' lead, and not even this in the 16mo books. Lastly, but by no means least, comes the position of the printed matter on the page. This should always leave the inner margin the narrowest, the top somewhat wider, the outside (fore-edge) wider still, and the bottom widest of all. This rule is never departed from in mediæval books, written or printed. Modern printers systematically transgress against it; thus apparently contradicting the fact that the unit of a book is not one page, but a pair of pages. A friend, the librarian of one of our most important private libraries, tells me that after careful testing he has come to the conclusion that the mediaeval rule was to make a difference of 20 per cent, from margin to margin. Now these matters of spacing and position are of the greatest importance in the production of beautiful books; if they are properly considered they will make a book printed in quite ordinary type at least decent and pleasant to the eye. The disregard of them will spoil the effect of the best designed type.

It was only natural that I, a decorator by profession, should attempt to ornament my books suitably: about this matter, I will only say that I have always tried to keep in mind the necessity for making my decoration a part of the page of type. I may add that in designing the magnificent and inimitable wood-cuts which have adorned several of my books, and will above all adorn the Chaucer which is now drawing near completion, my friend Sir Edward Burne-Jones has never lost sight of this important point, so that his work will not only give us a series of most beautiful and imaginative pictures, but form the most harmonious decoration possible to the printed book.

Kelmscott House, Upper Mall, Hammersmith. Nov. 11, 1895.

Chapter 1.1.3

The Studio: photomechanical reproduction and the changing status of design

Gerry Beegan

The 1890s marked the beginning of a new era in visual representation. It was during this decade that photographic images were first successfully incorporated alongside written texts in illustrated weekly and monthly magazines. Photo relief reproduction processes, which had been developed over the previous decades, were refined to a level where they became commercially viable and culturally acceptable. Line methods had been in use since the 1870s. They produced an image which was fixed onto a sensitized metal plate, and etched to produce a type-compatible relief block. The halftone techniques first developed in the 1880s transformed the continuous tones of an original into tiny dots, which then were etched in much the same way as photo relief line methods. Halftone techniques could duplicate photographs, paintings, and wash images, while line methods were widely used for the printing of pen and ink drawings. Collectively, these photographic approaches were known as "process." These techniques were able to challenge the existing reproduction technology of wood engraving, which had dominated the illustrated press up to this point. This essay looks at one particular aspect of this shift in the mass-produced image: the depiction of art and design. It examines *The Studio*, a monthly art magazine which was launched in London in April 1893, and which used only photomechanical methods to visualize an extended range of artistic practice. I examine the meanings and effects of the reproduction processes as they relate to the status of design.

Clive Ashwin has suggested: "*The Studio* was the first visually modern magazine to the extent that it adopted the reproductive medium which would dominate art publishing, indeed publishing in general, for the century to come."[1] Certainly, around this time, a number of English magazines were applying this new imaging technology. *The Sketch*, the first middle-class, photographically reproduced weekly was launched in February of 1893, just before *The Studio*. By the early–1890s, most magazines, including the specialist art monthlies, were using a mixture of reproduction methods including wood engravings and photographic halftones. So why did *The Studio* switch entirely to this new method? I will examine the early days of the magazine in some detail to analyse the significance of its image reproduction decisions.[2]

First published in *Design Issues*, 23 (4) (Autumn 2007): 46–61. © Massachusetts Institute of Technology.

Although Walter Benjamin famously suggested that the increased circulation of images of art resulted in the weakening or removal of the aura of the original, an examination of the art publications of this era reveals a complex situation in which reproduced images actually added to the allure of the real thing. The widespread diffusion of inexpensive mass reproductions was an element in the creation of a mystique around original paintings or sculptures, objects which often had not been visible at all up to this point. In addition, I would argue that the change in reproduction methods itself served to heighten the standing of the original. The wood engraving retained a status and a function independent of the original: it was clearly a translation into another medium—a medium with its own, long-established symbolic language. The halftone, on the other hand, was essentially a simplified, lesser, monochrome version of something superior, unaffordable, and apart.[3]

Yet, in the early days of *The Studio*, photomechanical reproduction operated in an egalitarian and inclusive manner since the fine and applied arts, both high and low, were reproduced in an identical way. In other art magazines, status was inscribed within the printed image by the reproduction method that was used. The more important the artwork, the more elaborate the reproduction techniques which were employed to produce a printable matrix. *The Studio*, on the other hand, treated all forms of art in the same way: a sculpture, a painting, a chair, a tapestry, a photograph, or a bungalow would be shown in an identical manner. This radical approach was associated with the magazine's founding editor, Joseph Gleeson White, who was one of the major figures in the discourse around decorative art and reproduction in the 1890s.

Early in 1893, Gleeson White was approached by his friend, Lewis Hind, regarding a new monthly magazine that intended to take an innovative approach to the depiction of art. The periodical would provide international coverage of contemporary developments in modern art and design, and it would do so using only photographic reproduction methods. Hind's project was being financed by Charles Holme, a wealthy businessman. Holme, having made a fortune in the textile trade, had retired at the age of forty-four to promote the new movement in design. Hind already had begun to commission articles when he was poached by Lord Astor to oversee his revamped process illustrated weekly, the *Pall Mall Budget*. Hind offered to find a replacement, and persuaded Gleeson White, an experienced writer and editor, to take over the job on short notice.[4]

The proposed magazine would be a radical, pioneering publication at variance with the conservative art world and established art periodicals. It intended to take a different approach from these existing monthlies in price, audience, content, and reproduction method. Although heavily illustrated, it was relatively inexpensive at sixpence per issue. Some of the established art monthlies cost three times that amount. Its price brought it within the reach of a younger readership, an audience not of connoisseurs and collectors, but of practitioners, students, and middle-class enthusiasts. *The Studio*'s intention was to visualize a wide spectrum of artistic practice. Its title referred not only to the painter's studio, but to the studio of the textile designer, the poster designer, the illustrator, the potter, the furniture maker, the architect, and the photographer. The magazine was intent on establishing art as a modern, everyday activity in which its readers could participate. Rather than dealing with the art of the past, it would show the work of its own time and deal with contemporary concerns. It also proposed to highlight younger artists, who might not yet have established a reputation. From the beginning, it was international in its scope: its aim was to spread awareness of developments in the English decorative arts through Europe and North America. To this end, *The Studio* printed an American edition as well as a bilingual French version.[5]

Established art magazines such as the *Art Journal* and *The Magazine of Art* catered to an affluent, upper-middle-class readership. They were expensive and conservative in their content, and featured much academic and historical art. By the early nineties, the mainstream magazines had adopted photo relief halftone technologies, but these were positioned at the lowest level of the hierarchy of reproductive techniques deployed within their pages. Halftones were used to depict paintings and sculpture, although mainly as small images documenting artworks within articles. These photographic images not only would have been cheap to replicate, but the "Old Masters" would have been copyright free.[6]

For its full-page images of paintings, *The Magazine of Art* often used highly finished wood engravings based on photographs. This approach to reproductive wood engraving had emerged through the American "New School" engravers who, from the 1880s, had produced increasingly fine tonal reproductions which captured the surface qualities of paintings in a pseudo-photographic manner. Photographs of paintings were fixed onto woodblocks and then painstakingly engraved using a small number of tools to produce an even tonal effect. As the "New School" aimed for mimesis rather than translation, why not simply use photo relief halftones to reproduce the originals? First of all, halftone processes were still unable to capture the subtleties of an original without considerable, expensive retouching. Second, and even more significant, the halftone image erased the handwork which still was an important element in the assignment of status to a printed image. The "New School" approach combined the factuality of photographic facsimile with the visible artistic labor of the engraver.[7]

In *The Magazine of Art*, the "New School" style reproductive prints were credited to their engravers. These wood engraved images were spatially separated from the editorial text. They occupied full pages rather than being placed within the text like the halftones. The fact that they were allocated an entire page was an indication of their importance—these were freestanding objects framed by the white margins of the paper in a manner similar to a painting. However, they still were subordinate to the text and were used as examples of a particular artist's oeuvre. They also were linked to the editorial text by being printed on the same paper stock.

At the top of the image hierarchy in the art press were the etchings and photogravure inserts, which were on thicker stock than the rest of the magazine.[8] These images, unlike the wood engravings or halftones, were not printed at the same time as the letterpress text, but were run off separately and then bound in. In order to emphasize their value, these inserts often appeared on stock which had colors and finishes that did not match the rest of the journal. In *The Magazine of Art*, each insert's subject matter and artistic merits were discussed in an essay on the facing page. The halftones and wood engravings illuminated the texts they accompanied, while, in the case of the etched or photogravure inserts, the written texts were subservient to the images.

The old-fashioned wood engraving and the high-class reproductive etching, which were such a feature of art magazines, were to be excluded from *The Studio*. Its radical modernity and democratic intentions were asserted by its commitment to using only photo relief processes. This signaled that the art which appeared in *The Studio* was to be less precious and more accessible.[9] As a shrewd businessman, and an outsider to publishing, Charles Holme also would have appreciated the economic advantages of photographic reproduction. He could not have afforded to bind in etchings if he hoped to sell his magazine at sixpence a copy. Photomechanical techniques helped to keep the price of his new venture relatively low, while providing readers with large numbers of images. *The Studio* contained the same amount of illustration as the existing art monthlies, only it did so at a greatly reduced cost.[10]

Although he had not been Holme's first choice, Gleeson White proved to be the ideal editor for his new venture. Gleeson White originally had been a bookseller by trade, but he combined this with literary editing and freelance writing on the decorative and fine arts. A progressive cosmopolitan critic, Gleeson White had a broad knowledge of the contemporary art and design world. Not only had he written on art, crafts, and illustration, he also had a strong interest in photography. Moreover, unlike his fellow English journalists, he had editorial experience on an art magazine illustrated mainly by process. Many of the innovations that appeared in *The Studio* had been anticipated by *The Art Amateur*, an American magazine on which Gleeson White had worked in 1890. *The Art Amateur* was a large-format, heavily illustrated popular magazine of decorative and fine arts. It used modern techniques of image reproduction with many line and halftone illustrations and large, lithographic supplements. Gleeson White moved to New York to work as its associate editor, and although his stay in the United States turned out to be short-lived, he gained invaluable editorial experience on a magazine which illustrated the spectrum of arts in an accessible and contemporary fashion.[11]

In 1892 after returning to England, Gleeson White engaged in the energetic promotion of modern illustration and decorative arts. His main employment was as art editor of George Bell and Sons. Here he wrote, commissioned, and designed many important books on illustration and reproduction. His "Ex Libris Series" on the art of the book included both Joseph Pennell's *Modern Illustration* (1895) and Walter Crane's *The Decorative Illustration of Books* (1896). Other titles in the series included books on bookplates, printer's marks, and bindings. Bell was highly regarded as an art publisher. In 1895, for instance, *The Art Journal*'s annual review of notable books on art and design concentrated almost entirely on works by George Bell.[12] Gleeson White also continued his freelance journalism, writing on photography in *The Photogram* and interviewing illustrators in *The Idler*.[13] He was deeply involved in issues of reproduction; he attend the meetings of the Royal Photographic Society's process section, and sent his son to study printing and process.[14]

The Studio's launch issue in April 1893 under Sir Gleeson White's direction was a dramatic demonstration of the possibilities of photographic reproduction. Within its forty pages were forty-seven illustrations in line and halftone. The two major articles dealt with Frederick Leighton's sculptures and Aubrey Beardsley's pen and ink drawings, both of which were ideal subjects for demonstrating what modern imaging processes could achieve. The Leighton article was illustrated by halftone photographs, while the Beardsley article used line processes.

The opening article started at the apex of the art establishment by way of an interview with Leighton, the president of the Royal Academy.[15] The piece was illustrated by nine large, retouched halftone photographs of his clay maquettes.[16] By launching its premiere issue with an interview, the epitome of new journalism, *The Studio* made its modern editorial stance clear. The conversation with Leighton begins: "You are early," were his first words. "I have so many engagements I am compelled to keep punctually to the exact time."[17] The magazine's interviews with artists in their studios emphasized the specific circumstances of the encounter between the interviewer and the subject. This was typical of the press interviews of the day, which included a great deal of information on the site in which the encounter between the subject and the reporter took place. This approach was particularly appropriate for a magazine of decorative art in which there was a strong sense that the individual and his or her surroundings were one.[18]

After the photographs of Leighton's sculptures, the next images the reader encountered were two Beardsley line drawings. This marked a dramatic transition from the most respected academic artist of the day to a totally unknown young illustrator. *The Studio* was demonstrating both its intention to spotlight emerging artists, as well as its commitment to a broad spectrum of art practice. At the foot of page ten was a one-and-a-half by six-inch Beardsley drawing of Joan of Arc. It formed the end piece to an article entitled "The Growth of Recent Art," which defended contemporary art against charges of eccentricity, decadence, and morbidity, the very accusations that soon would be leveled at Beardsley. The caption to the Joan of Arc illustration promised that a large seven inch by thirty inch lithographic reproduction would be included as a supplement in a later issue. This image demonstrated the ability of process to produce images in many sizes, and also underlined the magazine's commitment to the young Beardsley. The few supplements which appeared in the early years of *The Studio* often were lithographs, a process which had been associated up to this point with the commercial poster, but which was being established as a medium of artistic expression.[19]

Facing the Joan of Arc drawing on the recto page was a full-page image captioned "Siegfried, Act II. By Aubrey Beardsley (Reduced from the Original Drawing in Line and Wash.)" The caption underlined again the ability of photography to change the scale of images. Although there was a huge gulf in experience and reputation between Beardsley and Leighton, in terms of subject matter, these images were rather harmonious. Beardsley's *Siegfried* echoed the earlier images of Leighton's draped or naked mythological figures, particularly the *Andromeda* on page three, who also was shown with a winged dragon.[20] These images were just a foretaste, since they were followed not by the article on Beardsley but by a piece on sketching in Spain illustrated by Frank Brangwyn's tonal wash illustrations.[21] It was common in *The Studio* for illustrations to overlap into adjoining articles. Image and text were not always in step. Another Beardsley pen drawing *A Frieze from Malory's Morte d'Arthur* was dropped in at the foot of page thirty-three, in the middle of an article on the newly reopened Grafton Gallery. In all, the novice illustrator had thoroughly infiltrated the launch issue. Including the cover design, there was a total of nine of his images in *The Studio*, five of which were full-page.

The Beardsley article was evidence of *The Studio*'s commitment not only to new talent, but also to its new imaging processes. Both visually and textually, the article was a powerful demonstration of photomechanical reproduction. By removing the interpretive hand of the engraver, the photographic processes emphasized the artist's individual vision in a more intense way. The early years of the decade saw an explosion of pen and ink illustration reproduced by photo relief line techniques, from the realist social cartoons of Phil May to Beardsley's decorative fantasies. Before his departure, Lewis Hind already had commissioned Joseph Pennell, "the most vocal of critics," to write the piece on Beardsley.[22] Pennell, an acerbic American illustrator, was the acknowledged expert on pen and ink drawing, and a fervent supporter of photomechanical methods. The article he created was as much to do with process reproduction as it was with Beardsley. In fact, the essay was rather noncommittal on Beardsley's talent and his potential as an artist. Although Pennell often was credited with discovering Beardsley, he saw him as a young man very much at the beginning of his career, and he was unsure of Beardsley's future prospects or direction. In his three, short columns of text, he said surprisingly little about the illustrator himself, and made only a brief, surface analysis of his work. As Haldane Macfall, the art critic of *St. Paul's* and a friend of Beardsley's noted: "Pennell was writing for a new magazine of arts and crafts: and his fierce championship of process reproduction was as much part of his aim as Beardsley's art—and all of us who have been saved from the vile debauching of our line work by the average wood engraver owe it largely to Pennell that process reproduction won through—and not least of all to Beardsley."[23] As Macfall's comments make clear, the eventual success of process was a struggle, not a foregone conclusion, and the opinion of critics was necessary in the promotion of this new technology.

Pennell's article "A New Illustrator: Aubrey Beardsley" begins in the second column of page fourteen with a huge initial letter "I" drawn by Beardsley. Pennell launched his text: "I have lately seen a few drawings which seem to me to be very remarkable." The piece makes it clear that the drawings were as remarkable for their method of reproduction as for their content. He went on to say:

> It is most interesting to note, too, that though Mr. Beardsley has drawn his motives from every age, and found his styles—for it is quite impossible to say what his style may be—on all schools, he has not been carried back into the fifteenth century, or succumbed to the limitations of Japan; he has recognized that he is living in the last decade of the nineteenth century, and he has availed himself of mechanical reproduction for the publication of his drawings which the Japs and the Germans would have accepted with delight had they but known it. The reproduction of the *Morte d'Arthur* drawing, printed in this number, is one of the most marvelous pieces of mechanical engraving, if not the most marvelous, that I have ever seen, simply for this reason: it gives Mr. Beardsley's actual handiwork, and not the interpretation of it by someone else. I know it is the correct thing to rave over the velvety, fatty quality of the wood-engraved line, a quality which can be obtained from any process block by careful printing, and which is not due to the artist at all. But here I find the distinct qualities of a pen line, and of Mr. Beardsley's pen line, which had been used by the artist and reproduced by the process-man in a truly extraordinary manner.[24]

For Pennell, the *Morte D'Arthur* image proved that process could match the visual richness of wood engraving. Pennell's argument was particularly compelling because this section of his text was inserted within Beardsley's borders. As he wrote of the "velvety, fatty" line, his words were encircled by just such lines, reinforcing his point that these effects were possible with process. In fact, Beardsley's *Morte D'Arthur* designs were ersatz wood engravings. The book was a cheap photo line relief imitation of William Morris's hand-engraved and hand-printed Kelmscott Press books.[25] In the mid-nineties, there was a dramatic proliferation of books such as *Morte D'Arthur* which were inspired by the Kelmscott style, but which were reproduced by line process and printed on simulated handmade paper on mechanized presses. Their illustrations appeared to be wood engravings, but were pen and ink drawings in the style of woodcuts reproduced by much cheaper photographic methods.[26]

Not only could process match the richness of wood engraving as Pennell noted, what was crucial for him was that it could directly convey the artist's "actual handiwork." Beardsley was an ideal example of this claim. The images demonstrated that he was working with a number of styles. The "distinct qualities" of his pen line varied considerably from image to image in the illustrations that *The Studio* printed. In fact, this eclecticism is what was distinctive about Beardsley. His appropriation of styles was, paradoxically, an indication of the individuality of the person choosing and combining these various disparate approaches. The *Morte D'Arthur* image showed him using Burne-Jones's mock medieval tropes, but in "J'ai baisé to bouche Iokanaan" Beardsley already was experimenting with the stylistic mixture that would become known as "art nouveau." Photographic reproduction allowed image makers this hybrid freedom to mix and quote from other styles and other periods for the first time. Indeed, with its emphasis on the authorial hand, the move to process reproduction heightened an awareness of style. The individual was free to produce highly personal "grotesque" or "eccentric" work that ignored the principles of the Academy and the conventions imposed by wood engraving. Beardsley's work, which was constantly in flux, created an awareness that style is a choice and a construction.

The images in *The Studio* demonstrate Beardsley's move from using process to imitate wood engraving to his staking out a new territory for this technique, a new photomechanical aesthetic. The sinuous line that Beardsley used in his illustration for Wilde's *Salome,* which became typical of art nouveau, would not have been possible in wood engraving, or at least would not have been thinkable. Process gave Beardsley the freedom to extend his line in length and contract it in width to a degree that wood engraving would not have encouraged.

Pennell's article ended on a typically aesthetic elitist note, although it may have been an appropriate remark, given *The Studio*'s intention of appealing to an artistic readership: "Certainly, with the comparatively small amount of work which Mr. Beardsley has produced, he has managed to appeal to artists—and what more could he wish."[27] The article launched the young illustrator's career. *The Studio* claimed that Beardsley was known in Paris two weeks after the publication of its first issue, and that this was the most rapid international fame of any English artist. Paul Greenhalgh sees the publication of "J'ai baisé ta bouche Iokanaan" as the first seminal moment in the art nouveau movement, and notes its rapid international diffusion. Will Bradley, a young illustrator in Chicago, saw Beardsley's work in *The Studio* and immediately was inspired to take a new direction in his own illustration. With process reproduction, illustrators were able to see the work of their peers very quickly and directly. In the case of paintings, halftones were unable to convey the colors, scale, or subtleties of the distant and inaccessible original. But the pen and ink drawing was made with the intention that it would be mass-produced in books or magazines; the printed images were not lesser objects, but final pieces.[28]

From the first issues, *The Studio*'s readership was assured of the suitability of process as a means of reproduction by regular comments on the subject. Articles, book reviews, and editorials all dealt with the replication and printing of imagery.[29] Almost all of these texts supported photomechanical reproduction as an accurate and modern imaging method, and characterized wood engraving as old-fashioned and intrusive. Wood engraving's true role was now as a medium of artistic expression, as in the wood cuts of Lucien Pissaro.[30] In the second issue of *The Studio,* Gleeson White insisted that process reproduction was the only truthful way of showing artistic photographs. In an interview with H. H. Hay Cameron, the photographer son of Julia Margaret Cameron, Gleeson White requested some photographs for reproduction. "May I take some of them to show (in the paraphrase which photo-engraving alone offers) to the readers of *The Studio*, a proof that the praise I mean to set down is based on solid facts?"[31]

The Studio continued to feature reproduction and illustration extensively as part of its reporting on the decorative arts. The magazine included pen and ink process illustration as one of a range of modern image-making and image-reproduction practices which included photography, etching, poster illustration, and lithography. The common thread in this coverage was the individuality that the imagemakers brought to their task. In *The Studio*'s discourse on artistic value, the defining quality assigned to the artist/designer and his or her products was that of uniqueness. Speaking of the French poster designer Théophile Steinlen, Gleeson White asserted that " . . . in art, especially in design, personality and individual feeling are the chief things."[32] Furthermore, this personal quality was an innate aspect of the artist and designer himself or herself, rather than being something that could be instilled through education.[33] Photomechanical reproduction was praised for its ability to directly communicate these distinctive personal characteristics.

With the success of *The Studio*, other art magazines attempted to follow its lead, both in terms of content and reproduction techniques. However, any claims to modernity that these other magazines made were compromised in a number of ways. By 1896, the fine reproductive wood engravings which had been common in *The Art Journal* disappeared, and their place was taken by large, retouched, photographic halftones. However, the editorial support for new artistic developments was undermined by the highly conventional and sentimental nature of the majority of these photomechanical images.[34] *The Magazine of Art* continued to employ a reproductive hierarchy so that a range of techniques including halftones, etching, and wood engraving might all be used within the same article.[35] The various images that the publication printed using these different methods remained maudlin and trite.

Meanwhile, *The Studio* itself was changing and, ironically, becoming more like these conventional magazines. Fine art took an ever more prominent place in its pages. In its first volumes, the magazine reproduced halftones of three-dimensional pieces in preference to paintings. When it did feature two-dimensional work, rather than showing chromatic paintings, it preferred line images and pen and ink sketches or objects such as tapestries which had strong surface patterns. Volumes one to three covering 1893 and 1894 contained only a handful of paintings.[36] However, in 1895, a total of ninety-five appeared. By 1896, the fine arts had become the most visible element in the magazine. This change could be explained by the increasing sophistication of halftone techniques as finer screens produced images with sharper contrast. But this presumes that only technical considerations governed the content of the first years and, I believe, there are other explanations for the change.

Gleeson White stepped down as editor in 1895 to pursue his other publishing ventures, and Holme took over as both editor and publisher.[37] Although Gleeson White continued to contribute important articles to *The Studio* up to his sudden death in October 1898, he was no longer in charge. The subjects that he was particularly interested in promoting: black and white illustration, reproduction, and photography became less prominent. They continued to be covered, but with a much less-intense focus than in the first few years. Between 1893 and 1901, *The Studio* printed approximately 850 paintings, 60 posters, 144 illustrations, and approximately 90 photographs. Most of the photographs and the articles on photography appeared in the first five volumes, when Gleeson White was still exerting editorial influence.

As *The Studio*'s content subtly changed, so did the format through which it was expressed. Each issue now opened with an extended article on an artist, illustrated by large halftones of his or her work and occasionally by photographs of the artist in his or her studio.[38] The vast majority of *The Studio*'s articles were now on artists rather than designers. The magazine also became more conventional in that it established an imaging hierarchy. It did not change its reproduction methods, but photographically reproduced inserts of prints or sketches became a regular feature in the magazine. As in the established magazines, these were printed on thicker paper stock and blind-embossed to enhance their status and make them look like handmade autographic prints.

During his tenure, Gleeson White had promoted modern illustration not just as a valid art form, but as the most vibrant of the contemporary arts. His "Lay Figure" columns form a sustained argument for poster, book, magazine, and newspaper illustrations as the equals of painting. In a piece from "The Editor's Room" in 1895, the writer, most probably White, argued: "To those whose art domain is bounded by picture galleries and *éditions de luxe,* the mere mention of posters, daily newspapers, and current periodicals as new regions wherein it lurks, comes as almost treasonable laxity."[39] Gleeson White tried to open up new areas of design practice as valid domains for the collector. Indeed, poster collecting did become a rage in the 1890s with exhibitions, books, magazines, and dealers all devoted to preserving these ephemeral advertisements. *The Studio*'s launch issue contained one of the first important articles on the subject: Charles Hiatt's "The Collecting of Posters: A New Field for Connoisseurs."[40] However, there was clearly no commercial value in the collecting of contemporary newspapers and magazines. Decorative art, particularly furniture and other domestic and personal objects, for which there was an established market, retained an important place in the magazine. However, despite *The Studio*'s achievement in carving out a space for design, the superior position of fine art was, within a few years, reasserted through the editorial structures of the magazine itself. Indeed, the publication of halftones of paintings in magazines became a crucial aspect in the marketing of artists and their works. In contrast, Joseph Gleeson White's hope that process reproduction might make the everyday and the ephemeral worthy of equal consideration as art did not prevail.

Notes

1. Clive Ashwin, "The Founding of *The Studio* in High Life and Low Life: The Studio and the Fin de Siècle," *Studio International* Special Centenary Number 201.1022/1023 (1993): 5–10, quotation 8.
2. On *The Sketch* and for more details on photomechanical reproduction, see Gerry Beegan, "The Up-to-Date Periodical: Subjectivity, Technology, and Time in the Late-Victorian Press," *Time and Society*, 10 (2001): 113–34.
3. James Parton, writing in the *Atlantic Monthly* in 1869, suggested that reproduction would enhance the value of the original. See Mary Warner Marien, *Photography and its Critics: A Cultural History 1839–1900* (Cambridge: Cambridge University Press, 1997), 178. Walter Benjamin's ideas about mechanical reproduction and the death of the artistic aura have been questioned by many commentators. See Jaquelynne Baas, "Reconsidering Walter Benjamin: The Age of Mechanical Reproduction in Retrospect" in G. P. Weisberg, *The Documented Image: Visions in Art History* (Syracuse, NY: Syracuse University Press, 1987), 339–40. Elizabeth McCauley argues that the copy adds to the aura of the original in a cult of celebrity in *Industrial Madness: Commercial Photography in Paris 1848–1871* (New Haven, CT: Yale University Press, 1994).
4. Hind was the editor of *Pall Mall Budget* for three years, during which time he employed Beardsley as an illustrator. See Haldane Macfall, *Aubrey Beardsley: The Man and His Work* (London: John Lane, 1928). Some of Beardsley's drawings appeared in *The Pall Mall Budget* before *The Studio*'s profile. They had little impact.
5. The French edition featured an insert, which translated the text. Clive Ashwin suggests: "For *The Studio*, the central purpose of art was to make life more comfortable, convenient, and pleasant; not to challenge assumptions about the nature of experience or the facts of perception." Clive Ashwin, "*The Studio* and

Modernism," *Studio International*, 193 (1976): 103–12, quote 104. I think this interpretation misses some of what was genuinely new about *The Studio* and its agenda.

6. Harper stated that, although *The Magazine of Art* and *The Portfolio* used to show good work, by 1894, they were filled with photographs of paintings; especially old paintings because they weren't copyrighted. Charles Harper, *A Practical Handbook of Drawing for Modern Methods of Reproduction* (London: Chapman and Hall, 1894).

7. In the early 1890s, retouching costs ranged from one shilling and six pence per square inch for standard images to seven shillings and six pence per square inch for the retouching of paintings. The reproduction of the block itself cost one shilling and six pence per square inch. *British Printer,* 4 (24) (1891): 7. By 1896, a block that cost ten shillings to engrave might require retouching by hand costing 50 shillings. The elaborate hand engraving on a block in *Harper's* could cost £15. See W. Cheshire, "On the Touching of Half-tone Process Blocks," *Photographic Journal* NS, 20 (7) (1896): 181–6.

8. The photogravures were by the Berlin Photographic Company and by Goupil.

9. On the destabilizing effect of the introduction of photomechanical reproduction into art publishing, see Tom Gretton, "Signs for Labour-Value in Printed Pictures after the Photomechanical Revolution: Mainstream Changes and Extreme Cases Around 1900," *Oxford Art Journal*, 28 (3) (2005): 371–90. Gretton notes the conflicts in slightly later magazines such as *The Connoisseur* (1901–1992), which tried to add artistic value and status to photomechanical images through various strategies involving color printing, special paper stock, and finishing. These tactics attempted to combine the old with the new but, in Gretton's view, were unsuccessful. At this point, as he notes, *The Studio* also was engaging in similar tactics, including the use of tipped-in prints and blind-embossing.

10. *The Magazine of Art* cost one shilling and four pence.

11. "My Note Book," *The Art Amateur*, 23 (3) (1890): 109. This piece testily records a piece in *The Boston Globe* that stated Gleeson White was now the editor of *The Art Amateur*. Montague Marks insisted that he was still the editor, but affirmed: "It is a pleasure to add that Mr. Gleeson White is Mr. Mark's valued associate," Simon Houfe describes *The Art Amateur* as "a low-priced, rather brash production filled with line blocks and half-tones" in his *Fin de Siècle* (London: Barrie and Jenkins, 1997), 54. It appears, on the contrary, to have been a well-informed and progressive magazine, albeit aimed at a middle-class audience.

12. "Some Art Books of the Year," *The Art Journal* NS, 47 (1895): 376.

13. He also was very active in photographic criticism. He wrote for *The Amateur Photographer* and *The Photogram*. In *The Photogram*, as in *The Studio,* he promoted the homoerotic work of Wilhelm von Gloeden. On his involvement with *The Photogram*, see "In Memory of Gleeson White," *The Photogram*, 5 (1898): 371–4.

14. Ibid.

15. Although *The Studio* generally was critical of "academic art," the London art scene in the 1890s cannot be simplified into oppositions between the avant garde and the Academy. There were many connections between the arts and crafts movement, the aesthetic movement, and the Academy. On the complexity of the art scene, see Alan Staley, *The Post-Pre-Raphaelite Print: Etching, Illustration, Reproductive Engraving, and Photography in England in and around the 1860s* (New York: Columbia University Press, 1995).

16. "Artists as Craftsmen No. 1 Sir Frederick Leighton, Bart, P. R. A., as a Modeller in Clay," *The Studio*, I (I) (1893): 27.

17. Ibid., 5–6.

18. For examples, see "An Interview with Charles F. Annesley Voysey, Architect and Designer," *The Studio*, 1 (6) (1893): 231–7; "Afternoons in Studios: A Chat with Mr. Whistler," *The Studio*, 4 (21) (1894): 116–21; and E. B. S., "A Chat with Mr. And Mrs. Nelson Dawson on Enamelling," *The Studio*, 6 (33) (1895): 173–8.

19. The lithograph appeared as a supplement to the May 1893 issue, after which there were no further supplements for that volume. The use of supplements and tipped-in prints was something that became more common in

The Studio from its third volume, but for a while, the use of supplements remained an ad hoc, occasional promotional technique.

20. It was, it must be admitted, not a very good reproduction; the black areas were very mottled. This and two other Beardsley line and wash images were reproduced by a gelatin process which yielded poor results, compared to the line zino images. Beardsley, at first, had been unsure of the requirements of drawing for process reproduction, and in some images used a combination of wash and line that would have been very difficult to reproduce.

21. Frank Brangwyn, "Letters from Artists to Artists—Sketching Grounds. No. 1—Spain," *The Studio*, 1 (1) (1893): 12–14. The tone of this piece also is very much in a new, journalistic mode; taking the form of a chatty, anecdotal letter to a friend about a trip to Spain. This type of material continued to be used in the magazine.

22. Haldane Macfall, *Aubrey Beardsley: The Man and His Work* (London: John Lane, 1928).

23. Ibid., 36.

24. Joseph Pennell, "A New Illustrator: Aubrey Beardsley," *The Studio*, 1 (1) (1893): 14–18, quotation 15–17.

25. See Matthew Sturgis, *Aubrey Beardsley* (London: Harper Collins, 1999), 107–14, on the genesis of the *Morte d'Arthur* project.

26. Much of this was traced in *The Studio* itself. "The Editor's Room New Publications," *The Studio*, 4 (1895): xix, noted that decorative books were surprisingly popular in an age of music halls, trains, impressionism, and capitalism. "The Editor's Room New Publications," *The Studio*, 4 (1895): xxxi, argued that decorative illustration had been creating a sensation with European artists. "The Arts and Crafts Exhibition," *The Studio*, 9 (46) (1897): 262–85, suggested that the large number of books on display at the Exhibition demonstrated the popularity of decorative illustration.

27. Joseph Pennell, "A New Illustrator: Aubrey Beardsley," *The Studio*, 1 (1) (1893): 14–18, quotation 18.

28. "The Lay Figure at Home," *The Studio*, 3 (1894): xxii. In 1895, Charles Hiatt noted Beardsley's immedite influence on Will Bradley in the US, and on illustrators in England. Charles Hiatt, *Picture Posters; A Short History of the Illustrated Placard* (London: Bell, 1895); Paul Greenhalgh, *Art Nouveau 1890–1914* (London: V&A Publications, 2000), 24. Also see Houfe, *Fin de Siècle* (London: Barrie and Jenkins, 1997), 79–81 on the rapid international spread of Beardsley's influence.

29. Gleeson White contributed a monthly column "The Lay Figure Speaks," later retitled "The Lay Figure at Home," that dealt with current art topics in short paragraphs. The column invariably commented on illustration and reproduction. A selection of other important articles from the early volumes include: "Drawing for Reproduction: Outline Work and Tint Boards," *The Studio*, 1 (2) (1893): 65–72; Charles Harper, "Drawing for Reproduction by Process: Lithographic Chalk on Various Papers," *The Studio*, 2 (9) (1893): 99–100; "New Publications," *The Studio*, 2 (10) (1894): 143–6, which is a criticism of the use of wood engravings in G. H. Boughton's *Rip Van Winkle* illustrations, "Some Recent Volumes on the Printed Book and its Decoration," *The Studio*, 2 (10) (1894): 140–2; "Afternoons in Studios: A Chat with Mr. G. H. Boughton, ARA," *The Studio*, 3 (17) (1894): 131–6; Joseph Gleeson White, "Decorative Illustration, with Especial Reference to the Work of Mr. Paton Wilson," *The Studio*, 3 (18) (1894): 182–4; review of Henry Blackburn's *The Art of Illustration* in "The Editor's Room: New Publications," *The Studio*, 3 (1894): xxxiv; and J. M. Buflock, "Charles Dana Gibson," *The Studio*, 8 (40) (1896): 75–80. It also is worth noting that many of *The Studio*'s competitions, which were a popular feature of the magazine in its first decade, were for drawings reproduced by photomechanical process. On the competitions, see Barbara Morris, "*The Studio* Prize Competitions: The Early Years 1893–1900" in "High Life and Low Life: The Studio and the Fin de Siècle," *Studio International*, 201 (1022/1023) (1993): 80–4.

30. See "Reviews of Recent Publications," *The Studio*, 6 (34) (1896): 258, on Lucien Pissaro's *The Queen of the Fishes*. On wood engraving as an expressive art form rather than a reproduction method, sea "Reviews of

Recent Publications," *The Studio*, 14 (63) (1898): 10–16, review of A. L. Baldry. *The Future of Wood Engraving,* Gabriel Mourey, "Auguste Lepère, A French Wood Engraver," *The Studio*, 12 (57) (1897): 143–55; and Joseph Gleeson White. "The Coloured Prints of Mr. W. P. Nicholson," *Studio*, 12 (57) (1897): 177–83.

31. Joseph Gleeson White, "Photographic Portraiture: An Interview with Mr. H. H. Hay Cameron," *The Studio*, 2 (8) (1893): 84–9, quotation 89.

32. Joseph Gleeson White, "The National Competition: South Kensington," *The Studio*, 8 (42) (1896): 224–37, quotation 224.

33. "The Work of Miss Ethel Reed," *The Studio*, 10 (50) (1897): 230–6.

34. Trevor Fawcett suggests that the opportunities that cheaper reproduction and printing opened up led to a "visual anarchy" in most of the art magazines of the time. Across Europe, from *Jegend* to *The Studio*, to *The Connoisseur*, they became "overfilled with disparate illustrations, graphic and photographic, coloured and plain, originals and reproductions." Trevor Fawcett and Clive Phillpot, *The Art Press: Two Centuries of Art Magazines* (London: The Art Book Company, 1976), 57.

35. An example of this approach is an article on W. Dendy Sadler's sentimental "Georgian" genre pictures of monks and coaching inns. This is one of the first occasions on which *The Magazine of Art* featured a full-page reproduction of a painting by halftone rather than wood engraving: "The Widow's Birthday" facing page 267. But the magazine also illustrated the article with a full-page wood engraving of "A Hunting Morn" facing page 268. To add to the variety. "The Top of the Hill" facing page 272 is an etching printed on thicker stock. *The Magazine of Art* (1896): 265–73.

36. There are four wall paintings reproduced in Volume 1, and only three paintings reproduced in Volume 2.

37. These projects were more adventurous than *The Studio*. One of his major achievements was *The Pageant,* a beautifully illustrated and designed book that was published as an annual in 1896 and 1897. Contributors included Verlaine, Beerbohm, Whistler, Millais, Watts, Burne Jones, Housman, and Shannon. *The Magazine of Art* described it as "a genuine delight to those who take a vivid interest in the most modern manifestations of art and literature." *The Magazine of Art*, 20 (Nov. 1896–April 1897): 341. Gleeson White had been very involved with key members of *fin de siècle* homosexual culture from early in the decade including Charles Kains Jackson, Henry Scott Tuke, and Frederick Rolfe. On the homosexual content of *The Pageant,* see Laurel Brake, "Gay Discourse" and "The Artist and Journal of Home Culture" in *Nineteenth Century Media and the Construction of Identities*, Laurel Brake et al., eds. (Basingstoke, UK: Palgrave, 2000), 271–91. In 1898 on a long-planned trip to Italy with members of the Art Workers' Guild, Gleeson White caught typhoid. A couple of weeks after his return to London, he died on October 19 at the age of 47. His activities as a writer, editor, designer, and publisher had not been financially rewarding; the profits from the sale of his bookshop had dwindled, and his estate yielded only a few thousand pounds. His friends got together to contribute to a fund to support his widow and children. A glowing eulogy in *The Studio* praised him as hugely knowledgeable, energetic, and influential on an international scale. "His death not only removes a man of conspicuous importance in artistic circles, but deprives numerous branches of aesthetic energy of their controlling spirit and their active leader." "The Late Mr. Gleeson White," *The Studio*, 15 (68) (1898): 141.

38. The Index to the first twenty-one volumes listed monographs on two architects, nineteen illustrators and printmakers, fifteen designers, and eighty-four painters and sculptors. The painters began to dominate from volume 7 onwards. *The Studio* included two women painters in its lead articles on individual artists: Evelyn De Morgan and Marianne Stokes. Walter Shaw Sparrow, "The Art of Mrs. William De Morgan," *The Studio*, 19 (86) (1900): 221–32 and Harriet Ford, "The Work of Mrs. Adrian Stokes," *The Studio*, 19 (85) (1900): 149–56. An earlier piece on Elizabeth Stanhope Forbes showed her in her studio and also painting outdoors. E.B.S., "The Paintings and Etchings of Elizabeth Stanhope Forbes," *The Studio*, 4 (249) (1895): 186–92. Luise Hagen, "Lady

Artists in Germany," *The Studio*, 13 (60) (1898): 91–9, notes the prejudice against women artists in Germany, and records work by Bertha Wegmann and Jenna Bauck. Women were featured more often as designers and illustrators than as painters. Examples include: "The Work of Miss Ethel Reed," *The Studio*, 10 (50) (1897): 230–6; E. B. S., "Eleanor F. Brickdale, Designer and Illustrator," *The Studio*, 13 (60) (1898): 103–8; and Walter Shaw Sparrow, "Some Drawings by Mrs. Farmiloe," *The Studio*, 18 (81) (1899): 172–9. Women were particularly well represented in the discussions and surveys of decorative design. Gleeson White's article on The National Competition South Kensington illustrated twelve pieces by women students and five by men. Gleeson White, "The National Competition South Kensington, 1895," *The Studio*, 6 (31) (1895): 42–50. On the complexities of gender roles in the arts and crafts movement, see Anthea Callen, "Sexual Divisions of Labour in the Arts and Crafts Movement," 151–64, and also Lynne Walker, "The Arts and Crafts Alternative," 165–73, in *A View from the Interior Women and Design*, Judy Attfield and Pat Kirkham, eds. (London: The Women's Press, 1995).

39. "The Editor's Room New Publications," *The Studio*, 4 (1895): xvii. Not only are the sentiments very much in line with Gleeson White's, the piece was a review of a book by Pennell, with whom Gleeson White worked closely on a number of publishing projects.

40. Charles Hiatt, "The Collecting of Posters: A New Field for Connoisseurs," *The Studio*, 1 (1) (1893): 61–4. W. S. Rogers in *The Book of the Poster* (London: Greening and Co., 1901) claimed that Gleeson White was, in fact, the author of the article, and noted the importance of *The Studio* in focusing attention on posters. Rogers recorded Gleeson White's involvement in the first English poster exhibitions at the Royal Aquarium in 1895 and 1896. Gleeson White also lectured on posters in a series of talks at the Bolt Court School in 1896, which featured the key figures in contemporary printing and illustration: William Morris, Joseph Pennell, T. R. Way, Cobden Sanderson, and Emery Walker.

Chapter 1.1.4

Narrative problems of graphic design history

Victor Margolin

Narrativity becomes a problem only when we wish to give real events the form of a story.[1]

Introduction

In recent years scholars have devoted considerable attention to the study of narrative structures in history and fiction.[2] Central to their concerns are several key issues: notably what constitutes a narrative as opposed to other forms of temporal sequencing of actions and events and how a narrative makes claims to being true or fictive. Regarding the first issue, Hayden White has identified three kinds of historical representation: the annals, the chronicle and history itself. Of these, he argues, only history has the potential to achieve narrative closure.[3] By organizing our accounts of the past into stories, we attempt to "have real events display the coherence, integrity, fullness, and closure of an image of life that is and can only be imaginary."[4] While some theorists like White regard history as a narrative that refers to events outside itself, others, particularly those who define themselves as post-modernists, refuse to make a distinction between fact and fiction and, in effect, treat all history as fiction.[5] That is not the position I will take in this essay, but I mention it to acknowledge a climate in which the idea of history as objective reality is heavily contested.

The distinction that White makes between the messiness of events and the order that historians seek to impose on them is important because it denaturalizes the narrative itself and obliges us to interpret the historian's strategy as a *particular* attempt to order events rather than recognize the historical work as an objective account of the past. This brings to the fore the necessity of including an analysis of the historian's method in the discussion of a work of history, whether or not that method has been made explicit.

The problem of method in the construction of narratives is particularly acute in the field of design history which, since Nikolaus Pevsner's proto-history of design, *Pioneers of the Modern Movement* was

First published in *Visible Language*, 28 (3) (Spring 1994): 233–43. © Victor Margolin.

first published in 1936, has been highly charged with moral judgments that have conditioned the choices of subject matter and the narrative strategies historians have employed.[6] Adrian Forty, for example, in a response to an article I published on the relation of design history to design studies, claimed that the judgment of quality in design is central to the enterprise of design history.[7]

I do not believe that quality is the primary concern although it raises necessary questions about how different people give value to products. However, the question of what design history is about has never been thoroughly addressed or debated, which has resulted in considerable confusion in the field, a condition which the move to establish graphic design as a separate subject area of design history has been unable to escape.[8]

Issues in graphic design history

The first book on graphic design history to gain widespread recognition was Philip Meggs's *A History of Graphic Design*, first published by Van Nostrand Reinhold in 1983 and then in a revised and expanded edition in 1992. It has been extensively used as a text in design history courses and includes a wide range of material. In 1988, Enric Satué, a graphic designer in Barcelona, published *El Diseño Gráfico: Desde los Orígenes hasta Nuestros Días (Graphic Design: From Its Origins until Today)*, which appeared originally as a series of articles in the Spanish design magazine *On*. The most recent book on the topic is Richard Hollis's *Graphic Design: A Concise History*.[9] In addition, there have been supplementary works such as *Thirty Centuries of Graphic Design: An Illustrated Survey* by James Craig and Bruce Barton, which appeared in 1987, and *The Thames and Hudson Encyclopedia of Graphic Design + Designers* by Alan and Isabella Livingston, published in 1992.[10] We have as well various chronicles and histories of graphic design in particular countries such as *Visual Design: 50 Anni di Produzione in Italia*, by Giancarlo Iliprandi, Alberto Marangoni, Franco Origoni, and Anty Pansera; *The Graphic Spirit of Japan* by Richard S. Thornton; *Chinese Graphic Design in the Twentieth Century*, by Scott Minick and Jiao Ping; and *Graphic Design in America: A Visual Language History*, the catalog of the exhibition curated by Mildred Friedman at the Walker Art Center in 1989.[11]

While this plethora of publications is commendable for the attention it brings to the subject of graphic design, it has not led to any clarification of how graphic design has been constituted by the respective authors nor has it marked a satisfactory course for the fuller development of a narrative structure that can begin to explain graphic design as a practice. The term "graphic design," itself as it as it is applied in most books on the subject remains problematic. W.A. Dwiggins was the first to call himself a graphic designer, a title he used to characterize a practice that consisted primarily of typography and book design.[12] The term was subsequently adopted, beginning sometime after World War II, to replace such appellations as "commercial art" and "typographic art."

Some authors have used "graphic design" to account for all attempts to communicate with graphic devices since the beginning of human settlements. Writing in 1985 in a special issue of the *AIGA Journal of Graphic Design* on the topic of graphic design history, Philip Meggs noted the disagreement among experts on the historical scope of the subject:

Some advocate the short-sighted view and believe that graphic design is a new activity, born of the industrial revolution. Others advocate a farsighted view, believing the essence of graphic design is giving visual form to human communications, an activity which has a distinguished ancestry dating to the medieval manuscript and early printers of the Renaissance.[13]

When one considers Meggs's own book, it is clear that he has chosen the "farsighted view," in that he identifies the cave paintings of Lascaux as the beginning of a sequence that ultimately connects with the contemporary posters of April Greiman. Likewise, Craig and Barton argue in the introduction to their illustrated survey that:

Graphic design—or visual communication—began in prehistoric times and has been practiced over the centuries by artisans, scribes, printers, commercial artists, and even fine artists.[14]

Enric Satué takes a similarly long view, beginning his own narrative with an account of "graphic design in antiquity." The problem with the comprehensive accounts of graphic design history that Meggs, Craig and Barton, and Satué propose is that they assert a continuity among objects and actions that are in reality discontinuous. This makes it difficult, if not impossible, to disentangle the separate strands of visual communication practice and write a more complex account of the influence they have had on one another. To do so is to begin from a different position than those in the above mentioned texts. It means looking far more closely at the activity of designing as a way of understanding the specific moves by which designers expand the boundaries of practice. This strategy is addressed by Richard Hollis in the introduction to his history of graphic design:

Visual communication in its widest sense has a long history . . . As a profession, graphic design has existed only since the middle of the twentieth century; until then, advertisers and their agents used the services provided by "commercial artists."[15]

Hollis begins his own narrative in the 1890s with a discussion of the illustrated poster. His distinction between graphic design and other practices that produce visual communication is helpful in that it makes possible the tracing of separate strands of practice that sometimes intertwine within a professional category but also have their own trajectories.[16] By maintaining the separation, we can then look more deeply at the distinctive discourses within each practice such as advertising, illustration or typography and understand better how they are contextualized and recontextualized into new narratives.[17]

For example, the graphic projects of the poets and artists of the early twentieth-century avant-garde are usually incorporated within the history of graphic design even though they were frequently produced outside the client-practitioner relationship that normally characterizes professional design activity. The innovations of syntax and mixtures of typefaces such as we see in the futurist poet Filippo Tommaso Marinetti's book of visual poems *Parole in libertà* (Figure 1.1) were integral components of specific poetic texts which he wrote, just as the visual forms of concrete poems written by others years later were to be.

Similarly El Lissitzky's small book *Of Two Squares* originated as an argument for a new reading strategy which had implications in Lissitzky's thinking that went far beyond the formal order of the book page. When the book was assimilated into the discourse of the new typography by Jan Tschichold in 1925, it was recontextualized and its original meaning was altered from a new way to think about

Figure 1.1 *Parole in Liberta*. © 1915. Designer: Phillipo Marinetti. Courtesy of Beinecke Library.

reading to an argument for a modern design formalism. These shifts of intention and context tend to be suppressed when diverse graphic products are drawn together within an assimilationist narrative based on a theme such as modernity or innovation.

Meggs, looking farther into the past than the moment of the modernist avant-garde, writes about graphic design of the Renaissance and of the rococo era, thus blurring the various specialized strands of professional practice that, when delineated separately, form a constellation of distinct activities rather than a single generic one. In his article previously cited, Meggs identified several factors that have contributed to an interest in graphic design history. Among them is "the graphic design discipline's quest for professional status and recognition as an important activity requiring specialized knowledge, skill, and even a measure of wisdom."[18] While tracing graphic design's roots back to the printers and typographers of the Renaissance is an attempt to provide greater cultural legitimacy for the practice of graphic design, it also obscures the cultural and technical distinctions between the different practices such as printing, typography and advertising.

Another problem is the conflation of graphic design and visual communication as we see in the introduction by Craig and Barton. Graphic design is a specific professional practice, while visual communication denotes a fundamental activity of visual representation (I would include here coded body language and gestures as well as artifacts) in which everyone engages. Visual communication is a larger category than graphic design, which it includes. A history of visual communication also suggests a completely different narrative strategy from a history of graphic design. The former rightly begins with the cave paintings of Lascaux and Altamira and continues up to the present development of home multimedia systems. The emphasis in a history of visual communication is inherently sociological and does not exclude anyone on professional grounds. While such a history may focus as well on the semantic issues of how things transmit communicative intentions, its principal subject matter is the act of communicating itself.[19]

Conversely, if we are to adhere more strictly to the meaning of "graphic design" as a description of professional practice, we are obliged to consider the way such practice has been institutionalized in order to include some people and exclude others. This would certainly establish subject matter boundaries that leave out vernacular material done by non-professionals whose talents are considered inferior to those of professionals.[20] We would also have to address the ways that different forms of practice have been professionalized. Are typographers, calligraphers, art directors and illustrators to be considered graphic designers, even when they have their own societies, exhibitions, publications and the like?[21] Unless a history of graphic design honors the distinctions among these practices, there is no way of delineating how the profession has developed socially. Ironically, the cultural identity of the graphic designer will be strengthened more through such an approach than by conflating graphic design with all the other activities that produce visual communication.

Following the latter strategy, the texts by Meggs and Craig and Barton, in particular, result neither in a history of graphic design as a professional activity nor in a history of visual communication as an explanation of human communicative acts. Instead, they mystify the differences between the two, and suppress the distinctions among the images they incorporate, which range from Egyptian hieroglyphs to Ohrbach's advertisements.

Narrative strategies of graphic design history texts

We can now turn to the three major texts by Meggs, Satué and Hollis to better understand how they tell the story of graphic design. We should first note the different emphases that the authors give to the pre-industrial, industrial and post-industrial periods. Meggs makes the strongest argument for a continuity between these, giving the lengthiest account of the pre-industrial era. He establishes analogies between works in earlier and later periods on the basis of such characteristics as formal arrangement, and unifies communicative activities in different periods by attributing to them such common qualities as "genius" and "expressivity."[22] Satué moves in three brief chapters to the beginning of the nineteenth century while Hollis, as mentioned earlier, begins his history with the 1890s.[23] Regarding the material included for the nineteenth and twentieth centuries, the three authors have much in common, particularly in the sections that begin with the Arts and Crafts Movement and then continue through the European avant-gardes, the new typography in Germany, wartime propaganda, the émigré designers in America and the subsequent emergence of an American mass communications style, corporate identity, Swiss typography and its revisions, European pictorial posters and protest design of the 1960s.

It is worth noting here that all the authors were trained as graphic designers and share similar values about the canon of their profession. This canon has neither developed randomly nor was it institutionalized the way a literary canon was in academia. Rather it resulted from a selection process that has celebrated noteworthy designs in professional magazines such as *Gebrauschgrafik, Graphis* and *Print* as well as in numerous picture books and occasional museum exhibitions.[24] An important factor in the canonization of graphic design pieces is the visual satisfaction they give to the trained graphic designer. As the three books under discussion show, there is a considerable consensus among the authors regarding the visual quality of the work they include. What is generally missing, however, are accounts of work by lesser known designers who played important roles in the development of the profession. I think here of Fritz Ehmke in Germany or Oswald Cooper in the United States. Ehmke was important because he wanted to preserve design traditions at a moment when Jan Tschichold and others were promoting the new typography. In Chicago, Cooper was the best of the lettering and layout men who preceded the emergence of graphic design as we have come to know it.

One significant difference among Meggs, Satué and Hollis is the varying amount of attention they give to geographic areas outside the European and American mainstream.[25] Satué is considerably more aware than either of the other two authors of how graphic design developed in the Spanish-speaking countries as well as in Brazil. He devotes almost one hundred pages to this material while Meggs dedicates four pages to "The Third World Poster", a section that mainly refers to Cuban posters of the 1960s with a brief mention of posters in Nicaragua, South Africa and the Middle East. Hollis, by contrast, devotes a little less than two pages to Cuban posters in a section entitled "Psychedelia, Protest and New Techniques of the Late 1960s." In the texts of Meggs and Hollis, Japanese graphic design is discussed briefly, but the authors refer only to postwar activity. Satué does not talk about Japan at all. None of the authors make any reference to China or other Asian countries nor do they mention graphic design or vernacular visual communication in Africa.[26]

Although Meggs presents typographers such as Baskerville, Fournier and Bodoni, who worked in the eighteenth century, as geniuses, typography as a practice becomes merged with other design activities once he reaches the twentieth century, where he neglects, as do the other two authors, some of the most prominent modern typographers such as Victor Hammer, Jan van Krimpen, Giovanni Mardersteig and Robert Hunter Middleton.[27]

The authors' relation to other visual practices such as advertising vary somewhat. According to Hollis:

> However effective, such work [Hollis refers here to the early 20th-century German posters of Bernhard, Erdt, Gipkins, and Hohlwein] belongs to a history of advertising. Only when advertising has a single visual concept, as it developed in the United States in the 1950s . . . does it have a significant place in the history of graphic design.[28]

Meggs, by contrast, does not even identify these posters as advertising artifacts. He accounts for them in terms of a formal style which he calls "pictorial modernism." Satué too treats this work as exemplary of a modern visual style.

Of the three authors, Hollis is most attentive to the differences among visual practices, making reference, for example, to the calligraphic training of Edward Johnston, who designed an alphabet for the London Underground. He also mentions the contribution art directors in America made to the emergence of graphic design as a profession. At the same time he removes noteworthy practitioners, firms and work from the discourses in which their practice was embedded—such as the discourse of advertising—and inserts them into a different narrative. Hence, we encounter the "new advertising," not as a response to the limits of the old advertising, but as a contribution to the development of a sophisticated visual sensibility within the graphic design profession.

While none of the authors writes an exclusively connoisseurist history, each is particularly attentive to visual quality. This plays an important role in the construction of their stories, which are propelled along by changes in the look and form of designs as well as by other factors. I make this observation not to espouse a social history of graphic design that subordinates discussions of form to arguments about social meaning, but to stress that describing how artifacts look does not sufficiently address the question of why they look as they do. This can only be answered by extracting them from narratives that draw them together for the purpose of creating a tradition of innovation that never existed. The artifacts must be reinserted in the various discourses within which they originated—whether those be related to art, advertising, typography or printing—and then related in new ways.

Conclusion

What then might a history of graphic design that respected the varied discursive locations of visual design activity be like? It would preserve many elements of the narrative sequences established by Meggs, Satué and Hollis, but it would be more attentive to a close reading of professional practices in order to discriminate between the different types of work. As a result, we would understand better how graphic design practice has been shaped by borrowings and appropriations from other discourses instead of seeing it as a single strand of activity that embraces a multiplicity of things. By recognizing the many routes into graphic design from other fields and practices, we can learn to see it as more differentiated than we have previously acknowledged it to be. This will enable us to better relate emerging fields of endeavor such as information design, interface design and environmental graphics to what has come before.[29]

Clearly, the history of graphic design does not follow a neat linear path that can be characterized by a unifying theme such as innovation, excellence or modernity. Because there have been no shared standards that define professional development, nor has there been a common knowledge base to ground a definition of what graphic design is, its development has been largely intuitive and does not conform to a singular set of principles shared by all designers. While the scope of what we today call graphic design has considerably expanded from what it once was, it has not done so in any singular way.[30] Frequently individual designers have simply moved into new areas of practice and are then followed by others.

Not all graphic designers work on the same kinds of projects. Some specialize in posters and function like artists. Others are involved with strategic planning and draw more on management skills. And some designers specialize in information graphics which requires a strong knowledge of social science.[31] What a history of graphic design should explain is how the various activities that fall within the construct of graphic design practice are differentiated. It should acknowledge the tension that arises from the attempt to hold these activities together through a discourse of professional unity while designers continue to move in new directions. A recognition of this tension will ultimately teach us much more about graphic design and its development than the attempt to create a falsely concordant narrative of graphic design history.

Notes

1. White, Hayden, 1980, "The Value of Narrativity in the Representation of Reality," *Critical Inquiry*, 7 (1) (Autumn): 8.
2. The study of narrative forms is a distinct field of research called narratology. A useful introduction is David Carrier's article "On Narratology," in *Philosophy and Literature*, 8 (1): 32–42. For a full account of the subject, see Mieke Bal, *Narratology: Introduction to the Theory of* Narrative, translated by Christine van Boheemen. Toronto: University of Toronto Press, 1985.
3. White, "The Value of Narrativity . . .," 9.
4. White, "The Value of Narrativity . . .," 27.
5. Linda Hutcheon provides an account of this position in *The Politics of Postmodernism*, London and New York: Routledge, 1989. See particularly the chapter entitled "Representing the Past."
6. Pevsner, Nikolaus, 1936, *Pioneers of the Modern Movement from William Morris to Walter Gropius*, London: Faber & Faber. The book was subsequently republished in several revised editions as *Pioneers of Modern Design from William Morris to Walter Gropius*.
7. Forty, Adrian, 1993, "A Reply to Victor Margolin," *Journal of Design History*, 6 (2): 131–2. My article, "Design History or Design Studies: Subject Matter and Methods" was published in *Design Studies*, 13 (2): 104–16.
8. Arguments for a separate history of graphic design have been voiced for more than a decade. See Steven Heller, "Towards an Historical Perspective,' AIGA *Journal of Graphic Design*, 2 (4): 5, the special issue of the Journal, entitled "The History of Graphic Design: Charting a Course." Steven Heller, editor. AIGA *Journal of Graphic Design*, 3 (4) and Steven Heller, "Yes, Virginia, There is a Graphic Design History," AIGA *Journal of Graphic Design*, 10 (1): 4.

9. Meggs, Philip B., 1992, *A History of Graphic Design*, 2nd edn. New York: Van Nostrand Reinhold; Satué, Enric, 1988, *El Diseño Gráfico: Desde los Orígenes hasta Nuestros Días*,, Madrid: Alianza Editorial; and Hollis, Richard. 1994. *Graphic Design: A Concise History*, London and New York: Thames and Hudson. The books by Meggs, Satué and Hollis were preceded by several volumes that were essentially visual chronicles such as Karl Gerstner and Marcus Kutter, *die Neue Graphik*, Teufen: Arthur Niggli, 1959, and Josef Müller-Brockmann, *A History of Visual Commuunication*, Teufen: Arthur Niggli, 1971. A brief illustrated survey of contemporary graphic design is Keith Murgatroyd's, *Modern Graphics*, London and New York: Vista/Dutton, 1969.

10. Varying numbers of entries on graphic designers and firms have been included in other reference works such as *Contemporary Designers, The Conran Directory of Design*, and *The Thames and Hudson Encyclopedia of 20th Century Design and Designers*.

11. A shorter account of American graphic design history can be found in the 50th anniversary issue of *Print* magazine (November/December 1969), edited by Steven Heller with articles on each decade from the 1940s to the 1980s by different authors.

12. Shaw, Paul, 1984, "Tradition and Innovation: The Design Work of William Addison Dwiggins," *Design Issues*, 1 (2): 26.

13. Meggs, Philip B., 1985, "Design History: Discipline or Anarchy?" AIGA *Journal of Graphic Design*, 3 (4): 2.

14. Craig, James and Bruce Barton, 1987, *Thirty Centuries of Graphic Design: An Illustrated Survey*, New York: Watson-Guptill, 9.

15. Richard Hollis, *Graphic Design: A Concise History*, 7.

16. However, the problem with writing a progressive narrative that identifies illustrated posters as precursors for more conceptual design work is that it then makes the posters less accessible for other histories such as a history of illustration which does not have a similarly progressive character.

17. Howard Lethalin provides an excellent model for how separate strands of design practice might be researched in his article "The Archeology of the Art Director? Some Examples of Art Direction in Mid-Nineteenth-Century British Publishing," *Journal of Design History*, 6 (4): 229–46.

18. Meggs, Philip B., "Design History: Discipline or Anarchy?", 2.

19. An excellent example of a sociological approach to the history of communication is J. L. Aranguren, *Human Communication*, New York and Toronto: McGraw-Hill, 1967 (World University Library). Aranguren discusses both linguistic and visual communication as well as transmission instruments.

20. This does not preclude work that adheres to institutional standards of quality being considered within the canon even if its makers are not trained professionals. But it does exclude work that can be easily defined as vernacular because of its difference from work by professionals. In fact, graphic design is not a profession with a body of technical knowledge that can easily exclude non-professionals. If anything, the proliferation of desktop software makes it more and more possible for non-professionals to approximate, or at least appear to approximate, professional standards.

21. Specialized histories of these practices were among the building blocks that preceded Meggs's own more comprehensive history. Books by those engaged with typography such as Frederic Goudy's *Typologia*, Daniel Berkeley Updike's *Printing Types: Their History, Forms, and Use*, or Stanley Morison's *A Tally of Types* provide coherent accounts of how typographic design developed and also assert standards of quality. Frank Presbry's pioneering work *The History and Development of Advertising* is an account of professional advertising practice that describes the changes which led from selling space to comprehensive campaigns.

22. Thus Meggs applies the term "Spanish pictorial expressionism" to Spanish manuscripts of the tenth century which features letter-forms as pictorial objects, while "American typographic expressionism" refers to New York graphic design of the 1950s and 1960s.

23. For a discussion of Hollis's thoughts on graphic design and how they affected the writing of his book, see Robin Kinross's "Conversation with Richard Hollis on Graphic Design History," *Journal of Design History*, 5 (1): 73–90.

24. Martha Scotford discusses the problems of canonization in graphic design history in her article "Is There a Canon of Graphic Design History?" in *AIGA Journal of Graphic Design*, 9 (2): 3–5, 13. Among the points she makes is that women are noticeably lacking in the canon. This subject sorely needs more attention.

25. I refer specifically to American rather than North American work. Although Canada has a rich history of graphic design, including some outstanding designers in the postwar era, none of the authors mention it as a distinct site of graphic design practice. An excellent presentation on the history of graphic design in Canada was made by Peter Bartl at the ICOGRADA (International Council of Graphic Design Associations) Congress in Dublin in 1983.

26. See *Dialogue on Graphic Design Problems in Africa*, edited by Haig David-West, London: ICOGRADA, 1983. This publication reports on a 1982 conference held in Port Harcourt, Nigeria under the sponsorship of ICOGRADA.

27. This obscuring of the typographic tradition and the lack of sufficient recognition for twentieth-century typographers has been rectified to a large degree by the recent publication of Robin Kinross's *Modern Typography: An Essay in Critical History*, London: Hyphen Press, 1992.

28. Richard Hollis, *Graphic Design: A Concise History*, 31.

29. Gui Bonsiepe has recently proposed that a new designation, *information designer*, would more appropriately characterize the designer's ability to work in the emerging information environment. See his article "A Step Toward the Reinvention of Graphic Design," in *Design Issues*, 10 (1): 47–52.

30. Some designers and design educators now prefer the term "communication design."

31. For a critique of graphic design as an art-based profession, see Jorge Frascara, "Graphic Design: Fine Art or Social Science?" in *Design Issues*, 5 (1): 18–29. In this article, Frascara proposes to shift the definition of quality from the way things look to their effect on the intended audience.

Chapter 1.1.5

Elementary school

J. Abbott Miller

Once upon a time there was a school not far from the Black Forest. . . . The Bauhaus has become the opening chapter to the narrative of twentieth-century design. It is the most widely known, discussed, published, imitated, collected, exhibited, and cathected aspect of modern graphic, industrial, and architectural design. Its status as a founding moment of design has been strengthened by the adoption of its methods and ideals in schools throughout the world. The Bauhaus has taken on mythic proportions as an originary moment of the avant-garde, a moment when a fundamental grammar of the visual was unearthed from the debris of historicism and traditional forms. A central element of this "grammar" was—and continues to be ▲ ■ ● (see Figure 1.2). The repetition of this trio of basic forms and primary colors in the work of Bauhaus teachers and students evidences the school's interest in abstraction and its focus on those aspects of the visual which could be described as elementary, irreducible, essential, foundational, and originary. The understanding of the Bauhaus as a point of origin is an effect of its reception within the history of art and design, as well as a reflection of its own ideals: Johannes Itten, who taught in the early years of the school, used unconventional teaching methods, hoping to "unlearn" students and return them to a state of innocence, a point of origin from which true learning could begin. This interest in the clean slate, the first moment, is evident in Wassily Kandinsky's *Point and Line to Plane*: "We must at the outset distinguish basic elements from other elements, viz.—elements without which a work . . . cannot even come into existence."[1] From its inception, the Bauhaus was premised on the notion of a *return* to origins in hope of discovering a lost unity. The school's program, written by Walter Gropius in 1919, charted the institution's mission of recovery: "Today, the arts exist in isolation, from which they can be rescued only through the conscious, co-operative effort of all craftsmen. . . . The ultimate, if distant, aim of the Bauhaus is the unified work of art . . . . "[2] A woodcut of a Gothic cathedral graces the cover of Gropius's manifesto, invoking the historical moment when he felt this prior unity, fullness, and harmony had once been achieved.

For Gropius, this unity would be recovered through training that would develop within students a generalized competence in crafts, forming an "indispensable basis for all artistic production." This agenda was given institutional form in the *Vorkurs*, or Basic Course, which departed from traditional academies by erasing the boundaries between craft instruction and fine art training. The Basic Course

First published in *The ABC's of Bauhaus: The Bauhaus and Design Theory*, eds. Ellen Lupton and J. Abbott Miller, New York: Princeton Architectural Press (2000), 40–1. © J. Abbott Miller.

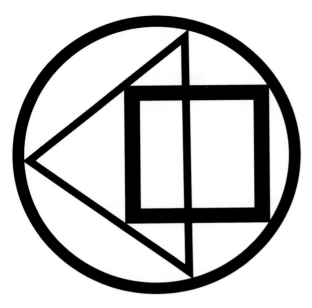

Figure 1.2 Symbol for Bauhaus Press (1923). Designer: László Moholy-Nagy. The mark combines the circle, square, and triangle into an arrow-like form. The design was used on stationery and advertising for the Bauhaus Press publications.

was a general introduction to composition, color, materials, and three-dimensional form that familiarized students with techniques, concepts, and formal relationships considered *fundamental* to all visual expression, whether it be sculpture, metal work, painting, or lettering. The Basic Course developed an abstract and *abstracting* visual language that would provide a theoretical and practical basis for *any* artistic endeavor. Since it was seen as the basis for all further development, the course aimed to strip away particularities in favor of discovering fundamental truths operating in the visual world. Thus ▲ ■ ● were paradigmatic of the formal laws considered to underlie all visual expression.

While the concept of a Basic Course is one of the greatest legacies of the Bauhaus, it was a notion that had many precedents in progressive educational reforms of the nineteenth-century, particularly in the *kindergarten,* as developed by its founder, Friedrich Froebel (1782–1852).[3] Froebel's greatest influence was the Swiss educator Heinrich Pestalozzi (1746–1827), whose concept of sensory education was an application of the Enlightenment ideals set forth by Jean-Jacques Rousseau (1712–1778). Rousseau's *Emile* (1762) argued that education is the cultivation of inherent faculties, rather than the imposition of knowledge. Taking this path, Pestalozzi recast the teacher as a protective figure who follows and stimulates the child's inherent intelligence. Pestalozzi sought a model of education that would build upon an evolving mastery of concepts and skills. Educational reformers often used the metaphor of the child as a "seed": education has the role of nurturing the seed to fruition. The "child garden" (*kindergarten*) was metaphorical as well as literal: early in his career as a teacher, Froebel discovered the importance of play in education, and made gardening a central part of his pedagogy. He also privileged drawing as a special mode of cognition.

Drawing had been a central part of educational reform since the publication of Pestalozzi's widely influential *ABC's of Anschauung*,[4] written with Christoph Buss in 1803. This manual established drawing—which carried connotations of a leisurely, aristocratic pursuit—as a legitimate area of children's education. Pestalozzi, Froebel, and others in German-speaking Europe at this time championed drawing as a form of *writing* parallel to alphabetic writing. Pestalozzi's *ABC* initiated the nineteenth-century interest in "pedagogical drawing," distinguished from drawing taught in the academy tradition by the fact that it begins at an early age and is conducted through exercises taught simultaneously to a group.[5] Pestalozzi's drawing method was based on his belief that "the square was the foundation of all forms, and that the drawing method should be based upon the division of squares and curves into parts" (Ashwin 1981: 56). Through a series of synchronized, repetitive exercises, the teacher would demonstrate the figure to be drawn, name it, and then question the child about its form. After drawing the form, the child was asked to locate it within the environment. The repertoire of forms was based on a spare grammar of straight lines, diagonals, and curves. As historian Clive Ashwin notes, Pestalozzi sought to "break down the complexity of nature into its constituent forms . . . to identify and 'elementarise' the underlying geometry of the visual world in a way which would make it assimilable for the child" (Ashwin 1981: 16).

Another drawing method based on the idea of creating a reductive graphic code, an "alphabet" for drawing, was published in 1821 by Johannes Ramsauer, one of Pestalozzi's colleagues. Ramsauer's *Drawing Tutor* is premised on the idea of *Hauptformen* (main forms), that "represent the abstracted essence of physical objects" (Ashwin 1981: 43). His typology consists of three main forms: objects of rest (further divided into standing versus lying objects), objects of movement (including the directional forms of arrows, swinging objects like wheels, and turning objects such as rising smoke), and objects which combine movement and rest (including floating forms such as a boat on the water, and hanging forms such as a tree branch). Each of the "main forms" is given a linear equivalent, an abstracted sign describing an object's "essential" character.

The method of pedagogical drawing adopted by Froebel drew upon two earlier methods called *Stygmographie* (dot drawing) and *Netzzeichnen* (net drawing). Dot drawing consisted of a grid of dots on the student's paper correlated to a similarly gridded slate used by the teacher. Net drawing extended the points to form a continuous grid across the page. The addition of numerals to the dots or the axes of the grid allowed the teacher to dictate drawings to the classroom. Dot drawing was based on the practice of learning to write by joining dots, indicating the degree to which educators saw writing and drawing as parallel disciplines. Unlike the grids employed by sixteenth-century artists, those used in pedagogical drawing methods were for transposing *flat designs* rather than three-dimensional objects. The forms and patterns that were the subject of pedagogical drawing exercises already conformed to the flatness of the gridded field. They were viewed as disciplinary exercises—often taught with the aid of rhythmical chanting—that developed dexterity and analytical skills that would benefit the student in all areas of endeavor, not just in visual representation (Ashwin 1981: 127–132).

Froebel's use of the graph or "net" for drawing is an extension of his belief that the process of perception is dependent upon the concepts of horizontality and verticality. Froebel believed that there is a natural correspondence between the squared surface (*Netzfläche*) of the grid and the way we receive images on the retina (*Netzhaut*). Froebel's teaching method was to draw geometric figures on a large gridded slate at the front of the classroom, while his students replicated these shapes on gridded paper or slates. Naturalistic or "true" representation was the ultimate aim; thus the gridded exercises were a way of reducing the complexity of the visual world into simplified components. As students gained a mastery of form, the grids and geometric elements which had been used for analysis

Chapter 1.1.6

Graphic Design History edited by Steven Heller and Georgette Ballance, and *Texts on Type: Critical Writings on Type* edited by Steven Heller and Philip P. Meggs

Michael J. Golec

Book reviews of *Graphic Design History*. Edited by Steven Heller and Georgette Balance (Allworth Press: New York, 2001) 352 pages; $21.95; paperback.

Texts on Type: Critical Writings on Typography. Edited by Steven Heller and Philip B. Meggs (Allworth Press: New York, 2001) 288 pages; $19.95.

In his recent collection of essays, *The Politics of the Artificial: Essays on Design and Design Studies* (Chicago and London: University of Chicago Press, 2002), Victor Margolin, among other topics, accounts for how the history of graphic design has been incorporated into the practice of graphic design. Beginning in the 1980s, according to Margolin, several symposia were organized under the auspices of engaging the field of graphic design from a historical perspective, Rochester Institute of Technology's "Coming of Age" (1983) and the School of Visual Art's "Modernism and Eclecticism: The History of American Graphic Design" (1987–1996) are two influential examples. The latter of the two series of symposia was organized by Steven Heller. During the past twenty or so years, the growing number of symposia and the increasing wave of texts written by professional graphic designers and design journalists that address the history of graphic design (Heller, Rick Poynor, Teal Triggs, Philip Meggs, Tibor Kalman, Andrew Blauvelt, J. Abbott Miller, and Ellen Lupton, to name a few) has resulted in a broadly felt awareness that graphic design's past is constitutive of its present and its potential future. That this is the case, as Margolin observes, has much to do with "the desire to create a professional identity for graphic designers [. . .]."[1]

First published in *Design Issues,* 20 (4) (Autumn 2004): 91–4. © Massachusetts Institute of Technology/Michael J. Golec.

Recently, the ongoing construction of graphic design's professional identity has been fortified by numerous texts published by Allworth Press, an imprint devoted to the "creative professional." A large percentage of Allworth's output of graphic design texts are edited by Heller, who in addition to writing and editing, is senior art director at the *New York Times* and co-chair of the graduate design program at the School of Visual Arts. In today's world of graphic design, there is probably no one more influential nor more prolific in his written output than Heller, whose bibliography will soon exceed, if it has not already, that of another influential art director, public relations man, and design writer D. C. McMurtrie.

A recent contribution from Allworth is *Graphic Design History*, a collection of articles that Heller co-edited with design educator and curator Georgette Ballance. *Graphic Design History* is organized into five sections, the most substantial of which is section three, "Designed Lives," which consists of eighteen articles on notable graphic designers. That the structure of *Graphic Design History* emphasizes this, what we might call, after the Reniassance artist and biographer Giorgio Vasari, the lives of the designers, certainly underscores Margolin's observation that the history of design has been put into the service of the profession. In addition to the five main sections, there is Heller's introduction and an epilogue that consists of Heller's interview with Louis Danziger, one of the first graphic design practitioners to introduce the history of graphic design to the practical design curriculum. Both Heller's introduction and his interview with Danziger tightly circumscribe the limits of what the editors contend that "graphic design history" offers to the profession it purports to document.

In "The Beginning of History," the introduction to *Graphic Design History*, Heller matter of factly states the role that graphic design history can play in the construction of the profession's identity: "Lest ignorance overshadow talent, graphic designers should be literate in graphic design history. Being able to design well is not enough. Knowing the roots of design is necessary to avoid reinvention, no less inadvertent plagiarism."[2] For Heller, the graphic design profession is progressive in the sense that its social-cultural value rests on the graphic designer's knowing capacity for innovation. If, as Heller claims, graphic design is "a significant component of mass communication, from producing advertising to defining zeitgeist," it is precisely because the profession views its own history as productive and understands the cumulative benefits of that production. How this understanding is expressed poses a significant problem for the profession's historical comprehension of and subsequent construction of itself.

Of course, the history of design has, in part, been the history of the designer's sometime successful and sometime failed attempts to convince other professionals that what he or she does is innovative beyond merely mediating information. This is exemplified in R. Roger Remington's "Lester Beall: A Creative Genius of the Simple Truth," the lead article in *Graphic Design History*'s "Designed Lives" section. In his article, Remington writes, "Creativity speaks to the heart of the process of graphic design." And, Remington continues, "Beall proved to American business that the graphic designer was a professional that could creatively solve problems and at the same time deal with pragmatic issues of marketing and budget."[3] Knowing that Beall had demonstrated to his employers that graphic design was a profession on par with other professions does more to bolster graphic design's conception of itself as a profession than it does to account for the social and cultural significance of the designer's work. After all, a critical history of graphic design—a history that acknowledges the broader social and cultural fabric in which graphic design is enmeshed—would have to account for non-creative aspects (or those aspects that are not relevant to the creative process) that constitute a high percentage of the graphic designer's work.

In this vein, Heller's article, "Advertising: The Mother of Graphic Design" attempts to critically account for the historical and institutional formation of the graphic design profession as it was modeled after advertising and commercial art. As he states, "In the 1930s the distinction between advertising art and graphic design was virtually nonexistent." Most penetrating, is Heller's observation that graphic design has repressed its roots and that the profession has maintained something of an historical false consciousness when it views advertising as an entity apart from the more loftier concerns of graphic design. Importantly, Heller points out a crucial error when histories of graphic design focus exclusively on formal developments and exclude "issues of consumerism and marketing." Heller is right to complain that graphic design's rejection of advertising-as crass commercialism and as vulgar marketing is deeply rooted in the practitioner-historian who writes a history of graphic design from the point of view that graphic design is somehow a more valuable, purer form of communication. And he warns, "if graphic design history does not expand to include advertising and other related studies, it will ultimately succumb to the dead-end thinking that will be the inevitable consequence of being arrested in a state of continual adolescence."

Heller directs his admonition to, what he refers to as "the graphic design history movement." By "the graphic design history movement," I can only assume that Heller means a movement within the profession of graphic design, primarily made up of graphic designers and design journalists, and not a movement in terms of scholarship produced by design historians who are conversant with critical research methods and exposition. To be sure, there are very few, if any, academically trained historians of graphic design, of art, of science, of business, of architecture, etc., that are not conversant in research methodologies that critically contest the shortsighted tendencies that Heller worries will impede graphic design history.

Indeed, *Graphic Design History* does reprint contributions by academically trained historians. Although they are journalistic in nature, these articles are conversant with historical research methods and thus deliver penetrating essays on formidable themes. Victor Margolin's "Construction Work" upends the knee-jerk assumption that art and design produced within the context of "repressive regimes" need be, or is necessarily aesthetically compromised. Ellen Lupton's "Post-*Saturday EveningPost*: Magazine Design and Its Dis-Contents" underscores the historical relation between magazine content and the concerns of advertising. Maud Lavin's "Heartfield in Context" fleshes out the political and social context of John Heartfield's photomontage work, correcting what she views as the dominant apolitical and merely aesthetical reception of Heartfield by designers. Importantly, she asserts that "Heartfield's art canonization [. . .] can be problematic when it threatens to upstage the history of the montagist's politics and mass-media involvement."[4] All three of these articles take advantage of the limited space allowed by *Graphic Design History* and cut straight to the bone.[5] By emphasizing historical concepts, like regime, economics, and mass-media all three authors jettison the idea of a history of graphic design as a history of exceptional personalities that make up the bulk of *Graphic Design History*.

These critically informed contributions are too few, however. I say this not to devalue the contributions made by many fine writers but to mark what is self-defeating in *Graphic Design History*, because it exemplifies what Heller cautions against. For example, both Veronique Vienne's "Alexander Liberman:

On Overcoming Aesthetics" and "The Brand Named Walter Landor: Historical View" are anecdotal, biographical, and autobiographical essays. Both essays are of the "great man" and the woman who admires them (despite their faults) genre. Granted, Vienne's essays provide the reader with a vivid snapshot of a moment in history; but this is more an effect of her articles having been written in the past tense rather than Vienne's having worked out how Liberman and Landor's works were embedded in the broadly complementary and competing discourses that dominated each designer's respective activities or how their works exemplified the nascent states of post-World War II mass-media, in Liberman's case, and marketing, in Landor's case. At the very least a history of graphic design is better served by, for example, an account of Landor's contribution to the incipient business of branding rather than a glimpse at his incorrigible womanizing. Of course, equally productive, both sociologically and historically, would be an examination of a lasciviousness reflected structurally within the power relations that are acted out between design principals, partners, or managers and their underlings.

This is not to say that history writing cannot be autobiographical, biographical, sociological, anthropological, intellectual, or any other method that can be appended to "-history." But, historical writing should not be so inclined in method that it obscures or neglects, what Heller acknowledges as, the "larger context wherein it functions.[6] As Heller rightly states, "[h]istory must show that graphic design is not the product of a hermetically sealed environment."[7] Nonetheless, historiography must likewise show that graphic design history writing is not itself the product of a hermetically sealed environment. Unfortunately, Heller's and Ballance's editorial decisions bear out the negative implications of the latter. Heller's interview with Louis Danziger instantiates an inherent inconsistency—the idea that graphic design is not isolated from larger social-cultural events and yet is resistant to those social-cultural events and seemingly opposing institutions (like the academy) that threaten graphic design's status as a profession. Danziger makes two illuminating statements that reflect this inconsistency and say much about the state of design history from the profession's point of view. (I do not mean that Danziger speaks for the entire profession, one hopes that he does not. Rather, I mean that because the Danziger interview appears as an epilogue—a conclusion—to a book on graphic design history I can only presume that it is intended by the editors to encapsulate all of the preceding articles.) When asked by Heller how he approaches the organization of his lectures on graphic design history, Danziger replies, "Although I believe in the importance of contexts and historical imperatives, I think that, particularly in design history, the idiosyncratic personality is of prime importance."[8] And, when asked, what he feels is the appropriate manner in which to teach design history, Danziger responds: "A discipline which conducts research, asks questions, gathers credible information, and leads to greater understanding of a subject is of value for general cultural and intellectual reasons irrespective of whom that material is addressed to or to what specific purpose that research is directed. Having said that, I think that in graphic design history particularly, the distinction between the academic historian and the practitioner-cum-historian presents problems."[9] Danziger means, as he goes on to explain, that the distinction between the academic historian and the graphic design "practitioner-cum-historian" is that the former lacks practical experience of the latter and that poses a problem. "I believe," he states, "they look at the same material with different eyes." What I take to be the main thrust of Danziger's distinction is that the "practitioner-cum-historian" has a greater appreciation for the visual/informational artifacts designed by the idiosyncratic personality and thus the history of graphic design should be a history of designers and the things designed.

Danziger's prescription adds up to nothing short of cultural isolationism; he assumes that graphic design can only be appreciated by the graphic designer who is best equipped to evaluate visual/ informational artifacts. This is, I will argue, an alarming position for two reasons. First, it presupposes that graphic design is produced for an audience of graphic designers rather than for those individuals or institutions who commission graphic design or those individuals who populate the demographic targeted by graphic design. Second, such a presupposition creates a hierarchy where a superior position is taken by designers who possess a cultivated standard of taste and an inferior position is occupied by those individuals who commission or consume what design has to offer and therefore lack cultivation and taste. This would seem to contradict Heller's own definition of what graphic design history should be or that it should not be isolated from the broader social-cultural context from where it arises. That Heller never presses Danziger on his isolationist view underscores the editor's tacit agreement, a principle that guides his and Ballance's selection, with the few exceptions already cited, of the majority of the articles in *Graphic Design History*.

Despite the above criticisms, I recommend that *Graphic Design History* is a valuable resource for graphic design historians and those practitioners interested in graphic design history. Rather than presenting a concise critical history, *Graphic Design History* exemplifies the current state of the graphic design profession in its ongoing construction of itself as such. The book is a historical document in and of itself; and its limits are the limits of the field of graphic design rather than the limits of what can possibly be recovered and represented as history.

The current state of graphic design as it is offered by *Graphic Design History*, and thus its status as an historical document, is echoed by another recent book from Allworth, *Design Issues: How Graphic Design Informs Society*, its subtitle succinctly registering the one-way bias of the profession. As the editor D. K. Holland explains in an attempt to come to terms with, for her, the inexplicable nature of design, "you can talk about everything that surrounds design, and in doing so, understand it as we understand the sun through the shadows and light it creates."[10] I happen to agree with the general intent here, but Holland's metaphor is, for me, question begging: Does graphic design inform society in ways that are comparable to the sun's illuminating rays? Or, to put it more pragmatically, does society inform itself, in part, through the mediating technologies of graphic design? (Contrary to Marshall McLuhan, it is not always, nor is it necessarily, the case that the medium or the media is the message.) If an affirmative answer to the former question is taken for granted by the profession, then the possibility of a critical graphic design history produced by graphic designers is uncertain.

Certainly, this need not be the case. No less ambitious, but less troubling in its format is *Texts on Type: Critical Writings on Typography*, a collection edited by Heller and practitioner-historian Philip Meggs.[11] Here we find a book that is more conventionally historical in its scope than *Graphic Design History* for the simple fact that it reprints nineteen primary documents, including essays by Frederic Goudy, Herbert Bayer, Paul Rand, and Stanley Morrison. Most importantly, Heller and Meggs have chosen two essays by the lesser known D. C. McMurtrie, once the publicist for the Ludlow Typograph Company in Chicago. "The Cult of Lower Case" and "The Philosophy of Modernism in Typography" (both from 1929) demonstrate that McMurtrie's interest in European modernism predated the arrival of the emigres who have been thought to be largely responsible for introducing modern typography to the United States.[12]

The construction of a professional identity is itself an historical subject, one that certainly deserves more attention within graphic design history. Paramount to such a project is the identification of those instances where graphic design struggles to establish itself as a coherent practice, where it claims that graphic design creates unified fields of understanding, or where it seeks to implement comprehensive projects towards some greater social good. All of this can be found in the pages of *Graphic Design History.* Therefore, a history of the ongoing development of the graphic design profession would certainly have to take into account the anxiety and the desires embodied here.

Notes

1. Victor Margolin, *The Politics of the Artificial: Essays on Design and Design Studies* (Chicago and London: University of Chicago Press, 2002), 139.
2. Steven Heller and Georgette Ballance, ed., *Graphic Design History* (New York: Allworth Press, 2001), viii.
3. Ibid., 75.
4. Ibid., 89.
5. Almost all of the articles are collected from a variety of trade journals and popular art and design magazines. Lupton's and Margolin's articles were first published in Print and Lavin's article originally appeared in Art in America.
6. Heller and Ballance, ed., *Graphic Design History* (2001), ix.
7. Ibid.
8. Ibid., 330.
9. Ibid., 331.
10. D.K. Holland, ed., *Design Issues: How Graphic Design Informs Society* (New York: Allworth Press, 2001), ix.
11. Steven Heller and Philip B.Meggs, eds, *Texts on Type: Critical Writings on Typography* (New York: Allworth Press, 2001).
12. Seemy "A Typography of Impoverishment: D. C. McMurtrie's Reception of European Modernist Typography and an American Depression," *Visible Language*, 34 (3) (2000): 264–2.

Section 1.2

Graphic design canon(s)
(1980s to present)

EF: I don't believe that at all. Those forms have to do with rationality and pragmatism and legibility. I don't see how they can ever go away. I don't see that people are going to make traffic signage or brain surgeon manuals that can't be read, to use the most ridiculous examples.

The form of graphic design has to function to carry the content. Look at Gran Fury's AIDS activist graphics: it looks like advertising. And rightly so, in order to reach people in a language they can understand. If you wanted to do pamphlets about access to government programs for the homeless and the indigent, you wouldn't do it in the Ray Gun style. I don't know if that's what Heller's afraid people would do, that they would somehow mix up these styles, that a Stop sign would appear in a disintegrated typeface you can't read. I always tell students to "stabilize the referent" when necessary.

We have courses in information design at CalArts. We want our students to understand typography as being appropriate to its content, and it has to be structured to further the message. But Heller's looking at a lot of cultural graphics, which don't necessarily have to do that.

One problem with Heller is, for example, he never quite figured out what *Output* was all about. He was looking at it in this naive Modernist context of a simple dichotomy between beautiful and ugly, good and bad, instead of seeing it in the context of the whole discourse that surrounds art practices and cultural practices. *Output* was a free play of endless printed stuff, signifiers that deliberately signified nothing. It's like Greenbergian formalism; it isn't about narrative or content, it's about paint-on-canvas. On the other hand, there's plenty of other precedents in art and literature for not being able to say anything, because the world is just too awful. You know: "How can there be poetry after the Holocaust?" And the Cranbrook students, whether they did this deliberately or not, were in that kind of tradition, that whole twentieth century Nihilism that says, "It's all hopeless, everything's inevitable, nothing can be done or even said."

So if Heller had understood that, then I could see how he could have attacked it. Then he could have said, "These silly students!" From a leftist or a socially conscious and activist position he could say, as I would, "That's a ridiculous statement to make: of course there's plenty to say. You've got to keep fighting all the time. And communicating. And no one more so than artists and designers."

MD: Steve also identifies himself as a leftist.

EF: I would assume he does. In his columns, he always talks about the '60s, like the time he got raided when he was the editor of *Screw* magazine. And he's done books on activist and protest graphics.

MD: Why do you imagine Steve's having trouble with the new work?

EF: I don't know why, to tell you the truth. It's possibly because it's easy to like all this old commercial art stuff—who wouldn't like Italian Art Deco graphics?—and it's difficult to understand the new stuff.

I also wonder if he feels a personal loyalty to Paul Rand, who's going down in his last hurrah. It's understandable, as pathetic as it is, for the poor old guy to make a last ditch effort to deny and denigrate everything that's going on now. All the reviews of Paul Rand's book basically say that. Even though everyone admires Paul Rand as a great designer of the past, they feel sad for his lack of understanding. But it's not understandable for someone like Steven Heller, who's got nothing at stake. In fact, it's just the opposite. He's the critic and the historian and the commentator. He should really understand the contemporary dynamic.

MD: Even if he feels a loyalty to Rand. . .

EF: I don't know that. I really shouldn't speculate on it. . .

MD: Well, wouldn't you think it's possible for critics to realize that Rand's work has been assimilated into the culture of design to the point that this new work is part of a continuum?

EF: I certainly feel that, yes. I would agree with you one hundred percent. That's why I don't understand why Paul Rand and Massimo Vignelli are so upset by this new work. That's why I'm not upset by it. That's why I love it, because it's the next generation. I don't think there's such a big break. Good solid work is always good solid work. That's why I don't see myself as a young Turk. I think my work is as carefully done and as "beautiful" as anybody's work from any previous time.

I don't like to use terms like "good," "bad," "beautiful," "ugly," because they continually take on different meanings. The eighteenth century thought that beauty was in the eye of the beholder, but it's in the culture of the beholder. Every culture has its own standards of beauty. Design has opened up to accept the high culture and the low culture, the vernacular, amateur art, outsider art, so-called primitive art and just about everything else you can identify or catalog: it's all part of the mix.

Chapter 1.2.3

An unbearable lightness?

Steve Rigley

Designers used to stand for beauty and order. Now beauty is passé and ugliness is smart.

(Heller, 1993: 52)

Introduction

For some academics, the contemplation of beauty may be just another dead-end discourse or "a door to confusion" (Townsend, 1997: 210). In 1921, the philosopher Moritz Geiger argued that aesthetics should be compared to a weather vane, turned around by any philosophical, cultural or scientific gust or wind of change. The debate surrounding beauty continues today with Craig Lambert's essay "The Stirring of Sleeping Beauty" (1999) where he notes that 'beauty has been in exile'. He writes:

> In American universities, beauty has been in exile. Despite its centrality in human experience, the concept of beauty has virtually disappeared from scholarly discourse. Oddly enough the banishment has been most complete in the humanities, home of literature, music and art. Criticized as an elitist concept, an ethnocentric creation of white European males, beauty has been stigmatized as sexist, racist and unfair.

Within this broad context, it comes as no surprise to see why Steven Heller—the eminent American graphic designer and writer—created so much controversy with his 1993 essay *The Cult of the Ugly* in which he claimed that certain graphic design educational courses were cultivating a new wave of ugly design. Heller introduced his argument by discussing a project entitled *Output* (1992) that had been recently produced by students of Cranbrook Academy of Art (Figure 1.3) and which he felt typified the work emanating from a number of American schools at that time and that had been created, he suggested, within "a laboratory setting and freedom from professional responsibility" (p. 52). Heller moved on to attack the work of Ed Fella and Jeffery Keedy—senior figures in such academic institutions, who also maintained their own professional practices—before finally focusing upon the Chicago-based company

First published in *Visual Communication*, 6 (3) (October 2007): 281–304. © 2007. SAGE Publications Ltd.

Figure 1.3 *Output*. © 1992. Designers: Richard Bates, David Shields, Brian Smith, and Susanna Stieff.

Segura, which Heller felt represented the 'professional wing of the hot-house sensibility' (p. 57). Heller's central tenet defined ugly as "the layering of unharmonious graphic forms in a way that resulted in confusing graphic images" (p. 53).

Not surprisingly, the essay struck a nerve: editor John L. Walters suggested this was probably the magazine's most controversial article,[1] whilst critic and former *Eye* editor Rick Poynor (2003) described it as "the most notorious and hotly contested attack" upon post-modern graphic design (p. 149). In the ensuing debate (1993), Kathryn McCoy—at that time the co-chair of the Design Department at Cranbrook—replied to *Eye* and suggested that whilst Heller's views were driven by nineteenth-century sources such as Ruskin, Emerson and Keats, beauty as such had never been a goal of twentieth-century high culture; she cited Picasso's *Les Demoiselles d'Avignon*, the ready-mades of Duchamp, and Chicago blues and jazz as examples of contemporary cultural forms with integrity and resonance. McCoy concluded that 'some paradigms work better than others. I prefer integrity and authenticity and quality and appropriateness. But these take a little more work than simple-minded beauty' (p. 3).

The fact that McCoy offered examples outside what we would call graphic design reminds us that it is itself a young profession with the term first coined in 1922 (Meggs, 1992: xiii). Whilst there are obvious differences between the goals of a graphic designer working to communicate a client's message and those of an artist or musician working towards self-expression, they nevertheless occupy the same zeit-geist. For that reason, it is possible—indeed important—to look outside the parameters of graphic design and its roots in printing and commercial art, and to seek parallels with other more established creative professions to build a more balanced picture.

Although Heller could have been guilty of a "simple-minded" polemic, he posed one pertinent, nagging question: could "ugly" design represent "a foundation for new standards based on contemporary sensibilities?" (p. 56). Had the pursuit of "integrity and authenticity and quality and appropriateness" in 20th-century cultural forms and communication ultimately lead to a new paradigm? In short, has ugliness become the new beauty? If this is the case, should we now consider classical notions of "beauty" to be superseded and redundant? Or could it be that the term "beauty" carries too many interpretations to be truly helpful? If so, how and on what basis can we continue to make value judgements that divide the beautiful from the ugly?

Heller's criticism was impassioned and carried a degree of certainty that many of his contemporaries would struggle to muster. So which individuals did he have in mind when he claimed that "designers used to stand for beauty and order"? When he railed against the 'fashionable ugliness as a form of nihilistic expression' (p. 56), where did his confidence come from and is it a valid basis for such criticism?

Modernism and beauty

The idea that beauty should be a goal or product of intent was a difficult concept that divided early modernist typographers and designers. From within the Arts and Crafts movement, William Morris had significant influence upon the development of modern typography with the work produced by the Kelmscott Press. Reflecting upon his reasons for starting this venture, he wrote:

I began printing books with the hope of producing something that would have a definite claim to beauty, while at the same time they should be easy to read and not dazzle the eye or trouble the intellect of the reader by the eccentricity of the form in the letters.

(Naylor, 1988: 225)

Morris acknowledged that utility and decoration could be competing components, yet he was firmly committed to finding a sensible line between the two: in short, a beautiful solution. For the type designer T.L. deVinne—himself a great admirer of Morris—the solution lay in "masculine printing" that instructed the reader as opposed to "feminine printing," which he considered to be overly decorative (Kinross, 1992: 41). Through the influence of figures such as Morris and deVinne, a changing notion of beauty came to be expressed through the gradual stripping away of ornament and excess; yet this found differing expressions in British and German modernism in the interwar years. In her celebrated lecture "The Crystal Goblet" (1930), publicity manager for the Monotype Corporation Beatrice Warde championed the notion of typographic transparency—the setting of type to be read rather than noticed—and famously likened the "modernist" to a connoisseur of fine wine.[2] Perhaps this came as something of a comfort to her colleagues in contemporary British literary circles, but this is a far cry from the modernism of Jan Tschichold's *The New Typography* (1955[1928]). For Robin Kinross (1992) this was "the difference between merely modern, set against a backward trade or ossified bibliophile context and the consciously modern or modernist" (p. 59). In Britain, Warde, Stanley Morrison and the "new conservatives" considered beauty to be the result of an evolution of common sense, whereas Tschichold and his followers demanded a revolution.

David Harvey (1980) identifies the influence of Nietzsche upon early twentieth-century modernism through his celebration of the Dionysian acts of "creative destruction" considered necessary to destroy traditional notions of beauty, which were now seen as either invalid or as a distraction on the road to progress (pp. 15–16). Tschichold's *The New Typography* (1955[1928]) was very much a child of this time. Writing at the age of 26, Tschichold saw fit to dedicate only one chapter to his forerunners: "The Old Typography 1440–1914." Of the aims of the "new typography," he concluded: "the essence of new typography is clarity. This puts it in deliberate opposition to the old typography whose aim was beauty and whose clarity did not attain the high levels we require today" (p. 66). Yet his confidence did not last. In the years leading up to the war, Tschichold was to gradually turn full circle and abandon the "new typography" which he now considered an expression of the German need for the absolute (Kinross, 1992: 106). His return to a more traditional typographic approach that acknowledged history through the use of serif fonts and symmetrical composition was welcomed in Britain in that he finally seemed to recognize—like Morris, Warde and the "new conservatives"—that beauty and clarity need not be mutually exclusive. It also served to confirm the belief that this union was most successfully realized through an informed understanding of classical proportion. For a book typographer, such as Tschichold, working specifically with numeric relations—page dimensions, margins and line length—the desire for "sound" principles could be readily satisfied by referring back to a period of greater confidence, a time when "designers used to stand for beauty and order" since the two were assumed to be mutually dependent.

Renaissance beauty

The Renaissance laid a powerful claim to the understanding of what at that time was considered to be "universal" beauty through the rediscovery of classical geometry and mathematics. Of particular influence was the Roman architect Vitruvius who saw the source of the beautiful as nature itself since nature conformed to what was perceived as a "divine order". This perfect order—as expressed through the proportions of the human body—could be measured, understood and applied as the ruling component in the design process, as demonstrated by the versal construction by Geofroy Tory from his Champfleury produced in Paris in 1529.

Inspired by Vitruvius, as well as by Pythagoras and Plato's *Timaeus*, Alberti (1991[1472]) developed his own theory of *concinnitas*—a blend of number, measure, proportion and arrangement—declaring that 'the very same numbers that cause sounds to have *concinnitas* (certain harmony) pleasing to the ears, can also fill the eyes and mind with wondrous delight' (p. 305). Working from this premise, the typographer, architect or composer could conclude that the main objective would be to get the numbers right. Beauty would occur once correct relations were secured; in the case of typography, these would be between page proportions, margins and type size. The classical perspective also saw these divine arrangements as inter-changeable, working equally successfully for a musical score, a building or a book. More recently Robert Bringhurst has strengthened claims to a ruling and universal order by suggesting that these same "pleasing proportions" are demonstrated in nature within the structure of molecules, flowers and mineral crystals as well as in manuscripts from the Tang and Song dynasties of China, early Egypt and pre-Columbian Mexico (Bringhurst, 2001: 144; see also Wittkower, 1973: 101, for further reading on this assumed relationship between architectural and musical proportion).

Fallen beauty one

Building upon the discoveries of Copernicus, Kepler and Galileo, the scientists and philosophers of the Enlightenment were confident that measurement and reason could deliver a greater understanding of this assumed relationship between science and beauty, so much so that Newton and Locke were seen as the "unveilers of the beautiful" (Landow, 1971: 116). For the rationalists, "disciplined critical rationality would overcome the untrustworthy information about the world given by the senses or the imagination" (Tarnas, 1991: 276). This aspect of Enlightenment thinking—namely to find the internal workings, laws and structures of the separate domains (Harvey, 1980: 12)—was reflected in the activities of those involved in the nascent printing industry, figures such as Joseph Moxon who, in 1684, was the first to define typography as a distinct discipline (Kinross, 1992: 15). The most concerted efforts to rationalize the design of letterforms at this stage was made by the French Académie des Sciences. Under the supervision of a specially appointed committee, a grid system was developed consisting of 2,304 small squares. This formed the basis of a new alphabet called the "Romain du Roi," which was cut by Philippe Grandjean in 1695. The alphabet was a genuine attempt to work from a purely rational base, but the crude methodology—which saw the development of sloped (italic) letterforms by skewing the angle of the grid—had limitations and lacked the subtlety achieved by the rather more conventional use of hand and eye. A little later, but very much in the confident spirit of early Enlightenment rationalism, came the work of Fournier and Didot in developing systems of typographic measurement (see Kinross, 1992: 17–24 for further reading on the development of typographic forms of classification and measurement in France and Britain).

Yet this scientific revolution, which brought a radical re-orientation for man within the cosmos, suggested that a greater understanding of beauty now required recognition of both the *experience* and the *perspective* of the particular viewer. With his outlook greatly broadened by his travels, Descartes (1596–1650) had already noted in his *Compendium Musicare* (1618) that differing notions of beauty existed in different epochs, countries and cultures (Bredin and Brienza, 2000: 77). Developing the theme, Hume (1711–76) was famously to suggest that "Beauty is no quality in things themselves; it exists merely in the mind which contemplates them; and each mind perceives a different beauty. One person may even perceive deformity, where another is sensible to beauty" (Hume, 1965[1757]: 86). Hume emphasized the superior role of the senses in shaping understanding over the superior role of the senses in shaping understanding over the "feeble, obscure and undefined" realm of abstract ideas (Bredin and Brienza, 2000: 78). Burke (1729–97) maintained that proportion—which he termed "the creature of understanding"—should be considered separate from the realm of the senses and the imagination, insisting that beauty "demands no assistance from our reasoning" (Burke, 1803: 99). Such pre-occupation with the sensory experience was reflected in the architect Boulée's (1728–99) sugges-tion that "circular bodies please our senses because of their smooth contours; angular bodies are displeasing because of their harshness of form. Bodies that crawl over the ground sadden us, those that rise in the sky delight us" (Pérouse de Montclos, 1974: 38). Similarly Goethe said of the Gothic script often termed "textura": "In its decoration German script is like Gothic buildings which can draw the eye upwards and fill us with astonishment and admiration" (Kapr, 1983: 62). This connection between typography and architecture is extremely revealing; reflecting upon Goethe's observations, Albert Kapr writes: "The soaring tendency of Gothic cathedrals was intended to show believers their powerlessness in the face of the world beyond; the dark type surface of the textura gives a foretaste of the sacred and the numinous in mysticism" (p. 62).

As a consequence of the shift towards empiricism and to the recognition of the temporal and subject-ive position of the viewer, it became increasingly difficult to pin down any exact definition of universal beauty. Kant (1724–1804) attempted to resolve this in his *Critique of Judgement* (1952[1781]), arguing that the aesthetic was subjective, yet in the determination of beauty it was also universal. This position assumed that all rational minds were structured alike in their cognitive faculties. However, the idea of a subjective harmony between subject and object could not survive, with Kant ultimately confirming "that all human knowledge is interpretive . . . the human being knows not the world, but the world as rendered by the human mind" (Tarnas, 1991: 417).

It was not until 1853 that an attempt was made to define "ugliness" as an aesthetic concept as opposed to purely an absence of beauty. Rosenkranz proposed that ugliness could be recognized by *Formlosigkeit* (lack of form or symmetry), *Inkorrektheit* (a mismatch between an idea and its physical expression) and *Verbildung* or defiguration (a qualitative property which includes the vulgar, the disgust-ing, the boring, lifelessness and bad taste) (Bredin and Brienza, 2000: 92). How these characteristics compare against the claims made in *The Cult of the Ugly* will be considered later.

Reacting against the purely rational mindset of Enlightenment scientists, the romanticists placed greater emphasis upon the subject and celebrated the role of intuition and the imagination in creating works considered to be beautiful. The art critic John Ruskin, although influenced by classicism, differed with Palladio and Alberti in that he saw beauty represented by *melody* rather than by *harmony*. This is an important distinction recognizing that beauty could be found not only in a re-creatable order, but also in the expression of the imagination "that surpasses reason" (Landow, 1971: 132). Ruskin was also critical of the perfectionist traits of classical architecture, preferring Gothic, which, he believed, allowed for human imperfection and a greater degree of personal expression (Naylor, 1988: 10). His second volume of *Modern Painters* (1883) identified what he felt to be four errant positions in the judgement of beauty, namely that beauty is the true and the useful, and that it is dependent upon custom as well as on the association of ideas. His strongest attack was aimed at the latter, termed as "associationism." Ruskin declared: "Associationism removes beauty from the heavens and places it within the changeable and limited territories of the human mind" (Landow, 1971: 132). However, later in life and with his Christian faith faltering, he was able to incorporate elements of associationism, recognizing the importance of the subjectivities that a viewer may take to a painting. The gradual emergence of relativism—epitomized in Ruskin's failure to dismiss associationism—helps us to understand the difficulty with which many received Heller's *The Cult of the Ugly*.

Fallen beauty two

In his rejection of radical modernism and return to classical typography, Tschichold probably shared the same conclusion as the architect Robert Venturi who a few years later bemoaned the fact that "functionalist architecture . . . represented function more than resulted from function—it looked functional more than worked functionally" (Venturi and Scott-Brown, 1984[1974]: 44). Venturi's observations seem equally suited to matters of graphic design and typography, in view of the strong similarities in the spatial, aesthetic and functional requirements considered by the designer. For the graphic designer, function is usually associated with effective communication, particularly in the setting of typography to be read clearly. The difficulty in resolving competing functional and aesthetic demands is clearly demonstrated in the various stages of development in Swiss typography. Of particular relevance is the hugely influential work of Wolfgang Weingart, who sought to extend the expressive potential of the then dominant Swiss or "International Style" through syntactical play. In *The Cult of the Ugly*, Heller seems to misunderstand the original intentions of Weingart and some of his successful students and therefore bundles him in with mid–1970s British punk rock.

> The current wave began in the mid–1970's with the English punk scene, a raw expression of youth frustration manifested though shocking dress, music and art. Punk's naive graphic language—an aggressive rejection of rational typography that echoes Dada and Futurist work—influenced designers throughout the 1970's and seriously tested the limits imposed by Modernist formalism. Punk's violent demeanour surfaced in Swiss, American, Dutch and French design and spread to the mainstream in the form of a "new wave," or what Gary Panter has called "sanitised punk." A key anti-canonical approach later called Swiss Punk—which in comparison with the gridlocked Swiss International Style was

menacingly chaotic, though rooted in its own logic—was born in the Mecca of rationalism, Basel, during the late 1970's. For the elders who were threatened (and offended) by the onslaught to criticise Swiss Punk as ugly was avoiding the issue. Swiss Punk was attacked not so much because of its appearance as because it symbolised the end of the modernist hegemony.

(Heller 1993: 54)

Yet despite the convenience of such a broad term as "new wave" to contain both Weingart and punk rock, and some of the similarities in the manner of working, the two need to be seen in context. The experimental work of the Basel School can be traced back to Weingart's own experiments in the 1960s with adjusting type size and spacing to enhance expression (Weingart, 2000: 271–303), and with lithography and film over-lays, which began in the early 1970s (pp. 350–67). The work therefore comfortably predates punk rock and the famous Sex Pistols" *God Save the Queen* single cover of 1977 in which a photograph of Queen Elizabeth's head is superimposed with "GOD Save THE QUEEN" across her eyes and "SEX PISTOLS" across her mouth. While it could be argued that Sex Pistols poster designer Jamie Reid had been working with cut and paste technique for the *Suburban Press* in the early 1970s, the two were operating with different intent: Weingart (the trained typesetter) hoping to "question established typographic practice, change the rules and to re-evaluate its potential" (p. 112), Reid (inspired by the situationists) operating as an "artist improvising with graphical techniques for political purposes" (Poynor, 2003: 40).

To suggest that the work emanating from Basel represented the end of the modernist hegemony seems a little unfair on Weingart who admits that his work would be "impossible without the classical Swiss typography, in that it is a logical development of it" (Weingart, 1987[1972]). Indeed his respect for thorough typographic grounding and his enthusiasm for logical development—in part afforded through the opportunities of new technology—should really position Weingart as a late modernist rather than as an early post-modern designer, as Poynor (2003: 19) suggests.

To avoid associating Heller's ugly design with what was a valid interrogation of modernist typography, it is necessary therefore to prise apart individuals grouped under the term "new wave"—Weingart from Reid, but also, I would suggest, from his influential protégés Dan Friedman and April Grieman, who combined the Basel principles with greater subjectivity and eclecticism (Meggs, 1992: 450–5). Unpicking the "new wave" helps us to understand that Heller's ugly design was a product of greater depth and complexity than a mere "stylish conceit" assimilated into popular culture (Heller, 1993: 54).

Equally important in this process is to recognize the difference between Weingart and the students of Cranbrook Academy of Art of the mid 1980s, whose activity was no doubt influenced by the syntactic experiments of Basel but also by post-modern critical theory. Students such as Jeffrey Keedy, Alan Hori and Ed Fella were far more committed to finding connections between their graphic design practice and semiotics, post-structuralism and literary criticism than their Basel contemporaries or indeed their professional peers. Whilst there is a genuine scepticism as to how successfully these texts were understood or applied by the designers (Poynor, 2003: 46) and whether they merely served to reproduce the rejections already worked through by the avant-garde of Dada and early new typography (Kinross, 1992: 140), they certainly articulated a post-modern loss of faith more explicitly than anything produced in Basel. Yet these are not the only sources for the rejection of balance and harmony that so concerns Heller (1993: 53). Consider the table compiled from a broader list by Charles Jencks and representing the paradigm shift from the modern to post-modern. Jencks is at pains to point out that these are not binary opposites and that the table represents an "ambiguous slide and shift" (Jencks, 1992: 33). However, the table clearly demonstrates the move away from classical thinking.

> Whereas Alberti and Palladio believed in the harmony of the spheres and that the world's order could be captured by simple ratios and musical harmonies, post-modernists coming after Einstein and the Big Bang theory of the universe could not believe in such a simple picture. Harmonies inevitably play a part within this new approach, but do not make up the whole picture. Thus when a post-modern artist or architect uses simple ratios and composed figures he will fracture this beauty in some respects, or place it in tension with counterforms. One will continually find in art and architecture the oxymoron of "disharmonious harmony," dissonant beauty and syncopated proportions, that is simple ratios which are set up and then consciously fragmented or violated.
>
> (Jencks, 1992: 28)

For Heller, such strategies have ultimately lead to *Formlosigkeit*. Yet it seems inevitable and necessary that new discoveries in our understanding of the cosmos should challenge our values and find their expression in the forms that we produce, whether architectural or typographic. This was certainly the case following the scientific revolution with the enthusiasm for systems of classification and measurement of type discussed earlier, almost as if typography was seeking to find its own place within the universe machine. The fragmentary nature of much post-modern design can be seen either negatively as the broken shards of a previously unified whole or, in a more positive light, as the many perspectives that now inform a more healthy and holistic worldview. Yet either way we have to agree with David Bohm and accept that when we approach the world in a fragmentary way, the response will be "correspondingly fragmentary" (Bohm, 1992[1988]: 390).

Jencks articulates a move towards a pluralistic and semiotic worldview in his table, a shift that prompts Tarnas (1991) to conclude that "every act of perception and cognition is contingent, mediated, situated, contextual, theory soaked" (pp. 418–19). So it comes as no surprise to find that a concept such as "pure communication" is too difficult for graphic design students and "universal beauty" is too difficult for many academics, hence the retreat from the curriculum. Camille Paglia links the decline of the study of beauty with the ascendancy of French theory—Derrida, Foucault and Lacan—within American humanities faculties in the early 1970s. "I was a Yale graduate student then; I saw it happen and felt the switch beginning away from the contemplation of art and objects of beauty themselves, to this Mandarin theorizing" (Lambert, 1999). What have been the consequences to the student designer? Has it resulted in less successful or indeed ugly design? Accompanying the piece entitled *No Sign* by Laurie Haycock Makela (1991) featured in *Emigré 19* (Figure 1.4), the designer vividly recalls the following:

> I was cranky and dehydrated. It was the morning after the party—the party of a thousand meaningless typefaces and dead-end discourses—I just didn't feel like getting up and making anything. Can't make anything out of aesthetic and philosophical fallout. Can't find anything new in the black hole of post-modernism. The chattering, so-called layering of vacant meanings and type-tick fetishes that make graphic designers speak nonsense to each other just make me want to leave the party.
>
> After prolonged theoretical dry heaving. I made this piece within a month of arriving at Cranbrook: NO FORM begins with an academic rejection of modernism. NO WORD is what I get if I call on literary theory to tell the story. NO SIGN is what I'm left with as Deconstruction steals the meaning from my experience and cuts it into little pieces. NO GOD is the endpoint of confusion and doubt in the post-modern world.
>
> (Haycock Makela, 1991: 18)

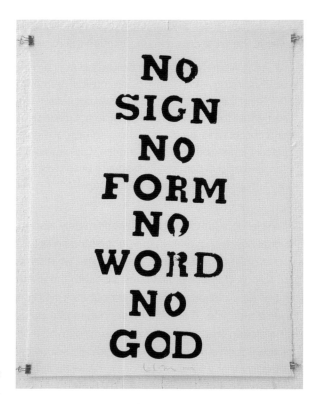

Figure 1.4 *No Sign*. © 1991. Designer: Laurie Haycock
Makela. Photographer: David Cabianca.

From a purely formal point of view, *No Sign* fails to meet the requirements of classical beauty. The typography, although almost classically centred, is intentionally warped and distressed. The arrangement appears to have fractured, suffering a form of subsidence, unable to hold together. If it fails to live up to the demands of classical beauty, we must then ask if this piece is ugly. Certainly Rosenkranz would argue that Makela's subtle neglect of true symmetry would qualify as *Formlosigkeit*. But what of Rosenkranz's *Inkorrektheit*, is there a mismatch between the idea and its physical expression? Considering the message—a rather chilling post-mortem for the Enlightenment—the design decisions, namely to warp and fracture the composition, seem entirely appropriate and a powerful expression of a broken worldview. This leads us to ask whether this "academic rejection of modernism"—that underpins so much of the work that Heller criticizes—has ultimately lead to the emergence of a different notion of beauty.

Beauty by mistake

If we survey graphic design magazines of the past decade it is no surprise to find that the layered, "car-crash" aesthetic and the splintered typographic forms of designers such as David Carson, Why Not Associates and others that characterized much of the early 1990s have given way to a succession of alternative stylistic approaches, each championed by a new generation of designers. In their place, we see the flowering of the neo-baroque, the low-fi bitmap and 70s retro-cool. Yet typographic fashions—whether expressed through the spacing of letters, choice of fonts or materials—are always open to the same influences that inform fashion, music and other areas of cultural production; for this reason, we must recognize that these are not necessarily value judgements specifically regarding typographic beauty. We must also remember how "classic" typefaces such as Baskerville or Bodoni initially struggled to find acceptance and that a broader recognition of beauty can be subject to a form of aesthetic time-lag. For some, this will be interpreted as the ongoing, ever-changing manifestation of the avant-garde, indeed Heller (1993: 56) quotes John Cage: "Where does beauty begin and where does it end? Where it ends is where the artist begins." Similarly the American sculptor David Smith says:

> The truly creative artist deals with vulgarity . . . to the creative artist it is his beauty, but to the audience, who will wait for the aestheticians" explanation, it is new and has not yet hammered its way into acceptance. It will not conform to the past.
>
> (Smith, 2003[1952]: 586–7)

Yet if we are prepared to dig deeper, below the commentaries on typographic trend, below the influence of new technology and the vagaries of fashion or the "shock of the new," we inevitably hit the bigger questions. The chilling observations of scientist David Bohm (1992[1988]) take us back to Haycock Makela:

> Clearly, during the twentieth century the basis of the modern mind has been dissolving, even in the midst of the greatest technological triumphs. The whole foundation is dissolving while the thing is flowering, as it were. The dissolution is characterised by a general sense of loss of meaning of life as a whole. This loss of meaning is very serious, as meaning in the sense intended here is the basis of value.
>
> (Bohm, 1992: 384)

The point is not lost on intelligent designers; Barry Deck suggested that "a fucked-up world gets fucked-up type" (Hall, 1993: 29). Crucially, does this fucked-up aesthetic represent a radically new and shared notion of beauty? Or is it merely a nihilistic reflection upon a deeper loss of meaning, a loss so deep that we find ourselves—alongside Haycock Makela—having lost the desire or confidence to make? It may be that it is a little of both. In his novel, *The Unbearable Lightness of Being* (1984), Kundera writes:

> Franz and Sabina would walk the streets of New York for hours at a time. The view changed with each step, as if they were following a winding mountain path surrounded by breathtaking scenery: a young man kneeling in the middle of the sidewalk praying; a few steps away, a beautiful black woman leaning against a tree; a man in a black suit directing an invisible orchestra while crossing the street; a fountain spurting water and a group of construction workers sitting on the rim eating lunch; strange iron ladders running up and down buildings with ugly red facades, so ugly that they were beautiful. . . . . . Franz said "Beauty in the European sense has always had a premeditated quality to it. We've always had an aesthetic intention and a long-range plan. That's what enabled Western man to spend decades building a Gothic cathedral; or a Renaissance piazza. The Beauty of New York rests on a different base, it's unintentional. It arose independent of human design, like a stalagmitic cavern. Forms which themselves are quite ugly turn up fortuitously, without design, in such incredible surroundings that they sparkle with a sudden wondrous poetry."

Sabina said: "Unintentional beauty. Yes. Another way of putting it might be 'beauty by mistake.' Before beauty disappears entirely from the earth, it will go on existing for a while by mistake. 'Beauty by mistake'—the final phase in the history of beauty."

(Kundera, 1984: 97–8)

For some, this is a cause for celebration. It certainly seems to be the same notion of the beautiful as captured by the designers featured in the 1999 show *Stealing Beauty* at the ICA in London. Curator Claire Catterall (1999) suggested that the show "was not so much about repositioning and re-contextualising the ordinary as about revealing beauty from the palette of everyday life" (p. 7). Alex Rich's *mistake font*, which featured in the catalogue, derives its form from the software automatically correcting an assumed error. In another of Rich's pieces, he asks each visitor to his father's hairdressing salon to draw a horse, the results of which he used to promote a record company. The work represented in *Stealing Beauty* shares a new aesthetic sensibility, yet is it beautiful? It is clearly not beautiful in the classical sense, it is not the result of long-term planning or careful mathematics, and it carries no claim upon divine inspiration or higher ideals. Yet for this reason it carries a certain resonance with our time. If this is a beauty, it is a tragic beauty, fragile, dysfunctional, unplanned and alienated. Essentially urban, this is beauty by mistake.

In his essay that accompanied the exhibition, Michael Horsham (1999) celebrates the blurring and confusion of traditional boundaries, claiming that formal beauty is no longer to be found in the elision of appropriate materials, proportions and significant form, and that "Art in all its artfulness knew and exploited the value of confusion long before design could even walk" (p. 13). For this reason, we may consider *Stealing Beauty* to be a typical modernist project, salvaging the forgotten and the everyday, inverting values and turning the tables on tradition: in this case, the ideals of both classical and high modernist design. It talks of that particular quality identified by the poet Theodore de Banville, who, at the funeral of his friend Baudelaire, offered the following tribute.

He [Baudelaire] accepted modern man in his entirety, with his weaknesses, his aspirations and his despair. He has thus been able to give beauty to sights that did not possess beauty in themselves, not by making them romantically picturesque, but by bringing to light the portion of the human soul hidden in them; he has thus revealed the sad and often tragic heart of the modern city.

(Berman, 1982[1867]: 132)

From such a perspective, familiar strategies within contemporary graphic design—such as Ed Fella's celebration of the vernacular, the dysfunctional and the naive—can be seen to possess greater resonance and depth. The inherent fragility and vulnerability rendered in part through a rejection of classical form reveal and reflect human fragility and therefore offer empathy to the viewer. In an uncertain and rapidly changing world we are able to *identify with* rather than *aspire to* qualities found within the composition. It is this shift, from confidence to doubt, from strength to weakness, which essentially characterizes the new aesthetic sensibility that Heller speculates upon.

Future discourse

The success of the *Stealing Beauty* exhibition confirms that the contemplation of beauty is certainly not redundant. Indeed, it offers a vital means of understanding the concerns and values of the society in which we live. For this reason, Moritz Geiger's weather vane analogy should be seen in a positive light as a valuable *recognition* rather than a *criticism*.

Within academia, the contemplation of beauty may be making something of a comeback. Deconstruction theory fuelled the layered aesthetic of the 1990s, and once again literature is leading the way. Lambert (1999) notes a shift in interest from context (surrounding social, historical and economic circumstances and meanings) towards the text (examination of the structure, language and rhythms of literary works themselves). Harvard Professor of Aesthetics Elaine Scarry talks of the positive benefits to the recognition of beauty, claiming in her book *On Beauty and Being Just* (1999) that beauty "assists us in our commitment to justice" and confers upon us the gift of life. Scarry quotes Simone Weil who identifies the value of beauty "de-centering" the viewer, a process which Iris Murdoch referred to as an "un-selfing" (Scarry, 1999: 57–124 for a full description). Whilst this terminology is suggestive of a return to early Ruskin, it seems pertinent to a society increasingly caught up in the vanities of career and appearance.

In contemporary design is it possible to find the confidence that Heller demonstrated? In what seems essentially to be a return to Vitruvian values, the psychologist Nancy Etcoff goes so far as to suggest that universal standards of human attractiveness do actually exist and serve "Darwinian ends," making it more likely that fertile and genetically sound individuals will reproduce themselves (Lambert, 1999). Yet we need to ask if it is possible to be more specific, whether we can define what these qualities might be and if they possess an exclusive claim to beauty.

The architectural theoretician Christopher Alexander (2002) confidently claims to have arrived at an objective basis for identifying beauty through the recognition and consideration of the "immense orderliness" that governs the world around us (p. 9). He declares all space and matter, organic or inorganic, to be less or more "alive," that there exists a discernible, living energy that we all perceive but have been educated by our overly mechanistic society to ignore, and that this energy contributes to "wholeness" which we experience as beauty. This notion of beauty determined by degrees of life certainly confirms Rosenkranz's assertion that the ugly or *Verbildung* is characterized by lifelessness. Alexander is highly critical of much twentieth-century architecture and suggests that the loss of beauty in contemporary design is due to the fragmentation caused by a shared mechanistic worldview. He traces this worldview back to an overly literal application of Descartes" model of the universe as machine that has made the making of beautiful buildings "all but impossible" (p. 8) since it is unable to recognize or articulate harmony or order (p. 15). Similarly, the physicist Bohm (1992[1988]) proposes an "unbroken wholeness," which could bring about a reality that is "orderly, harmonious and creative" but warns that it would demand a "thoroughgoing end to fragmentation." Bohm's theory claims that we are not separate from the world but rather that we are "enfolded inseparably in the world, with no ultimate division between matter and consciousness" and that "*meaning and value are as much integral aspects of the world as they are of us*" (pp. 390–1, original emphasis).

It is with similar confidence that Alexander (2002) attempts to build a theory of order that identifies the role of what he terms "centres" and "fields" in building life and how these adhere to 15 fundamental properties.[3] In tones resonant of Morris, he believes these principles are capable of resolving the ongoing conflicts of function versus ornament and interior versus exterior reality (p. 22). To support his theory he examines responses to a wide variety of objects including barns, palaces, cars, calligraphy and household objects. Alexander is confident that the general consensus observed in many of the experiments does indeed prove that varying degrees of life can be recognized. His examples of successful design draw heavily from eastern religions and Islamic architecture to demonstrate the benefits of a less mechanistic and more holistic worldview. In doing so, Alexander reveals the role of religious faith in shaping and expressing a positive worldview; an observation he shares with Scarry (1999) who notes that "a special problem arises for beauty once the realm of the sacred is no longer believed in or aspired to" (p. 47).

In contrast, Tarnas (1991) places less emphasis upon faith and looks to the "wholeness" to which Scarry, Alexander and Bohm aspire as being achieved by a "profound and many levelled marriage" of the previously dominant but now alienated rational masculine self with the previously repressed feminine (p. 444). He suggests that for this marriage to take place, first the male must undergo the "ego death." This begs the question of how this ego death may be secured. It would seem that this could indeed be achieved by finally acknowledging that a singular and exclusive definition of beauty is now impossible and that beauty may exist by *intent* and also by *mistake*. In this recognition, the rational male—representing both classicism and high modernism—gives up the exclusive claim to the knowledge of beauty in order to share with the previously repressed female, who may be seen to represent the intuitive, the accidental and the neglected.

Conclusion: looking to the weather vane

In conclusion, despite the controversy, Heller's *The Cult of the Ugly* did reveal the difficulty of making aesthetic judgements in isolation from context. Indeed, as McCoy (1993) asks, when the primary goal is communication, "why should graphic design's highest visual expression be defined as beauty or harmony?" (p. 3). Yet we have to acknowledge that this communicative process—achieved through the designer's deployment of formal properties of typeface, size, space and colour—inevitably elicits a response in the form of an aesthetic judgement, whether passive or, in the case of Heller, highly impassioned.

It is clear that we are labouring under terminology that carries too many historically loaded associations. How do we interpret the word "beauty"? Does it represent—as the classicists would have us believe—a manifestation of the divine through numeric order, is it the product of an act of genius or merely the current taste of a particular individual? Aesthetic judgements are informed by worldview and so carry different meanings in different epochs. As a consequence, the singular terms "beautiful" and "ugly" cannot be trusted to present historically consistent value, so in one sense they are redundant. Nevertheless, to engage in the contemplation of things considered to have positive aesthetic value remains valid. Nancy Etcoff claims that "the idea that beauty is unimportant or a cultural construct is the real beauty myth. We have to understand beauty or we will always be enslaved by it" (Lambert, 1999). Understanding beauty need not necessarily mean trapping it within dogma, but rather acknowledging the complex factors that shape and inform judgement over time. As Helen Vendler suggests, relativism ultimately gives way to a coherent judgement, as borne out by our continued approval of Shakespeare, Rembrandt and Vermeer, so we are in a better state to decide a hundred years later whether something is beautiful (Lambert, 1999).

If aesthetics can be compared to a weather vane—essentially as an indicator of cultural movement over time—then it clearly has a positive use for those not discomforted by change. It seems logical therefore that discussions on aesthetics should take their place within graphic design courses, certainly at post-graduate level, and that these should find space alongside other areas of critical theory to present a historically and culturally balanced picture. Within such an environment it is likely that future speculation and discourse can only be enriched by the recent contributions from other disciplines coming from Scarry, Alexander and Bohm. It may be the case that we are subsequently "assisted in our commitment to justice," that we sense a degree of healing and find a new understanding of wholeness. This would inevitably be reflected in the way that we consider the design process, and a renewed confidence in making may threaten our current embrace of the found or accidental. Beauty by mistake may not be the "final phase in the history of beauty," as Kundera suggests.

Notes

1. Telephone conversation between the author and John Walters, editor of *Eye* magazine, July 2003.
2. The excerpt below from Warde's lecture of 1930 entitled "The Crystal Goblet, or Printing Should Be Invisible" clearly articulates the belief that typography was essentially concerned with function:

    Imagine that you have before you a flagon of wine. You may choose your own favourite vintage for this imaginary demonstration, so that it be a deep shimmering crimson in colour. You have two goblets before you. One is of solid gold, wrought in the most exquisite patterns. The other is of crystal-clear glass, thin as a bubble, and as transparent. Pour and drink; and according to your choice of goblet, I shall know whether or not you are a connoisseur of wine. For if you have no feelings about wine one way or the other, you will want the sensation of drinking the stuff out of a vessel that may have cost thousands of pounds; but if you are a member of that vanishing tribe, the amateurs of fine vintages, you will choose the crystal, because everything about it is calcu-lated to reveal rather than hide the beautiful thing which it was meant to contain . . . Now the man who first chose glass instead of clay or metal to hold his wine was a "modernist" in the sense in which I am going to use that term. That is, the first thing he asked of his particular object was not "How should it look?" but "What must it do?" and to that extent all good typography is modernist.
3. Alexander's "Fifteen Fundamental Properties" are:

    1. Levels of Scale; 2. Strong Centres; 3. Boundaries; 4. Alternating Repetition; 5. Positive Space; 6. Good Shape; 7. Local Symmetries; 8. Deep Interlocking and Ambiguity; 9. Contrast; 10. Gradients; 11. Roughness; 12. Echoes; 13. The Void; 14. Simplicity and Inner Calm; 15. Non-Separateness. A fuller description and practical examples can be found in Alexander (2002: Ch. 5, pp. 143–242).

Chapter 1.2.4

Is there a canon of graphic design history?

Martha Scotford

A *canon*, defined by the *American Heritage Dictionary* as it might relate to graphic design, is a basis for judgment; a standard; a criterion; an authoritative list (as of the works of an author or designer). The word was originally used to designate the books of the Bible officially recognized by the Church. The concept of *canon* is under debate right now in literary/educational circles, as its existence is alleged to produce a culturally narrow and elitist university curriculum, among other cultural problems.

Having followed the discussion about the problems arising from the study of literature produced mainly by Western white males, it occurred to me that the study of graphic design history, coming out of its infancy, may be producing its own canon, perhaps unintentionally and unconsciously. What would such a canon consist of? Are there designers and works that are used to represent whole periods, styles, and theories in graphic design history? Are some designers' works more revered than others? Why? Judgments are implied when certain designers and works become better known than others; is this process wholly legitimate and deserved? What is it based on? What problems will it cause for the future study of graphic design history?

Premise

I want to make it very clear at the outset that in suggesting a canon here, I do not wish to perpetuate one; only to show one may exist for the purpose of discussion. Given what I believe is its unintentional nature, it may be that there are 'mistakes': this could be *a* canon, but not *the* canon of graphic design. It could very well be that some designers and their work do not belong here or that others have been overlooked.

If a canon of graphic design exists, or is developing, how can this be proved? The specific period I am discussing here, modern graphic design, is broadly dated as beginning in 1850. Given the visual nature

First published in AIGA *Journal of Graphic Design,* 9 (2) (1991): 37–44. © Martha Scotford.

of the subject, it is most strongly established and communicated in a visual way, i.e., by reproduction, especially in books. Exhibitions and poster reproductions could also be studied, but books seem the most widely available and least ephemeral source at present to explore the presence of a canon.

Method

Five books were chosen for the study; these represent the best known general historical surveys of the past twenty years. The following is a description, alphabetical by author, of each volume and explains the criteria cited by the authors (with page reference noted) used for the inclusion of design works in each of the volumes. It also includes the limitations, if any, of each for the purposes of this study.

1. James Craig and Bruce Barton, *Thirty Centuries of Graphic Design* (New York: Watson-Guptill Publications, 1987), 224 pages; 10 pages for study period; 400 black-and-white illustrations. The subtitle, 'An Illustrated Survey,' accurately describes the prolific use of reproductions over text. The text is more in outline form than prose, and is often in the form of timelines, lists, and technical sidebars. The book starts with prehistory and includes more discussion and reproductions of the fine art concurrent with graphic design than do the other books in this study. "Designers and illustrators have been carefully selected to show diversity and to create a feel for a specific period" (p. 9).

2. Alan Fern and Mildred Constantine, *Word and Image* (New York: Museum of Modern Art, 1968), 160 pages; 138 pages devoted to study period; 211 illustrations, 30 in full color. The most limited resource, in subject matter, for this study because it is restricted to posters and to those in the MoMA collection. However, it is critical because posters, collected and saved, have always been one of the most prominent and important media in graphic design and its history. In addition, this particular collection is large and well regarded. It must be accepted that there have been judgments at all levels: what was selected for the collection and then what was chosen for inclusion in the book (about ten percent of the collection). Critical selection is what makes a canon. The preface to the book states that works for the collection have been 'selected primarily for their aesthetic quality, but also include work of mainly historical or social significance" (Constantine, p. 6).

In his essay's introduction, Fern states that the book "is a brief history of the modern poster (and its close typographical relatives) as an art form. I have limited my investigations to those designers who have approached the poster as a means of expression as well as communication, and have explored graphic design and typography as serious creative media" (p. 11).

3. Steven Heller and Seymour Chwast, *Graphic Style: From Victorian to Postmodern* (New York: Harry N. Abrams, 1988), 238 pages; 233 for study period; over 700 illustrations, 225 in color. This is the most recent publication and covers exactly the period under discussion. The book is a survey like the others, but makes no attempt at scholarly analysis. Rather, it "is primarily concerned with the images, not the image maker . . . we consistently emphasize the formal, emblematic visual characteristics of a design period . . . we are tracing nothing less than the evolution of the popular tastes of the period" (p. 12).

This is the only volume among the five to concentrate on visual form. It is notable for its many anonymous pieces and for the breadth of its visual offerings.

4. Philip B. Meggs, *A History of Graphic Design* (New York: Van Nostrand Reinhold, 1983), 511 pages; 335 pages on study period; over 1,000 illustrations, all black-and-white. The first survey published in the United States, this book appeared just as many design programs were incorporating graphic design history into their curricula. It has become the textbook for such courses and the standard reference for design professionals. The author expresses the necessity for the understanding of the past so "we will be better able to continue a cultural legacy of beautiful form and effective communication" (p. xi). The survey begins with the invention of writing after the pictograph and petroglyphs of prehistoric times.

5. Josef Müller-Brockmann, *A History of Visual Communication* (Switzerland, Niggli/Teufen, 1971), 334 pages; 214 for study period; 570 illustrations, 6 in color. The only European publication among the five, this was the first historical survey of the subject to be published. It explores the wide scope of the field that its well-known author/designer considers more accurately termed *visual communication* than *graphic design.* He states that the survey is not complete, but he has "concentrated on those aspects of particular interest to me: factual advertising, experiments which influence our thinking, and artistic works which set the stylistic trend" (p. 6). The book begins its discussion with prehistoric cave paintings and early writing forms.

Criteria for analysis

Having selected these books for study, what are the criteria for tabulating what is published in them? One, of course, is the visual imprint—how certain works and designers are made more memorable than others by differences controlled by size, color, and repetition. A caveat is in order: I have no pretensions to being a social scientist and have developed the tabulation system here as a way to prove relative rather than absolute presence of designers and works. I have been as accurate as possible with the tabulation, and the numerical interpretation (using the median and setting the categories) is governed by my desire to be inclusive. It is hoped that no one will waste time recounting the numbers. That is not the point.

The study began with the creation of a list (alphabetical by author), tabulating each reproduction of a design work and noting whether that reproduction is black-and-white or color, and its relative size to other work in the book. In general, small is any size up to one-quarter page; medium is one third to two thirds of a page; large is two thirds to full page. Once this list of 286 designers/partners was compiled for each book, and the information from all books was combined, the list was edited to cull a list of all the designers (205) who were represented at least twice among the five books: either a single work reproduced in two different books, or two different works shown in one or two books. The list was then studied to discover what patterns of appearance might exist among the designers and the works that could prove a canon existed. It could then describe what it contained. Once this tabulation was complete, these findings were broken down even further, to study other criteria for each designer:

1. Total number of individual works reproduced.
2. Total number of all works reproduced.

3. Number of repeats (#2 minus #1).

4. Total number of large reproductions.

5. Total number of medium reproductions.

6. Number of large and medium reproductions (#4 plus #5).

7. Total number of color reproductions.

8. Total number of large reproductions in color.

9. Total number of single works reproduced four times (four books).

10. Total number of single works reproduced three times.

11. Total number of single works reproduced twice in color.

12. Country of birth/significant practice.

13. Gender.

14. Born before 1900.

15. Born 1900–1919.

16. Born 1920–1929.

17. Born 1930–1939.

18. Born after 1940.

19. Deceased.

From the edited list of 205 designers, a smaller list (63) was made of designers/partners who had a significant appearance in at least one category of the first eleven. *Significant* was defined as having a number two-below the median for that category or higher. The results of this operation were studied and the absolute lack of women was duly noted. I decided to include on the list those women designers (6 out of 14) having the highest frequency of reproduced works. As well, a very few other well-known designers were allowed, whose numbers were just below the cutoff point and were interesting in relation to the others. I fully realize this might be a canon trap in itself; my reasoning is that one instinctively looks for certain designers and would want to see these numbers for comparison. I think these inclusions strengthen the example.

Discovering the canon

The table gives the corresponding numbers for the sixty-three designers/partners and each criterion (see Figure 1.5). These are not scores or ratings; this is not a contest. These numbers reveal the relative weight/importance that these specific five books have placed on certain designers and works.

The numbers in bold are those that are considered significant for the final cut of the list; these fall at or above the median for each category. This again seems the broadest way to include individuals. You will notice a range in the amount of bold numbers among the designers. There are eleven categories; it was decided that if a designer had bold numbers in five or more categories (that is, a significant showing

	Total # individual works reproduced	Total # works reproduced	Total # repeats	Total # large	Total # medium	Large & Medium	Total # in color	Total # large & in color	Total # × 4	Total # × 3	Total # × 2 and in color	Born before 1900	Born between 1900–1919	Born between 1920–1929	Born between 1930–1939	Born between 1940	Deceased	Country of birth/significant practice
DESIGNER MEDIAN	*18*	*23*	*5*	*3*	*8*	*11*	*3*	*1*	*1*	*2*	*1*							
Baumberger	4	4	0	3	1	4	1	*1*	0	0	0	•	•	•	•	•	•	Switzerland
Bayer	**30**	**40**	**10**	**4**	**17**	**21**	**0**	**0**	**2**	**1**	**0**		•				•	**Austria/Germany**
Beardsley	16	16	0	1	3	4	1	0	0	0	0	•					•	Great Britain
Beggarstaff	5	8	3	3	2	5	0	0	0	1	0	•					•	Great Britain
Behrens	11	17	6	1	6	7	0	0	*1*	0	0	•					•	Germany
Bernhard	9	12	3	2	2	4	3	*1*	0	1	*1*	•					•	Germany
Bill	15	19	4	3	9	12	0	0	0	1	0		•				?	Switzerland
Binder	5	9	4	0	2	2	0	0	*1*	0	0	•					•	Austria
Bonnard	3	6	3	1	4	5	1	0	0	1	0	•					•	France
Bradley	*18*	19	1	0	6	6	1	0	0	0	0	•					•	United States
Brodovitch	14	15	1	0	5	5	1	0	0	0	0	•					•	Russia/France/US
Carlu	5	9	4	2	3	5	2	*1*	*1*	0	0		•				•	France
Casey*	4	4	0	0	2	2	0	0	0	0	0			•				United States
Cassandre	**19**	**27**	**8**	**6**	**12**	**18**	**7**	**2**	**0**	**3**	**1**		•				•	**Russia/France**
Cheret	11	15	4	1	7	8	2	0	0	2	0	•					•	France
Chermayeff & Geismar	15	15	0	0	5	5	0	0	0	0	0				•			Great Britain/US
Erdt	2	4	2	1	1	2	1	0	0	1	0	•					•	Germany
Glaser	11	12	1	1	1	2	0	0	0	0	0			•				United States
Golden	5	7	2	0	2	2	0	0	0	1	0		•				•	United States
Grasset	8	10	2	0	3	3	0	0	0	1	0	•					•	France
Greiman*	8	9	1	1	2	3	0	0	0	0	0					•		United States
Heartfield	*19*	19	0	0	5	5	2	0	0	0	0	•					•	Germany
Hofmann	**11**	**12**	**1**	**1**	**3**	**4**	**2**	**0**	**0**	**0**	**0**			•				Switzerland
Hohlwein	12	17	5	2	10	12	3	0	0	1	0	•					•	Germany
Huber	7	1	2	2	4	0	0	0	0	0	0		•					Switerland/Italy
Huszar	7	10	3	0	4	4	1	0	0	1	0	•					•	Netherlands
Kamekura	10	12	2	1	2	3	0	0	0	1	0		•					Japan
Kauffer	16	20	4	*4*	4	8	5	*2*	0	0	0	•					•	US/Great Britain
Lissitzky	**39**	**49**	**10**	**6**	**17**	**23**	**4**	**3**	**1**	**4**	**1**	•					•	**Russia/Germany**
Lubalin	*21*	21	0	0	5	5	0	0	0	0	0		•					United States
Macintosh	5	9	4	0	8	8	2	0	0	1	0	•					•	Great Britain
Marinetti	6	10	4	0	2	2	0	0	0	1	0	lb					•	Italy
Matter	**16**	**25**	**9**	**4**	**9**	**13**	**3**	**1**	**1**	**1**	**0**		•				•	**Switzerland/US**

	Total # individual works reproduced	Total # works reproduced	Total # repeats	Total # large	Total # medium	Large & Medium	Total # in color	Total # large & in color	Total # × 4	Total # × 3	Total # × 2 and in color	Born before 1900	Born between 1900–1919	Born between 1920–1929	Born between 1930–1939	Born between 1940	Deceased	Country of birth/significant practice
Moholy-Nagy	*18*	23	5	1	*11*	12	2	*1*	0	1	0	lb					•	Hungary/Germany/US
Morris	9	13	4	3	3	6	0	0	0	0	0	•					•	Great Britain
Moscoso	5	6	1	0	3	3	*4*	0	0	0	0				•		•	United States
Moser	16	7	0	7	7	2	0	*1*	1	0	0	•					•	Austria
Mucha	12	12	0	1	5	6	2	0	0	0	0	•					•	Czechoslovakia/France
Müller-Brockmann	**14**	**23**	**9**	**3**	**12**	**15**	**4**	**1**	**0**	**3**	**1**		•					**Switzerland**
Neuberg	7	7	0	2	2	4	1	*1*	0	0	0		•				?	Switzerland
Philips	5	5	0	1	0	1	5	*1*	0	0	0	•					•	United States
Rand	*24*	28	4	2	7	9	0	0	0	0	0	•						United States
Ray	5	3	2	0	4	4	0	0	0	1	0	•					•	US/France
Rodchenko	*18*	18	0	1	7	8	5	0	0	0	0	•					•	Russia
Roller	6	8	2	0	3	3	1	0	0	1	0	•					•	Austria
Rudin*	5	5	0	2	4	5	0	0	0	0	0			•				Switzerland
Schelmmer	3	5	2	0	2	2	0	0	0	1	0	•					•	Germany
Schuitema	7	7	0	2	3	5	0	0	0	0	0	•					•	Netherlands
Schmidt	8	13	5	0	7	7	0	0	*1*	0	0	•					•	Germany
Schultz-Neu	1	3	2	0	2	2	1	0	0	1	0	•					•	Germany
Schwitters	11	13	2	2	2	4	3	*1*	0	0	0	•					•	Germany
Sutnar	23	25	2	0	7	7	0	0	0	0	0	•					•	Czechoslovakia/US
Thompson	10	10	0	0	5	5	1	0	0	0	0		•					United States
Tissi*	5	6	1	0	0	0	1	0	0	0	0				•			Switzerland
Toulouse-Lautrec	11	17	6	2	*12*	14	5	2	0	0	1	•					•	France
Tschichold	*20*	20	4	2	8	10	1	*1*	0	1	0		•				•	Germany/Switzerland
Van de Velde	6	9	3	0	5	5	1	0	*1*	0	0	•					•	Belgium
Van Doesberg	9	12	3	1	3	4	4	*1*	0	1	0	•					•	Netherlands
Vivarelli	7	10	3	1	6	7	0	0	*1*	0	0		•				?	Switzerland
Weingart	14	14	0	0	3	3	2	0	0	0	0					•		Switzerland
Wyman & Terr	7	8	1	*3*	5	8	0	0	0	0	0				•			United States
Yokoo	7	8	1	1	2	3	*4*	*1*	0	0	0				•			Japan
Zwart	**21**	**29**	**8**	**1**	**14**	**15**	**0**	**0**	**0**	**1**	**0**	•					•	**Netherlands**

Boldface = Canon   *Female   (Median) numbers in italic

Figure 1.5 Results of the analysis of a possible canon. Author's image.

in eleven criteria), that designer had been consistently "featured" by the majority of the books and could be considered part of the canon of graphic design. The table here produces a canon of eight designers (in alphabetical order): Herbert Bayer, Afonse Mouron Cassandre, El Lissitzky, Herbert Matter, Laszlo Moholy-Nagy, Josef Müller-Brockmann, Henri de Toulouse Lautrec and Piet Zwart.

Interpreting the canon

What do we notice about this group? First, and more about this later, the canon is all male. They were all born before 1920, several before 1900, and all but one (Müller-Brockmann) are deceased. They are all native Europeans: two are from Eastern Europe (Lissitzky and Moholy-Nagy; Cassandre was born in Russia to French parents, but left Russia to attend school); two are French (Cassandre and Toulouse-Lautrec); two are Swiss (Müller-Brockmann and Matter); one is Austrian (Bayer); and one is Dutch (Zwart).

Are there surprises here? Perhaps the only surprise is Toulouse-Lautrec, who, though considering him important to poster history, most would not expect to make the graphic design canon. One should question the inclusion of Müller-Brockmann because he is the author of one of the books; however, records seem to indicate he has been approximately as generous to himself as was Meggs.

More surprises in the inclusion area: chauvinistically, we might murmur, "What, no Americans?" And there are several poster "masters"—you can fill in your favorites—who might be expected on the list. Each period/style has its heroes, but, across the broad survey period, it is difficult for these individuals to stand out consistently. There are also several designers who have very respectable showings in the category of "number of reproductions," but who have not been set apart by size or color of such.

A possible explanation for some of these exclusions may be the nature of the work. For instance, Armin Hofmann's revered posters are originally in black and white, so featuring him by a color category is difficult. (This is one example of the possible disservice to individual designers by the criteria used for this list.) Another designer in a similar situation is William Morris. He worked as a graphic designer primarily in book design; books are mostly printed in black and white.

Other designers, working mainly with typography, are using smaller formats that are seldom reproduced in a large format.

One case struck me as a serious misrepresentation of the designer's work, not in the number of reproductions, but the nature of them. Cheret's posters were and are important for their pioneering use of color, both technically in historical terms and aesthetically for the richness of the effects he achieved in lithography. Yet, these five books present only two of his works in color.

Interestingly, after the initial curiosity of discovering the canon's identity, the rest of the list shows how different designers are represented in the books, and brings to mind those designers who have not made the edited (and amended) list of 63. Here, in my opinion, are the more intriguing cases of inclusion and exclusion.

The most obvious distinction, about which I do not intend to get polemical, is that of gender. There are no women in this canon. There are six women represented on the edited/amended list, four of them independent designers. (Margaret and Frances McDonald were part of the Mackintosh group and had less to do with graphics than other design formats.) The numbers for the independent four indicate they are poorly represented in all categories. There may be explanations, but not many excuses: the women are all younger than the men (two of the women born in the 1920s, one in the 1930s, one in the 1940s) and therefore have had shorter careers (less production is not always a correlation). But even comparing the two oldest, Casey and Rudin, with male designers of their generation, Glaser and Hofmann, produces a serious discrepancy. And the youngest woman, Greiman, is reproduced more frequently than the rest, but not featured as well as the second youngest, Tissi. Once we have passed into the post Second World War generation, there are many more female designers from which to choose, but this option has not been exercised. Possibly, there are problems with critical distance, yet the contributions of Muriel Cooper, Barbara Stauffacher Soloman and Sheila Levrant de Bretteville (among others) have been recognized elsewhere.

As stated before, I believe the canon that exists was unintentionally created. That is, each book in the study is an individual set of decisions. But what were all those decisions based on? Aesthetics? Economics? And who made the decisions? Authors? Publishers? Book designers? Clive Dilnot pointed to this problem in 1984, before several of the books used for this study were published:

> At present, there is no real discipline of design criticism, but a canonical list of 'important' design and designers is rapidly being established, despite that the critical arguments for their inclusion in such a list remain almost unstated. We are seeing this sharp differentiation into "important" and "unimportant" design works, which is tending to exclude the unimportant works from the definition of design and to restrict the material we actually discuss.[1]

Each book is a different and separate case, and no specific research has been done by me on this aspect. But one anecdotal piece of evidence leads me to suspect the general logic I would otherwise credit to the authors: the relative and real sizes of the reproductions in each book are related to the design format of that book. One assumes the authors of each are selecting the pieces to be reproduced, and that they have some reasonable idea of what they consider more or less important for their particular presentation—and would seek to express this by size and color. However, Philip B. Meggs has told me that the publisher's designer did the layouts for his book and, as that particular inexperienced designer was not a historian, the design works were used to fill six pages as needed. For purposes of the canon, this is the reality that the reader finds, assuming there are few other resources for the beginning graphic design student.

There may be some other practical issues affecting the canon. The availability of works for reproduction is affected by several factors. Some works that a conscientious author would want to show are not available due to collection restrictions, or the cost of permission is prohibitive. There may be copyright restrictions. In many cases, where no source is given for the work, it is from a private collection that may also be that of the author. How does this affect selection? In only one area might it be salutary: the increased inclusion of anonymous work.

What about color? Two of the five books have no color reproductions at all; one (Müller-Brockmann) has very few. The decision is mainly about economics, the trade-off being the ability to print more black-and-white illustrations rather than fewer in black and white plus a few in full color. A cursory inspection of *Word and Image* shows that the appearance of a poster in color may have more to do with its location relative to page imposition than with aesthetics or critical importance. Looking through *Graphic Style* also reveals that specific pages in each signature are available for color; it is hard to assess how much this dictates to the authors and how much they will work within this production limitation. *The History of Visual Communication,* with so few reproductions in color (only six), may be the only book to express an accurate opinion with color.

Does this dismiss color as a criteria? Yes and no. Since it is my belief that this canon and the list it generates are unconsciously created, we need not be concerned with the lack of control on the author's part over color, but we do need to deal with the reality of the reader. Not knowing and/or not concerned about bookmaking, the reader may naturally assume color has significance and will pay more attention to and remember works shown in color. If we consider color a non-category, given this discussion, what happens to the canon if color is removed as a criterion? Left with eight criteria (the median then becomes four), are there significant changes? No, the eight designers remain and no one is added. The color categories remain.

As I have mentioned, many designers' works have been reproduced in healthy numbers; that is, the books have provided a reasonably broad presentation of the possible designer pool (exceptions as noted). Some designers you might have expected in the canon have a strong presence in the books, based on frequency of appearance: Beardsley, Bill, Bradley, Brodovitch, Chermayeff & Geismar, Heartfield, Hohlwein, Kauffer, Lubalin, Rand, Rodchenko, Sutnar, Tschichold and Weingart. If this group is added to the Canon Eight, we get a much broader selection by geography/nationality and by generation (but still no women).

You will undoubtedly have thought of some designers you consider important and will have attempted to find them on the list here. Lustig and Danziger are two that come to mind. They both have considerable western US connections. Is there bias for the East Coast in this list? De Harak and Vignelli are two others who do not appear on the final list. It is true that it takes time for judgments of historical and contemporary importance of individual designers to be made. This is the most obvious reason we see so few postwar generation designers represented: careers are not long enough yet; the time-distance is not sufficient, and there are so many more to choose among than in the case of earlier generation designers. The same cannot be said for the generation born in the twenties and thirties; they are quite sparse on the list here and have certainly developed their work/careers sufficiently for us to assess it.

The canon and the list are Western biased (First and Second worlds). Some of the books have sought to partially redress the imbalance with some work from the Far East and Third World nations. Japan, as the Eastern nation with the most highly developed (in a Western sense) graphic design, is represented by two designers: Kamakura, of the first generation to adapt Western/Swiss design, and Yokoo, much younger and influential here in the early 1970s. They are better represented than any of the women.

Other questions and comparisons will occur to you. Feel free to use the table to satisfy your curiosity. There are even some silly discoveries: accounting for variations among languages, the most popular name for a designer is William (eight); the second most popular is John, and the third is a tie between Herbert and Henry. For national chauvinists, looking at geographical distribution and birthplace, we find the US with 13, Switzerland with 11, and Germany with 10. Consider population size.

Problems for the future

Is the existence of a canon a problem? Is this canon a problem? A canon creates heroes, superstars, and iconographies. In singling out individual designers and works, we may lose sight of the range of communication, expression, concepts, techniques, and formats that make up the wealth of graphic design history. As we attempt to become more objective and critical, it will also be harder to assess the 'stars'.

The existence of a graphic design canon, so early in the development of graphic design history and criticism, may focus too much attention and research in certain areas, to the exclusion of others equally significant. A canon reduces a lot of material (designers, works, facts, biographies, influences, etc.) to a smaller and perhaps more manageable package. Fewer names and works may make it easier to teach and learn and even to imitate, but reduces the rich, complex, and interrelated history that truly exists. If we narrow the field now, it will take much longer and be much more difficult to properly study and understand our cultural and professional heritage. For students new to the study of graphic design, a canon creates the impression that they need go no further; the best is known, the rest is not worth knowing. This is unfair, dangerous, and shortsighted.

The existence of a canon is the result of a natural reliance on art history (and on the example of architectural history) as a model for studying graphic design history. There are other ways of looking at, and exploring, graphic design history. These may well result in other ways of understanding and categorizing design works: by explicit and/or implicit content, by communication intent, by communication concept, by audience, by visual/verbal language, etc. The master/masterpiece approach also dismisses the existence (and possible importance) of anonymous works. How can the study of ephemera ignore the significance and influence of this category of works? Graphic design work will always, and finally, reveal its cultural origins. These origins need not be a particular person to be appreciated and understood; the origins can well be a specific time and place and people. With a perspective closer to *cultural* history than to *art* history (with its implied elitist flavor), we might come closer to a realistic and meaningful evaluation of our design cultural heritage.

Whether we agree that there should be a canon or not, I submit one exists and is being created, and that this process will continue at an increased pace as graphic design history develops further through publications, exhibitions, scholarship, and collections. We need to evaluate and control the process; if we need a canon, if we really need to label and separate, we need to assess better what canon exists and to amend it to make it intentional, conscious, responsible, and truly meaningful for all.

Note

1. Clive Dilnot, "The State of Design History, Part II: Problem and Possibilities," *Design Issues* (1.2) (Fall 1984).

Chapter 1.2.5

Good history bad history[1]

Tibor Kalman, J. Abbott Miller, and Karrie Jacobs[2,3]

It's been over a year since the end of the '80s. This gives us some distance, some perspective. The '80s are now, officially, History.

The '80s were a decade of comebacks: suspenders, miniskirts, Roy Orbison, Sugar Ray Leonard. . . . But the really big comeback was history. We got rid of history in the '60s; saw what the world looked like without it in the '70s; and begged it to come back in the '80s.

And it did; it came back with a vengeance.

In design, history came back as well. Suddenly, there were countless books—big, glossy, oversize volumes—and starchy[4] little[5] journals[6] devoted to the history of design. Careers were constructed around this fascination. Conferences, too.

And there's nothing wrong with studying the history of design. In fact, it's healthy and smart, especially for design professionals. At the same time, the indiscriminate use of history has produced some really bad, unhealthy design. History in itself isn't bad, but its influence can be.

There are two problems with design history. The first is how design history is written, for how history is written affects how the past is seen and understood. How history is written also affects how the past is used. And that's the second problem: Most design history is not written, it's shown. There's a lot to look at, but not much to think about. Maybe this is because designers don't read. That particular cliché (which, like most clichés, has a basis in truth) provides a good excuse for a lot of hack work in publishing: collections of trademarks, matchbooks, labels, cigar boxes, you name it—volumes and volumes of historical stuff with no historical context. And since these artifacts are mostly in the public domain, unprotected by copyright, such books are a bargain for the publishers and a godsend to designers who are starving for "inspiration."

We seem to be locked into a self-fulfilling prophecy: Designers don't read, so design writers don't write.[7] Let's amend that: They write captions. Sometimes they write really long captions, thousands of words that do nothing but describe the pictures.

Books of design history that are packaged for a supposedly illiterate audience only engender further illiteracy. Visual literacy is important, but it isn't everything. It doesn't teach you how to think. And an enormous amount of graphic design is made by people who look at pictures but don't know how to think about them.

First published in *Print*, 45 (1991): 114–24, 132–5. © Karrie Jacobs, Tibor Kalman, and J. Abbott Miller.

The study of design history is a way of filtering the past; it's a way of selecting what's important to remember, shaping it and classifying it. It's also a way of selecting what's important to forget.[8] In a way, historians are inventors. They find a design movement, a school, an era, and if it doesn't already have a name, they make one up: Depression Modern. The American Design Ethic. Populuxe.

Design historians construct a lens through which they view design—and we view design. This lens is selective: It zooms in on a subject and blocks our peripheral vision. What we see is a narrow segment of design history: one period, one class of designers within that period. What we don't see is the context, both within the design profession and within real history.[9]

Design history provides us with terminology, a shorthand for thinking about the design of an era. We come across phrases like the "New York School," under which Philip Meggs, in his *History of Graphic Design*, groups innovators like Paul Rand, Bradbury Thompson, Saul Bass, Otto Storch, Herb Lubalin, Lou Dorfsman, and George Lois. The New York School is made up of designers about whom we've reached a consensus: Most of us believe they were the great designers of the '50s and '60s. Even so, looking at their work gives us a very stilted, narrow view of those decades. If we remember the '50s and '60s, then we know that most things did not look as if they were designed by Bradbury Thompson or Herb Lubalin. We know how elite the design represented by the term "New York School" is. And we know first-hand how selectively design history remembers.

The historical lens is both a way of seeing (or including) and a way of not seeing (or excluding). When we look back at eras that are beyond personal experience and memory, we become more dependent on what we see through the lens. What we don't see, in effect, didn't exist.

Meggs uses another term, "Pictorial Modernism," to describe graphics of the '10s, '20s, and '30s that were inspired by certain movements in Modern painting—Cubism, for instance—but that did not depart altogether from the conventions of representation. We look through the lens of Pictorial Modernism and we see work by Lucian Bernhard or A.M. Cassandre, design we now think of as great. What we don't see is the angry, frightening graphics of a tumultuous era. We see a Modernism that's deceptively cool, deceptively pretty. Even Ludwig Hohlwein's posters for the Nazis are neutralized by a lens that isolates only esthetic qualities.[10,11]

Through this lens, we see Western European design, and design that was used primarily for selling expensive but tasteful luxury products—design that can be put to those same uses today. What we see through this lens becomes the design we know, and remember, and admire.[12]

Our ideas about what we see through the lens shape our ideas about contemporary design. A restricted view of the past creates an equally restricted view of the present. If we see the past as a series of artifacts, then we see our own work the same way.[13]

Graphic design isn't so easily defined or limited. (At least, it shouldn't be.) Graphic design is the use of words and images on more or less everything, more or less everywhere. Japanese erotic engravings from the 14th century are graphic design, as are 20th-century American publications like *Hooters* and *Wild Vixens*. Hallmark has as much to do with graphic design as Esprit does. Probably more. The Charter paperback edition of *Eden's Gate* is as much a part of graphic design history as Neville Brody's book.

Graphic design isn't so rarefied or so special. It isn't a profession, it's a medium. It's a mode of address, a means of communication. It's used throughout culture at varying levels of complexity and with varying degrees of success. That's what's important about graphic design. That's what makes it interesting. And it is at work every place where there are words and images.

But design history doesn't work that way; it operates with a restrictive definition. Graphic design, says History, is a professional practice with roots in the Modernist avant-garde. Design history creates boundaries: On this side is high design; on that side is low design. Over here is the professional and over there is the amateur. This is what's mainstream, that is what's marginal. Preserve this, discard that.

For design history to be worth anything, it has to have a more inclusive definition of graphic design and a more inclusive way of looking at graphic design. Graphic design has artistic and formal qualities, and much of what's written about design focuses on these qualities. Design history becomes a history of esthetics, of taste, of style. But there is another, more important history. It is the history of graphic design and its audience. It tells how political images have been crafted, how corporations have manipulated public perceptions, how myths have been created by advertising. This other history is the history of design as a medium and as a multiplicity of languages speaking to a multiplicity of people.

In focusing on its artistic and formal qualities, history has neglected graphic design's role as a medium. It has presented design as a parade of artifacts, each with a date, a designer, and a place within a school or movement. But each artifact marks more than a place in the progression of artistic sensibility. Each also speaks eloquently of its social history. All you have to do is learn the language.

Don't misunderstand. The formal evaluation of objects is okay, but it's tricky to evaluate objects from another era intelligently. Our esthetic standards are different from those of the past. What looks cool to us today may have been embarrassing, regressive, offensive, or just run-of-the-mill in its own day. To look at artifacts without knowing what they were in their own time is to look into a vacuum.

We try to use contemporary language and standards to talk about design from the past. But do we mean the same thing by "modern" as designers did in the first half of the century? What was modernity in the 19th century? What did the Museum of "Modern" Art mean by the phrase "good design" in the 1950s? When and where did the term "white space" come into use? Did they have it in the Renaissance? Did it mean the same thing?

The lack of critical commentary in design and design history has produced an ambivalence toward language. Writing about design sometimes seems pointless or suspect, and design as the expression of the written language has been seen as a less-than-"artistic" pursuit. Design becomes the composition of purely pictorial elements rather than the manipulation of both image and language. Design becomes mute. Anyone who has tried to design with dummy copy knows that hypothetical situations don't inspire brilliant work. Some of the best designers—Paul Rand, Herb Lubalin, Saul Bass, Alvin Lustig—are those who consistently engaged the editorial and textual dimensions of design.

The key word in bad design history is de-contextualization. A history of design artifacts is only interested in constructing an evolutionary chain of progressive design styles. In order to do this, the object must be extracted and abstracted from its context. The abstraction occurs because abnormal and stylistic features are discussed apart from the content of a given work.

One symptom of this tendency has been the production of graphic design in which style is a detachable attribute, a veneer rather than an expression of content. This is nowhere clearer than in the so-called historicist and eclectic work which has strip-mined the history of design for ready-made style. And this brings us to the second part of the problem: the use and abuse of history.

Designers abuse history when they use it as a shortcut, a way of giving instant legitimacy to their work and making it commercially successful. In the '80s and even today, in the '90s, historical reference and down and outright copying have been cheap and dependable substitutes for a lack of ideas. Well-executed historicism in design is nearly always seductive. The work looks good and it's hard not to like it. This isn't surprising: Nostalgia is a sure bet; familiarity is infinitely comforting.

So this criticism has nothing to do with whether the execution is good or bad, but with the question of use and abuse. The image in the left column of the preceding spread falls under the heading of "Modernism." You'll recognize it; is a well-known work by a Modernist designer. The image in the right column represents "jive Modernism." You'll recognize this work, too; it is a well-known work by a contemporary designer.[14] [Eds. note: see original essay]

There's a lot of confusion about Modernism these days, mostly engendered by the use and abuse of the term "Postmodernism." Jive Modernism is not post-Postmodernism. In a way, it's the opposite. In architecture, Postmodernism has come to mean the habit of affixing pre-Modernist stuff—classical ornament—to the facades of otherwise Modernist buildings. In graphics, the term has been used to mean just about anything, at least anything that departs from the most austere, Swiss-born, corporate-bred Modernism.

Jive Modernism is not a departure from Modernism. It's a revival, a way of treating Modernism as if it were something that was thought up by the ancient Romans, something dead from long ago. And in reviving Modernism, jive Modernism is a denial of the essential point of Modernism, its faith in the power of the present, and the potential of the future. Modernism was an attempt to jettison the confining aspects of history. It replaced the 19th century's deep infatuation with the past with a 20th-century optimism about the present and the future. Our infatuation with Modernism—jive Modernism—is now an infatuation with the past.

The Modernists invented new formal languages that changed not just how things looked, but how people saw. Modernism was a heartfelt attempt at using design to change the world.[15] It succeeded. And it failed.

Modernism was optimistic about the role of design. Even the pissiest Modernists, the Dadaists and Futurists, believed that design has a responsibility to carry a new message. Modernism believed in itself, in its contemporaneity: It believed in the present.

Clearly, the esthetic part of the new message was carried forward successfully. And that is Modernism's failure. We've learned the esthetics of Modernism by rote, and we repeat these lessons as faithfully and with as little thought as a school-child repeating the Pledge of Allegiance.[16] Modernism failed because the spirit of it, the optimism, was lost. Modernism without the spirit is Trump Tower. It's a fake Cassandre poster advertising Teacher's Scotch.

The contemporary work shown here has a parasitic relationship to the past. Modernism is the host organism and jive Modernism is the parasite that feeds off it. The relationship is one-sided and opportunistic. Like a real parasite, jive Modernism doesn't care about what the host organism thinks. It doesn't care about Modernism's politics or philosophy or anything that might be below the surface of the look.

Jive Modernism[17] gains—prestige, instant style, clients, awards—while real Modernism loses. Jive Modernism has invoked Modernism as nostalgia. It's pessimistic about the present, which it rejects in favor of the past. Jive Modernism is very useful in graphic design, in politics, in advertising, in fashion,

Figure 1.6 Winterferien—Doppelte Ferien, Schweiz advertisement (1936). Designer: Herbert Matter. © 1943, photo, Scala, Florence. ©2015, digital image, The Museum of Modern Art, New York/Scala, Florence 2015.

Figure 1.7 Swatch advertisement (1982). © 1986. Designer: Paula Scher. What's going on here? Theft? Cheap shots? Parody? Appropriation? Why do designers do this? Is it because the designers don't have new ideas? Is it a glorification of the good old days of design? Is it a way to create a sense of old-time quality in a new-fangled product? Are the designers being lazy, just ripping off an idea to save time and make for an easier client sell? I can only speak for the last example. It was designed by M&Co. in 1982; and in this case, the answer to the questions above is yes.—Tibor Kalman.

in films. It feeds into prevailing Reaganesque conservatism in America, which seeks solace in images whose familiarity is comforting. Modernism, which was once radical, is now safe and reassuring. And the amazing thing about jive Modernism is, unlike other, sloppier, more sentimental forms of nostalgia, such as Art Nouveau, you can use it and still seem hip.

Jive Modernism succeeds to the extent that it does because our conception of the bygone era it invokes is based on a stock of fuzzy, out-of-context imagery. We think of the '20s as the Jazz Age and the '30s as the Streamlined Decade. We know what we know mostly from Hollywood movies, television, and selected graphics. The vernacular, the eccentric, the marginal, and the minority have been filtered out of our collective memory.

Jive Modernism turns up in some odd places, places where it shouldn't even be: Ralph Lauren advertising, for example. These ads generally involve a cast of characters who seem to have success- fully colonized some third world nation and have now turned their attention to lawn tennis. But here they use what Meggs calls Pictorial Modernism. The look is an amalgam[18] of Ludwig Hohlwein, Lucian Bernhard, and Joseph Leyendecker, mixed with some nonspecific heroic realism. It's not even very Modern (except when compared with most of Lauren's graphics). Mostly, it's jive.

But let's just suppose that the image below, which was designed in the late 1980s, really is a histor- ical object: What kinds of questions should we ask if it were designed in 1927, and what should the questions be if it were designed in 1987? For starters, we should ask: *Who played golf in 1927, and what did it signify as a social activity?* [Eds. note: see original essay]

Upper-class white men being exclusive.

And then we should ask: *Who played golf in 1987, and what did it signify as a social activity?*

Middle- and upper-class white people, including a growing number of female executives, being exclusive.[19]

What did the artist of 1927 intend by rendering the image in this high-contrast style?

Here we can answer that, in 1927, it was a progressive, state-of-the-art style. It was also a way of incorporating color and the look of photography without the expense of photography.

What did the artist of 1987 intend by rendering the image in this high-contrast style?

Here we can answer that it was a way of achieving a retro look by referring to what was once a progressive, state-of-the-art style. The decision not to use a color photograph carries with it certain anti- technological associations. These associations are useful because they support the sense of Ralph Lauren products as hand-crafted rather than machine-made.

What did the image of the airplane signify in 1927?

Progress.

What did the image of the airplane signify in the late 1980s?

Quaintness.

Jive Modernism thrives on our collective memories of the past. The Ralph Lauren design works because it plugs into an existing network of personal associations and recollections. It's effective. It's also a cheap shot.

Is this a problem? Well, if jive history is so successful that it replaces both the past and the present, then future historicist design will be double-jive-history, twice removed from the original reference.

We'll be living in hyper-jive.

Bad historicism reduces history to style. We learn no more about the historical forms being used than we learn about music from a lounge musician playing note-for-note reproductions of the hits. Bad historicism reduces Cassandre, Lissitzky, Mondrian, Schlemmer, and Matter into names to be dropped or designer labels to be conspicuously displayed. The history of design becomes a marketplace where we shop for style—the proverbial marketplace of ideas. We pull a style off the rack, we try it on. If it fits, we take it.

Now, the point of this article is not to argue against appropriation of ideas. And it's certainly not to argue against influence. Designers can borrow ideas from other media, contemporary ideas or historical ideas, and transform them into good design ("transform" is the key word here).[20] Cross-pollination is an important and legitimate aspect of how culture works.

What we're arguing against is design that cashes in on history. We object to contemporary designers who take ideas that might have been radical 70 years ago but have since become legitimate—more than that, endearing and very, very safe—and reuse those ideas without even reinterpreting them. We're not opposed to historical reference: Just as there is good history and bad history, there is good historical reference and bad historical reference. Reference means just that: You refer to something. It gives you an idea. You create something new.

Real Modernism is filled with historical reference and allusion. And in some of the best design today,[21] historical references are used very eloquently. But those examples were produced with an interest in re-contextualizing sources rather than de-contextualizing them.[22]

There's an important difference between making an allusion and doing a knock-off. Good historicism is not a lounge act. It's an investigation of the strategies, procedures, methods, routes, theories, tactics, schemes, and modes through which people have worked creatively. If we have any monuments in the history of design, they should be the basis for critical evaluation. We need to learn from and interrogate our past, not endlessly repeat its recipes. What we can learn from Constructivism is not type placed at 45-degree angles and the reduction of colors to red, white, and black, but freedom with word order and the lack of strict hierarchies in the typographical message. We need to look not at the stylistic tics of Modernism but at its varied strategies. We should focus not on its stylistic iterations but on its ideas.

How can we change bad history into good history? How can we change bad historical reference into good historical reference? We need fewer coffee table books and more ambitious design writing. We need as much time spent on the editorial conception of books as is spent on sexy layouts and glossy photography. We need to ask the right questions. After all, good history is a matter of asking good questions.

While we have access to the individuals who have been influential in graphic design, we should ask the questions that can't be answered by the work alone, questions that can't be addressed directly or empirically, but are elusive and genuinely historical. They are questions such as: What is it about this piece of design that we can't understand because we are not part of the culture in which it was produced? What did the style of this image communicate to its audience? What was the relationship of the designer to his or her client? If this object is an example of good design at the time, what was considered bad, or banal, or mediocre? What aspects of the image have become transparent to the eyes of a contemporary viewer?

Good design history is interested in the finished product not as a point of perfection bound for the Museum of Modern Art but as the culmination of a process. Because of this, good design history pays attention to the fringes of design as well as the mainstream, and to the rejects and failures as well as the award-winning examples.

We need design history that does not see itself in the role of a service to the design profession, but as a history of ideas. Such a design history would tell us not only who produced something when and for whom, but would situate the object in a historical moment and would reveal something about the way design works on its audience.

A good history of design isn't a history of design at all. It's a history of ideas and therefore of culture. It uses the work of designers not just as bright spots on the page but as examples of the social, political, and economic climate of a given time and place. This isn't really much of a stretch. Good history in general presents ideas in context in a way that teaches us more than how things once looked. It is not just a roster of names, dates, and battles, but the history of how we have come to believe what we believe about the world. Likewise, good design history is not just a roster of names, dates, and objects; it is the history of how we have come to believe what we believe about design.

The biggest difference is this: Bad design history offers us an alternative to having ideas. Bad design history says, here, this is nice, use it. Good design history acts as a catalyst for our own ideas. Good design history says, this is how designers thought about their work then, and this is how that work fits into the culture. Now, what can *you* do?

Notes

1. The title should tip readers off to the fact that this is a polemic: more concerned with *having* an argument than *making* an argument. In keeping with this strategy, the authors exploit appealingly succinct, unqualified pronouncements that are the hallmark of devil-may-care glibness.—JAM

2. This speech was written slowly and painfully by Tibor Kalman and J. Abbott Miller. It was then rewritten in great haste by Karrie Jacobs. The finished product, the speech given by Kalman at last year's "Modernism & Eclecticism" symposium (sponsored by the School of Visual Arts in New York City in February 1990), was full of highly debatable points. But since Tibor delivered the speech, he took the flack. The rest of us were able to sink down in our seats and watch from a safe distance. Now, in PRINT, all of our names are attached, so we are doing the only prudent thing. We are qualifying and modifying. We are writing footnotes.—KJ

3. Too many cooks spoil the soup, but can the same be said of designers and writers? The three of us set out to challenge this old adage by concocting a stew. After several days of toiling in our respective crock pots, the three recipes were combined into a fine kettle of fish. This "eclectic" mix was the soup du jour that was dished out by Tibor Kalman in his keynote address to the "Modernism & Eclecticism" conference. To Kalman's taste, the mixture required more spice, especially salt rubbed in several wounds. Such are the prerogatives of the chef invited to table his comments.

    After Kalman's presentation, some members of the audience were simmering and others felt left out in the cold from the rough draft that filled the room. The version of the talk published here is no less rough, yet it includes annotations which clarify, modify, qualify, deny, reiterate, and eliminate aspects of the original.—JAM

4. This little word seemed to cause consternation during the discussion period following the presentation. Perhaps this is the perfect moment to check [Webster's] dictionary:

    starch n (15c) 1: a white odorless tasteless granular or powdery complex carbohydrate $(C_6H_{10}O_5)x$ that is the chief storage form of carbohydrate in plants, is an important foodstuff, and is used also in adhesives and sizes, in laundering, and in pharmacy and medicine 2: a stiff formal manner: FORMALITY 3: resolute vigor | —MTK

5. *Journal of Decorative and Propaganda Art* (circulation: 5,000, trim size: 7¼″ by 10″); *Design Issues* (circulation: 1,500, trim size: 7″ by 10″); *The Journal of Design History* (circulation: 750, trim size: 6″ by 8½″); *TV Guide* (circulation: 15,800, trim size: 5″ by 7.375″).

   Well, maybe this could be understood as a negative reference. It's not intended that way. If the journals were less starchy, they might not provide the kind of pure academic study that's actually needed in this area. If they were physically larger, chances are they'd only get glossier with bigger and better-reproduced artwork, which isn't the point, either. If the circulations were larger, these journals would be taking ads, worrying about their "reader profiles." and probably lowering their standards. None of this is desirable. In short, we think these journals are pretty good, and we like them.—TK

6. One man's starch is another man's complex carbohydrate. The journals designated by Kalman as "starchy" are not part of the same commercial enterprise as "big, glossy, oversize volumes." Academic journals—particularly *Design Issues*—represent, in fact, alternative models to the kinds of history writing criticized here. In its first year of publication (1984), *Design Issues* published Clive Dilnot's two-part essay "The State of Design History," which laid out many of the crucial problems facing the development of design history. Specifically, Dilnot called attention to the narrow focus on professional design activity, the emphasis on solitary genius-creators, and the fetishization of design as a "value" expressed through style.

   Apart from the forum such journals provide to designers, writers, and academics, they are a means through which design and design history may be recognized by other disciplines as a worthwhile arena of study. The status of design in relation to other established disciplines matters if one hopes to affect the institutional structure of design education and design within general education.—JAM

7. There are, of course, exceptions.—KJ

8. It's inarguable that the influential texts on graphic design history (Meggs's *A History of Graphic Design*, Remington and Hodik's *Nine Pioneers of Graphic Design*, Müller-Brockmann's *A History of Visual Communication*) have focused on the sunnier side of the street. The persistent forgetting of (refusal to notice?) the "shady" side of the street (advertising, propaganda, forced obsolescence, the designation of "vernacular" forms, the relationship between designers and the client class they serve) needs to be viewed critically, and in relation to the way in which the expanding image bank of design history is being put to use.—JAM

9. The line of argumentation throughout this essay finds its "low sodium/high carbohydrate" antecedent in Clive Dilnot's statement that "the essential field of design's meaning and import . . . is *not* the internal world of the design profession, but the wider social world that produces the determining circumstances that lead to the emergence of designers" (Dilnot, "The State of Design History," *Design Issues* [Spring 1984]: 14). In our presentation, we tried to bring this theoretical point home through specific examples of graphic design and references to what we think are familiar texts on design.—JAM

10. These references to Hohlwein seem to have gotten Phil Meggs, author of *A History of Graphic Design*, into a nettle. You'll no doubt be reading his spirited response in a forthcoming issue of PRINT. However, the authors stand by this analysis and suggest a re-reading of the aforementioned tome's pages 299–300 (including captions) to better enable the reader to decide which analysis is correct. Perhaps future editions of Meggs's book might be revised to include a broader discussion of not only Hohlwein's pro-Nazi views, but the development of the most powerful logo ever: the swastika, which apparently was designed (presumably for a big fee) by a local corporate identity firm.—TK

11. Philip Meggs considers Ludwig Hohlwein's career (including his involvement with Nazi propaganda) within the overarching framework of "Pictorial Modernism." The question remains: Are stylistic features an adequate means to describe the role of design in society? Or is Hohlwein and the style of graphics he helped to establish better understood as an especially important part of a historically evolving relationship between images of

power and governmental sponsorship of such images. What about the recurrence and resonance of this style in American mass media then and now?—JAM

12. Between all these lines we are asking: What about all the other design? The newspapers, the ads for hemorrhoid products, retail handbills, license plates, signs, diplomas—all the stuff people saw every day. Where is that history?—TK

13. In fact, this is exactly the way we look at our own work, as artifacts out of context, reproduced in annuals.—KJ

14. This is a mistake we've all made. Students of art and design are taught to copy as a way of understanding a process so they can better understand the way to evolve their own styles. But you're *supposed* to outgrow this. A 1982 M&Co. project for Jerry Harrison (Fig. 12) is included by way of purging our own guilt about a cheap-shot copy.—TK

15. This remarkably general discussion of "Modernism" rhetorically lumps together an actually divergent set of ideas and practices, not all of which are so utopian. Not all Modernists were (and are) of the Howard Roark variety (see Gary Cooper as Howard Roark as Frank Lloyd Wright in King Vidor's version of Ayn Rand's *The Fountainhead*). Other facets of Modernism were melancholic, dystopian, and deeply pessimistic. Yet this pessimism still reserved a role for art and design as a mode of criticism. For a discussion of different aspects of Modernism's critical potential, see Peter Bürger's *Theory of the Avant-Garde* (Minneapolis: University of Minnesota Press, 1984).—JAM

16. Actually, I think it's more complicated than this. I think there are several levels of historicism. On one hand, there is a self-conscious use of Modernist style, and on the other, there is a use of Modernism that occurs almost naturally because Modernist style has been incorporated into the generic language of design.—KJ

17. And every other nostalgic device.—KJ

18. Confidential to TK: e-māl' gem.—KJ

19. People play golf for many reasons, yet the decision to market clothing by associating it with golf highlights the popular understanding of golf as a country-club activity.—JAM

20. "Transform" is the key word on any side of a debate about the use of historical sources. The argument rests on opinions about how effectively, creatively, or cleverly historical sources are "transformed" by the designer. The very same set of comparisons we've used here to make our point about the abuse of history could, in the hands of someone else, be used to argue the vitality of contemporary designers' use of historical sources. This essay attempts to distinguish different varieties of and motivations for using historical sources: It argues for a self-consciousness about what it means to "transform."—JAM

21. E.g., by Tom Bonauro, Rick Valicenti, the photographers Geof Kern and Bruce Weber, *Spy* magazine, etc.—TK

22. There is an almost automatic sense of indignation when a vanguardist, political form of art, design, or language is used in a different context and for different (typically commercial) ends. The indignation arises from the fact that the original meaning gets lost, subsumed, or sugar-coated under the pressure of the new context. In architecture, preservation councils protect buildings considered significant so that new construction and planning do not violate the buildings' original contexts. We don't have such things in graphic design: Trademarks and packages are updated without regard for their status as icons of our consumer landscape. This is partly why there is so much nostalgia in design and design history.

But the anxiety about style as a detachable attribute—the uneasy feeling that in much design, form is cleanly separable from content—relates to the fundamentally ephemeral status of graphic design as a sign system. Graphic design is a medium enabled by the possibility of making new signs out of existing verbal and visual elements. Thus, recontextualization and decontextualization are at the heart of the enterprise. Design functions because signs of any sort (colors, textures, typefaces, etc.) do *not* retain meaning across contexts, but are adaptable, mutable, unstable, and vulnerable.—JAM

Chapter 1.2.6

Out of the studio: graphic design history and visual studies

Rick Poynor

Introduction: the reluctant discipline

Twenty years ago there was considerable optimism about the possibility that graphic design history would become a fully-fledged academic discipline, despite some unresolved questions about its purpose. Although there has been some progress toward this goal in the past two decades, these developments have taken place at a slower pace than might once have been expected.[1] As a discipline—if this is even the right term to use—graphic design history is still in a state of becoming, and there are good reasons to ask whether, on its present course, it will ever achieve the maturity that some observers hoped for.

This lack of progress might be measured in various ways. Most obviously, in Britain, where I write, there is no such thing as a first degree in graphic design history. Even design history studied as a clearly defined degree subject concerned with largely non-graphic forms of design remains a rarity.[2] The subject is usually combined with art history and sometimes with film history.[3] Art history established itself several decades ago as a coherent academic discipline and as a subject for study with a broad appeal to non-practitioners. Design history has a long way to go to achieve the same stature or pulling power.

The situation is not much better when it comes to graphic design history writing—which is not surprising because the need for such research is inevitably linked to the amount of study taking place in higher education. The key indicator of the discipline's health is book publishing. Although academic papers about aspects of graphic design history are delivered at conferences and surface in publications such as *Design Issues* and *Journal of Design History*, we should be wary of mistaking these occasional expressions of interest in graphic design history for signs of much activity in the field. Perhaps the most striking example of this shortfall is the three issues of *Visible Language* published in 1994–5, which set out to explore the possibility of new "critical histories of graphic design."[4]

This ambitious project appeared to promise a dawning era of intellectually challenging, revisionist graphic design history writing that would in time have a significant effect on the field of book publishing—even transforming perceptions of what such writing could be; but this promise did not come to fruition.

First published in *Design Observer*, January 10, 2011. © Rick Poynor.

Only a minority of the 15 *Visible Language* contributors went on to make substantial contributions to graphic design history, in terms of scholarly research that led to the publication of original, authoritative, subject-redefining books.[5] This is not to say that there have been no other significant additions to the graphic design history bookshelf during the past decade, but even in a good year, the additions never amount to more than a few titles.[6] When this patchy output is placed beside the numerous books produced by scholars working in, for instance, the fields of art, architecture, or film, as it is in any visual arts bookshop, it becomes obvious that graphic design history as a terrain for intensive and sustained research and study barely exists at all.

The reasons why graphic design history has failed to develop—and, without a change of direction, will most likely continue to fail to develop—are sometimes acknowledged in passing but are not addressed with any persistence or rigor, perhaps because they point to some unwelcome conclusions for the subject as it is currently situated and being taught. In an attempt to see the problem more clearly, this essay revisits some of these perspectives. The essay's second aim, arising from this review, is to propose an alternative site of production for graphic design history, albeit one that is interdisciplinary in essence rather than located within its own clearly delineated departmental borders. Graphic design history's best chance of development now lies in an expanded conception of the rapidly emerging discipline of visual culture or visual studies.[7] Although this proposal is also problematic, for reasons that will be explored, only in visual studies might graphic design history be able to establish the interdisciplinary connections necessary for it to fulfill its early promise and to grow.

Graphic design history is for graphic designers

Almost all of the early arguments about the need for graphic design history were made from within the discipline of graphic design by informed observers, often graphic designers, who felt that knowledge of graphic design's history and development was essential for any practitioner. This grounding would allow graphic designers to avoid plagiarism and pointless reinvention; it would supply "inspiration" and give them a legacy on which to build. Steven Heller sets out this position in his introduction to *Graphic Design History*, a book of essays about design history subjects intended for graphic design students:

> A compelling case has been made through conferences, magazine articles, and books, for the centrality of graphic design history in the education of all graphic designers. During this formative period in the digital age, when new media is altering traditional notions of graphic design practice, it is even more important that designers have the grounding provided by historical knowledge.[8]

Andrew Blauvelt, editor of the three "critical histories" issues of *Visible Language*, put the issue even more strongly; writing two years after the trilogy appeared, he went so far as to assert that the only plausible use for graphic design history was as a tool for educating graphic designers more effectively:

> The notion of design as a field of study without practical application is unlikely and undesirable. After all, it is the practice of graphic design—no matter how wanting or limiting—that provides the basis for a theory of graphic design. [. . .] The calls for graphic design to be a liberal art—a quest for academic legitimacy—need to be supplanted by strategies which foster "critical making," teaching when, how, and why to question things.[9]

Indeed, at least one call for design to be considered as a liberal art had been made, but this tendency hardly needed to be supplanted because the design-history-is-for-designers point of view has always dominated discussion.[10] This design studio orientation is only to be expected because those who write about the possibilities of graphic design history are usually graphic designers who, if they also teach, are almost always situated within graphic design departments. However, the idea that design history, pursued as an academic end in itself, could lead to estrangement from the methods and goals of design practice has also been proposed by professional historians who might seem to have every reason to wish to construct design history as a separate enclave. Guy Julier and Viviana Narotzky note "a yawning gap between the desires of design historians and the actions of designers," suggesting that design history might have made itself redundant as a contributor to essential principles of practice.[11] They conclude: "We do not question the value of history as discourse [. . .] But we do ask design history to return to its roots and bed itself with practice."[12] Whatever relevance this request might have had for historians concerned with industrial design, for graphic design it could be taken as little more than a warning for graphic design history to stay where it was already situated—in bed with practice.

However, this location was by no means as secure, congenial, or productive for the incubation of graphic design history as it might sound. In the way that they are usually constituted and administered, graphic design departments have some profound limitations as homes for historical study. As Heller observes, most American design schools do not use dedicated teachers of design history; in fact, most design history teachers are "practitioners who have entered the field through the back door," without experience in historical research and publishing, and most design schools, even if they offer a few graphic design history courses, do not have the finances to maintain a dedicated history program.[13]

Louis Danziger, described by Heller as one of the first "historian-cum-practitioners" to introduce a class in graphic design history, is frank about the limitations of his own design history teaching, acknowledging that it is neither academic nor scholarly and is primarily concerned with helping students to enhance their performance as designers. Danziger claims that practitioners cannot be good historians because their experience "inevitably introduces biases," and they "cannot be objective."[14] The British design educator Jonathan Baldwin has expressed similar concerns about the situation in Britain, where design history is often taught by part-timers on hourly contracts, and studio staff and students see design history as disconnected from the practical side of their courses. "If [design history] is so unimportant that staff are paid by the hour and only during term-time, it's obviously not [seen as] important at all," he writes.[15]

All of these perspectives begin to explain why, despite the energetic and optimistic support of a few notable proponents, graphic design history has progressed so slowly. For the most part, the subject remains essentially an afterthought, a comparatively minor adjunct to the design studio, conceived by its apologists as a means of molding better-rounded graphic designers but still seen as irrelevant by many students obliged to take these classes, and permanently undernourished by a lack of institutional support.

Publishers are fully aware of graphic design history's lack of presence and status as an academic subject, and the small number that are prepared to take the risk and produce books about graphic design history know from experience that the market for these studies remains small. Such books can only do well if they are placed on course reading lists, but the more specialized the subject matter, the less likely this placement is to happen, leading publishers to favor bland visual surveys with the widest possible appeal. At the same time, the number of teachers with the motivation, talent and pressing career reasons to undertake ambitious research projects is tiny compared to other, better established and more academically grounded visual arts subjects. Graphic designers with commercial practices to maintain, in addition to their teaching duties, have little time to engage in protracted historical research and writing, even if they possess an aptitude for it.

Visual studies' mysterious blind spot

With graphic design history still not fully formed as a subject, it might seem that continuing calls to reform it, to introduce "new perspectives" and "new views," can only fall on stony ground, no matter how well intentioned. Who is to do the reforming, and to what end? Is there any reason to suppose that the personal and institutional factors that have inhibited graphic design history's growth in its unre-formed state will not continue to inhibit any widespread adoption and application of new thinking within the field? Or will these new impulses by their very nature somehow succeed in lifting graphic design history—still positioned where it always has been as a studio add-on—to a higher plane of perceived relevance, productivity and academic attainment?

The primary contention of the critiques originating within design is that it is not enough for design history to concern itself with the evolution of graphic styles as seen in the work of a canonical list of heroic (white, male) designers. Meggs' *A History of Graphic Design* (1983) is generally cited as the work that enshrines this Pevsnerian view of graphic design history.[16] Many design teachers have drawn atten-tion to the limitations of this approach; two examples will suffice. Baldwin suggests that the slideshow parade of "great" historical moments, with its emphasis on long lists of unfamiliar names, facts, and dates that must be committed to memory, is thoroughly off-putting to students, who fail to see its rele-vance to their studio-based studies and future activities as designers. Instead, he suggests, design history should adopt what he calls "history-less history," which looks at history as a series of causes and effects with particular emphasis on the systems of production and consumption of design. This perspective allows us to bring in social studies, cultural studies, psychology, audience studies, politics and issues that are often ignored: ethics and human ecology.[17]

Prasad Boradkar, writing in *The Education of a Graphic Designer*, likewise moves the emphasis to the contexts of graphic communication's production, arguing that this theme be "situated within a variety of venues, including cultural, social, political, environmental, and economic contexts."[18] Similarly, he invokes a list of adjacent disciplines and areas of study that could function as valuable resources, including visual culture, media and cultural studies, anthropology, material culture and sustainability studies.

Although any of these disciplines might offer methods, perspectives, and insights for understanding graphic design history, most of them are clearly unsuitable as alternative resting places for the discip-line's study. As Robin Kinross has remarked with obvious irony, in the early 1990s it seemed that, at least in Britain, cultural studies would "take care of graphic design, seeing it as just one more item in the total menu of 'culture.'"[19] In the past decade, however, visual studies, rather than cultural studies, has emerged as the discipline with aspirations to take care of every aspect of the visual realm, and it might have seemed inevitable that graphic design's outputs, as omnipresent phenomena in this realm, would fall under its gaze. However, this has not as yet happened. It is rare for books about visual culture to include even the briefest discussion of design, while graphic design usually goes entirely unremarked—an omission that can only be described as astonishing, bearing in mind visual studies' overarching ambitions.[20]

Perhaps the most emblematic example of this oversight is *The Visual Culture Reader*, edited by Nicholas Mirzoeff. This much-reprinted title finds no space for any discussion of graphic design among the 60 texts that fill its 740 pages—not even in the section concerned with "spectacle and display."[21] Not a single writer associated with graphic design history, theory, or commentary contributed to the book. When visual culture writers summarize the areas that concern the new discipline, graphic design is not one of them. Martin Jay writes that visual culture is "located somewhere at the crossroads of traditional art history, cinema, photography, and new media studies, the philosophy of perception, the anthropology of the senses, and the burgeoning field of cultural studies . . . ."[22] Margaret Dikovitskaya sees it as arising from the convergence of art history, anthropology, film studies, linguistics and comparative literature after they encountered poststructuralist theory and cultural studies.[23] On the rare occasions when specifically graphic forms of visual culture are discussed, the new discipline's leading lights can sound oddly distant and uncertain, as though they have little precise contextual awareness of the object of study:

> [W]hen I look through certain magazines, I am always struck by the manner in which the impact of what is on a page seems to be more due to the images and the typeface and glaring visual stimuli, than to the substance of the arguments and the meanings of the words themselves. However, too much post-modern writing seems to hide itself behind the pyrotechnics of postmodern visuality. This may be generational: younger people seem more comfortable with it than older people, since perhaps their greater exposure to computer games and other modern mass media has made them a little more visual.[24]

For anyone located within design, visual studies' failure to acknowledge and address the central role of graphic design as a shaper of the visual environment, alongside the forms of visual culture that it does acknowledge—art, film, television, photography, advertising, new media—must seem unaccountable. What could explain this peculiar blindness among a group of academics hyper-attuned to most forms of visuality?

One point that is immediately clear is that the oversight duplicates a wider public oversight—the oft-remarked "transparency" or "invisibility" of graphic communication—that has long been a source of concern among designers. It is still unusual for graphic design to be discussed anywhere other than in professional publications and a few academic journals; in addition, oversight by the media begets over-sight by the public (even by academics in neighboring disciplines), so that the vast majority of people are not accustomed to thinking of graphic design as a vital part of culture worthy of continuous (or even sporadic) comment.[25]

Even more significant, however, are the departmental factors discussed earlier. Many of visual studies' leading figures come from art history and evidently lack even the most basic knowledge of design history. Graphic design history's compromised location as an adjunct to the design studio—its lack of full departmental status—denies it the appearance of academic legitimacy. In addition, the inward-looking nature of graphic design history writing and other forms of design discourse, and the continuing assumption among designer writers that the ultimate purpose of such commentary is professional improvement, has created a body of writing that appears from the outside, when it is noticed at all, to be merely of professional interest. If graphic design history books are being consulted by academics working in visual studies, they certainly are not being cited regularly. Before graphic design history writing can connect with a wider academic readership, it needs to orient itself differently—no small task at even the most elementary level of distribution. Bookshops struggle with the idea of interdisciplinarity when it comes to classifying and shelving a book. Even design titles purposefully aimed in part at cultural studies or visual studies readers can end up in the design section, where they are less likely to be encountered by readers who are not designers.[26]

Does visual culture have a history?

Unpromising as its resistance to design might sound, visual studies nevertheless has the potential to offer the most propitious base, outside the design studio, for new critical approaches to graphic design history. To understand how graphic design might fit into visual studies, we need to consider its underlying principles. Any view can only be provisional because, as a new subject, visual studies is in a state of flux and because, despite many shared assumptions, its proponents differ on some key questions. One point they tend to agree on is that culture has taken a "visual turn": that the visual is ever more dominant in contemporary society, both as a means of communication and as a source of meaning.[27] While this process began with industrialization and accelerated throughout the 20th century, digital technology pushed the production, dissemination, and use of imagery to a new level of reach and saturation. The fusion of media made possible by digital technology mandates the convergence within visual studies of critics, historians and practitioners who reject the received ideas of the established disciplines they come from.[28] Visual studies directs its attention to the visual as a place where, in Mirzoeff's words, "meanings are created and contested."[29]

Julier has characterized visual studies as occupying "the enervated position of the detached or alienated observer overwhelmed by images."[30] But this complaint underplays the fact that the images are already out there circulating and disregards the possibility that they might be problematic. According to Mirzoeff, "visual culture is a tactic with which to study the genealogy, definition, and functions of postmodern everyday life from the point of view of the consumer, rather than the producer."[31] Far from encouraging enervation, the educational aim of visual studies is, then, essentially positive: to produce active, skeptical viewers equipped to respond critically to the visual imagery that surrounds us. This viewpoint immediately puts the analytical emphasis exactly where many critics of graphic design commentary and history say they wish it to be. Instead of focusing on the designer, a visual culture approach to design would focus on the effects of design as everyday, visual communication on its audiences. As Mirzoeff explains, visual culture is not concerned with the structured, formal viewing that takes place in a cinema or art gallery, but rather with the visual experience in everyday life: "from the snapshot to the VCR and even the blockbuster art exhibition."[32]

Although this brief list typically privileges forms of visual material (e.g., photography, film, art) that tend to predominate in visual studies, we might just as plausibly add wall posters, magazine layouts, luxury goods packaging, or postage stamps. Graphic design has been overlooked precisely because it forms the connective tissue that holds so many ordinary visual experiences together. We don't usually view a professional photograph in isolation: We view it as part of a page, screen, billboard, or shop window display in relationship with other pictorial, typographic and structural elements determined in the design process. These frameworks and relationships are an indivisible part of the meaning.

Where the theorists of visual studies sometimes part company is in their view of the extent to which the field should concern itself with history. Irit Rogoff is emphatic in distinguishing between her work on visual culture and her early approach as an art historian:

> The field that I work in [. . .] does not function as a form of art history or film studies or mass media, but is clearly informed by all of them and intersects with all of them. It does not historicize the art object or any other visual image, nor does it provide for it either a narrow history within art nor a broader genealogy within the world of social and cultural developments. It does not assume that if we overpopulate the field of vision with ever more complementary information, we shall actually gain any greater insight into it.[33]

Such a view might be welcomed by supporters of "history-less history," but it poses some problems for graphic design history. As Dikovitskaya notes, an academic field is defined by three criteria: "the object of study, the basic assumptions that underpin the methods of approach to the object, and the history of the discipline itself."[34] Compared to art history, the project of graphic design history is still at a formative stage, and this is one reason why the subject has low visibility for people in visual studies. Only in recent years, more than two decades after the arrival of Meggs' history, have several similarly scaled rival volumes emerged.[35] By the time radical art historians developed the new art history in the 1970s, with its emphasis on the social production of art, the art libraries of the world were already stocked with conventional art histories. In other words, there was already a structure of basic information and an interpretive framework in place for the new wave of historians to revise.[36]

In the graphic design field, however, historical information is still lacking about even the most notable subjects, "narrow" as such scholarship might appear. Many significant but lesser known figures are overlooked.[37] Given the difficulties of publication already outlined, the arrival of any well-researched volume of graphic design history signifies a triumph against the odds. Rogoff argues persuasively that it is "the questions that we ask that produce the field of inquiry and not some body of materials which determines what questions need to be posed to it."[38] Nevertheless, she also acknowledges the danger that casting aside historical periods, schools of style, and the possibility of reading objects through conditions of production might entail losing a firm sense of "self location."[39] Divesting graphic design of its historical sign posts and landmarks would be enormously risky for a subject that is shakily located and barely apparent to those outside the field in the first place.[40]

Mirzoeff notes that graduate students approaching visual studies are sometimes worried about what body of material they are supposed to know; their concern instead, he asserts, should be with the questions they want to generate. The focus then moves to finding the most appropriate methods to answer those questions and to locating the sources that can lead to discovering the answers.[41] In a field as broad, provisional and unstable as visual culture, where visual media and their uses change all the time, the traditional pursuit of encyclopedic knowledge is no longer tenable. The history of modern media must be understood collectively rather than as a series of discrete disciplinary units, such as art, film and television (or for that matter, graphic design).

Nevertheless, in Mirzoeff's view, historical inquiry remains central to an understanding of visual culture because signs are always contingent and can only be understood in their historical contexts.[42] If art history, film studies and media studies are going to be taught together under the heading of visual studies, then new integrative histories of visual media must be written, necessitating much new research. W.J.T. Mitchell, one of visual studies' most influential figures, is similarly committed to the idea of a defined and teachable history, wanting students who take his courses to understand that "visual culture has a history, that the way people look at the world and the way they represent it changes over time, and that this can actually be documented."[43] According to Mitchell, the idea that visual studies seeks to take an unhistorical approach to vision is a myth.[44]

Conclusion: history leaves the studio?

It should be clear even from this brief overview that there is no intrinsic reason why graphic design history (and graphic design studies) should not form part of visual studies' purview. Every indication suggests that visual studies will become increasingly well established in the years ahead. Economic factors to do with student preferences cannot be ignored, and in the United States, the subject attracts students who are not necessarily interested in the specialized forms of knowledge offered by traditional visual disciplines.[45] Visual studies connects with visual media experiences familiar to everyone in a way that art history does not. Its burgeoning introductory literature attests to its popularity, as well as its intellectual vigor. For teachers coming to visual studies from other disciplines, it offers ways of understanding visual media more closely related to the overlapping, interlocking, hybrid nature of contemporary visual experience. It would be a strange oversight—to the point of undermining visual studies' claims of integrative purpose—if its theorists were to continue to overlook and thereby discount graphic communication's central participation in the creation of the image world.

This proposal is not to suggest that graphic design history does not have a place in the studio as an essential part of any graphic design student's understanding of the discipline. History-conscious teachers of graphic design no doubt will continue to argue that the subject be taken seriously and given adequate funding and support within design schools, and they are right to do so. However, a view of graphic design history that sees it as being only, or even primarily, for the purpose of educating graphic designers and that seeks to confine it to the design studio will continue to restrict the development of the subject in the ways described here. If graphic design is a truly significant cultural, social, and economic force, then it has the potential to be a subject of wider academic (and public) interest, but it will need to be framed and presented in ways that relate to the concerns of viewers who are not designers—that is, to most viewers. As habitually inward-looking custodians of their own history, few graphic design educators have proven to be effective at this outward-looking, viewer-oriented style of writing and public address.[46]

Design educators need to foster this ability because until graphic design teachers with historical and theoretical insights begin to build a bridge toward visual studies—by writing for its journals and presenting papers at its conferences, and by demonstrating graphic design's interest and significance through the strength of their scholarship—there is little prospect that visual studies will expand to include it. Although there are comparatively few academically trained design historians who concentrate on graphic design history (which is also a matter for concern), they, too, could redirect some of their output toward visual studies.

In the short term, this movement toward visual studies would not mean abandoning graphic design departments as places of "self location," but it would certainly require self-questioning and self-reinvention, starting with a close engagement with the thinking and literature of visual studies, which has barely been mentioned to date in historical and critical writing about graphic design. There are reasons, in any case, as we have seen, to anticipate that less designer-centric and fact-heavy ways of addressing the subject and investigating its social meanings would make graphic design history more appealing and useful to design students. Only when graphic design as an existing object of study becomes more visible will visual studies scholars who have come from other disciplines begin to see it as a potential field of inquiry alongside more clearly perceived visual media. The study of graphic design surely would benefit from opening itself up to these new interdisciplinary perspectives and investigations from the outside.

It might be argued that the partial absorption of graphic design history by visual studies would involve a crucial loss of autonomy. Art historians have certainly voiced fears that the renegade proponents of the new visual studies risk undoing their discipline.[47] In the case of graphic design history, however, there isn't a unified discipline to undo. Graphic design history exists between the cracks. It is not likely to achieve independence as a department in most institutions anytime soon, and, as things stand, it will continue to camp out in the studio. It is a late-starter with a lot of catching up to do.

Visual studies is an even newer arrival, although it has an energy and sense of purpose that comes from soaking up the strength of other disciplines with a long pedigree and deep theoretical foundations. Yet visual studies also exists in the gaps between other less adaptable fields of study, with an uncertainty, a lack of firm adhesion, that only makes it feel more timely and relevant. If graphic design history could find a second outpost within this territory, the making of the subject could prove—at last—to be a possibility.

Acknowledgment

Thanks to the Royal College of Art, London, where a research fellowship made this research possible, and to Teal Triggs at the London College of Communication for inviting me to speak at *New Views: Repositioning Graphic Design History*, the starting point for this essay.

Notes and links

1. See, for instance, *Journal of Design History*, 5 (1) (1992), a special issue devoted to graphic design history.
2. In the United Kingdom, Brighton University offers a well-established BA in History of Design, Culture, and

Society. The Royal College of Art, in association with the Victoria and Albert Museum, offers a well-established MA in History of Design.

3. Examples of combined BA courses in the United Kingdom include: History of Art, Design, and Film (Kingston University), History of Art and Design (Manchester Metropolitan University), History of Modern Art, Design, and Film (Northumbria University).

4. *Visible Language*, special issues: "New Perspectives: Critical Histories of Graphic Design," Andrew Blauvelt, guest ed. 28 (3) (1994), 28 (4) (1994), 29 (1) (1995). See also Andrew Blauvelt, "Designer Finds History, Publishes Book," *Design Observer* (2010).

5. See Victor Margolin, *The Struggle for Utopia: Rodchenko, Lissitzky, Moholy-Nagy 1917–1946* (Chicago and London: University of Chicago Press, 1997), Deborah Rothschild, Ellen Lupton and Darra Goldstein, *Graphic Design in the Mechanical Age: Selections from the Merrill C. Berman Collection* (New Haven and London: Yale University Press, 1998), Martha Scotford, *Cipe Pineles: A Life of Design* (New York: W.W. Norton, 1999).

6. Since 2005 see, for instance, Michel Wlassikoff, *The Story of Graphic Design in France* (Corte Madera: Gingko Press, 2005), Stanislaus von Moos, Mara Campana and Giampiero Bosoni, *Max Huber* (London and New York: Phaidon Press, 2006), Richard Hollis, *Swiss Graphic Design: The Origins and Growth of an International Style* (London: Laurence King Publishing, 2006), Kerry William Purcell, *Josef Müller-Brockmann* (London and New York: Phaidon Press, 2006), R. Roger Remington and Robert S.P. Fripp, *Design and Science: The Life and Work of Will Burtin* (Aldershot: Lund Humphries, 2007), Laetitia Wolff, *Massin* (London and New York: Phaidon Press, 2007), Steven Heller, *Iron Fists: Branding the 20th-Century Totalitarian State* (London and New York: Phaidon Press, 2008).

7. I shall follow W.J.T. Mitchell's distinction and use "visual studies" for the field of study and "visual culture" for the object or target of study. Some writers on visual culture, including Mitchell, prefer to use "visual culture" interchangeably. See Mitchell, "Showing Seeing: A Critique of Visual Culture" in *The Visual Culture Reader*, Nicholas Mirzoeff ed. (London and New York: Routledge, 2nd ed. 2002), 87. On visual culture, in addition to the other works cited here, see Block Editorial Board and Sally Stafford, *The Block Reader in Visual Culture* (London and New York: Routledge, 1996), John A. Walker and Sarah Chaplin, *Visual Culture: An Introduction* (Manchester: Manchester University Press, 1997), Malcolm Barnard, *Approaches to Understanding Visual Culture* (Basingstoke: Palgrave, 2001), and James Elkins, *Visual Studies: A Skeptical Introduction* (New York and London: Routledge, 2003).

8. Steven Heller in *Graphic Design History*, Steven Heller and Georgette Ballance, eds. (New York: Allworth Press, 2nd ed. 2001), viii.

9. Andrew Blauvelt, "Notes in the Margin," *Eye*, 6 (22) (1996): 57.

10. Gunnar Swanson, "Graphic Design Education as a Liberal Art: Design and Knowledge in the University and the 'Real World'" in *The Education of a Graphic Designer*, Steven Heller ed. (New York: Allworth Press, 2005), 22–32.

11. Guy Julier and Viviana Narotzky, "The Redundancy of Design History" (Leeds Metropolitan University, 1998).

12. Ibid.

13. Heller, "The Case for Critical History" in *Graphic Design History*, 94.

14. Louis Danziger, "A Danziger Syllabus" in *The Education of a Graphic Designer*, 333.

15. Jonathan Baldwin, "Abandoning History," *A Word in Your Ear* (2005). Baldwin delivered a paper on this theme at New Views: Repositioning Graphic Design History (London College of Communication, 27–29 October 2005).

16. Philip B. Meggs, *A History of Graphic Design* (New York: John Wiley, 3rd ed. 1998, 4th ed. 2005).

17. Baldwin, "Abandoning History."

18. Prasad Boradkar (1998), "From Form to Context: Teaching a Different Type of Design History" in *The Education of a Graphic Designer*, 85. For further discussion of the problems arising from the "varied discursive locations

stress on abstraction, the grid's association with the world of outer appearances loosens. As the rules elaborated in the *Discourse* made clear, appearances are suspect, and a problem (or, in visual terms, a field) is to be divided into its smallest component parts. This geometric, reductive operation is, of course, a mental process. The grid thus comes to represent not only the structural laws and principles behind physical appearance, but the *process* of rational thinking itself. So timely is this conception that, by the late seventeenth and early eighteenth century, the concepts of Nature and Reason achieved the status of leading ideas and came to be used interchangeably.[15] Signs of this reciprocity are evident, for example, in the application of the Cartesian grid to the exterior landscape, as in the case of the great French geometrical gardens.

Yet it is at the end of the eighteenth century that we find one of the best examples of the Cartesian grid bearing such symbolism. The intellectual climate at this time was characterized by deism, a movement which was a well-established by-product of rationalism. The latter is a theory that rejected formal religion and the concept of supernatural revelation but argued that the logic of nature demonstrated God's existence. Conceived as the Great Clockmaker, God had designed the world as a machine run by natural laws and then had abandoned it to run by itself. This mechanistic determinism informed the use of the grid by the French neoclassicist painter Jacques Louis David in his painting *The Death of Socrates* of 1787. In the charcoal study of this painting, David used the grid not merely as an illusionistic tool for transferring the drawn figure of Socrates from paper to canvas; rather, the rigid network of horizontals and verticals, evident in the wall behind Socrates, is represented in the finished painting as well.[16] The grid, which invades and integrates itself into the figure's very gestures, signifies the rational, impersonal, and inevitable character of natural law, which deterministically controls the structure of the material world and of events within that world. Indeed, the main theme of David's painting is the syllogistic inevitability of Socrates's death by his own hand as a consequence of his rigid adherence to the laws of rational thought and logically determined behavior.

The modern grid

By the second decade of the twentieth century, the full development of the Cartesian grid was realized. The dual emphasis on appearance and structure that had characterized the symbolism of the grid during the Renaissance, scientific revolution, and Enlightenment now moved strongly toward structure and away from appearance and the illusionistic depiction of external phenomena. The architectonic and constructive values so central to the early twentieth-century modernist canon were inherited from the preceding century. Violet-le-Duc's or Joseph Paxton's promotion of exposed iron structure in buildings, Christopher Dresser's functional Arts and Crafts design of teapot handles based on bird and fish skeletons, or art nouveau's rejection of the applied surface decoration of Victorian design were all nineteenth-century expressions of this exodus from a belief in surface appearance as an esthetic end in itself.

The Cartesian tradition in France continued to act as the major stimulus for the grid as it assumed its modernist embodiment. For practical purposes, the process may be said to begin with Paul Cézanne's initial move away from Renaissance illusionism toward the abstraction and geometricization of nature and an emphasis on the flat field of the picture plane. This impulse continues through the faceting of the picture plane by synthetic cubism to produce an overall effect, and it peaks when Piet Mondrian takes up the pictorial grid of synthetic cubism to explore and purify it in virtual isolation from other pictorial elements. Under cubism's influence, Mondrian's naturalistic subject matter became progressively abstracted until, in 1915, he could paint a circular field of short horizontal and vertical bars and title it *Pier and Ocean*. His paintings in the years immediately following continued to employ vertical and horizontal bars, sometimes colored and usually not touching, on a white field. Often these bars appear to continue off the edge of the canvas, suggesting that the field extends infinitely in all directions although the viewer sees only that portion visible within the "window" of the canvas. By 1920, Mondrian's pictorial vocabulary is established and consists of a white field through which travel continuous black horizontal and vertical bars that bound intermittently occurring rectangular zones of primary color. The composition still implicitly extends beyond the borders of the canvas, and (according to Mondrian) the bars cross one another and overlap, but do not actually intersect. The resulting grid is of the *line-based* type and is thoroughly Cartesian in its presentation of an unchanging regular and isotropic universal field, ruled by logic and by the mathematical law that underlies the world of external appearance. The same conception is expressed in three dimensions in the *Red and Blue Chair* of 1917 by Gerrit Rietveld, who, like Mondrian, was associated with the Dutch de Stijl movement. Each axial structural member of the chair bypassed rather than abutted its neighbor and was painted black, with the exception of the exposed yellow end which signified it as an arbitrary terminus for an otherwise infinitely extending axis.

This concept of an axially-defined field in infinite extension brings the symbolism of the Cartesian grid to its highest stage of development by linking it with the concept of a universal continuum drawn from contemporary physics.[17] The de Stijl grid visualized this physical spatial continuum not so much in material terms, but rather in terms of the mathematical laws that rule matter, space, and time. Mondrian's two-dimensional composition and Rietveld's chair were thus subsets of a larger universal field described by the grid. Also, because the modern grid was synonymous with the continuum itself, it may be defined equally well as a set of continuous axes or as a never-ending series of modules. The modern grid thus continued to be a field-based matrix predicated on the line and module.

The modernist principle of continuousness was applied as much to space as to material. The exploded form of Rietveld's chair partially dematerialized the object by dispersing it into the spatial field; space was thus allowed to circulate uninterrupted through the chair. This field-centered approach, which sought to oppose the object- or possession-centered ideals of the Victorian bourgeoisie (as expressed in their dark, massive, and closed furniture forms) was also to become the ideal of modernist interior space. Examples of this are the flowing spaciousness of Mies van der Rohe's interiors and the "free plan" of Le Corbusier, as are the reductive furniture forms they developed based on skeletal line and supporting plane, which subordinated the piece of furniture to the greater realities of streaming space and light.

But although the concept of the modern grid as a representation of the ubiquitous and invisible field of universal physical law was not too different in general meaning from that of the Cartesian grid of the eighteenth century, its specific meanings were closely tied to early twentieth-century events and ideas which informed the modern grid and, later on, the postmodern grid. A basic characteristic of twentieth-century conceptions of the field is the de-emphasis of the point coordinate or individual unit (not unlike the de-valuation of the point which occurred in the shift from the late medieval to the Renaissance grid). This de-emphasis was an implicit feature, for example, of the homogeneous continuum of Einstein or of the anti-object paradigm of the Rietveld chair's exploded form. The pro-field, anti- or neutralized-point paradigm also characterized leading conceptions of the *person-environment relationship* during this period. For example, in the fields of sociology and psychology, Durkheim, Freud, and Watson described human behavior as environmentally or statistically determined. In the sociopolitical realm, socialist, communist, and collectivist writings and experiments placed great emphasis on groups and on relationships between groups, thereby deemphasizing the importance of the autonomous individual. And in the sphere of design, the artists and designers affiliated with de Stijl and the Bauhaus felt that the passionate individualism at the root of the competing nationalisms which had caused World War I must be countered by an international impulse in architecture and design that would transcend national styles and differences.[18]

It is therefore not surprising that an anti-individualist vision expressed itself in the entire spectrum of innovations which accompanied the use of the Cartesian grid in European graphic design in the late 1920s. The underlying, invisible matrix of the grid guided the placement not of manually produced letterforms or expressive gestures, but of clean and geometric sans serif typography. Horizontal and vertical bars and rules were also used to subdivide the page space and corresponded to certain axes of the underlying grid. The leading innovators to employ this family of elements included El Lissitzky (*The Isms of Art*, 1925), Herbert Bayer, and László Moholy-Nagy (Bauhaus publications), culminating in the formulaic expression of the philosophy and method of this approach by Jan Tschichold in his 1928 book, *The New Typography*. The field axiom behind this form of graphic communication was also evident in factors beyond the use of the grid and of copy that was factual and impersonal. For example, the asymmetric distribution of typographic elements on the page created an overall visual tension that converted the negative white space from a passive to an active value. The entire visual field was thus dynamically brought into play. The tension of this field was due as well to the use of sans serif typography, which *decreased* visual interaction between different letterforms and between letters and white space.[19] This lack of interaction between the individual letter and its neighbors was another example of the element of the impersonal. In addition, the preference for principally lowercase letters—even to the point of occasionally refusing to use uppercase initials for proper names or sentence beginnings[20]— reveals an antihierarchic disposition that disdained the elevation in status of the individual (be it a person's name or other proper noun) above an otherwise *homogeneous* field.

The subsequent generation of Swiss graphic designers expanded the applications of the mathematically drawn grid and brought it to a level of perfection and elegance, without, however, altering its basic use as a tool for rationally structuring and delivering factual information. Representative designers of the Swiss school included Theo Ballmer, Emil Ruder, and Joseph Müller-Brockmann, who acted as the movement's chief theorist and spokesman. The movement proved to have much international influence in the 1950s and 1960s, although the grid itself retained the same meaning it had in the 1920s; that is, as the continuous field of rational law which underlay the physical universe much the way the grid itself remained invisible "beneath" the final design composition. As Müller-Brockmann's own book, *Grid Systems,* made clear, the modern Swiss grid retained all the Cartesian symbolism it had possessed during the early modernist era and remained a rational, universally valid, objective, and future-oriented design tool.[21]

The postmodern grid

The modern Swiss grid enjoyed its heyday during the decade of the 1960s. But during the 1970s a number of graphic designers began to overthrow the conventions of modernist graphics and use the grid to new ends. The representative work of Yale graphics instructor Dan Friedman (Figure 1.9), or that of former Emil Ruder student and Basel School of Art graphic design professor Wolfgang Weingart, illustrate the changed use and features of the grid within postmodernist graphic design. The postmodernist grid no longer acted as the invisible logic "behind" the composition, but was often visually exposed and used as a subordinate decorative element. The grid was sometimes tilted and made to express antirationality and randomness. It was often coupled with other seemingly accidental marks or manually applied gestural (signature) elements, in stark contrast to the impersonal and overly rational compositions of Swiss modernism. Usually the grid was established and then violated (ignored) or fractured along with the surface plane it defined. Both grid and composition departed radically from modernism's functionalist ethic, sometimes to the point of sacrificing the clarity, legibility, and readability

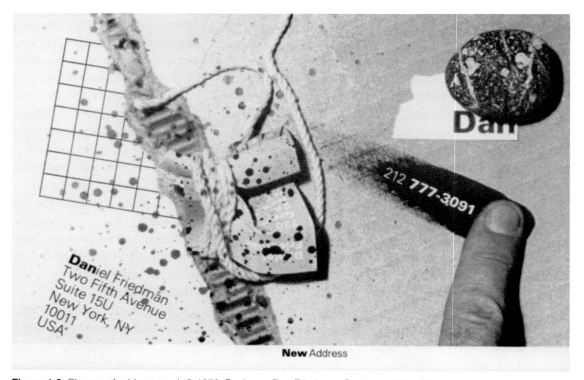

Figure 1.9 Change of address card. © 1976. Designer: Dan Friedman. Courtesy of Ken Friedman.

miniaturist were the same person was even more strongly supported in one instance by the presence of prick marks at page top and bottom to vertically establish the placement not only of text and margins, but of the painted illumination as well.

4. In designing this page, the artist innovated a visual counterpart to the practice of scriptural exegesis, a method of critically reading and comparing Biblical passages to discover hidden patterns of correspondence planted there by God. The discovery of these patterns could be accompanied by various forms of spiritual illumination, as was consistent with the anagogical principle holding that certain physical events or objects (in addition to scripture) contained the impress of the divine. When properly understood through contemplation, one's consciousness would be led from the object to its transcendent source in God.

5. The use of the point as a focus for contemplative consciousness, or the concept that it could be a threshold between physical and spiritual realities, was a standard feature of spiritual education in the Middle Ages. For example, in the twelfth-century treatise on Noah's mystical ark by Hugh of St. Victor, a mandala-like diagram guides the Christian meditator in the construction of a sequence of mental images until, arriving at the center-point of the figure, a concentration and transformation of consciousness occurs with an attendant passing into the Godhead (see Grover A. Zinn, Jr., "Mandala Symbolism and Use in the Mysticism of Hugh of St. Victor," *History of Religions,* May 1973). The allusion to Noah's ark in the title of the treatise may help to explain the unique psychotechnics of this meditation. On a metaphorical level, the Biblical account of the flood represents a plant-like process of world death and rebirth: the contraction of life to a seed-point (into the ark), the passage and survival of that point through the obliteration of the surrounding senseworld (the flood), and the subsequent re-expansion or blossoming of that point on the "other" side.

6. Robert Campin's triptych, *The Merode Altarpiece* (c.1426), which is contemporary with the birth of St. John, uses the same devices to the same ends. The altarpiece is based on an underlying grid with key symbols and dramatic points of action sited at strategic coordinates and intersections, and a sashwork cross in a window represents the only place in the pictorial program where the grid is revealed to the viewer (see the author's master's thesis, *The Meaning of the Merode Altarpiece,* Ann Arbor: University Microfilms, 1982, 350pp).

7. The cross was but one of a host of symbols that represented Christ as the conjunction of the heaven and earth. Another such symbol, also popular in Christian religious art, was the almond-shaped *mandorla* in which was placed the seated or standing figure of Christ. The shape was formed by overlapping two circles that represented the spheres of heaven and earth. As the link between both, Christ occupies the area of their conjunction.

8. The coordinate's shift from a spiritual to a physical meaning is well exemplified in the radical alteration of environmental space which occurred in Lyon, France, when the city passed from Catholic to Protestant rule in the sixteenth century. The widespread iconoclasm which accompanied the takeover eliminated numerous sacred grottoes, churches, and similar spiritual "hotspots" through which the divine was felt to vertically penetrate the space of the mundane world from above. Once destroyed, a more horizontally oriented environmental network of secular and commercial activities took its place. A homogeneous cityscape thus displaced one that was qualitatively differentiated. Natalie Zemon Davis, "The Sacred and the Political in Sixteenth Century Lyon," *Past and Present* 90 (February 1981): 40–70.

9. In major respects, the page grid undergoes few significant alterations in its development during the five-hundred-year period between Gutenberg and modernist graphic design. As with Gutenberg, the modernist grid is a field defined by either large zones created by perpendicular axes and/or by small zones in the form of individual typographic modules. In the interest of historical accuracy, it must be conceded that it is perhaps unlikely that the character-based typographic grid which typifies high-modernist graphics was consciously correlated by Gutenberg with his simple guidelines grid. Nonetheless, Gutenberg's grid *was* based on the rule which, like

the entire printed field of the page itself, was undoubtedly conceived in terms of the individual typographic unit. That these two field conceptions of the page may not have overlapped in Gutenberg's mind did not, however, prevent the fact of its being grasped and utilized by his successors.

10. Earlier world maps treating spiritual in addition to physical geography often featured Jerusalem at the center. Operating as the *axis mundi,* a concept derived from earlier "world tree" mythologies that posited a spiritual connection (trunk) between heaven (branches) and earth (roots), Jerusalem was highest in qualitative status, other geographical locations being measured in value by their proximity to it. Considered alternately as a "world navel," a similar umbilical-like connection between earth and heaven was implied.

11. The use of the grid as a device for transferring drawings from one surface to another, and from one scale to another, dates back to ancient Egypt and seems to have been in fairly continuous use by artists ever since (see James W. Davis, "Unified Drawing Through the Use of Hybrid Pictorial Elements and Grids," *Leonardo* 5 (1972): 1–9, especially the section on "Grid Structures in Western Art").

12. That this combination was both unique and representative of a new concern entering Western culture at that time is suggested, using the example of perspective painting, by the many artists using perspective to achieve a novel effect versus the few who used it chiefly as a method not of representation, but of investigation.

13. Early examples include, at the turn of the seventeenth century, Leonardo da Vinci's dissection of cadavers in order to understand the nature of bone, muscle, and tissue and the effect of these on external bodily form and movement. Also, at century's end, the first compound microscope was developed, thus opening a window onto material phenomena lying below the threshold of the unaided physical senses.

14. In the *Discourse*, Descartes presents four rules for acquiring knowledge, which may be paraphrased as follows: (1) doubt all that is not clearly evident to be true and do not accept surface appearance, (2) always begin by dividing each problem into its smallest component parts, (3) always conduct thoughts in logical order proceeding from that which is most simple to that which is most complex, and (4) reason rigorously and geometrically and never skip a logical step. Robert Nisbet, *The History of the Idea of Progress* (New York: Basic Books, 1980), 116.

15. John Herman Randall, Jr., *The Making of the Modern Mind* (New York: Columbia University Press, 1926/ 1976), 255.

16. Jean Clay, *Romanticism* (New Jersey: Chartwell Books, Inc., 1981), 35.

17. In his influential "Special Theory of Relativity" of 1905, Einstein had defined the infinite as merely the finite in extension. The medieval concept of a qualitatively differentiated, two-tiered universe consisting of physical and superphysical dimensions was thus collapsed into a nonhierarchic, physical universe conceived of as being in continuous extension. In terms of Mondrian's work, the reference to the sea in his early use of the grid in *Pier and Ocean* (1915) suggests that the continuum paradigm was established well before his mature works of the 1920s.

18. The most representative design example of this is the Weissenhof Housing Project, done for the Deutsche Werkbund exhibition of 1927 and directed by Mies van der Rohe, and generally regarded as the first official expression of the International Style in European architecture. The project sought, through the rational standardization of building forms and materials, to achieve a uniformity of vision and expression.

19. Frances Butler, "Modern Typography," *Design Book Review*, 3: 96. The organic letterforms of art nouveau, on the other hand, carried on an intimate visual conversation with the surrounding white space. Open, sinuous, or seemingly undulating art nouveau letters often sent the surrounding space swirling in eddies in and around themselves and one another. This expressive relationship between letter and page was a carryover from art nouveau's sculptural treatment of wall or surface planes in the design of interiors and domestic artifacts. In such instances the surface was conceived of as a mobile, living membrane with an inner being out of which expressive forms would manifest themselves in low sculptural relief. Thus, in the case of extremely organic art nouveau

letterforms (e.g., Henri Van de Velde's initials for *Van Nu en Straks* of 1893, or Otto Eckmann's *Fette Eckmann* typeface of c. 1902), the white of the page was seen as a generative surface out of which grew (as with the surface of nature upon which this surface was modeled) living forms. Naturally, these living forms were closely tied to the *environmental field* of nature from which they sprang. The geometric and thus inorganic sans serif letterform understandably lacked this living relationship to its environmental context: the empty white space of the Cartesian plane. More precisely, the white space of the Cartesian field signified the deserted spatial field of the deists made final in the continuum of Einstein. The estrangement of the sans serif letterform from its field was in truth a symptomatic expression of the increasing alienation of modern rational man from the world (as reflected in the pro-field, anti-individual paradigm already discussed). It was therefore not coincidental that, during the decade of the 1920s in which this visual language of modernist graphics was being articulated, the same message was being verbally expressed in the existentialism of the German philosopher Martin Heidegger, (professor at Marburg 1923–28, Berlin 1928–33) in his 1927 book, *Being and Nothingness.*

20. Leading examples of this include Bayer's "universal" lowercase alphabet of 1925 and Tschichold's "single case" alphabet of 1929.

21. In the chapter entitled "Grid and Design Philosophy," Müller-Brockmann states, "The use of the grid as an ordering system is the expression of a certain mental attitude inasmuch as it shows that the designer conceives his work in terms that are constructive and oriented to the future. This is the expression of a professional ethos: the designer's work should have the clearly intelligible, objective, functional, and esthetic quality of mathematical thinking. . . . Working with the grid system means submitting to laws of universal validity." And finally ". . . [The grid] fosters analytical thinking and gives the solution of the problem a logical and material basis." Josef Müller-Brockmann, *Grid Systems* (New York: Hastings House, 1981).

22. Weingart's cover designs for the 1974 spring and summer issues of the journal *Visible Language* offer extreme instances of over- and underexposed typography in which recognition of words and individual letters is often impossible.

23. Representative examples of futurism's infatuation with electrical phenomena include Umberto Boccioni's painting *Forces of a Street* (1911), an early example of the "lines-of-force" theory (also associated with "atmospheric electricity" or lightning); his painting *Matter* (1912), in which material reality becomes transparent to reveal a ubiquitous field of powerful forces which overwhelm both the woman in the picture and the viewer (Boccioni wrote about some people's clairvoyant ability to visually penetrate the opacity of material bodies, in the manner of X rays); and the futuristic cities of the movement's architect, Sant' Elia, in which electrical generating complexes and powerhouses were the favored building type.

24. The sense of an unseen, hidden menace also characterized an important aspect of the 1950s in American society. The "red scare" of the cold war years, the profusion of 1950s science fiction monster films, and the post-Sputnik rash of backyard fallout shelters all expressed the anxious sense that an unseen menace lurked at the edges of the familiar world accessible to the rational mind.

25. Freudian and structuralist Jacques Lacan asserted that a person's speech, far from expressing the thoughts of the conscious self, was the medium through which the "Other" self expressed itself. This "Other" was a being prior to and more real than a person's conscious self. Lacan maintained that rationality, like the conscious self, was also surface illusion. Following Lacan, structuralist Michel Foucault extended the concept of the subrational "Other" still further in 1966 with his "end of man" doctrine. See Peter Caws, s.v. "Structuralism," *Dictionary of the History of Ideas* 4 (New York: Charles Scribner & Sons, 1973), 329.

26. The drug culture which arose to assist the flight from the unpleasant realities of this period likewise represented a quite forcible destruction of rational consciousness, and the substitution of a consciousness of or by some "other" self.

27. The tilted, floating grid represents free-floating or disembodied consciousness. Although it may signify human consciousness loosed from rational or "earthly" applications, the tilted grid has been most commonly used in association with computers and high-tech advertising. This is appropriate inasmuch as the computer is the ultimate externalization (disembodiment) of human rationality.

28. The result of this collection of fragmented planes was that the "picture space" abounded with a profusion of edges. The same abundance of edges characterizes much of postmodern architecture as well. Take, for example, Charles Moore's *Piazza d' Italia* of 1975–79, in which layers upon layers of false facades stand on the periphery of an open circle of space. The theme of the vacated center, of attention focused on the periphery and on the edges of things, is typical of postmodernism in general. Architecture, graphics, furniture, and interiors abound with color-differentiated planes continually "popping away" from another. Postmodernist scholarship is characterized by a dilettantish love of peripheral or fringe topics rather than mainstream issues, a looking at phenomena from odd angles, and the rejection of sustained and centered treatment of material in favor of eccentric digressions. This search for "otherness" in the freakish and bizarre within postmodernist writings is criticized in Robert Darnton, "Pop Foucaultism," *The New York Review of Books* (October 9, 1986): 15ff. In popular culture, the Steve Martin and "Nerd" films about social misfits are similar expressions of postmodernism's "off-center" interest. This off-center theme of the late twentieth century was prophesied by W.B. Yeats in his poem *The Second Coming*: ". . . Things fall apart; the centre cannot hold;/Mere anarchy is loosed upon the world. . . ." The poem was composed in 1919, the first year the atom was smashed.

29. The 1975 movie *Jaws,* which spawned a rash of similar movies, featured a mammoth killer shark which lurked beneath the placid water surfaces of swimming beaches, etc., only to burst upward and pull someone back down at unexpected moments.

30. Michael Bonifer, *The Art of Tron* (New York: Simon and Schuster, 1982).

31. A series of books were written in the late nineteenth century that dealt with descending to the center of the earth, such as *Alice's Adventures Underground* (later titled *Alice in Wonderland*), *Journey to the Center of the Earth,* and *20,000 Leagues Under the Sea,* many of which were turned into American movies in the 1950s. French filmmaker Jean Cocteau's films *Blood of a Poet* (1930) and *Orpheus* (1950) represented similar descents—now into the irrational underworld of the self—by having the main character pass through the threshold of a mirror.

32. This is well exemplified in the anthropomorphic symbolism which abounds in the bureaus, shelving units, and lamps of the Italian Memphis group. The staccato angularity of these figures refers to electrical phenomena (see, for example, Ettore Sottsass's *Ashoka Table Lamp*, figure 6, page 13, *Design Issues* II(1) (Spring 1985), and may draw from the earlier Italian futurist conception of the human being based on subphysical electrical forces.

Chapter 1.3.2

Gebrauchsgraphik as an early graphic design journal, 1924–1938

Jeremy Aynsley

Introduction

Gebrauchsgraphik, Monatschrift zur Förderung künstlerischer Reklame (Commercial Graphics, Monthly Magazine for Promoting Art in Advertising), which was published in Berlin from 1924 until 1944, was one of the first-generation graphic design journals in Europe. It followed the poster movement and typographic reforms associated with German *Jugendstil* and their respective literature in the pre–1914 years and developed them in new directions. *Gebrauchsgraphik* published some of the first reviews of an activity still to be termed "graphic design," together with articles on book design, advertising, publicity and packaging. In the years before the Second World War, *Gebrauchsgraphik* established itself as a successful bilingual (German–English) publication, with a hiatus between 1944 and 1950. Then it was relaunched from Munich where it is still published under the revised title of *novum Gebrauchsgraphik*.[1]

This article will examine the nature of *Gebrauchsgraphik* in the years up to 1938. Besides offering a case-study of the magazine I shall suggest that its editorial policy and overall format could be considered one model for the representation of graphic design in magazine form, which proved successful and was repeated and adapted in the magazine's own history and used by other contemporary magazines as well.[2] Thus I shall examine various aspects of *Gebrauchsgraphik*: its layout design, editorial policy and critical evaluation of graphic design. I shall also consider the place of *Gebrauchsgraphik* in the context of other graphic design journalism in Europe at the time.

In relation to much more recent material, Dick Hebdige has argued for the "reading" of magazines to be considered as a process of negotiation, a multi-layered and variable process, in which a preferred and contested or negotiated reading can coexist.[3] In the light of this, it is perhaps worth indicating that the first stage for a history of the literature surrounding the emergence of *Gebrauchsgraphik* still needs to be written in order to indicate that preferred reading, before we can move to the historically more difficult question of contested readings.

First published in the *Journal of Design History*, 5 (1) (1992): 53–72. It is republished here with the kind permission of Oxford University Press on behalf of The Design History Society and the *Journal of Design History*. © OUP/Jeremy Aynsley.

In 1924 *Gebrauchsgraphik* might have been regarded as relatively innovative in its focus on advertising design. Ten years earlier, Paul Ruben had edited a significant and comprehensive two-volume study of advertising, *Die Reklame: Ihre Kunst und Wissenschaft,* with short chapters on types and scale of advertising from trademarks and press inserts to street hoardings. It included guides to copyright laws for designers, discussion of the relation of art to industry, and a brief review of the relationship between German and American advertising.[4] This book was illustrated with examples of posters by the groups of designers associated with the prominent lithographic printers in Germany, which generally aligned it with the design reform movement of the late *Jugendstil* period. It could be regarded as setting the overall agenda for a magazine such as *Gebrauchsgraphik* to pick up, although when it came to the latter's launch in 1924 neither Ruben nor other contributors to his book wrote for the magazine.[5]

It is important to acknowledge that the journal *Gebrauchsgraphik* was not representative of all graphic practice in the period under review: specialist journals on typography, books, arts, advertising and the new techniques such as offset lithography were published alongside it. Thus the historian interested in charting a wider view of graphic design may find it necessary to explore a more representative quotidian production.[6]

In its title *Gebrauchsgraphik* used the new generic term, which encompassed design for publication, advertising and typographic design. Apart from *Gebrauchsgraphik* the literature in the area of graphic design in the early 1920s in Germany tended to reflect pre-1914 divisions of activities. Hybrid labels were still used to classify what a graphic and typographic artist working for industry might do. From the previous generation the terms Buchkünstler (book artist) and Plakatkünstler (poster artist) were still current in the 1920s. An example of the latter was Ludwig Hohlwein, who resisted more modern definitions of graphic activity and continued to design figurative posters in lithography as prestigious campaigns for German and American companies.[7]

In other cultural arenas of Weimar Germany, the prefix "Gebrauch" was used to signify a functionalist, non-élitist, usually marxist approach, as in Hanns Eisler's "Gebrauchsmusik,"[8] This was akin to Bertolt Brecht's functional transformation, when everyday subject-matter could be included in compositions. In poetry this was reflected in the use of everyday speech, and in music the distinction between high art instruments and rhythms and popular or commercial was collapsed. However, it would appear that "Gebrauchsgraphik," both as magazine title and generic label, carried an underlying assumption of a ready acceptance of capitalist application of design for improved economic performance. The radical end of graphic practice was represented instead by those artists or designers who advocated "Tendenzkunst" (tendency art) and propaganda, among them John Heartfield, Heinrich Vogeler, Jan (iwan) Tschichold, who turned to their own publications for more extensive polemical intervention and for whom a magazine such as *Gebrauchsgraphik* was no doubt a more pragmatic trade interest.[9]

In the area of the avant-garde publications a synthesis of design approaches across diverse media was more likely. Interest in typographical layout and imagery was part of a broader advocacy of "die neue Wohnkultur." Additionally, in the terms "die neue typografie" and "die neue fotografie," the prefix "Neu" signified internationalist intentions and alliance to photomechanical processes, photomontage and compositional asymmetry, their single case setting and use of the "f" instead of "ph" denoting this.[10] They advocated "typophoto," the combination of mechanically derived word and image, on the basis that it adapted the newest reproductive means to convey its message photographically, incorporating object photography, montage and negative. This was most succinctly argued for by Laszlo Moholy-Nagy in *Malerei–Foto–Film* in 1925.[11]

Gebrauchsgraphik's background

In July 1924 the *Gebrauchsgraphik* started publication in Berlin, and by 1926 it had become a regular monthly journal. The editor was Professor H. K. Frenzel (1882–1937), who worked from Berlin. Frenzel was a significant force in defining the newly emergent roles of designer for industry in the years until his unexpected death in 1937, contributing to major events in Germany as well as other European countries and the United States.[12]

Frenzel, born in Silesia, had trained in scientific draughtsmanship, painting and graphic art at Leipzig Academy for Graphic Arts after 1900.[13] He then worked for a newspaper press before 1914 in Berlin. A founder member of the Bund Deutscher Gebrauchsgraphiker (BDG; Association of German Commercial Graphic Designers) which was established in 1920, he went on to organize exhibitions on its behalf and, on the perceived success of the Gothenburg 1923 exhibition, the title of Professor was conferred on him by his contemporaries.

His major emphasis in his writing was on the improvement of German advertising. Having spoken out against the level of design and displays of excess and bad taste at the Berlin 1925 *Reklamemesse* (Advertising Fair), he was appointed to head the Reichsverband Deutscher Reklamemesse (Reich Association of German Advertising Fairs), which culminated in the International Advertising Congress held in Berlin in 1929 and which was particularly highly regarded because it encouraged contributions from across the Atlantic.[14] Frenzel also had links with art directors in the United States, visiting in 1924 and 1926 and carrying out interviews for *Gebrauchsgraphik,* which will be considered in this article.[15]

A main source of material on British poster and advertising design for *Gebrauchsgraphik* and an introduction to contributors on various aspects of British work was provided through Frenzel's collaboration with Sir William Crawford. Crawford established a Berlin branch of his progressive London advertising agency Crawfords around 1926.[16] Frenzel acted as German adviser to them and through this exchange someone like the designer Ashley Havinden was introduced to a German readership, especially his work on the Chrysler cars advertising campaign.[17]

Frenzel was German representative at the Milan International Advertising Congress of 1933, by then under the National Socialist Fachgruppe Reichskammer der bildenden Künste (Professional Subject Division of the Reich Chamber of Fine Arts). He was also an occasional contributor to the *Penrose Annual* and *Modern Publicity–Commercial Art Annual.*[18]

From this brief account it becomes apparent that Frenzel was a significant internationally established figure, who would use *Gebrauchsgraphik* as his mouthpiece for ideas about graphic design. After one year of publishing an indication of Frenzel's main objectives for the magazine was given in an editorial in July 1925:

> Strong endorsements from all parts of the world should goad us on to even greater achievements. As previously, it will be our aim to further the value in work of commercial graphic design. We hope we shall

succeed in giving our specialist area a particular place of attention and thereby be useful to the salesman and the whole of economic life.[19]

Frenzel's basic driving force was for quality of work in his areas of interest:

The works reproduced by me in *Gebrauchsgraphik* are entirely in accordance with the idea which I have adopted as the policy of my periodical. I wish to circumscribe a circle covering what can be regarded as good present day graphic art. If I were to take to publishing only what satisfies me completely I should have to adapt a certain policy, and the periodical would no longer reflect the actual present state of graphic art.[20]

In the same issue *Gebrauchsgraphik* also announced a formal relationship with the BDG. This was the national professional association with regional divisions interested in improving codes of practice and links between German industry and designers of advertising and publicity. The agreement was that Frenzel would maintain overall editorial control while the BDG published a supplement in each issue reporting on its events, exhibitions and meetings. Naturally this relationship guaranteed a readership for *Gebrauchsgraphik* and it could be said that it also reinforced the identity of the magazine, as well as the BDG, as one of the significant professionalizing agencies for the new "graphic designer" at this time in Germany.

Gebrauchsgraphik began its life with a series of special issues. The aim at this stage was to promote the role of the advertising designer, typographer or illustrator to industrial patrons. Consequently issues were devoted to "The Poster," "Illustrators," "The Office," "German Typefoundries," and "Official Graphic Design," either areas of practice or aspects of business and commercial life, in which a designer might be used.[21] In these issues links were argued between patronage of good design and economic well-being. The editorial approach can be seen to be generally compatible with the stabilization of the currency and recuperation of the German industrial base between 1924 and 1930.

Interpretations of German design history have indicated that these years saw progressive forces in favour of industrial cartels and amalgamations of German large-scale companies at their most vocal, concerned to keep up with advances in the United States. Gert Selle in *Geschichte des Design in Deutschland von 1870 bis Heute* has argued:

Between the end of inflation and the world economic crisis of 1929–32 in Germany there still existed sufficient industrial and economic foundations for a socially functional mass product culture [to develop].[22]

Indeed, Selle quotes Tomás Maldonado's concern to map the history of modern design in Germany directly on to political and economic life.

Maldonado (1963), who makes the attempt to interpret Bauhaus development coupled with the history of the Weimar Republic, sketches three historical sections: "1919 to 1924, chaos, unemployment, political assassinations. 1925–1929/30, the deceptive prosperity of the Dawes Plan, international credit and industrial rationalization. 1930–33, once again chaos, unemployment and political assassination."[23]

However, it would be mistaken to associate the Weimar years with unproblematically internationalist and therefore modernist characteristics. Joan Campbell, in *The German Werkbund: The Politics of Reform in the Arts,* has indicated that conservatives and nationalists held a strong lobby against modernism and internationalism and, as Jeffrey Herf has shown in *Reactionary Modernism: Technology, Culture and Politics in Weimar and the Third Reich,* there was no necessary relationship between modern attitudes towards mechanization and efficiency in industrial production and leftist or radical political beliefs.[24] A reading of *Gebrauchsgraphik* seems to support this view, on the evidence of articles in which attention was given to publicity and advertising design for the large industries with international objectives. On the other hand, tensions of practice were reflected—competing modes of "modern" practice were offered. Arguments to embrace modern or up-to-date attitudes towards mechanical setting and use of advanced printing processes were made, without necessarily advocating stylistic modernism.[25]

Gebrauchsgraphik's coverage

The regional nature of German printing and book and newspaper publishing and wider industrial organization was signalled early on in *Gebrauchsgraphik.* Among the special issues referred to above were those focused on established centres of printing and regional capitals of industry.[26] The usual pattern was for a feature article to be on a designer or design school of the region and they would contribute a cover and back page advertisement in conjunction with a local, high-profile printer. Such was the case for "Werbebau," the association of Johannes Canis and Max Burchartz when the first photomontaged cover was used on the magazine (Figure 1.10).[27] All regional issues were published bilingually in German and English, a policy that would be followed subsequently for selected articles throughout the period concerned. These issues were accompanied by advertisements of regional typefoundries, printers and paper manufacturers, as well as small announcements (Inseraten) for local illustrators, graphic designers and poster artists.

The national and city emphasis may be characterized by the special issue on Berlin, which featured a main article on prospectuses and brochures produced by Berlin's major electrical companies as well as graphic and information design for the city's transport systems, stressing the commercial character of the city and the users of design. A city such as Leipzig, by contrast, was given focus as a centre for typographic design, books and publishing, where a strong tradition of specialist production existed.[28]

Important German industrial and trade fairs were usually reported in the magazine, such as the two Berlin advertising fairs mentioned above, the 1927 Leipzig "Internationale Buchkunst Ausstellung" (International Book Arts Exhibition) and 'Pressa' in Cologne of 1928, a vast international press and publishing convention and exhibition, which was first announced and then reviewed in *Gebrauchsgraphik.*[29]

A characteristic coverage from a single issue from 1926 shows an article "Rules on the Standardisation of Paper Formats," dealing with Deutsche Industrie Normen (German Industrial Standards) recommendations, the development of the *Pelikan* poster, by Wilhelm Grabow, Max Burchartz on "handschrift-type-zeichnung-foto" ("lettering-type-drawing-photography"), and a feature on "Berlin's Advertising on the Elevated and Underground Railways."[30] This represents a range running from a profile of Gunther Wagner, prominent Deutscher Werkbund member, who had commissioned Ludwig Hohlwein, El Lissitzky and Kurt Schwitters, among prominent designers to work on publicity for *Pelikan* stationery and artists'

Figure 1.10 *Gebrauchsgraphik*, vol. 3 (8) cover (1926). © 1926. Designer: Fritz Lewy. Courtesy of SLUB Dresden.

materials, to more straightforward informative articles which provided codes of practice for jobbing designers.[31]

What was the critical or discursive language and how was evaluation made in *Gebrauchsgraphik*? The editorial policy of *Gebrauchsgraphik* was catholic throughout the period 1924–33, covering reviews of type designs, book design, advertising, packaging, exhibition display. Writers for the magazine included the editor H.K. Frenzel, members of the BDG, and a regular house-journalist, Traugott Schalcher. Success was often assessed in terms of stylistic resolution, novelty or formal coherence. Scale of work and its impact were taken into account, while skill and technique especially regarding illustration, intaglio printing and bibliophile work were also recognized.

A move towards providing an international coverage was made from 1927 when the editorial announced:

Beginning with Volume four, 'Gebrauchsgraphik' is to carry the subtitle of "International Advertising Art." In adopting this we feel that we are following the line of natural development which our periodical has hitherto undergone in what it has achieved in the service of art in advertising. The great attention which has been paid to "Gebrauchsgraphik" in every part of the world has confirmed in us the conviction that Commerce in the proportions it has assumed today is something that passes beyond all national boundaries and is now assuming the character of world economics, thus also necessitating an international understanding in advertising, its most valuable means of expression. We assume this concept consciously and it is our aim and desire to mirror the face and features of international trade propaganda.[32]

There followed three issues devoted to a range of poster design, advertising and typography in Germany, America, Belgium, England, Holland and Switzerland. The definition of "international," then, was in fact North America and Western Europe, although later in the year an article on Japanese advertising art appeared.[33] By contrast, little interest was shown in the pages of *Gebrauchsgraphik* in the Soviet Union, with the exception of the work of El Lissitzky, who was resident in Germany throughout most of the Weimar period, where he was responsible for designs of Soviet contributions to German displays and exhibitions.[34]

In 1930 the ripples from the Wall Street Crash of the previous autumn were discussed and more overt detail of the economy and its implications for design was included. Frenzel opened the year with "Where Is Advertising Going?" a plea for German industries to use advertising and publicity designers, in which one of his examples of the benefits of advertising was work by Moholy-Nagy for a Berlin chain-store.[35] A direct response to the critical economic situation came when a regular section began, "Wirtschaft und Werbung" (The Economy and Publicity). This provided statistical and demographic analyses of German markets, under such headings as "Income and Consumption," "The Automobile Market in Germany" and "Growth of Unemployment in Germany."[36]

By 1930, graphic design was interpreted as affecting all walks of life in *Gebrauchsgraphik*. In one issue, for example, a review "El Lissitzky Moskau" by Traugott Schalcher was followed by "30 Years of Ullstein 1897–1927," looking at the design record of one of the most prolific publishing houses, whereas "50 Years of Typography" presented a qualified attack on the New Typography. "The Window Display as Educator" stressed the familiar argument that retail design might infiltrate a public's awareness of good design and Rudolf Gabrie reviewed German contemporary book covers from a French standpoint.[37]

Although there was a change in emphasis throughout the period from national to international concerns, in its coverage of graphic designers, *Gebrauchsgraphik* was always sufficiently pluralist to be able to give focus to traditionalist and modernist alike. The tradition of poster art was featured with examples such as Ludwig Hohlwein and Jean Carlu. Modernist designers such as Herbert Bayer were less often covered. Designers who would adapt their style according to the type of publicity, advertising or company design identities they were working on were frequently profiled, figures such as Otto Arpke, Gerhard Marggraff, and Otto Hadank.[38] This list not only indicates the stylistic diversity of the profiles but furthermore that there was no evolutionary progress in coverage from traditionalist to modernist in the magazine's chronology.

The layout design of *Gebrauchsgraphik*

The layout design of the magazine was carried out by the editor, who would liaise with the printer, Phönix Illustrationsdruck und Verlag, Berlin, rather than employ an art editor. In its first years the design of title-page of the magazine varied greatly, with calligraphic, typographic and 'new' typographic solutions all used. The text itself was initially set as book typography, a conventional approach for this time with a body of text separated from carefully placed illustration, a small typeface used with little design emphasis and all organized around a centre point. In 1926 came the change to a modern magazine-oriented design approach, with an integrated layout for an article by Max Burchartz, for example, and by 1928 title-page and lead articles were presented in a consistent typographical style, perhaps based on Frenzel's American art direction (Figure 1.11). Integrated layout became usual, illustrations counter-balanced by a body of text and headlines in geometrical arrangements, often in the same typeface as the main editorial content.

Fellow journalist Eberhard Hölscher wrote of Frenzel's approach:

> But very few can imagine how much inventiveness and gift for composition he had to expend in always making his periodical fresh and animated. He had an unusually versatile technical talent for this, and anyone privileged to watch him doing this work was directly infected by indefatigable and seemingly almost childlike delight he displayed in experimenting with the arrangement of his pages, testing different plans, gumming and building them up, till everything had been arranged to his satisfaction.[39]

Although this implies the design was subject to similar personal intuition as the editorial process described above, there are sufficient significant parallels in the changes the magazine went through when it is compared with other publication design of the time to suggest that it was an informed as well as a subjective approach.

A comparison with the second series of *Die Form,* the Deutscher Werkbund magazine started in 1925, indicates this.[40] The redesign of both magazines can therefore be placed within the period when editorial content embraced internationalizing tendencies. Although *Die Form* had begun in a modern cover, with sanserif letterforms and photographic panel, the interior of the magazine had been book format until 1928 when it was redesigned. In the same year *Gebrauchsgraphik* was printed with Paul Renner's Futura for its main typeface. Renner's type design was very recently available and quickly

trend of *Gebrauchsgraphik* under its new publishing conditions. On the contrary, being essentially a commercial art journal serving trade and industry, and the promotion of art in advertising, it will exhibit the same objectivity and open-mindedness as in the past when dealing with the important problem of form as applied to widely differing spheres of everyday life. Fully aware, moreover, of its cultural responsibilities *Gebrauchsgraphik* will not refrain from criticizing mistakes or abuses inimical to culture which, in its opinion, require to be remedied. This is not a new program. It is simply a re-statement of the journal's traditional principles that will certainly secure approval of its old readers, and, it is hoped, will appeal to others who are seriously and actively engaged in promoting the commercial art of today.

Appendix B

"Introducing *Graphis*," *Graphis—International Advertising Art* (Werbegraphik), Zurich, vol. 1, no. 1, October 1944.
The war has entered its decisive phase, and the spirit of reconstruction is already abroad. Plans made for an uncertain future can now begin to taken on solid form. European culture revives from the ordeal of war; and for this revival it is essential that there should be some centre at which the truly creative forces can unite and find coordination.

Lying at the meeting point of several cultures and itself a synthesis of three of them, Switzerland is ideally placed for the encouragement of that atmosphere which is salutary, if not indispensable, for intellectual discussion and the exchange of cultural and artistic ideas. It is in the hope of providing some such European focus in artistic fields that *Graphis* now appears, a magazine published in Switzerland and concerned with all problems attaching to free and applied art.

The aim which *Graphis* sets itself is that of enriching practical life with the seeds of creative inspiration; of helping to bring art into touch with everyday life, and enduing (*sic*) the forms of that life with the artistic significance and value. Our articles and criticism will deal not only with pure art, not only with the graphic arts in a narrower sense, but also with every sphere of applied art. Collaborators, artists and writers, scholars and experts here and abroad will give their views in these pages on all vital problems of the artistic world.

Graphis sets out, in short, to provide stimulating material for all who by inclination or profession have to do with art. Richly and tastefully illustrated and produced with the greatest typographical care, it will appear for the time being every two months in the form of a double number of about one hundred pages.

The Publishers
Editors Dr Walter Amstutz and Walter Herdeg

Notes

1. This article arises from my thesis "*Gebrauchsgraphik*: Style and Ideology in German Graphic Design 1910–1939," submitted for Ph.D. examination in 1989 to the Royal College of Art, London. I am grateful for comments

received from the members of the Editorial Board of the *Journal of Design History* at an earlier draft stage of this article and especially to Charlotte Benton and Gillian Naylor for their advice.

2. As the conclusion to this article indicates, the magazine *Gebrauchsgraphik* was relaunched in 1950, by which time *Graphis* was published from Zurich. If a comparison between these journals is made by referring to their overall editorial intentions and characteristic contents, similarities in approach are apparent. It is not possible at the time of writing to ascribe influence from *Gebrauchsgraphik* to *Graphis* or to connect the journals by anything more than this similarity, but the suggestion that *Gebrauchsgraphik* was a model is nonetheless possible.

3. Dick Hebdige, "The Bottom Line on Planet One: Squaring Up to the Face," in *Hiding in the Light*, London: Comedia/Routledge, 1988.

4. Paul Ruben, *Die Reklame: Ihre Kunst und Wissenschaft*, 2 vols, Berlin: Verlag für Sozial Politik, 1913.

5. Other writers in *Die Reklame* included Ernst Gröwald, E.E.H. Schmidt, Dr Ludwig Lindner, and Dr Hugo Waldeck.

6. For a journal defined by technique, see the monthly *Offset, Buch und Werbekunst*, subtitled "the magazine for printers, advertising specialists and publishers," editor Siegfried Berg, nos. 1–16, Leipzig: Offset Verlag, 1924–1939. Literature on the poster included the journal *Das Plakat*, published by Dr Hans Sachs, Berlin Nikolassee, on instruction from the Verein der Plakatfreunde, 1912–1921. A specialist typographical magazine was *Typographische Mitteilungen*, Haus und Fachorgan der Typograph GmbH, Berlin, 1901–1933.

   Although not my focus here, an example of how collections of posters and archive material reflect the selection principles of graphic design journalism and the same clusters of significant figures' work tend to form major museum collections is apparent at the Berlin Kunstbibliothek Graphische Sammlung. This has teaching collections of student and master work from major art and design schools' typographic and graphic courses in Germany, among them Rudolf Koch, Joost Schmidt and Max Hertwig. Material for the exhibition, "Wohin Geht die Neue Typographie?," organized by MoholyNagy in Berlin in 1929, is also held there. To go beyond what might be considered to be designers talking to other designers, to find design which is more representative of general graphic practice, rather than paradigms of official taste, the historian would need to consult material collected for other criteria, which might coincidentally indicate design patterns and thinking. Moves in this direction were made in the work at the Zurich Kunstgewerbemuseum, in response to the concept of "Alltagskultur" (culture of everyday life) and anonymous design. Graphic design then becomes of interest for its currency, rather than for its links with a design profession and the process of its identification and legitimization. See the catalogue *Werbestil 1930–40. Die Alltägliche Bildersprache eines Jahrzehntes*, Zurich: Kunstgewerbemuseum, 1981.

7. H.K. Frenzel, *Ludwig Hohlwein, Sein Leben und Werk*, Berlin: Phönix Verlag, 1924.

8. Hanns Eisler, *A Rebel in Music*, Berlin: Seven Seas, 1978.

9. Their work was not covered in *Gebrauchsgraphik* except within surveys of bookcover design, illustration and typography respectively. For consideration of this radical context, see the catalogue, *Wem Gehört die Welt? Kunst und Gesellschaft der Weimarer Republik*, Berlin: Neue Gesellschaft für Bildende Kunst, 1977.

10. The spelling indicated a modern approach and very often advocacy of single case setting, "Kleinschreibung." On terminology, "Entwerfer," broadly translated as designer, was also very often used in the captioning of illustrated work, for instance in *Gebrauchsgraphik*. Finally, "Werbegestalter" (advertising designer) was used by a group of functionalist designers, the "Ring Neuer Werbegestalter," who in their choice of name signified a matter-offact approach to the activity and rejected the masquerade of art, as indicated in the book by H. and B. Rasch, *Gefesselter Blick* (The Fixed Gaze), Stuttgart: Wissenschaftlicher Verlag, 1931. Arguments for the New Typography were made in the Deutscher Werkbund journal *Die Form*, see: Paul Renner, "Die Schrift Unserer Zeit," *Die Form*, 11 (1927): 10–12, and Jan Tschichold, "Zeitgemässe Buchgestaltung," 116–23; Willy Lotz, "Werkbundausstellung Film und Foto 1929," *Die Form*, IV (1929), and Werner Gräff, "Es Kommt der neue Fotograf!," 252–5, and L. MoholyNagy, "Fotogramm und Grenzgebiete," 256–9. For English language commentaries on this movement

see: Otto Bettmann, "Elements of the New Typography in Germany," in *Penrose Annual*, 32 (1930): 116–21, and G. Stresow, "German Typography Today," in *Penrose Annual*, 39 (1937): 60–4.

11. L. MoholyNagy, *Malerei–Fotographie–Film*, Albert Langen, Munich, 1925, Bauhaus Book no. 8, reprinted and translated as *Painting–Photography–Film*, Lund Humphries, London, 1969.

12. I have not found much biographical detail on H.K. Frenzel during this research beyond published sources. Instead, his writings indicate his activities. According to the present archivist of Bruckmann Verlag, Munich, publisher of *novum Gebrauchsgraphik*, no archive material remains from the pre-1939 Berlin stage of *Gebrauchsgraphik*, presumably as a result of the upheaval of war and the move to Munich.

13. The main source of this biographical information on Frenzel was an obituary section in *Gebrauchsgraphik*, 14 (11) (November 1937).

14. On the Reichsreklamemesse, see H.K. Frenzel, "Betrachtungen zur Reichsreklamemesse," *Gebrauchsgraphik*, 1 (9) (1924–25): 1–5. On the 1929 exhibition, see the catalogue, *Reichsreklameschau*, Berlin: Messehalle-amFunkturm, 1929.

15. See H.K. Frenzel, "New York after Two Years," *Gebrauchsgraphik*, 5 (9) (September 1928). The New York office of *Gebrauchsgraphik* was established in 1928, listed as the Book Service Club of New York. By 1930, to this were added English, Italian and French distributors. During this research no other specific information has come to light concerning circulation figures or the print run. This would be necessary, for example, for a more conclusive evaluation of the magazine's impact in the United States to be made.

16. "Crawfords Reklame Agentur" was announced in *Gebrauchsgraphik*, 7 (8) (August 1930). William Crawford contributed an article reviewing poster design in many countries, "Das Plakat," *Gebrauchsgraphik*, 2 (5) (1925).

17. Havinden's campaign was highly regarded for its combination of abstraction and detailed copyline, as the influence on the work by Max Bittrof for Opel cars indicated, *Gebrauchsgraphik*, 5 (12) (December 1928).

18. He contributed to the *Penrose Annual*, 38 (1936): 23–6, with the article "The Influence of Market Fluctuations on the Demand for Advertising." An obituary to Frenzel was published in the *Penrose Annual*, 40 (1938).

19. H.K. Frenzel, *Gebrauchsgraphik*, 2 (1) (July 1925), original translation.

20. Reported in *Gebrauchsgraphik*, 14 (11) (November 1937), original translation.

21. Special issues on these areas included in 1925 "Schrift und Schriftschreiber," no. 1, "Amtliche Graphik des Reichs," no. 2, two issues on the poster nos. 4 and 5 and illustrators in no. 6. In 1926 the emphasis was on cities; however, the business prospectus, no. 5, and travel posters, no. 9, were also subjects of special issues.

22. G. Selle, *Geschichte des Design in Deutschland von 1870 bis Heute: Entwicklung der industriellen Produktkultur*, Cologne: Verlag M. Du Mont Schauberg, 1973, 94–5, my translation.

23. T. Maldonado, "ist das Bauhaus aktuell?," in *ulm—Zeitschrift der Hochschule für Gestaltung*, quoted in G. Selle, op. cit., my translation.

24. J. Campbell, *The German Werkbund: The Politics of Reform in the Applied Arts*, Princeton University Press, Princeton, 1978, and J. Herf, *Reactionary Modernism, Technology, Culture and Politics in Weimar and the Third Reich*, Cambridge: Cambridge University Press, 1984.

25. Articles which argued for conservatism in typographic style in *Gebrauchsgraphik* included: H. Wieynck, "Neue Typographie," 5 (7) (July 1928): 28–9, and "Leitsätze zum Problem zeitgemässer Druckschriftgestaltung," 8 (2) (February 1931).

26. Dresden was the first city profiled in *Gebrauchsgraphik*, 2 (3). This was followed by Munich in January 1926, Hanover in April, and the RheinRuhr region in August, and finally Leipzig in December 1926.

27. The RheinRuhr issue of *Gebrauchsgraphik*, 3 (8) (August 1926). "Werbebau" was established in 1924, based in Bochum. They worked for the iron and steel amalgamation "Bochumer Verein" using advanced techniques of

photomontage and asymmetry in their designs of publicity booklets. Max Burchartz, an exponent of the new typography, contributed "Auswertung Neuzeitlicher Techniken" in *Die Form*, 1 (1925). He also wrote a short essay for Kurt Schwitters' *Merz*, 11, on "Typoreklame."

28. Special issue on Berlin, *Gebrauchsgraphik*, 3 (5) (May 1926); special issue on Leipzig, *Gebrauchsgraphik*, 3 (12) (December 1926).

29. "Pressa" was announced in *Gebrauchsgraphik*, 4 (4) (April 1927), and reviewed in *Gebrauchsgraphik*, 5 (7) (July 1928).

30. *Gebrauchsgraphik*, 3 (8) (July 1926).

31. See the catalogue, *Das Frühe Pelikan Plakat 1898–1930*, Göttingen: Städtisches Museum, 1975.

32. *Gebrauchsgraphik*, 4 (1) (January 1927), original translation.

33. "Japanische Reklame" in *Gebrauchsgraphik*, 4 (5) (May 1927).

34. S. LissitzkyKuppers, *El Lissitzky: Life Letters Texts*, London: Thames & Hudson, 1968. For a consideration of El Lissitzky's changing style to meet changed Soviet requirements, see B. Buchloh, "From Faktura to Factography," in *October*, 20 (Fall 1984): 83–118.

35. H.K. Frenzel, "Where is Advertising Going?," *Gebrauchsgraphik*, 7 (1) (January 1930).

36. The main author, Dr W. Puttkammer, contributed articles on "The Development of Consumption," no. 1, "Dwellings and Housekeeping," no. 4, "Income and Consumption," no. 7, and "The Clothing Retail Trade," no. 9, all in the first year of this column in *Gebrauchsgraphik*, 7 (1930).

37. *Gebrauchsgraphik*, 7 (7) (July 1930).

38. For Jean Carlu, see 12 (1) (January 1934); for Ludwig Hohlwein, see the *Gebrauchsgraphik* monograph, op. cit. Herbert Bayer was the subject of a profile in 15 (6) (June 1938), Otto Arpke, 7 (12) (July 1929), and 12 (1) (January 1934), Gerhard Marggraff in 15 (10) (October 1938), and Otto Hadank in 16 (7) (July 1939).

39. E. Hölscher, obituary of H.K. Frenzel, in *Gebrauchsgraphik*, 17 (11) (November 1937).

40. *Die Form: Zeitschrift für Gestaltende Arbeit*, Berlin: Organ des Deutschen Werkbundes, 1925–1934.

41. Renner's Futura for photomontage was advertised in *Gebrauchsgraphik*, 7 (11) (November 1930). For Renner's own writings on typography see P. Renner, *Typografie als Kunst*, Munich: Georg Müller, 1922, and P. Renner, *Mechanisierte Grafik*, Berlin Reckendorf, 1931.

42. In *Offset Buch und Werbekunst Das Blatt für Drucker, Werbefachleute und Verleger*, no. 3, Leipzig: Siegfried Berg, 1924, my translation.

43. This was the case, for example, in the prestigious printing annual *Penrose Annual*, London, 1890–.

44. A range of articles on the United States in *Gebrauchsgraphik* would include: "Amerikanische Reklamemethoden in Europa," 2 (3) (1925–6); "How American Advertising Agencies Advertise Themselves," 7 (5) (May 1930); "Wrappings and Boxes of the Wards Company, Chicago," 11 (3) (March 1934); and "Container Corporation of America," 15 (7) (July 1938).

45. The *Annual of Advertising and Editorial Art*, New York, 1922–. The first was published as a catalogue "for the first Annual exhibition of Advertising Paintings and Drawings held by the Art Directors Club of New York." The twelfth annual was advertised *Gebrauchsgraphik*, 11 (2) (February 1934).

46. B.W. Randolph, "Amerikanische Universitätsausbildung in Reklame und Marktkunde," *Gebrauchsgraphik*, 3 (2) (February 1926).

47. See H.K. Frenzel, "Vorwort," *Gebrauchsgraphik*, 3 (10) (October 1926), my translation.

48. Ibid.

49. H.K. Frenzel in a conversation with Frederic Suhr, *Gebrauchsgraphik*, 5 (10) (October 1928).

50. Ibid., original translation.

51. Ibid.

52. *Arts et Métiers Graphiques*, director Charles Peignot, editor Bertrand Guégan, published from 3 Rue Séguier, Paris, 1927–39.
53. *Arts et Métiers Graphiques* 2: 357–64.
54. *Arts et Métiers Graphiques*, 19: 46–54, and *Arts et Métiers Graphiques*, 15: 909–13, and 21: 135–9.
55. For the New Objectivity in photography, see the special issue of *Arts et Métiers Graphiques*, 16 (1930). The catalogue, *Film und Foto der zwanziger Jahre*, Württembergischer Kunstverein, 1979, which marked the fiftieth anniversary of the Stuttgart division of the Deutscher Werkbund exhibition, "Film und Foto Internationale Ausstellung des deutschen Werkbundes," organized by Hans Hildebrandt, Bernhard Pankok and Jan Tschichold, with collaboration from Otto Baur, Mia Seeger, L. MoholyNagy, Edward Weston, Edward Steichen, Piet Zwart, F.T. Gubler and Siegfried Giedion. The original exhibition travelled to Zurich, Berlin, Danzig, Vienna and Agram during 1929 and 1930. Later parts of the exhibition were used for another photographic exhibition, "Das Lichtbild," which originated in Munich and travelled to Hamburg, Essen, Düsseldorf, Dessau and Breslau.
56. *Gebrauchsgraphik*, 10 (1) (January 1933).
57. Ibid.
58. B. Hinz, *Art in the Third Reich*, Oxford: Blackwell, 1979, 13.
59. In *Gebrauchsgraphik*, 10 (8) (August 1933), my translation.
60. It would appear that Eberhard Hölscher stepped in as *Gebrauchsgraphik*'s main journalist and possibly its editor from 1938, but at the time of writing this cannot be confirmed. Apart from published articles in *Gebrauchsgraphik*, I have found no further detail on Hölscher.
61. See A. Fleischer and F. Kämpfer, "The Political Poster in the Third Reich," in B. Taylor and W. van der Will (eds), *The Nazification of Art*, Winchester Press, 1990, and F. Kämpfer, *Der Rote Keil: das politische Plakat Theorie und Ideologie*, Berlin: Gebr. Mann Verlag, 1985.
62. P. K. Schuster (ed.), *Die Kunststadt München 1937: Nationalsozialismus und "Entartete Kunst,"* Munich: Prestel Verlag, 1987.
63. J. Heskett, "Art and Design in Nazi Germany," *History Workshop Journal*, 6 (Autumn 1978): 139–53, and "Modernism and Archaism in Design in the Third Reich," in *Block*, 3 (1980).
64. G. Selle, op cit.
65. The impact of "Gleichschaltung" on daily reportage and photojournalism, which underwent this process, is considered in D. Kerbs et al., *Gleichschaltung der BilderPressefotografie 1930–1936*, Berlin: Frölich & Kaufmann, 1983.
66. C. FischerDefoy, "Artists and Art Institutions in Germany 1933–45," *Oxford Art Journal*, 9 (2) (1986).
67. By official is meant those articles dealing with exhibitions organized by the NSRDW or when *Gebrauchsgraphik* gave space to notices from the Reichskammer Fachgruppe Gebrauchsgraphiker.
68. For example, *Die Rechtlichen Grundlagen der Werbung in Deutschland* in *Gebrauchsgraphik*, 10 (11) (November 1933). Another example would be recommended charges for press advertising at standardized rates, announced in *Gebrauchsgraphik*, 10 (12) (December 1933).
69. "Deutsche Werbung," Essen, was reviewed in *Gebrauchsgraphik*, 13 (10) (October 1936): 16–32.
70. For a review of the design for the Olympic Games, see *Gebrauchsgraphik*, 13 (7) (July 1936). See also the profile on the 1938 exhibition, in which Otto Arpke had a significant part, "International Handicraft Exhibition," *Gebrauchsgraphik*, 15 (7) (July 1938).
71. As well as articles resulting from H.K. Frenzel's visit to Milan in 1933, there was a major profile of Italy in October 1937, covering advertising art, periodical publications, exhibition design and typography, *Gebrauchsgraphik*, 14 (10).

72. The profile on Herbert Bayer was in *Gebrauchsgraphik*, 15 (6) (June 1938). His cover design for *Gebrauchsgraphik* was later that year, in October. Magdalena Droste, *Herbert Bayer: das künstlerische Werk 1919–1938*, BauhausArchiv/Gebr. Mann Verlag, Berlin, 1982, provides the fullest discussion to date of Bayer's work of this period.

73. For O.H.W. Hadank, see *Gebrauchsgraphik*, 16 (7) (July 1939).

74. For an overall approach to art in exile, see *Kunst im Exil in Großbritannien 1933–1945*, catalogue, Berlin: Neue Gesellschaft für Bildende Kunst, 1986. For a specific consideration of graphic design in particular, see R. Kinross, "Emigré Graphic Designers in Britain: Around the Second World War and Afterwards," in *Journal of Design History*, 3 (1): 35–59.

75. I originally was introduced to *Gebrauchsgraphik* when Humphrey Spender, designer and photographer, spoke about its influence on his generation; interview with the author, January 1980.

76. *Penrose Annual*, 40 (1938).

77. *Graphis*, 1 (1) (October 1944).

Chapter 1.3.3

Zombie Modernism

Mr. Keedy

This is a very scary essay. It's about death and denial. But you don't have to be afraid to read it, because it's just language, and meaning is arbitrary. At least that is what those nasty postmodernists and deconstructivists want you to believe. But we know better. There is a right way and a wrong way to do everything. A good way and a bad way, a rational way and a crazy way, a clear way and a chaotic way, the modern way and the modern way. In graphic design, there is no alternative to modernism. To predate modernism is to be a commercial artist, printer or scribe, not a designer, because the designer was born out of modernism. To postdate modernism is equally incomprehensible for most designers, because it exists outside their realm of comprehension.

In most areas of cultural production such as art, architecture, music, and literature, modernism was just one more event in a continuing life cycle. Graphic design, on the other hand, did not have sufficient time to develop a mature sense of self—the umbilical cord had not been severed yet. So when modernism died, many designers' ideology died with it. However, they did not go peacefully into that dark night. They refused to acknowledge their own ideological demise, and they continue to haunt the living, moaning and groaning because they no longer belong to this world. That is the fate of the Zombie Modernist, the living dead who design among us.

In the beginning, when modernism was young, it was a radical idea that positioned itself in opposition to a more conservative traditionalism. As time went on, the modernist ideology spread into all areas of cultural production, eventually becoming the dominant esthetic ideology. Design was an extremely effective tool in converting the masses to modernity; it spread modernism from a few liberal thinkers to a conservative majority. Consequently, designers defined design as a modernist practice, and design's history and theory exist almost exclusively within the modernist paradigm.

Unfortunately, design's modernism is an ill-considered version of art modernism, one that is based on an Enlightenment faith in progress and singular answers, reinforced by a rationalist universalism. Modernist design theory has developed little beyond the reiteration of modernist platitudes that are endlessly repeated but that are not expanded, questioned, or adjusted to meet the needs of design theory and practice.

Only in the past few years has there emerged a sufficient amount of work and writing to challenge the hegemony of design modernism. This has prompted some modernist designers to re-evaluate and re-define modernism. They want to appear relevant, without giving up the privileged position that a

First published in *Emigre*, 34 (Spring 1995): 17–31. © Jeffery Keedy.

universalist dogma constructs. These last ditch efforts superficially pay lip service to, and subsequently disavow, the importance, complexity, and diversity of contemporary culture.

Design modernism's hegemony reveals itself in its countless annual shows and publications that primarily function to establish a universal standard of "excellence" by a contrast canonizing of "modernist masters" in design,[1] the absolutist, rationalist, obsession with, "problem solving," "clarity," and "legibility," and the paranoid attacks against anything that is pluralistic, de-centered, or new.

The core philosophy of modernist design is in instrumentalist, or pragmatic thought. "Pragmatism is America's only native philosophy."[2] It is goal oriented, practical, and distrustful of all things metaphysical. Paul Rand frequently quotes John Dewey: "In Deweyan pragmatism there is no ecstasy, no Dionysian muse, no charismatic illumination."[3] It is this pragmatism that is at the root of America's "down to earth" but decidedly "cranky" tone in criticism (this essay not excluded).

In Europe we find, not surprisingly, that design critic Robin Kinross's philosophical hero is the neo-pragmatist, Jürgen Habermas, the German hyperrationalist whose faith is that "language, however distorted and manipulative, always has consensus or understanding as its inner *telos*,"[4] and that "the truth of statements is linked in the last analysis to the interpretation of the good and the true life."[5]

Habermas's and Dewey's pragmatism is not an unlikely source of interest for designers, particularly die-hard modernists. I wonder how our pragmatist critics overlooked Richard Rorty, America's best known (neo-pragmatist) philosopher, who makes use of the ideas of Dewey and Derrida. Many designers are disturbed by the Marxist and leftist politics of postmodern theorists, but absolutely nothing has been said of the right-wing conservatism of the modernist theorist. Is that simply because design consists of a silent conservative majority? Following the historical model of early, classical, and late periods, I would categorize modernist ideology in graphic design as: starting with the (early) pragmatic, art historical dogma of Paul Rand, ossifying into the (classical) traditionalist, hyper-rationalism of Robin Kinross, only to dissipate into the (late or rococo) decorative, modernism of Dan Friedman.[6]

Although the work of these modernists differs greatly, the message is the same: "I am the voice of clarity and reason," "I am the voice of authority and progress," and "I am in charge of this family's values." From the Bauhaus to our house, this "father-knows-best" baloney has always passed for design theory. Graphic design's alleged birth place, the Bauhaus, has, from the start, been idealized and mythologized by designers. "The pathos of such idealism has been revealed by subsequent events. The fact that the school was destroyed by Fascism may have enhanced its credibility in post-war Europe and the United States, but its ideal of universality was a myth and mirage, shattered by the war, politics and the demands of consumer society."[7]

Creation myths die hard, if at all. The Zombie Modernist refuses to let go of modernism at any cost.

For the Zombie Modernist, everything outside of modernism is chaos, superficial, trendy, of poor quality, and just an empty formal style. It became increasingly difficult for designers to keep the myth alive. Gropius himself, in an effort to recuperate modernism in design said in 1968: "The complexity and psychological implications, as we developed them at the Bauhaus, were forgotten and it [modernism] was described as a simple-minded, purely utilitarian approach to design."[8] The fact is, for the most part, it was a simple-minded, purely utilitarian approach that continues to be taught the same way today. Likewise, the Granddaddy of all Zombie Modernists, Paul Rand, complains in his latest book that "The

Bauhaus, into whose history is woven the very fabric of modernism, is seen as a style rather than as an idea."[9]

Echoing that sentiment, the radical Zombie Mod Dan Friedman says in his latest book, "Many in design think of modernism as a style that began in the Bauhaus in the 1920s and fell into disrepute in the 1960s. But modernism means different things and is traced to different origins by different people. Philosophers, for example, trace it to the seventeenth century and the dual influences of rationalism and humanism."[10] I am not sure exactly what the point is, but I'm sure there is one. The important thing is that modernism is not a style.

That's right, modernism is no longer a style, it's an ideology, and that ideology is conservatism. Modernism, unarguably design's greatest asset, has become its greatest liability because it is inextricably bound to conservative dogma. As such, design has become primarily an ideologically conservative practice. In *Design, Form, and Chaos,* Paul Rand quotes A. N. Whitehead: *"Mere change without conservation is a passage from nothing to nothing.* Mere conservation without change cannot conserve." (The emphasis on the first sentence is Mr. Rand's.) This quote is instructive not only as an illustration of Mr. Rand's usual harping against change, but also for its assumed goal to "conserve." Modernist designers believe the function of design is to "conserve" universal values in designed objects. I suspect most designers are comfortable with that idea, even though few of them will admit it publicly. Most designers claim to be very liberal, or even radical, like their early modern art heroes. But this is 1995, not 1925, and we are formulating design practice, not art history. Recently I interviewed design critic Rick Poynor, and I asked him if he was a modernist or a postmodernist. He said, "The problem I have with postmodernism is the relativism and nihilism that follows it."[11] Understandably, many design critics are reluctant to give up the absolute values of modernism because that is what makes design criticism an easier, right or wrong proposition.

By contrast, the contextual postmodern approach is "relative," because the discourse is relative to the subject at hand. This greater demand for specificity and complexity is often dismissed as "nihilism" or "chaos." Mr. Poynor went on to say, "So I recognize what you say; that there is, at times, in the way I write and in the areas that interest me, a split between those two areas of thinking (modernism and postmodernism)—an acknowledgment of one, and maybe a hankering after the other."[12] It is precisely this fearful and nostalgic "hankering" for modernism that has retarded the intellectual growth of design theory and criticism, and has hidden a deep seated conservatism.

My aim in this essay is to examine modernism in design, not make a case for postmodernism. If you would have told me ten years ago that I would still be making a case for postmodernism in design in 1995, I probably wouldn't have believed it because the political imperative that drives modernism-at-all-cost in design was not as evident to me then, and I assumed design would move along with other cultural practices.

How, then, should postmodernism in general be evaluated? My preliminary assessment would be this: That in its concern for difference, for the difficulties of communication, for the complexity and nuances of interests, cultures, places, and the like, it exercises a positive influence. The metalanguages, metatheories, and metanarratives of modernism (particularly in its later manifestations) did tend to gloss over important differences, and failed to pay attention to important disjunctions and details. Postmodernism has been particularly important in acknowledging "the multiple forms of otherness as

they emerge from differences in subjectivity, gender, and sexuality, race and class, temporal (configurations of sensibility) and spatial geographic locations and dislocations."[13]

Zombie Modernists survive by eating the living flesh of Postmodernism

The Zombie Modernist's biggest enemies are postmodernism and deconstruction because they reveal
that the simplistic, rationalist/universalist modernism of design is long dead and starting to stink.

> We know the world only through the medium of language. Meaning is arbitrary. Meaning is unstable
> and has to be made by the reader. Each reader will read differently. To impose a single text on the
> readers is authoritarian and oppressive. Designers should make text visually ambiguous and difficult to
> fathom, as a way to respect the rights of the readers.[14]

This is the "straw man" of postmodernism that Robin Kinross props up so he can knock it down with
his universalist, rationalist, truth-seeking, neo-con rant titled *Fellow Readers*.

That we understand the world through language, that meaning is unstable, and that people tend to
interpret things differently are hardly radical or wacky ideas. What is wacky is Kinross's hilarious interpretations of how postmodernist designers react to this condition. It does strike me as a bit "authoritarian"
and "oppressive" to "impose" a single *anything* on any one. I like choices. People who believe in democracy are nutty that way. However, *assuming* a single reading from a text is just plain stupid (even
Mr. Habermas has failed to make a convincing argument). Given that multiple readings are inherent in
most texts (too relativist an idea for Kinross because "truth" loses its absolutism), it doesn't make any
sense to make the text even more "difficult to fathom" unless you absolutely hate the reader.

But Mr. Kinross already knows that the whole point of his ridiculous characterization of poststructuralist theory is to insist that without modernism all is chaos, obscurantism, lies, and nonsense meant to
draw attention to megalomaniac designers (**like me, me, me**).

Robin Kinross is an Enlightenment Era throwback who has taken it on himself to be the quality
control officer of our "common society." He goes about this task with a decidedly "un-common" set of
ideological and formal values that never seem to make their way beyond the posh and precious world
of limited edition, fine, collectable books. As one of society's "common folk," let me be the first to say,
"Gee, thanks, Robin!"

I have included Mr. Kinross as the European representative of fundamentalist, modernist thinking.
There are others, but he presents the most compelling argument, such as it is. As with most cultural
concerns, the "European version" is "classier" than the "American version," but the political strategy is
the same. The usual party line of the far right is: We are being led astray by "bad people" (academics,
pinkos, perverts), and they are steering us away from the "truth" (family values, Jesus, order, clarity) for
their own "selfish gain" (wealth, fame, power). We must get back on the "right track" (throw the bums
out, vote for me, buy my vision).

Modernism in design went from a radical idea to a liberal ideal only to stagnate as conservative
dogma. Because the Zombie Modernist doesn't want to come to terms with the fact that their ideology
is dead, they are always trying to *rationalize* away (they think they own exclusive rights to everything that

is rational) the postmodern condition the rest of us know as reality. That is why postmodernism must be discredited and exposed as empty formalism (a style), and one should never "attempt to go beyond Modernism." Typically, it goes something like this: "It (postmodern design) concentrates on visual techniques and individual solutions rather than on cultural context. Much of this 'Postmodern' design uses a visual vocabulary pioneered by the 1920's avant-garde, yet without the critique of cultural institutions that informed the found-object collages of Kurt Schwitters, the typographic havoc of the Futurists, or the socially engaged design of the Constructivists. Our attempts to go beyond Modernism are often realized by referring to visual techniques that we have been taught represent radicality: avant-garde design of the 1910s and 1920s."[15]

Like the smooth "double talk" of Ronald Reagan, this makes sense if you don't think about it in any detail or any *actual* context. But the idea only makes sense in a contextless void, where there is no distinction between art and design or past and present—in the "metacontext" of design modernism. Even if we accept the dubious claim that art movements like dada and constructivism were effective as critical social discourse (as if Lissitzky's prouns and Schwitters' collages really enlightened the mostly illiterate masses who somehow had the luxury of visiting art galleries and museums from 1910 through the 1920s), whoever said it was design's ambition to "critique its cultural institutions, or its clients"? The strategy of subversion is an art world pretension that has little relevance to design practice. To criticize design for its lack of "cultural critique" makes about as much sense as criticizing art for its inability to "solve problems." Art exits outside (above) society and is expected to be critical of it. Design exists inside (below) society and is expected to serve it. Many young designers today refuse to accept that simple distinction, or any distinction between art and design, because they think art is somehow "better" than design (I think it has something to do with the fact that design is taught in ART schools). Actually, most postmodern design was and is engaged in a critique of a cultural institution. Obviously, postmodern design is very critical of modern design—design's cultural institution. The effectiveness of its criticism is evident in how afraid the modernist designers today are of postmodernism.

The other half-baked idea, expressed in the quote above, is how those postmodern designers stole their forms from early modernist artists and are therefore less original (Never mind that the modernist designers also stole their forms from modern art). The modern art paradigm of originality or—Who Did it First?—assumes to be the most important factor in evaluating design (even though the art world itself has discredited that as a primary criteria years ago). Obviously the art world did it first because, at the time, graphic design as a discipline didn't even exist. So if we judge design by modern art standards (as most of our so-called design critics do) then the design can't possibly go beyond (art) modernism. It can only catch-up, at best. Using art world paradigms for graphic design criticism not only renders postmodern design useless, but the validity of design practice itself is always in question.

If the Zombie Modernists can't discredit postmodernism, then they try to co-opt it. Whatever threatens to be new, or different, must immediately be subjugated to modernism. In an essay about Neville Brody's new project, *Fuse,* Michael Rock writes: "While the forms assume the variegated surface of post-modernism, the underlying issues indicate that projects such as *Fuse* are deeply rooted in Modernist goals of avant-garde experimentation and artistic originality."[16] Sounds familiar? Michael Rock points out that *Fuse* is just continuing in the modernist tradition (art tradition, that is. Never mind that *Fuse* exists in the design context). He then goes on and uses (Art critic) Rosalind Krauss's postmodern critique (of modern art) to lambaste the whole project. Is he advocating postmodernism? Art criticism? Of course not. The main point he feels compelled to make is that *Fuse,* like everything else in design, is still just "good ol' modernism."

Mr. Rock continues: "The stranglehold of a single, homogeneous Modernist theory is a designer's fantasy." As proof of the fact, he offers that "Even a cursory glance through a type house manual or popular magazine from the last thirty years should dash the idea that the world ever tottered on the brink of Global Helvetican domination."[17] But is that proof an alternative *theory* to modernism?

I know I will be accused of portraying modernism in design too narrowly and simplistically, particularly now that we have entered the revisionist-modernist era, when issues raised by postmodernism are routinely claimed as modernist by dredging up obscure precedents in modern art practice. It is no fantasy that there have been very few voices reaching the entire design community. The ones that have, however, are modernist ones ("Oh, but the times, they are a-changin'!").

If the hegemony of modernist design theory is a fantasy, where are all the essays and books on postmodern design theory? Where should we look for them? Certainly not in *I.D.* magazine, where Ralph Caplan has been dispensing his "good-old-boy," "commonsense," modernist pap for years, only to be replaced by Mr. Rock's own, "pedantically correct," "middle-of-the-road," modernism. Sounding a lot like *previous* Yale professor Paul Rand, Michael Rock writes in the *AIGA Journal:* "Perhaps the most socially *irresponsible* work is the overdesigned, overproduced, typographic stunts that serve no real function, speak only to other designers and the cultural elite, and through opulence and uselessness revel in a level of consumption that glorifies financial excess."[18]

I doubt if Mr. Rock would complain about architects, doctors, engineers, and scientists speaking only to themselves. Of course they talk to themselves; they are experts, specialists, and professionals. Because design is not a profession,[19] designers do not understand that professionals have a responsibility to each other to keep practicing at the highest level. That is how they protect the credibility and the value of their profession.

Designers, however, have the trade mentality that the more accessible their work is, and the greater the number they can service (over one billion served daily!), the more secure their jobs will be. This trade mentality is ironic coming from someone like Michael Rock who is not a professional as a designer, but as an educator, a degreed, accredited, professional.

One can only guess who this "champion of the people" and current Yale professor considers the "cultural elite,"[20] but the fact that design critics pick up the rhetoric of the far right should come as no surprise. Whether it is politics, economics, aesthetics, or design, conservatism is still conservatism.

Most of the current debate in graphic design is characterized as a generational split between the older modernist and the younger postmodernist. As I have pointed out in this essay, there are more than a few vocal young modernists, as well as a few older postmodernists (Ed Fella, for example). It would be more accurate to characterize our current situation as the backlash of an entrenched conservatism against a real, or perhaps only imagined threat, of a relativist/liberal agenda. Design is certainly big enough to hold designers with conservative and liberal agendas, but I guess it's just a bad time for liberals everywhere now.

Ask yourself this question: If Newt Gingrich and Rush Limbaugh were graphic designers, would they be:

(A) Complaining about the "visual pollution," "typographic stunts," and the many shortcomings of deconstruction and postmodernist design in centrist publications like *ID, Print, CA,* and the *AIGA Journal*?

Or would they be:

(B) Writing about new ideas and work in smaller circulation publications like *Émigré,* and academic publications like *Visible Language, Design Issues,* or ACD's *Statements*?

Hmmm?

As it became embarrassingly obvious that there were fundamental flaws in modernism as it traditionally functioned in design, some designers started to redefine modernism as a one-ideology-fits-all metaphilosophy.

"I view modernism in design as a broad, potentially open-minded, and inexhaustible way of thinking that began in the mid-nineteenth century and continues today among the majority of us who believe that we should use all existing means to understand, improve, change, and refresh our condition in the world."[21] Sounding suspiciously similar to the ingratiating speeches made by beauty pageant contestants, as in ". . . and I wish for world peace," modernist designers try to prove that their ideology is still *universally* relevant through a new (trendy?) commitment to good citizenship.

"Modernism ran out of steam over a decade ago. But at its core is an ethic—the responsibility that a designer has to actively contribute to, indeed enhance, the social, political, and cultural framework— that continues to inform even the most diehard Postmodernist."[22] Wow, I had no idea that the whole concept of being a productive, responsible citizen was invented by modernism! I thought it was just something modernists used to justify their aesthetic self-indulgence (I guess that's just the nihilistic, postmodern cynic in me).

"Although the rhetoric proclaimed better goods or living conditions, the intended consumers, the public, had little chance to influence or shape Bauhaus ideology. The public became a misunderstood and mostly unwilling participant, blamed for its lack of worldly perspective and aesthetic-value discrimination."[23] Maybe the Bauhaus doesn't represent the "ethical core" of modernism. But then, what does? That's the great thing about modernism: you can pretty much take your pick from the past six decades.

In an effort to avoid change, contemporary modernist designers indulge themselves in a pathetic, kinder, gentler, morphing ideology that is virtually meaningless. The only connection that the current modernism has to what was once understood as modernism is that it is now *rationally* and *universally* useless. This "new" or "late" modernism is an exhausted modernism that the designers prefer to a vibrant but uncertain postmodern future.

The myth of universal modernist values is so pervasive in design, that it swallows up even the possibility of an alternate ideology. "The fact is, it's foolish to deny that anyone who seriously explores the outer limits and inner soul of visual communication is not in some way a Modernist. Or as Pogo's Walt Kelley said: "We have met the enemy and it is us."[24] I believe it would be more accurate to say "We have *reinvented* the enemy and it is us." By co-opting all change and difference into a simplistic modernist paradigm, we prohibit design from ever growing up and leaving its conservative modernist home.

Imprisoned in a dilapidated old house built by modern art, design is unable to strike out on its own and make a place for itself in the world. Thus design's "outer limits and inner soul" is immobile, caught between heaven and earth, in a no-place, we call purgatory—the zombies' fate.

"Today no designer or design organization could or would contemplate universal solutions to the problems of design for the real world. We are still in search of a theory, social commitment is still elusive, so we indulge in our fantasies, ironies and pastiche, which are more comforting (and more profitable) than that respect for 'stern realities' that Gropius demanded from architecture and design."[25]

Designers should stop "hankering" after a mythical modernist ideal, or pretending that art theory is a viable theoretical model for design. We don't need to "conserve" our past and resist change. We need to construct our future theoretical discourse, carefully, around the particular and exciting context of design. We must allow ourselves to look at design in new and challenging ways, we must look for—ourselves.

Notes

1. Books on design can be divided into two types, "serious" monographs on famous modernist masters (the canon), and "fun" collections of vernacular ephemera (the "other").
2. John Patrick Diggins, *The Promise of Pragmatism: Modernism and the Crisis of Knowledge and Authority* (Chicago: University of Chicago Press, 1995).
3. Ibid.
4. Terry Eagleton, *The Ideology of the Aesthetic*, Oxford: Basil Blackwell, 1990.
5. Quoted in Thomas McCarthy, *The Critical Theory of Jürgen Habermas* (London, 1978), 273.
6. Dan Friedman is not a designer. "I have chosen to define my position as that of an artist whose subject—design and culture—affects all aspects of life." However his new book, *Dan Friedman: Radical Modernism,* has been reviewed and received as a design book (I found it in the design section of my local bookstore), and he continues to be a design educator, so I am treating him here as a designer. His impact on design was substantial; his impact on the art world has yet to be seen.
7. Gillian Naylor, *The Bauhaus Reassessed* (E. P. Dutton, 1985), 180.
8. Ibid.
9. Paul Rand, *Design, Form, and Chaos* (New Haven and London: Yale University Press, 1993), 212.
10. Dan Friedman, *Dan Friedman: Radical Modernism* (New Haven and London: Yale University Press, 1994), 114.
11. Rick Poynor, "An Interview with Rick Poynor," by Mr. Keedy, *Émigré,* 33 (Winter, 1995): 35.
12. Ibid.
13. David Harvey, *The Condition of Postmodernity* (Oxford: Blackwell, 1990), 113.
14. Robin Kinross, *Fellow Readers: Notes on Multiplied Language* (London: Hyphen Press, 1994), 5.
15. Mike Mills, "The (layered) Vision Thing," *Eye,* 8 (2) (1992). The title is a reference to George Bush. Ironic, Huh?
16. Michael Rock, "Beyond Typography," *Eye,* 15 (4) (Winter 1994): 31.
17. Ibid., 27.
18. Michael Rock, "Responsibility: Buzzword of the Nineties," *AIGA Journal,* 10 (1) (1992).
19. A professional is someone who has a specialized knowledge, skill, and training that is regulated by their peers. Professionals establish standards of employment and advancement, practice, research, development, and education to further that practice. Although most practicing designers today receive degrees from accredited universities, there is absolutely no necessity to have a degree to practice, and there are no regulated standards

for practice or teaching. Design educators are, however, the only professionals in design, because they are professional educators.

20. "Newt Gingrich, the new Speaker of the House, promises to furnish many ingenious demonstrations of ways to dress authority in the rhetoric of anti-elitism. So far, his handling of his status as a former professor has proved the most instructive. When he first made his ill-fated appointment of a new House historian, Gingrich explained in a public appearance that he was, in fact, a pro. 'As a Ph.D. in history,' he said, 'I think I have the right to select an academic who has legitimate credentials . . . I think I may be peculiarly, of all the people who have been Speaker, in a legitimate position to make a selection that I think will be helpful in re-establishing the legitimacy of history.'

    "But when at the same appearance he was asked about his qualifications for teaching his course on American history at Reinhardt College, he was quick to put his anti-professionalism on display. 'I teach a course which is an outline of my thoughts at fifty-one years of age, based on everything I've experienced, which is, frankly, rather more than most tenured faculty,' he noted. 'I haven't written twenty-two books that are meaningless.' He's not a professional academic after all. He's a citizen professor. We're going to see more of them." Louis Menand, "The Trashing of Professionalism," *New York Times Magazine* (March 5, 1995), 43.

21. "Dan Friedman, *Dan Friedman: Radical Modernism* (Yale University Press, 1994), 114. I consider the consistently favorable news of *Radical Modernism* as emblematic of the myopic, New-York-based design press, and the general dumbing down of America.

22. Steven Heller, "Design (Or Is It War?) is Hell," *Émigré,* 33 (Winter 1995): 48.

23. Dietmar R. Winkler, "Morality and Myth: The Bauhaus Reassessed," *AIGA Journal*, 7 (4) (1990).

24. Steven Heller, "Design (Or Is It War?) is Hell," *Émigré,* 33 (Winter 1995): 48.

25. Gillian Naylor, The Bauhaus Reassessed (E.P. Dutton, 1985), 180.

Chapter 1.3.4

The Global Style: Modernist typography after Postmodernism

Mr. Keedy

As a reaction to the postmodernism of the 80s, and 90s, modernism reasserted itself (did it ever really go?) with a new-ish style of typography that has become ubiquitous in cultural institutions around the world. The good old International Style has been upgraded to a bigger and better (or at least easier) Global Style.

Over the course of about thirty years the various radical and experimental modernist styles coalesced into the Swiss Style of typography. Which grew and spread across Europe and to the Americas and was renamed the International Style. It was *the* style for typography for three more decades until the late 80's when postmodernism deconstructed its hegemony. But postmodernism set too many designers adrift, up a creek without a paddle (not enough rules), and their nostalgia brought them back to the safer and familiar shores of modernism.

The International Style designers turned their backs on local and regional traditions and created a new universal visual language that became the default style of corporate capitalism. It gave impersonal companies an identity so they could be easily recognized but not really known (that would come later with branding). To this day the International Style is still in full force at most airports, and government offices of western superpower nations.

History does not repeat itself but it rhymes.

What the International Style was to commercial corporations, the Global Style is to cultural institutions. It is the new typographic style of institutional art and cultural production. You can see it at your local museums and art galleries, or at just about any arts institution of any kind, anywhere in the world. Thanks to the internet it is more wide spread than the International Style ever was, and it is becoming a universal visual language on a global scale.

For most graphic designers Modernism is not an unfinished project, it's an unending one. Where postmodern typography was a fragmented, de-centered, self-regulating (some might say self-defeating) system, for making meaning, the Global Style, like the International Style before it, is a prescriptive,

Originally published in *Slanted* 22—Art Type (Autumn/Winter 2013/2014): 190-195. © Jeffery Keedy.

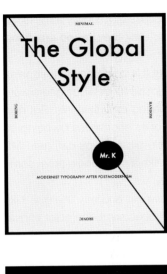

Figure 1.12 Posters generated with trendlist.com's "Trend Generator" app. Designer: Mr. Keedy.

language of specific formal compositional rules that when followed will successfully convey a message while expressing a specific mood or emotional response. These rules that elicit the desired emotional response are what constitutes the style.

The emotional response that one has to the old International Style is that it is contemporary, sophisticated, cool, calm, and rigorously logical. And that is exactly how it's supposed to feel. Designers wore lab coats at Unimark, to show that they were not artists, they were calculating professionals. But now after half a century the International Style is pretty familiar. It's lost some of its snootiness by being so pervasive in the corporate and commercial world. Helvetica starred in a bio-pic and you can get PMS color chips on a coffee mug or t-shirt. Today the International Style is more like a posh uncle (from some exotic European metropolis). He's distinguished and cool, but he's old!

By contrast the Global Style looks new, but still familiar. In fact it radiates newness and very little else. Like the International Style before it, the Global Style is easy to assimilate and is obedient to the point of near transparency. On an emotional level it sublimates quotidian boredom into a contemporary expression of cool, ironic, ennui. It is as if the lab-coat wearing designer/scientist of Unimark has been replaced by an App.

Most of the formal and aesthetic attributes of the new Global Style are lifted directly from the International Style. White space backgrounds, sans serif typefaces, minimalist asymmetrically balanced compositions with limited color palate. No extraneous decoration, ornament or complex patterns. A love of simple geometric shapes. The one notable exception is the grid.

It's not that the grid is no longer there it's that the grid is no longer visible or even detectable. It is embedded in the 0's and 1's and x and y coordinates of digital space. Just like the movie *Tron* the digital environment is built on a grid (it just doesn't glow like neon). So it is understandable why designers would stop fussing with grids when it is the ground beneath us, the water we swim in and the air we breathe in our virtual/digital world.

But back in the old days, the International Style designers ground their blue lead pencils to a razor-sharp point that they used to inscribe a bespoke grid structure into the picture plane. This was the scaffolding or framing on which the typography would hang. The grid was the starting point that determined more than anything what the relationship between the typography and the space it existed in would be. So the designer took great care to make sure that the grid they devised would accommodate the space they were creating to the concept they wanted to communicate.

Grids were something you learned about in school. Competent use of a grid is one of the things that showed you were a pro. Creative transgression or "breaking" of the grid, showed that you wanted to be more than just good. The analog world of the International Style was grounded in the laws of physics. Paper was cut and scored to a quantifiable and very determinate size. Type came in at limited sizes of lead or photo-film strips. Within these finite restrictions the designer asymmetrically composed carefully scaled text into architectonic compositions that conveyed a concept that embodied the message. Transforming the simple 2D space of the printed graphic into an abstract deep space that seemed to extended from the poster to the wall and worlds beyond.

By contrast the Global Style's typographic composition does not explicitly refer to the rectangle or object in which it exists, nor to anything in the real world. It may be on a poster or book or website, but it is not an integral part of an object occupying a specific space or size. It could be a large poster that someone is holding in their studio or just a thumbnail JPEG of someone holding a poster. It makes no difference to the design. Because the design is not size, site, nor media specific. When you gaze upon a Global Style composition you don't imagine what is happening outside of the picture plane, because you know the answer is nothing. The typography doesn't delineate space, it just fills it.

Space in the Global Style is flat to the point of non-existence. Although there is almost always some layering of a tedious geometric shape on top of an insipid block of text, the effect is still one of simultaneity and flatness as the overlap is usually transparent. The picture plane is not composed it is just temporarily occupied. The hierarchy of forms is designed so that everything within the composition is of more or less equal unimportance. Some words go this way some go that way, here it is, easy to read, easy to look at, everything in place filling the page up nicely. Since the page is so evenly filled we read it instantly as "complete" or "done" it requires very little of the audience in terms of interpretation or participation (who has the time). Like a child's drawing there is a charming dumbness to it. It feeds on our nostalgia for a long lost simplicity and purity that never existed. It functions like cultural "wallpaper" it is easy to ignore.

The International Style used typographic trickery to animate the flat picture frame with the illusion of depth and space. Borrowing from music and video, the Global Style uses the 4th dimension of time, or rather a reference to time, to animate the 2D space. It accomplishes this by looking like it was a single frame taken out of an animated sequence. One can easily imagine many different iterations before and after the one we are currently seeing. The overlap of disparate imagery looks like "screen burn" or "ghost images" that would make more sense seen individually and sequentially. In this way the Global Style extends beyond itself forward and backward in time but not in space. It is very emblematic of our transient culture, it's a move that hits the zeitgeist right on the head. Making it more relevant than the old International Style with its analog abstraction of 2D space.

What the Global Style took from Postmodernism is a taste for the vernacular, the quotidian, the punk inspired anti-aesthetic and an interest in language. That is where the "ugly" font and color choices come from as well as the squashed type and the frames around the outside and the frames within frames, the overt use of language and diagrammatic symbols, the slash the underline etc. Center axis typography, was used as a historical referent in postmodern typography, but in the Global style it is simply an easy (auto) default setting, randomly deployed.

It also appropriated the aura of theory, or at least it insinuates theoretical motivations, even though there is to-date little tangible evidence of any theory. That so many designers would utilize a single prescribed style almost exclusively in service to cultural practices and yet be so uncritical or self-reflecting of that style is curious indeed.

Designers of the postmodern era were accused of aesthetic self-indulgence with all the computer stunts, historical quotation, formal contortions and time consuming complexity. No one can accuse the designers of the Global Style of aesthetic self-indulgence since pretty much anyone can design like that, and do it quickly. Obviously their self-indulgence is not an aesthetic one but a social one. Forget about print, digital, motion, environmental, or interactive media, because it's social media that has the biggest impact on design today.

Does it really take a studio of 3 or 4 designers to design a Risograph art catalog or silk-screened poster consisting of an <u>ALL CAPS HEADLINE</u> (with underline) and coarse half-tone photos for a friend's "art" show? Should design studios really put the bulk of their efforts into "projects" of their own devising that are of no use or interest to anyone but themselves and a few underemployed friends? Feeding your blog, Instagram, Tumblr, and Twitter account is self-promotion, but is it design? The fact that you are busy doing design doesn't mean you are a designer, anymore than the fact that you are busy cooking makes you a chef.

Design is for somebody besides you!

I say this as someone who argued, back in the day, for designers to be recognized as making culturally significant contributions and not just be seen as problem solving commercial tools. Today it is taken for granted that graphic designers have a cultural role to play. We won that battle, we have our autonomy. But is this how we want to use it? Replicating art world practices, and recycling old styles for each other? Is being an institutional servant somehow better than being a commercial one? Better for who?

The Global Style like the International Style before it, will be with us for some time to come. It is the new normal, or base from which a multitude of stylistic iterations, and reactions will evolve. Every era and culture gets the style it deserves. What did we do to deserve this?

Or maybe it's something we didn't do?

whatever gods we choose, to celebrate artifice, to construct our selves in fiction and fantasy, to play in the blank, empty spaces of the now.

One of the most currently influential of Second World strategists, Jean Baudrillard, has gone further still, declaring that appearances can no longer be said to mask, conceal, distort or falsify reality.[6] He claims that reality is nothing more than the never knowable sum of all appearances. For Baudrillard, "reality" flickers. It will not stay still. Tossed about like Rimbaud's "drunken boat" on a heaving sea of surfaces, we cease to exist as rational *cogitos* capable of standing back and totalising on the basis of our experience.

The implication is that "we" never did exist like that anyway, that there never was a "behind" where we could stand and speculate dispassionately on the meaning of it all. Thus the 'I' is nothing more than a fictive entity, an optical illusion, a hologram hanging in the air, created at the flickering point where the laser beams of memory and desire intersect. The subject simply ceases . . . this is the Post Modern Condition and it takes place in the present tense. Rimbaud's *bateau ivre*, in fact, is too ecstatic and too bohemian a metaphor to encapsulate the drift into autism that the Baudrillard scene[7] entails—end of judgement, value, meaning, politics, subject-object oppositions.

A more fitting analogy for what it's like to live through the "death of the subject" might involve a comparison with the new reproductive technologies. Baudrillard's position on what life on Planet Two is like amounts to this: like the heads on a video recorder, we merely translate audio and visual signals back and forth from one terminus (the tape) to another (the screen). The information that we "handle" changes with each moment—all human life can pass across those heads—but we never own or store or "know" or "see" the material that we process. If we live in the Second World, then our lives get played out of us. Our lives get played out for us, played out in us, but never, ever *by* us. In Baudrillard's anti-system, "by" is the unspeakable preposition because it suggests that there's still time for human agency, for positive action; still some space for intervention and somewhere left to intervene. But this is an inadmissable possibility in a world where politics—the art of the possible—has ceased to have meaning.

For Baudrillard, standing in the terminal, at the end of the weary European line, the music of the spheres has been replaced by the whirring of tape heads. As far as he is concerned, we are—all of us—merely stations on the endless, mindless journey of the signifier: a journey made by nobody to nowhere . . .

The suggestion that we are living in the wake of the withering signified may well sound like science fiction or intellectual sophistry but there are those who argue that all this is linked to actual changes in production[8]—that the flat earth thesis (what Fredric Jameson calls the "disappearance of the depth model"[9]) finds material support in the post-War shift from an industrial to a "post-industrial", "media" or "consumer" society. These terms have been coined by different writers to signal the perceived move from an industrial economy based on the production of three-dimensional goods by a proletariat that sells its labour power in the market into a new, qualitatively different era of multi-national capital, media conglomerates and computer science where the old base-superstructure division is annulled or up-ended and production in the West becomes progressively dehumanised and "etherealised"—focused round information-and-image-as-product and automation-as-productive-process.

According to some Post people, the tendency towards acceleration, and innovation, to programmed obsolescence and neophilia which Marx saw characterising societies dominated by the capitalist mode of production—where, to use his own words, "all that is solid melts into air"[10]—has been intensified under contemporary "hypercapitalism"[11] to such an extent that a kind of rapturing has occurred which has "abstracted" production to a point beyond anything Marx could have imagined possible. New commodities untouched by human hands circulate without any reference to vulgar "primary needs" in a stratosphere of pure exchange.

In such a world, so the argument goes, not only are signifiers material but a *proper* materialist (e.g., Marx himself were he alive today) would proclaim—even, some suggest, celebrate[12]—the triumph of the signifier. A materialist proper would welcome the coming of the flat, un-bourgeois world: a world without distinction and hierarchy, a society in which—although growing numbers of people are without permanent, paid employment—more and more (of not necessarily the same) people have access to the means of *r*eproduction (television, radio, stereo, hifi, audio and videocassette recorders, cheap and easy-to-use cameras, Xerox machines if not portable "pirate" radio and television transmitters, record-ing facilities, synthesisers, drum machines, etc.). A world where although many may be "trained" and few educated, everyone—to adapt Benjamin again—can be an amateur film, television, radio, record, fashion and photography critic.

Meanwhile, the relations of knowledge and the functions of education are transformed as models of knowledge based on linguistics and cybernetics move in to subvert the epistemological foundations of the humanities, and the university faces a crisis as it is no longer capable of transmitting the appropriate cultural capital to emergent technocratic and bureaucratic elites. The proliferation of commercial labor-atories, privately-funded research bases, of data banks and information storage systems attached to multi-national companies and government agencies, amplifies this trend so that higher education can no longer be regarded—if it ever was—as the privileged site of research and the sole repository of "advanced" knowledge.[13]

At the same time, recent refinements in telematics, satellite and cable television threaten to erode national cultural and ideological boundaries as local regulations governing what can and can't be broadcast become increasingly difficult to implement. As the related strands of social and aesthetic utopianism, the notions of the Radical Political Alternative and radicalism in Art[14] are unravelled and revealed as untenable and obsolescent, advertising takes over where the avant garde left off and the picture of the Post is complete.

According to this scenario absolutely nothing—production, consumption, subjectivity, knowledge, art, the experience of space and time—is what it was even forty years ago. "Experts" equipped with narrow professional and instrumental competences replace the totalising intellectual with *his* universal categories and high moral tone. "Weak thought",[15] paradoxology and modest proposals in the arts replace the internally consistent global projections of marxism and the romantic gestures or grand (architectural) plans of modernism (". . . we no longer believe in political or historical teleologies, or in the great 'actors' and 'subjects' of history—the nationstate, the proletariat, the party, the West, etc. . . .".[16]) The consumer (for Alvin Toffler, the "prosumer"[17]) replaces the citizen. The pleasure-seeking *bricoleur* replaces the truth-and-justice seeking rational subject of the Enlightenment. The now replaces history. Everywhere becomes absolutely different (doctrine of the diverse v the dictatorship of the norm).

Everywhere—from Abu Dhabi to Aberdeen—becomes more or less the same (first law of the level earth: lack of gravity = end of distinction *or* the whole world watches *Dallas* ergo the whole world is Dallas).

This is where *The Face* fits. This is the world where the ideal reader of *The Face*—stylepreneur, doleocrat, Buffalo Boy or Sloane—educated, street-wise but not institutionalised—is learning how to dance in the dark, how to survive, how to stay on top (on the surface) of things. After all, in 1985 with the public sector, education, the welfare state—all the big, "safe" institutions—up against the wall, there's nothing good or clever or heroic about going under. When all is said and done, why bother to think "deeply" when you're not *paid* to think deeply?

Sur *le face*

Sur-face:
1. The outside of a body, (any of) the limits that terminate a solid, outward aspect of material or immaterial thing, what is apprehended of something upon a casual view or consideration.
2. (geom) that which has length and breadth but no thickness. (*The Concise English Dictionary*)

A young man with a haircut that is strongly marked as "modern" (i.e., 1940s/1950s short) is framed in a doorway surrounded by mist. He carries a battered suitcase. The collar of his coat is turned up against the cold, night air. He walks towards the camera and into a high-ceilinged building. A customs official in a Russian-style military uniform stops him, indicating that he intends searching the young man's bag. A shot-reverse-shot sequence establishes a tense, expectant mood as eyelines meet; the stylish boy confronts the older-man-in-uniform. One gaze, fearful and defiant, meets another diametrically opposed gaze which is authoritarian and sadistic. The bag is aggressively snapped open and the camera discloses its contents to the viewer: some clothes, a copy of *The Face*. The official tosses the magazine to one side in a gesture redolent of either disgust or mounting anger or a hardening of resolve. The implication is that his initial suspicions are confirmed by the discovery of this "decadent" journal.

At this, the crucial moment, the official's attention is diverted as a VIP, an older, senior official dressed in a more imposing uniform marches past between a phalanx of severe, grim-faced guards. The customs man, eyes wide with terror, jerks to attention and salutes, indicating with a slight movement of the head that the young man is dismissed. The sequence cuts to the young man, still in his coat, standing in a cramped, poorly furnished room. He opens the case, emptying the contents hurriedly onto a table or bed. The camera sweeps in as his trembling hands close around the forbidden article, the object of desire: a pair of Levi jeans.

The confrontation which provides the dramatic structure for the micro-narrative of this, the latest Levi jeans television and cinema commercial, is the familiar one between, on the one hand, freedom, youth, beauty and the West and, on the other, the cold, old, ugly, grey and unfree East. The commercial quotes visual and thematic elements from the spy thriller genre in order to sell a multiple package: the idea of rebellious-youth-winning-through-against-all-odds; the more general myth of the young Siegfried slaying the dragon of constraint; *The Face*; Levi jeans; the image of the "self-made man" constructing himself through consumption and thereby embodying the spirit of the West. The articulation of commodity consumption, personal identity and desire which characterises life under hypercapitalism has here been universalised. There is nowhere else to go but to the shops. For in a flat world there is an end, as well, to ideology. The only meaningful political struggle left is between the individual body and the impersonal, life-denying forces of the state (whether nominally capitalist or communist).

However, this is not just another bourgeois myth that can be turned inside out and demystified (and hence deactivated) by the methods proposed by the early Roland Barthes, because the fictional scenario upon which the commercial is based has, in its turn, some foundation in fact. Rumour has it that Levi jeans go for high sums on the Russian black market and, according to issue no. *61,* "in Moscow old copies of *The Face* are reported to change hands for upwards of £80." On a flat world, a commercial becomes a social (if not a socialist) realist text. It documents the real conditions of desire in the East and its claims to "truth" are not challenged by the fact that the copy of *The Face* used in this ad is not, in a sense, "real" either. It is, according to issue *61,* just a mock-up, a cover, a ghost of a thing, a skin concealing absent flesh. Thus, on the Second World, a cover can stand in for a whole magazine (the face of *The Face* for the whole *Face*). A magazine can stand in for a pair of jeans and the whole package can stand in for the lack of a "whole way of life" which on a flat earth is unrealisable anywhere under any system (capitalist or otherwise).

But even the shadow of a shadow has a value and a price:

> The rarest issue of *The Face* consists of only one page—a cover designed at the request of Levis for use in a new television and cinema commercial. There are only four copies in existence.
>
> (*The Face* no. *61*, May, 1985)

Rarity guarantees collectability and generates desire which promises an eventual return on the original investment. One day, one of the three copies of the copy that we saw all those years ago on our television screens may be auctioned off at Sotheby's and end up in the V&A, the Tate or the Ghetty Collection . . .

. . . Do you remember John Berger speaking from the heart of the First World in the television version of *Ways of Seeing* in 1974 as he flicked through a copy of the *Sunday Times* Colour Supplement moving from portraits of starving Bangla Deshi refugees to an advertisement for Badedas bath salts? "Between these images," he said and goes on saying on film and videotapes in Complementary Studies classes up and down the country, "there is such a gap, such a fissure that we can only say that the culture that produced these images is insane." *The Face* is composed precisely on this fissure. It is the place of the nutty conjunction.

In the exhibition there is one panel of selected features from *The Face* presumably displaying the inventive layout and varied content. A photo-documentary account of a teenaged mod revivalist at a scooter rally entitled "The Resurrection of Chad" is placed alongside photographs of the Nuba of Southern Sudan above a portrait of Malcolm McLaren, inventor of the Sex Pistols, and Duck Rock, a pirate of assorted black and Third World (Burundi, Zulu, New York rap) musical sounds against an article on Japanese fashion and an interview with Andy Warhol.

More facetious (a First World critic might say "unwarranted" or "offensive") juxtapositions occur elsewhere. A photograph by Derek Ridgers of the Pentecostal Choir of the First Born Church of the Living God shot outside a church (?) in a field in hallucinatory colour is placed next to a glowering black and white portrait of Genesis P. Orridge and friend of the occult/avant garde group, Psychic TV, after they had just signed a £1,000,000 contract. The malevolent duo are posed in front of a collection of metallic dildoes alongside the original caption: "Which are the two biggest pricks in this picture?" Insolent laughter is, of course, incompatible with a high moral tone. Where either everything or nothing is significant, everything threatens to become just a laugh and, as one look at television's *The Young Ones* will tell you, *that* kind of laughter is never just or kind . . .

On a flat world, it is difficult to build an argument or to move directly from one point to the next because surfaces can be very slippery. Glissage or sliding is the preferred mode of transport—sliding from a television commercial to the end of ideology, from the Bill Brandt Room to a Picture of the Post, from *The Face* exhibition to *The Face* itself . . .

All statements made inside *The Face,* though necessarily brief are never straightforward. Irony and ambiguity predominate. They frame all reported utterances whether those utterances are reported photographically or in prose. A language is thus constructed without anybody in it (to question, converse or argue with). Where opinions are expressed they occur in hyperbole so that a question is raised about how seriously they're meant to be taken. Thus the impression you gain as you glance through the magazine is that this is less an "organ of opinion" than a wardrobe full of clothes (garments, ideas, values, arbitrary preferences: i.e., signifiers).

Thus, *The Face* can sometimes be a desert full of silent bodies to be looked at, of voices without body to be listened to not heard. This is because of the terror of naming.

As the procession of subcultures, taste groups, fashions, anti-fashions, winds its way across the flat plateaux, new terms are coined to describe them: psychobillies, yuppies, casuals, scullies, Young Fogies, Sloane Rangers, the Doleocracy, the Butcheoise—and on a flat earth all terminology is fatal to the object it describes. Once "developed" as a photographic image and as a sociological and marketing concept, each group fades out of the now (i.e., ceases to exist).

The process is invariable: caption/capture/disappearance (i.e., naturalisation). (". . . information is, by definition, a short-lived element. As soon as it is transmitted and shared it ceases to be information but has instead become an environmental given . . .".)[18] Once named, each group moves from the sublime (absolute now) to the ridiculous (the quaint, the obvious, the familiar). It becomes a special kind of joke. Every photograph an epitaph, every article an obituary. On both sides of the camera and the typewriter, irony and ambiguity act as an armour to protect the wearer (writer/photographer; person/ people written about/photographed) against the corrosive effects of the will to nomination. Being named (identified; categorised) is naff; on Planet Two it is a form of living death. A terrifying sentence is imposed (terrifying for the dandy): exile from the now.

And in the words of Baudelaire who preceded Godard in the Second World as Christ preceded Mohammed; as Hegel did Marx in the First:

> The beauty of the dandy consists above all in his air of reserve, which in turn arises from his unshakable resolve not to feel any emotions.[19]

To live ironically is to live without decideable emotion; to be ambiguous is to refuse to "come out" (of the now). It is to maintain a delicate and impotent reserve . . .

. . . The aversion to direct speech is also apparent in the tendency to visual and verbal parody. At the exhibition, Robert Mapplethorpe contributes a self-portrait in which he masquerades as a psychotic,

1950s juvenile delinquent. The staring eyes, the bulging quiff, the erect collar, the flick knife laid against the face, all suggest a mock-heroic sadomasochistic fantasy directed at him "self". Here the camera discloses no personal details as the body becomes the blank site or screen for the convocation of purely referential signs: *West Side Story*; doowop, "New York"-as-generalised-dangerous-place, the "Puerto Rican type": the banal and flattened forms of homoerotic kitsch . . . Annabella, singer with Bow Wow Wow sitting on the grass in the nude surrounded by the other (clothed) male members of the group glumly contemplates the camera and us in an exact reconstruction of Manet's *Déjeuner sur l'herbe* . . . Marilyn and Boy George stand outside the Carburton Street squat where they once lived, the mundane context and milk bottles in ironic counterpoint to their exotic, camp appearance: Hollywood and *The Mikado* come to *Coronation Street* . . . The high-key lighting, the braces, suits and picture ties, Duke Ellington moustaches and cigarette smoke in a black and white studio shot of Lynx are direct quotations from *film noir* and from 1930s/1940s promotional pics for black American jazz artists.

The past is played and replayed as an amusing range of styles, genres, signifying practices to be combined and recombined at will. The then (and the there) are subsumed in the now. The only history that exists here is the history of the signifier and that is no history at all . . .

. . . I open a copy of *The Face*. The magazine carries its own miniature simulacrum: a glossy five-page supplement commissioned by Swatch, the Swiss watch company which is aiming its product at the young, professional, style and design conscious markets. Like a Russian doll, the hollow *Face* opens to reveal a smaller, even emptier version of itself: *International Free Magazine No 2*. The black and red *Face* logo box is reproduced in the top left-hand corner with the words "Swatch o'clock" in white sans serif caps across it. The host magazine is mimicked and parodied by its guest. A photograph of a model wearing watch earrings—her face reduced to a cartoon with a few strokes in "wild style" with a felt tip pen—pouts out above a caption reading "Art o'clock, look chic but rare". A double page spread reveals a "hunky" man in leather posing with a bow and arrows in a wood. The captions read: "Homme Swatch. Outdoor, ton corps, ta Swatch". The "Swatch" mock-editorial "explains":

> *Parlez vous* Swatch? To look or not to look? That is the question. *Sommaire.* Summer 85: let's go, *l'été,* come on in Swatch, *aujourd'hui la mode o'clock est entrée dans ma tête* . . . etc.

This is a parody of a parody. As the primary objection to advertising on Planet Two is aesthetic rather than ideological—a matter of the signifier and not the signified—potential advertisers can be educated to commission designs compatible with editorial preferences . . .

Advertising—the *eidos* of the marketplace—is pressed into the very pores of *The Face*. For advertisers as for *The Face,* sophists and lawyers, rhetoric is all there is: the seizure of attention, the refinement of technique, the design, promotion, marketing of product (ideas, styles; for lawyers, innocence or guilt depending on who pays). *The Face* habitually employs the rhetoric of advertising: the witty one-liner, the keyword, the aphorism, the extractable (i.e., quotable) image are favoured over more sustained, sequential modes of sense-making. Each line or image quoted in another published context acts like a corporate logo inviting us to recognise its source—the corporation—and to acknowledge the corporation's power.

The urge to compress and condense—to create an absolute homology of form and meaning which cannot be assimilated but can only be copied—is most pronounced in Neville Brody's sometimes barely legible typefaces. It is as if we were witnessing in the various trademark scripts and symbols he devises, a graphic depiction of the power shift from Europe to Japan as the phonetic alphabet takes on before our eyes a more iconic character. The occidental equivalent of Japanese or Chinese script is to be found here in *The Face* in the *semiogram*: a self-enclosed semantic unit—a word, graphic image, photograph, the layout of a page—which cannot be referred to anything outside itself. In the semiogram, *The Face* capitulates symbolically to the empire of signs, robots, computers, miniaturisation and automobiles—to Japan, which has served as the first home of flatness for a long line of Second World orientalists including Roland Barthes, Noel Birch, Chris Marker, David Bowie and, of course, the group Japan. The pages of *The Face,* like a series of masks in an occidental Noh play, act out a farce on the decline of the British Empire. The name of this production: "[I think] I'm going Japanese" . . .

Renouncing the possibility of challenging the game, Baudrillard has formulated a series of what he calls "decadent" or "fatal" strategies (where decadence and fatalism are seen as positive virtues). One of these he names "hyperconformism". *The Face* is hyperconformist: more commercial than the commercial, more banal than the banal . . .

Behind *The Face*: the bottom line on Planet One

Vietnam was first and foremost a war in representation.

(Jean Luc Godard)

What are Chile, Biafra, the 'boat people', Bologna or Poland to us?

(Jean Baudrillard, Sur le nihilisme)

The Tatler: the magazine for the other Boat People.

(Advertising slogan for The Tatler accompanying an image of a
group of the "beautiful rich" aboard a yacht.)

Many people of my generation and my parents' generation retain a sentimental attachment—in itself understandable enough—to a particular construction of the "popular"—a construction which was specific to the period from the inter-War to the immediate post-War years and which found its most profound, its most progressive and mature articulation in the films of Humphrey Jennings and on the pages of *The Picture Post.* We hardly need reminding that that moment has now passed.

The community addressed by and in part formed out of the national-popular discourses of the late 1930s and 1940s—discourses which were focused round notions of fair play, decency, egalitarianism and natural justice now no longer exists as an affective and effective social unit.

Forty years of relative affluence, and regional (if not global) peace; five years of Thatcherite New Realism and go-gettery, of enemies within and without, and of the dream of the property-owning democracy, have gradually worn down and depleted the actual and symbolic materials out of which that earlier construction was made.

At the same time, the popular can no longer be hived off from Higher Education as its absolute other ("innocent", "spontaneous", "untutored") because those same forty years have seen more and more ordinary people gaining some, admittedly restricted, (and increasingly endangered) access to secondary, further, higher and continuing education. It is neither useful nor accurate to think about the "masses" as if they were wrapped in clingfilm against all but the most unsavoury of new ideas.

There have, of course, been positive material advances. To take the most important example, feminist concerns, idioms and issues have become lodged in the very fabric of popular culture even in those areas from television sit-com to working men's clubs where the implications of feminist critique have been most actively and hysterically resisted. It's also clear that the mass media—whatever other role(s) they may play in social reproduction—have served to democratise, at least to circulate on an unprecedented scale, forms and kinds of knowledge which had previously been the exclusive property of privileged elites.

The Face should be seen as functioning within this transfigured social and ideological field. Whilst I would not suggest that *The Face* is the *Picture Post* of the 1980s, I would go along with the claim asserted in the accompanying notes that *The Face* exhibition "is about looking at popular social history in the making". *The Face* has exerted an enormous influence on the look and flavour of many magazines available in newsagents up and down the country and has spawned countless imitations: *I-D, Blitz, Tomorrow, Etcetera,* etc. The repertoire and rhetoric of photographic mannerisms, devices, techniques and styles in the fashion and music press have been fruitfully expanded and the studio has been rediscovered, in a sense re-invented as a fabulous space—a space where every day the incredible becomes the possible. But *The Face*'s impact has gone far beyond the relatively narrow sphere of pop and fashion journalism dictating an approach to the visible world that has become synonymous with what it means for a magazine today to be—at least to look—contemporary. The gentrified cut-up has found its way into the inaptly named *Observer* "Living" supplement and the *Sunday Times* has followed *The Face* into the continental 30.1cm × 25.3cm format.

Amongst its other services, *The Face* provides a set of physical cultural resources that young people can use in order to make some sense and get some pleasure out of growing up in an increasingly daunting and complex environment. It has been instrumental in shaping an emergent structure of feeling, a 1980s sensibility as distinctive in its own way as that of the late 1960s (though how resilient that structure will prove remains to be seen). But in any case, it does no good to consider the readers of *The Face* as victims, culprits, dupes or dopes, as "kids" or *tabulae rasae* or potential converts. Their world is real already even when the sensibility which *The Face* supports and fosters seems to bear a much closer and more vital relationship to the anomic Picture of the Post that I outlined earlier than it does to the "social democratic eye" of Hulton's classic photojournal weekly.

The Face reflects, defines and focuses the concerns of a significant minority of style and image conscious people who are not, on the whole, much interested in party politics, authorised versions of the past and outmoded notions of community. The popular and the job of picturing the popular has changed irrevocably out of all recognition even since the 1950s.

It should also be borne in mind that Nick Logan is not Jean Baudrillard and that *The Face* is infinitely better, more popular, significant, influential and socially plugged in than *The Tatler* is or ever could be. It's also clear that the photography, design, and a lot of the writing are, by any standards, good and on occasion attain levels of excellence which are still rare in British pop journalism. And, finally, it is as well to remember that a text is, of course, *not* the world, that no one *has* to live there, that it is not a compulsory purchase, that no one has to pay, that no one has to even pay a visit.

I'm well aware that only a gossip columnist, a fool or an academic could find the time to undertake a close analysis of such self-confessed ephemera or would set aside sufficient energy to go chasing round those circles where, as George Eliot puts it, "the lack of grave emotion passes for wit".[20] Yet, despite such reservations, I cannot escape the conviction that something else, something deeper is at stake, not just here in this talk of signifiers, surfaces, post-modernism, but in the broader streams of social life and practice, and in all personal and political struggle, irrespective of where it takes place and irrespective, too, of how these terms and the relations between them get defined.

Something that really matters is at stake in this debate. At the risk of alienating the reader with an analogy already stretched to breaking point, one last battle in the War of the Worlds may help to clarify the issue . . .

. . . I was about to leave *The Face* exhibition feeling vaguely uneasy about the ambivalence of my response when—not for the first time—the beautiful, clear, soulful voice of Chrissie Hynde came drifting across from the video installation in the corner of the room. The promo tapes were on some kind of a loop so that I had heard her sing the same song at least three times as I meandered round the photographs, the layout and typography panels, the cases containing Crolla and Bodymap clothes. As I moved towards the door, that voice rose once more singing over and over the same agonised refrain:

It's a thin line between love and hate . . .

And words like "love" and "hate" and "faith" and "history", "pain" and "joy", "passion" and "compassion"—the depth words drawn up like ghosts from a different dimension will always come back in the eleventh hour to haunt the Second World and those who try to live there in the now. This is not just pious sentiment. It is, quite simply, in the very nature of the human project that those words and what they stand for will never go away. When they seem lost and forgotten, they can be found again even in—especially in—the most inhospitable, the flattest of environments. John Cowper Powys once wrote:

We can all love, we can all hate, we can all possess, we can all pity ourselves, we can all condemn ourselves, we can all admire ourselves, we can all be selfish, we can all be unselfish. But below all these things there is something else. There is a deep, strange, inaccountable response within us to the mystery of life and the mystery of death: and this response subsists below grief and pain and misery and disappointment, below all care and all futility.

That something else will still be there when all the noise and the chatter have died away. And it is perhaps significant that the quotation came to me courtesy of one of my students who included it in a deeply moving essay on how the experience of personal loss had transformed his response to photos of his family. He in his turn had found it in an advertisement for a group called The Art of Noise designed by Paul Morley, arch *bricoleur* and publicist, the mastermind at ZTT behind the Frankie Goes to Hollywood phenomenon last year.

Whatever Baudrillard or *The Tatler* or Saatchi and Saatchi, and Swatch have to say about it, I shall go on reminding myself that this earth is round not flat, that there will never be an end to judgement, that the ghosts will go on gathering at the thin and bitter line which separates truth from lies, justice from injustice, Chile, Biafra and all the other avoidable disasters from all of us, whose order is built upon their chaos. And that, I suppose, is the bottom line on Planet One.

Notes

1. Northrop Frye, *The Great Code: The Bible and Literature* (New York: Harcourt Brace Jovanovich, 1981).

2. See, for instance, Paul Virilio and Sylvere Lotringer, *Pure War* (New York: Semiotext(e) / Foreign Agents series, 1983); Felix Guattari, *Molecular Revolution, Psychiatry and Politics* (Harmondsworth, UK: Penguin, 1984); Felix Guattari and Gilles Deleuze, *Anti-Oedipus: Capitalism and Schizophrenia* (Minneapolis: University of Minnesota Press, 1983); Meaghan Morris, "Room 101 or a Few Worst Things in the World," in André Frankovits (ed.), *Seduced and Abandoned: The Baudrillard Scene* (Glebe, NSW: Stonemoss Services, 1984); Meaghan Morris, "des Epaves/Jetsam", in *On the Beach* 1 (Autumn, 1983); André Gorz, *Farewell to the Working Class* (London: Pluto Press, 1983); André Gorz, *Paths to Paradise* (London: Pluto Press, 1985); Rudolf Bahro, *From Red to Green* (London: New Left Books, 1982).

3. See Roland Barthes, *The Pleasure of the Text* ((London: Jonathan Cape, 1977). For a more condensed, programmatic manifesto of post-structuralist aims and objectives, see R. Barthes, "Change the Object Itself" in S.Heath (ed.), *Image-Music-Text* (Harmondsworth, UK: Penguin, 1977).

4. The phrase the "impossible class" was originally coined by Nietszche in *The Dawn of the Day*, 1881 (New York: Gordon Press, 1974): ". . . the workers of Europe should declare that henceforth as a class they are a human impossibility and not only, as is customary, a harsh and purposeless establishment . . . [They must] protest against the machine, against capital and against the choice with which they are now threatened, of becoming, of necessity, either slaves of the State or slaves of a revolutionary party . . ." The phrase has since been appropriated as a self-description by certain anarchist groups, by situationists, urban Red Indians, radical autonomists, etc. (see, for instance, the anarchist pamphlet Riot Not to Work on the 1981 riots).

5. This is a mutated echo of the title of an article by Jean Baudrillard (see note 6 below): "The Precession of Simulacra" in which he postulates that the "social body" is being mutated by the "genetic code" of television in such a way that psychotic planar states of drift and fascination emerge to supplant social and psychic space (the space of the subject). In this way, reality is supposedly replaced by a "hyperreality" (an eventless imaginary). See "The precession of simulacra" in *Art & Text* 11 (Spring, 1983).

6. For an excellent introduction, summary and critique of Baudrillard's work read André Frankovits (ed.), *Seduced and Abandoned: The Baudrillard Scene* (Glebe, NSW: Stonemoss Services, 1984). To retrace Baudrillard's trajectory (for given his flatness it can hardly be a descent) from a (ed.), op. cit. (1984). Confronted with the terminal condition of culture in the West, Baudrillard relinquishes the rôle of surgeon (radical, dissecting analyst) and tries homeopathy (paralogic) instead . . . more decadent than the decadent . . .

7. See Frankovits, op. cit. (1984).

8. See, for instance, Alain Touraine, *The Post-Industrial Society* (London: Wildwood House, 1974); A. Gorz, op.cit. (1983, 1985); Daniel Bell, *The Coming Post Industrial Society* (New York: Basic Books, 1973); Alvin Toffler, *The Third Wave* (London: Bantam, 1981); for post-modernism, see Hal Foster (ed.), op. cit. (1985); Jean-François Lyotard, "Answering the Question: What is Postmodernism?", in *The Postmodern Condition: A Report on Knowledge* (Manchester: Manchester University Press, 1984); Fredric Jameson, "Post modernism or the Cultural Logic of Late Capitalism," in *New Left Review*, 146: 1984. For New Left and neo-Marxist critiques of postmodernism, see Perry Anderson, *Considerations on Western Marxism* (New York: New Left Books, 1976), and "Modernity and Revolution", in *New Left Review* 144 (March to April, 1984); Dan Latimer, "Jameson and Post Modernism", in *New Left Review* (November to December, 1984).

9. Jameson quoted in Latimer, op. cit. (1984).

10. This phrase from The Communist Manifesto is taken by Marshall Berman as the title of his book, *All That's Solid Melts into Air* (New York: Simon & Schuster, 1983). The book deals with the dialectics of modernisation—the process of social, demographic, economic and technological change associated with the rise of capitalism—

and modernism—the answering innovations in the arts. For a discussion of Berman's account of the "experience of modernity," see P. Anderson, op. cit. (1984) and M. Berman, "The Signs in the Street: A Response to Perry Anderson", in *New Left Review* 144 (March to April, 1984).

11. This neologism is used by Jean-François Lyotard in "The Sublime and the Avant Garde" in Art Forum, April, 1984.

12. See Baudrillard, also Latimer, op. cit. (1984). Latimer suggests that Dick Hebdige adopts the celebratory stance in "In Poor Taste: Notes on Pop." He writes: "'We cannot afford', says Jameson, 'the comfort of "absolute moralizing judgements" about post modernism. We are within it. We are part of it whether we like it or not. To repudiate it is to be reactionary. On the other hand, to celebrate it unequivocally, complacently, is to be Dick Hebdige . . .'" Whilst agreeing with Jameson on the facticity of certain aspects of the post modern condition, the present author would distinguish himself from the "Dick Hebdige" referred to here.

13. See Jean-François Lyotard, *The Postmodern Condition: A Report on Knowledge* (Manchester: Manchester University Press, 1984); Edward W. Said, "Opponents, Audiences, Constituencies and Community," in Foster (ed.) op. cit. (1985); Herbert Schiller, *Communication and Cultural Domination* (New York: Pantheon, 1978), and *Who Knows: Information in the Age of the Fortune 400* (Norwood, NJ: Ablex, 1981).

14. See, amongst many others, Herbert Marcuse, *One Dimensional Man* (Boston: Beacon Press, 1966); Jean-François Lyotard, "The Sublime and the Avant garde", in *Art Forum* (April, 1984).

15. The Italian school of "weak thought" was invoked by Umberto Eco in conversation with Stuart Hall in the opening programme in the current series of *Voices*, Channel Four, 1985. Weak thought refers to new, more tentative and flexible styles of reasoning and argumentation developed to avoid the authoritarian and terroristic tendencies within "classic" (social) scientific theorising.

16. Fredric Jameson, Foreword to Lyotard (1984).

17. Alvin Toffler, op. cit. (1981). Toffler argues that information technology and home computing are rendering "second wave" (i.e., industrial) patterns of work, leisure, family structure, etc., obsolete. Commuting electronically from her/his "electronic cottage", the prosumer is the new (a)social subject, working, playing, and shopping by computer and thus synthesising in his/her person via her/his terminal the previously separate functions of production and consumption.

18. Lyotard, *Art Forum,* op. cit. (1984).

19. Charles Baudelaire, "The Painter of Modern Life," in J. Mayne (ed.), *The Painter of Modern Life and Other Essays* (London: Phaidon Press, 1964).

20. George Eliot, *Daniel Deronda*, 1876 (Harmondsworth, UK: Penguin, 1967). This final note provides a late opportunity for me to point out that whilst this article is ostensibly about *The Face* and postmodernism, it is also in part an indirect critique of certain aspects of my own work. For instance, *Subculture: The Meaning of Style* (London: Methuen, 1979)—especially the insistence in that book on ambiguity and irony both as subcultural and as critical strategies. This is not a retraction but rather a modification of an earlier position. This note may also explain the subtitle of the present article: "Squaring up to *The Face*." By squaring the circular logic of those hermeneutic analyses which concentrate exclusively on the world of the (photographic/written/cultural) "text" I have sought to find a bottom line—a point of departure and return—from which it becomes possible to draw on some poststructuralist, postmodernist work without at the same time being drawn into the maelstrom (male strom?) of nihilism, epicureanism and Absurd Planer "logic" associated with some Post strands. After the ironic modes of "cool" and "hip," and studied self-effacement, a speaking from the heart: squarer than the square . . . The student's essay referred to in the text is *Paper Ghosts: A Phenomenology of Photography* by Steve Evans.

Chapter 1.3.6

A brave new world: understanding Deconstruction

Chuck Byrne and Martha Witte[1]

When it comes to aesthetic theory, designers today perceive themselves as originators, not followers, and most are loath to admit that they are influenced by much of anything other than their own inner creative resources.

To suggest that there is a link between new directions in design and ideas or developments taking place in contemporary society ought not to give offense to this ideal of creative individualism. Believing it does is a relatively new phenomenon and one that many respected figures in the history of graphic design would probably find puzzling. For the seeds of many a historic movement in graphic design are found in contemporaneous literature, painting, philosophy, politics, and technology.

In a January/February 1960 *Print* article, "The Bauhaus and Modern Typography: The 'Masters' Liberate the Typographic Image," Sibyl Moholy-Nagy discusses the relationship of the designer to culture and technology. She points out that one of the most significant reasons for the success of the Bauhaus was its artists' abilities to make creative use of the inventions of the time. Under the aegis of a fundamental group philosophy, Bauhaus designers were able to capitalize on new, and seemingly alien, construction procedures and materials, exploiting them for their production and esthetic advantages. They did not resist change, but embraced it and engaged in meaningful discourse about it.

Today, the technological changes taking place in typography have been brought about by the personal computer. Relatively inexpensive and easy-to-use desktop publishing equipment and software have given those designers choosing to take advantage of them direct control over typographic arrangements which were previously dependent upon expensive typesetting techniques or laborious handwork.

The ability of the computer to allow variations at low cost gives the designer the freedom to experiment until the page seems "right," whereas previously, tried-and-true formulas were necessary in order to predict the outcome more certainly, and avoid undue expense at the typesetter. Today's seemingly boundless freedom precludes the need for many typographic conventions and even brings into question the need for that most sacrosanct of mid-twentieth-century graphic design devices—the grid.

First published in *Print,* 44 (Nov/Dec 1990): 78–87. © Chuck Byrne and Martha Witte.

Grids are but one means of organizing visual material—a means to an end, not an end in themselves. Ostensibly, the best grids are based on a general evaluation of content and reflect the particular character and presentational requirements of that content. Besides being useful to designers from the Middle Ages to the present as visual organizers, they are useful to those designers who, because of the expense involved, are unable to visualize or mock-up accurately more than a small amount of the total material that will be controlled by the grid. Based on this sampling, the designer using the subsequent grid, with its inherent regimentation, can predict the visual outcome of the entire body of the material. At the same time, however, general assumptions about all or portions of that material are made that may not be specifically responsive to the content, nor in its best interpretive interests.

The computer permits the designer to view all the material that needs to be organized at one time. It does this by allowing the designer to place into the machine, and then maneuver and accurately view, the actual copy and images before even the most rudimentary of design decisions are made. This versatility includes the particulars of the page itself, the style, size, character, and position of type; as well as the size, shape, position, and other features of all kinds of imagery. Just as important, the designer is able to experiment freely with the relationship of these elements one to another—left to right, top to bottom, and even front to back. These capabilities allow the designer to organize empirically, that is, from within the actual environment of the material thus permitting the development of a more responsive grid, or the exploration of other means of visually organizing materials, or quite possibly eliminating the need for any kind of restrictive structure. The grid may be dead, and if so, the computer will have been the culprit.

But while the computer provides the technical ability to accomplish a seemingly new look in typographic design, it is certainly not the only inducement to aesthetic innovation.

The evolutionary temperament of general culture is capable of producing an atmosphere that stimulates a variety of creative disciplines to respond simultaneously, sometimes similarly, sometimes dissimilarly. And designers often find concepts and images generated by disciplines remote from design seductive and worthy of appropriation.

Sibyl Moholy-Nagy writes that two of the most dynamic revolutions in twentieth-century typography, Futurism and the Bauhaus, were fueled by the excitement of ideas generated by such seemingly unrelated developments as the automobile, Einstein's theory of Relativity, and Freud's theories of the self. According to Moholy-Nagy, the inventive quality in all of these ideas had to do with motion, and so typography, "in it's age old function of filtering the great artistic movements down to a residue of simple communication, then took upon itself this restlessly evolutionary trend . . ."

Within the last few years, typography and design in general have been influenced, either directly or indirectly, knowingly or unknowingly, by the concept of "deconstruction."

Most designers moving in deconstructionist directions vehemently deny any knowledge of deconstruction, much less admit to being influenced by this encroaching concept from critical thought and philosophy. But design does fall under its influence, if for no other reason than because designers live in the culture that gave birth to deconstruction. We live in a deconstructed world, a world agitated by more and more complexity, where the attention span diminishes hourly (turning us into a society of information grazers), and values appear to change weekly. It is inevitable that heretofore clear and supposedly resolved notions about what design does and the way it does it will begin to blur and ultimately reshape themselves.

Deconstruction, which began as an avenue of literary criticism, involves the examination of texts in terms of the language and ideas of which they are composed. Evolutionarily, deconstruction (also referred to as post-structuralism) grew out of—but later disputed—an earlier movement called structuralism, which, led by the linguist Ferdinand de Saussure, sought to establish language study as a science in and of itself. Deconstructionist ideas were first introduced in the U.S. by the French philosopher and critic Jacques Derrida, who, in 1966, was invited to speak at Johns Hopkins University. Beginning in the late sixties, Derrida's writings, including *Of Grammatology, Writing and Difference,* and *Dissemination,* became available in English and are now widely read, albeit with some difficulty.

As the word itself suggests, "deconstruction" refers to the breaking down of something (an idea, a precept, a word, a value) in order to "decode" its parts in such a way that these act as "informers" on the thing, or on any assumptions or convictions we have regarding it. Its intention, revolutionary insofar as critical thinking is concerned, is to activate the discussion of ideas by demonstrating how their interpretation is influenced less by their actual meaning than by the amount of play in the fabric that holds them together.

For example, think about deconstructing the word "whole." We think of a whole as one complete thing, but in actuality we never understand any one thing except in terms of its parts, and at the same time our understanding of the details is conditional, or informed by an idea of how they are a part of and make up a totality. In concept therefore, "wholeness" is inherently incomplete. Its meaning depends on the multileveled, mental play of the parts that hold it together. This kind of deconstructive thinking has moved philosophy away from meaning-centered discourse and into a sort of flirtatious game-playing *around meaning,* or with multi-meaning.

One deconstructs something for a variety of reasons, which may be political, artistic, philosophical, or otherwise expressive. Political/cultural positions such as feminism and Marxism work deconstructively when they uncover aspects of our society which, while appearing to be universally humanistic, actually suppress the needs of one social group while serving those of another.

While several branches of art and design, most notably the practice of architecture, have been heavily influenced by deconstructionist ideas, typographic design is probably the most logical *visual* extension of deconstruction because of its basis in words and text. Deconstructionist writings are linked with the visual world, in that their authors often utilize graphic nuances in order to illustrate difficult concepts or subtle contradictions in meanings. Derrida, in the essay "Différance," demonstrates *in print* the concept of something being present and absent at the same time, by cleverly inserting a "rogue" vowel to replace one of the correct characters in the French word *différence.* The new word reads *différance,* in which the "a" is a misspelling—in French, this change is visible (present) but inaudible (absent). Thus the distance between two seemingly contradictory concepts, presence and absence, is remarkably abbreviated, collapsed into one typographic solution.

Similarly, deconstructionist Jacques Lacan, a French psychoanalyst and structuralist, uses an illustration of two side-by-side, identical lavatory doors, over one of which is the sign "ladies" and over the other, the sign "gentlemen." With this simple picture, he attempts to show the impossibility of there being only one point of reference or "meaning" for any one word or concept. The difference again is graphic: The lavatory doors look the same, but the designation over them—and each viewer's reference point to either sign—is different.

The deconstructionist view asks that a reader comprehend and account for complex differences in signification, at one level meaning one thing and at another level meaning its possible opposite—to point out that "meaning" is an elusive business. For designers, using different layers to create a sort of comparative visual vocabulary in order to present the evolution of a particular idea has become a fairly common, and sometimes arbitrary, practice. But when the deconstructionist approach is applied to design, each layer, *through the use of language and image,* is an intentional performer in a deliberately playful game wherein the viewer can discover and experience the hidden complexities of language. While this approach is effective when the purpose of the game is to extend or enhance the message being conveyed, it can be a communications paradox when merely used for stylistic purposes.

The intricacy of this kind of work virtually requires the designer to participate in the writing process, if not actually be the writer, something more and more designers seem willing, able, even anxious to do.

Some graphic designers may be inclined to think of a process like deconstruction that is so deeply involved in theory as absurd and remote. But the very essence of contemporary typography-driven design lies in the process of determining the characteristics and arrangement of type relative to the interpretation or presentation of the text or words in order to enhance communication or expression. With this in mind, it is easy to realize the susceptibility of typographic design to this kind of deconstructionist visual discourse.

The Modernist movement advocated simplicity, and so it is understandable that many of today's designers view the visual complexity found in much de-constructionist design as extraneous and alien. Far from being the mere application of style, however, deconstructionist design potentially clarifies or extends certain aspects of communication that the uniform treatment of elements inherent in Modernism has a tendency to obscure. Some signposts of deconstructionist design are: empirical page design and juxtaposition of elements based on context rather than traditional presuppositions (for example, the entire character of a particular page being determined by the subject of that page alone); typographic coding and modulation arising from content and language rather than convention (for example, articulating the content/context of significant words in the text by visual or literary punning); and/or meaningful layering and contrast to create discourse rather than adornment (for example, superimposing selected portions of text directly over the appropriate area of a related photograph, in order to comment on or emphasize aspects of their association).

Throughout the history of graphic design, there have been reinterpretations of the contextual assumptions concerning the typographic page, and it is possible to find isolated examples of fascinating deviations from the norm that rival in typographic intricacy anything being done today. But for the most part, until the revolutionary explosions of the early twentieth century, and much later the work of Wolfgang Weingart in the late sixties and the seventies, changes have been evolutionary rather than revolutionary.

The way was prepared for the introduction of deconstruction to graphic design by the reissuing in 1982 of *Pioneers of Modern Typography*, first published in 1969, and the publication of *The Liberated Page* in 1987, both by Herbert Spencer. These books made it possible for designers to see a substantial collection of the work of those twentieth-century innovators, the Dadaists, Futurists, De Stijl artists, and Constructivists through examples by designers such as Filippo Marinetti, El Lissitzky, Piet Zwart (who often wrote his own copy), Kurt Schwitters, Herbert Bayer, László Moholy-Nagy, Jan Tschichold, and Theo van Doesburg.

Spencer points out that the visual interpretation of the meaning of words to provide emphasis, and even the portrayal of the sounds of words, was of interest to both Dadaist and Futurist typographers. The Futurist Marinetti proposed a revolution against formulaic design, and began by refuting the uniform integrity of the text block: "My revolution is aimed at the so-called typographical harmony of the page, which is contrary to the flux and reflux, the leaps and bursts of style that run through the page. On the same page, therefore, we will use three or four colors of ink, or even twenty different typefaces if necessary."

Regardless of whether Marinetti might reconsider the idea of using twenty different faces on a page upon seeing the progeny of the average "desktop publisher," his work and ideas as well as those of his contemporaries have had a direct impact on work from the studios of Rick Valicenti, Neville Brody, Ross Carron, Katherine McCoy, Nancy Skolos, Gordon Salchow, Rudy VanderLans, Tom Bonauro, Stephen Doyle, Lucille Tenazas, Tibor Kalman, and others. Some of these designers also reflect the influence of the turn-of-the-century French poet Guillaume Apollinaire and the American concrete poets of the sixties, writers who understood the importance of the visual presentation of words and chose to make typography an extension of poetry by taking direct personal control of it. The work and ideas of these designers is in strong contrast to the aloof minimalist typography generally seen in the fifties, sixties, and seventies.

Deconstructionist design continues to collapse traditional typographical harmony even further than Marinetti's claim. The visual coding accomplished by style, size, weight, and position of each typographic element on a page, from initial caps, text, and headlines to captions, has begun to disintegrate. Evidence of this can be seen in the new work of Joel Katz, Michael Mabry, David Carson and Joe Miller, where what are still obviously initial caps are distorted or appear in unexpected places, or the contrast, in weight, of a portion of the text causes the eye to begin reading in a non-traditional location.

In graphic design as a whole, formulaic structures seem to be blurring in favor of a kind of empirical context for the page that serves to create a new relationship between form and content specific to an individual piece of work. Although pages from different issues of *Emigre* bear a family resemblance to one another, for example, the resemblance does not spring from traditional graphic structure. John Weber's work exploits these methods not only in traditional print graphics, but also in type animations that take place on a computer screen, or in video, where the relationships between typographic elements constantly change.

At the MIT Visible Language Workshop, designers are experimenting with the very nature of the perception of typographic information. Their work goes so far as to tamper with presumptions about the eye moving from the top to the bottom of a body of information. Here, powerful computers allow the viewer to control interactively the sequence or movement *through information,* rather than over it. Moving a pressure-sensitive pen up or down, left or right, and in or out, causes text and images on the screen to be moved or selected, indicating to the computer the interests of the viewer. The computer reacts with the new information in the form of new type and visuals on the screen.

Deconstruction brings into question and reshapes the entire typographic vocabulary, the orientation of the page, whether there should be a page, and whether type itself should do more than perform its basic historical function of being readable.

Discussing legibility, both Rudy VanderLans, designer and publisher of *Emigre,* and Tibor Kalman of M&Co are quick to point out that there are many ways to approach reading and that type and text can have a purpose other than to be read.

While saying so might seem heretical to some, type can have purposes which are illustrative, atmospheric, interruptive, and expressive in addition to, or beyond, mere legibility—what Sibyl Moholy-Nagy refers to as "the non-communicative function of type." Designer Paula Scher, who occasionally uses typography executed by hand, maintains, "The legibility of type is dependent upon the goal: If it's supposed to be legible, it should be. If it's not supposed to be, it shouldn't be." With this observation, she clearly points to the need for the designer to understand the reason for a particular approach rather than merely engaging in meaningless stylistic mimicry.

If the computer has been an important influence on typographic design, it promises to challenge equally the traditional use of photography in design. With the new-found ability to capture images, manipulate, crop, and mask them on a screen, designers are beginning to rediscover the power of the photographic image. Photography is being used less and less to isolate rectangles of "reality," and is instead becoming more fully integrated in the "reality" of the entire page—a circumstance that quite naturally serves deconstructionist ideas about the discourse and play between language and image achieved through positioning and layering. The visual expression of these ideas can be seen in the work of April Greiman, Lorraine Wild, Chuck Byrne, Katherine McCoy, Rudy VanderLans, Ross Carron, Lucille Tenazas, Edward Fella and Jeffery Keedy.

Sibyl Moholy-Nagy states that her husband's special contribution to his era was the integration of photography with typography. He would surely have recognized and appreciated the significance of the introduction of the computer into the two, and the potential for that relationship to be more synergistic. Doubtless, Laszlo Moholy-Nagy and his contemporaries would have embraced the computer with a passion.

The most extreme deconstructionist reassessments of design precepts tend to distinguish themselves clearly from other forms of reinterpretation, such as those of the early twentieth century. A recent issue of *Emigre,* titled "Heritage," is devoted to the state of Swiss design today. In it, Richard Feurer, a founder of the studio Eclat, states the goals of his work in a discussion with other young designers. "To me, it's neither a question of bringing across a significant message, nor of being 'understood.' I don't expect to be understood in the way that I myself understand my visual message. . . . My task is to generate an effect. You can't define what exactly, or how, the viewer will take in your visual message. There are an endless number of possible ways of looking at it. The only thing I can do as designer is to animate the person through my message. He himself should act, should analyse, and reproduce the visual message for himself."

These designers, as do most, grouse at the suggestion that what they are doing involves deconstruction. But the new thinking behind their work stands in strong contrast to Modernist concepts of visual clarity and reduction of complexity and reflects the introduction of deconstructive ideas, directly or indirectly, into graphic design.

While some critics feel that these ideas are a moral transgression of the designer's commitment to clear visual communication, it can't be denied that reading and the perception of visual information is a learned skill the practice of which can be altered. Interestingly, many designers who find great fault with the legibility of this kind of typography tend to forget the hue-and-cry that was raised concerning read-ability when the use of small-size, unjustified, sans-serif type was introduced in the early 1960s—the model held up today as the ideal of readability! The pages of *Emigre,* and many of its mainstream visual imitators, are not only widely admired, they are even read—suggesting that human perception, or at least young human perception, is more flexible than it seems.

Some designers are more closely tuned than others to the world of ideas outside design, and the educators and writers among them are beginning to disseminate these ideas in the classrooms and various design publications. But these designers, too, respond cautiously when it is suggested that deconstructionist characteristics originating in fields such as literary theory, semiotics, linguistics, and philosophy are apparent in their work.

Hans Allemann, an instructor at University of the Arts in Philadelphia, finds that training in semiotics is a useful "tool" for graphic designers, but warns against the complexity of "signs" brought from the vernacular environment distorting communications on the printed page. Allemann argues that, for the most part, it is still a designer's responsibility to communicate clearly, regardless of his or her facility with complex language. In discussing the influence of literary theory and criticism on graphic design, Katherine McCoy at Cranbrook is similarly cautious. "Some of these ideas," she says, "fit the role of art better than design, since designers have an implicit agreement to accept the client's message as their primary content."

The ultimate effect on graphic design of deconstruction and computers can't be known. What is apparent is that even though they tend to isolate themselves from its philosophical origins, many designers today are engaged in deconstructive design. That they should wish to isolate themselves from the origins of a philosophy so intertwined with the visual is unfortunate, as it seems to be the source for a significant change in graphic design. They should instead follow the example of the early pioneers of twentieth-century design: seek to understand these sources and engage them.

Note

1. Many of the ideas and much of the thinking contained in this article were suggested by the poet and scholar David Orr, who died during the summer of 1989 while preparing research for a book to be titled *The Ecology of Information*.

Part 1: Further reading

Breuer, G. and J. Meer, eds (2012), *Women in Graphic Design (1890–2012)*, Berlin: Jovis Verlag.

Chantry, A. (2015), *Art Chantry Speaks: A Heretic's History of 20th Century Graphic Design*, Port Townsend, WA: Feral House.

de Bondt, S. and C. de Smet (2012), *Graphic Design: History in the Writing (1983–2011)*, London: Occasional Papers.

Drucker, J. and E. McVarish (2008), *Graphic Design History: A Critical Guide*, Upper Saddle River, NJ: Prentice Hall.

Eames: "The Architect and the Painter" (2011), [Film] Dir. Jason Cohn and Bill Jersey, USA: First Run Features.

Engholm, I. (2002), "Digital Style History: The Development of Graphic Design on the Internet." *Digital Creativity* 13 (4): 193–211.

Eskilson, S. J. (2007), *Graphic Design: A New History*, New Haven: Yale University Press.

"Graphic Means" (2017), [Film] Dir. Briar Levit, USA: History of Graphic Design Productions.

Heller, S. (2010), *POP: How Graphic Design Shapes Popular Culture,* New York: Allworth Press.

Hollis, R. (2001), *Graphic Design: A Concise History* (World of Art), revised edn, London: Thames & Hudson.

Hollis, R. (2006), *Swiss Graphic Design: The Origins and Growth of an International Style 1920–1965,* new edn, London: Laurence King.

Lzicar, R. and F. Davide, eds (2016), *Mapping Graphic Design History in Switzerland*, Göttingen: Triest.

Poynor, R. (2003), *No More Rules: Graphic Design and Postmodernism*, New Haven: Yale University Press.

Stein, J. (2016), *Hot Metal: Material Culture and Tangible Labour*, Manchester: Manchester University Press.

Thomson, E. Mazur (1997), *The Origin of Graphic Design in America: 1870–1920*, New York: Yale University Press.

Triggs, T. (2011), "Editorial: Graphic Design History: Past, Present and Future," *Design Issues, Special Issue: Forms of Inquiry* 27 (1): 3–6.

Vanderlans, R. and Z. Licko (1994), *Emigre, the Book: Graphic Design into the Digital Realm*, New York: Wiley.

Part 2

Education and the profession

Part 2: Introduction

Graphic design education and professional practice are shaped by the dispositions of political, social, technological, and economic conditions, such as the complexities of globalization, the impact of mobile and social media technologies, and the challenges of social transformation. The advent of the Apple MacIntosh computer in the early 1980s, for example, prompted a renewed cottage-industry in which designers created their own fonts, set their own type, and printed their own work. A subsequent backlash in contemporary design against digital technologies, along with an interest in independent publishing, led designers to revive old techniques such as letterpress and risograph printing. And the increased need for communication in a variety of media has been a catalyst for new approaches—such as service and social inclusion design, in which designers work directly with customers to address issues. Graphic designers are also contributing to human-centered design, in which the human perspective drives problem-solving processes, and transition design, in which design plays an active role in the transition to sustainable futures.

In these contemporary kinds of design, graphic designers use methodological approaches that emphasize interconnectedness among people and things, or that underscore transitions to sustainable environments. Contemporary graphic designers explore how both conventional and novel modes of practice square with these circumstances. The essays in this Part, "Education and the Profession," consider how design negotiates various social, technological, and cultural concerns, and how the outcomes of these negotiations contribute to current developments in design education and practice.

Educators often both practice and teach design, and they train practitioners and educators. The interrelatedness of education and practice is vital to the development of graphic design as a bona fide subject, and their interrelationships have an impact on how graphic design is both taught and practiced. The first Section, "Graphic Design Education," shows how key educators have led the development of innovative approaches to curricula and classroom practices. The essays introduce specific moments in which shifting political, social, and economic contexts gave rise to new ways of thinking about design teaching. As discussed above, contemporary graphic design evolves in response to changing cultural contexts; the essays in this Section enumerate past practices that could inform how we engage with interdisciplinarily focused and socially responsive graphic design. First, Katherine McCoy explores what kinds of education and qualifications are needed to produce professional graphic designers in the 1997 essay "Education and Professionalism or What's Wrong with Graphic Design Education?" McCoy recommends shrinking the number of graphic design programs, which she explains would lead to higher standards in the remaining programs. She considers the ramifications of this for graphic design program accreditation and licensing for professional graphic designers.

The next essay "England: The Working Party on Typographic Teaching," presents findings from a British study of typographic education by the organization Working Party on Typographic Teaching. This 1969 report—which was commissioned by the Society of Industrial Artists and Designers to address the quality of typographic education at the time—advocates for stronger professional, liberal arts, and technical coursework. The report also considers the social role graphic designers play in the community, as do Damian and Laura Santamaria. The two authors discuss how their interest in social design was shaped both by Argentinian political history and their studies at Universidad Nacional de La Plata (UNLP) in the late 1980s and early 1990s in "A Journey Toward *Sublime*: A Reflection on The Influence of Education Values in Design Practice" (2018). In this essay, they consider how the program at UNLP was inspired by the German Hochschule für Gestaltung in Ulm (HfG) philosophy that design is methodologically applied social science. They relate ways that they have adapted their interest in social and collaborative design to their practice in the UK. Both essays, one from the 1960s and the other contemporary, stress the critical social roles that designers and design can play in society.

Considering contemporary pedagogy, Yoko Akama suggests ways to bring human-centered design practice into design education. In "Scaffolding a Human-Centered Practice in Graphic Design" (2018), Akama describes her experience working with the Australian government Bushfire Co-operative Research Centre (CRC)—an interdisciplinary research team that investigates how communities prepare for fire events. She argues that "scaffolding," information structures that facilitate candid problem exploration, help graphic designers to consider audience and stakeholder perspectives for a design.

Michael Worthington and Yasmin Khan next contemplate the interrelationships between design education and practice. Their two-spread "family tree" visual essay "Future Issue" (2011) lays out the complicated educational and professional interrelationships among twenty graphic design educators under 30 years old, demonstrating how infographics can reveal otherwise obscure information. Using primarily visual media, the authors present an instant and accessible starting point for the study of a rich history of education and practice.

Taken together, these five essays show how graphic design has embraced both individual-based practices in which designers produce artifacts in response to specific needs, and team-based practices in which designers collaborate with other stakeholders to address broad sets of needs in a holistic fashion. In either case, graphic design education needs to take into consideration the idea that designers do not just make things. Rather, they tackle complex issues by first understanding what is required to address unresolved needs or situations, then conceptualizing what might be done to resolve them, and finally bringing viable solutions to fruition.

The second Section features essays about "Postgraduate Education and Graphic Design as a Profession." Sharon Helmer Poggenpohl's essay, "Design Literacy, Discourse and Communities of Practice" (2008), considers design literacy and practice. Helmer Poggenpohl reflects upon the differences between tacit knowledge—learning by doing and by imitation—and explicit knowledge—learning through explanation, analysis, and transformation. Tacit knowledge, she contends, may be fine for undergraduate education, but graduate education requires both tacit and explicit knowledge to create a community of practice and to move design discourse ahead. In "What is Worth Doing in Design Research?" (2018) Meredith Davis discusses the implications of design research for PhD students at a moment in the mid–2000s when there were many more PhD students than available academic positions. In response to this fact, she suggests four trends that should be considered for academic design research: interdisciplinary teams and new methods should be required for complex design problems, design tools and systems should address participatory aspects of contemporary culture, changes in technology should suggest new kinds of sense-making, and economies based on ordinary service projects should shift to an economy that encourages "clustered creative industries."

In "Locating Graphic Design History in Canada" (2006), Brian Donnelly likewise deals with design research and the profession. He describes Canadian graphic design history as an unwritten "oral history" that needs to be "gathered." He considers the historical evidence that can be evinced by memory—as a "scan" of graphic design work across Canada. Donnelly concludes that the oral histories and archives of Canada's vernacular design canon, while not always "truthful," inevitably frame a history of the profession.

In a similar fashion, the next three authors frame various trajectories for design practice. In "French Graphic Design: A Contradiction in Terms?" (2009) Véronique Vienne extols the virtues of French graphic design (although she observes that French design does not seem to get enough recognition). Vienne describes how French graphic designers would rather tell visual stories than communicate coded messages. In "The Importance of the Dutch Football Club Ajax and Total Football (totaalvoetbal) to the Sport of Graphic Design" (2011), Elliott Earls compares successful graphic design education and practice to the training methods of the Dutch soccer club Ajax, in which each player develops skills to play all positions. Earls encourages graphic design education and practice to evolve away from a focus on the needs of clients and commercialism and toward an interpretive discourse based on graphic design making and objects. Jorge Frascara argues that design is first and foremost communication within a societal context in "Graphic Design: Fine Art or Social Science?" (1988). In contrast to Earls' call for an interpretive discourse and Vienne's enthusiasm for visual stories, Frascara maintains that focusing principally on the experimental side of design, and losing sight of how design communicates effectively, undermines the effective practice of graphic design.

The themes that emerge from these essays—the significance of design for social needs, the role of visual narrative and storytelling, the plurality of history and design discourse, the philosophy of interdisciplinarity, and the importance of in-depth, investigative design research—need to be part of the development of professional practice and education. These have been, and still are, vital components of graphic design.

Section 2.1

Graphic design education

Chapter 2.1.1

Education and professionalism or what's wrong with graphic design education?

Katherine McCoy

We refer to ourselves as professionals all the time. And we want our clients to respect us as professionals. But the US government sees us differently. The Department of Labor publishes the *Occupational Outlook Handbook*, the legal source that defines the nature of graphic design in this country. There is no section on "graphic designers" in this book. "Graphic artists" are under the category of VISUAL ARTISTS, parallel to "Fine artists." There is also a section on DESIGNERS which includes industrial designers, interior designers, furniture designers, fashion and textile designers, and even floral designers. But apparently we aren't designers. On page 191 of the 1996 edition the books says, "Graphic artists use a variety of print, electronic, and film media to create art that meets a client's needs." This is distinguished from fine artists who "sell their works to stores, commercial art galleries, and museums, or directly to collectors." In the section on training requirements, it states "demonstrated ability and appropriate training or other qualifications are needed for success. Evidence of appropriate talent and skill, displayed in an artist's portfolio, is an important factor used by art and design directors in deciding whether to hire or contract out work to an artist."

The portfolio is the most important factor in getting a job, and this book implies that a person with a good portfolio but no education could succeed in the graphic arts. They do note that, more often, "Assembling a successful portfolio requires skills generally developed in a post-secondary art or design program, such as a bachelor's degree program in fine art, graphic design or visual communications."

The goal of a college education here seems to be the production of a good portfolio. Now, I realize many of our field would probably agree with that. But this view of graphic design and design education neglects the conceptual side of our field. And it's the conceptual elements of design—research, analysis, problem-solving, innovation—that are what make us competitive in an increasingly sophisticated marketplace and effective with a very diverse range of audiences.

This description of our field's educational requirements is very muddled, cobbled together and modified over the years. Odd that a student would go to school in graphic design to become a "graphic

First presented at How We Learn What We Learn Conference, New York City, April 5, 1997. © Katherine McCoy.

artist." But the handbook is very clear when it says that industrial design "requires a bachelor's degree," and that a professional degree in architecture is necessary.

What is wrong with this picture? Our name, first of all, is totally confused. The government does not know what our name is—but then we do not either. Visual communications, visual design, communications design, graphic design, advertising design, commercial art and layout are just a few of the names we hear. The Department of Labor's description of our practice is terribly naive and superficial, stressing manual skills and intuition. Graphic design is defined as the production of a decorative commodity rather than a professional service. Education is underplayed and the emphasis is the development of the skills and the "hardware" of a designer—the portfolio.

Contrasted to this are the *Handbook*'s descriptions of architecture and industrial design—these read beautifully. They are good, clear, accurate descriptions of these fields. There is no reason that graphic design's description cannot be better. In reality graphic design professionals have very high expectations of entry level designers and consider a four-year degree the basic requirement to enter the profession. The vast majority of AIGA and ACD members under 50 (postwar babies) have at least a four-year degree. But none of our professional organizations have effectively insisted that the Department of Labor make an accurate description of graphic design. Architecture and industrial design's professional organizations have established relationships with the Department of Labor and have seen to it that good descriptions are published.

Because this description does not stress professional services, intellectual activity or higher education, the government is reluctant to recognize graphic design as a profession. They see us as a mixture of tradesmen, technicians, craftsmen and hobbyists. The Department of Labor recognizes a 4-year degree as a basic requirement to be considered a professional. A kindergarten teacher is a professional in the eyes of the government, but we are not.

Why is this important? It was important to Colin Forbes of Pentagram when he applied for his green card 15 years ago. He had to masquerade as an industrial designer to be considered a professional under US immigration law. He asked me to write him a reference letter when I was president of the IDSA to convince US Immigration that because he engaged in package design, he was an industrial designer and therefore a professional.

I know many educators around the country are frustrated when our outstanding foreign graduates struggle for permission to practice in the US. If it wasn't such a painful memory for the current president of the American Institute of Graphic Arts—a highly celebrated graphic designer—we could ask her to tell the sad tale of her difficult experience obtaining a work permit.

The *Occupational Outlook Handbook* is in every high school library and every public library in the US. This is the career reference for high school counselors. It is the main source for potential students of graphic design to learn about our field.

But the problem with the government's confused definition of graphic design goes deeper than that—it reflects our own confusion and failure to establish standards of excellence beyond the beauty pageants in the magazines. It promotes the idea that talent alone is sufficient—that only those without enough talent have to go to school to become a graphic designer. There is very little mention of the conceptual aspects of graphic design—the software of our profession, the intellectual process that distinguishes design from a craft or trade.

The Department of Labor's casual attitude towards graphic design education is not shared by graphic design professionals. It's from professionals that we hear the most complaints about design education.

How often do we hear our colleagues lament the sorry state of the entry level applicants they interview for design staff positions? This familiar refrain is sung daily in design offices across the country. Complaints include graduates with weak conceptual skills or poor typography, graduates that can barely write or speak clearly to clients, graduates with no grasp of business practices and unrealistic expectations of the field. But graphic design education has become far more professional in the past fifteen years and a number of graphic design schools have achieved real excellence.

So why the continuing lack of professionalism in so many entry level college graduates from design programs? The answer lies in a graphic design educational community totally out of control. The number of schools has grown wildly in response to societal change and a technological communications revolution. We have a huge number of graphic design programs, doubling over the past 10 years, with rapidly growing enrollments. A tidal wave of vocationally-minded college students see graphic design as a practical way to apply their visual arts talents in a rewarding career. University art departments are eager for graphic design programs to build their enrollments, whether they are prepared or not. Most of these art departments are openly using graphic design programs as cash cows to support fine arts programs with shrinking enrollments. As a result, entrenched fine arts faculty are teaching graphic design in many university design programs. These same fine artists generally see graphic design as simply the commercial application of fine art principles and typically hold very negative attitudes towards design, as well as being woefully unequipped to teach the discipline. Equally problematic are the start-up graphic design programs that hire one fresh-out-of-graduate-school MFA with no professional experience to teach an entire graphic design program.

Many university programs offer a graduate degree in graphic design as well. Sadly, most of these programs are remedial in nature with no faculty dedicated solely to graduate study, and pursue no in-depth research or experimentation. Many of our country's graduate students in graphic design are simply staying on in school for two more years to make up for what they failed to get in their insufficient undergraduate experiences.

In addition, there are over 1,500 2-year programs also claiming to teach "graphic design," promoting the idea that a graphic design education can be accomplished in two years. In reality these programs teach only software skills and graphic arts techniques. The graphic design profession must make it clear that at least a four year degree is necessary for a professional base of preparation. "Graphic arts technology" would be a more correct term for 2-year programs.

The new field of multimedia complicates the situation still further. Programs are popping up everywhere in universities, as well as 2-year schools—in computer science, in communications, in technical writing, in film, in photography, in journalism. Yet multimedia is visual communications design, adding sound, motion and interaction design to our traditional design elements. Our field will quickly lose our legitimate claim to expertise in multimedia if we do not take control of its education.

The result is a great number of entry level graduates unprepared to compete in a very rigorous field. The drop-out rate is extremely high in the first years after graduation, and studios find few graduates prepared for the responsibilities and realities of professional practice.

Over 2,000 schools in the United States claim to teach graphic design as an area of emphasis. This includes community colleges and two-year art schools. In professional practice, there are fewer than

10,000 graphic designers in our professional organizations. So we have 2,000 plus schools for just 10,000 professionals comprising the core for our field.

In contrast, landscape architecture has 12,000 practicing members in their professional organization, and they have only 56 accredited schools in the entire US. Yet these schools supply their field with a sufficient number of landscape architecture graduates to keep the discipline advancing on a high level. Interior designers have 30,000 certified professionals and have 116 accredited schools. Architecture has 56,000 either registered or in the track to become registered architects, and they have 120 schools in the entire country. In the United States, there are 900,000 licensed attorneys. Do you know how many schools they have? 180.

Why does graphic design need 2,000 schools? The answer is that we do not. We need fewer, bigger and better design programs. In fact there is an inverse relationship between the number of professional schools and the quality of those schools—the fewer the schools, the better the schools.

Why are fewer schools better? Fewer programs would allow us to concentrate our resources into larger and more comprehensive programs that achieve a critical mass in each program. This allows highly qualified faculty to focus in-depth on their particular area of specialization, and more extensive facilities and resources available to students. It is time for us to insist on no more one-faculty or two-faculty programs, of which there are hundreds.

Does each state really need more than one state university graphic design program, one regional university program, and one private art or technical university program? Even with this, the United States would have 150 graphic design schools. Where did we get the idea that a prospective student should have to drive no further than an hour from their birthplace to receive a professional graphic design education? This is certainly not the case in any of the other design professions.

How can we reduce the numbers of schools and improve the quality of our education? Accreditation is a process used successfully by all the other design professions to determine which schools are qualified to offer programs and to control the number of programs. In addition, there are mechanisms to support excellence, as well as minimum standards.

Graphic design needs to establish these baselines and minimum standards of professional practice and education. In a sense, we need to draw a circle around the discipline to clarify what is and what is not quality graphic design. Amazingly enough, this is a controversial statement. Some designers have a strong suspicion of formalizing either the practice or the education of graphic design. Some find the idea elitist and exclusionary. Some fear that in raising the baseline, we may eliminate the peaks. And that by insisting on—or even just advocating—a quality education as preparation for design practice, we will somehow exclude our geniuses and individualists. And some designers fear that national school accreditation standards would result in boring predictability. But there are workable methods to include the exceptional exceptions while excluding the unqualified. Other professions do this very effectively.

Remember that graphic design is in the midst of a life cycle, a state of evolution. In the United States after World War II, we were in our infancy, gaining the first traits of professionalism. At that time there were virtually no educational programs.

Early graphic designers in the twentieth century through the 1950s were generally trained in neighboring disciplines, often fine arts, and applied their past experiences to this new field of advertising design and "commercial art". Their emphasis was on the sender component of the communications equation of sender– message– receiver. They were dedicated to advancing the clients' sales goals and using the tools of fine art based on self-expression and intuition—the big idea, aha! school of design. As the field progressed into the 1960s, the lessons of the Bauhaus as developed in Zurich, Basel and Ulm put the emphasis on the message, the center component of this equation. Functionalism, rationality, and some rudimentary communications theory from semiotics were applied to analyse information content and to structure hierarchies. The result was far clearer and objective communication of messages. As more theory was explored, adapted and absorbed by our field, graphic design has moved on to include the right side of this equation. Post structuralism, reception theory and even market research are helping us understand increasingly diverse and segmented audiences.

I would say that graphic design has moved from infancy in the early twentieth century to a vigorous childhood in the 1950s to adolescence—and some would say a self-absorbed one—in the 1980s, and now to late adolescence or early adulthood. We're inching toward maturity as a discipline.

But we compare our field with the other design disciplines we look very adolescent, with more to be accomplished to rank as an equal with a field like architecture, for example. We do have a number of excellent schools, a fledgling community of journalists, critics and historians, and many high level professionals. Now it is time to take the final steps towards early maturity—this includes definition, standards and exclusion.

This is a transitional phase, as well, rather than an end point. Full maturity of a discipline allows the opportunity to relax some standards and encourage more deviation from established professional norms, something architecture—which some would describe as "overly mature"—is challenged to consider. But they have been a discipline since the Renaissance.

There are two formalized steps other professions employ to promote a high level of professional discourse and practice. One is the accreditation of schools, and the other is the licensing or certification of professionals. The latter ranges from voluntary certification to legally-required licensing for professional practice. Lawyers and doctors have some of the most stringent licensing requirements, regulated by state laws. On the other end of the spectrum, interior designers have upgraded their field substantially by offering a voluntary examination to qualify for full professional status in the ASID. In addition, 16 states regulate the use of the title interior designer. This means that only those interior designers that have passed the national interior design licensing exam and have practiced for several years are legally allowed to call themselves interior designers in 16 states—any others calling themselves interior designers are subject to state fines.

Professions that involve public risk from shoddy practitioners and malpractice, such as structural engineering and medicine, have the most imperative for licensing. Since graphic design is a less technical and relatively subjective field, a certification test to evaluate a graphic designer's capability could be difficult to develop. After all a falling poster has never killed anyone, although its message might have. But licensing isn't just for the elite or risky professions: a directory of occupational licensing lists over 130 fields ranging from aircraft pilots and accountants to taxi drivers, plumbers, umpires and cosmetologists. Also, many have asked if it is possible to test objectively for conceptual innovation and aesthetic quality. These seem very subjective. However, methods already exist; the architecture and interior design exams' design sections seem quite effective.

In actuality, any form of legally required licensing for graphic design is highly unlikely in our era of downsizing government and de-regulation. A voluntary self-certification program administered by a professional graphic design organization remains a possible future option.

But let's turn to accreditation of graphic design programs in higher education. Accreditation is a very applicable process to the concerns of excellence in graphic design. And is much more immediately achievable.

Accreditation typically defines baselines for curriculum standards, faculty numbers and qualifications, and facilities and equipment. More specialized design faculty and a generous number of courses create a broader and more balanced professional education. The thoroughly educated student needs to experience so much in undergraduate school: a complete liberal arts and sciences education, art and design history, communications theories, methods of research, analysis and problem-solving, form giving, typography, image-making, drawing, photography, interaction design, multimedia, production technologies, business skills, marketing, sociology and psychology, plus a comfort level with key software programs.

By describing these requirements for the undergraduate level, we would define the boundaries of a basic graphic design education. An initial part of this process is the definition of several paradigms of undergraduate graphic design education that respond to the broad types of design practice. For instance, advertising design, graphic design, multimedia/ interaction design and design planning. The intention is not to make all programs identical.

Once accreditation standards and a process are agreed upon by the participating organizations—the AIGA and the Graphic Design Education Association in conjunction with an organization like the National Association of Schools of Art and Design—graphic design programs will be invited to initiate an accreditation review. This process is extremely useful to the school. The central part is a self-study in which the program defines its goals and how it reaches them. Deficiencies become clear even before the visitation team arrives for an on-site review. Although this might sound a bit brutal, it is actually a valuable tool, providing design faculty effective leverage with their administration as they lobby for better resources. Accreditation standards also give nonqualifying programs goals toward which to strive.

One of the most important offshoots of accreditation will be accurate career information for high school students. AIGA will publish a list of accredited schools to guide prospective students to make an informed choice of school that fits their personal career goals. The situation we have now remains nearly as abysmal as in 1963 when I compared Michigan State's course listings to Pratt's, and could perceive no difference. They read the same on paper—and I went to Michigan State. Today the typical high school student still has little guidance from poorly informed career counselors.

The good news is that at the Spring 1996 AIGA Chapter Retreat in Nashville, AIGA announced a Task Force chaired by Meredith Davis to begin the organization of graphic design education accreditation. Meredith asks, "What sort of long term accreditation structure can we create that will have the flexibility to respond to the evolution of the field and its diversity of practice? We want to raise the ceiling of curricular and faculty performance, as well as encourage innovation and excellence."

Graphic design is a rapidly growing discipline with a recognized body of history, theory and method. Society is in the middle of a great expansion of communications, and business is increasingly

results in mere stylishness which disguises a complete absence of original thinking. Consequently, many extremely important but unspectacular areas of typography and graphic design, such as educational books and other visual aids, scientific papers, government regulations, reports, instructions, forms, and directional systems, all of which play an important part in our lives, are usually either not designed at all or are designed very badly.

2.4 *Economic considerations for the country.* We believe that, on economic grounds alone, this country cannot afford to tolerate bad design education any longer. Our concern here is with the role of the typographer, which is perhaps rather a special one since printing and other visual communication systems are central to the machinery of government, industry, trade, transport, education and scholarship. The efficient working of all kinds and levels of society depends to a large extent on communication by means of the printed word. We cope with an enormous quantity of material of this kind, the effectiveness of which depends to a large extent on the ability of the typographer to understand its content, order it meaningfully, and find a suitable medium for it. A pattern of design education based primarily on cultivating personal expression does little to come to terms with this problem. Most students leaving colleges of art and design this year will be ill-equipped to face up to the needs of industry today, let alone the future.

3 The Work of the typographer

As stated earlier, we believe that design method in general is best studied through a specific industrial design discipline, and as far as graphic design is concerned we believe that typography is the ideal one.

The function of the professional typographer is to communicate specific information as efficiently as possible within the limitations imposed by his brief. In the first place the typographer must be capable of analyzing "copy" and, if need be, re-ordering its structure. A thorough understanding of the use of English is essential for him to handle efficiently any material given to him. He must equally be able to advise a client as to the appropriate means of communication. A general knowledge of systems of communication as a whole is therefore necessary, together with an understanding of the psychology of perception. The need to be able to discuss and analyse projects and problems with keen minds from business and industrial fields suggests that the typographer needs to be articulate as well as literate.

Because the typographer must produce creative and compelling solutions to the problems that are put to him, we must stress at this point the importance of stimulating the student's imagination as well as training his analytical powers. A course which neglected this in favor of purely scientific and technical studies would be grossly unbalanced. We recommend that any complementary studies designed to avoid this imbalance should be connected where possible with the student's main field of study. To quote a single example, an historical topic can on its own be a disciplined and imaginative field of study, but when related to the typographer's other activities it can enrich and expand his appreciation of them.

Having studied a client's requirements and having, from his experience in this field, arrived at an efficient and creative solution to the problems raised, the typographer will next advise the client on production methods in relation to such factors as costing, budgeting, quality control, and allocating priorities. The typographer, and thus the student of typography, has to be informed of every aspect of the printing and allied industries—methods of typesetting, printing, and binding, materials, processes, trade services, and so forth. The typographer will be acting as planner and co-ordinator of a multiplicity of processes and the link between them and his client. He must therefore be conversant with the theory and practice of them all.

Summing up, the practice of typography is not only a matter of intuition or flair, but essentially a discipline and a combination of skills and functions capable of analysis. On this basis typography can be taught in a way that can be professionally and educationally valuable, while at the same time demonstrating the principles of design practice as a whole.

4 Related disciplines

We do not propose a rigid structure of studies relating to graphic design, but it is very clear that many new disciplines need to be introduced, and that they would open up the possibility of worthwhile advanced work in a variety of fields. The desirability of introducing new disciplines naturally has some bearing on the plans to incorporate many graphic design courses into the educational work of polytechnic institutions. We believe that the following subjects are amongst those which have a direct relevance to the education of typographers and graphic designers, and indeed most other designers: English, mathematics, management studies, psychology, linguistics, cybernetics, technical studies, history of design.

4.1 *English*. Any designer needs to be capable of writing and speaking clearly and objectively on various aspects of design. The preparation of visuals, storyboards, process artwork, and working layouts has to be augmented by concise, but comprehensive, written and oral data. A designer who is responsible for fact finding in relation to a project must be able to present his findings in a form in which they can be used by others. Furthermore, the typographer is closely involved with editorial decisions and must have a clear understanding of the meaning of his copy before he can begin to order it. For these reasons we recommend that all courses in typography include provision for students to develop fluency and clarity of expression in written and spoken English and that, where possible, this should be linked with practical work in design.

4.2 *Mathematics*. Calculations and measurements are normal routines of typography and demand a competence in simple mathematics. The preparation of specifications is an important aspect of design, and students of typography must be familiar with methods of calculating costs and quantities and ways in which these can be expedited by the use of formulae and slide-rules. The typographer is also concerned with communicating statistical data, and this means that he must be able to understand the general principles of statistics and statistical graphs. Descriptive geometry, augmented by practice in technical drawing, is clearly of value to graphic designers who frequently work in three dimensions. Particular areas of mathematics, such as mathematical logic, analogue geometry and binary notation, are linked with cybernetics. We believe that mathematics is as central to typography as it is to many other areas of design and technology.

4.3 *Management studies.* Definitions of management are often synonymous with definitions of design. The functions of management have been defined as planning, organizing, directing, co-ordinating, and controlling. These are also important functions of the designer, and it is commonplace for designers to fulfil executive roles in organizations. Training in the principles and techniques of effective management, administration, and planning is valuable to the young designer because such principles are analogous to those of good practice in design. In a number of colleges students of graphic design are already being taught the principles of particular management techniques of analysis and planning. Through such studies students can be helped to develop their own design philosophies; they can learn something about organizational structure, acquire insight into the roles and activities of managers, and learn to appreciate that implementation of a project is equal in importance to, and more complex than, its visualization. Management studies, including matters of finance, law, and modern techniques of planning should be integrated with the study of professional practice in typography and graphic design courses.

4.4 *Psychology.* We believe that the study of the processes of conceptual thought, learning, perception, memory, cognition, and other aspects of human behavior are of great importance to the typographer and graphic designer and should be included in his education. In particular, all students should have some understanding of perception in relation to reading and should be familiarized with work that has been done in the field of legibility and allied problems.

4.5 *Linguistics.* The typographer is primarily concerned with ordering verbal information and ideas. Until recently the traditional ways of ordering such material had changed very little, but the development of algorithmic methods for the presentation of information during the last decade has opened up entirely new approaches which should be very much the concern of the typographer. Similarly, the typographer has much to learn from the new discipline of linguistics, which is concerned with the study of the function and structure of language in general. Typography can legitimately be seen as "visual linguistics" and should be studied in relation to the wider use of language.

4.6 *Cybernetics.* The interrelated fields of cybernetics, computing, and automatic data processing are the leading edge of contemporary technology and are central to a large and important sector of typographic engineering. Unless students of typography are introduced to the principles of cybernetics, they run the risk of becoming redundant within a few years of leaving college. Access to a computer is desirable but not essential in order to train students in the principles of computing and programming. Such simple apparatus as a typewriter and stencil-duplicator can be used for a communication system which can provide a basis for introductory experience in the disciplines of systems analysis and systems programming.

4.7 *Technical studies.* For many reasons this is perhaps the most difficult kind of study to implement in full-time education. We are conscious that some teachers attach little or no importance to technical studies, and we know that many teachers are largely ignorant of technical matters and are not in touch with recent developments. We believe that technical studies in typography should not be limited to the operations of printing but should extend into other areas of the communications industry. It seems to us absurd that design students in any field should be uninformed of relevant equipment, materials, processes, standards, conventions, and terminology.

4.8 *History of design and technology.* We believe that students of design are most likely to be interested in an historical study arising from their practical work. The typographer and graphic designer should study some aspects of the history of graphic communication, design, and technology in relation to social, economic, political, and intellectual developments. A study of the history of letterforms could increase a student's sensitivity to typefaces in use at the present time and help him to come to terms with future developments. We do not accept that analysis of history is irrelevant to the education of designers and believe that such a study can play a valuable part in opening up fields outside a student's immediate experience. It is also a means of making students aware of the elementary tools of scholarship and of encouraging critical judgment.

5 Implications for higher education

As mentioned above, this document is not concerned with making specific proposals relating to the implementation of courses, but more with general conclusions that have emerged from our discussions.

5.1 *Entry requirements.* We do not wish to state categorically which subjects should be required of students who enter design courses, or what level of achievement should be expected, but we do believe that some requirements will have to be made. We make three general observations.

First, there is at present a tendency for good applicants with scientific interests not to look in the direction of design. Ways must be found to change this situation if students with such potential are to come forward.

Secondly, the new approaches to teaching science and mathematics in primary and secondary education are particularly relevant to the thought processes which will be required of designers, especially in relation to the inter-disciplinary character of design operations demanded by new technological developments and managerial techniques. We are certain that unless students have a foundation in these disciplines at school, higher design education cannot properly fulfil its role.

Thirdly, design education must provide opportunities for mature students who need to change direction. We believe that provision for such students must become a feature of design courses, and that high level studies will benefit from an infusion of maturity (as was shown during the immediate post-war period in many areas of further education). Clearly, entry requirements demanded of this type of person would not be solely dependent on formal academic qualifications.

5.2 *Equipment.* A generous supply of elaborate and expensive equipment is no substitute whatsoever for a sound, imaginative approach to teaching typography and graphic design. Many of our members have been disturbed by the undue emphasis placed on prestige equipment in some schools and have found that this can so easily obscure some of the more essential thought processes of design education. Machinery and other major items of equipment can, and ideally should, play an important part in the education of students of typography and graphic design, but the first priority should be to discover what they are needed for. Only then will it be seen what kind of equipment can be most satisfactorily used to serve the educational purposes in mind.

5.3 *Links with industry.* We are very much in favor of forging strong links between educational establishments and the printing and allied industries. Such co-operation would go some way to solving the problem of familiarizing students with modern industrial processes without the need for schools and colleges to incur enormous and unnecessary capital costs. It would also help students to understand some of the social and organizational problems of industry. Students should spend some part of their vacations working in a variety of branches of the printing and allied industries, and ways must be found for students to spend periods working under supervision in industry as part of their courses.

5.4 *Staffing.* The re-training of existing staff and the appointment of suitable new staff (including some with industrial experience) are clearly major issues arising from these proposals. We are only too aware from our own discussions over the last two years of the inadequacies of our own education and training which, in the majority of cases, has been visually oriented. The contribution made by professional designers from industry to Working Party meetings has been particularly valuable, and we are sure that industry itself must be prepared to encourage the involvement of its personnel in the overall pattern of design education. There is, however, no substitute for full-time teachers, and the profession must be prepared to come to terms with many new disciplines which may perhaps be foreign to its nature and past experience.

6 Urgency

We welcome the current re-appraisal of design education and cannot overstress the urgency of dealing with these problems.

Postscript: international dialogue

This report is adapted from the first Interim Report of the Working Party, published at its third study conference at Stafford in November 1968; earlier conferences were held in 1967 and 1968 in London and Manchester. The Working Party's steering committee is preparing pictorial documentation of approaches to typographic teaching for publication in a subsequent issue of the *Journal,* and the Working Party is interested in exchanging views with educators in other countries. Correspondence should be addressed to the secretary: Miss Gillian Riley, "ma," 9 South Villas, Camden Square, London NW1, England. The Interim Report is available in booklet form (single copies $2.00, bulk orders above 30 copies $1.00, prepaid) from the secretary.

Chapter 2.1.3

A journey toward *Sublime*: a reflection on the influence of education values in design practice

Damian and Laura Santamaria

In 1994 we came to the United Kingdom from Argentina as young design professionals in search of opportunities our country could not provide due to a prolonged period of political and financial instability. At the time, little did we know that our educational heritage would color and guide the development of our design practice in the UK throughout the years to come. Ours is a journey of lineage, beginning with the worldviews and teachings that were first introduced at the Hochschule für Gestaltung in Ulm (HfG), and then advanced at the Universidad Nacional de La Plata (UNLP) in Argentina where we studied.

The philosophy of Ulm had a great influence on design education and design discourse in Latin America (Fernández 2006). During the 1960s and 1970s, design in Argentina (and other Latin American countries) was at the center of a socio-political project for economic autonomy that sought to stimulate rapid development through industrialization, in order to decrease fiscal deficit by reducing imports. To achieve this, it was necessary to create skilled jobs; and consolidating the design profession (both practice and education) became crucial if the country was to become this kind of economically competitive nation.

At that time, the HfG was advancing the notion of "design leadership" as a way to push for systemic change, dismissing the idea that design was purely an applied form of aesthetics (which was felt diminished the role of the designer) and advocated for design to be viewed as an applied human and social science (Findeli 2001). As such, the Ulm model was seen as highly relevant to the Argentine context because it offered an operative, concrete and systematic way to implement the independence-through-industrialization that Latin America was seeking (Fernández 2006). Emerging university departments and programs in design across Latin America were keen to adopt this view of design as "a science that could support industrialisation," which was regarded as instrumental to the continent's social, cultural, and economic success (Fernández 2006).

However, this vision for socio-economic autonomy was never fulfilled, due to the political turbulence that Argentina (and the continent) suffered during the 1970s and early 1980s.

Starting in 1975, Argentina endured a long, dark period of harsh, consecutive authoritarian military governments that culminated with the Falklands War in 1983. During the "de facto" (dictatorship) years, educational institutions became highly politicized as students and staff persistently engaged in public protests and demonstrations, demanding the reinstatement of a democratic government. In an attempt to control dissent, the "junta" (a military group leading the authoritarian government) implemented deep reforms within the universities, thwarting critical thinking by closing down those departments in the arts and social sciences they considered to be threats. Hundreds of students, staff, and other intellectuals—including journalists, writers, rights activists, and artists—were relentlessly targeted during the "dirty war." Many were assassinated, abducted, or forced into exile (Moyano 1995).

Our student years at UNLP

By 1987, the year we begin our journey as design students, democracy was still young and political stability was unpredictable. In the city of La Plata, students from the Fine Arts college had been abducted and tortured just a few years earlier, following a peaceful demonstration for reduced bus fares—the infamous *Noche de los Lápices* (Hernández 2011). For us, even enrolling in the Visual Communication Design course at UNLP during this time was a risky political act. Ahead of us lay not only a five-year multidisciplinary course in design, but also hopes for the reconstruction of our country's identity and trust in its political institutions. We were "freshers" in the university, but also in a whole new era in Argentine history.

In contrast, the Design faculty at UNLP was well established (Figure 2.1), and our course was celebrating its 25th anniversary that year. Founded at the University in 1963, it was said that "the seeds of the Bauhaus had germinated in Argentina" but the program and style of study at UNLP drew heavily on the views and methods of the HfG in Ulm (Rollie 1987). The Ulm-UNLP connection was made

Figure 2.1 Courtyard and corridors of the Facultad de Bellas Artes, Universidad Nacional de La Plata, Argentina. Image courtesy of UNLP/Santamaria Media.

through a direct link between the founding professors and the visionary Argentine painter and philosopher, Tomás Maldonado, who held the post of rector at the HfG between 1956 and 1966. Maldonado's affiliation with both institutions meant a fluid exchange took place between the HfG and the design school at UNLP. Argentine students who visited Ulm returned to Argentina with new ideas. Faculty members of the HfG established contacts with Latin American universities; they participated in programs at UNLP and other Latin American universities, and helped shape an emerging design profession throughout Latin America (Fathers 2003; Fernández 2006).

For example, German designer Gui Bonsiepe collaborated closely with Maldonado at the HfG, and in 1964 he was invited to work with him in Argentina:

> I was invited to Argentina by my teacher, friend, and intellectual mentor, Tomás Maldonado, whom I considered one of the most important design theoreticians of the twentieth century—a real giant, though his works weren't widely known outside the Spanish and Italian language context.
>
> (Fathers 2003: 44)

Bonsiepe moved to Chile in 1968, following the closure of the HfG, and he worked extensively in Brazil, Argentina, and Mexico for over four decades. Along with Maldonado, Bonsiepe is considered one of the most important figures associated with the HfG influence on Latin American design discourse and education (Fathers 2003).

At UNLP, the Ulm influence was rooted in three fundamental concepts, which shaped Maldonado's tenure at the HfG, and also resonated with the emerging socio-cultural context of Latin America:

- Technology and its impact on how we conceive of and practice design

- The relevance of culture and the social sciences in design education

- Design ethics—the relationship between design and consumer society

These concepts permeated and shaped the design curriculum at our school (Fernández 2006).

The Visual Communication Design course was implemented as a five-year program of study. During the first three years, Visual Communication Design students shared most course modules with students from Product Design, and some with Stage Design and the Fine Arts. Along with the core Visual Communications Workshop module, which ran throughout the five years, we were taught Drawing, Visual Literacy, Design Methods, Technology and Materials, and History of Design, and a modern European language (French, Italian, German or English). These were complemented by subjects that developed philosophical and critical thinking skills, such as History of Argentine Philosophy and Introduction to Cultural and Media Studies.

Silvia Fernández, our senior lecturer and mentor (who later married Gui Bonsiepe) was among the founders, and central to the development of the Visual Communication Design program. In an article published in 1987 by *tipoGráfica* magazine celebrating the degree's 25th anniversary, she recounts:

> We believe that the breadth of teaching staff should reflect the broadness of the Visual Communication Design degree; a pioneering concept determined by the visionary founders of this school. For that reason, the team includes, for example, professionals in cinematography, who introduce new variables

to the visual field: time and motion, key elements in the visual expression of today, arising from the application of new technologies.

> (Fernández 1987: 4; all translations from the Spanish by the authors)

As at Ulm, there was little interest in the "artistic" dimensions of design. Instead, the "scientific" content of the curriculum was emphasized. Subjects such as Physics, Mathematics, and IT were included, but the main contributions came from the Human and Social Sciences—Gestalt Psychology, Semiotics (the study of signs and symbols as communication) and Ergonomics, as well as Systems Thinking and Philosophy of Science (Neves and Rocha 2013).

In practical terms, the design thinking method upon which the workshop activities were developed was based on an understanding of design as a problem-solving activity:

> The constant problem framing, research and synthesis cycle followed by the students, either working individually or in groups, comes to shape the learner's own method, tailored by the student herself to fit her own view and vision, and refining it along the entire course by applying it to varying degrees of complexity.
>
> (Fernández 1987: 5)

This statement emphasizes a methodological, non-artistic approach. However, this "scientific" approach was not based on pure rationalist thinking, because it acknowledged other ways of knowing such as intuition and lived experiences.

> We cannot rely on rational knowledge only, but we must also appeal to sensitive memory and intuition, which are inseparable components of our nature as individuals. Design thinking is certainly not linear, it is holistic, and resorting to the sensory world stimulates an exchange between reality and the designer's own sensory experience of it, thus enriching the outcome.
>
> (Fernández 1987: 5)

Also, the methodological approach was instrumental to a goal, which was to develop in students the ability to "read" and transform our local reality as future design professionals.

> Our role is to focus on and frame the local problematic so that we can better serve our communities. Therefore, in the field of communications, the aesthetic decisions we make are not arbitrary—they must emerge from a deep understanding of the process of signification, which, of course, can only be conceived within a contextualized and concrete socio-cultural reality.
>
> (Fernández 1987: 5)

Therefore, the learning objectives were aimed at the formation of character, rather than the development of technical skills or abilities alone.

> We understand that freedom, knowledge of one's identity, knowledge of reality and the ability to transform it, are the main learning objectives that contribute to form our graduates' 'social being' and ethics. The way to achieve these goals is none other than that of 'teaching to learn'. Hence, we encourage self-knowledge, a creative attitude and build transformational capacity. The students then become the protagonists of their own training, which tears apart the traditional model where that role is played by the professor. The teacher, now, is a mentor who guides the process of 'being-and-doing' while the students methodically self-exercise *thought* and *action*.
>
> (Fernández 1987: 5)

This ideology was supported pragmatically through the promotion of teamwork, mentorship, and interdisciplinarity.

> We believe that the practice of visual communication design is, by nature, an interdisciplinary activity. Be it in the analysis and diagnostic of the problematic or in the development of solutions, it is necessary to engage interdisciplinary teams. We know that, due to budgetary constraints, the economic situation in our country prevents us from conducting our practice in this manner. However, this does not change the intrinsic nature of our practice.
>
> (Fernández 1987: 4)

Collaborations and close relationships were fostered, and as students we felt nurtured and valued as individuals—a real challenge in practical terms, considering the large size of our classes. The Design Workshops, for example, could include up to 200 students at any one time. Claudio Pousada, a former graduate, recalls:

> Acknowledging that memory is selective, I insist in thinking that perhaps it's that special microclimate floating in the classroom that ultimately sums up the particular characteristic of this course.. . . It was that close relationship between teacher-student (not always idyllic) that nurtured the learning experience, which even today, with a fabulously multiplied student roll has not been lost.
>
> (Pousada 1987: 6; translation from the Spanish by the authors)

Although our design activities engaged with the local context, the university ensured that we did not operate in silos. The workshop activities were enriched by encouraging students to continually build connections with other areas of knowledge; various guest speakers were invited to inspire students to forge new relationships and connections that contributed to the development of our projects. Jorge Frascara and Norberto Chavez were among the regular visiting lecturers, and the university facilitated access to exhibitions in Buenos Aires—Shigeo Fukuda, Alan Fletcher, and Milton Glaser among others—to ensure that our local practice and education were situated within the global design discourse.

The final year was dedicated to the development of an elective specialism—Corporate Identity, Packaging, Editorial Design, or Audio-visual (Film) Studies—which took the form of a practice-based research project and a written thesis with oral defence. The important requirement here was that it should be rooted in a 'real life' problem.

> In the final year, the student faces the solution of a problem of communication detected at the national, regional or local level. This project must be inserted in reality, with an established public or private commissioner, who should contribute to oversee the feasibility of the solution provided, in all aspects of implementation.
>
> (Fernández 1987: 4)

By 1992, we graduated holding what we felt—and still feel—is a visionary, ambitious and pioneering degree from a non-fee-paying university. This course had not only prepared us to approach design as a methodological (as opposed to a "black box") creative discipline, but those formative years had also taught us how to take an active part in the reality we were in, engaging in both action and intellect.

Two former students in their final year at the time reflect:

We lived the instability of a transitional period of normalization that has not yet ended—learning to participate as active citizens in a fledgling democracy, with its problematic of national reality, such as teacher strikes, into which our faculty is inserted. But at this stage, what we are most concerned about is the near future: our insertion in a society that barely recognises our profession. We are well aware of the vast knowledge we have gained during this time—hard going and, at times, more full of criticism than praise. A question worth asking is perhaps, have we learned this through the course, or alone, by necessity? Perhaps the distinction doesn't matter anyway. We can confidently say that these five years' experiences have borne some fruit. However, we know, despite the uncertainties we face, that we are prepared to face the reality 'on the street'.

(Alimenti and Christiansen 1987: 6; translation from the Spanish by the authors)

Leaving the course as young graduates, we were idealistic, full of hope and ready to work and bring about change, but the socio-economic climate in Argentina was highly volatile. Argentina's inflation rate had reached breath-taking proportions, giving rise to a wave of food riots in 1989 when inflation peaked at over 20,000 per cent (March 1989—March 1990) (Brooke, 1989; Cavallo and Cavallo, 1996). Ronald Shakespear, founder of one the most respected design consultancies in Buenos Aires, recalls: "Printers' estimates were only good for a few hours. Estimating the cost of jobs for clients required impossible strategic skills, political and economical knowledge, and a huge nose to assess the future. Getting paid was just as difficult" (Shakespear 2009).

Even middle-class families were struggling to make ends meet. For young design graduates like us, job prospects were extremely limited. Feeling overqualified and constrained, we decided to leave Argentina for a while and explore opportunities abroad.

Living our values: our work as design practitioners in the UK

The mid 1990s in the UK was, in our eyes, "design heaven." In 1994, the British Design Council celebrated its 50th anniversary. There was economic prosperity and the value of design to the economy in the UK was formally acknowledged with the term "creative industries" (Flew 2012). For us, it was an ideal context in which to gain the much-needed work experience for our CVs.

Since we were going to be contributing our skills and time pro bono, we chose to volunteer for Wycliffe, an international charity that focuses on supporting literacy programs to protect endangered languages (Figure 2.2). We were immediately captivated by the multicultural vibrancy of our new surroundings and the exciting opportunities that were open to us. We had state-of-the-art equipment at our disposal, and 24/7 access to the studio since we worked and lived at the organization's headquarters. This self-contained, family-like environment proved ideal for us to adapt to a new culture, see our skills in a new light, and gain confidence in our future as design professionals.

During this time, we kept in touch with colleagues in Argentina, and contributed articles to the Argentinian magazine *TipoGráfica*. This work opened doors for us into the London design scene, and we were able to gain insight into the UK design industry from influential figures like Seymour Powell, Wally Ollins, and institutions such as the Design Council.

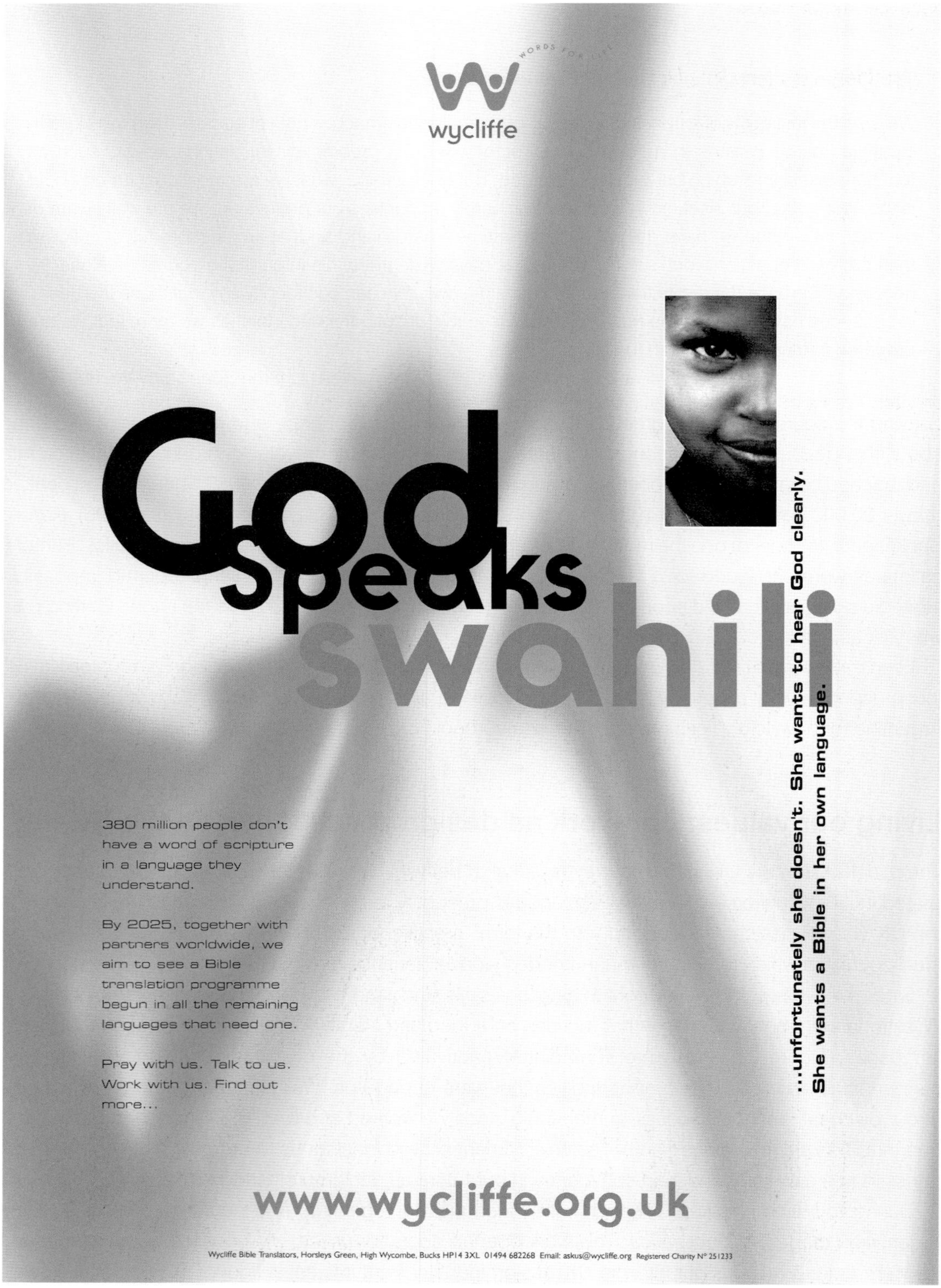

Figure 2.2 *God Speaks Swahili* (1996). Poster designed for Wycliffe's fundraising. Santamaria Media.

Humble beginnings

In the year that followed, embracing the British lifestyle, we set up our own micro-consultancy (meaning we bought our first Apple Mac and we were working from home). These were booming times for design in London, but some people thought we were overconfident: we had limited local market experience and were not following the conventional design start-up path (i.e. we had neither the investment capital nor a portfolio with an impressive client list).

However, our education gave us grounds to feel well-equipped: we had been given solid professional skills and methods to be able to tackle a diversity of design projects—after all, as students we had learned to cope with a complex, unpredictable context and solve real-life problems by relying more on ingenuity than on resources. But, most importantly, we were given something that, for most, comes only after years of professional experience: the ability to view our profession and ourselves critically and reflectively, to be self-aware of our particular design philosophy (our purpose and our own way of seeing and acting in the world).

Although we set up our workspace at home, and regularly had clients over for supper, our commitment to standards remained intact, and we were able to offer a personable, yet highly professional service (see Figure 2.3). This friendly and non-corporate approach to client liaison is common in Latin

Figure 2.3 "All in the Family," feature article on Santamaria, *Blueprint* magazine, no. 188 (October 2001). © 2001. Santamaria Media.

America. However, in the UK the concept of creative living/working spaces was just starting to develop, and in this context our approach was perceived as rather refreshing. It also proved successful, and our commissions grew from graphic design projects to planning communication, branding, and new product development strategies. We pitched for projects, often going against the grain to win a client, in competition with iconic agencies such as Saatchi & Saatchi, or being subcontracted for special projects by Ogilvy One, among others.

Ultimately, what characterized our work was not the uniformity in aesthetic style, but our consistent, methodological and contextual approach to the design process that our tutors had imprinted on us. Our interest was to reach people in meaningful ways, and we purposely sought to develop our work by digging deep into the essence of each project in order to ground our aesthetic decisions on the client's core values, making manifest its uniqueness through design representation.

At the time, we knew little about methods of participatory design and co-creation. However, we were keen to involve clients in our process, and presented them with at least three choices, finished to a high standard; understanding that our role was not to impose or invent, but to envision what clients could not readily articulate for themselves. This reflected our intention to engage them in dialogue and reflection; in a way, presenting them with "mirrors" so they themselves could guide the process by choosing what resonated most with them.

As these methods and concepts became clearer to us, we published a design book in 2001, entitled *Santamaria—identity* (Figure 2.4). In this publication we put forward our conceptual approach to

Figure 2.4 Santamaria Identity © 2002. Authors/Designers: Damian and Laura Santamaria. Publisher: Art Books International. Santamaria Media.

design: "identity comes from within," by reflecting on the parallels between a person's identity and that of a company or brand. The book helped to place our consultancy on the map of the UK design industry. But for us, it was an exercise of reflection that attempted to explore and make sense of two aspects of our professional reality: how to reconcile the design philosophy we inherited from our years of education (design as critical reflection and emancipation) and our commercial practice in the UK (an aesthetic preoccupation for market differentiation), which provided the financial means for our existence?

In search of meaning and identity

> Even while working for industry, designers must continue to assume their responsibilities to society. In no circumstances may their obligations to industry take precedence over their obligations to society.
>
> (Maldonado 1977: 70; translation from the Spanish by the authors)

Although we had gained valuable experience and insights during our years of commercial design consultancy work, a conflict of interest started to emerge. We were good at what we were doing—i.e. the methods were consolidated, but the concept of design as an emancipatory, transformational discipline was still missing: the very basic premise that was foundational to our education in Argentina had given way to the need to make a living. We wondered: what sort of value are we creating and for whom? What kind of social project are we contributing our skills to? Is this "responsible practice?"

As we became increasingly interested in seeking ways to create meaningful societal value (Frascara, Meurer, van Toorn, and Winkler, 1997), we invested time and effort into helping charities and non-profit organizations to bring their communications up to date by developing business-like strategies so they could fundraise more effectively. At the same time, we advised commercial clients to be bolder when communicating their purpose and values, so they could engage more meaningfully with their customers and employees. We found ourselves connecting both sides of the coin: trying to put a heart into commercial companies, and giving a strategic brain to non-commercial organizations. Thus, a new chapter opened for us out of the realization that both strands—strategy and social value—are needed to create meaning.

The social design discourse pioneered by Tomás Maldonado and Victor Papanek in the 1970s re-emerged in the new millennium. Maldonado had called for a new "design hope" (Maldonado 1970), advocating for the social responsibility of designers. And once again, issues on design ethics, ability, and the creation of social value were coming to the fore in design discourse as key aspects of the designer's role to bring about systemic change (Findeli 2001; Frascara et al. 1997; Manzini 1999; van Toorn 1998). By 2005, we were fully involved in developing brand and communication strategies for the emerging new wave of fair trade, ethical, and sustainable enterprises. We felt that we had finally found our footing again, and that the cognitive dissonance between our values and design practice was gone.

In the flow

If you want to change the world, first you have to change the media.

—Damian Santamaria

While we realized creating brands and strategies for social and pro-sustainability enterprises was a step forward in our responsible design practice, we felt there was still potential for us to engage more deeply in societal change. As Papanek had stated: "design can and must become a means for young people to take part in the transformation of society" (Papanek 1971). We were prompted to reflect once again on the meaning that statement held for us, and to ask ourselves "what can we do, as visual communicators, to magnify the impact of an emerging contemporary social and sustainability discourse that is full of hope for societal transformation?" How can we contribute to the transition of society from a culture of consumption to a culture of sustainability? (Ehrenfeld and Hoffman, 2013).

The values that were initially fostered by Maldonado, and which inspired UNLP staff—critical thinking, ethical responsibility, and an enduring commitment to the betterment of society—left a lifelong imprint on us that could not easily be disregarded. Following our interest in ethical and social issues, we embarked on the next challenge: to develop our own media platform that united design,

Figure 2.5 *Sublime* issue 7 (2008). *Sublime* is a lifestyle magazine for the "new economy." Its mission is to inspire influencer readers to advance social and environmental sustainability. www.sublimemagazine. com. Santamaria Media.

Section 2.2

Postgraduate education and graphic design as a profession

Chapter 2.2.1

Design literacy, discourse and communities of practice

Sharon Helmer Poggenpohl

No graduate program can cover all of design, successful programs seek to differentiate themselves and they do so with their mission statement and philosophy. It is within this context that programs develop a particular literacy and discourse. This conversation is not only internal, it is increasingly an international conversation with like-minded individuals and programs—some call this a community of practice—and in design there are many such communities. Building a community of practice depends on faculty and student attention to issues and research of concern. How are perspectives and new knowledge shared? Do graduate students read as a way to contextualize and extend their work? Do faculty read in order to stay abreast of changing ideas in their area of interest, bringing relevant inform- ation to studio critique and seminar discussion? And if they read and write—what do they read and where are their writings published?

Designers are slow to embrace more scholarly information that requires reading and critical thinking; they are more inclined to viewing. Is this a problem? This paper addresses the following questions. What is design literacy and how does this relate to discourse and community building? How can an existing discourse within a program be identified and examined? How can a particular discourse be supported? Where can designers participate in sharing scholarly information? What peer-reviewed and other scholarly journals are available to assess the state of knowledge building in design. Why is this important? The paper concludes with the ways in which design education and practice is changing.

Tacit and explicit knowledge

A long tradition of learning by doing permeates design education. It is even possible that students who learn best through practical exercise are initially drawn to the design field. While this is an effective way to learn, it is only one of many ways and it is based on a context of design that is fairly stable. The most

First published in *Visible Language,* 42 (3) (September 2008): 213–36. © Sharon Helmer Poggenpohl.

natural outcome of this approach is teaching based on a master-apprentice model. The master has exceptional skills that s/he attempts to pass on to the student through demonstration followed by the students' skill imitation with projects that are defined to bring the learning to fruition. Much undergraduate learning with regard to basic skills and visual sensibility are taught in this way through presentation of a model solution or tightly constrained criteria with limited development options. Trial and error and tacit exposure to skill development result in a gradual growth of sensibility. Another dimension of this form of learning is examination of trade magazines as they also provide master models of current design trends in form making. Assessment of learning is often measured imitatively against what the master would do.

In *The Tacit Dimension*, Michael Polanyi (1966) discusses the basis of knowledge as encompassing aspects that are practical (tacit) and theoretical (explicit). His focus on practical, tacit knowledge reveals the basis of the master-apprentice model in learning. Many trades have been taught in the master-apprentice mode. Polanyi and others (Lave and Wenger, 1991) have given interesting and diverse cases of such learning. Tacit skills are learned through the doing of them, by repetition and fine tuning of performance. These skills resist being made explicit; they reveal an affinity for performance, a felt 'rightness' in execution that is context dependent with many interacting variables. Much undergraduate teaching depends on tacit knowledge. However, some things can be made explicit, i.e., they can be made plain through language, explanation, method, process or identification of recurring or related patterns. Yet even these explicit ideas must be brought into design action and performance. Knowing the theories or principles alone is insufficient; they must be adopted and adapted through performance. They become more abstract guides that assist performance. It is not that tacit elements disappear or are devalued; the context of design becomes more differentiated in that the ideas that can be made abstract and explicit are stated and the ones that rely on tacit sensibility, a kind of physical touch, remain so with both working together. This enhances the designer's performance. Moving from the tacit to what can be explicit is also an indication that a field is moving from its craft origins to a discipline.

Explicit description of design actions as principles, theories and methods sets the stage for another powerful learning strategy—transformation. Here the limitations of imitation are challenged with a complementary increase in creativity and control on the part of the designer, supporting a more open exploration of the design problem or its possible solutions. This is a more analytical and exploratory approach to design that uses analogies, metaphors, critical perspectives, alternative methods and representations to open issues and development with less constraint and more reflection on process. Development of the design in question is heightened, bringing students to reflective practice (Schön, 1983). This is an appropriate strategy in graduate education.

Many would argue that explicit, transformative learning has a place in much earlier education too. Early in the 20th century, John Dewey, a pragmatist and still controversial educational reformer in the United States, made a distinction between apprentice-based and laboratory-based learning (referenced in Shulman (2004): 524–5). According to Dewey, apprentice-based learning looked backward to the demonstration and exercise of known "best practices" that are particular in nature. Laboratory-based learning is transformative and requires a critical and experimental approach to new practices and ideas; it looks forward to improvement in the well accepted and preferred mode of the research university. Despite the dichotomy set up here by the author or others that sets apprenticeship against transformative (laboratory-like) learning, both are essential and have a role in developing the next generation of designers.

Within tacit learning and its master-apprentice model, there are communities of practice; sometimes very strong communities that center on a particular master. Certain ideas may also form a center around which practitioners gather. Examples can be drawn from design history, the Bauhaus for example; or art history, Futurism or Fluxus for example; or contemporary design process with its user studies, interaction or experience design for example. In all these cases there are some core concepts or processes that give shape to the community and its concerns. Within explicit approaches to design, such communities of practice are even more evident as they tend to publish cases, theories and research in their attempt to develop knowledge and transform its practical extension into design performance.

Locating three key terms

A few terms and their interrelationships need to be sorted out for clarity. Design literacy underpins a discourse that becomes the focus for a community of practice. Design literacy refers to knowing the history, seminal writings and objects, practitioners and current controversies that establish continuity and change in design. This is less about knowing the fleeting fashion of design and more about understanding cultural shifts that push design to re-evaluate and re-think its position. Such literacy is behind the development of a discourse that is an ongoing—internal conversation within a faculty, but increasingly also an international conversation with like-minded individuals, programs and practices. It is this discourse that brings into being, defines and sustains a particular community of practice.

Design literacy depends on the publication and dissemination of ideas through writing, image documentation, museum exhibition, conference and seminar. It looks through time, from the past to the future in its concerns. It provides a panorama in which a particular discourse resides. The discourse relies on the same vehicles just mentioned, but it is a connected set of particular ideas in either media publication or artifact that supports a community of practice—and there are many such communities in design. Some elements of design literacy coalesce to form a linked discourse that is sustained and developed by a community of practice.

It is difficult, maybe impossible, to cover the breadth of design in general. Identifying a discourse of interest provides entry to a community that shares design performance values. The diversity among communities is interesting, there is design management, design and emotion, design research, creativity, human-computer interaction, design science—to mention only a few. Together they reveal the multifaceted nature of design.

Identifying the existing discourse

A simple, if crude, way to see what is the current discourse in one's education program is to ask students what are the keywords they hear over and over from various faculty in different subjects. Their answers may be surprising. Of course they'll identify the ideosyncracies of some of the more dramatic faculty members, but they will also reveal the repetitions (even if the exact words or the emphasis shifts a bit) that highlight the conceptual threads that pull the program together. This simple exercise can deliver a broad understanding of what is essential in a program and it can reveal useful information about the focus of either undergraduate or graduate programs. It may also be useful to ask faculty for the keywords that identify their particular learning objectives and then see the comparison between student and faculty responses. A more rigorous approach would be to perform a network analysis (Scott, 1991) that delivers a more dimensional view of the themes, their overlaps and the people that interact around them. Such interpersonal networks can be examined based on the quality of reciprocity, intensity and durability in their relationships. People come together based on shared interests and ideas to form a community of practice.

Understanding changes in design practice

Reliance only on the tradition of a master-apprentice learning mode, with its implicit concreteness and stable learning environment, no longer functions very well. The context in which we live and work is more dynamic with unpredictable change, that sometimes occurs quickly on many fronts. For example, technological change continues to alter how we communicate and what we expect from information, environments and products. Business sometimes sees design as a value creation center that requires better overall planning and integration, while end users of products and services become subjects for observation and investigation, or even participants in the design process. These few examples demonstrate the fact that contemporary design work goes beyond form-making and aesthetic decisions to the earliest stages of developing a possibility, addressing a felt need for something that does not yet exist, that could be made better or that could form a core business idea. These ideas stimulate change in design education, the scope it needs to cover and how learning opportunities are delivered.

Building an explicit discourse in graduate education

If we agree that the undergraduate years are best suited to developing tacit skills, particularly in their earliest years, then more explicit knowledge needs to be developed in later years, largely in graduate education. It is these later years that are the focus of this paper. In particular, graduate programs seek to differentiate themselves by developing a particular community of practice, based on ideas that are evolving and subject to research and refinement. No graduate program can cover all of design, it necessarily sets its focus to develop some ideas while it ignores or downplays others. The faculty has their own particular interests, but in a focused graduate program, they share a philosophical underpinning for their educational goals and overlap to some degree in their interests. This promotes development and cohesion in what is a poorly organized, emerging discipline. These shared ideas become a discourse that runs through a graduate experience and colors the work of the students and the expectations of those with whom they'll later work professionally. Some programs become known for their discourse. For example, Cranbrook was known for its post-modern discourse; the Rhode Island School of Design for its semiotic interest and application as well as its attention to process and materiality; the Institute of design, IIT for its interest in planning and the design/business symbiosis: Milan Polytechnic for its interest in sustainability—the list could go on. Today, graduate programs are turning to an interest in design research within professional as well as in research-oriented programs. But research possibilities are expansive in a poorly defined field such as design, so programs focus on a set of carefully defined research interests that match faculty interest and university capability. Program focus also depends on a philosophical position and faculty with shared, but not necessarily identical interests, who are actively engaged in building a discourse that supports a community of practice.

Building a community of practice depends on faculty and student attention to issues and research of concern. This goes beyond what someone does in design practice, to how they think about and express ideas, making them explicit, connecting them to the work of others. The result may be a new perspective, a more complete synthesis of existing work, or new knowledge—all of these outcomes need to be shared. Presumably the faculty in a graduate program is reading to stay abreast of changing ideas in their area of interest; writing and publishing papers on their work as they need to bring new knowledge to studio critique and seminar discussion. Here the graduate faculty diverges from the undergraduate faculty; rather than be design practitioners who demonstrate tacit knowledge and its application in practical performance, they need to be design scholars who are focused on extending the limits of design thinking and performance in their area of concern.

In 2002, some doctoral students and I decided to try to find out what design faculty members and doctoral students were reading in order to understand the importance of certain ideas and see how widespread their influence was. A broad list of books was posted online with an invitation to a PhD list-serv to participate. People were asked to indicate whether they read a particular book, were aware of it or its author, and to add any notable books they thought were missing from the list. The results from this survey were discouraging—it appeared that the respondents read little.

Because of this we were forced to take another approach by contacting known design scholars who read and to ask them to add to our list and annotate selections. The participants in this were an informal community of practice who shared attitudes and perspectives on design scholarship. The outcome of this was a special issue of the journal *Visible Language* titled An Annotated Design Research Bibliography: by and for the design community (Chayutsahakij et al., 2002). Edited by doctoral students, it contained 90 books ". . . selected through two analytical approaches: the essentialness of the book determined through a design community on-line ranking survey and the discipline distribution through keyword analysis (Chayutsahakij, p.109). Besides an overview of process, there were three sections that listed the annotated entries: philosophy and theory of design, principles and methods of design research, and discourse between design theory and practice.

While the first study was based on books, the most recent investigation, presented here, is concerned with journals. If design faculty read and write, what might they read and where can their writing be published?

The process to identify a range of design journals was based on the author's attention to and experience with such journals over several decades. An online search using the keywords 'design journal' was undertaken in April 2007. Other online lists of journals from university sources and individual compilers were also consulted (see Designophy, Media Lab, Usernomics in the References). The twenty-nine journals represented in Table 1 demonstrate a range of scholarly interest in Design. Their data, with very few exceptions, covered the categories the author sought to present: journal title. ISSN number, URL, statement of focus (greatly abbreviated) and start date. No claim is made that this list is exhaustive or complete, however the twenty-nine representative journals offer a window on developing research and scholarship in Design. For example, if the start dates for these journals are examined by decade from the 1960s to the present, one notices the following: only 2 journals began in the late 1960s,

1 journal in the late 1970s, 3 journals in the 1980s, 11 journals in the 1990s, and 12 journals so far in the first decade of the twenty-first century. The trend clearly demonstrates increased optimism regarding the need for and availability of more in depth scholarship in Design—more explicit information to guide design performance as a transformative practice. Another way to understand this is through the average start date spanning forty years with 1967 (the earliest journal) and 2007 (the latest); the average date is 1995, demonstrating how young this effort is.

Journals begin and sometimes disappear in a few years for a number of reasons; they are: unable to find their audience (either authors, readers or both), unable to sustain themselves financially or unable to generally define their mission and capture interest. Not all the new journals will survive despite the best effort of those involved. University libraries largely supply access to these journals and their use is often monitored as universities seek to contain their operating costs. It is doubtful that any of the journals listed make a profit. They exist as a social good to extend scholarship and are sustained by a community of practice. Two journals on the original list (see Table 1 discussed later) were folded into other journals, largely disappearing no doubt for financial reasons. One, *Information Design Journal,* with a heritage from 1979 and respected by many, became part of *Document Design* when it moved to a new publisher. This demonstrates the fragility of such publications.

Building communities of practice

Design is a vital collection of ideas not all of which are compatible. Not only the broad ideas, but their fittingness to a region or locale are important. Which ideas fit the specific faculty, students, institution and professional practice? Identification of core ideas and competencies need not be monolithic or dogmatic, but they need to fit their environment and be shared. Some ideas lean toward social action with an emphasis on respect for people and their cultural forms; some lean toward science with an emphasis on logic, problem and solution, or evaluation; and some lean toward art and aesthetics. The philosophical bases for each of these is different and the values present in their performance lead to different kinds of assessment. One set of ideas is not superior to another—they are simply different. Design has no singular story; it has many stories and perspectives. As argued, these perspectives become a focus for a community of practice and this is particularly important in graduate programs. How does this work?

Literacy is a very broad concept that encompasses everything design might care about. Within this overarching literacy are specific kinds of discourse that might be big and well developed or small and at an early stage of development. The various forms of discourse might be isolated from others, design as art for example; or related to others, user studies and participatory design for example; or overlap another, sustainability and ecological design for example.

A community of practice that provides energy and ideas sustains a discourse. It encompasses programs, faculties and students that represent the teaching and learning of the discourse; practitioners who represent the practical performance of the discourse and who may be former students or current faculty. Faculty and practitioners can both do research that investigates the development and performance of the discourse, sharing their results and critical ideas with others through journal articles that help establish and expand literacy within the discourse, thereby coming full circle.

Table 1 A sample of current design journals

JOURNAL TITLE	ISSN	URL	FOCUS	START
Art, Design and Communication in Higher Education	1472 2273X	http:/www.ovid.com	Interest in research in arts and media based subjects in educational institutions; fine art practice-based education, theoretical studies of media, cultural studies, art, design history	2003
Artifact*	1749 3463 1749 3471	http://www.tandf.no/artifact	Explores relevant topical themes for design researchers, practising designers, manufacturers to promote transdisciplinary connections	2006
Asia Design Journal	1738 3838	Unknown	Promotes design's ethical responsibility toward human life and society as well as a vision for the future environment	2004
Co-Design*	1571 0882 1745 3755	http://www.tandf.co.uk/journals	Reports new research and scholarship in principles, procedures and techniques relevant to collaboration in design	2005
Computer-Aided Design*	0010 4485	http://www.elsevier.com	Presents research and development in the application of computers to the design process	1969
Design Issues	0747 9360	http://www.mitpressjournals.org	Presents design history, theory, and criticism	1984
The Design Journal*	1460 6965	http://www.ashgate.com	Covers design practice, theory, management and education; encourages discussion between practice and theory	1998
Design Management Review (formerly Design Management Journal)	Unknown	http://www.dmi.org	Explores articles and case studies on design (products, communication, environments) as an essential resource contributing to long-term success and profit	1990
Design Research Quarterly*	1752 8445	http://www.drsq.org/Issues	Focuses on knowledge and its production in the design fields	2006

(Continued)

Table 1 Continued

JOURNAL TITLE	ISSN	URL	FOCUS	START
Design Philosophy Papers	Unknown	http://www.desphilosophy.com	Explores aspects of design as an object of philosophical inquiry in its relation between beings/worlds as they shape each other	2003
Design Studies*	0142 694X	http://www.elsevier.com	Provides an interdisciplinary forum for development and discussion of design activity and experience fundamentals	1980
Document Design	1388 8951 1569 9722	http://www.benjamins.nl	Covers communication studies, electronic/multimedia products, linguistics, and psychology	1999
Ergonomics in Design (formerly Human Factors)	1064 8046	http://www.hfes.org/publications	Reports on usability of products, systems, environments	1998
International Journal of Art & Design Education*	Unknown	http://www.blackwellpublishing.com	Disseminates ideas, research, case studies with attention to social and cultural values that inform education	1997
International Journal of Design*	1991 3761 1994 036X	http://ijdesign.org	All fields of design research; industrial, visual communication, interface, animation, games architecture, and related fields	2007
International Journal of Design Computing*	1329 7147	http://www.intute.ac.uk	Supports research and technology transfer in design computing through publication of interaction and multimedia	1997
Journal of Computer-Aided Environmental Design and Education	Unknown	http://scholar.lib.vt.edu/ejournals/JCAEDE	Research and teaching in CAD, computer-enhanced instruction and digital technology in design	1995
Journal of Decorative and Propaganda Arts	0888 7314	http://www.jstor.org	Fosters new scholarship for the period 1875 to 1945 in decorative and propaganda arts	1986
Journal of Design History	0952 4649 1741 7279	http://jdh.oxfordjournals.org/	Covers design history (including crafts and applied arts) and studies of visual and material culture	1988

JOURNAL TITLE	ISSN	URL	FOCUS	START
Journal of Design Research*	1748 3050 1569 1551	*http://inderscience.com/jdr/*	Interdisciplinary, emphasizes human aspects as central issue of design though integrative studies of social sciences and design disciplines	2001
Journal of Visual Culture*	1470 4129 1741 2994	*http://vcu.sagepub.com*	Promotes research, scholarship, and critical engagement with all forms of visual culture	2002
Journal of Sustainable Product Design*	1367 6679	*http://www.cfsd.org.uk/journal/*	Covers economic, environmental, ethical, and social issues in product design and development	1997
New Media & Society	1461 4448 1461 7315	*http://www.sagepub.com/ journals*	Draws on interdisciplinary theoretical and empirical research to discuss new media development	1999
Planning Theory & Practice	1464 9357 1470 000X	*http://www.tandf.co.uk/journals*	Presents research, review, and analysis regarding spatial planning and public policy	2000
Point Art and Design Research Journal	1360 3477	*http://www.point.ac.uk/index.htm*	Offers a context for the presentation and discussion of research in art and design	1999
Research Issues in Art Design and Media	1474 2365	*http://www.biad.uce.ac.uk/ research/rti/riadm*	Reflects on research process, particular methods or techniques, new and emerging themes and topics.	2000
Scandinavian Journal of Design History	0906 3447	*http://www/designhistory.dk/ index.asp*	Supports articles on arts and crafts, decorative arts, industrial design, graphics art, interiors, etc.	1991
Visible Language* (formerly Journal of Typographic Research)	0022 2224	*http://www.visiblelanguage journal.com*	Presents interdisciplinary research and scholarship on typography and visual language in digital media and beyond	1967
Working Papers in Art & Design	1466 4917	*http://www.herts.ac.uk*	Supports practice-based research in art and design	2000

Notes: *designates peer reviewed; First ISSN is print, second ISSN is electronic version. Author's image © 2008.

Why is design discourse and community building important now? As mentioned nearly a decade ago at the First Doctoral Education in Design Conference (Poggenpohl, 1998, p.104). "Not surprisingly, design [information] is invisible, dispersed within other classifications." Our literature and discourse are scattered; we publish opportunistically in ACM (American Computing Machinery) or IEEE (Institute of Electrical and Electronics Engineers) publications or other journals that are respected, but not quite directly in our field. In this way we add to knowledge broadly, but not necessarily in our own field as the information is hidden and not attributed to design in any direct way. The design journals with longer history cited in Table 1 are interdisciplinary—covering many design sub-disciplines and even disciplines somewhat aligned but tangential to design. When scholarly design information or research is not actively or broadly sought after by students, faculty or practitioners, a broad publishing agenda is a survival strategy. This is where building discourse and communities of practice with their underpinning literature intersect. It is such communities of practice that will create a mature design discipline and support more focused journals.

In October of 2007, the university where I teach (Hong Kong Polytechnic) requested all schools to submit a list of important high quality journals that support the various subject areas and discourse present in research and taught programs (table 1 is the author's list not the more extensive list prepared for the university). Identification of these journals and the grading of them according to their quality support the formal research assessment exercise that determines allocation of research money and support for research students. The sciences, engineering and social sciences can easily prepare such a list based on well developed and easily accessible citation indices. This is more problematic for design as it has no citation index; design lacks much of the typical infrastructure that other disciplines take for granted. While design has been something of an outlier on university campuses, this request for a journal list is a clear indication that some universities are trying to bring design into a tighter and more accountable relationship with the university and that design's agenda must go beyond teaching to research and the development of new knowledge in design.

Both design practice and education are changing. A look at the growth of PhD programs indicates that design research is now more present within universities worldwide. Table 2 is taken from a recent PhD

Table 2 Distribution of PhD design programs worldwide

11	AUSTRALIA	1	HONG KONG	4	PORTUGAL
1	BELGIUM	3	INDIA	1	SINGAPORE
1	BRAZIL	2	ITALY	4	SWEDEN
2	CANADA	1	JAPAN	3	TAIWAN
3	DENMARK	1	MEXICO	6	TURKEY
2	FINLAND	2	NETHERLANDS	29	UNITED KINGDOM
5	GERMANY	3	NEW ZEALAND	11	UNITED STATES
		2	NORWAY		

listserv (see Melles, 2007). Here are ninety-eight programs across the world and more in the planning stages. You may be surprised to see emerging nations such as Brazil, India, Mexico and Turkey on the list. From an economic perspective, many emerging countries understand the connection between design and economic development. To this we can add the pressure from universities that encourage design programs to engage in knowledge building and to conform to the university mission to openly create and disseminate new knowledge, such as previously mentioned at Hong Kong Polytechnic University. In this way design is invited to take its place among other more established disciplines that balance professional preparation with knowledge generation. Design practice itself is becoming ever more multidisciplinary due to technological developments and the need for human-centered advocates with broad skills in synthesis. Crossing disciplinary boundaries requires explicit knowledge regarding what is known, how it is known, what constitutes evidence for what is stated and how other disciplines can accept or refute such information. Designers need an epistemological understanding of their own field and those of others with significantly different bases of knowledge in order to effectively interact and collaborate on multidisciplinary teams. As argued, this goes beyond tacit knowledge but does not negate it.

Changes in design practice and education challenge the status quo and call for both explicit and tacit knowledge. The following six principles, taken from Lee Shulman, president of The Carnegie Foundation for the Advancement of Teaching, identifies "authentic and enduring learning" (2004: 493–4, author italic additions):

The subject matter to be learned is generative, essential and pivotal to the discipline or inter-discipline under study, and can yield new understandings and/or serve as the basis for *future learning* of content, processes and dispositions.

*

The learner is an *active agent* in the process, not passive, an audience, a client or a collector. Learning becomes more active through *experimentation and inquiry,* as well as through *writing, dialogue and questioning*.

*

The learner not only behaves and thinks, but can '*go meta*'—that is, can reflectively turn around on his/her own thought and action and analyse how and why their thinking achieved certain ends or failed to achieve others. . . .

*

There is *collaboration* among learners. They can work together in ways that scaffold and support each other's learning, and in ways that supplement each other's knowledge. . . .

*

Teachers and students share a *passion* for the material, are emotionally committed to the ideas, processes and activities and see the work as connected to present and future goals.

*

The process of activity, reflection and collaboration are supported, legitimated and nurtured within a *community* or culture that values such experiences and creates many opportunities for them to occur and be accomplished with success and pleasure. . . .

*

These more general principles for learning support the argument offered here that learning prepares one for the future and its uncertainties through experimentation and inquiry born of explicit learning that may be sharable through critical writing, visual reflection and the development of a literature. The active teacher or student can reflectively analyse (meta-cognize) their performance as a way to learn. Social learning, both formally and informally in a community of practice, supports collaboration and pursues design knowledge and performance with passion. Graduate programs in design need to stake out their territories for development through building a particular literacy, discourse and community of practice.

The implication for this argument in favor of design literacy, discourse and communities of practice goes even further. For example, languages that are used only orally, that lack a writing system, are likely to disappear. Robust languages have not only a writing system, but also typographic development and extensive creative use. They continue to change and develop—they live. Likewise, design's limited explication of itself is cause for concern. It's infrastructural shortcomings put it at risk as other disciplines discover its methods of thinking and development and perhaps presume to poach on its intellectual and creative territory. Design learning and performance encompass border-crossing activities—between tacit and explicit, logic and intuition, artfulness and science, technology and human behavior, business and the social good. As such it is hard to pin down and this has prevented an easy or clear classification or reference. We have a serious stake in developing design literacy, discourse and communities of practice now.

Chapter 2.2.2

What is worth doing in design research?

Meredith Davis

My brother has a PhD in organic chemistry. A good many of his six years of doctoral study were spent figuring out what had not been done in his chosen field. And like others in the sciences, he pored over existing research to settle eventually on a topic of investigation. The search for original territory is not the problem in design research. Compared to the sciences and humanities, little design research has been done and our real task in design schools and universities is to determine what is worth doing—deciding among all the concerns of the discipline and practice, what actually matters in the grand scheme of things.

If our discipline were medicine, we could look to the practice for guidance. For example, how many patients have been discharged from hospitals with Type II Diabetes as part of their diagnoses tells us something about the urgency of the obesity epidemic. There is some agreement in the field and in society that this issue is important and funding opportunities reflect that consensus. The standards for judging the quality of research, whether in the social or basic sciences, are in place. And the outcomes of such research are reported to the public and guide the recommendations of practicing physicians. But design has no common understanding within the field of what is meant by research, no unified theory guiding practice, few research methods that haven't been borrowed whole-cloth from other disciplines and little recognition by practice and the public of the value of design research findings.

In a 2005 *Metropolis Magazine* survey of 1,051 US design professionals, faculty, and students (Manfra), respondents' definitions of design research ranged from studies of user behavior to selecting colors from ink swatches. For most undergraduate students, research means library retrieval only. When asked whether there should be a unified theory of design guiding research, the overwhelming majority of respondents said, 'No'. And when ranking potential research topics by importance to the field, respondents selected "sustainability" as their number one priority, but ironically, placed 'systems theory' at the bottom of their list. Clearly, the field—at least in the US—is confused about what might constitute a research agenda and, if the trade magazines are indicators, what role research degrees and doctoral education should play in the evolution of the design disciplines.

As an emerging research culture, therefore, every dissertation by a doctoral student in design contributes to shaping exactly what people think design research is about. The topics our students choose and the methods they employ matter in defining for the field and the public the potential of design to make a difference in the quality of life and the environment.

First presented at the Doctoral Education in Design Conference, Hong Kong Polytechnic University, May 23-5, 2011. © Meredith Davis.

Many are tempted to legitimize design research through quantitative studies that satisfy a counting and measuring culture. Not long ago, I reviewed the work of a PhD graduate who compared the recognition of Cook and Shanosky's 1974 travel symbols for the US Department of Transportation by readers of ideographic and phonetic languages. The sample size was too small to be generalizable, the differences in recognition were negligible and the methods were unremarkable. But the bigger question for me was what significance the researcher thought the findings of this study held for the design of symbol systems, global communication or our understanding of cognitive processing. Why was recognition of these symbols outside their intended context important and where in travel situations was it possible to separate ideographic and phonetic readers? On what basis was it assumed that interpretation of these pictograms could be attributed to the native languages of the readers or that the subjects of the study were innocent of all prior experiences with such symbol systems? And while this shaky quantitative study yielded several articles in scholarly journals, it is difficult to imagine how it might further the future work of other researchers. Are we simply counting things because it is easy to do, or should numbers really tell us something about how design works?

From a humanities perspective, in one year there were no fewer than six calls for papers for scholarly journals and conferences devoted exclusively to the critical analysis of *Mad Men*, an American television melodrama about advertising in the 1960s. Presumably these discussions deconstruct the role of media in society, but it seems a stretch to think that this single product of Hollywood was deserving of so much intellectual attention. And any subscriber to Design Studies Forum—a listserv for people interested in design history, theory, and criticism—must marvel at the number of conferences framed around topics so specific that it is hard to imagine how they all find audiences. This raises questions concerning the value of design research. Are we generating studies to populate conferences and fill journals in support of academic degree requirements and tenure cases, or are we doing important work that truly helps people make sense of the world through writing about design?

Now I didn't choose these examples as indictments of individual inquiry or to suggest that all knowledge generation should be about immediate application in practice. But I am concerned about what these and similar investigations I've encountered add up to as the output of doctoral programs and consequences for the discipline and culture. Where in the preparation of PhD students do we ask 'What is worth doing?' and how do we ensure that, as in other fields, design research projects lay a foundation for others to build upon in addressing the challenges of our time? Are we simply talking to ourselves in conferences and journals or do others really care about and make use of what we discover about design and its influences? And what is the special obligation of doctoral universities at this particular moment in the early practice of doctoral research?

I would argue that we've begun this design research enterprise at a time in history that places special responsibilities on university programs to look at the larger implications of what doctoral students do. In fact, the very notion of doctoral studies is under attack, as in the December 2010 issue of *The Economist* ("The disposable"). *The Economist* article reported that since 1970 the number of doctorates produced in the United States has doubled and that between 1998 and 2006 the number of diplomas handed out in all OECD countries grew by 40 percent. In a book by Queens College professor Andrew Hacker and *New York Times* writer Claudia Dreifus, the authors reported that the United States produced more than 100,000 doctoral degrees in this period but that there were only 16,000 new professorships. Canada conferred 4,800 doctoral degrees but hired only 2,600 new faculty. Only China and Brazil seem to find a shortfall in PhDs (Hacker *et al.* 2010).

The salary premium for a PhD is also shrinking, according to *The Economist*. In engineering, architecture, and education, students with PhDs actually command less money than those with master's degrees. And overall in all subjects, PhDs earn only 3 percent over those with master's degrees. The OECD study also showed that as many as 60 percent of PhDs in some countries are still on temporary contracts five years after graduation and as many as one-third take jobs totally unrelated to their fields of doctoral study.

For those who argue that employment is not the goal of doctoral education, the statistics on PhD dropout rates are sobering. In the United States, only 57 percent of doctoral students will have a PhD ten years after their first dates of enrollment. Humanities students fare less well as a group at 49 percent and hang on longer without graduating than those in the sciences. And while it is easy to think of this work as a love of learning, nearly one-third of British PhD students admitted that they were undertaking a doctorate to put off job hunting or to continue their student status. Half of engineering students admitted the same. It is little surprise, therefore, that studies show people with more education than their work requires are less satisfied and less productive than others. I would argue, therefore, that there needs to be some larger goal for developing doctoral research in design than simply raising the entry qualifications for a limited number of university faculty positions or preparing students for an intellectual life that could be financially unsustainable.

But figuring out what is worth doing isn't easy. And it is especially difficult under the rapidly changing world context and for disciplines whose territory is unclear. But there are a few trends with long arcs that might suggest areas of possible research, or at the very least, conditions under which the relevance of design research topics might be judged.

One trend is that design problems are increasingly complex and require the work of interdisciplinary teams and new methods for their solution

Nearly fifty years ago, J. Christopher Jones wrote about a hierarchy of design problems with components and products at the bottom and systems and communities at the top. He challenged the design professions to develop methods appropriate to the complexity of problems at the upper levels of the hierarchy, which he believed characterize life in post-industrial society (Jones 1970). It is difficult today to think that most design research problems aren't nested within complex webs of social behaviors, cultural values, cognitive challenges, environmental consequences, technological affordances and economic imperatives. On Core 77—an internet site for articles, portfolios, and discussions of industrial design—cognitive psychologist Don Norman echoes Jones' opinion that design has failed to develop methods appropriate for research and practice at this scale. He suggests that our position in colleges of art and architecture hamper our ability to meet today's research demands and our understanding of the work by important collaborators from other fields ("Why design").

So, the question for doctoral programs is whether we scale our research efforts to the traditional problems and methods we already know or borrow from other fields, or address the more ambitious agenda presented by the contemporary context for professional design and critical interpretation? Do we confine ourselves to the more familiar territory of craft and sensory experience, or do we participate in the grand challenges presented by a complex world that calls for broader insight? And if the latter, who do we need as partners in research investigations that, by their very complex nature, cross disciplinary and geographic boundaries?

Another trend is the participatory nature of contemporary culture that argues for the design of tools and systems

The history of design has been largely about crafting physical artifacts. But the complexity of today's problems demands that we develop tools and systems that support people in crafting their own experiences. Not only is this a change in the scale of our work as designers, but it also recasts our relationships with others. Gerhard Fischer and Liz Sanders describe a move from designing for people to designing with people; from thinking about consumers and users to thinking about participants and co-creators. Human Computer Interface professor Fischer challenges us to recognize situations in which people want to be designers in personally meaningful activities and are forced to be consumers, and when they want to be consumers in personally irrelevant activities and are forced to be designers (Fischer 2012). Think about software that requires extra work on the part of users to subvert automated formatting and manuals that describe components and features instead of tasks. Design researcher and cognitive psychologist Sanders makes a case for the development of convivial tools through which we study not only what people do and say, but also what they make (Sanders 2006).

We're only beginning to understand what it means to work at the level of systems—at the complex intersections between people, activities, places and things. Apple Computer, for example, has a well-defined service system. Purchasing an Apple Product provides access to content through iTunes and its retail stores allow people to touch and use computers on the showroom floor; access components through self-service packaging that reveals the product; pay for purchases without queuing up at a cash register; and sign-up for repair appointments online before they leave their homes or while shopping in a mall. Systems are not void of compelling artifacts—the physical and functional attributes of Apple's products and store environments are integral to its success—but the value of artifacts lies in the contributions they make to people's overall experiences with Apple and the changes they introduce in the culture.

We have yet to fully comprehend how systems adapt organically to differences in people's behavior and what it means to have an end state that is 'good enough for now' because there will always be a new iteration or condition. And we have much to learn about the nature of experience: about what philosopher John Dewey called the structure of 'doing and undergoing'.

A third trend is the rapid, unstoppable evolution of technology that encourages new forms of sense-making

MIT literature professor David Thorburn, in describing the history of technology, says that 19th century technology arrived to meet the needs expressed by industrial society, while contemporary technology develops before we really comprehend what it is good for. It is clear that the proliferation of information and new technological tools and systems demand new interpretive behaviors.

The Knowledgeworks Foundation and the Institute for the Future talk about social media and collaborative tools leaving 'data trails' as traces of people's interactions; about collective sense-making that defines new forms of knowledge and assessment by digital citizens; and about sensors and global positioning technology that are less about interacting with visual representations than about responding to unconscious action ("2020 Forecast"). Writer and former interface designer Adam Greenfield goes further to describe our current condition as one of information processing dissolving into behavior (Greenfield 2006).

How people adjust to new tools and new forms of information and what they mean to decision-making is ripe for investigation. What can design research tell us about technology enhancing human understanding rather than simply automating human activity? How can we mine data for sentiment as well as statistical pattern? How can mobile technology deliver instruction, healthcare, counseling and other essential services? The questions are endless, yet we see hundreds of PhD applications from people who simply want to make the next cool thing. In some fundamental way, we are failing at communicating the power of design research at the precise moment when others recognize the power of design.

A fourth trend is the shift from an economy defined by routine service work to one of clustered creative industries

Thomas Friedman's 2005 book proclaimed *The world is flat*. Friedman asserted that technology and economic shifts in the distribution of production and manufacturing have leveled the global playing field. Economist Richard Florida disagreed and in a 2005 article in *Atlantic Monthly* stated instead that 'The world is spiky', that there are hills and valleys in the distribution of economic potential and that we cannot think of places as being homogenous in their culture or opportunities. Florida describes three sorts of places in the world that have less to do with geopolitical boundaries and more to do with potential in the confluences of resources: (1) those that can attraction global talent and create new products; (2) those that manufacture the world's goods and support its innovation engines; and (3) those with little connections and few immediate prospects (Florida 2005).

So is it any longer possible, if it ever was, to separate a concern for the social from a concern for the economic? And if the health of the economy depends on the social, then what is the nature of collaboration and workflow technology that allows people with different incentives, cultural behaviors, and values to collaborate successfully? And what responsibility does design research have to those who live in the valleys?

So, I'm a pragmatist and it is my hope that we develop the collective will among educators and practitioners to shape the future of design research in ways that assert the contemporary relevance of design for those outside our small community. That our debates over definitions, methods, and ideology are grounded by good work and the consequences of things worth doing. And that we see communicating the value of these things to the profession and public.

Chapter 2.2.3

Locating graphic design history in Canada

Brian Donnelly

The study of graphic design in Canada suffers from a scarcity of written sources and collecting institutions. Interviews conducted by one researcher suggest that, far from preventing the formation of an active design industry or any sense of an historical canon, Canadian designers draw on international examples from a variety of sources and pass values on in a largely unrecorded fashion, almost like that of an oral tradition itself. Canadian designers have a largely coherent and shared, if vernacular, sense of which works and individuals are of historical importance. Because the process of gathering and recording graphic design history in Canada currently leans heavily on recording oral histories, it is framed by many designers' memories and collections, in interaction with critical and practical analysis of what design history is. The implications of the theory and practice of oral history for design are explored, as is the importance of maintaining the difference between memory and history. Locating that existing, vernacular canon, it is suggested, is the best way to locate and study the post-war history of graphic design in Canada.

Appropriately, this article will begin with a variation on a story I have told before: Harold Kurschenska (1931–2003) was a typographer and book designer, and he began working as an apprentice at the University of Toronto Press in 1957. I interviewed him at his small apartment in Toronto in 1999, just before he moved on to retirement in British Columbia. As always with designers, my interview with Harold was lively, wide-ranging, and surprising. The biggest surprise, however, came as I was leaving: Harold asked me if I would take his papers. He had collected, sorted, filed, and labeled the highlights of a long career—in effect, his life's work—and packed them in seven boxes. Now, he insisted that I load them in the trunk of my car.[1]

Kurschenska was the designer of, among many other books, the first edition of *The Gutenberg Galaxy* (University of Toronto Press, 1962; see Figure 2.7), Marshall McLuhan's aphoristic pastiche on print and technological change, subtitled *The Making of Typographic Man*. Although Kurschenska worked at the centre of print culture in Canada, and with one of its gurus, it seems no one else had ever come to talk about his work, and there was apparently no institution willing to take the written records of his history. This is not because Kurschenska was a 'minor' figure in a design history being actively

First published in *Journal of Design History,* 19 (4) (2006): 283–94. It is republished here with the kind permission of Oxford University Press on behalf of The Design History Society and the *Journal of Design History*. © OUP/Brian Donnelly.

written about other, more important, careers. Except for his careful act of self-archiving, his story is typical: there literally was no place for his history.

For the past ten years, off and on, as time and funding provided, I have been engaged in a process of interviewing graphic designers in Canada, almost a hundred to date, about their history, their work and their understanding of the post-war development of design. Without thinking of it as such, this has involved conducting an oral history project among articulate, educated and literate professionals working at the fulcrum of print culture. The individual designers chosen have all proved very willing to talk, but only a scant few have had work collected somewhere, or themselves preserved representative archival records of their work, much less written about In the near-complete absence of any collecting institutions dedicated to graphics and the paucity of other sites of memory such as written texts, the material history of graphic design, although reproduced in mass quantities in the recent past, has almost disappeared from view, or just disappeared altogether.

Beyond the obvious irony to be found in producing an oral history of the very designers of our massive print culture, there is another twist in my story. This research has been supported by several different grants and funding initiatives, all of which have been for digital and online projects, funded by governments and organizations wanting to swim with the electronic current by stimulating production of digital information on Canadian culture. The history of 'typographic man', at least in Canada, is being captured largely by "pre"- and "post"-print technologies—that is oral and digital, but not in print itself—because the printed and written basis for compiling a written history of print is so rare as to be almost non-existent.[2] The graphic design tradition in Canada, then, could be said to be an oral tradition in two senses: it has been informally transmitted, primarily through studios, schools and periodicals, without having been permanently collected, curated or canonized in print or by institutions, and it is only now being gathered up again as an oral history from the practitioners themselves.

In considering design history in Canada as an oral history, then, we encounter some interesting questions, not primarily about "who" made this history or when it occurred, but rather where our history is. Canadian communications theorist Harold Innis noted that some social media were based in time: lasting sculptural or architectural monuments, for example, or religious and educational institutions that draw their meaning from their endurance over the years. He distinguished these from media that were highly mobile and diffuse, working across—having a bias in, or being bound by—space. Foremost among these was print culture, ascendant since Gutenberg.[3] (Innis was an important influence on McLuhan, his University of Toronto colleague, in both style and content.) Graphic design extends this notion further, because it is not a medium at all, but a practice that reaches across several media, from print to screen to digitization, each of which accelerates this spatial bias by moving faster through broader channels and across greater distances. The state of design history in Canada, then, remains dispossessed because it has not been formally established or preserved through time. (In this sense the medium of print, in the form of canonical texts, can provide relative permanence and a bias toward time.) Further, it has evolved as a result of many different determining factors drawn from several influences and traditions, many of which are not Canadian at all. Its location, then, is radically decentred, and this paper will look at what theories of oral history and memory can do to help us locate this history.

After 1945, graphic design in Canada developed as part of the general, international design discourse, shared in particular among more industrially developed nations. Because of the relative lack of design studies in Canada, however, design institutions here never established broadly ideological

Figure 2.7 *The Gutenberg Galaxy* cover. © 1962. Author: Marshall McLuhan. Designer: Harold Kurschenska. Reprinted with permission of the publisher: University of Toronto Press.

claims regarding this country's unique or national design culture, as was so often the case elsewhere and in other fields (such as literature or art). Canada, in other words, has never merited a chapter in Meggs.[4] A recent economic study done in the province of Ontario, *Design Matters*, suggests that, in all fields (including architecture and industrial, interior and graphic design), there are some 40,000 designers in Ontario alone.[5] These industries, with the arguable exception of architecture, function largely without written record of their own history. (Architecture, like painting and sculpture, is studied in art history departments and has more of a published and preserved record.) Obviously, all those designers are working with a clear picture of what they believe design is; where do they get it?

Oral evidence suggests that the picture designers have of their own national disciplines comes from the few national trade magazines (in graphic design, Applied Arts has played this role in English; a number of publications, including *G* and *grafika*, have served in French); from whatever local histories are preserved in the companies they work for, in the form of portfolios and self-promotional material; particularly from whatever few Canadian images they have exposure to in schools (often haphazardly captured in the form of an individual instructor's slide collection; small wonder that students attend so closely to the passing flow of contemporary images in advertising and the media). Although Canada possesses a highly developed professional and institutional framework of companies, professional associations, competitive exhibitions, contemporary publications and educational institutions, nonetheless the retained historical record of all that design has depended largely on the unrecorded self-understanding and self-selection of its practitioners. Oral history, then, does have an appropriate role to play in a country where much design history is, by default, transmitted in an informal, largely oral tradition.

One interesting fact of design in Canada is that the dominant visual influences—what designers see in print and construe as the canonical basis of their profession— have come from outside the country, largely from the USA and Europe. To note this is not to adopt a nationalist perspective, to raise the flag or posit some crisis of identity or loss in urgent need of salvage and redress. It is to assess the objective reality that the history of design in Canada is not entirely, or even fundamentally, a Canadian history. This can be seen, positively, as the realization of the internationalism and idealism that marked graphic design thinking generally in the post-war period. Remarkable international exhibitions held here after 1945, such as *Typomundus 20*, held in Toronto in 1966, and Expo 67 in Montreal, were defining moments for Canada's designers—many of whom were trained in and emigrated from Britain, West Germany, Austria, or the USA in any event. Thus, the national (or perhaps notional) space of 'Canadian' design is, quite literally, an arbitrary line around parts of a much larger intellectual and visual territory.

Scanning is one interesting metaphor for how history might approach this vast space. Scanning emerged from Cybernetic theory in the 1950s, and Claude Shannon's original idea was itself based on a spatial metaphor for communicating information: divide up a surface into discrete blocks and average out the visual information in each of them, thereby reducing the smooth surface of the world to manageable, defined, digital pixels. Scanning also implies, however, that the results obtained will depend on the algorithm that defines in advance what is scanned and how. One of the few historical texts, *Great Canadian Posters* (1979) by Canadian designer Theo Dimson,[6] employs a chronology that goes from the early days of colour lithography through to the early 1940s, but then jumps to the late 1960s. In other words, it skips twenty-five years, missing the 1950s completely. Dimson had great success as an illustrator of fantastic, lively fantasies in that decade, and his later work is associated with a highly recognizable, very sophisticated, neo-Art Deco style. It appears though that the style of the 1950s, which he did so much to define, was (at least when he wrote this book) no longer to his taste; he therefore scanned accordingly.

Throughout history, aesthetic judgements like these have often been used to erase not the detail of images (all scanning involves choices, sampling, lowering the resolution of the picture), but eliding entire parts of the image. A scan, however, bears a resemblance to the original only to the extent that it attempts to average across all of what is there. Scanning does not involve making judgements or digitizing only selected areas. In instances such as Dimson's book, when a designer's aesthetic and design thinking have been captured in print, the result tends to appear very conservative and selective. Possibly the clearest example of this is Canadian typographic writer Robert Bringhurst, whose book, *The Elements of Typographic Style* (2004; see Figure 2.8), speaks romantically of the deep roots of the dense forests of type and stresses many highly technical rules for the use of hanging punctuation, titling figures and so on.[7] In my experience, design students use this advice in the most enlightened way possible: not as the literal rule, nor even as a set of generally helpful guidelines, but as a manifesto of an individual's historically over-determined and highly specific taste.

In contrast to such highly selective, aesthetically based historical scans, there is a broader and more positive example of a selection process, the one that has been employed directly by designers themselves. When asked to be interviewed about their careers, designers all reach for their 'book', their portfolio of designs, a working tool carefully edited over time and containing largely those works that have been in exhibitions, won awards, drawn the most attention when shown to prospects, clients or other designers, or simply those that felt like the best and most sturdy examples over time. The time spent by individuals, working collectively in design firms or assembling personal slide libraries in design schools, refining and reconsidering the best (or most readily available) examples of the history, is in fact a large, highly diffuse and self-defining process on which to base the visual history of graphic design in Canada. This heteroglossia, or diverse set of practices, with its complex and multiple kinds of codes and purposes, is both more and less than a fixed language or grammar. It is more, in that it permits, stimulates or even requires a high level of creative originality from its practitioners; but it is also less, as it does not presume to contain any binding rules, or any notion of a "correct" grammar for visual images.

(For this reason, it is misleading to suppose that a "visual language," per se, exists at all.) Further, this diversity suggests that the visual culture of graphic design is, in practice, located too broadly for a focused, selective scan to capture. A broadly inclusive oral history project, therefore, seems the only way to record this work and map it into an accurate history.

These memories, narratives and, above all, self-curated professional collections of graphic design show that such a history can define and create itself (as it has) without having occurred in, and without having been directed from, any single place. The memories of designers in Canada have clearly been organized and shaped in comparison with a vast range of images and reproductions. The early efforts of art historians, beginning in the nineteenth century, focused on the identification and collection of the most important images, on the assumption that only specific standards of beauty merited display, in museums, as reproductions in books, or as slides in school libraries. Given the present rate of digitization of virtually every fragment of visual culture, however, the very success and scale of this enterprise creates new and different opportunities. Susan Buck-Morss discusses the potential of a visual memory

Figure 2.8 *The Elements of Typographic Style* (first edition) cover. © 1992. Designer: Robert Bringhurst. Publisher: Hartley and Marks Publishers.

that escapes local containment: Images are the archive of collective memory. The twentieth century distinguishes itself from all previous centuries because it has left a photographic trace. What is seen only once and recorded, can be perceived any time and by all. History becomes the shared singularity of an event. The complaint that images are taken out of context (cultural context, artistic intention, previous contexts of any sort) is not valid. To struggle to bind them again to their source is not only impossible (as it actually produces a new meaning); it is to miss what is powerful about them, their capacity to generate meaning, and not merely to transmit it.[8]

Precisely because it is not thus bound within national boundaries, nor to any single, dominant narrative or aesthetic, Canadian graphic design might be said to be a powerful generator of meaning and one which opens several questions about the very location of histories and meanings.

Memory and history

My intention in recording and teaching this history is to attempt to lengthen professional memories, beyond immediate experience of the contemporary environment and beyond individual preferences or available business records. Writing and lecturing about that history inevitably shapes memory; the production of new meaning alters existing meanings, changing their metaphorical valence or voltage. History changes how designers and students consider the past by getting beyond their pasts, and thus changes how they imagine their future. But memory, importantly, is not history; history must act as the collective reconsideration and reflection upon the written and remembered record. At a recent conference, "New Views: Repositioning Graphic Design History," at the London College of Communication, a number of participants very clearly asserted that memory and history were not identical; in the words of Judith Williamson, 'memory masquerades as history'.[9]

Others have written about this important distinction, notably Pierre Nora. In his studies of France's many *lieux de mémoire*, its realms or sites of memory, Nora examines the way that ideas and values adhere to things, both material and immaterial—locales, images, buildings, symbols and so on. His work analyses "the construction of representations,"[10] the richly symbolic stories that make up the imagined, remembered community of a place. This process comes about, he argues, because "there are no longer any . . . settings in which memory is a real part of everyday experience."[11] The loss of memory, of lived, daily ritual and continuous shared traditions unique to any single place, results in a mania for the past, for collecting and hoarding things, in an attempt to fill the void left by "churches, schools, families, governments [that] no longer transmit traditional values as they once did."[12]

Nevertheless, however important the study of such ideological sites—the Eiffel Tower, a painting by Delacroix, a tri-coloured flag—in suggesting that history is a pale substitute for living memory other, greater problems arise. Nora suggests a specific metaphor for memory: "memory is life, always embodied in living societies."[13] This is a dangerous choice of words, as though a national "body," or any body, were some natural, authentic or organic site for memories, or that memory might be outside history, prior to those social institutions or collections which only sever memory from its original, true site. (Anyway, do we want "traditional values" transmitted as they once were?) Tony Bennett suggests that "the opposition at work here is profoundly disabling."[14]

He argues instead that "all memory is necessarily archival and technical."[15] While carried in the body, it is nonetheless shaped and socially organized by the media, mechanics and technologies of memory in any given society (and the prevailing powers that employ them). This is not entirely a limitation or loss, either, for it is "only through their detachment from an immanent tradition that cultural artifacts can become the objects of self-conscious theoretical attention."[16]

For this reason, memory and history must be kept distinct. Yet, they need not be seen as strictly opposed; because they work to frame and shape each other, a collected, or contested, but above all public historical account should be seen as the realization of memory, generating common visible traces that in turn provide the armature for further remembering.

Graphic design history in Canada, in its oral, uncollected state, might be said to be apocryphal: not false, but not yet publicly captured or verifiable either, questionable or dubious, perhaps, but not simply wrong. Edward S. Casey distinguishes between kinds of human memory: individual memories (which may be unique, but not created in isolation from or with-out reference and responsibility to other kinds of memory); social memories (shared by a linked group, without necessarily having wide dissemination); collective memories (broadly shared by several individuals without any conscious link or proximate relationship) and public memories (which include all of the above in an active, open, shared and above all 'contested' resource).[17] In its unformed state, graphic design history in Canada leans rather more toward the former two than the latter pair. Only the last, public memory, by virtue of its openness, is capable of generating history. It will be through the creation and expansion of the public institutions and technologies of collection and history that designers' memories can be made public, placed within an historical narrative, theorized and kept "alive."

Given that a public sharing of memories is the key to establishing their historicity, there is also a body of collectively developed principles for assessing the historical truth of what oral historians record. Is a given statement valid, does it stand comparison with other known, external sources? Is a given source internally reliable, is it consistent with itself? Is the information verifiable, can it be authenticated or checked? Are the memories from direct, first-hand experience, or are they hearsay? Is the speaker generally of sound mind?[18]

Finally, though not least, what was the role of the interviewer in shaping the questions, as this inevitably introduces an entirely new set of variables? How have the questions been framed? (It is worth noting in this context that large corporate research firms, in addition to polls and surveys, have begun tracking the vast range of unasked opinion that mushrooms daily on the Web, in chat rooms and blogs, because "participants in discussion groups can say anything they like, whereas people answering a survey answer only the questions that researchers think to ask."[19]) Histories, unlike memories, must be open to the active cross-examination of all these issues. As Paul Thompson notes, one can ask a farmer "precisely how he handled his horses while ploughing, and it will be very, very rare for him to be wrong."[20] Professional details and specifics of the trade are not likely to be subject to intense scrutiny or hotly contested; what matters is the historical framework that emerges when writing oral memory into design history.

Of course, despite our best efforts to establish veracity, memories vary. The distinction between different kinds of memory is parsed out by Elizabeth Loftus in her essay "Tricked by Memory."[21] Semantic memory, for example is the recollection of specific details and factual information, such as times tables, and is generally more heavily reinforced and reliable. Episodic memory, by contrast, is the narrative flow of a life or career and, while also reinforced over time, tends to be altered or polished by repeated reflection, in consideration of an individual's changing needs and in light of later events. Different kinds of memory require different reconsideration. There is also the (mis)shaping of memory by the desire to write a certain kind of history. The story is often told of how the Canadian National railways (CN) logo, a totemic image in the Canadian modernist narrative, was drawn on a napkin in a moment of inspiration by Allan Fleming. Sketches in the National Library confirm another story: that the design involved many rough and intermediate sketches, by Fleming and others, in a process art directed by James Valkus, a designer brought in by CN from New York. Fleming played an important design role, but the napkin anecdote must finally be said to be folklore. As such it is, finally, not true; but the story can play more than a negative or obstructive role nonetheless. It is a perfect example of a *lieu de mémoire* in Nora's sense, and its mythical status usefully points to widely held ideas about design, throwing common beliefs—about the sanctity of the creative individual, or the highly personal nature of creativity—into sharp relief. In discussing the work of Fernand Braudel, Bill Schwarz notes that certain interior memories or narrative explanations might be studied in the same way as shamanism or mysticism: they might "become the object of history, but never the means by which history itself is explained."[22] The story of the CN logo-on-a-napkin tells us about how design sees its history, but does not tell us the history itself.

In "Believe it or Not: Rethinking the Historical Interpretation of Memory,"[23] Paul Thompson refers to collective memory as the means by which literate societies record, shape and reuse events (and non-events, such as Fleming's imagined moment of solo genius), and he equates this process to the oral traditions of non-literate societies. He defends oral history, arguing that memory is not simply shaped to serve the needs of the present (or by such needs in the past, whence memories come). Functional or instrumental distortions of memory can be overcome with sufficient application to detail, he argues. Memories play an important part in the construction of history, as remembered events and traditions do have genuine links to the past in ways that make them useful to the historical record. Thompson gives the example of apprentice bakers recounting years of hardship, while those who become masters tell of their wonderfully useful and productive training. This suggests that different accounts of history may come from the same general experience, depending on the outcome and the present perspective of the narrators, without either being false. History must capture both of these lived spaces.

Those graphic designers whose work is singled out by other designers in Canada for recognition and historical importance are, of course, the masters (both male and female) of their trade, and their narrative accounts will be similarly affected, whether denigrated or enhanced. Reading back against the grain of what is actually said, checking it against other sources, recognizing the subject position of the source, paying attention to specific factual details and getting beyond personal myth and received ideas are all essential to assembling such interviews and opinions into a more reliable historical record. Alex Callinicos describes history as "provid[ing] a framework within which [culture] can be understood, not as a free-floating process, but as the ways in which human beings located in contradictory relations of production seek to make sense of the world, and develop strategies for coping with, and sometimes for changing it."[24]

Issues in oral history

Oral history in design is motivated by different circumstances from those found in histories of folklore, which make up the majority of oral histories. Folklore is that set of common practices, everyday inform-ation and habit spread by informal communication, but which specifically excludes professional or mass-produced, popular cultures (and hence the study of design).[25] Design history is hardly a history of the illiterate or the oppressed, but of individuals highly literate in both verbal and visual means. Indeed, in some accounts of oral history, professional graphic design is counted among the enemy. If oral history is defined as a political tool that finds a voice for marginalized groups, "a tool for clarifying the past and reshaping the present,"[26] then design's easy proximity to mass media make it, to some, part of the problem. As Michael Riordan sees it, the battle to establish a dominant mode of vision is imbalanced: "in a media-soaked culture, they simply stupefy us."[27] So oral history, in its application to design, must take into account that its subject places it outside some of the most common purposes for which oral history is employed.

Nonetheless, there are also useful similarities among otherwise very different uses for oral history. In discussing *The Artists Behind the Work*, a Study of Four Alaskan Artists, William Schneider notes that "Native art has a social, ceremonial, and utilitarian role that is different from Western art,"[28] which is overly concerned with display and spectacle. He contrasts this with the practical, hands-on and every-day uses of Native Alaskan media such as masks, blankets and beadwork. Artists in small-scale communities display a continuing interest in such concerns as craft or manual skill, the use of objects as gifts and exchange or of such exchanges as markers of status and symbols of identity, and a pref-erence for group standards and collaborative assessment, rather than competition over individual creativity or innovation. Interestingly, Schneider might here be said to be inadvertently also describing many of the values retained in the practice of contemporary designers. The strong affinity of design with such visual cultures marks it as an applied, non-art, something to be used, in common, and through openly commodified exchanges of visual and material value. This description also captures how design, like the traditional arts of small-scale cultures, is best understood as positioned outside the dominant visual discourse, that of the fine arts.

Nonetheless, despite all similarities, it must be accepted that the scale and nature of modern mass media have changed the usual goals in the gathering and recording of oral traditions. The ethnography of Franz Boas, to take on originary example, was known for its extraordinary cultural relativism and inclusiveness and for breaking open the collecting habits of Western museums. Design studies research, on the contrary, can all too easily demonstrate an enormous visual variety. Variety is precisely what profes-sional marketing and communications demand, and the design field is indeed highly varied. Neither can design in any way be described as a "vanishing" culture, as has often been the case with anthropological studies. (The idea of small-scale cultures as "primitive" or in need of isolation or preservation has been strongly rejected in any event.[29]) Design history is, to borrow a term from Eric Hobsbawm and Terence Ranger, evidence of an invented tradition, one which claims a long and antique history (from cave walls and Mesopotamian markings to Renaissance Europe), but which is, instead, largely a relatively recent product of the industrial revolution, mass marketing and the enormous rise in technological scale of the last century and a half.[30] It does not fit neatly with the goals of even a progressive anthropology.

Because design is a profession, collecting such oral histories could perhaps best be described as "elite oral history," a category discussed by Eva M. McMahan.[31] She observes that such interviews are transactional, subject to the willful intent of both interviewer and subject. Political or cultural elites do command social position and power, such that they can create and foster 'a lore that justifies their attempts to control society'.[32] The elite subject cooperates in order to control interpretation. McMahan notes that interpretation is central to human existence; however, in the "new hermeneutics"[33] that she applies, neither the researcher nor the narrator controls the "real" meaning. The search is not for authorial intention as the final, correct interpretation: the researcher/author of the history and the narrator/author of the original designs probably have differing, even opposing, intentions in any event.

There are also important implications in the values inherent in designers' descriptions of their own work. Like an ethnographer's system of ethnopoetic notation, designers share a formal language to describe the visual: terms such as "freshness," for example, or "originality," which both mark the extraordinary importance of innovation in the design field. This loose verbal system makes frequent reference to shared markers, in particular the work of other well-known designers (many of whom are international, of course), and above all the single great reference point for the description of post-war design, the International Style, which still figures prominently even in the memories of those designers born long after its eclipse. Such terms and their transcription into history provide an opportunity to critically examine the normative biases built into language. For example, could post-war graphic design in Canada be usefully described and historicized without any reference to the "modern"?

Modernism has been seen as many things, of course: as the inevitable aesthetic response to capitalist modernity; as the best means of rebuilding a better, brighter, more functional world or as the nightmare of a technocratic and monolithic class culture imposed from above. Nonetheless, its primary use in contemporary visual cultural studies remains as a marker of historical originality and canonical importance. The most "advanced" work is assumed to be the most original and the most important. Interestingly though, the concepts of "modernism" and the term "modern" do not figure prominently, if at all, in the interviews I have conducted. This is not to say that we are lacking any consensus on who are the most important designers. The same local and Canadian names recur in designer's recorded narratives, within cities but also across the country. This has been confirmed to me by the steady repetition of particular names—"oh, have you interviewed . . .?"; "do you know the work of . . .?". It speaks to a continuing, immanent process of canon formation, one which is, crucially, more than the product of individual or centred, institutional judgements of taste or quality. The canon of Canadian design, in other words, is not bounded by any simple, clearly stated principle, such as "modernism," or its relative state of "advance." It would logically follow that we require a broad process of discovery to locate it.

There is, then, even within the limitations of memory and oral tradition, an extensive shared vocabulary and canonical consensus within the country about the main players in that history. This consensus is also shared to a remarkable degree between English-speaking Canada and the distinct national culture of Quebec. Such a broadly agreed, largely oral tradition also goes a considerable way towards establishing a history based on something more stable than aesthetic choices. It suggests a mutual assessment of importance based on many factors, a collective judgement or even just grudging acknowledgement that draws on more than visual standards of pleasure: knowledge of others' clientele, jobs and positions held; their role in educational or other institutions; those with whom they worked in the past; the success of their designs for their clients' purposes and so on. The history that emerges from the memories and oral accounts of Canadian designers itself suggests that design is inherently an important counterpart to the concerns and practices that have shaped visual collections and institutions to date. Because it forms the basis of cultural capital in the profession of design, and because it establishes and enforces actual markers of social position, identifying a visual canon is a necessity, one recognized and defended as such by Canadian designers, however unconsciously, in their verbal narratives.

The canonical visual record of modern design is often selected for its simplicity, or its disciplined control of typography, forms, shapes and images. Since the idea of the modern as simplicity[34] does not adequately cover our understanding of the present, it should be possible, in fact necessary, to write a history of design, post–1945, which does not use the terms "modernist" or "modernism," (As a term for the dominant social fact of our age, it cannot similarly dispense with "modernity.") It could simply be argued, however, that design history is made up of a succession of professionally selected, abstract visual devices, historically determined but with no particular logic of their own. It should be possible, in effect, to "sample" the field as the designers themselves have sampled it, as a heteroglossia, locating as significant those works that practitioners themselves have found significant for a variety of reasons. These will not be necessarily the most obviously avant-garde works, nor those that best represent the aesthetic of simplicity, difficulty or any other single visual value. Any canon does reduce the field, but it need not be filtered through any single aesthetic, nor even, in all cases, through the aesthetic per se, at all. The method of visual cultural studies, in design as in any visual production, must be to place aesthetic affinities in their context, not to exalt or isolate them (which is only to distort the aesthetic in any event). To do so, we must be "meticulously attentive to the local, the contingent, and the conjunctural."[35]

Conclusion

As a method of investigation, oral history attends quite closely to the local, even as it works to understand it in its increasingly global context. It reports on the judgements of interest and importance as formulated by a diverse and broad association of practitioners—in the case of design, by designers consciously sharing a tradition and a profession, often at a distance from each other, but living in the shared space of design, professionally linked across the borders of any one country. It is therefore necessary to use oral history to sample the visual field of design history as broadly as possible, to arrive at a widely inclusive and plural history. The assumption that extraordinary, difficult, avant-garde practices might be the only oppositional space in culture, powerful as it has been, remains a fantasy.[36]

In trying to locate Canadian graphic design, then, the process has necessitated a reconsideration of the methods of visual culture and some reflection on the location and meaning of memory and history. Understood for its apocryphal content, the stories told by designers are not necessarily always true (although most are), but they do yield evidence that points to important truths. The best means for the study of design is close attention to the forms it takes and the understandings of its practitioners, their arbitrary visual selections and their supporting myths. Such ideas are all evidence of design's usefulness, its location—even its absolute necessity—for the reproduction of capital in a world of images. In scanning across the surface of graphic design in Canada, we can get a picture, albeit in somewhat reduced resolution, of a space far larger than just design.

Notes

1. B. Donnelly, "Reading Kurschenska: On the Centres and Boundaries of Design History," unpublished paper delivered at the Universities Art Association of Canada annual conference, Montreal, October, 2001.
2. It should be noted that the province of Québec, with its distinct national history, has produced some important exceptions, in particular *L'Affiche au Québec*, Montréal, Les Éditions de l'Homme, 2001, and the section on graphic design in *Le design au Québec*, Montréal, Les Éditions de l'Homme, 2003, both by Marc H. Choko, director of the Centre de design at the Université du Québec à Montréal. Posters, in particular, have been covered; see R. Stacey, *The Canadian Poster Book: 100: Years of the Poster in Canada*, Methuen, Toronto, 1979. There have been a number of focused historical articles, which usefully go beyond posters (and beyond Québec), particularly in the journal *DA* (Devil's Artisan), the trade journal *Applied Arts and the Graphic Design Journal*, published by the Society of Graphic Designers of Canada.
3. Besides Innis's own late works on communication, notably *Empire and Communications* (1950), and *The Bias of Communication*, (1951), an excellent short introduction is provided in "The Communication Thought of Harold Adams Innis (1894–1952)," ch. 3 of R.E. Babe, *Canadian Communication Thought: Ten Foundational Writers*, University of Toronto Press, Toronto, 2000.
4. P. Meggs, *Meggs' History of Graphic Design*, 4th edn, Toronto: John Wiley & Sons, 2005.
5. Design Industry Advisory Committee, DIAC Design Industry Study, Toronto, 2004, www.dx.org/diac.html
6. T. Dimson, *Great Canadian Posters*, Toronto: Oxford University Press, 1979.
7. R. Bringhurst, *The Elements of Typographic Style*, 3rd edn., Point Roberts, WA: Hartley & Marks, 2004.
8. S. Buck-Morss, 'Visual Studies and Global Imagination', *Papers of Surrealism*, no. 2, Summer 2004, www.surrealismcentre.ac.uk/ publications/papers/journal2
9. Author's notes, from panel discussion on "Memory and History," including Anne Bush, Judith Williamson, Val Williams, and Kerry William-Purcell, Saturday, October 29, 2005.
10. P. Nora, *Realms of Memory*, Lawrence D. Kritzman (ed.), trans. Arthur Goldhammer, New York: Columbia University Press, 1996, p. xxi.
11. Ibid., p. 1.
12. Ibid., p. 2.
13. Ibid., p. 3.
14. T. Bennett, "Stored Virtue: Memory, the Body, and the Evolutionary Museum," in S. Radstone and K. Hodgkin (eds.), *Regimes of Memory*, New York: Routledge, 2003, p. 41.
15. Ibid., p. 52.
16. Ibid., p. 42.
17. E. Casey, "Public Memory in Place and Time," in K. Phillips (ed.), *Framing Public Memory*, Tuscaloosa: University of Alabama Press, 2004, pp. 17–44.
18. W. Schneider, . . . *So They Understand: Cultural Issues in Oral History*, Logan: Utah State University Press, 2002, p. 129.
19. Technology Quarterly (supplement) (2006), 'Listening to the Internet',*The Economist*, March 11, 2006, p. 8.
20. P. Thompson, *The Voice of the Past: Oral History*, 3rd edn., Oxford: Oxford University Press, 2000, p. 158.

21. E. Loftus, "Tricked by Memory," in J. Jeffrey and G. Edwall (eds), *Memory and History: Essays on Recalling and Interpreting Experience*, Lanham, MA: University Press of America, 1994, 17–32.

22. B. Schwarz, "'Already the Past': Memory and Historical Time," in S. Radstone, and K. Hodgkin, op. cit., p. 141. Schwarz notes that, for Braudel, memory was to be seen not only as distinct from history but also as its enemy.

23. P. Thompson, "Believe It or Not: Rethinking the Historical Interpretation of Memory," in J. Jeffrey and G. Edwall (eds), op. cit., pp. 1–16.

24. A. Callinicos, "Marxism and the Crisis of Social History," in J. Rees (ed.), *Essays on Historical Materialism*, London: Bookmarks, 1998, pp. 25–40.

25. M. C. Sims & M. Stephens, *Living Folklore*, Logan: Utah State University Press, 2005, pp. 1ff.

26. M. Riordan, *An Unauthorized Biography of the World: Oral History on the Front Lines*, Ontario: Between the Lines Press, 2004, p. 6.

27. Ibid., p. 2.

28. W. Schneider, 2002, op. cit., pp. 95ff.

29. See J. Clifford, T.M. Trinh, and V. Dominguez, "Of Other Peoples: Beyond the 'Salvage' Paradigm," in H. Foster (ed.), *Discussions in Contemporary Culture*, New York: Bay Press, 1987, pp. 121–50.

30. While their examples tend to the social, as, for example the British monarchy or Scottish tartans, it is a concept usefully applied to design. It might be especially useful in understanding what great significance is assumed to be attached to contemporary design by tracing its roots to the shapes of ancient alphabets and other pieces of distant or pre-modern history. See E. Hobsbawm and T. Ranger (eds.), *The Invention of Tradition*, Cambridge: Cambridge University Press, 1983.

31. E.M. McMahan, *Elite Oral History Discourse: A Study of Cooperation and Coherence*, Tuscaloosa: University of Alabama Press, 1989.

32. Ibid., p. xiv.

33. Ibid., p. 2.

34. This narrative has been recently and cogently summarized by Paul Greenhalgh in *The Modern Ideal: The Rise and Collapse of Idealism in the Visual Arts*, London: V&A Publications, 2005.

35. Ibid., p. 39.

36. This argument has recently been remade by Hal Foster, in *Design and Crime*, New York: Verso, 2002.

Chapter 2.2.4

French graphic design: a contradiction in terms?

Véronique Vienne

As someone only recently acquainted with the latest cultural intricacies of the old continent, I am still striving to evaluate the work of French graphic designers by my American standards. But it feels like trying to fit a square peg in a round hole. It cannot be done. In fact, I am beginning to wonder whether there is (or ever was) such a thing as French graphic design. I have come to the conclusion that "French" and "graphic design" are two mutually exclusive propositions.

Let's face it, the French have never truly embraced graphic functionality. Historical circumstances having to do with the Catholic Church's censorship of books during the Counter-Reformation have flattered the French's preference for pictorial expression. The reason French graphic designers are unable to gain international recognition is systemic. To this day, before you can be admitted into most graphic design programs in the best French art schools, you have to learn to draw. If you cannot render a pretty good likeness of the Venus de Milo, you need not bother.

Don't get me wrong: I am not a harsh critic of French design, far from it. I often feel like Miss Conviviality compared with my blasé and disgruntled French colleagues. Last May, at the 20th edition of the International Poster and Graphic Design Festival of Chaumont—a venue for a yearly ritual that brings together students and professionals from France, Holland, Germany, Italy and Spain for a weekend of show and tell—I was the only person walking around with a big grin on her face. The reason for the knitted brows, I found out later, was the perception that the main event, a grand retrospective of the last 20 years of French poster design, looked paltry compared with a concurrent show of more than 100 contestants from all over the world. French graphic design, it turns out, is so unlike any other that it almost does not make sense when viewed in a competitive environment.

I would like to argue that what I saw there was evidence that French graphic design is not behind, but on the contrary ahead of its game. Its pictorial approach, far from looking quaint, is exhilarating. Its imagery, for the most part, steers clear of clichés. Its creativity is not dampened by commercialism. But there is more: What became obvious to me at the Chaumont retrospective is that French designers seemed more interested in telling visual stories than conveying coded messages. Across the board,

First published in *AIGA Voice*, July 7, 2009. © Véronique Vienne.

they showed the greatest disregard for the sacrosanct Conceptual Image. To this popular, tried-and-true design solution, they seemed to prefer the flourishes of a narrative style.

To replace conceptual images, French graphistes are proposing compositions that subvert the now-universal (and safe) graphic language of codes and tropes. They take chances with unconventional imagery in an attempt to provoke an emotional release, a gut-level reaction, something not unlike a *coup de cœur*. Selected for the Chaumont retrospective were numerous examples of what is sometimes called "French organicity." For a 2004 poster for an independent film about Los Angeles, the celebrated M/M duo—Michael Amzalag and Mathias Augustyniak—created a brilliant typographical staccato of diffracting images set against a mundane LA streetscape. For a 2005 self-generated project, Christophe Jacquet, alias Toffe, compared digital bits to sardines—yes, sardines—building around the slimy imagery a complex visual discourse à la Baudrillard (see Figure 2.9).

But what really got many Chaumont festival attendants upset was a strikingly beautiful poster by Mathias Schweizer. Looking at first glance like a personal project, the poster, representing a majestic waterfall as seen from the entrance of a cave, made a strong reference to Marcel Duchamp's famous installation *La chute d'eau* (The Waterfall). However, unlike other similar experimental work by designers-as-authors, the image did not include any typographical element. "If only there had been a logo for an electrical company on it, you could have called it 'graphic design,'" remarked a flustered visitor, "but this is an exercise in self-indulgence. It doesn't belong in this retrospective." People were shaking their heads. What is the matter with French graphic designers? Don't they know their place? Aren't they supposed to communicate?

If indeed all it took was a logo in the corner of a painting to turn it into a legitimate graphic artifact, we could all be rich and famous. Schweizer, it turned out, is not rich, but he is famous for his iconoclastic yet effective design solutions. His waterfall poster was not a *caprice d'artiste*. It was an assignment to promote a contemporary art show called Le travail de rivière (River Work), a collection of odd pieces on the theme of the excavation of memories. It did function as a regular poster does, its haunting evocation of raging water jumping over rocks arousing people's curiosity and drawing them to the event. Like the river itself, one had to do a little digging around to find out what the image was all about. Eventually, a week or so before the opening, the same posters, but with pertinent information overprinted, were seen around town. The campaign had done more than just announce the exhibition, it had conspired with it.

Far from being anti-functional, graphic designers in France are embracing a much larger functionality. Schweizer and his contemporaries see the role of graphic design as "branding" ideas (though they would never, ever use this crass term to describe what they do!). A likeminded fellow designer is Vincent Perrottet, who works in collaboration with Anette Lenz to develop the graphic identity of a number of small theatrical companies located in provincial towns. Together they've come up with a series of upbeat poster campaigns that reaffirm, season after season, the personality of the various theaters. But just as critical for them is the emotional connection these posters create with the public. Their visual appeal, their inventiveness, their complexity even are qualities that serve to establish an ongoing dialogue with the various communities whose members, for the most part, would rather go to a soccer game than attend an avant-garde play. Whether abstract compositions, photomontages or graphic puzzles, the posters perform in their environment as signs—as signs of intelligent life on earth. Their goal is not to sell seats but win minds.

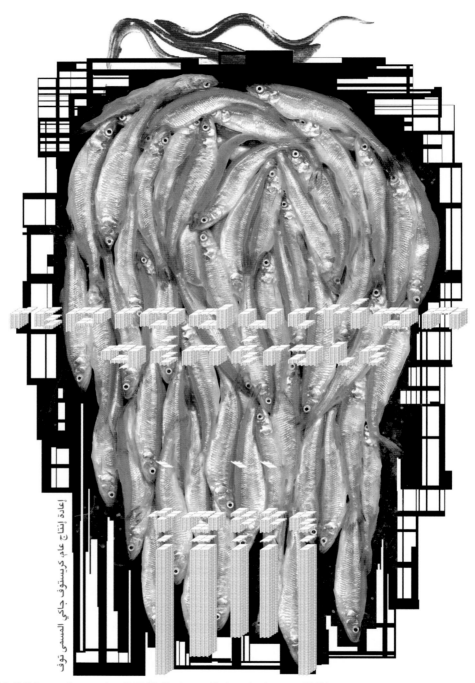

Figure 2.9 Toffe's sardine poster. © 2005. Designer: Christophe Jacquet (Toffe).

French designers are known to argue with their clients to redefine objectives to include not only the more lofty values of the institutions they serve, but the best interest of the public as well. It's an uphill battle as clients, even those in the cultural field, are under increasing pressure from the market economy to focus on short-term growth. "But working in graphic design means taking a stand," write Pierre Bernard in the introduction to the Chaumont catalogue. "Graphic design is the opposite of media communication," he insists. Alex Jordan, who, with Bernard and Perrottet, is one of the leading instigators of the festival, concurs: "A mark on a piece of paper is never benign nor innocuous." In theory, one can only applaud their attitude, but "how come, after 20 years of fighting to be heard, there is no evidence that we are making any sense other than to ourselves?" asks Perrottet.

They are making sense to me. But then again, my endorsement of their fine ideals might be a warning sign that I am about to go native. Next thing you know, I'll be writing paragraph-long sentences.

Chapter 2.2.5

The importance of the Dutch football club Ajax and Total Football (*totaalvoetbal*) to the sport of graphic design

Elliott Earls

Give me your tired, your poor

Your huddled masses yearning to breathe free

Precariously situated between commerce, art and communication technology, graphic design[1] as a practice has the potential to be one of the most commanding forms of cultural engagement. Graphic design as a practice should be refocused to serve as a powerful form of Nietzschean Hammer, testing our culture for the hollow ring of false idols.[2] And yet like a methane-bloated raccoon corpse precariously buoyant in the summer sun, the culture of graphic design needs to be poked with a stick so that from its fecund corpse a thousand flowers may bloom. Sixty some odd years of formalized graphic design education has produced a highly commercialized field with deep links into the flaming soul of capitalism, but has failed to yield a substantive critical culture, nor yield a significant body of work outside of overt commercial concerns.

In Ovid's *Metamorphoses,* Daedalus the father of Icarus was a cunning craftsman and artisan who designed the labyrinth which was used to imprison the gruesome Minotaur. And because Daedalus constructed the labyrinth so cunningly that none but he could escape, Daedalus and his son Icarus were locked in a tower in order to prevent this knowledge from spreading. Daedalus, the cunning craftsman, fashions two pairs of wings in order to escape their tower prison. In preparation for flight Daedalus warns Icarus to fly neither too high near the sun, nor too low near the sea because of the attendant dangers.

As we know, Icarus did not heed his father's warning, flew too high and drowned in the sea. Often this allegory focuses on Icarus and is used to illustrate the dangers of overreaching, as in the nature of this essay. But more importantly and often overlooked in this story is the simple fact that unlike Icarus, a grieving and overwrought Daedalus gained his freedom by arriving safely at his destination. One of the many allegorical points of this story being that Daedalus, through the strength of his will, depth of his intellect

First published in *Graphic Design Worlds/Words*, ed. Giorgio Camuffo, Milan: Mondadori Electa (2001), 172–85. © Elliott Earls.

and Its Significance: An Anthology of Aesthetic Theory edited by Stephen David Ross is a collection of writings dealing with aesthetic theory from Plato through Sol LeWitt.[8] Clearly if it is possible to excerpt and provide an overview of this discourse in a 500-page book, it is more than possible to deal with this subject matter in a comprehensive and rigorous manner over a four-year period.

The third primary component of this undergraduate education would be discussion groups to make tangible the connection between the philosophical component and the formal component of the education. These loosely structured discussions would track the development in the studio and in the reading, and would attempt to drive home the correlation between form and content, between Aesthetics and form. This would be set up in order to mercilessly ensure that intellectual connections are drawn between the current material under discussion in the Aesthetics component and the work being done in the Form component. Undergraduate education should be a studio-based experience broken into three core elements: the Fundamentals of Form, the Fundamentals of Aesthetics, and the connection between the two. On a more detailed level, the Fundamentals of Form and Aesthetics should be focused as follows:

1. The Fundamentals of Form:

    i.   Drawing

    ii.   2D design

    iii.   3D design

    iv.   4D design (motion)

    v.   Photography

    vi.   Software instruction

    vii.   Typography and layout

2. The Fundamentals of Aesthetics:

    i.   A historical survey of Aesthetics and the tangible relationship to Form

    ii.   Art history

    iii.   Design history

The goal behind undergraduate education in graphic design should be to produce a Total Footballer. In order to achieve this, a student absolutely must posses the ability to produce compelling form nearly at will. The "formal monster" quickly becomes the sophisticated designer once that ability to make form is brought under the control of the intellect. This is the job behind the philosophical component to the education.

With this as a foundation, graduate education in graphic design would then be free of remedial bullshit. Foundation studies are so named because one is laying the foundation for future work. All too often post-graduate education cannot contend with the real issues that it should be contending with because it is forced to deal with remedial issues. In far too many instances re-training the graphic designer supplants the heavy lifting that should be taking place. De-training, un-training and counter-training should be the real goal of graduate school, but this is only possible if the necessary groundwork has been laid. One cannot forget what one never knew.[9]

The single most important activity in graduate school should be critique. Unfortunately the manner in which critique is practiced in the vast majority of design schools does little to actually aid the student. As a matter of fact the "defensive model" of design school critique represents the single biggest impediment to the effective education of the designer.

As a kind of schematic,[10] the typical design school critique is based upon the primacy of the thesis. In other words nearly all design critiques involve placing a student in a defensive posture in relationship to the work shown and to their "idea." Typically a student will present his/her work and then be asked a series of questions by the instructor and by their fellow students. The unstated goal (the *a priori*) of the critique is to suss out logical inconsistencies between what the student says is his "idea" and the work presented. Both the instructor and the students' peers are looking for logical inconsistencies in the "idea" (as communicated by the one showing work) and between the idea and the actual work. Like this, "could you discuss this red horse that I see here in your design?" The student then responds with something like this: "As you know my piece deals with domestic violence, and the red horse here is meant to represent man's Id, his basic desires and drives." In this scenario if the instructor finds that the student's answer makes sense, based upon what the instructor knows about Freud, the Id and horses then the item can "stay" in the design. If on the other hand the instructor thinks the answer makes no sense, then the student must remove the item from the composition in order for conceptual harmony to be restored. Critique needs to be refocused around an interpretative critique methodology that focuses on close reading the object. Critique within design school should be focused on the power trio of interpretation, theorization and assessment.

In brief, the problems with this begin with the simple fact that in this method the actual work as an object is sublimated in deference to the work maker's language. In this form of critique, the critique is actually dealing with what is being communicated verbally. It is not primarily looking at the work, and attempting to understand it as a discreet object. Further, in this form of critique the logical consistency of the "idea" becomes the litmus test for the work, not the logical consistency of the object (the work). Often powerful work establishes an internal logic structure that may not conform to linguistic logic. The illogical possibilities of the visual realm are its own form of logic. The third major problem in this form of critique is the simple fact that it forces a kind of reductionist simplicity as a conceptual through line for the work. Because the student is always forced to defend the work, the work out of necessity becomes simplistic, logically bound and linguistically driven.

A simple prescription for the restructuring of critique around an interpretative methodology:

1. The goal of critique is to call the work into crisis, and is based upon the principle that all work can be called into crisis.

2. The maker of the work does not speak about the work.

    a.   The work speaks for itself.

    b.   Questions are not directed at the maker.

3. Work must be completed at least 48 hours prior to critique.

4. A peer is required to write a comprehensive criticism of the work focused on Morris Weitz categories prior to critique.

5. The written critique must attempt to call the work into crisis from multiple theoretical vantage points.

6. The written criticism is read to begin the critique.

7. A free ranging conversation follows which attempts to understand what the work is actually "about," following from the principle that all work has an "aboutness," it is the residue of human labor and unlike a rock or tree, it is "about" something.

8. The internal fault lines of any given work are exposed and broken apart.

9. The work maker reads a prepared statement at the end of critique addressing salient issues.

Graphic design as a practice will finally be invested with its full measure of power when its culture is able to incorporate and sustain a number of characteristics. It must be able to sustain and nurture a rich critical discourse focused on the products of graphic design. The criticism produced concerning these products must be interpretative in nature, not simply limited to description, and evaluation. Those products as a whole must transcend the simple transubstantiation of corporate values into visual form. Its practitioners must come to an understanding that instrumentalist work decoupled from positive social ramifications is nothing more than base consumerism. Further the field must be flexible enough to incorporate hybrid forms of work that are largely based upon graphic design principles, history and methodology but eschew traditional designer–client relationships.

Without the institutional incorporation of these forms, graphic design ends up marginalizing its most powerful form of cultural output. Hybrid forms of work which rely heavily on graphic design methodology, history and training need to be fully embraced by the field. The many possible histories of graphic design include powerful figures like John Heartfield, El Lissitzky and Kurt Schwitters. And while the field as a whole during the education of the graphic designer, seems to acknowledge a deep debt to this kind of work, contemporary examples are not simply missing but almost tacitly forbidden. (Evidence for this supposition resides in the ridiculously vacuous nature of the fields' professional awards.) And here in a nutshell is both the problem and the promise of graphic design as a contemporary practice.

Historically the most powerful articulations of graphic design as a cultural practice have been pushed to the margins or assimilated by other disciplines. John Heartfield, possibly the single most important graphic designer in history, is a marginal figure at best within graphic design and is a far more important figure within the "Art" world. Contrast Heartfield's cultural profile and "importance" within contemporary graphic design with that of Paul Rand and it becomes clear that commerce trumps humanities.

There is no immutable law that states that in the great panoply of important dead men, Paul Rand must be lionized before John Heartfield. Maybe if we specifically did the opposite—that is if we recognized and embraced the contribution of designers like Heartfield—the field would strive to cultivate this kind of work.

Notes

1. The discipline to which I refer is variously called graphic design, visual communication or communication design. For the sake of simplicity hereafter it will simply be called "graphic design."

2. "Refocused?" In 1935 the German proto-graphic designer John Heartfield produced *Hurrah, die Butter ist Alle!* (Hurray, the Butter is Gone!) which directly challenged Adolph Hitler and the unchecked rise of German

nationalism. It is perhaps a specious claim to suggest that the cycloptical eye of graphic design was ever truly focused on John Heartfield. But the "refocusing" also implies a turning away from its current focus.

3. M. Weitz, *Hamlet and the Philosophy of Literary Criticism,* Chicago: University of Chicago Press, 1964.

4. The dangerous naiveté of this argument is not what it may seem. The various histories of graphic design are replete with examples of designers, educators and design writers being very much aware of the most sophist-icated linguistic and communication theories. And not only being aware, but monkeying with the notion of the designers' agency within this equation. Historically schools like Cranbrook Academy of Art and Cal Arts, and magazines like *Emigre* have all played important roles in foregrounding these issues. Further, they have played a critical role in de-educating and re-educating the designer with regard to these issues. And that may be the point. When we essentialize, when we attempt to understand what lies at the core of graphic design by examin-ing the structural relationships within our culture, what are we left with? In other words by getting "real" for a moment and taking a hard look at what the vast majority of graphic designers do on a day to day basis, we can finally glimpse behind the veil and understand its *raison d'être*. In this light we can see that the postmodern agency of the designer within the communication equation is not so much a sham but rather a simple fact that has been thoroughly co-opted by corporate consumerist agendas. As a simple example I refer you to Sony's botched 2005 guerilla marketing campaign for the PSP game system where Sony hired graffiti artists in major cities to spray paint totemic images of kids playing with the unit. This campaign was widely derided as an attempt to buy the street credibility. Further we can understand the historical role of Cranbrook Academy of Art, Cal Arts, *Emigre* magazine, and a number of the writers and educators associated with these institutions as renegade de-educators and de-programmers. By their very existence they in fact "prove" (test) the rule.

5. Determining causality within any complex system is extremely difficult if not practically impossible, but this does not mean that one should not try. In fact attempting to come to a deeper understanding of the possible ramific-ations of one's actions is nearly a pre-requisite for self-actualization.

6. The most direct way to attempt to destroy the merits of this entire argument is to simply perform a kind of regres-sion analysis. Regression analysis in philosophy "is understood by the critical realist explication as a *post hoc* attempt to identify a restricted closed system." In other words, the merit of this entire essay swings on an attempt to delineate the field of graphic design in a certain way, to essentialize it. So an opponent to this essay would simply say: "You have defined a closed system. Your definition is too narrow. Your argument fails because you have excluded the diversity of approaches to graphic design education and you have excluded the infinite professional possibilities for the practicing designer." But what I am really doing here is asking, "What kind of concept is graphic design?" and this essay attempts to characterize that concepts' problems, promise and remedies.

7. J. Ladefoged, "How a Soccer Star is Made," in *The New York Times,* June 6, 2010, http://www.nytimes.com/201%6/06/magazine/06Soccer-t.html?pagewanted=all.

8. State University of Binghamton (NY): New York Press, 1984.

9. Forgetting is quite possibly one of the most important skills that an artist, designer or craftsman must learn. Knowledge, craft and technique once fully assimilated must become automatic and must be forgotten.

10. This entire essay is an attempt to create a kind of conceptual map. This map is a schematic representation of an actual territory: design and art school. Out of necessity in this process of mapping certain details and territories are left out. The goal is not to faithfully recreate the actual terrain, but to simplify and produce a productive schema. This again speaks to both the nature of maps, and regression analysis. I am not suggesting that there are not a number of different critique methodologies in place in design school. I am suggesting that there are certain commonalities that permeate design (and art school education), and the goal is to think critically about them.

Chapter 2.2.6

Graphic design: fine art or social science?

Jorge Frascara

Toward a theoretical backbone for graphic design

Graphic design has existed long enough for its role in society to be easily understood. However, unlike architecture, literature, or the fine arts, it has developed without much theoretical reflection. It has evolved into a sophisticated practice in a piecemeal fashion, with scattered efforts aimed at the development of subareas, such as posters or books, but without either the critical apparatus in literature or the discussion present in architecture.

The aspect of graphic design that has attracted some discussion is visual style. But this discussion of style has several flaws:

- It overemphasizes the importance of the visual structure within an esthetic context.

- It omits problems of appropriateness.

- It leaves out certain areas of graphic design, such as signage, forms, timetables, maps, and educational material.

- It omits the importance of ideas in the communication process, not distinguishing between visual creation and visual manipulation.

- It avoids problems of performance related to visual perception.

- It omits problems related to the impact that graphic communication has on the public's attitudes and ideas.

These flaws have led to several distortions, the most important brought about by the praise of modern avant-garde typography. How long will the praise of El Lissitzky continue? True, he made a strong impact on a few typographic designers whose work in graphic design was closely related to the practice of art and looked very similar to their paintings or the paintings of avant-garde artists of the time. However, was Lissitzky's contribution really positive? His visual language was tremendously abstract,

First published in *Design Issues,* 5 (1) (Fall 1988): 18–29. © MIT/Jorge Frascara.

as inappropriate to mass communication as Schwitters's graphics using Pelikan ink motives were inappropriate for the product. Pelikan ink, used for line drawing and calligraphy, was presented surrounded by geometric typography, black and red bars, and rectangles. Not only did that imagery not express the product, but it did not even relate to the logo or the label. Why did Schwitters's designs include Pelikan ink bottles when the designs really related to constructivism, not to Pelikan?

Lissitzky was interested in improving communication, as his writing shows. This article, however, questions the apparent success of his works reproduced in design history books. He and other avant-garde artists made a major impact in the visual development of graphic design, but they also raised the importance of their esthetic approach to a point where the communication link with the common denominator they were addressing broke down. They seem not to have been aware that communication requires the sharing of codes. Although designers need not rely totally on the stereotypes, they cannot disregard the codes of the public; they should work with the public and improve its visual and conceptual language as much as possible, without breaking the communication link.

Lissitzky worked on a wide range of projects, some of them possibly less flashy and more useful than others, but the Lissitzky worshiped by many contemporary designers and design historians is the person who produced the quasi-abstract, constructivist, red and black pieces.

Although the quality of Lissitzky's, Schwitters's, and van Doesburg's designs in their own exhibitions, ideas, and publications can be praised, the fact that they failed to realize that their visual language was not appropriate in all possible cases must be acknowledged. The same is applicable to other artists who did some graphic design. Joan Miro was perfectly skillful in the promotion of his own exhibition, but Albers's promotion for a Lincoln Center Film Festival says a lot about Albers and little, if anything, about a film festival.

The excessive importance given to the avant-garde movement in the context of graphic design history is based on the failure of theory to recognize graphic design as something other than an art form. Furthermore, as an art form, graphic design is viewed only from an esthetic perspective, without enough consideration of communication and social significance. Surely, esthetics is important, but it is by no means the sole measure for quality.

Discussion should start with a working definition. Graphic design is the activity that organizes visual communication in society. It is concerned with the efficiency of communication, the technology used for its implementation, and the social impact it effects, in other words, with social responsibility. The need for communicative efficiency is a response to the main reason for the existence of any piece of graphic design: someone has something to communicate to someone else. This involves, to a greater or lesser extent, a perceptual and a behavioral concern.

The perceptual concern involves visual detection problems sometimes and communication problems all the time. Problems of detection and communication include visibility, legibility, and esthetics. The behavioral concern has to do with the way graphic communications affect the attitudes and conduct of their audiences. Advertising design is expected to make people buy products or services; political or ideological propaganda is expected to affect people's beliefs and actions; regulatory signs on highways are intended to organize the flow of traffic; teaching aids are supposed to improve learning performance; bank notes are designed to make forgery difficult and identification of one denomination from another easy. This is the real measure of the performance of any and every piece of graphic design

ABCDEFGHIJKLMNOPQRSTUVWXYZ
Abcdefghijklmnopqrstuvwxyz
&£1234567890.,;:-!?' ""/()

Figure 2.10 Railway type (1916). A no-nonsense typography for signage. A step ahead in communication at a time when ornament and self-expression were the common alternatives. Designer: Edward Johnston. Sourced from the International Typeface Corporation.

and the proof that graphic design cannot be understood in isolation but only within a communication system.

Social responsibility in graphic design is the concern for the following:

- The impact that all visual communication has in the community and the way in which its content influences people.

- The impact that all visual communication has in the visual environment.

- The need to ensure that communications related to the safety of the community are properly implemented.

This brief summary shows that the practice of graphic design transcends the realm of esthetics. Pursuing the identification of the pioneers of graphic design in this context and seeing in what way El Lissitzky compares to Edward Johnston (Figure 2.10) or to Jan Tschichold is therefore worthwhile. Interesting results might also be derived from comparisons between the contributions of Armin Hofmann and Giovanni Pintori when the focus of attention moves from a specific esthetic conception to communication efficiency. Although Hofmann created a beautiful style, Pintori had a greater flexibility and a better understanding of the importance of appropriateness and created a feeling for Olivetti that still existed after 30 years (Figure 2.11).

Although the concepts of communication and technological efficiency are common denominators for all areas of graphic design, several internal differences, depending on the subarea, need developing. The things graphic designers should know to promote the sale of cookies are very different from those they need to know to teach a five-year-old how to read. Every time a graphic designer really wishes to achieve the objectives of the communication proposed, the cross-disciplinary nature of the profession becomes apparent.

Graphic designers are always in need of active dialogue with their clients and with other professionals—be it with an editor, a manager, a marketing expert, or an educator—to really make the best of their practice. This certainly has important implications in relation to the evaluation of graphic design quality and to the education of graphic designers.

The problem of quality in graphic design

Further to the working definition of graphic design advanced above, a definition for quality in graphic design is also necessary: Quality in graphic design is measured by the changes it produces in the audience. The movement away from esthetics and stylistic innovation as determinants of quality started when investigations related to perceptual psychology, particularly the Gestalt school, provided some theoretical concepts for visual fundamentals courses in art schools. These concepts replaced intuitive

Figure 2.11 Poster for Olivetti Diaspron 82 typewriter (1958). Technological precision and modern elegance in the development of a successful corporate identity. © 1958. Designer: Giovanni Pintori. Courtesy of Associazone Archivio Storico Olivetti, Ivera, Italy.

rules for what was called composition. This involved a rationalization of part of the design process and was parallel to developments in the study of legibility. The studies in legibility were the expression of an interest that went beyond the esthetic structure of the visual field and stepped into a concern for communication efficiency.

This concern represented a new factor in the measurement of quality in design. The 1950s and 1960s saw a growing interest in communication throughout the field. The works of Paul Rand and Josef Müller-Brockman are two different expressions of this concern. Research on labeling of equipment, instruction strategies, and information panels, developed by the United States armed forces since World War II introduced a concern for communication efficiency simultaneous with the development of information theory, communication theory, and semiotics. Signs became signage systems and logos became corporate identities. Buildings, fashion, and life-styles started to be analysed in communication terms. In addition, the receivers of graphic design messages were then discovered as an active part of the communication process. However, these receivers initially were perceived basically as decoders.

The objective of graphic designers was to produce clear communications. Only designers in the advertising business were concerned with other elements in the performance of their designs: namely, sales. At least as far back as the 1950s, it became clear that clients' accounts depended on clients' success and that advertising design was a contributing factor to the success of a business. The concern for sales and persuasion in the advertising field led to the constitution of multidisciplinary teams of managers, writers, sociologists, psychologists, and designers who contributed to the establishment of marketing as an indispensable component of the advertising field.

Although understanding the importance of changes in public attitudes as a consequence of design has so far been limited to advertising, a closer look at the whole field of graphic design might suggest that specific changes in attitudes and behaviour are, indeed, the final aim of graphic design in most areas. It has been said many times that the designer is a problem solver of visual communications and of clients' needs. But the solution to a client's need is not the production of the visual communication; it is the modification of people's attitudes or abilities in one way or another. This modification can be a change, as in switching from one product to another or in quitting smoking; a reinforcement, as in the case of exercising more, giving more money to charities, or drinking more milk; or a facilitation, as in the case of reducing the complexity of reading, operating a machine, or orienting oneself in a new place.

The quality of the designs produced in relation to the above examples will be determined by the number of people who switch to the desired product, who quit smoking, and so forth. Clarity and beauty do not necessarily determine objective achievement, whereas they usually contribute to success. If graphic designers wish to be recognized as problem solvers, it is indispensable that they concern themselves with the results of their work measured by achievement of the objectives that generated the need for the production of the visual communication in question.

I am not advocating the demise of esthetics. Esthetic appropriateness and quality are certainly of high importance, both as factors that affect performance and as responsibilities designers have to the community. My proposition is to place the concept of quality in context and to establish its relativity, as well as to clarify that the esthetic quality of a design does not determine its overall quality.

This thesis has wide implications both in terms of the practice of the profession and of education for it. In the case of practice, specialists other than graphic designers are required to interpret public responses, to evaluate design performance, and to advise regarding appropriate modification of the communication strategies when better results are desired. The experts required for this task may vary from one professional area to another, but, in general, they should presumably come from the fields of marketing, sociology, psychology, and education, disciplines whose main concerns are the behavior of individuals and groups, and the problems of interpreting, quantifying, and qualifying information, as well as to a greater or a lesser extent, applying the information to practical ends.

The implications for graphic design education are just as obvious: the traditional art school cannot provide a full answer. Obviously, the thesis here contends that the designer's job is not finished when the design is produced and delivered, but that evaluation must be an integral part of the design process. In a safety symbols project, for example, the design problem is not the production of symbols but the development of an effective communication strategy for the prevention of accidents. It is not enough for the symbols to be beautiful, clear, and visible; these are useful factors, but the real measure of the quality of the design lies in its contribution to the reduction of accidents.

At best, these considerations will make the evaluation of design quality clearer and will better equip designers to contribute more efficiently to the solution of clients' problems. And not just communication problems, because as already indicated, the final objective of every communication design is some kind of behavioral change in a target population that occurs after the communication has taken place.

The education of graphic designers

A basic duality of graphic design becomes apparent when the formation of practitioners is considered: what skills do they need to develop? Graphic design is both a rational and an artistic activity. The decision-making process in graphic design alternates between the consideration of objective information and intuitive leaps. The goal of practitioners should be to base their decisions as much as possible on objective information, but the nature of the field always requires a certain degree of artistic intuition, that is, of decisions made by designers on the basis of experience that is difficult to quantify or explain rationally. (Graphic design in this case is comparable to marketing or psychoanalysis. All are activities in which a body of knowledge has to be applied to specific situations that relate to human behavior.)

The balance between artistic and rational elements in the practice of graphic design poses an interesting challenge to design educators, a challenge that calls for the development of visual sophistication and intuitive abilities to express concepts visually, along with a rational capacity for processes of analysis and synthesis. In addition, graphic designers need skills to listen and interpret the needs and concepts of people in other fields and enough flexibility of mind and visual resources to produce efficient communications.

No school could attempt to deal with all of these requirements in every area of professional practice. Advertising, information, illustration, editorial, signage, and education design are areas that demand different backgrounds, training, and aptitudes and require both specialized instructors and motivated students for each. Reducing the scope of a program to include only some of the professional areas would be admissible. A school might choose not to deal with three-dimensional design, that is, packaging, signage, and exhibitions; another might concentrate on advertising, which might be excluded by still another.

Whereas, making the above choices would be desirable, removing any of the concerns that should be present in all graphic design work would not be advisable. The teaching should represent all levels of the activity, that is, the emotional and the rational, the communicative, the technological, and the awareness of the social context. In most cases, emphasis has been placed on the visual aspect in education. There has also been a focus on education as a process of transmission of information and the development of personal skills and style. This trend has led to a reduction of the concerns appropriate to graphic design.

In this context, an important distinction can be made between undergraduate and graduate education in graphic design. Undergraduate education must be centered on developing individual student's skills; graduate education should do the same at a higher and more conceptual level, while also contributing to the advancement of knowledge in the field.

Research and advancement of knowledge in graphic design require the support of senior educational institutions. Professional practice does not usually allow for research time, and, when research is developed, practitioners do not share information with others. Market research in advertising is very common, but it is case specific and difficult to apply to different situations. Perception psychologists develop basic and applied research of wider application, but many times psychological research is so removed from reality that placing its results in applied contexts requires additional research efforts.

I am not supporting the idea that universities should directly serve industry, but that those interested in the advancement of knowledge cannot expect from industry inquiries other than those connected to its immediate benefit. It therefore follows that visual communication problems that relate to noncommercial human needs have only the university as a resource for developing solutions. There is a need to work on several fronts:

- Reference centers where existing information can be stored and retrieved should be developed.
- More information should be generated through two kinds of research activities: experimental, and critical discussion of both present and past work.
- Communication networks should be developed among researchers, leading, at best, to coordinating efforts and, at worst, to avoiding duplication.

Graduate programs in graphic design should either work along the preceding lines or generate design solutions for specific projects that clearly surpass the usual level of quality in the professional field and that become models of excellence for practicing graphic design. This practical work however, should be developed hand in hand with a sound, theoretical analysis of design solutions.

Although due regard should be paid to visual sophistication, and although design solutions cannot be based solely on the rational organization of objective information, the profession needs to move away from being a purely artistic endeavor toward becoming one in which visual solutions are based as much as possible on explicable decision processes.

In order to direct graduate graphic design studies toward the development of new knowledge, educators should conceive them as qualitatively different from undergraduate studies and not as mere continuation, whatever the increased degree of complexity and ambition might be. In undergraduate studies, the teachers instruct and create learning situations that help students make discoveries and develop their skills, but those discoveries and that development do not necessarily expand either the knowledge of the instructors or the advancement of the profession as a whole. Students can make new, surprising, and exciting syntheses, and teaching at the undergraduate level is therefore not necessarily repetitious, but the central task is the learning process of the students who require some years before they can make significant contributions to the profession. Nevertheless, undergraduate studies should not be seen as a mere preparation for integration into industry; in other words, undergraduate studies should not be merely job training, nor is it possible to believe that four years is all that is needed for a professional education. Undergraduate programs should aim at graduating persons who are ready to begin a professional career and whose conceptual preparation will allow them to progress rapidly and to enrich the practice of the profession.

Developing an awareness of the essential problems of graphic design in undergraduates is important. Graphic design is first and foremost human communication. A graphic designer is a person who constructs a pattern in order to organize the communication link between the piece of design and the viewer. In most cases, graphic designs are meant to be seen or read. These activities happen in time, as well as in space. Although designers work in two dimensions or in sequences of two-dimensional pieces for the most part, the enactment of these pieces occurs over time. As with the playwright or the composer, the designer produces a piece (score, play) that only comes into full existence when the communication with the audience takes place.

My emphasis on this aspect shifts the designer's center of attention from the interrelation of visual components to that between the audience and the design, recognizing the receiver as active participant in the construction of the message. It follows that decisions relating to visual aspects of the design should be based not only on compositional concerns, but also, and chiefly, on the study of human communication. This emphasis on the receiver within the conventional scheme of transmitter-receiver opposition places visual communication design opposite to the romantic conception of art as self-expression, thus avoiding one of the distorting conceptions of the profession.

Given the above, the time has come to understand that the education of designers cannot be satisfied by the resources of traditional art schools and that several branches of psychology, verbal communication, sociology, computing science, marketing, and other disciplines should be called upon to develop in students the required awareness. This seems to be the only choice if a theoretical understanding of graphic design is to develop and if the field is to take on the responsibility for the conception and production of effective and conscientious communications and for the education of graphic designers. This specific operational dimension must be qualified by a concern for professional and social responsibility that includes ethics and esthetics.

Part 2: Further reading

Andersen, M. (2017), "Why Can't the U.S. Decolonize Its Design Education? What truly diverse + inclusive international programs can teach Americans," *AIGA Eye on Design* 2 January. Available online: eyeondesign. aiga.org/why-cant-the-u-s-decolonize-its-design-education/ (accessed 15 June 2017).

Bennett, A. and O. Vulpinari (eds) (2011), *Icograda Design Education Manifesto 2011*, Montreal: International Council of Graphic Design Associations.

Bennett, A. (2012), "Good Design is Good Social Change: Envisioning an Age of Accountability in Communication Design Education," *Visible Language*, 46 (1–2): 66–79.

Biesele, I. G. (1981), *Graphic Design Education,* Winter Park, FL: Hastings House.

Bonsiepe, G. (1994), "A Step Towards the Reinvention of Graphic Design," *Design Issues*, Spring 10 (1): 47–52.

Dabner, D., S. Calvert, and S. Stewart (2014), *Graphic Design School: A Foundation Course for Graphic Designers Working in Print, Moving image and Digital Media*, London: Thames & Hudson.

Davis, M. (2017), *Teaching Design: A Guide to Curriculum and Pedagogy for College Design Faculty and Teachers Who Use Design in Their Classroom*, New York: Allworth Press.

Design is One: A Documentary about Lella and Massimo Vignelli (2013), [Film] Dirs. Kathy Brew and Roberto Guerra, USA: First Run Features.

Downs, S., ed (2012), *The Graphic Communication Handbook*, London: Routledge.

Fontine, L. (2014) "Learning Design: Thinking by Designing Learning Experiences: A Case Study in the Development of Strategic Thinking Skills through the Design Interactive Museum Exhibitions," *Visible Language* 48 (2): 49–69.

Frascara, J. (2005), *Communication Design: Principles, Methods, and Practice*, New York: Allworth Press.

Graphic Means (2016), [Film] Dir. Briar Levitt. USA: Briar Levitt.

Griffen, D. (2014), "Moving Beyond 'Just Making Things': Design History in the Studio and the Survey Classroom," *Visible Language* 47 (3): 7–27.

Griffin. D. (2016), "Survey Paper: Doctoral Education in (Graphic) Design", *Dialectic,* Winter I (I). Available online: http://quod.lib.umich.edu/d/dialectic/14932326.0001.109?view=text;rgn=main (accessed 4 June 2017).

Heller, S. (2004), *The Education of a Typographer,* New York: Allworth.

Heller, S. (2015), *The Education of a Graphic Designer,* 3rd edn, New York: Allworth.

Heller, S. (2017), *Teaching Graphic Design: Course Offerings and Class Projects from the Leading Graduate and Undergraduate Programs*, 2nd edn, New York: Allworth Press.

Over, P. C. and, B. Predan, eds (2015), *Design Education: What Do You See? What Do You Think About It? What Do You Make of It?*, Ljubljana: University of Ljubljana.

Reinfurt, D. and R. Wiesenberger (2017), *Muriel Cooper,* Cambridge: MIT Press.

Shaughnessy, A. (2010), *How to be a Graphic Designer without Losing Your Soul*, expanded edn, New York: Princeton Architecture Press.

Shaw, P. (2014), "Graphic Design: A Brief Terminological History," Available online: www.paulshawletterdesign. com/2014/06/graphic-design-a-brief-terminological-history/ (accessed 4 June 2017).

Sutherland, I. (2004), "Paradigm Shift: The Challenge to Graphic Design Education and Professional Practice in Post-Apartheid South Africa," *Design Issues* 20 (2): 51–60.

Swanson, G. (1994), "Graphic Design Education as a Liberal Art: Design and Knowledge in the University and the 'Real World'." *Design Issues* 10 (1): 53–63.

The Happy Film (2016), [Film] Dirs. Hillman Curtis, Ben Nabors, and Stefan Sagmeister, Germany: Ben Nabors.

Van der Waarde, K. and M. Vroombout. "Communication Design Education: Could Nine Reflections Be Sufficient?" (2012) in S. Poggenpohl (ed), Special Issue of *Visible Language: Envisioning a Future of Design Education*, 46 (1–2): 8–35.

Vaughan, L., ed (2017), *Practice Based Design Research*. London: Bloomsbury.

Winkler, D. (1997), "Design Practice and Education: Moving Beyond the Bauhaus Model," in J.Frascara (ed) *User-Centered Graphic Design: Mass Communications and Social Change*, 129–135, London: Taylor and Francis.

Part 3

Type and typography

Part 3: Introduction

Many of the most critical transformations in graphic design thinking and practice have been instigated in the typographic realm. These investigations are often carried out in response to new printing techniques and technological advances, or in reaction to the conventions of language during typographic experimentation. Both how we apprehend and how we make type have an impact on typographic interpretation and meaning. In fact, renewed interest in the craft of typography has fostered re-evaluation of the materiality of typographic form. This interest in craft also tends to spotlight production technologies—such as the printing press, risograph, or digital media. Attention to technology also highlights the environments in which type is experienced—on the page or screen, or in spatial or immersive environments. Digitally produced generative type, for example, which is programmed to evolve along with the data it represents, expands the experience of reading and designing with type. This Part of the book highlights the relationships between the exploration of content and experimentation with form, and it underscores the critical role that typography plays in both historical and contemporary graphic design discourse.

The first Section, "History of type and typography," includes essays from various historical periods that address novel or controversial approaches to typography and typographic form. In "A brief history of type historians" (2018), Caroline Archer presents a historical chronology of writings by typographers and printers. Archer begins by noting that seventeenth-century English printer Joseph Moxon's practical publications about typefounding, composition, and presswork set the tone for future printing history writing. Beginning in the nineteenth century, though, new technologies, such as metal and steam-powered presses, motivated printers to write about printing and typographic history, theory, and practice. The twentieth century brought typographic innovation, typographic journals—including Herbert Spencer's influential magazine *Typographica* (1949–1967)—and a "printing renaissance" that turned to typefaces designed by artists and historical revival of typefaces. Archer also discusses the original editor of *The Monotype Recorder*, commentator Beatrice Warde, the author of the next essay in this section. Warde's seminal essay, "The crystal goblet or printing should be invisible" (1932), was first given as a lecture, entitled "Printing Should Be Invisible," to the British Typographers' Guild in 1930. In both essays, Warde argues that typography should, like a crystal goblet containing fine wine, be an invisible carrier of textual content. Warde's essays had a profound effect on twentieth-century typography. New developments in typography, whether in previous centuries or today, are often associated with pioneering treatises, inventive technologies, and experimental practices.

Contemporary dynamic and generative typography has antecedents in the experimental work of the early twentieth-century European avant-garde (e.g. Futurism, Constructivism, Dadaism, and Modernism). The act of experimentation can be understood as a process that challenges the conventions of tradition and the fundamental notions of function and aesthetics. In "*FUSE* 1–20: Wreckers of typographic civilisation" (2011), Adrian Shaughnessy reveals how Neville Brody and Jon Wozencroft's radical typographic publication *FUSE* tests accepted practices. The software Fontographer, Shaughnessy explains, made it easy to experiment, striking down "hallowed notions" of typography as concealed craft and an '"invisible' vessel tasked only with imparting linguistic meaning (the 'crystal goblet' of typographic lore)"—a reference to the ideas in Beatrice Warde's essay. *FUSE* was a collaborative "designer/author" undertaking in which Brody and Wozencroft's typefaces, design, and writing functioned together as a "wrecking ball" for traditional typography.

Peter Bil'ak next considers the term "experimentation" and what this suggests for typography in two short essays written five years apart. In the first piece "Experimental typography. Whatever that means." (2005), Bil'ak observes that experimentation is not used the way it is in science, in which experimentation attempts to prove (or disprove) a hypothesis. Bil'ak then examines two commonly held notions of experimental typography: that experimentation is about the formal novelty of the resulting outcome and, that experimentation refers to an open-ended unfettered creative process. He discusses several provocative typography projects—including *FUSE*—that both challenge and validate aspects of these two notions about experimentation with typography. Bil'ak's second essay, "Conceptual type?" (2010), asks how type can be "conceptual," when the term typically refers to semantic versus applied entities. He proposes that "conceptual" typography is instead about the ideas that underlie its design. Type designer Tobias Frere-Jones next considers the ideas underlying grunge typography in "Towards the cause of grunge" (1994). Writing at the height of the 1990s popular grunge craze, Frere-Jones looks back at the experimentation that occurred in reaction to new typographic technology in previous historical periods. He then points out that grunge type is, in part, a response to the abundant mediocre computer produced fonts in the 1990s, and he notes the wry humor in the notion that grunge fonts utilize such a "precise tool" to "spout dirt" in rebellion against the "default" design of these computer fonts.

"About the making of *The Telephone Book*" (2006) spotlights letterpress technology. In this essay, typesetter Michael Jon Jensen discusses the inventive designs that designer Richard Eckersley produced for philosopher Avital Ronell's 1989 book *The Telephone Book*. Eckersley designed his typographic solutions with close attention to the content of this book—which investigates the function of the telephone in philosophical terms. To do justice to Ronell's text, Eckersley created devices such as typographic "rivers" cut into text blocks that represented cuts in communication, and "typographic representations of circuits" using hair-line rules that extend out of black box shapes, which also functioned as telephonic "visual connectors" with other pages.

Dietmar Winkler likewise considers the connections between visual form and its conceptual underpinnings in the 2010 essay "Helvetica, the film and the face in context." He complains that adaptations of Swiss design, including Helvetica, neglected the historical and theoretical bases of the movement—"as though design exists in a vacuum." He explores the practical and philosophical Swiss design context for both Helvetica the typeface, and *Helvetica*, the movie. Winkler also discusses how Helvetica type made its way into American design practices, and he offers his perspectives on the pros and cons of graphic design (and typographic) education in the US and Switzerland in the 1960s and 1970s. Together the essays in this Section offer contemporary designers food for thought about the cultural contexts behind, and the thinking and making processes for, experimental design.

The final Section, "Dimensional, physical, digital, and kinetic typography," traces graphic designers' move away from typography as solely a two-dimensional printed form, and toward typography as a time-, space- and motion-based medium. In the groundbreaking 1996 project "Dimensional typography," J. Abbott Miller investigates three-dimensional sculptural aspects of individual letterforms (versus letters that move in three-dimensional spatial or temporal environments). He presents techniques by which individual flat letterforms can become dimensional: extrusion, in which letterforms are multiplied in three dimensions like the pages in a book; rotation, in which the letterform is rotated around an axis; tubing, which is similar to rotation (but rotation is only performed upon the stroke or surface of the letterform); shadowing, which uses implied light sources; sewing, in which letters resemble ribbons or stitching, threading, and lacing; modular construction, in which letterforms are come from building blocks or "kits of parts"; and bloating, in which letters appear to be made of soft bloated organic forms. Miller then presents case studies of several letterforms that have been designed using one or more of these techniques. "Dimensional typography. The unbearable flatness of being" (2010) considers immersive dimensional typography. Relating this design to the typography in Abbott Miller's "Dimensional Typography," Leslie Atzmon suggests that the projects in Miller's book may be compared to early photography—a momentary representation of the physical world—while the new dimensional typography that she discusses here is like early cinema—an immersion in a representation of the physical world. Atzmon illustrates this point further with work from an exhibition held in Chicago in 2009, with examples that include physical letterform structures based on a brick and mortar paving pattern metaphor, room-filling connected matrices that mold outline letters out of wire, and Akzidenz Grotesk letters to which a z-axis is added and then removed to create a new two-dimensional set of letters. Atzmon argues that this typographic work translates sensibilities from the digital realm into physical spaces or hybrid digital and physical environments.

Michael Worthington discusses how, in virtual space, type in motion balances text and subtext, voice and message, in "The new seduction: movable type" (1998). He points out that although readers access print typography using time and motion as they read it, in digital time-based media both the reader's eye and the media surface are in motion. The "rules, metaphors, and processes" of print typography, Worthington argues, don't precisely fit type in motion. Designers will need to write, design, and think differently to create the expressive character of type in motion—and they must understand how to use technology to enhance this kind of typography. Jessica Helfand similarly considers the grammar of screen-based typography in the 1990s as a time-based, interactive visual language in "Electronic typography: the new visual language" (1994). She cites twentieth-century examples of the visual expression of spoken language, and of type as "medium (structure), message (syntax), and muse (sensibility)." How we design with static typography will need to be recontextualized for type in motion. Rather than turning to traditional design or linguistic theories, Helfand suggests, we need to think "outside the box" to find unexpected and dynamic models for this new visual language. In the last essay of this section, Javier Candiera interviews Casey Reas and Ben Fry about the benefits of designers learning to write code in "Working the art process by typing in computer code" (2006). Fry explains that he uses programming to create work that needs to be made using personalized software. Reas notes that he and Fry transferred their training, in which they do lots of sketches and then contemplate these sketches, to their processing in which they create many small programs and analyse them. The essays in this Section set the stage for contemporary multi-dimensional and dynamic typography.

Today, open-source software is fostering innovative approaches to typography; at the same time, debates about the conventions of reading and writing practices are emerging in contemporary design discourse. Generative typography—in which a code-driven algorithm renders a typeface that constantly evolves with the data it represents—expands experiences of reading from a two-dimensional page to immersive and spatially enhanced environments. This shift suggests new hybrid typographic processes, such as typeforms that become performative in response to their readers and environments. Aspects of our experiences of materiality in physical craft and spatial experience are transplanted into these digital spaces. The work in this section demonstrates that typographic experimentation was, and continues to be, at the vanguard of what is possible in our field.

Section 3.1

History of type and typography

Chapter 3.1.1

A brief history of type historians

Caroline Archer

Printing has a history that spans nearly six centuries, and literature about printing has been around for almost as long. Individuals who were concerned with designing type and reproducing words have also often been interested in writing. Their unmitigated involvement in printing and typography has led them to research, write, and publish their findings on the subject. This essay, therefore, takes a brief look at the history of type historians from their earliest writings to the twentieth century.

Ever since Gutenberg established his printing press in the mid-fifteenth century, printing has had its documenters: men who itemized books that had been printed; listed the dates on which they had been published; registered the places where they were produced; and recorded the names of printing proprietors. This information provides a rough compendium of the trade at the time, and a useful vista of the landscape of early European printing.

It was not until the seventeenth century, however, that any attempt was made to describe the techniques of printing craft, or to write a purposeful history of printing. Joseph Moxon, an English printer of mathematical books and maps, was the first in a line of practical printers to write about his trade. Moxon's *Mechanick Exercises on the Whole Art of Printing* (1683) was an attempt to produce an account of contemporary practices in typefounding, composition, and presswork: it was an instruction manual of the techniques used by seventeenth-century printers and a publication that influenced future printing historians.

Printers' manuals continued to be issued throughout the eighteenth and nineteenth centuries—many were derived, to a greater or lesser extent, from the *Mechanick Exercises*. The first of Moxon's successors was Scottish printer James Watson, whose publication *The History of the Art of Printing* (1713) was an account of the invention and progress of printing, complete with the names of famous printers, the places of their birth, and the works that they printed. Watson's *History* was followed by John Smith's *Printers' Grammar* (1755), which, according to the original title page, "exhibited and examined and explained the superficies, gradation and properties of the different sorts and sizes of metal types cut by letter foundries." Smith dealt exclusively with the work of setting type, which was performed by men known as compositors, and his detailed descriptions indicate that this book drew largely upon his own experiences. Another notable eighteenth-century printing manual was Philip Luckombe's *Concise History of the Origin and Progress of Printing* (1770), which was issued in two parts. Part one provided a concise account of printing from its invention up to the eighteenth century, including specimens of printing types of all sizes and languages, musical types, flowers, and ornaments, while part two was a practical manual of printing.

At the start of the nineteenth century there was a revolution in printing techniques. The wooden screw-press gave way to the iron press, and developments in steam power enabled Koenig's cylinder printing machine to increase production speeds. These advances in the trade made printing a popular topic for early nineteenth-century printer-writers who produced a rash of books devoted to its history, theory, and practice. The earliest work of a practical nineteenth-century printer was Caleb Stower's *Printers' Grammar* (1808). *Printers' Grammar* featured an introduction to the art and history of printing that was accompanied by a description of improvements in trade practice made over the previous fifty years. Other nineteenth-century printers who wrote about their craft likewise included accounts of the new machinery and the changes it brought to the industry. John Johnson, a master printer with the Lee Priory Press, produced *Typographia* (1824), which is perhaps the most familiar of all the standard works on printing in the English language. *Typographia* was published in several formats, and contemporary reviewers mentioned Johnson's highly ornate typography and use of engravings more than they referred to the book's contents (Figure 3.1).

The first volume—in which Richard Thomson, Librarian of the London Institution assisted Johnson— covers the history of printing. This volume lists printers working in England up to the end of the sixteenth century, along with bibliographical details of their known publications. Much of Johnson's knowledge of printing history, however, is largely derived from secondary works, particularly those of Moxon. The second volume of *Typographia* is purely practical and gives a description of types, and directions for composing, for press, and of warehouse work. This volume is particularly rich in foreign alphabets, a feature for which it gained a reputation and for which it became a printer's classic.

Contemporaneous with Johnson was the parliamentary printer Thomas Curson Hansard, whose fascination with the art of printing led to the publication of *Hansard's Typographia* (1825) in which Hansard acknowledges his debt to earlier authors such as Moxon and Stower. This important and clearly written study of the history and practice of printing is a valuable source of information for students and historians of the subject. Originally aimed at both young printers and amateurs, it explains all of the different aspects of running a printing business. The book is particularly valuable for its discussion of contemporary developments in printing technology and lithography, and for details about the business and financial side of the trade. Part one contains the historical background and details of typefounding and typefaces; part two contains details of printing machinery, organization, and lithography. The final book of note during this period is *Dictionary of the Art of Printing* (1841), written by William Savage, printer to the Royal Institute. The dictionary was compiled between 1822 and 1832 from notes that Savage gathered throughout his career. It is an exceptional reference book, which offers a comprehensive account of the state of the printing industry in England in the first part of the nineteenth century. Savage touches upon all the aspects of the trade from technical to legal and provides a few lively glimpses into the busy workshops, habits, and customs of the workers.

All of the writers so far mentioned were working printers with little interest in type design. In 1866, however, Talbot Baines Reed, a partner in the typefounding firm of Sir Charles Reed & Sons, published his *A History of the Old English Letter Foundries*, a valuable and scholarly work on typographic history. The dissemination of printed information and learning is crucial to this history, and Reed is particularly

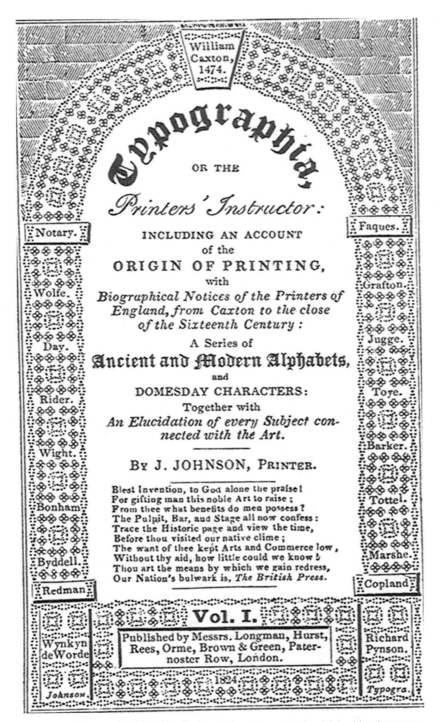

Figure 3.1 *Typographia* (1824),"edited by John Johnson and published by Longman. The title page displays a myriad of typographic ornaments in which are embedded the names of eminent printers through history.

conscious of the debt his contemporaries owed to the early typographers such as William Caslon and John Baskerville. Reed's appreciation for these early typographers is evidenced throughout his work in his careful and liberal account of their artistic exploration and expression. Reed's book affords many technical and historical insights for the modern reader, and his style of writing and presentation of information is fresh and engaging. In 1875, Reed's work was followed by that of the printer and bibliographer William Blades who published a *Catalogue of Type Specimen Books of England, Holland, France, Italy & Germany*, for which he wrote a persuasive foreword. The respective works of Reed and Blades demonstrated that printers could write eloquently about type, but also that these non-academic historians had also begun to define typographic history and delineate it as a specialist area of research.

Both Reed and Blades paved the way for the work of American printer Theodore Low De Vinne whose four-volume *Practice of Typography* provided the first serious analysis of letterforms (Vol. 1: Plain Printing Types, 1900) and the first appreciation of the title-page as display (Vol. 3: A Treatise on Title Pages, 1902). With De Vinne, the printing historian was finally starting to provide qualitative commentary on typography and type design. The opening decades of the twentieth century witnessed a period of startling typographic growth, and something of a printing renaissance. There was an emphasis on providing a choice of novel typographic material such as typefaces designed by artists, newly imported typefaces from Continental Europe and recently revived historical typefaces from rich and varied sources. It was also an era that saw the introduction of new production techniques that were capable of providing high quality work at competitive prices. Letterpress was giving way to offset lithography, hand setting was usurped by machine setting, and printing was moving from a craft-based to technology-led industry. This shift was reflected in excitement about the unprecedented number of books and periodicals that were devoted to the subject of printing.

In 1911, Daniel Berkeley Updike, master printer at the Merrymount Press, Boston, was invited by Harvard University to deliver a series of lectures on "Type and composition." Later these lectures were published in a two-volume book *Printing Types—Their History, Forms and Use: A Study in Survivals* (1922). *Printing Types* was far removed from the usual manual-cum-history of printing and not like anything hitherto written on the subject, for as well as being instructional it was also a cultured body of writing—it was a work of literary merit that was considerably more polished than anything written by earlier printing historians.

Updike wrote his book according to a structure that dealt systematically with printing in one country after another. He allocated to each country a separate chapter for its incunabula period,[1] followed by a chapter that considered type developments in each country between 1500 and 1800. The book included 365 full-page illustrations, as well as many examples from typefounders' specimens. *Printing Types* was a landmark publication that, according to Stanley Morison, made it possible for the first time "to view printing types in relation not merely to changes of technique and fashion, but also in relation to artistic, social and political movements" (quoted by Ellic Howe, in Harling [1936], *Typography*, pp. 10–12). *Printing Types*, however, dealt exclusively with the period of movable type and did not cover hot-metal type; and some of Updike's statements in the book were both subjective and partisan. Despite these flaws, *Printing Types* was, and remains, an essential guide for anybody wishing to have a panoramic view of the subject. *Printing Types* continues to be one of the most formative texts on typographic history.

Specialist typographic journals also emerged in the twentieth century concurrent with these canons of printing history. In 1923 the first number of *The Fleuron* appeared. Founded in London by Stanley

Morison,[2] Francis Meynell,[3] Holbrook Jackson,[4] Bernard Newdigate,[5] and Oliver Simon,[6] *The Fleuron* was a yearly review that discussed the problems of both contemporary and historical type design. Between 1923–30, *The Fleuron* published a series of articles on printing types that were written by the most eminent and influential names in the typographic field at the time. These articles were more rigorous than previous writings, and included a number of articles that added to—or questioned—some of the information given in *Printing Types*. For example, Paul Beaujon's[7] examination of the Garamond types used scientific methods to disprove the claims that the Imprimerie National in Paris possessed the original Garamond punches and matrices. Beaujon showed beyond a doubt that the assumed sixteenth-century punches were, in fact, the work of a seventeenth-century craftsman (1926, pp. 131–79). Stanley Morison's work on the ancestry of Old Style typefaces was another example of a developing critical approach to typographic history, for while printing historians of the past worked on a rather small scale, Morison's research extended over three centuries with evidence culled from countries across Europe. Morison's article for *The Fleuron* was later extended and published as *Four Centuries of Fine Printing* (1924). Typographic historians were starting to understand the need to exercise independent judgement rather than simply to accept and repeat the writings of the past; the purely historical approach favored by Updike was being usurped by scientific methods, and an exact terminology was beginning to be established.

The typographic debates started by *The Fleuron* in the 1920s were continued by *Typography* (1936–39), a quarterly magazine edited by Robert Harling that ran for just eight issues (Figure 3.2). *Typography* became one of the most significant and sought after English design publications of the period. With *Typography*, Harling set out to create a journal that considered historical aspects of typography and type design alongside reflections on recent typographic developments—and as with *The Fleuron*, contributors included such illustrious commentators as Harry Carter, John Betjeman, Imre Reiner, and Stanley Morison. Articles on Eric Gill and Jan Tschichold could be published next to features on railway timetables or tram tickets because *Typography* made no distinction between high- and low-end cultures, or between fine bookwork and cheap ephemera. Harling's journal was both revolutionary and unique in this way.

Concurrent with both *The Fleuron* and *Typography* was the French periodical *Arts et metiers graphiques* (1927–38), one of the most entertaining and visually satisfying graphic arts magazines of the period. Charles Peignot, director of the Deberny & Peignot's Parisian typefoundry, was the impresario behind the publication. Peignot was assisted by typographer and publicist Maximilien Vox, along with a coterie of au courant French designers. *Arts et metiers graphiques* was concerned with the French book trade, and it offered articles both on printing history and on contemporary developments in the typographic trade. A patriotic publication, it aimed to raise the profile of French designers and French printing history. Later editions of *Arts et metiers graphiques* were expanded to include articles on advertising and publicity, and attempts were made to include new ideas from abroad. Although it did not overtly promote the trade interests of the parent company, *Arts et metiers graphiques* was a wonderful piece of publicity for Deberny & Peignot. Its true success, however, lay in its ability to understand and showcase the emerging modernism and new industrial techniques that came to dominate communication—new printing processes and photography, film and animation.

While male commentators dominated printing history for nearly three hundred years, in the first half of the twentieth century, one female commentator arguably climbed above her male counterparts,

Figure 3.2 *Typography* (Summer 1939), edited by Robert Harling and published by James Shand at the Shenval Press, Hertford, UK. The bold cover reflected the confident editorial which covered subjects as diverse as lettering in the environment, parliamentary printing, and the book decorations of Rex Whistler.

created a lively debate, enriched understanding of typographic history and helped shape the discourse in the subject. Her works continue to be influential today. Beatrice Warde was an American typographic expert who was the publicity manager for the Monotype Corporation in England and editor of the *Monotype Recorder* and *Newsletter* for most of her career. Well known for her essay "The crystal goblet" and the broadsheet "This is a printing office," she was also a prolific writer, researcher, and public speaker. "The crystal goblet" was first delivered as a lecture, called "Printing should be invisible" given to the British Typographers' Guild in 1930 at the St Bride Institute, London. The essay advocated clear typography and the straightforward presentation of content, and immediately after her address the lecture appeared in the *British & Colonial Printer & Stationer*, and it was also reprinted as a pamphlet in 1932 and 1937. In 1955 it was once again reissued, and the essay reached its widest audience in a book called *The Crystal Goblet: Sixteen Essays on Typography*, which is now a significant text in typography and graphic design. Beatrice Warde was much more than a typographic historian; she was an intellectual who wrote and lectured on a huge variety of topics, from typesetting poetry, to points of grammar, from renaissance typography to letters in lights. Warde was an educator and a communicator who had a profound effect on a whole generation of printers and typographers. Beatrice Warde was a beacon in the pre-war landscape that continued to glow well into the post-war era.

Only some of the journals that were founded before the war survived into the post-war period. Of those publications that did persist, however, three are particularly noteworthy: *Penrose*, *Signature*, and *Typographica*. The first post-war survivor, *The Penrose Annual* (1895–1982), was edited in succession by William Gamble, Richard Bertram Fishenden, Allan Delafons, Herbert Spencer, and Clive Goodacre. Initially intended as a record of technological printing developments, it soon evolved to include essays on design and typography, photography, illustration, and the social and historical aspects of printing. Articles were authored by Noel Carrington, Harold Curwen, John Gloag, Allen Lane, Stanley Morison, Moholy-Nagy, Nikolaus Pevsner, and Beatrice Warde, among others. The content in *The Penrose Annual* was significant in bridging the gap between the technical aspects of printing and the artistic facets of design, and in uniting the disparate areas of the trade. *Penrose* remains of interest today because its influential articles—monographs on individuals, and articles on various matters of typesetting, illustrators and photographers, and histories of type—still have reference value.

The second post-war survivor was *Signature: A Quadrimestrial of Typography and the Graphic Arts* (1935–40; 1949–54), which was edited by Oliver Simon. *Signature* achieved a high level of design that was matched by the quality of its content. While it was obviously aimed to appeal to printers and typographers, it was also intended to capture the attention of artists by introducing them to the work of contemporary designers, and by marrying typography with artistic versus technical aspects of the subject (Figure 3.3).

The 1950s saw great changes in the printing industry: the transition from letterpress to offset lithography, from metal composition to computer-generated type, as well as new processes, papers, and principles that all influenced production. *Typographica* (1949–67)—which featured boundary-blurring, sumptuous, and tactile pages, and which merged tradition with modern experimentation in type and image—did more than any other title to lead the emerging generation of designers and printers through the big changes in the industry. *Typographica* was launched in 1949 by the printing and publishing firm of Lund Humphries, Bradford. It was the brainchild of Herbert Spencer: a twenty-five-year-old

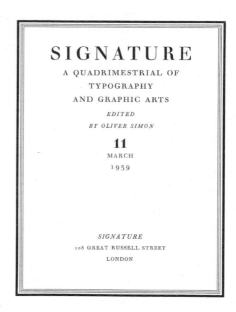

Figure 3.3 *Signature* Signature (March 1939), edited by Oliver Simon and printed by the Curwen Press, London. Title page and the facing verso, which is illustrated by Edward Ardizzone. The publication contained articles by renowned typographic historians Stanley Morison, Ellic Howe, and Holbrook Jackson.

designer-editor-writer who guided the publication for eighteen years. Those typographers who subscribed to *Typographica* were influenced by its news, discoveries, and teaching. They were also inspired by the publication to bring energy and ideas to their work, which helped create a genuinely contemporary genre of design. Herbert Spencer, Lund Humphries, and *Typographica* were undoubtedly pioneers of British typographic design and history.

The second half of the twentieth century witnessed two typographic revolutions: machine printing surrendered to offset lithography, which then gave way to digital printing; and phototypesetting finally usurped metal composition, which then was superseded by desktop publishing and the digital revolution. This recent history has yet to be fully documented, but two good resources about this period are Lawrence Wallis's *Modern Encyclopedia of Typefaces, 1960–90* (1990) and *A Concise Chronology of Typesetting Developments, 1886–1986* (1988). It remains to be seen what typographic historians of the future will make of our present and recent past.

All the publications mentioned in this chapter are readily available either in their original editions in specialist libraries such as St Bride Library, London, as re-editions or facsimiles from online or high-street book shops; some are available online as Google books. This list is far from exhaustive, but gives a reasonable introduction to four centuries of typographic writings.

Notes

1. Editors' note: Incunabula are books that were printed between the invention of letterpress printing in the 1450s and 1501.
2. Typographical advisor, Monotype, and designer of Times New Roman.
3. Printer, Nonesuch Press.
4. Writer and publisher.
5. Typographer, Arden Press, Shakespeare Head Press.
6. Printer, typographer, and manager of the Curwen Press, London.
7. Paul Beaujon was the pen name of Monotype's publicity manager Beatrice Warde.

The crystal goblet, or printing should be invisible

Beatrice Warde

Imagine that you have before you a flagon of wine. You may choose your own favourite vintage for this imaginary demonstration, so that it be a deep shimmering crimson in colour. You have two goblets before you. One is of solid gold, wrought in the most exquisite patterns. The other is of crystal-clear glass, thin as a bubble, and as transparent. Pour and drink; and according to your choice of goblet, I shall know whether or not you are a connoisseur of wine. For if you have no feelings about wine one way or the other, you will want the sensation of drinking the stuff out of a vessel that may have cost thousands of pounds; but if you are a member of that vanishing tribe, the amateurs of fine vintages, you will choose the crystal, because everything about it is calculated to reveal rather than to hide the beautiful thing which it was meant to contain.

Bear with me in this long-winded and fragrant metaphor; for you will find that almost all the virtues of the perfect wineglass have a parallel in typography. There is the long, thin stem that obviates fingerprints on the bowl. Why? Because no cloud must come between your eyes and the fiery heart of the liquid. Are not the margins on book pages similarly meant to obviate the necessity of fingering the type-page? Again: the glass is colourless or at the most only faintly tinged in the bowl, because the connoisseur judges wine partly by its colour and is impatient of anything that alters it. There are a thousand mannerisms in typography that are as impudent and arbitrary as putting port in tumblers of red or green glass! When a goblet has a base that looks too small for security, it does not matter how cleverly it is weighted; you feel nervous lest it should tip over. There are ways of setting lines of type which may work well enough, and yet keep the reader subconsciously worried by the fear of "doubling" lines, reading three words as one, and so forth.

Now the man who first chose glass instead of clay or metal to hold his wine was a 'modernist' in the sense in which I am going to use that term. That is, the first thing he asked of this particular object was not "How should it look?" but "What must it do?" and to that extent all good typography is modernist.

Wine is so strange and potent a thing that it has been used in the central ritual of religion in one place and time, and attacked by a virago with a hatchet in another. There is only one thing in the world that is

---

First presented as an address to the British Typographers Guild at the St. Bride Institute, London, 1932. Reprinted in *Monotype Recorder*, 44 (1) (Autumn 1970): 24–5. Out of copyright.

Experimental typography.
Whatever that means. (2005)
2010 Conceputal Type?

Peter Bil'ak

2005 Experimental typography. **Whatever that means.**

Very few terms have been used so habitually and carelessly as the word "experiment." In the field of graphic design and typography, experiment as a noun has been used to signify anything new, unconventional, defying easy categorization, or confounding expectations. As a verb, "to experiment" is often synonymous with the design process itself, which may not exactly be helpful, considering that all design is a result of the design process. The term experiment can also have the connotation of an implicit disclaimer; it suggests not taking responsibility for the result. When students are asked what they intend by creating certain forms, they often say, "It's just an experiment . . .," when they don't have a better response.

In a scientific context, an experiment is a test of an idea; a set of actions performed to prove or disprove a hypothesis. Experimentation in this sense is an empirical approach to knowledge that lays a foundation upon which others can build. It requires all measurements to be made objectively under controlled

Figure 3.5 *aa* and *gg* (Karloff type). © 2010. Designer: Peter Bil'ak.

Experimental typography. Whatever that means." first published in *Items*, no. 1 (2005).
Conceptual type? first presented at the conference *Conceptual Type-Type Led by Ideas* in Copenhagen, November 2010.
© Peter Bil'ak.

Figure 3.6 "Process" in *Ortho-type*. © 2005. Designers: Enrico Bravi, Mikkel Crone Koser, and Paolo Palma.

conditions, which allows the procedure to be repeated by others, thus proving that a phenomenon occurs after a certain action, and that the phenomenon does not occur in the absence of the action.

An example of a famous scientific experiment would be Galileo Galilei's dropping of two objects of different weights from the Pisa tower to demonstrate that both would land at the same time, proving his hypothesis about gravity. In this sense, a typographic experiment might be a procedure to determine whether humidity affects the transfer of ink onto a sheet of paper, and if it does, how.

A scientific approach to experimentation, however, seems to be valid only in a situation where empirical knowledge is applicable, or in a situation where the outcome of the experiment can be reliably measured. What happens, however, when the outcome is ambiguous, non-objective, not based on pure reason? In the recent book *The Typographic Experiment: Radical Innovation in Contemporary Type Design*, author Teal Triggs asked thirty-seven internationally recognized designers to define their understandings of the term experiment.

As expected, the published definitions couldn't have been more disparate. They are marked by personal belief systems and biased by the experiences of the designers. While Hamish Muir of 8vo writes: "Every type job is experiment," Melle Hammer insists that: "Experimental typography does not exist, nor ever has." So how is it possible that there are such diverse understandings of a term that is so commonly used?

Among the designers' various interpretations, two notions of experimentation were dominant. The first one was formulated by the American designer David Carson: "Experimental is something I haven't tried before . . . something that hasn't been seen and heard." Carson and several other designers suggest that the nature of experiment lies in the formal novelty of the result. There are many precedents for this opinion, but in an era when information travels faster than ever before and when we have achieved unprecedented archival of information, it becomes significantly more difficult to claim a complete novelty of forms. While over ninety years ago Kurt Schwitters proclaimed that to "do it in a way that no one has done it before" was sufficient for the definition of the new typography of his day—and his work was an appropriate example of such an approach—today things are different. Designers are more aware of the body of work and the discourse accompanying it. Proclaiming novelty today can seem like historical ignorance on a designer's part.

Interestingly, Carson's statement also suggests that the essence of experimentation is in going against the prevailing patterns, rather than being guided by conventions. This is directly opposed to the scientific usage of the word, where an experiment is designed to add to the accumulation of knowledge; in design, where results are measured subjectively, there is a tendency to go against the generally accepted base of knowledge. In science a single person can make valuable experiments, but a design experiment that is rooted in anti-conventionalism can only exist against the background of other— conventional—solutions. In this sense, it would be impossible to experiment if one were the only designer on earth, because there would be no standard for the experiment. Anti-conventionalism requires going against prevailing styles, which is perceived as conventional. If more designers joined forces and worked in a similar fashion, the scale would change, and the former convention would become anti-conventional. The fate of such experimentation is a permanent confrontation with the mainstream; a circular, cyclical race, where it is not certain who is chasing whom.

Does type design and typography allow an experimental approach at all? The alphabet is by its very nature dependent on and defined by conventions. Type design that is not bound by convention is like a private language: both lack the ability to communicate. Yet it is precisely the constraints of the alphabet which inspire many designers. A recent example is the work of Thomas Huot-Marchand, a French post-graduate student of type design who investigates the limits of legibility while physically reducing the basic forms of the alphabet. Minuscule is his project of size-specific typography. While the letters for regular reading sizes are very close to conventional book typefaces, each step down in size results in simplification of the letter-shapes. In the extremely small sizes (2 point), Minuscule becomes an abstract reduction of the alphabet, free of all the details and optical corrections which are usual for fonts designed for text reading. Huot-Marchand's project builds upon the work of French ophthalmologist Louis Émile Javal, who published similar research at the beginning of the twentieth century. The practical contribution of both projects is limited, since the reading process is still guided by the physical limitations of the human eye; however, Huot-Marchand and Javal both investigate the constraints of legibility within which typography functions.

The second dominant notion of experiment in *The Typographic Experiment* was formulated by Michael Worthington, a British designer and educator based in the United States: "True experimentation means to take risks." If taken literally, such a statement is of little value: immediately we would ask what is at stake and what typographers are really risking. Worthington, however, is referring to the risk involved with not knowing the exact outcome of the experiment in which the designers are engaged.

A similar definition is offered by the *E.A.T. (Experiment And Typography)* exhibition presenting thirty-five type designers and typographers from the Czech Republic and Slovakia. Alan Záruba and Johanna Balušíková, the curators of *E.A.T.*, put their focus on development and process when describing the concept of the exhibition: "The show focuses on projects which document the development of designers' ideas. Attention is paid to the process of creating innovative solutions in the field of type design and typography, often engaging experimental processes as a means to approach unknown territory."

An experiment in this sense has no preconceived idea of the outcome; it only sets out to determine a cause-and-effect relationship. As such, experimentation is a method of working which is contrary to production-oriented design, where the aim of the process is not to create something new, but to achieve an already known, pre-formulated result.

Belgian designer Brecht Cuppens has created Sprawl, an experimental typeface based on cartography, which takes into account the density of population in Belgium. In Sprawl, the silhouette of each letter is identical, so that when typed, they lock into each other. The filling of the letters, however, varies according to the frequency of use of the letter in the Dutch language. The most frequently used letter (e) represents the highest density of population. The most infrequently used letter (q) corresponds to the lowest density. Setting a sample text creates a Cuppens representation of the Belgian landscape.

Another example of experiment as a process of creation without anticipation of the fixed result is an online project. Ortho-type trio of authors Enrico Bravi, Mikkel Crone Koser, and Paolo Palma describe ortho-type as "an exercise in perception, a stimulus for the mind and the eye to pick out and process three-dimensional planes on a flat surface. . . ." Ortho-type is an online application of a typeface designed to be recognizable in three dimensions. In each view, the viewer can set any of the available variables: length, breadth, depth, thickness, colour, and rotation, and generate multiple variations of the model. The user can also generate those variations as a traditional 2D PostScript font.

Although this kind of experimental process has no commercial application, its results may feed other experiments and be adapted to commercial activities. Once assimilated, the product is no longer experimental. David Carson may have started his formal experiments out of curiosity, but now similar formal solutions have been adapted by commercial giants such as Nike, Pepsi, or Sony.

Following this line, we can go further to suggest that no completed project can be seriously considered experimental. It is experimental only in the process of its creation. When completed it only becomes part of the body of work which it was meant to challenge. As soon as the experiment achieves its final form, it can be named, categorized, and analysed according to any conventional system of classification and referencing.

schools in which composers for type houses were trained together with graphic designers. Also, all the way into the sixties, European designers had to apprentice in professional printing and typesetting plants before certification. There may have been some schools in New York or Chicago that had state of the art typography facilities, but most type-shops were undernourished.

Even the technical teaching literature was very sparse. In contrast, in Switzerland, continuously since 1933, *Typographic Monatsblätter*, a journal of typography, writing and visual communication, instructed professional designers. In Germany, *Der Druckspiegel* and its archive of many years, referenced the work of prominent European designers before some of the professional design journals did. Both journals were available to students. The fact is, that until the introduction of photo and digital typesetting, there were no earth-shaking typography instructions delivered at US art/design schools. The programs dealing with letterform used standard texts from the holdings of bibliophiles or of disciplines like calligraphy, lettering and type rendering. Editor and historian Max Hall writes in *Harvard University Press: A History* of three courses in printing and publishing, given by the Harvard Business School intermittently from 1910 to 1920, organized with the help of The Society of Printers, depending on distinguished lecturers like D. B. Updike, Bruce Rogers and William A. Dwiggins. There was nothing equivalent at art/design schools. US designers of that period learned the use of type on the job in agencies and studios. Dwiggins died in 1956. In 1960, Harvard was still considered a center for typography, not so much for practice, but for the extensive library holding of documents of typographical history; likewise, the Anne Mary Brown Memorial Library at Brown University with an extensive collection of the Incunabula.

It is odd to think that the credit for Swiss Design or Helvetica should go to Americans or anybody of another nationality. The true contribution to the field cannot lie in active plagiarizing or copying the inventive work of Swiss designers. Even though Unimark and Container Corporation of America should be credited with popularizing Helvetica, most American designers of that time had little notion of the arduous discipline of modular typography. Swiss designers did not see the process as completed. There was always the need to push investigations further. For example, Thérèse Moll brought the new disciplined design methods to MIT in 1958, invited by John Mattill, then director of the Office of Publication, to instruct his untrained design staff by direct example. Ms. Moll designed a series of recruitment folders for MIT's budding Summer Session Program, which was distinctly recognizable because of its highly integrated design quality. However, she had to substitute another gothic typeface for Akzidenz Grotesk, because none of the type houses in Boston carried it, and New York houses dealing mostly with advertising agencies were too expensive and the mail-process too slow.

Even then, it took a long time for systemic typography to find sure footing. Muriel Cooper, an art education major, and Jacqueline Casey, graduating with a fashion design/illustration degree, were not even trained in any traditional design techniques. Their typographic knowledge was very sparse. Both would travel to the Mead Library of Ideas in New York to procure quality design examples. They then would take tear sheets of typographical arrangements they liked and attach them to manuscripts as style guides for typesetters to follow. Although untrained in design, they were quick understudies; both were enthusiastic design autodidacts, learning quickly from Thérèse Moll as well as Paul Talmann, a Swiss minimalist artist, and George Teltscher, a former student of the Bauhaus, who also were in the office.

The designer who was more instrumental in fostering minimalist typography and design was Ralph Coburn, very much overlooked by American professional design history. While enrolled at MIT in the

School of Architecture, through his studies alone, he was introduced in depth to work by Mondrian and de Stijl, and exposed to work by Max Bill, Karl Gerstner, Josef Müller-Brockmann as well as Joseph Albers. He also worked in the MIT Office of Publications, first part-time then fulltime. Ralph Coburn insisted that the use of Helvetica should not be seen as a style fad. He backed up his arguments with his own visual work as a minimalist artist. Coburn began a lifelong friendship with Ellsworth Kelly, the minimalist painter, who had been a student at the Museum School in Boston. He and Kelly discussed, explored and collaborated on numerous concepts hoping to resolve them into a "concrete" language. Ralph Coburn did not just adopt Swiss Design. He explored and expanded it, melding what he had learned into a very personal approach. The many visits by Müller-Brockmann, Hofmann and Gerstner to the office, the MIT Press and later to the Media Lab, strengthened the understanding and commitment to structural graphic design. For several decades Helvetica became the identity of the university, because most other institutions mimicked the classical style of Harvard.

The world is always confusing for the uncommitted. For them design is not linked to any specific philosophy of life. It is much more like picking a winner—out of context. When the King gets demoted to Commoner, what happens to the camp followers?

Section 3.2

Dimensional, physical, digital, and kinetic typography

Chapter 3.2.1

Dimensional typography

J. Abbott Miller

Typography has historically been conceived as the art of designing letters: DIMENSIONAL TYPOGRAPHY adds a spatial and temporal concern to the traditionally "flat" and static province of the letter. From early carved inscriptions to neon signs, numerous experiments in the history of typography and signage have interpreted letters as physical, spatial entities.[1] With the advent of motion pictures, animation and movie titles have explored the temporal possibilities of letters moving through space and time. By now, the spectacle of the dancing, decorated, and three-dimensional letterform is common in both print and electronic media.

Developments in graphic design and multimedia have suggested two directions for dimensional typography: on the one hand, "normal" letterforms are agents in an increasingly complex layering of information; the pioneering work of Muriel Cooper at the M.I.T. Media Lab is a prime example of this direction.[2] In these experiments, readers navigate textual displays through spatial paradigms that represent depth. This vein of inquiry replaces the small-to-large hierarchy of traditional print media with a near-to-far SPATIAL AND TEMPORAL dynamic—an eloquent transposition that maps neatly onto our sense of reading as a process of moving deeper and deeper into a document. This direction in dimensional typography investigates the spatial disposition of "flat" letterforms: depth is represented through the layering of successive planar surfaces.

Dimensional typography can also be understood as an investigation of the SCULPTURAL AND THREE-DIMENSIONAL FORMS of individual letters.[3] This line of inquiry assumes that the ability to think of letterforms as having spatial and temporal dimension brings with it new obligations and opportunities to augment the visual and editorial power of letters. In its focus on the individual letterform, this direction is akin to the concerns that preoccupy type designers. Rather than looking at how typography is arranged within a spatial construct, this vein of research looks at the formal, visual properties of individual characters.

Yet these two avenues of research need not be thought of as exclusive of one another: presumably, concern for the SPATIAL aspect of *navigation* and the SCULPTURAL aspect of *individual forms* will converge in a new approach to typography that fuses these two spheres of interest. Both directions suggest an expanded field for design. Readers and viewers are increasingly able and willing to navigate texts and

First published in *Dimensional Typography: Words in Space,* New York: Princeton Architectural Press (1996). © J. Abbott Miller.

Figure 3.11 *Dimensional Typography* cover. © 1996. Designer: J. Abbott Miller. Publisher: Princeton Architectural Press.

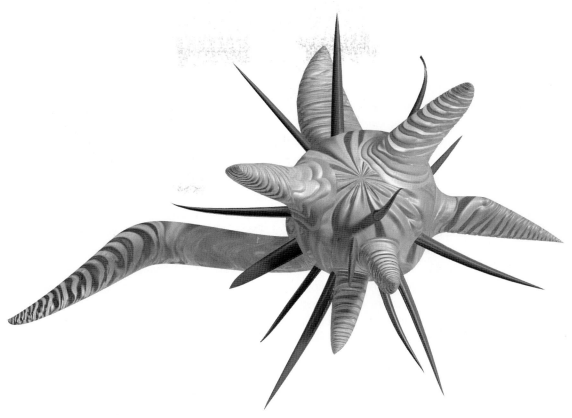

Figure 3.12 Copyright page. © 1996. Designer: J. Abbott Miller.

negotiate challenging textual and visual environments, whether they are the physical spaces of exhibitions or the virtual environments of new media. Designers accustomed to dealing with the flat, pictorial paradigms of print are now dealing with the architectural, ergonomic, and cinematic paradigms of environmental, immersive media.

Historical precedents in lettering, typography, and signage exert a strong influence on how we think about what three-dimensionality in letters might look like. Among the ways in which letters have been rendered dimensional, EXTRUSION is probably the most prevalent. It is a direct transposition of the ordinarily flat world of letters into objecthood. The effect is of a letterform multiplied and stacked in depth, like pages in a book. Nineteenth-century wood type explored illusionistic depth through elaborate perspective constructions.[4] Perhaps because of its deep roots in the history of ornamental and display typography, extrusion remains the most enduring strategy of dimensional typography today. Extruded letters signify monumentality, as in the *20th-Century Fox* logo, by rendering letterforms weighty and material. New software programs automatically "dimensionalize" fonts by extruding them and rendering them in simulated stone, glass, and chrome.[5]

Extrusion is a predictable yet powerful expression of dimensional typography. Its utter obviousness and widespread use tends to occlude the variety of other ways letterforms may become dimensional. For instance, the ROTATION of a letter yields classical forms: spheres, columns, and cones. As a formal operation, performed digitally or on a woodworker's lathe, rotation is as basic as extrusion. But because it transforms the signature silhouette of a letter into a solid, often closed form, it is rarely seen in dimensional typography (even rarer is rotation along vertical, rather than horizontal axes). Rotation generates less automatically legible forms, yet it suggests ways of introducing three-dimensionality that escapes the conventions of extrusion.

TUBING is related to extrusion and rotation, but it limits the "lathing" operation to the stroke of the letter rather than the overall shape of the character. Novelty fonts like *Frankfurter,* or vernacular letters based on pipes, are figurative versions of tubing. Neon signs are an obvious three-dimensional application of tubing which has, in turn, become the basis for the display fonts like *Neon* and *Electric* and others.

Many letters evoke three-dimensionality through SHADOWING or the use of implied light sources.[6] This was another persistent motif of nineteenth-century wood type. But shadow fonts were also of interest to designers at the Bauhaus, who were attracted to the relationship of shadow letters to the "new vision" offered by photography. The design and photography of Joost Schmidt and Laszlo Moholy-Nagy incorporated the cast-shadows of letters, and Herbert Bayer developed an alphabet which relies exclusively on the cast shadow to delineate the letterform.[7] A similar strategy was used by the American type designer R. H. Middleton in his 1932 font called *Umbra*. Shadows have become such a standard technique that a "drop shadow" option is incorporated into most typesetting and page layout software, accessed as easily as *italics* or **boldface**.

Two dimensional letters resembling ribbons and those created with reference to stitching, threading, and lacing, comprise a genre linked to SEWING. In paintings from the Renaissance onward, curling ribbons are shown bearing letters. In ceremonial documents the letters themselves—rather than a supporting surface—are represented as undulating ribbons. The linked forms of many script fonts, such as Matthew Carter's 1966 *Snell Roundhand*, interpret the stroke of the letter as if it were formed from a continuous strand of ribbon. The possibilities of twisted, folded, and pleated letterforms suggests that the logic of sewing could fruitfully inform the construction of dimensional typography.

Another strategy with resonance for both two- and three-dimensions is MOLECULAR CONSTRUCTION: letters that are built from similar, small-scale units to form a larger whole. Individual units may be identical—as in the brick-like formation of bit-maps that comprise Zuzana Licko's fonts *Oakland* and *Emperor*—or merely similar in scale.

Another formal principle that builds larger forms out of smaller, although not necessarily identical components, could be termed MODULAR CONSTRUCTION. Such letters are built from a discrete vocabulary of often interchangeable parts, a notion inherited from the language of industrialization. The rationalist ethos of modularity has funded a number of investigations in twentieth-century type design, including Theo van Doesburg's 1919 geometric font, Josef Albers's 1925 stencil font, and Herbert Bayer's 1925 *universal*. Common to all of these approaches is an interest in reducing alphabetic forms to a limited vocabulary of repeatable marks.

A more complex interpretation of modular construction may be seen in the ingenious *Fregio Mecano*, designed in Italy in the 1920s.[8] It reduces the alphabet to a sequence of curved, straight, and transitional forms, a kit-of-parts that can yield a tremendous variety of heights, widths, and thicknesses. *Walker*, a 1995 font by Matthew Carter is not a strictly modular font, but it shares the constructive logic of modularity by employing detachable slab-serifs. Accessed through optional keystrokes, the serifs may be applied as one might add a finial to a post.[9]

Another operation in this expanding, imprecise system of classification that now further challenges the nomenclature of typography,[10] may be awkwardly described as BLOATING. Bulbous, organic, corpulent, inflated, and biomorphic are all adjectives that come to mind when trying to describe letterforms that exhibit mutable, ductile qualities. Bloated letterforms are reminiscent of both the way skin envelopes a skeletal understructure, and the shapes produced by the expansion and contraction of membranous materials. Thus the associations of bloated forms range from the organic, vegetal, and bodily, to the balloon-like and tensile. A range of display fonts produced in the 1960s and '70s exhibit cartoon-like forms that bear the influence of the Pop appreciation of toys, kitsch, and vernacular objects. Pop art directly engaged letterforms and numbers as part of its inventory of everyday life. The soft sculptures of Claes Oldenburg, which presented letters and numbers as soft, pillow-like constructions, have directly and indirectly informed the sensibility of 1960s and 70s novelty lettering.

In the case studies that follow, "dimensional typography" is explored at the micro-level of individual letterforms. We have interpreted historic and contemporary typefaces by transposing their two-dimensionality into volumetric and planar forms. Thus most of what follows builds on existing typefaces by historic figures like Ambroise Didot as well as contemporaries who have become our unwitting collaborators. The letters represented here are snapshots of "objects" constructed in digital environments: each letter could potentially be "output" as a three-dimensional artifact from the information used to describe them digitally. However, their physical manifestation is not a final objective: their exact role in either physical and virtual environments was bracketed off from their formal and conceptual development.

Many people were directly and indirectly involved in the conceptualization, production, and publication of this project. Thanks are due to Paul Carlos, Luke Hayman, Ji Byol Lee, and Jane Rosch of Design/Writing/Research; to Kevin Lippert, Kerry Fitzpatrick, Kim Lee, and Clement Paulsen of Design Systems, who contributed time and ingenuity in realizing CAD-generated images; to Rick Valicenti for his patience; to Gilbert Paper whose generous *Friends of Gilbert Paper* program enabled this publication; to Eduardo Dunphy and Guy Williams; to Claudia Gould, who invited me to show our work at Artists Space in early 1996; to Suzanne Salinetti of Studley Press; and finally to my partner Ellen Lupton and my radiant son, Jay Lupton Miller, my kindred spirits.

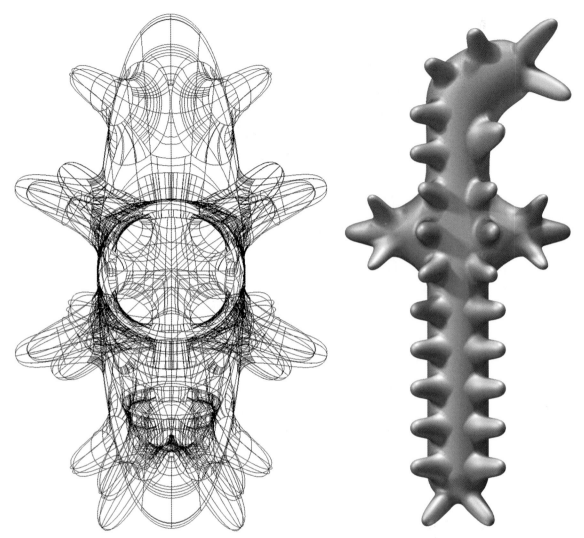

Figure 3.13 Polymorphous letterform. © 1996. Designer: J. Abbott Miller

Figure 3.14 Polymorphous letterform. © 1996. Designer: J. Abbott Miller.

Case studies

Rhizome

A secularized adaptation, *Rhizome* exchanges nature for religion and interprets the prickly silhouettes of *Jesus Loves You* as a botanical motif. The lowercase letter *j* is seen from overhead. [Eds. note: please see page 51 of the original publication].

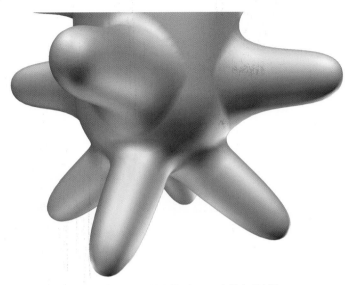

Figure 3.15 Polymorphous letterform. © 1996. Designer: J. Abbott Miller.

Figure 3.16 Rhizome letterform. © 1996. Designer: J. Abbott Miller.

In name and spirit, *Rhizome* recalls the writings of French philosophers Gilles Deleuze and Félix Guattari, who distinguish two logics of the root or radical. The root proper is a singular, linear origin which bifurcates into the ordered, mirroring complexities of both the system of roots below ground and the plant above. The rhizome, on the other hand, is a curly, bulbous network with no single point of origin: "The rhizome itself assumes very diverse forms, from ramified surface extension in all directions to concretion into bulbs and tubers. . . . The rhizome includes the best and the worst: potato and couch-grass, or the weed."[16] From *A Thousand Plateaus*, 1987. [Eds. note: This text refers to Figures 3.16, 3.17].

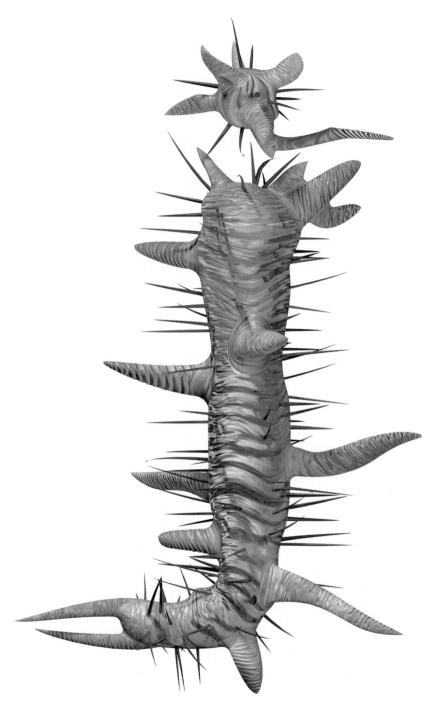

Figure 3.17 Rhizome letterform. © 1996. Designer: J. Abbott Miller.

3-didot

Letter constructions based on the classic font *Didot* (upper left), designed by François Ambroise Didot in 1784. The thick and thin variations of Didot are interpreted as functions of perspective and the position of planar elements. [Eds. note: This text refers to Figures 3.18. 3.19. 3.20, 3.21].

Figure 3.18 3-Didot Box 1. © 1996. Designer: J. Abbott Miller.

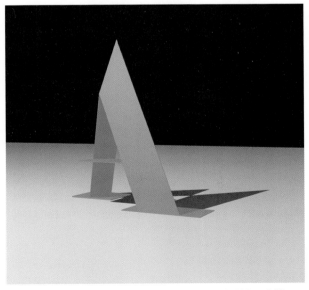

Figure 3.19 3-Didot Box 2. © 1996. Designer: J. Abbott Miller.

Figure 3.20 3-Didot Box 3. © 1996. Designer: J. Abbott Miller.

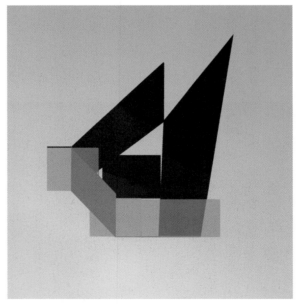

Figure 3.21 3-Didot Box 4. © 1996. Designer: J. Abbott Miller.

Notes

1. For a useful survey of lettering that includes signage and inscriptions, see Nicolete Gray, *A History of Lettering: Creative Experiment and Letter Identity* (Boston: David R. Godine, 1986). *Alphabet 1964: International Annual of Letterforms*, R.S. Hutchings, ed. (Birmingham, UK: The Kynoch Press) includes several useful historical articles on letters in the environment.

2. For an interview with Muriel Cooper, see Jan Abrams, *Muriel Cooper's Visible Wisdom*, in *I.D.*, 41 (5): 48–55 (Sept.–Oct. 1994). (Vol. 41, No. 5): 48–55.

3. Various artists and designers have explored this terrain, notably in the posters and sculptural constructions of graphic designer Takenobu Igarashi. Related investigations appear in the "word-as-image" approach of Herb Lubalin, Milton Glaser, and others.

4. For an excellent survey of the different types of such 19th-century typefaces, see Rob Roy Kelley's *American Wood Type, 1828–1900* (New York: Da Capo Press, 1977).

5. Three-dimensional type programs are reviewed by David Berlow in "The Shape of Things to Come," *Publish* (January 1993): 34–38.

6. The phrase "implied light source" is from Kimberly Elam, who provides a useful discussion of three-dimensional typography in *Expressive Typography: The Word as Image* (New York: Van Nostrand Reinhold, 1990).

7. For Bauhaus designers, see Hans M. Wingler, ed. *The Bauhaus: Weimar, Dessau. Berlin, Chicago* (Cambridge: MIT Press, 1978).

8. The "Fregio Mecano (Carattere scomponibile)" is reproduced in *Alphabets and Other Signs,* ed. Julian Rothenstein and Mel Gooding (London: Redstone Press, 1991). The text indicates only that it was designed by "an unknown Italian in the 1920s."

9. For a review of this remarkable typeface, see Moira Cullen's article "The Space Between the Letters," in *Eye* (No. 19, Vol. 5) 70–77.

10. Technology is challenging the already difficult system of typeface classification. Catherine Dixon provides a useful discussion in her article "Why We Need to Reclassify Type," in *Eye*, 19 (5): 86–87.

Chapter 3.2.2

Dimensional typography: the unbearable flatness of being

Leslie Atzmon

"One evening Harold decided to go for a walk in the moonlight. But there wasn't any moon, and Harold needed a moon for a walk in the moonlight. Fortunately, he had brought his purple crayon. So he drew a moon. He also needed something to walk on. So he drew a path." Thus begins Harold's illuminating adventure in the children's book *Harold and the Purple Crayon* (by Crockett Johnson, 1955). Harold is the consummate designer. He uses a purple line to imagine into being a variety of "material" objects. Harold takes no notice of the differences between two- and three-dimensional experiences. He first fashions and then steps into the two-dimensional line drawing environments he creates.

Like Harold, many contemporary graphic designers have produced inventive tactile and environment-sited two- and three-dimensional work. The books *Paper Graphics* (2001) and *Touch: Graphic Design with Tactile Appeal* (2001), for instance, feature work that reconfigures the run-of-the-mill print design medium, paper. *Touch This: Graphic Design That Feels Good* (2006) and *Fingerprint: The Art of Using Hand-Made Elements in Graphic Design* (2006) are volumes that present projects made from "you can't print on that" materials including ceramic tiles, fur, and cut up auto tires.[1]

It seems to me, though, that over the past two years some tactile or dimensional graphic design has gone beyond print media that capitalizes on creative paper configurations or unusual materials. Of this design, I've found the dimensional typography to be particularly provocative. Like Harold, these type designers create imaginative work that allows them—and their audiences—to enter into and participate in fabricated environments. Some of this design lifts letterforms right off page or screen and plants them firmly in the material world. This work isn't limited to real-world typographic forms made from unconventional substances, though. There are projects that aspire to pull viewers into virtual spaces in which they come face-to-face with shape-shifting letters or letter-like forms. Whether they are physical, virtual, or both, these thought-provoking typographic experiments require audiences to interact with typography as if it were a physical commodity.

Dimensional letterforms made from unique materials are clearly "hot" in contemporary typographic design. Although, as designer Jack Featherstone notes, making 3D type from unorthodox stuff can at times be "just another technique", I believe that it is invaluable to consider what work this design does for our discipline. These dimensional projects stretch the definition of graphic design. They add fresh substance to the decades-old debate about whether the moniker "graphic" design is appropriate to what we do. This dimensional typography highlights novel twists on design processes, new angles on matters of surface versus depth, and unique takes on issues of legibility versus illegibility. This work also expands the range of possibilities for the making of meaning. When these designers do decide to "flatten" their work, for example, the transformation from three-dimensional construction to two-dimensional print media is more than just expedient—the transition becomes an opportunity to enrich the work's metaphorical meaning.

Physical phases and digital versions of these projects typically flow effortlessly into one other. This dimensional type is just as likely to culminate in one-off, three-dimensional pieces as in reproducible two-dimensional design—and both genres transgress the line between art and design. I don't mean the sort of blurring of boundaries between art and design we've seen again and again over the past 100 years; this new dimensional stuff is not merely graphic design that champions personal expression. Some work featured in the books *Tactile: High Touch Visuals* (2008) and *Stereographics* (2008), for example, would have unquestionably been considered "art" just a few years ago. These constructions are now nonchalantly labeled graphic design by the books' authors.

The previous observations bring up some provocative questions. If dimensional formats or unconventional media—or even the design process itself—inadvertently render type unreadable, is it still communication? How is visual meaning made in this work? If illegible three-dimensional typographic work can be mass-produced, what are the ramifications of mass-producing it? What is lost and what is gained in our discipline when reproducibility, a hallmark of traditional graphic design, is traded for uniqueness? What are the implications when designers move seamlessly among three-dimensional and two-dimensional versions and physical and virtual iterations of one piece? What do we get if what we used to call art is now impulsively dubbed graphic design? Is this just a question of renaming, merely calling this work graphic design instead of art, or does this signal a change in what we deem communication design?

Consider work from the show *Dimension and Typography: A Survey of Letterforms in Space and Time*, which spotlights dimensional typographic work done by twenty designers. This exhibition ran in the I space Gallery in Chicago from 9 January to 7 February 2009. According to co-curator Ryan Molloy, this work is a direct result of the fact that designers from various disciplines influence each other "instantly" via "blogs, photo tagging sites like Dropular, Ffffound, [and] social networking sites . . . like Behance".[2] One result of this cross-pollination is that many of the projects in *Dimension and Typography* eschew familiar information systems. In the 1980s and 1990s, some designers likewise rejected traditional information systems; they challenged the limits of legibility and readability by deconstructing typography in print media. Testing the boundaries of legibility was one goal of this work. A number of the pieces in *Dimension and Typography*, on the other hand, introduce alternative information systems that engage unusual metaphors and contend with issues of surface versus depth. In the process, their letter-like forms may end up coincidentally illegible.

Geoff Kaplan's digitally created font *Letter(s) to Ed (Fella)* (Figure 3.22) is one such alternative information system. Kaplan's approach is based in systems theory, an interdisciplinary field in which human-made phenomena—such as letterforms—are considered to be interrelated components that

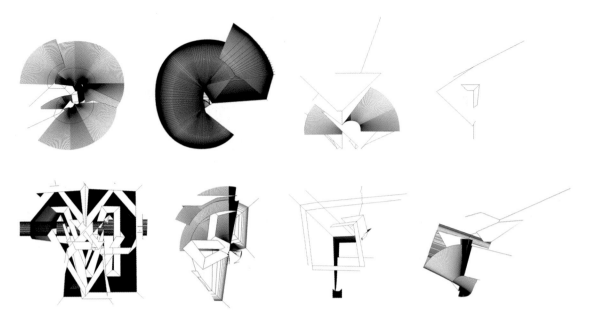

Figure 3.22 The letters A, C, H, L, M, R, T and Y from Letter(s) to Ed (Fella). Designer: Geoff Kaplan/General Working Group.

execute specific processes—such as written languages. Kaplan believes that two-dimensional letter-sets are closed systems. That is, according to Kaplan the information systems that structure two-dimensional fonts are mostly unaffected by other systems or external forces. With these ideas in mind, Kaplan added a z-axis to two-dimensional uppercase Akzidenz Grotesk letterforms—a process that he believed would destabilize the closed system. Kaplan then removed the z-axis and to see if he'd get back "any degree of the original [two-dimensional] data set [Akzidenz Grotesk]."[3]

The final product is the set of letter-like forms called *Letter(s) to Ed (Fella)* (Figure 3.22).[4] Kaplan wonders if these characters become a three-dimensional language system. He also speculates that the original Akzidenz letters are destabilized by the disruptive z-axis. Kaplan sees both possibilities as "simultaneous realities," which is why he believes that "these marks live between page and screen."

That *Letter(s) to Ed (Fella)* is illegible is not the point of Kaplan's project; rather, it is a byproduct of his inserting and then removing a three-dimensional axis in virtual space. Kaplan's final letter-like forms were printed on paper and several of these characters were featured in *Dimension and Typography*. It is interesting to me that the transitional three-dimensional form of Kaplan's font is virtual—the three-dimensionality is rendered in screen-based media—while the final two-dimensional form of this font is physical and printed on paper. In the end, we are left with a set of 26 gorgeous grotesques and a cascade of thought-provoking questions about the impact of forcing other dimensionalities on to stable two-dimensional communication systems.

In a similar vein, Jim Stevens and Ryan Molloy translate two-dimensional letterforms into a three-dimensional communication system. But their font La Robia, which was printed on a Zcorp 3-D printer that utilizes plaster with chromatic binder, is decidedly concrete. Their collaboration was spurred by a

Figure 3.23 *La Robia*. © 2009. Designers: James C. Stevens and Ryan Molloy. Photographer: Jimmy Luu.

conversation about the ways both Architecture and letterforms can function as street art. Stevens, who is an architect, worked out the tectonics for La Robia, and Molloy, who is a graphic designer and an architect, devised the letterforms. Loosely based on a brick and mortar paving pattern metaphor, *La Robia* (Figure 3.23) melds the modular aspects of letterforms with the modular pattern of Della Robbia-style masonry.

Stevens and Molloy followed certain ground rules to create their font: they devised red "brick" letterform units and gray "mortar" connector and ball joint units to facilitate reading in various directions, and they made sure that individual characters bore some resemblance to roman letters. To prevent confusion among letterforms, each character also had to be visually distinct since letters that mirror each other (such as d, p, q, and b) may be confused in three-dimensional space. Finally, Stevens and Molloy decided that each character "should have rotational symmetry along at least one axis," which allows each letter to be "recognized from multiple vantage points."

The piece Stevens and Molloy installed in *Dimension and Typography* reads: "Escape from the architectural ghetto". Knowing this—and that the letterforms are the red parts—makes recognizing the letterforms fairly easy. It is also important to note that La Robia letterforms can be mass-produced, and like the letterpress process, their units can be disassembled and reassembled to create any text.

In the past, type based on an architectural metaphor would likely have remained on the printed page or the computer screen. If this type happened to be built out of three-dimensional material, in the end it would probably be "flattened" in graphic or photographic form. La Robia, on the other hand, challenges the two-dimensional mindset that is still prevalent in our field. The composition of the units and the structural system they devised allow Stevens and Molloy to build on their architectural metaphor. Stevens explains that ultimately, "for the piece to be fully successful it will need to be installed in an environmental context." Molloy too envisions La Robia as "a building unit . . . a public space created by letterforms: a built environment in which . . . navigation and content could be both written and experienced." They intend to use La Robia to create structures in which letterform, textual content, and built form merge.

In a similar fashion, Jack Featherstone's piece *Play with Type* melds type and toy. Each letter in his brightly colored cut paper font is divided into three flat pieces. These pieces, which are created on the computer, have slits by which the letter parts can interconnect to create an expressive tinker toy-like construction. The three-dimensional piece entails a "toy" metaphor. Featherstone's design process, though, conveys a "play" metaphor. The tinker toy-like construction is flattened once again on the computer, and then cut out for use in another three-dimensional piece. This circular process loops continually from paper to three-dimensional construction to computer screen, amalgamating three distinct ways of playing. Featherstone, who purposely intended to "blur the line between art and typography" in *Play with Type*, explains that "different pieces or sections of the type can be picked up and felt[,] then rearranged to create new versions from the same word".[5] Again, illegibility is not a goal of this piece, it is an artefact of Featherstone's process. Remixing, though, is integral to Featherstone's concept of type as plaything—and the audience is encouraged to participate.

The audience also becomes immersed in Denise Gonzales Crisp's room-filling puzzle-like project *Prototype*. The piece begins with basswood jig units, which are the understructures for all the letter designs. The jigs—which have standardized slots and extensions that fit with those on other jigs—function as molds for strands of typographic information. The jig letters "snap" into place to form a line of letters (Figure 3.24). As with *La Robia*, Gonzales Crisp's unit forms can be disassembled and reassembled to create any text.

The face of each jig features a two-dimensional rendering of its letter that is shaped by a lush letterform pattern. Gonzales Crisp's two-dimensional pattern is not merely a decorative surface, however; it provides detailed visual information about each letter. In a process reminiscent of the way DNA units come together as a template for protein production, a second layer of wood functions as a matrix around which wire can be wrapped to outline the letter. When the jig letters are removed, full-text wire traces remain. Gonzales Crisp did not consciously intend this DNA metaphor. Nevertheless, it is intriguing that *Prototype* suggests a bodily "communication" process that depends upon the interaction of surface matrices to produce physiological "information."

The letters come together in a ribbon of wire text that is suspended from the walls and ceiling of the gallery. Gonzales Crisp's text documents her thoughts at a visit to the hardware store when she began working on "Prototype": "I ASK FOR BASSWOOD & HE LEADS ME TO TOWERING PLANKS & I SHOW HIM THE JIG & HE WITH EYES THAT MEASURE RIGHT ANGLES TRUE SAYS LASERCUTTER BUT I PREFER THE REAL THING & I SAY THAT WOULD TAKE FOREVER & HE

Chapter 3.2.3

The new seduction: movable type

Michael Worthington

Should there be a new system of communication for new media? The prospect that typography and the written word can evolve into something more (i.e., that motion and sound can become an integral part of the basic alphabetic system) is extremely seductive. Imagine a new, magical form of communication, born of a new, expanded "alphabet" that combines twenty-six letterforms with selected sound bytes and motion options. Then again, why use type at all when you can have video feeds, computer animation, streaming audio, icons, and digital imagery that merge into a mass of navigable space, all live and online?

Over the course of the last 500 years, writing systems—and the tools that enable them to become visually manifest—have reflected the perpetually evolving state of technology, from stone carving to the mechanization of printing and beyond. Writing has given us the ability to reconstruct images, enhance meaning, chronicle events, and communicate globally from an essentially abstract platform across space and time. While the letterforms themselves (and their means of production and dissemination) have altered wildly, the "magic" of the written word as communication has remained. At the same time, the relationship of word to image has perhaps grown equally complex. But while we understand the permutations and possibilities afforded us with respect to words and picures, the advent of additional media challenges our notions of designed communication—its process, its function, and in the long term, its ultimate promise.

Complex ideas may be depicted by a series of images or icons, but they have nowhere near the specificity (or speed of understanding) that text has to offer. True, there are situations when type is the logical choice and situations when non-typographic media are more suitable. Indeed, language itself can be either highly specific or open to interpretation. The poetics of language can act as a gateway to myriad meanings, or can be specific enough to feel personal to an individual.

The functionality and poetic possibilities of the alphabetic system in general suggest that while the written word is not likely to disappear in new media, its purpose demands of the designer new and complex considerations—considerations that embrace the multiple options afforded by (and in some cases, restricted by) time-based and interactive media. The key lies in understanding how such notions affect and advance the role of typography.

Typography's role—or, to put it in tangible terms, its voice—is most evident in the form of the letters themselves. Set in a certain typeface, words are delivered with great specificity: a "dog," for example, can be tail-wagging when set in Keedy Sans; vicious in Crack-house; a mongrel in DeadHistory; or a

First published in *AIGA Journal of Graphic Design*, 16 (3) (1998): 9–10. © Michael Worthington.

thoroughbred in Baskerville. The words themselves have character because they are read visually as well as literally. In this context, such readings of the expressive qualities of type extend our understanding beyond the mere selection of a typeface. In print we read the composition, observe the format, and absorb the context—in some cases, before we even get to the content itself. We hear the tone of voice before we understand what it is saying. These elements come into play on the screen, too— although in screen-based typography we are given ancillary information through the relationship the text has to time and motion. In a time-based medium, type has additional expressive qualities, additional layers of significance: the great advantage of motion is that it brings words to life, giving them character, emotional resonance, and depth.

Yet, haven't time and motion always been present in print design? Well-designed print typography typically addresses issues of hierarchy and composition to create a rhythm of seeing. The difference is that on screen, both the reader's eye (the seeing device) and the media surface (the screen) are in motion. Here the design negotiation is creative as well as custodial: the designer is both choreographer and cop, balancing creativity with functionality. Motion, in this view, is both an asset and a trap. It introduces possibilities for a three-dimensional typographic environment, fully navigable and interactive, into which, if it is to succeed, language (read "typography") must be successfully integrated.

At present, creating such hyper-typographic environments is both time-consuming and complicated. This is the land of gratuitous devices, flying type, and spinning logos. But understood in its relation to time, motion can be a persuasive conveyor of complex information—balancing text and subtext, articulating voices, orchestrating messages through the subtle articulation of timed movement. Wordplay can be layered over time, critical or supportive subtexts can be hidden one moment and revealed the next, and different voices can be simultaneously represented, tweaked, or finessed. Content can be shaped, manipulated, and transformed. In this multifaceted forum, readers can participate, reciprocate, and engage in dialogues that are at once visual and verbal.

Unlike print, too, such communication rarely has a discernible beginning, middle, or end. Because by its very nature it is an iterative process, new media develops in an exponential manner. Through repeated interactions and a kind of collaborative, shared authorship, there is a reciprocity between sender and receiver, a kind of perpetual back-and-forthness to this environment that is its own form of motion. Here, where design and typography are laid bare—open to alteration, manipulation, rampant (even wrong!) interpretation—a better model may be for designers to try to orchestrate readable experiences rather than to control scripted spaces. The thinking and conceptualizing of such spaces has more to do with defining the parameters and permutations than designing the infrastructure and filling in the details: indeed, such controlled intentions are virtually useless in this arena. Just as we must reconsider the role of the letterform (its intention, its behavior) and the responsibility of the designers (their purpose, their practice) so, too must we rethink the end user: this is an audience of active participants. It is they who are in control now—not us.

As new media moves away from mimicking print and toward establishing its own unique territory, it becomes clear the rules, metaphors, and processes of print cannot be imported wholesale into the interactive realm. Understanding the fundamental principles of expression and hierarchy, contrast and composition, tone and nuance, appropriateness and innovation remain essential criteria for evaluating, understanding, designing, and working with type. That said, creators of new media will have to learn to write differently, to design differently, perhaps even to think differently. Mostly, they will have to learn to approach technology differently, to expand typography's expressive voice. This is the next step for typography as it advances into the twenty-first century: type on the screen can fracture and flutter and fly on by.

Perhaps, in the end, Gutenberg's dream of movable type has finally become a reality. Indeed, it may never sit still again.

Chapter 3.2.4

Electronic typography: the new visual language

Jessica Helfand

As advances in technology introduce more complex creative challenges, screen-based typography must be reconsidered as a new language with its own grammar, its own syntax, and its own rules. What we need are better models which go beyond language or typography to reinforce—rather than restrict—our understanding of what it is to design with electronic media. This essay traces some of the experimental precursors to contemporary electronic typography—from Marinetti's *Parole in Libertà* to George Maciunas's Fluxus happenings—and looks at language as part of a more comprehensive communication platform: time-sensitive, interactive, and highly visual.

In 1968, Mattel introduced Talking Barbie. I like to think of this as my first computer. I remember saving up my allowance for what seemed an eternity to buy one. To make her talk, you pulled a little string; upon its release, slave-to-fashion Barbie would utter delightful little conversational quips like "I think mini-skirts are smashing" and "Let's have a costume party."

If you held the string back slightly as she was talking, her voice would drop a few octaves, transforming her from a chirpy soprano into a slurpy baritone. What came out then sounded a lot more like "Let's have a cocktail party."

I loved that part.

What I loved was playing director—casting her in a new role, assigning her a new (albeit ludicrous) personality. I loved controlling the tone of her voice, altering the rhythm of her words, modulating her oh-so-minimal (and moronic) vocabulary. I loved having the power to shape her language—something I would later investigate typographically, as I struggled to understand the role of the printed word as an emissary of spoken communication.

Today, my Macintosh sounds a lot like my Barbie did then—the same monotone, genderless, robotic drawl. But here in the digital age, the relationship between design and sound—and in particular, between the spoken word and the written word—goes far beyond pulling a string. The truth is that the computer's internal sound capabilities enable us to design with sound, not just in imitation of it. Like it or not, the changes brought about by recent advances in technology indicate the need for designers to broaden their understanding of what it is to work effectively with typography. It is no longer enough to design for

First published in *Print*, 48 (3) (May/June 1994): 98–103. © Jessica Helfand.

readability, to suggest a sentiment or reinforce a concept through the selection of a particular font. Today, we can make type talk: in any language, at any volume, with musical underscoring or sci-fi sound effects or overlapping violins. We can sequence and dissolve, pan and tilt, fade to black, and specify type in Sensurround. As we "set" type, we encounter a decision-making process unprecedented in two-dimensional design: unlike the kinetic experience of turning a printed page to sequence information, time now becomes an unusually powerful and persuasive design element.

Today, we can visualise concepts in four action-packed, digital dimensions. Interactive media have introduced a new visual language, one that is no longer bound to traditional definitions of word and image, form and place. Typography, in an environment that offers such diverse riches, must redefine its goals, its purpose, its very identity. It must reinvent itself. And soon.

Visual language, or the interpretation of spoken words through typographic expression, has long been a source of inspiration to artists and writers. Examples abound, dating as far back as the incunabula and extending upwards from concrete poetry in the 1920s to "happenings" in the 1960s to today's multicultural morass of pop culture. Visual wordplay proliferates, in this century in particular, from Filippo Tommaso Marinetti's *Parole in Libertà* to George Maciunas's Fluxus installations to the latest MTA posters adorning New York subway walls. Kurt Schwitters, Guillaume Apollinaire, Piet Zwart, Robert Brownjohn—the list is long, the examples inexhaustible.

For designers there has always been an overwhelming interest in formalism, in analysing the role of type as medium (structure), message (syntax), and muse (sensibility). Throughout, there has been an attempt to reconcile the relationship between words both spoken and seen—a source of exhilaration to some and ennui to others. Lamenting the expressive limitations of the Western alphabet, Adolf Loos explained it simply: "One cannot speak a capital letter." Denouncing its structural failings, Stanley Morrison was equally at odds with a tradition that designated hierarchies in the form of upper and lower-case letterforms. Preferring to shape language as he deemed appropriate, Morrison referred to caps as "a necessary evil."

Academic debate over the relationship between language and form has enjoyed renewed popularity in recent years as designers borrow from linguistic models in an attempt to codify—and clarify—their own typographic explorations. Deconstruction's design devotées have eagerly appropriated its terminology and theory, hoping to introduce a new vocabulary for design: it is the vocabulary of signifiers and signifieds, of Jacques Derrida and Ferdinand de Saussure, of Michel Foucault and Umberto Eco.

As a comprehensive model for evaluating typographic expression, deconstruction has ultimately proved both heady and limited. Today, as advances in technology introduce greater and more complex creative challenges, it is simply arcane. We need to look at screen-based typography as a new language, with its own grammar, its own syntax, and its own rules. What we need are new and better models, models that go beyond language or typography per se, and that reinforce rather than restrict our understanding of what it is to design with electronic media.

Of course, learning a new language is one thing, fluency quite another. Yet we have come to equate fluency with literacy—another outdated model for evaluation. "Literacy should not mean the ability to decode strings of alphabetic letters," says Seymour Papert, Director of the Epistemology and Learning Group at the MIT Media Lab, who refers to such a definition as "letteracy." And language, even to linguists, proves creatively limiting as a paradigm. "New media promise the opportunity to offer a smoother transition to what really deserves to be called literacy," says Papert. Typography, as the physical embodiment of such thinking, has quite a way to go.

The will to decipher the formal properties of language, a topic of great consequence for communication designers in general, has its philosophical antecedents in ancient Greece. "Spoken words," wrote Aristotle in Logic, "are the symbols of mental experience. Written words are the symbols of spoken words." Today, centuries later, the equation has added a new link: what happens when written words can speak? When they can move? When they can be imbued with sound and tone and nuance, with decibel and harmony and voice? As designers probing the creative parameters of this new technology, our goal may be less to digitise than to dramatize. Indeed, there is a theatrical component that I am convinced is essential to this new thinking. Of what value are typographic choices—bold and italics, for example—when words can dance across the screen, dissolve, or disappear altogether?

In this dynamic landscape, our static definitions of typography appear increasingly imperilled. Will the beauty of traditional letterforms be compromised by the evils of this new technology? Will punctuation be stripped of its functional contributions, or ligatures their aesthetic ones? Will type really matter?

Of course it will. In the meantime, however, typography's early appearance on the digital frontier does not bode well for design. Take email, for example. Gone are the days of good handwriting, of the Palmer Method and the penmanship primer. In its place, electronic mail which, despite its futuristic tone, has paradoxically revived the antiquated art of letter writing. Sending email is easy and effortless and quick. It offers a welcome respite from talking, and, consequently, bears a closer stylistic resemblance to conversational speech than to written language. However, for those of us with even the most modest design sense, it eliminates the distinctiveness that typography has traditionally brought to our written communiqués. Though its supporters endorse the democratic nature of such homogeneity, the truth is, it is boring. In the land of email, we all "sound" alike: everyone writes in system fonts.

Email is laden with many such contradictions: ubiquitous in form yet highly diverse in content, at once ephemeral and archival, transmitted in real time yet physically intangible, it is a kind of esthetic flatland—informationally dense and visually unimaginative. Here, hierarchies are preordained and nonnegotiable: passwords, menus, commands, help.

Software protocols require that we title our mail, a leftover model from the days of interoffice correspondence, which makes even the most casual letter sound like a corporate memo. As a result, electronic missives all have headlines. (Titling our letters makes us better editors, not better designers.) As a fitting metaphor for the distilled quality of things digital, the focus in email is on the abridged, the acronym, the quick read. Email is functionally serviceable and visually forgettable, not unlike fast food. It is drive-through design: get in, get out, move on.

And it is everywhere. Here is the biggest contribution to communication technology to come out of the last decade, a global network linking millions of people worldwide, and designers—communication designers, no less—are nowhere in sight. Typography, in this environment, desperately needs direction. Where to start? Comparisons with printed matter inevitably fail, as words in the digital domain are processed with a speed unprecedented in the world of paper. Here, they are incorporated into databases or interactive programs, where they are transmitted and accessed in random, non-hierarchical sequences. "Hypertext," or the ability to program text with interactivity—meaning that a word, when clicked upon or pointed to will, in fact, do something—takes it all a step further: here, by introducing alternate paths, information lacks the closure of the traditional printed narrative. "Hypertextual story space is now multidi-mensional," explains Robert Coover in the magazine *Artforum*, "and theoretically infinite."

If graphic design can be largely characterized by its attention to understanding the hierarchy of information (and using type in accordance with such understanding), then how are we to determine its use in a non-linear context such as this? On a purely visual level, we are limited by what the pixel will render: the screen matrix simulates curves with surprising sophistication, but hairlines and serifs will, to the serious typophile, appear inevitably compromised. On a more objective level, type in this context is both silent and static, and must compete with sound and motion—not an easy task. Conversely, in the era of the handheld television remote, where the user can—and does—mute at will, the visual impact of written typography is not to be discounted.

To better analyse the role(s) of electronic typography, we might begin by looking outside: not to remote classifications imported from linguistic textbooks, or even to traditional design theories conveni-ently repackaged, but to our own innate intelligence and distinctive powers of creative thought. To cultivate and adequately develop this new typography (because if we don't, no one else will), we might do well to rethink visual language altogether, to consider new and alternative perspectives. "If language is indeed the limit of our world," writes literary critic William Gass in *Habitations of the Word*, "then we must find another, larger, stronger, more inventive language which will burst those limits."

In his book *Seeing Voices*, author and neurologist Oliver Sacks reflects on the complexity of sign language, and describes the cognitive understanding of spatial grammar in a language that exists without sound. He cites the example of a deaf child learning to sign, and details the remarkable quality of her visual awareness and descriptive, spatial capabilities. "By the age of four, indeed, Charlotte had advanced so far into visual thinking and language that she was able to provide new ways of

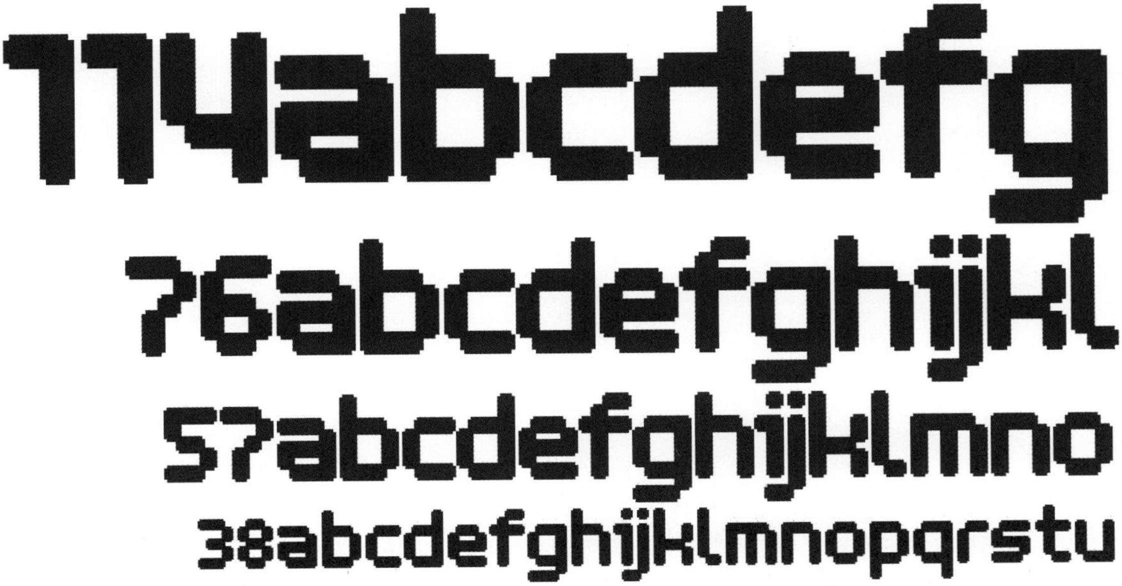

Figure 3.26 Interact font. The font is designed for screen use at four fixed sizes. The construction of the font is governed by 45-degree corner elements that provide a degree of optical modulation toward more familiar letter shapes. © 1993. Designer: 8vo. Publisher: Lars Müller Publishers/MuirMcNeil.

thinking—revelations—to her parents." As a consequence of learning sign language as adults, this particular child's parents not only learned a new language, but discovered new ways of thinking as well—visual thinking. Imagine the potential for interactive media if designers were to approach electronic typography with this kind of ingenuity and openmindedness.

William Stokoe, a Chaucer scholar who taught Shakespeare at Gallaudet College in the 1950s, summarised it this way: "In a signed language, narrative is no longer linear and prosaic. Instead, the essence of sign language is to cut from a normal view to a close-up to a distant shot to a close-up again, and so on, even including flashback and fast-forward scenes, exactly as a movie editor works." Here, perhaps, is another model for visual thinking: a new way of shaping meaning based on multiple points of view, which sees language as part of a more comprehensive communication platform—time-sensitive, interactive, and highly visual. Much like multimedia.

Addendum: In gathering research for this article, I posted a query on Applelink's typography board. I received the following response:

As a type designer, I am sort of surprised to find myself NOT VERY CONCERNED with how type is used in the fluid context of multi-media. In a way, type is as flexible as photography or illustration in a mm context . . . i.e., it's a whole new ballgame for everyone.

Though my link-pal claimed not to be concerned, he did take the time to respond. And as I read his reply, I realized how important it will be for all of us to be concerned: not merely to translate the printed word to the screen, but to transcend it.

Then I found myself wondering: what would Stanley Morison have thought of all those CAPS?

Chapter 3.2.5

Working the art process by typing in computer code

Casey Reas and Ben Fry
(in discussion with Javier Candeira)

In his essay "Processing Processing," the New York-based writer and designer Paul Ford declares his passion for "languages like Processing—computer languages which compile not to executable code, but to esthetic objects, whether pictures, songs, demos, or websites."[1] Most designers, musicians and moviemakers are used to working with visual tools that imitate the eye-to-hand coordination of working with physical tools, but the computer languages that Paul Ford extols (Processing for interaction, CSound for music and sound, TeX and LaTex for typographically consistent documents, POV-RAY for 3D, and so on) require that the artist work on the more abstract level of code, typing out letters that, when interpreted by the computer, will yield their visual or aural results.

In the contemporary world of art as concept, this is simultaneously a time-honoured practice (that of the artists' concepts being executed by craftspeople) and a strange harking back to the practice of art as craft. Code is one of the fundamental media of interactive works (the other one being hardware), and artists and designers writing their own code are immersing themselves in their own work in a much more intimate manner than those who have to use programmers and engineers as intermediaries. Thus it is not strange that designers are at the forefront of the practice of writing their own damn code, with "high" artists bringing up the rear at a slower pace.

The interest in this hacking of the artistic process by writing code is literally written on the wall, as art and design schools all over the world are offering courses teaching programming as a tool for exploring and conveying meaning.

And practitioners are certainly using the tools for expression afforded by programming. In the 2005 edition of Barcelona's Online Flash Film Festival, a design conference centred on motion graphics and online design was taken over by designers and artists who use code as their medium. Amit Pitaru presented his 3D drawing tools and the Sonic Wire Sculptor installation based on them. Jared Tarbell gave a mini-seminar on the algorithmic techniques he uses for his work. The clever buggers from Soda presented their animation-tool-for-children Moovl. Even Joshua Davis, the punkmeister of Flash design,

First published in *Visual Communication*, 5 (2) (2006): 205–17. © SAGE/Casey Reas/Ben Fry.

sang the praises of algorithmic manipulation of graphical work in his showcase-and-tell session about his collaboration with his programer partner Branden Hall.

Many of these artists use Processing, the Java-based Open Source programming environment and language initiated by Casey Reas and Ben Fry from their work at MIT. In 2005, Reas and Fry received the prestigious Golden Nica award from Ars Electronica in the category for Net Vision. Two days after receiving the prize, they answered these questions for *Visual Communication*.

VCJ: Do you think that everyone should learn to code? Is that the focus of Processing?

Reas: I do think that in a way, but it is a personal belief, not something that is behind the creation of Processing. Right now Processing is a great tool for people who want to find their way into a more professional mode of programming.

If the Processing project had been about teaching anyone, from children to grandparents, across many contexts, I think we would have made different choices. But as the majority of professional and even semi-pro and hobbyist graphics now are done in languages that are C-like and Java-like, I think it is a good service to them to learn this sort of syntax in Processing in a manageable way, and then go into these large languages like Java and C.

Another important side of Processing is that being based on Java makes it easy to export the programs, show them off the web and share the source-code; it is a wonderful way of people sharing programs and learning. Processing is so web-friendly as a result of it being based on Java.

VCJ: You have read the Paul Ford quote about "languages that compile to aesthetic objects." As makers of tools for coders of aesthetic objects, who do you feel are your peers?

Reas: Because we don't deal much in sound, we don't know much about that, but I find the PD/PureData community very interesting. I did a panel last year with Miller [Puckette, at ISEA] and it was fascinating to hear his stories about his community. MAX-MSP is also a very nice system and I have had nice conversations with people writing it. Also I see the Drawbot people and [typographers] Just [van Rossum] and Erik [van Blokland] at Letterror in Holland; we see their work as really interesting ways to work with design and code.

VCJ: And you are artists who are influencing art not only by making work but by making the tools other artists use. Your tool is not only a tool, like Photoshop or Illustrator, but a tool for artists to make their own tools. How far are you imbuing the art mainstream with this computer science-inspired pattern of "make tools that make tools"?

Reas: Actually the "make tools" attitude is very prevalent in the arts, we have that in film all the time. In Barry Lyndon, Kubrick wanted to shoot with low light, but the lenses weren't able to do that, so he commissioned special lenses so he was able to shoot by candlelight. So he had an artistic vision that he was able to satisfy through commissioning a new piece of technology. In the same way, I see programming as getting beyond what commercial software tools provide; if you have the power to build your own tools, then you can create your own infrastructures and be able to create tools to build better tools to build better tools, and so on. There are lots of other precedents in the arts; like Sol LeWitt's "machine that makes art," and Duchamp inventing his own physics, and there are many examples of people making systems in which to work, but . . .

Fry: The early starts of photography and cinema were very technical out of necessity because people had to figure out how to make images and how to make things that made them; it was not so much that they were interested in the science or the technology of it, but that they had a specific artistic goal in mind. For me, programming has to do with the fact that many of the things that I want to make can only be made through software. I set out to work on Processing in order to make tools I could use. I go down my wish list of things I wished I could do very quickly and just make happen. But it is very specific to my own work, and lots of other people might not want to create that kind of work . . .

Reas: The reason some people make things in software is because software allows you to do a certain category of experiences or work that other media don't allow. As there are lots of precedents of people innovating the technology in other media in order to fulfill their needs, so we are trying to innovate tool-building in the art domain, in order to satisify our needs within software.

VCJ: Processing is not only about programming or about graphical programming, but about a certain style of programming. In Processing, programs are called 'sketches'. Is Processing an enabler of sketching in coding?

Fry: Actually, that is something very different from how programming is typically done. With C++ or Java it is very top-down; people sit down and think about structures and object hierarchies and how to properly structure the whole project. I think those are fine things, but it is closer to big-time software engineering and not how artists work. Our approach is closer to scripting languages, where you can make something small, write a piece of code that does something for you, but doesn't require a very large structure.

Reas: The way I teach programming with Processing, it is about getting your hands dirty in the material as soon as possible. I come from an arts background where I am used to picking up a pencil and drawing something bit by bit till the structure appears. That is the way I like to program as well: write a few lines, test it, write a few lines, test it, and that way you always have something that works, you always have something to show.

Ben and I come from a background where if you want to do something you do a lot of sketches, you put them up on the wall, you look at them for a few days, you see what's working and what's not working, and that is an idea that we have included in Processing: you do a lot of small programs, and then you look at them and analyse them, and then decide where you want to go from there. Sketching comes from traditional arts pedagogy.

Fry: The idea of it being informal and based on sketches also came from [John Maeda's] Design By Numbers. With that environment one of the things that came up with students is that they weren't able to collect sketches well; there is no concept of a sketchbook, or being able to share sketches around, and that was one of the things that we wanted to address.

There's also lots of stuff that would be sort of "nice to have," but that is tougher than I would like to be able to get into Processing, like importing 2D and 3D geometry into processing, or taking a sketchbook and being able to actually draw something first and have that relate to the code, or work back and forth between that. There is a whole different level of stuff that we could have to make it more like sketching.

VCJ: You are both teachers. What are your impressions from using Processing with your students?

Fry: I have been teaching at the art department at Harvard about doing Data Visualization, and the idea was to pull together people from very different departments and teach them Information Visualization from complete scratch, so there were six people of whom four had never done any programming at all, they came from Government, History, Economics, and two of them were Computer Scientists.

It was interesting because my premise going into it was that artists and designers have dropped the ball in terms of being able to understand and deal with information. One significant role of artists is to be able to break down complex ideas for a wider public, as we are living in a very information-oriented time, but artists do not have the tools of programming for dealing with the more complex sorts of data that are out there. It was very interesting that the most succesful students were the ones who had the least programming background in the past, and they were able to pick it up by grabbing little titbits out of their own fields.

Reas: Picking up on that, one thing that I have enjoyed about Processing is that it is an equalizer. Usually one has to teach a class where there are people with a lot of programming experience and a lot of people without. Students typically—and this is unfortunate—are either conceptually and aesthetically advanced or they are technically advanced, and it is rare to have someone who is both. So the job for the class is to get each group to have empathy and an understanding of the other group's discipline.

Because Processing is a text-based programming environment the programmers are familiar with it, and because it is geared to making visual things, there is also a way in for people who are esthetically inclined or conceptually inclined. And when you have a class split like that, they rapidly learn from each other, which is fun.

At UCLA, where I teach Processing, it is done very differently at the undergraduate level and at the graduate level. For undergraduates, it's the first time they are reading texts about interactivity, and for some of them it is the first time they have looked at computer code. And on the graduate level, we do these kind of quick projects, for instance a one-week computer vision project where they hook up a camera in some sort of context and make a quick application. So Processing can be used in any teaching environment. It can be used in a very basic and didactic overview for issues of software, the arts and interaction. And it can also be used as a tool for making quick prototypes for a conceptually driven graduate project.

VCJ: What about the community of Processing developers? I don't mean those who develop with Processing, but those who develop the Processing system itself. Yesterday you commented that you two were more visually oriented and the people not visually oriented were doing the other parts of Processing for you.

Reas: Well, not "for us," they do it for everyone! Some people love MIDI, whereas Ben and I have never used MIDI for a project, so it is other people who write MIDI libraries, and Open Sound Control libraries, and sound libraries, and that way it helps the project to be more well rounded. The other thing is that as I am not an expert in sound, I shouldn't be the person writing the sound API (Application Programming Interface) for Processing anyway, whereas regarding the graphics APIs, we had a lot of experience in writing languages for making graphics, so we felt really solidly that we were making the right choices.

VCJ: You have also commented that most of the work done by others happens not in the core of the langauge but in its modules. Is it because you didn't open it enough, because you didn't need it, or because Processing is so well made that it doesn't really need any changes?

Fry: Not that last one, certainly. I think Processing got fairly complicated fairly quickly, in terms of how it works internally, and I think we underestimated some of how difficult it is to jump onto a project and start hacking away. But I also think it is more interesting for people to carve out their own piece of the project, and just to be able to work on that and have their own domain.

For instance, there are people who did video input libraries, and rather than saying "we'll work on the video library for Processing itself," instead they got together and made their own video library, which is fine, because as a group they are more motivated. They have their ownership, and [the rest of us] have this community structure of it where they post the work and share it with other people. They treat it the way that we treat the rest of the code.

VCJ: In a way they are helping you not only to code the project, but also to manage it by decentralizing it?

Fry: Exactly. We are realizing there is only so much coding and there are only so many hours in the day for Casey and I, and any way that we can hook people in and motivate them to carve out their own niche winds up being very important.

VCJ: What do you think is missing and what is the next thing that is going to be implemented?

Fry: There is a very interesting piece of Processing that hasn't emerged yet, and that's the tools menu. The tools menu will be a place where people will be able to write their own . . . they are not extensions, but tools. For instance, there can be a bezier editor where people can point and click and edit their curves in, and the code for the bezier tool that generates Processing code will just be added to the Processing codebase.

VCJ: So what work do you like that has been done with Processing?

Fry: The stuff that I like for Processing, the things that I get more excited about are seeing what people without design backgrounds do when they approach code and the difference in how they interpret things compared to others, like the REM video [Animal] by Motion Theory.

Reas: There was a young person working at Motion Theory, a young hacker who just got excited about Processing, and the boss there is so openminded and savvy that he just let him go with it. They are really good at using technology; that company uses the right tool for the right reason and they have integrated Processing into their complex workflow.

Also, there are many examples on processing.org and on Tom Carden's Processing blog.

VCJ: What about your own work? What's the relationship of Processing to your own artistic work?

Fry: For my own work, I see how my needs are driving the capabilities of Processing. For the Haplotype block[2] genomic data display that was later shown on the cover of Nature,[3] I needed to output to screen, and then to vectorial formats and to print output, so Processing has evolved as a direct result of my needs, in this case to express insights about data by information visualization. As to the "sketching" aspect, Zipdecode[4] is a piece I did before Processing (and then reworked under Processing) that shows the "quick sketch" type work that I wanted a tool like this for.

Reas: Processing's very name tells something about the nature of the work I do with it: it is about the process of making art with code. As a tool it allows me to cast my ideas into physical form and then refine them through a process of iteration. As an artist I am very interested in melding together the worlds of conceptual art and software, and I have been inspired by Sol LeWitt's wall drawings, where

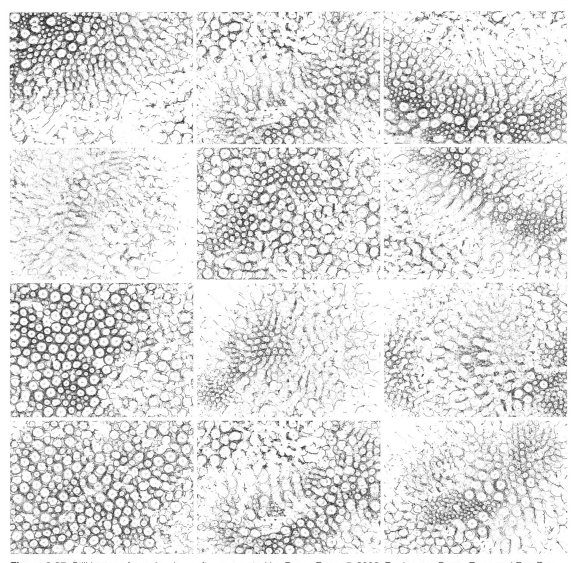

Figure 3.27 Still images from drawing software created by Casey Reas. © 2006. Designers: Casey Reas and Ben Fry.

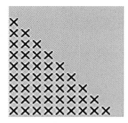

```
for (int y = 1; y < 100; y += 10) {
    for (int x = 1; x < y; x += 10) {
        line(x, y, x+6, y+6);
        line(x+6, y, x, y+6);
    }
}
```

Figure 3.28 Processing example code with for loops that draw a grid of shapes. © 2006. Designers: Casey Reas and Ben Fry.

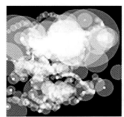

```
void setup() {
    size(100, 100);
    background(0);
    fill(255, 102);
    noStroke();
}

void draw() {
    float s = abs(mouseX-pmouseX) + 2;
    ellipse(mouseX, mouseY, s, s);
}
```

Figure 3.29 Processing example code that uses the position of the mouse to draw circles. © 2006. Designers: Casey Reas and Ben Fry.

```
strokeWeight(12);
strokeJoin(BEVEL);
rect(10, 20, 15, 60);
strokeJoin(MITER);
rect(40, 20, 15, 60);
strokeJoin(ROUND);
rect(70, 20, 15, 60);
```

Figure 3.30 Processing example code that shows the details of drawing the corners of shapes. © 2006. Designers: Casey Reas and Ben Fry.

he would specify an image to be drawn on the gallery's wall through a few sentences. In that process the English words are the "program" and the "computer" is a skilled draftsperson.

In my work,[5] I see the computer more as a mind-expanding collaborator than as a tool. In my former work, the program was computer code and was executed by a machine; in my new way of working, the program is English text, which is interpreted by a skilled programmer and then executed by a machine. Putting the emphasis of my processes on the English text rather than the computer code creates the opportunity for multiple interpretations of the work and gives the flexibility to not feel constrained by the current state of computer technology.

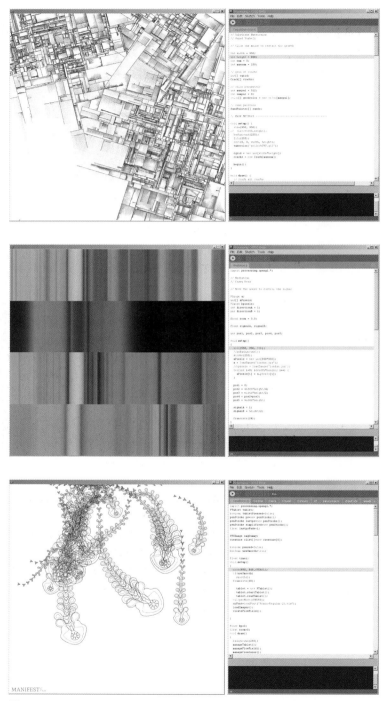

Figure 3.31 The Processing Development Environment (PDE) on the right with images on the left created with code written by (from top to bottom) Jared Tarbell, Casey Reas, and Michael Chang. © 2006. Designers: Casey Reas and Ben Fry.

Notes

1. http://www.ftrain.com/ProcessingProcessing.html
2. http://benfry.com/isometricblocks/
3. http://www.nature.com/nature/journal/v437/n7063/index.html
4. http://acg.media.mit.edu/people/fry/zipdecode/
5. http://reas.com/

Part 3: Further reading

Baines, P. and A. Haslam (2002), *Type and Typography*, London: Laurence King.

Binghurst, R. (2002), *The Elements of Typographic Style*, 2nd edn, Vancouver: Hartley & Marks.

Blankenship, S. (2003), "Cultural Considerations: Arabic Calligraphy and Latin Typography," *Design Issues*, 19 (2): 60–3.

Boutros, M. (2017), *Arabic for Designers: An Inspirational Guide to Arabic Culture and Creativity*, London: Thames & Hudson.

Brownie, B. (2014), *Transforming Type: New Directions in Kinetic Typography*, London: Bloomsbury.

Chahine, N. (2017), "Singing in Arabic," *Design Observer*, 31 March. Available online: designobserver.com/feature/singing-in-arabic/39544 (accessed 13 June 2017).

Drucker, J. (1997), *The Visible Word: Experimental Typography and Modern Art (1909–1923)*, Chicago: University of Chicago Press.

Drucker, J. (2008), "Letterpress Language: Typography as a Medium for the Visual Representation of Language," *Leonardo,* 41 (1): 66–74.

Garfield, S. (2012), *Just My Type: A Book About Fonts*, reprint edn, New York: Gotham.

Gill, E. (2013), *An Essay on Typography* (Penguin Modern Classic), London: Penguin.

Helvetica (2007), [Film] Dir. Gary Hustwit, USA: Swiss Dots.

Hyndman, S. (2016), *Why Fonts* Matter, London: Virgin Books.

Kinross, R. (2008), *Modern Typography: An Essay in Critical History*, 2nd rev. edn, London: Hyphen Press.

Kinross, R. (2011), *Unjustified Texts: Perspectives on Typography*, rev. edn, London: Hyphen Press.

Lupton, E. (2010), *Thinking with Type: A Critical Guide for Designers, Writers, Editors, and Students*, 2nd rev. edn, New York: Princeton Architectural Press.

Malsy, V. and L. Müller (eds) (2007), *Helvetica Forever: Story of a Typeface*, Baden: Lars Müller Publishers.

McClean, R. (1995), *Typographers on Type: An Illustrated Anthology from William Morris to the Present Day*, New York: Norton.

Mullaney, T.S. (2017), *The Chinese Typewriter: A History*, Cambridge: MIT Press.

Noordzij, G. (2005), *The Stroke: Theory of Writing,* trans. P. Enneson, London: Hyphen Press.

Pressing On: The Letterpress Film (2017), [Film] Dirs. Andrew P. Quinn and Erin Beckloff, USA: A Bayonet Media Film.

Purvis, A.W. (2010), *Type: A Visual History of Typefaces & Graphic Styles, 1901–1938* (v. 2), Cologne: Taschen.

Ruder, E. (2009), *Typography: A Manual of Design,* 4th edn, Salenstein: Verlag Niggli.

Sassoon, R. (ed.) (1993), *Computers and Typography 2,* London: Intellect.

Sassoon, R. (ed.) (2002), *Computers and Typography*, London: Intellect.

Schmid, H. (2016), *Typography Today*, Tokyo: Seibundo Shinkosha.

Shaw, P. (2011), *Helvetica and the New York Subway System: The True (Maybe) Story*. Cambridge: MIT Press.

Shaw, P. (ed.) (2015), *The Eternal Letter: Two Millennia of the Classical Roman Capital*, Cambridge: MIT Press.

Shaw, P. and P. Bain (1998), *Blackletter: Type and National Identity*, New York: Princeton Architectural Press.

Simeone, L. (2011), "Learning from Interstitial Typography," *Leonardo* 44 (5): 466–7.

Smeijers, F. (1996), *Counterpunch: Making Type in the Sixteenth Century; Designing Typefaces Now*, London: Hyphen Press.

Spiekermann, E. and E.M. Ginger (2002), *Stop Stealing Sheep & Find Out How Type Works*, 2nd edn, San Francisco: Adobe Press.

Triggs, T. (2003), *The Typographic Experiment: Radical Innovation in Contemporary Type Design*, London: Thames & Hudson.

Tschichold, J. (1991), *The Form of the Book*, London: Hartley & Marks.

Typeface (2009), [Film] Dir. Justine Nagan, USA: Kartemquin Films.

Typography Papers. Department of Typography & Graphic Communication and Hyphen Press.

Walker, S. (2000), *Typography & Language in Everyday Life, Prescriptions and Practices*, Harlow: Longman.

Weingart, W. (2014), *Typography*. Baden: Lars Müller.

Part 4

Graphic design, critical writing, and practice

Part 4: Introduction

Part Four surveys the ways in which graphic design practice has been, and still is, informed by discourses in criticism and theory, critical writing, and critical practice. In the 2000s, universities began to offer new courses in design criticism and design writing. Some programs remained true to kinds of writing that are associated with traditional criticism. Other programs developed curricula that incorporate experimental critical practice, echoing an emerging interest in the pragmatic applications of criticism and theory to practice. Reflective practice—in which designers scrutinize their work and reiterate based upon critical reflection—has recently re-emerged as an essential way for designers to approach practice. Co-design and participatory design likewise embrace diverse voices and discourses in ways that inspire critical approaches to practice. Contemporary graphic design criticism also offers designers a plurality of voices and processes that reinforce critical reflection. The essays in this Part signal that the evolution of graphic design as a profession calls for earnest engagement with theory and criticism, and with reflective and critical practice.

Graphic design emerged from fine art and commercial art traditions. Contemporary graphic design, however, has evolved practices that draw from various scientific, social scientific, and humanistic disciplines. Some in these other disciplines have likewise incorporated design thinking and design processes into their practices. This interdisciplinarity belies the traditional role of the design critic, who served as an arbitrator of taste—determining whether design was "worthwhile" to culture. In contrast, some contemporary design critics are critical storytellers, writing about their own and others' practices outside of the commercial domain. This critical storytelling embraces practice as a means for critical reflection and evaluation. Some texts in this Part show how designers integrate theory and criticism with design work as a way of understanding practice. Other texts reveal a desire for a range of diverse critical discourses. Many of the authors in this Part (like many of the contributors to the *Reader*) are both writers and designers who provide dual perspectives on critical writing and practice.

The first Section, "Graphic design theory and design culture," aims to explore the designer-critic as rhetorician and the ways in which theory might frame practice. In particular, the essays present theoretical approaches that reveal how content is generated when design is created and used. In "Deconstruction and graphic design" (1994), Ellen Lupton and J. Abbott Miller discuss the origins of the term "deconstruction" as it was first used in graphic design. Deconstruction is based on certain oppositions such as inside/outside, original/copy, and mind/body. The authors point out that, although deconstruction became a "period style" in 1980s and 1990s graphic design, it is, in reality, a methodology of critical form making.

In "Visual rhetoric and semiotics" (1995) Edward Triggs contemplates rhetoric, which is the art of persuasion, and semiotics, which is a theory that considers the relationships between things and meaning. Triggs investigates how both rhetoric and semiotics function in the print-media tripartite visual form of picture–headline–text. In a similar fashion, Ann Tyler closely reads persuasive arguments in the visual forms of various graphic design projects in "Shaping belief: the role of audience in visual communication" (1992). She contends that design inevitably references beliefs, and that new beliefs can be shaped by the choices designers make during projects. Arne Scheuermann also considers design as rhetoric in "Graphic design as rhetoric: Towards a new framework for theory and practice in graphic design" (2018). He maintains that understanding graphic design as rhetoric—as a practice in which designers analyze ideas surrounding design projects—reveals that theory and practice, and analysis and production, are interrelated. In the final essay, "Theories to understand graphic design in use: The example of posters" (2018), Jan-Henning Raff presents three theoretical frameworks that explore the relationships between design artifacts and those who use them: Distributed Cognition, Activity Theory, and Actor-Network Theory. All three approaches, he argues, advance the interconnections between graphic design theory and practice because they locate designed objects among people in their social and cultural contexts. The essays in this Section demonstrate how design theory relates to graphic design practice and artifacts.

The next Section features essays about "Writing, practice, and graphic design criticism." In the first essay in this Section, "What is this thing called design criticism?, I & II," Rick Poynor and Michael Rock discuss the need for a critical discourse about graphic design. In part I (1995), they astutely suggest that cultural theory has not been especially relevant to professional practice. They then call for an informed, thoughtful, and skeptical critical discourse that is likewise relevant to graphic design practitioners. In part II (2011), they acknowledge that there has been scattered, fragmented growth of graphic design criticism in print media and in blogs and social media venues. They conclude that critics should turn to a close reading of designed objects to reveal the roles they play in social, cultural, economic, and political contexts. In "Criticism and the politics of absence" (1995), Anne Bush argues against the stance that Rick Poynor and Michael Rock present in the above essay: that is, that graphic design criticism should be geared to practitioners. Gearing criticism to practitioners, she maintains, tends to center on internal questions in which design is only important to itself and discrete from the social and cultural environments in which it functions. As evidence and background for her argument, Bush presents a succinct history of critical approaches in the West since the eighteenth century. Kenneth FitzGerald alleges in "Quietude" (2003) that graphic design practitioners and educators are interested in the visual, conceptual, and commercial aspects of design work, and have little investment in graphic design criticism. Graphic design publications, according to FitzGerald, reflect what is valued in the field, so he considers what various book projects reveal about the state of graphic design. More recently, Francisco Laranjo argues, in "Critical graphic design: critical of what?" (2017), that the idea of critical graphic design is not taken seriously, and that a substantive discourse is imperative for the development of the field. Laranjo then offers three possible models for graphic design criticism: designers become self-aware about what they do and why, designers challenge disciplinary paradigms, and designers address design's role in pressing social issues.

The next three essays consider design writing, and the ways that text may be used to introduce new ideas and approaches in design practice. In "The march of grimes" (2018), Michèle Champagne uses American philosopher Harry G. Frankfurt's treatise *On Bullshit* (2005) as a basis to explore the bullshit in design, which she defines as highly persuasive ideas that are not concerned about truth. Champagne next elaborates upon three designations of Frankfurt's bullshit—"No Proof Bullshit," "Too Vague Bullshit," and "Hidden Tradeoff Bullshit"—using examples from design. In the 2009 essay "Discourse this! designers and alternative critical writing," Denise Gonzales Crisp considers how graphic design alternative critical writing allows authors creative freedom to explore topics without the constraints of academic or journalistic writing. Gonzales Crisp discusses several examples of critical fiction, including William Morris's *News from Nowhere*, both versions of the "First Things First" manifesto (which are included in this anthology), and design fiction written by Putch Tu (Diane Gromala). Anna Gerber and Teal Triggs, on the other hand, explore how fiction writers play with typographic elements in "Acrobat reader" (2006). The authors cite lipograms, in which one or several letters are consistently left out of a text, as one of the oldest forms of word play. Triggs and Gerber juxtapose twentieth- and twenty-first-century word-play projects with those done by experimental artists and designers to reveal the role "linguistic mischief" can play in design.

The last group of essays in Part 4 show how critique in graphic design is practiced in podcasts, in communities of practice, or in traditional curating for museums. In "How and why *Design Matters*" (2018), Debbie Millman reflects on the origin and mission of her graphic design podcast *Design Matters*, and on podcasts in general. In "Inquiry as a verb" (2018), Director of DesignInquiry, Margo Halverson, portrays DI's intensive, immersive gatherings in which participants come together to think about, discuss, and make design. Each gathering has a topic, and Halverson presents case studies of and examples from several DesignInquiry sessions. In "Graphic design in the collection of the Museum of Modern Art," (2004) Paola Antonelli, Senior Design Curator at the Museum of Modern Art in New York City, contemplates the museum's design collection, explaining that the graphic design collection needs to be brought up to date. An updated graphic design collection, Antonelli points out, should include projects that are both from a range of design media and directed toward those who encounter or use this design. Since the original publication of this essay, MoMA has expanded its collection to include more graphic design and new categories of graphic design, including video games (e.g. Pac-Man and SimCity).

The essays in this Part of the book demonstrate that graphic design theory and criticism have the capacity to engender change. We function in complex economic, political, social, cultural, and economic environments, and graphic design criticism can play a significant role in directing design practice to productive outcomes in these environments. Theory, criticism, and critical practices are central to how we define graphic design, but they are also essential for exploring ways that we can push the boundaries of the field. Design writing is also a practice, and for us it is integral to the shape of productive making and critical thinking.

Section 4.1

Graphic design theory and design culture

Chapter 4.1.1

Deconstruction and graphic design

Ellen Lupton and J. Abbott Miller

Since the surfacing of the term "deconstruction" in design journalism in the mid–1980s, the word has served to label architecture, graphic design, products, and fashion featuring chopped up, layered, and fragmented forms imbued with ambiguous futuristic overtones. This essay looks at the reception and use of deconstruction in the recent history of graphic design, where it has become the tag for yet another period style.

We then consider the place of graphics within the theory of deconstruction, initiated in the work of philosopher Jacques Derrida. We argue that deconstruction is not a style or "attitude" but rather a mode of questioning through and about the technologies, formal devices, social institutions, and founding metaphors of representation. Deconstruction belongs to both history and theory. It is embedded in recent visual and academic culture, but it describes a strategy of critical form-making which is performed across a range of artifacts and practices, both historical and contemporary.

Jacques Derrida introduced the concept of "deconstruction" in his book *Of Grammatology*, published in France in 1967 and translated into English in 1976. "Deconstruction" became a banner for the advance guard in American literary studies in the 1970s and 80s, scandalizing departments of English, French, and comparative literature. Deconstruction rejected the project of modern criticism: to uncover the meaning of a literary work by studying the way its form and content communicate essential humanistic messages. Deconstruction, like critical strategies based on Marxism, feminism, semiotics, and anthropology, focuses not on the themes and imagery of its objects but rather on the linguistic and institutional systems that frame the production of texts.

In Derrida's theory, deconstruction asks how representation inhabits reality. How does the external image of things get inside their internal essence? How does the surface get under the skin? Western culture since Plato, Derrida argues, has been governed by such oppositions as reality/representation, inside/outside, original/copy, and mind/body. The intellectual achievements of the West—its science, art, philosophy, literature—have valued one side of these pairs over the other, allying one side with truth and the other with falsehood. For example, the Judeo-Christian tradition has conceived the body as an external shell for the inner soul, elevating the mind as the sacred source of thought and spirit, while denigrating the body as mere mechanics. In the realm of aesthetics, the original work of art traditionally

First published in *Visible Language*, 28 (4) (1994): 346–66, a special issue on graphic design history edited by Andrew Blauvelt. This is an earlier version of the essay "Deconstruction and Graphic Design," published in *Design Writing Research*, London: Phaidon Press, (1999). © Ellen Lupton and J. Abbott Miller.

has carried an aura of authenticity that its copy lacks, and the telling of a story or the taking of a photograph is viewed as a passive record of events.

"Deconstruction" takes apart such oppositions by showing how the devalued, empty concept lives inside the valued, positive one. The outside inhabits the inside. Consider, for example, the opposition between nature and culture. The idea of "nature" depends on the idea of "culture," and yet culture is part of nature. It's a fantasy to conceive of the non-human environment as a pristine, innocent setting fenced off and protected from the products of human endeavor—cities, roads, farms, landfills. The fact that we have produced a concept of "nature" in opposition to "culture" is a symptom of our alienation from the ecological systems that civilization depletes and transforms.

A crucial opposition for deconstruction is speech/writing. The Western philosophical tradition has denigrated writing as an inferior copy of the spoken word. Speech draws on interior consciousness, but writing is dead and abstract. The written word loses its connection to the inner self. Language is set adrift, untethered from the speaking subject. In the process of embodying language, writing steals its soul. Deconstruction views writing as an active rather than passive form of representation. Writing is not merely a bad copy, a faulty transcription, of the spoken word; writing, in fact, invades thought and speech, transforming the sacred realms of memory, knowledge, and spirit. Any memory system, in fact, is a form of writing, since it records thought for the purpose of future transmissions.

The speech/writing opposition can be mapped onto a series of ideologically loaded pairs that are constitutive of modern Western culture:

Speech/Writing
Natural/artificial
Spontaneous/constructed
Original/copy
interior to the mind/exterior to the mind
requires no equipment/requires equipment
intuitive/learned
present subject/absent subject

Derrida's critique of the speech/writing opposition locates the concerns of deconstruction in the field of graphic design. We will return to the speech/writing problem in more detail later, but first, we will look at the life of deconstruction in recent design culture.

The design history of deconstruction

Deconstruction belongs to the broader critical field known as "post-structuralism," whose key figures include Roland Barthes, Michel Foucault, Jean Baudrillard, and others. Each of these writers has looked at modes of representation—from literature and photography to the design of schools and prisons—as powerful technologies which build and remake the social world. Deconstruction's attack on the neutrality of signs is also at work in the consumer mythologies of Barthes, the institutional archaeologies of Foucault, and the simulationist aesthetics of Baudrillard. The idea that cultural forms help to fabricate

represent? Key among these marks, which Derrida has called "graphemes," are various forms of spacing—negative gaps between the positive symbols of the alphabet. Spacing cannot be dismissed as a "simple accessory" of writing: "That a speech supposedly alive can lend itself to spacing in its own writing is what relates to its own death" (p. 39). The alphabet has come to rely on silent graphic servants such as spacing and punctuation, which, like the frame of a picture, seem safely "outside" the proper content and internal structure of a work and yet are necessary conditions for making and reading.

Derrida's book *The Truth in Painting* unfolds the logic of framing as a crucial component of works of art. In the Enlightenment aesthetics of Kant, which form the basis for modern art theory and criticism, the frame of a picture belongs to a class of elements called parerga, meaning "about the work," or outside/around the work. Kant's parerga include the columns on buildings, the draperies on statues, and the frames on pictures. A frame is an ornamental appendix to a work of art, whose "quasi-detachment" serves not only to hide but also to reveal the emptiness at the core of the seemingly self-complete object of aesthetic pleasure. In Derrida's words, "The parergon is a form that has, as its traditonal determination, not that it stands out but that it disappears, buries itself, effaces itself, melts away at the moment it deploys its greatest energy. The frame is in no way a background. . . . but neither is its thickness as margin a figure. Or at least it is a figure which comes away of its own accord" (p. 61). Like the non-phonetic supplements to the alphabet, the borders around pictures or texts occupy an ambiguous place between figure and ground, positive element and negative gap.

Spacing and punctuation, borders and frames: these are the territory of graphic design and typography, those marginal arts which articulate the conditions that make texts and images readable. The substance of typography lies not in the alphabet per se—the generic forms of characters and their conventionalized uses—but rather in the visual framework and specific graphic forms which materialize the system of writing. Design and typography work at the edges of writing, determining the shape and style of letters, the spaces between them, and their positions on the page. Typography, from its position in the margins of communication, has moved writing away from speech.

Design as deconstruction

The history of typography and writing could be written as the development of formal structures which have articulated and explored the border between the inside and the outside of the text. To compile a catalogue of the micro-mechanics of publishing—indexes and title pages, captions and colophons, folios and footnotes, leading and line lengths, margins and marginalia, spacing and punctuation—would contribute to the field which Derrida has called grammatology, or the study of writing as a distinctive mode of representation. This word, grammatology, serves to title the book whose more infamous legacy is deconstruction.

Such a history could position various typographic techniques in relation to the split between form and content, inside and outside. Some typographic conventions have served to rationalize the delivery of information by erecting transparent "crystal goblets" around a seemingly independent, neutral body of "content." Some structures or approaches invade the sacred interior so deeply as to turn the text inside out, while others deliberately ignore or contradict the internal organization of a text in response to external pressures imposed by technology, aesthetics, corporate interests, social propriety, production conveniences, etc.

Robin Kinross's *Modern Typography* (1992) charts the progressive rationalization of the forms and uses of letters across several centuries of European history. Kinross's book characterizes printing as a prototypically "modern" process, that from its inception mobilized techniques of mass production and precipitated the mature arts and sciences. The seeds of modernization were present in Gutenberg's first proofs; their fruits are born in the self-conscious methodologies, professionalized practices, and standardized visual forms of printers and typographers, which, beginning in the late seventeenth century, replaced an older notion of printing as a hermetic art of "black magic," its methods jealously guarded by a caste of craftsmen.

If Kinross's history of modern typography spans five centuries, so too might another history of deconstruction, running alongside and beneath the erection of transparent formal structures and coherent bodies of professional knowledge. Derrida's own writing has drawn on forms of page layout from outside the accepted conventions of university publishing. His book *Glas*, designed with Richard Eckersley at the University of Nebraska Press, consists of parallel texts set in different typefaces and written in heterogeneous voices. Glas makes the scholarly annotations of medieval manuscripts and the accidental juxtapositions of modern newspapers part of a deliberate authorial strategy.

A study of typography and writing informed by deconstruction would reveal a range of structures that dramatize the intrusion of visual form into verbal content, the invasion of "ideas" by graphic marks, gaps, and differences. [Eds: Illustrations from the original version of this essay of] pages of late fifteenth-century book typography, represent two different attitudes towards framing the text. In the first, the margins are a transparent border for the solid block dominating the page. The lines of classical roman characters are minimally interrupted—paragraph breaks are indicated only by a wider gap within the line, preserving the text as a continuously flowing field of letters. The second example draws on the tradition of scribal marginalia and biblical commentary. Here, typography is an interpretive medium; the text is open rather than closed. The first example suggests that the frontiers between interior and exterior, figure and ground, reader and writer, are securely defined, while the second example dramatizes such divides by engulfing the center with the edge.

Another comparison comes from the history of the newspaper, which emerged as an elite literary medium in the seventeenth century. Early English newspapers based their structure on the classical book, whose consistently formatted text block was designed to be read from beginning to end. As the newspaper became a popular medium in nineteenth-century Europe and America, it expanded from a book-scaled signature to a broadsheet incorporating diverse elements, from reports of war and crime to announcements of ship departures and ads for goods and services. The modern illustrated newspaper of the twentieth century is a patchwork of competing elements, whose juxtaposition responds not to rational hierarchies of content but to the struggle between editorial, advertising, and production interests. While the structure of the classical news journal aspired to the status of a coherent, complete object, the appearance of the popular paper results from frantic compromises and arbitrary conditions; typographic design serves to distract and seduce as well as to clarify and explain. Dictionaries of page design featuring schematic diagrams of typical layouts have been a common theme in twentieth-century design. Such visual enactments of theory include Jan Tschichold's

1934 manifesto "The Placing of Type in a Given Space," which charts a range of subtle variations in the placement of headings and body copy, and Don May's 1942 manual 101 Roughs, which catalogues various types of commercial page design. While Tschichold charted minor differences between clearly ordered elements, May accommodated the diverse media and competing messages found in advertising. Both theorists presented a series of formal containers for abstract, unspecified bodies of "content," but with a difference: Tschichold's structures are neutral frames for dominant textual figures, while May's patterns are active grounds which ignore conventional hierarchies in favor of such arbitrary rules as "Four point: The layout touches all four sides of the space once and only once", or "Center axis: The heading copy, illustration, and logotype flush on alternate sides of axis."

If one pursued the study of "grammatology" proposed by Derrida, the resulting catalogue of forms might include the graphic conditions outlined above. In each case, we have juxtaposed a coherent, seemingly self-complete literary artifact with a situation where external forces aggressively interfere with the sacred interior of content. A history of typography informed by deconstruction would show how graphic design has revealed, challenged, or transformed the accepted rules of communication. Such interventions can represent either deliberate confrontations or haphazard encounters with the social, technological, and aesthetic pressures that shape the making of texts.

In a 1994 interview in *The New York Times Magazine*, Derrida was asked about the purported "death" of deconstruction on North American campuses; he answered, "I think there is some element in deconstruction that belongs to the structure of history or events. It started before the academic phenomenon of deconstruction, and it will continue with other names." In the spirit of this statement, we are interested in de-periodizing the relevance of deconstruction: instead of viewing it as an "ism" of the late-80s and early-90s, we see it as part of the ongoing development of design and typography as distinctive modes of representation. But deconstruction also belongs to culture: it is an operation that has taken a name and has spun a web of influence in particular social contexts. Deconstruction has lived in a variety of institutional worlds, from university literature departments to schools of art and design to the discourse of popular journalism, where it has functioned both as a critical activity and as a banner for a range of styles and attitudes. We will close our essay with two examples of graphic design that actively engage the language of contemporary media: the first confronts the politics of representation, while the second remakes design's internal language.

Vincent Gagliostro's cover for NYQ, a gay and lesbian news magazine, was designed in November, 1991, in response to Magic Johnson's announcement that he is HIV+. Gagliostro imposed NYQ's own logo and headline over a Newsweek cover featuring Magic Johnson proclaiming "Even me," his upheld arms invoking saintly sacrifice and athletic vigor. "He is not our hero," wrote NYQ over the existing cover. While Gagliostro's layering and splicing of type and image are shared with more aestheticized, individualized gestures found elsewhere in contemporary design, this cover does not aim to trigger an infinite variety of "personal" interpretations but instead explicitly manipulates an ideologically loaded artifact. Gagliostro's act of cultural rewriting is a powerful response to the ubiquity of normative sign systems, showing that the structures of mass media can be reshuffled and reinhabited. The NYQ cover reveals and exploits the function of framing as a transformative process that refuses to remain outside the editorial content it encloses.

The manipulation of existing media imagery is one activity in contemporary design that can be described as deconstruction; another is the exploration of the visual grammar of communication, from print to the electronic interface. Designers working in hypermedia are developing new ways to generate, distribute, and use information—they are reinventing the language of graphic design today, just as typographers reacted to the changing technologies and social functions of printed media in the past. A leading pioneer of this research was Muriel Cooper, who founded the Visible Language Workshop at MIT in [the mid-1970s]. In the wake of her death in the spring of 1994, her students are continuing to build a concrete grammar of three-dimensional, dynamic typography. Cooper called the basic elements of this language "geometric primitives," defined by relationships of size, brightness, color, transparency, and location in 3-D space, variables which can shift in response to the user!s position in a document. Cooper and her students have worked to restructure the internal language of typography in four dimensions.

Spacing, framing, punctuation, type style, layout, and other nonphonetic marks of difference constitute the material interface of writing. Traditional literary and linguistic research overlook such graphic structures, focusing instead on the Word as the center of communication. According to Derrida, the functions of repetition, quotation, and fragmentation that characterize writing are conditions endemic to all human expression—even the seemingly spontaneous, self-present utterances of speech or the smooth, naturalistic surfaces of painting and photography. Design can critically engage the mechanics of representation, exposing and revising its ideological biases; design also can remake the grammar of communication by discovering structures and patterns within the material media of visual and verbal writing.

Chapter 4.1.2

Visual rhetoric and semiotics

Edward Triggs

Persuasive messages are presented most often in the print media as a tripartite structure of picture, headline and text, visually unified through axial symmetry. This ubiquitous, easily identifiable form has prevailed for over a century and has become synonymous with messages intending to sell a product or service, or to propagandize a position on some issue. A questioning of this convention leads to an investigation of the system of rhetoric and the theory of semiotics. Presented here is a discussion of these concepts as they relate to the development of an alternative form, one which emerges organically when an argument the designer has determined is given visual form.

Introduction

Messages in the print media represent intentions and ideas through the selection and organization of visual elements known to or comprehend-ible to a reader. Some of these messages intend to inform, others to instruct, identify, entertain or persuade. Persuasive messages are those which intend to influence the purchase of a product or service, as in advertising, or to encourage acceptance of a position proffered on an issue or topic, as in propaganda.[1] Of concern here are those messages which intend to influence choice or redirect thought. An investigation of the rhetorical system and semiotic theory suggests an expanded role for the designer responsible for developing persuasive messages, and also, a way of actively engaging readers in the message. The art director/designer traditionally establishes a concept for a picture and determines appropriate typography for the headline and text. These three elements, picture, headline and text, are then organized into a conventional visual structure, usually symmetrical, which maintains the identity of each element. Rhetoric and semiotics provide an opportunity to forego the model of conventional form and allow form to grow organically as an effective integration of the visual and verbal languages which, as a unit, declares a graspable idea.

First published in *Communicating Design: Essays in Visual Communication,* ed. Teal Triggs, London: B.T. Batsford (1995), 81–6. Reproduced with kind permission of B.T. Batsford, part of Pavilion Books Company Ltd. © Edward Triggs.

Rhetoric and its system

Rhetoric, simply defined, is the art of persuasion. Devised by the ancient Greeks and expanded into a system of interrelated activities by the Romans, rhetoric assists the development of a speech intended to persuade the listener to accept a position or opinion proffered by its speaker.[2] To be effective, Aristotle believed that a speech must appeal to the emotions of the listener, establish a favourable impression of the speaker's character, and prove the truth of statements made.[3] The speech, operating in a culture favouring ideas, oratory and aesthetics, had to exhibit a high degree of both intrinsic and extrinsic value through the choice of arguments, their organization and presentation. Although the classical system of rhetoric does not provide for the use of visual elements, selected concepts of the system can assist in making decisions affecting the structuring of ideas, choice of representational images and typeface— all of which determine a message's form and character. A speech unfolding over time allows the use of a host of rhetorical devices to argue its position and to establish a favourable character for the speaker. On the printed page where the "speech" resides in its completeness as a tangible visual thing, the element of time is absent. The visually presented speech, as a graphic display, is an organic complex of inert words and pictures, colours and textures, whose meaning is dependent on the active participation of a reader. To achieve participation, the graphic display must first assert its presence and stimulate its reader to enter a mode of objective thought.

In his treatise on human knowledge, Karl Popper proposes that the human world is composed of three distinct, interrelated sub-worlds. The first world, "the world of physical states," is where we speak of what we see; the second world, "the world of mental states," is where we speak of our emotional reaction to what we observe; and in the third world, the world "of ideas in the objective sense," we speak of the significance of what we have observed.[4] Following Popper's theory, we can say that identifying a thing as a message involves the first world; by enjoying the aesthetics of its visual form or being interested in what it says, we have brought the message into the second world. A message intended to persuade a reader to accept a new position on an issue cannot dwell in the emotional state of the second world, rather, it must be propelled into the third world where the idea it presents can be intellectually established, its value judged, and a decision made to agree with or reject the position proffered.

The ubiquitous tripartite form of picture–headline–text traditionally used to present persuasive messages in print is so familiar and easily identified as "selling something" that its use as a triggering mechanism is counter-productive. What is needed to open the reader's third world is an accessible graphic display perceived as being a significant idea—an intelligible, objective thought. Using the concept of rhetoric, the designer is afforded an opportunity to establish a position or opinion of the content. It is in offering visual evidence to prove the designer's opinion that a non-traditional visual form will emerge.

Rhetorical arguments

A rhetorical argument used in speech or writing is a course of reasoning unfolding over time which intends to achieve agreement that a stated or implied proposition is true or accepted as being true. The components of an argument are most often based on premises acknowledged as being true, or on acceptable examples of similar cases.[5] In printed form, where the 'speech' is before the reader in its entirety, the rhetorical argument provides either a visual demonstration or visual evidence which proves the truth of an opinion the designer has of the proposition presented in the text. As an example: a proposition that a reader should send money to supply food for children starving in a certain country might lead the designer to establish an opinion that "these children are vanishing." Visual demonstration of the truth of this opinion might be a photograph of children evidencing malnutrition screened to about 40 percent of black with text copy surprinted on the photograph.

Semiotics

Aristotle put forward the notion that each part of a natural thing has the potential of the complete thing of which it is part.[6] Relating his observation to printed communication, we can say that the recognition of a representation of a part of a thing points to the idea of the complete thing. A photograph of bark is both an imitation of natural bark and a suggestion of the complete tree.[7] This concept of a representation pointing to something other than itself is seen in the theory of semiotics, where a representation is not the physical thing itself but an indicator of ideas one might associate with that which is represented. Triggering awareness that an expression of a significant structured thought exists on the page is one of the aims of the designer being discussed. The reader must realize that a graspable, objective idea exists, one that is more than a description of things or a construction of persuasive utterances. Semiotics, being concerned with the relationship of things and meaning, provides assistance when selecting and configuring communication elements.

Semiotics is a broad, complex theory concerned with how meaning is attached to and derived from things in a given context.[8] The theory centres on the semiotic sign, a mental construction which arises when there is recognition of a correlation between an expression (signifier) and its content (signified).[9] For there to be a sign, someone must perceive an expression as referring to something other than itself. The recognition of something as standing for something else requires a stimulus external to the representation. The stimulus can be almost anything, such as one's desire to perceive things as signs, the context in which something appears, or the relationship one intended sign has to another. In the design of persuasive messages, it is the relationship between intended signs which activates 'sign-ness' and points to meaning. Signs, not being tangible objects *per se,* are suggested through the use of sign-vehicles, which have either a verbal form (words) or a non-verbal form (such as pictures, colours, arrows).[10] A pictorial sign-vehicle produced by photographic means is considered to be more immediately accessible to a reader than a representation produced by hand. Photographs have a desirable "neutral rhetoric" as they continue to be perceived by the casual reader as representing a non-interpreted reality. Hand-constructed representations exhibit a value-laden rhetoric peculiar to the artist which impedes or redirects a reader from immediately perceiving what is denoted in its representation.

Traditional form

The role the art director/designer plays in preparing persuasive messages for the print media has changed little over the past 100 years, when advertising agents first employed artists to oversee the production of pictures and their addition to headlines and text. In this respect, the designer's involvement in the effectiveness of a message is limited to the creation of a visual rhetoric which projects value for the message and good character for its originator through the choice of typeface, colour and art direction of the photograph. All of this is done, of course, using the conventionalized message form of picture–headline–text. This familiar form becomes a message in itself which says, "I am going to sell you something." It is viewed here as being an obvious sign which often impedes or discourages reader participation. The alternative is a naturally derived form, one having a neutral rhetoric because the form develops organically from the selection, configuration and linking of elements necessary to present an argument established by the designer.[11] A neutral rhetoric is considered to exist when factors other than the argument are not an issue. This is similar to the concept of transparency and opacity in typography, where a word's visual form must not be so evident that access to its content is restricted.

The synthesis

Decisions affecting the selection, configuration and linking of sign-vehicles follow concepts offered in semiotics and rhetoric. Using the proposition given in the previous example, that children of a certain country are in need of monetary assistance, a photograph of children evidencing malnutrition is selected as the major element to demonstrate the designer's opinion that "the children are vanishing." The photograph represents "real-ness," visible evidence of starving children, and from the rhetorical side, "starving children" is an emotional appeal. The configuration of this pictorial image must be such that evidence of starvation and of children is immediately before the reader by removing all but essential information. The image must dominate the page, but not bleed off the page, as definition of the rectangular shape of a photograph assists in signalling 'sign'.[12]

Activating a sign

A sign is realized when activated by something other than itself. The fact that technology is used to reproduce a photograph on a page is not of sufficient importance to a casual reader to affect the switch from "photograph" to "sign." Physically altering the image, such as screening it to 40 percent of black, modifying its boundary or putting type on it, increases the chances of sign awareness on the part of the reader.[13] Color also affects the perception of sign. In contrast to a full colour reproduction which reinforces the reality which existed in front of the lens, the translation of reality into black and white is a step away from "real-ness" and a step toward "sign-ness." The reproduction of a photograph as a single color halftone, say magenta, is an example of an undesirable rhetoric of aesthetics unless the color chosen reinforces the argument (red for passion, green for coolness or envy, for example).

the subject), or finds it unintelligible. The audience is viewed as involved in no deeper engagement than that of decoding references to the subject. A grammatical approach thus emphasizes the scientific over the esthetic aspects of design. In addition, since the audience brings nothing particular to the process, it is not particularized in any way; it is both a *nonspecific* and a passive audience.

Semiotics, a third and closely related view, recognizes the specificity of the audience. An audience holds or recognizes certain beliefs and reads messages based on these beliefs. In Roland Barthes's "Rhetoric of the Image,"[8] denotation and connotation distinguish the literal and symbolic messages within visual communication. The audience reads the literal message while also interpreting the signs which express the "iconic message."[9] The potential readings of these signs outside the communication device are multiple, but the interpretations are particularized within the design through their combination with other signs and the denoted messages.[10] The audience, with its cultural beliefs and understanding, is also involved in particularizing the symbolic (connoted) message,[11] thereby becoming an active reader.

Yet another view, to be explored in depth here, is a rhetorical analysis of design.[12] Within a theory of rhetoric the audience is not characterized as a reader but as a dynamic participant in argument. In this rhetorical view, visual communication attempts to persuade a specific audience through argument as opposed to making a statement within a grammatical structure or conveying a message within the dynamics of semiotics. Designers utilize existing beliefs to induce new beliefs in the audience. It is the use of existing beliefs, as much as the attempt to induce new beliefs, that contributes to maintaining, questioning, or transforming social values through argument. Designers persuade an audience by referencing established or accepted values and attributing those values to the new subject.[13] The specific audience's experiences within society and its understanding of social attitudes are an essential aspect of argument and necessary to the communication goal.

The selection of examples of design within this essay, though not comprehensive, shows the use of devices and strategies to construct argument, the use of existing beliefs in argument as a strategy to induce new beliefs, and the role of the audience in accomplishing communication goals. The formal devices in each example are discussed in terms of the primary deal[14] of the design: to induce action, to educate, to create an experience.

Persuading the audience to act

Persuading an audience to attend an exhibit, travel to another country, or invest in a company is inducing that audience to take an action. In an attempt to persuade, the designer develops an argument within the two-dimensional space that defines and represents an audience's future experience. The argument becomes a promise: if one attends A, one will feel B; if one goes to C, one will see D; if one uses E, one will become F.

The goal of the first example is to persuade the audience to visit the New York Aquarium. The poster's argument, made through formal devices, defines the audience's future experience at the aquarium: if you go to the aquarium, you will have an emotional experience based on a friendly, intimate relationship with members of the animal kingdom. Intimacy between audience and mammal is created through scale. The mammal takes up most of the space, creating the appearance that it is close to the viewer.

Personal contact is also suggested because the mammal appears to make eye contact with the audience. Standing in such close proximity to a large animal could be frightening rather than intimate, but any feeling of confrontation is avoided through the dreamy, soft quality of the image, the profile position of the mammal (it is not coming directly toward the viewer), and the friendly expression on its face (it appears to smile).

The formal devices suggest the nature of the aquarium experience by referencing and reinforcing beliefs regarding the relationship between individuals and nature—i.e., nature is friendly toward human beings and animals enjoy being the object of our attention. Although the word "aquarium" indicates confinement, the image defines it as vast, showing no cage or boundaries.

While the aquarium poster promises the audience an experience based on an emotional relationship with the subject, the PanAm travel posters offer a future experience predicated on distance and observation. The communication goal is to persuade the audience to travel to Bali or Japan. The posters argue that the audience will have an esthetic experience in these countries. The first poster, of Bali, is a rural scene of a terraced agricultural area and the second, of Japan, features a sunset and two figures in traditional clothing. Like the aquarium poster, both travel posters use monumental imagery. But the large-scale imagery in these travel posters, combined with other formal devices, makes a very different argument. The PanAm images are architectural in nature: the terraced land forms a contrasting figure/ground pattern; the two people standing with their backs to the audience become shapes against the sky. People and land become objects of beauty. Distanced from the scene through perspective and the lack of any reference back to the viewer, the audience thus remains "outside" a beautiful, tranquil scene. Landscape and people are frozen in time for the audience to view as they choose—as in a museum of artifacts. Both posters promise the audience an esthetic, *nonparticipatory* experience if they travel to these distant lands.

The travel posters have transformed these foreign countries and people into art, referencing a paradigm which says that art is to be observed, not experienced. The posters reinforce a belief that these cultures are static and removed from the audience's own experiences. This is achieved through formal devices that create the appearance of a nonparticipatory audience relationship. The audience appears in the role of observer, yet they do participate by bringing cultural beliefs about beauty and art to the argument.

The final example of design that persuades an audience to act is an annual report. The primary communication goal of annual reports is to persuade the audience either to invest or to maintain their investment in a company. Designers persuade the audience by making an argument that represents the company's philosophy, achievements, and financial solidity. The argument is often made through the company's employees or people using their services; in this way, the audience attributes the values embodied in these individuals with the institution they represent.

The Caremark Inc. 1985 Annual Report makes its argument through Dominick Petone, an individual benefiting from the company's services. The design argues that Mr. Petone, and therefore Caremark, has strong, moral values; he is hardworking, trustworthy, and straightforward. The dominant image is a photograph of a hardworking man in working-class clothing with his tools in the background. The audience knows he is hardworking because he is wearing a T-shirt, is slim, and appears to be serious in the workplace. The written text states that, though ill, Mr. Petone continues to work. From this information we can gather that work and self-sufficiency are important to him. He is also a rugged individualist: the lighting highlights and accentuates his facial features. He is portrayed as a role model, a hero. The portrait is isolated on the page as in an art catalogue; the borders around the photograph are the same proportions as in traditional art matting while the small serifed type of the written text reinforces the serious and classical image. Yet Dominick Petone is approachable: he makes direct eye contact with the audience, his gaze is open, not aggressive, and he gives the audience a "Mona Lisa" smile.

Although Mr. Petone is separated from the investor audience by his economic class, the audience identifies with him through the shared moral values of responsibility, honesty, and stability. These values are also intended to represent the institution and are shared by the image (Mr. Petone), the producer (Caremark), and the audience (investors). The beliefs represented by Dominick Petone are values that bind the culture, values that the audience recognizes and then attributes to Caremark.

Educating the audience

The second communication goal is to educate the audience or to persuade the audience to accept and interpret information. Information can be seen as valueless, as not reflecting a particular belief system. But all communication involves an interpretation of information,[15] an interpretation based on data, perspective, analysis, and judgment. Educational materials are no exception; information is interpreted and communicated according to the paradigms of academic communities. Educating the audience often includes making an argument that the information is "fact," that it is "true."

The map and guide to the Congaree Swamp is intended to educate the audience about the swamp's ecosystem. The argument suggests that nature has an inherent logical order and that the information provided is scientific, i.e., rational and factual. For information to appear factual, it must seem stable, unchangeable. Various formal devices such as detailed illustration techniques, minor changes in scale, and a lack of tension in margin and spacing mitigate against an emotive response by the audience, while a heightened sense of order is achieved through the clearly visible organizational grid system. The brochure is basically a diagram—codified information without expressive characteristics that might suggest individual authorship. Information, such as this, is presented as data and appears to be communicated through an omniscient voice. When the omniscient voice of science is used, the audience seems to be nonparticipatory. The audience is, apparently, only a reader. This dynamic is similar to that of the travel posters, but here the image lacks a sense of drama or emotion, eliminating the appearance of interpretation or perspective. In sum, the organization of facts in the Congaree Swamp brochure is an argument relying on a scientific paradigm. While learning about the swamp's ecosystem, the audience's belief in the rational order of the universe is also reinforced.

The goal of educating an audience also occurs within communication from the business community and through objects not generally classified as educational materials. Corporate and institutional logos are an example of design that attempts to educate.[16] The logo defines the company and persuades the audience that the qualities of the logo are also the qualities of the institution it represents. The audience includes both the company employees and those who come in contact with the company. Audience identification with the values of the organization serves the goals of management as well as those of public relations.

Simplified, geometric logos became the symbols of large corporations and dominated design in the 1960s and 1970s. These reductive icons were developed to represent the "modern" corporation as a large, anonymous entity driven by technology and the values attributed to science—rationality and objectivity. The icons reference science through formal devices such as diagrammatic imagery, an efficient use of line and shape, and an emphasis on positive and negative space. As in the swamp brochure, the elimination of individuality and emotion suggests an omniscient voice and the presentation of fact. Geometric simplification of form continues to be applied to logos, but the 1980s also saw the reintroduction of more formally complex shapes and "naive" representation. The icons began to take on some of the qualities of folk art imagery by referencing individual (handmade) characteristics. These new logos reflect the same communication goal: educating the audience by defining the organization. Rather than referring to the values associated with science and distancing the audience, these logos communicate a more emotional relationship with the audience. The quotidian quality of the logos represents the company not as an anonymous institution but rather as an organization comprised of individuals like the audience. The audience's relationship to the organization is based on self-identification. Though not overtly participatory, an argument involving personal identification recognizes the audience's existence.

In the previous examples, existing beliefs are transferred to the subject to create new beliefs. In posters within an exhibition titled "Visual Perceptions," existing beliefs are replaced with new beliefs. The goal of the posters is to educate the audience regarding the stereotyping of African Americans within the print and broadcast media.[17] Several posters in the exhibition invoke stereotypical images and racist values and then refute those beliefs within the argument. Beliefs are not only a strategy of argument but the subject of the posters as well and so must be clearly visible to the audience.

"Triptych," a series of three posters in the exhibition, alters the audience's relationship with and interpretation of the information over time. The first interpretation is ambiguous and may lead to a stereotypical conclusion, while the information received later exposes that stereotype. For example, in the last poster of the series, the audience first sees a blurred figure of an African-American man running juxtaposed with the headline "CRIME." The photograph suggests anonymity through cropping, motion, and soft focus; this is a man portrayed without individual characteristics. The large type screams like a tabloid headline and a label. Both the image and headline are ambiguous in meaning. Did the man commit a crime? Was a crime committed against him? The audience can only read the small type after coming closer to the poster, after the opportunity to form a stereotype has presented itself. The small type, contrasting in size and detail, shifts the ambiguity and tells the audience how to interpret the poster. ". . . Seeing my color makes me a criminal. But what is my crime?" Through the text the man must now be seen as an individual trapped within the context of racial stereotyping. By making the audience aware of their participation in the argument, the poster challenges the audience to recognize and confront their own beliefs and assumptions as well as those of the media. The formal devices that divide the audience's interaction into two clearly defined segments are merely expressions of a deeper engagement by the audience. Through this device, it is revealed that the *audience* holds or understands the beliefs demonstrated in the argument and that the *audience* is attributing those beliefs to the subject.

Chapter 4.1.4

Graphic design as rhetoric: towards a new framework for theory and practice in graphic design

Arne Scheuermann
Translated from the German by Chris Walton

1. The death of the graphic designer as we know her

Once upon a time, our towns were host to a multitude of milliners, saddlers, furriers, and farriers. They worked leather, fashioned saddles and hats and shod horses. These professions have largely disappeared from our latter-day townscapes because they have become superfluous. Hats are out of fashion, horses have been replaced by cars and the activities of many artisans have today been taken over by automated production lines in far-outlying factories.

Print workers, too, are enduring a similar fate. From a historical perspective even the profession of the graphic designer will be just as transient a phenomenon as that of the blacksmith, and, in fact, of far briefer duration. Since the 1990s, laymen have been making use of all those communication media from the realm of graphic design for which a team of specialists had hitherto been necessary. They take photographs with their mobile phones, typeset their texts on their laptops, print on their own laser printers at home, and publish through online media. Even the actual design work that today still depends on expert knowledge—such as digitally retouching fashion photographs—is often no longer undertaken by trained graphic designers. Design work is outsourced by agencies to specialized technical assistants in low-income countries. One does not need much imagination to conclude that in about forty years, the professions of graphic and communication design as we know them will probably have ceased to exist.

Yet we should consider the disappearance from our towns of hats, horses, and lead type from a different angle, for most of humankind's basic needs and activities are not as changeable as we often think they are. Even if horses, broadsheets, and hats fall out of fashion, people still want to be properly attired, they want to get quickly from A to B, and they want to give their fellow men and women food for thought—just as has always been the case. We simply do these things differently from how they were done four hundred years ago. We don't wear feather hats, we don't take hansom cabs to get about, and we don't print broadsheets any more—we wear sneakers, take a plane, and write blogs. But this changes very little about our fundamental human needs.

So if we take a broad historical view of things, it strikes us that what graphic designers did in the twentieth century—communicating with text and images—was also done in previous centuries by printers and illustrators, and before then by scribes and illuminators, and before then by priests and master builders. In forty or four hundred years from now, there will be new professions in which learned people will be communicating with text and images and mediating in the affairs of humankind.

For here we have the real heart of the matter: even if graphic design as a discipline and a profession is a historically ephemeral phenomenon, its contents stretch far back into the past and forward into the future—namely the possibilities and procedures for communicating through images and text. This is the case even if we expand the concept of "graphic design" to include visual communication and communication design using moving images and sound. Graphic design is thus, in historical terms, merely a specific means of designing media—a subsection of a far more comprehensive and historically varied profession.

If we make this shift in perspective, disregard what is *specific* to the discipline of graphic design, and instead attend to the overarching nature of graphic design practices, then we may arrive at a new order. And, as I propose to illustrate below, we also arrive at an expanded mode of both thinking about and producing graphic design. From this new vantage point we focus neither upon the individual disciplines—illustration, typography, photography, etc.—nor the individual media—posters, books, mobile apps, etc. Instead, we consider intentional actions conveyed through media. Why do people communicate through media in the first place? They do so typically to prompt others to action. And how do they do this? They do so most often by instructing others, and by moving them and delighting them. Yet this "new" perspective on graphic design is, in fact, almost 2,800 years old.

2. New Times Romans

When the first tentative forms of democracy developed in Ancient Greece in about 800 B.C.E., public speech acquired special significance: citizens used words to put their ideas in competition with each other in public places. Words were used to convince people of their own rightness, to elect candidates, to go to war, and to condemn traitors. The Ancient Greeks rapidly recognized that the art of convincing others with words represented an important technique for a successful democracy. The Greeks founded schools of oratory, and an elaborate system of sciences was formed that taught people how to plan a speech, how to memorize it, how to structure it effectively, and how to deliver it in a way that would move an audience. They learned when to give what type of speech, what they should avoid saying, what sorts of things would generate reactions, how to stimulate the emotions of their audience, and what emotions can lead to certain actions. By the time of the Roman Empire, this system of sciences had become a core element of education, and we know it as "rhetoric."

The basic concern of rhetoric is its intended impact: one acts with intent in order to achieve a specific effect in one's audience—for example, to convince or to persuade others to adopt a specific opinion or take a specific action (the Latin word *persuadere*, fittingly, can mean both at the same time). The different means (*modi*) of achieving this are: instructing (*docere*), moving (*movare*), and delighting (*delectare*) those who are listening. The primary criterion for choosing a means of achieving the preferred outcome is doing that which is apt or appropriate (*aptum*, *decorum*). An orator, or *rhetor*, will adapt her rhetorical means to her topic, to the occasion, and to the audience in order to achieve the desired effect. And this process is carried out according to a set formula. What is appropriate in a whimsical speech at the birthday party of a friend is inappropriate in a serious speech about treason that is delivered before parliament, and vice versa. Practice makes perfect, and over time a *rhetor* becomes better acquainted with the emotional responses that she aims to prompt. The more she listens to speeches of other *rhetores*, and the more speeches she makes, the more secure she will become in her choice of rhetorical means.

Now something fascinating happened in the ancient world: Because all people who were active in media had interiorized rhetoric as a core school subject, not only did they make speeches themselves, but they also transferred the notions of rhetoric to other aspects of life. Images, buildings, and music were, therefore, also conceived in rhetorical terms and they were used to instruct, to move, and to delight. The means by which this persuasion was achieved (in the color of sculptures, the floor height of court buildings, and the musical intervals in songs) were adapted to the topic in question according to their appropriateness (*decorum*). Even the strength of the "affect" (that is, the emotion or mood or passion) that the rhetor applied was judged according to this same system.

When ancient works of art and ancient texts on rhetoric and art were rediscovered during the Renaissance, their whole package of design production and analysis was adopted along with its rhetorical framework. Thus the European history of ideas after 1300 is connected to those ancient practices in which rhetoric provided a framework for the production of media. Renaissance artists, book printers, and architects learned rhetoric as a school subject during their humanistic education. From Leon Battista Alberti's Palazzo Rucellai to Albrecht Dürer's copper engraving *Melencolia I* to Orlando di Lasso's St. Matthew Passion—the books that were written, the drawings that were made, the buildings that were constructed, and the music that was composed were all indebted to the rhetorical ideas of intention of impact, communication of affect, and appropriateness, and they followed the ideals and rules of rhetoric. At this time, enormous collections of rhetorical figures—that is, individual structural rules—were developed for all genres of art and design. These aesthetic instructions for production and design brought together knowledge about individual forms of media, their impact, and their means (Heinen 2008). This instruction process was offered in detail, down to a micro-level: specific small-scale impact goals were described (such as evoking affect in the audience), as well as the means to achieve them (such as writing a particular musical interval that was believed to be able to bring an audience to tears).

This practice was applied comprehensively across all of Europe until new aesthetic ideas began to supersede rhetoric in about 1750 (Mühlmann 1996). Supported by the ideas of theorists and writers like Baumgarten, Lessing, and Kant, artists wanted to determine by themselves how they should work, and they wanted to create their art freely, as they saw fit. The rulebooks of rhetoric were now seen as a "rigid corset"—as "shackles" to artistic expression. New concepts such as "beauty" and "truth," the "genius," and the "sublime" took center stage. This re-evaluation process took on a radical slant about 1800. Rhetoric was eliminated from school curricula, and the question of appropriateness, *decorum*, no longer played a significant role in art (Ueding and Steinbrink 1994). Industrialization in the nineteenth century was one important factor that led to design becoming a discipline. The twentieth century trans-formed typesetters and illustrators into graphic designers, and by this time rhetoric as a school subject had already been forgotten. Meanwhile, the above-mentioned aesthetic theories of idealism dominated thinking about design and retained their sovereignty from the 1750s until the 1980s—under the guise of Classical Modernism, Bauhaus, and Ulm—until they were watered down by postmodern trends. They are currently in an advanced stage of dissolution.

In parallel to this development, rhetoric was rediscovered in the 1920s and 1930s. New mass media, such as the radio, shifted attention to political oratory and to the massive impact that it could have on society. This fuelled a new interest in rhetoric. In the Anglo-American sphere, a "new rhetoric" emerged that developed along similar lines to the emerging field of cultural studies; in the Francophone world, a "rhétorique générale" evolved that was oriented to philosophy and logic; and in Germany, historians and philologists worked on an "allgemeine Rhetorik" (general rhetoric). But "rhetoric" in these new forms meant analysis above all, and seldom encompassed production practices (Ueding and Steinbrink 1994: 165–71). Hardly anyone in the second half of the twentieth century read the speeches of famous men and women in school in order to learn how to become better orators themselves. Instead, speeches were analyzed mainly in order to discern their rhetorical figures, to understand them better and, if necessary, also to be better forearmed against their techniques of manipulation. Thus the ancient and early-modern (Renaissance) notion that listening to speeches and giving speeches must always be interlinked, has in modern times been replaced by the belief that media can be understood in an exclusively passive manner by adopting an analytical stance. To this end, the rhetoric of film, industrial design, and graphic design began to be analyzed in the twentieth century: we sought and found rhetorical figures in feature films (Clifton 1946, 1949, 1983), advertisements (Bonsiepe 1965; Forceville 1996; Messaris 1997), furniture (Buchanan 1985), and posters (Ehses 1984), all with the goal of being better able to interpret and understand these media (Kenney and Scott 2003). A time traveler from the Renaissance, however, would rub his eyes in aston-ishment at this practice and ask: how can one speak of graphic design if one has never designed a poster oneself?

It was in the 1980s that a new view of the relationship between design and rhetoric began to emerge. One of the issues that came to the fore was that the training to become a graphic designer emphasizes the same feedback loop as did Classical rhetoric: designers, too, study media in order to design media better (Kostelnick 1989). Theory and practice—or analysis and production—are not separate entities in the realm of design; they are interrelated in everyday design practice. Designers analyse the designs of others in order to become better designers themselves. They make assumptions about the impact intended by the actions of others, they speculate about what others' goals might have been, they analyze the means that have been employed to reach these goals, and they ponder the design "tricks" that have been utilized. In short, designers can be envisioned as the *rhetores* of today (Buchanan 1985; Hardison 1967; Joost and Scheuermann 2006; Mainberger 1989; Scheuermann 2009). The ancient mechanisms that build the intended impact of an argument are still in effect under the surface in graphic design, and these mechanisms are developed and passed on. In the future, even after the end of graphic design as we know it, these mechanisms will remain effective. But what does this all mean for graphic design today?

3. Please ask your graphic designer or communication designer about the risks and side effects

If designers are *rhetores*, then there is a series of consequences, both for design theory and for design practice. Some of the consequences are banal and have already been stated elsewhere, in other contexts (Atzmon 2011; Hill and Helmers 2004; Joost and Scheuermann 2008; Scheuermann 2013). Nevertheless, I would like to present them once more in this essay.

First, our perspective is altered with regard to the artifacts of graphic design—advertisements, posters, websites, and books. We are surrounded by thousands of lookbooks, yearbooks, competitions, and blogs that present us with excellent examples of graphic design. There is a whole industry of picture books and databases that have no goal other than to present "exceptional" graphic design. They are organized according to illustration styles and paper formats, and customer groups and agencies. Readers can analyze them according to their motives and styles, their clients and their functions. But if graphic designers want to become better designers by observing graphic design in the fashion of *rhetores*, then lookbooks would need to answer a very different set of questions than they currently do: What was the assignment? What was the intent? What impact was borne in mind? And observers should be able to derive from this process the answers to the following questions: What rhetorical means were used to reach these goals? And were they successful?

For trained designers it suffices to know the occasion and the brief, to see the means utilized in the artifact with their own (increasingly experienced) eyes, and then to refer them to each other. In this way, it can be observed if and how the means utilized are in accord with the given brief. Thus, for the analysis of graphic design the rule is: we have to understand the assignment given to the designer if we are going to be able to talk about the different qualities of a poster, such as its composition, its effectiveness of communication, or the context of its content.

Second, our perspective on graphic design as rhetoric allows us to recognize overarching patterns and commonalities in design that go beyond individual style or an individual hand. Dealing with graphic design in this rhetorical manner sometimes initially offends students, but after a time most students come to see that this analytical method has advantages. Looking through the lens of rhetoric, whoever believes that their individual style and brilliant thinking are responsible for the quality of their work will realize otherwise. Even the graphic design for an illegal underground dance event follows a series of patterns of intention that align with the project brief. This kind of reading does not merely open a window into the discipline for cultural studies, but in a highly practical sense it also opens graphic designers' eyes so that they are able to consider other styles of graphic design, other epochs in graphic design, and other approaches to graphic design. Their own design gains richness because they can draw from a larger repertoire.

Third, the framework of graphic design as rhetoric draws our analytical view, in general, away from artifacts and to the design process that leads to the artifacts. Nearly every design process is driven by a brief. The rhetorical principle of appropriateness—*decorum*—refers to the here and now, to the relationship between the object of a speech and its audience, to the appropriate point in time and to the appropriate means by which the intended goal is to be achieved. These criteria make it possible for graphic designers to engage with their assignments in a differentiated fashion, and to compel them to scrutinize their briefs within the framework of these rhetorical dimensions. If a graphic designer as *rhetor* is commissioned to design a poster, she first asks: Why a poster? What exactly is the poster meant to communicate? She does so, because perhaps what is needed is a website or an advertisement and not a poster at all.

The result is an expansion of designers' terms of reference. Besides design practitioner, she assumes the role of a counselor who advises the client above and beyond communication design by supervising certain management activities, such as decision-making processes. This extended activity requires both conversational techniques (which are often neglected in contemporary graphic design education), and also an ethical stance toward the client that should be learned and rehearsed. This means approaching the client free of prejudice, trusting the client's own specialist knowledge, and advising her without bias. Basic knowledge of conversation techniques for non-directional counseling also enables designers to develop an ethical approach in their work.

Fourth, it is interesting that the insistence on developing a recognizably ethical approach was also an integral aspect of Classical rhetoric. After Classical rhetoric was accused of being merely a means of unethical manipulation, schools of rhetoric drafted an ethical framework that would allow a *rhetor* to behave properly and honorably. This framework required that *rhetores* be proficient in politics, know both sides of an issue, and treat the public with respect. The rhetorical techniques, however, remained untouched: one and the same rhetorical figure can speak for something or for its opposite—it is the *rhetor*, thanks to his complementary training in ethical behavior who employs these rhetorical figures to benefit the general public interest.

This matter of arguing for both sides of an issue is also an interesting one for graphic design in which the same pictorial means can solicit either for one thing or its opposite. Developing ethical approaches to their work therefore plays an important part in graphic design training, and brings up questions such as: in what sort of society do we wish to live ten years from now? How can design contribute to justice, peace, and ecological change in our towns? How can graphic design support democracy? These questions resonate in every design commission, regardless of the client or the location, or the size of the design office.

The four previous observations about graphic design do not necessarily require rhetoric—but since they are *also* derived from rhetoric, they can make clear the broad context in which graphic design can be conceived as a form of rhetoric.

4. Empiricism strikes back

If we look at the instructional aesthetics of applied rhetoric, namely its books of rules, then we can observe more specific aspects. Until well into the eighteenth century, these instruction books regulated the production of media down to the smallest detail. But graphic design developed at a time when the early Modernist aesthetic had the guiding principle: "Good graphic design follows no rules—it breaks rules!" So what role do rules actually play in graphic design?

To be sure, most designers are right when they insist that distinguished graphic design cannot be achieved with rules alone. And this widespread mistrust of design "recipes" is often confirmed by mediocre design that is the result of working to a prescription. Rejecting recipes, however, ignores the fact that there are indeed rules in graphic design, especially when it comes to design basics. Whether it's a matter of the paper format, the reading speed, or the contrast of logos—graphic designers know a whole series of rules that make their design processes simpler. It's just that there are no rulebooks any more. These rules are usually only committed to paper when teaching beginners; professional designers have already interiorized them, and are in no more need of instructions.

This debate on rules becomes pertinent when one investigates the effectiveness of graphic design using methods that are traditionally employed in the natural sciences, such as collecting physiological data of people's reactions to graphic design. In recent decades there has been some discussion about whether design is (or should be) a science, and if so: how (Jonas 2012; Schneider 2006; Schultheis 2005). There are good reasons for and against. It seems that the desire for the scientification of the discipline remains roughly balanced against the feeling that design is simply not a science (Romero-Tejedor and Jonas 2010).

But if we want to regard design as a discipline—in order to apply for funding for design research, or to convince education policy-makers of the necessity for tertiary institutions for design, for example—then design practices (along with other aspects of design) should be empirically or even quantitatively investigable. And there's the rub. If someone wishes to investigate the neurophysiological aspects of basic patterns of perception of posters, for example, we find ourselves confronted with a methodological dilemma: a poster is too complex for us to undertake a quantitative investigation of its overall perception. There is no point in measuring the neurophysiological reactions of people who first look at one poster and then at another, because two posters are different on too many levels. Errors in most measurements would be too great to secure any substantial data about the design being evaluated. In order to get accurate data, researchers would have to test small variants—posters that are identical in every way, for example, except for one or two delimited factors such as color or font. All that can be derived from this analysis, though, are statements about these small design factors—about colors or fonts. But it is typically the overall impact of graphic design that is at work, however, so this small-scale knowledge is essentially useless for practitioners. Furthermore, this sort of minor data is seldom new; it largely serves to confirm the design fundamentals of which the practitioner is already aware. Here we see the point and the pointlessness of the scientific examination of design: its subjects are as a rule either too small (e.g. red as opposed to green) for them to be interesting for designers, or too large (the interdependency of all elements on the poster) for them to be investigated reliably by means of quantitative methods. As an answer to this dilemma, design research is typically qualitative, using methods from the social sciences, hermeneutics, and cultural sciences, and employing methods that are derived from design itself such as sketching or experience prototyping, and newly developed methods of artistic research such as experimental collaborative drawing or cultural probes.

Rhetoric offers a new method for design analysis. It allows us to proceed empirically because its relationship to empiricism is different from that of the natural sciences. Scientific investigation aims for measurable, generalizable knowledge about a subject that is generally independent of its practice. While the subject of rhetorical science and the practice of rhetoric are intertwined, rhetoric relies on the interplay of theory and practice, analysis, and production as a repository of knowledge.

For in rhetoric, it is the orator who is the "researcher." When they encountered specific rules for rhetoric, the *rhetores* of the Early Modern period wrote them in a little book called a *collectaneum*. Over the course of their lives, this *collectaneum* enabled them to observe, try out, apply, alter, and categorize a series of rhetorical rules. They did not perform these activities based on *why* these rules were effective; they were interested in *what* was effective, *when*, and *how*; in other words, what had proved itself in practice. When applied to graphic design, this mindset can lead to empirical design research methods. Collecting effective design rules and discussing them, studying reports by graphic designers about their briefs, analyzing and understanding interpretations of projects by experienced graphic designers—all of these factors together help us to utilize, both in theory and in practice, the practical knowledge and experience of designers. In this setting, designers are the researchers—they use a methodological mix in which they interrelate their own knowledge with others' experience. Like *rhetores*, they collect and observe the effective mechanisms of design, condensing them into specific patterns, discovering commonalities and differences, and reconciling this knowledge with their own practices.

In rhetoric, then, there is a hidden approach by which we can understand graphic design as a discipline in which theory and practice, and analysis and production, may be interrelated in a mutually beneficial manner. With this knowledge about design and rhetoric, graphic design can face its future dissolution with equanimity: the world will always need *rhetores* who can skilfully unite image and text in order to achieve specific communication goals. In other words: graphic designers.

The design lesson here is that for posters to become tools they must exploit existing activity systems. Posters and their locations have to be designed around such activity systems so that they may reinforce or contribute to a change in systems of social activity.

Actor-Network Theory: artifacts are delegates of humans

Actor-Network Theory was conceived by anthropologists and sociologists Bruno Latour, Michael Callon, and John Law in order to blur the distinctions between intentional subjects and inert artifacts. According to Actor-Network Theory the world is populated with human actors and non-human actors, such as public messages or technical artifacts that have different degrees of agency. Actors, which include both people and inanimate artifacts, may (or may not) work together, and their cooperation can result in stable networks. People are only one sort of actor in these networks.

How can artifacts around us have agency? Crucial here is the concept of "delegation to nonhumans" (Latour 1992: 232). When people produce an artifact, it becomes delegation; they delegate tasks to a non-human actor. Metaphorically, the non-human actor follows a "script" that the human actor has written for it. This is the reason that Actor-Network Theory designates non-human *actors* and is interested in this new actor's behavior. Actor-Network Theory is open about how to define an actor, and it investigates the behavior of non-human actors. How do non-human actors react to interactions with people? Which actions do they allow? Finally, which scripts do non-human actors impose upon human actors? Latour argues that "[t]he nonhumans take over the selective attitude of those who engineered them." (Latour 1992: 233). He provides as an example an "unfriendly" door that replaces a human doorman. The door closes automatically with a speed and force that is a problem for elderly users. The prescriptions imposed by non-human actors on human actors are physical constraints, but they also carry with them beliefs about how the world should be: non-human actors are also moral actors. The automatic door whispers to the aged: "What are you doing here? This is no place for you." The world is full of these sorts of delegated actors that can be compared to humans. Actor-Network Theory invites us to imagine artifacts as our counterparts. When artifacts are conceptualized as partly social beings, they are not only waiting to be used, but taking part in social relationships as well. As with people, such relationships may be strong or weak, hierarchical, intimate, etc.

How can we transfer these ideas to a graphic design artifact like a poster? We may begin by asking: Which tasks have been delegated to a poster? What would a human actor do in place of a poster? Let's imagine this for a moment. A person replacing a poster would probably wave at us, beckoning us to approach. When we're within speaking distance he or she would invite us to an event, or advertise a product. This behavior is more obtrusive than the behavior of a poster. Indeed, an individual poster, however visually aggressive, is nice and quiet compared to its human counterpart. But the individual poster's modesty is outweighed by its omnipresence. Another copy of the poster is waiting for us around the corner: The poster is a stalker.

We see now how human work has been delegated to the poster: the chore of standing and waiting for passersby has been entrusted to a visual plane that is typically made of paper that can be attached almost anywhere. While the poster performs this task more reliably than people do, it is rather unskilled when it comes to addressing passersby personally. On the other hand, the poster prescribes behavior on us: it requires us to approach. If we really want to absorb its information then we have to stop and look or read. But stopping in the flow of passersby is sometimes difficult, and people may criticize us for "hanging around" (Goffman 1966). That means socially accepted behavior toward a poster often happens only when a passerby absorbs the poster's information while passing by "*en passant.*" Posters are typically posted laterally to the direction that people walk, so their messages are usually disclosed at an acute angle. The best viewing angle commonly happens when a person's body is oriented orthogonally to the poster. But this posture requires people to turn their heads, distracting them from the goal of getting to their destinations. We see here that posters are contradictory actors. They demand our attention, requiring us to approach, and inviting us to contemplate their content. Within the actor-network of the city, however, posters reinforce another behavior: to quickly absorb the information while moving. That is to say, posters stipulate that passersby are busy people.

Indeed, standing before a poster is only acceptable when we make our behavior "visibly-rational-and-reportable-for-all-practical-purposes, i.e. 'accountable'" (Garfinkel 1967: vii) as waiting. Longer exposure to a poster typically happens in environments in which idling is expected: on railway platforms, in subway trains, etc.

We can see that posters imply modes of use that go beyond the constraints that its more obvious visual attributes prescribe. Posters are actors in a network: the city and its unwritten laws are reinforced by the "morality" of the poster. Posters' promotional content situates the passersby as consumers. Furthermore, as an actor in the city, posters position passersby as busy people who are solicited by potentially unwanted offers.

In summary, Actor-Network Theory invites us to imagine the human counterpart of an artifact; and reconstructing how human work is delegated to an artifact helps us to imagine this counterpart. This process unveils the sociality of artifacts, and the more or less acceptable prescriptions that artifacts impose on human behavior, to the point that they reveal the "morality" of artifacts and how artifacts can strengthen certain socially accepted behaviors.

Working with the theories in design practice and research

The three theoretical frameworks I discussed above provide new perspectives on how graphic design plays a part in everyday life. *Distributed Cognition* offers a concrete way to understand how graphic design artifacts are used as external resources that facilitate cognitive processes. Distributed Cognition's focus is on the optimization of cognitive processes by enhancing the roles of artifacts that are engaged by people. *Activity Theory* offers plausible concepts with which to model human activities, and investigates how these sorts of activities are mediated by artifacts. Artifacts can be evaluated as more or less adequate tools in these activities. The developmental perspective of Activity Theory, in particular, invites us to study and reflect upon how such tools evolve and eventually disappear. Finally, *Actor-Network-Theory* points to the agency of these artifacts and their possible participation in socio-material structures. As it conceptualizes the power of artifacts to prescribe uses, Actor-Network-Theory also unveils their "morality".

These three approaches move away from a product-centered perspective toward a broad view of the role of graphic design in everyday life. Even though these three approaches do not explore use processes in the typical sense of users handling artifacts, graphic design practice can derive implications for design from them beyond the example of the poster.

Distributed Cognition's concept of "offloading" cognitive effort to an artifact, for instance, is easily applicable to other graphic design artifacts. It guides designers to be attentive to the cognitive effort that the graphic design work imposes on its users. Thinking of graphic design as a tool, as Activity Theory suggests, helps to identify the different aspects of its use. In which context, for example, is it worth considering the spine of a book to be a tool? Such questions help to relate all aspects of a graphic design to meaningful use. Finally, with Actor-Network-Theory, graphic design may be examined for ways that it engages in social interaction: Is it a good replacement for a human? Is the tone well chosen? What must be made clearer? This extended perspective on use helps to inform design decisions based on actual use. The laboratory-like design studio, and the graphic design class in which use concepts are evaluated for the first time, may benefit from considering contexts of use that are inspired by these theories.

The theories I discuss here can also offer guidance to begin design research. First of all, they offer a productive distance from predictable graphic design products. Even seemingly old media like posters can be rethought by engaging these concepts. It is clear that graphic design and its use must be studied engaging users. Real contexts with real users are the most adequate to begin with, because we can gain the most insights and are pointed quickly to shortcomings of the design and the research question. Suitable methods to study use are observation and interviews. In the "wild," observation is problematic because the researcher must respect the user's privacy. Therefore, instead of using video cameras for observation, taking "field notes" like ethnographers do is more appropriate. In combination with interviews this creates data with behavioral and subjective aspects. Such early studies with few users may be later refined in more controlled settings when the research question gets focused. Then, more experiment-like study designs that result in quantitative data may be employed.

Ethnographic methods, like observation and interviews, should result in detailed descriptions of the practices around the graphic design artifacts. This data then has to be abstracted, categorized, and represented somehow to formulate more general evidence. As for the exploratory nature of such design research, Grounded Theory seems particularly useful for this part of the research (Corbin and Strauss 2008). Grounded Theory means that by closely examining the data and carefully abstracting from it, general evidence can be gained. This is done by "coding," e.g. labeling data with concepts and categories (Corbin and Strauss 2008: 160). This, of course, is an abstract outline of a possible research process that must be detailed by taking into account the specific graphic design artifact and the questions towards it.

Conclusion

Summing up, these concepts enable a critical perspective on graphic design. They help us to move away from a narrow approach to graphic design issues by forcing us to consider visual artifacts in their broad social contexts. The use of graphic design artifacts can be explored in new ways when their functions are situated within social contexts. What efforts do graphic design artifacts leave to their users? What questionable practices do graphic design artifacts promote? Which social behaviors do they sanction? The theories that I've discussed in this essay extend an invitation to critical practice and research in graphic design.

Section 4.2

Writing, practice, and graphic design criticism

Chapter 4.2.1

What is this thing called graphic design criticism? Parts I & II

Rick Poynor and Michael Rock

Part 1: 1995
Rick Poynor

Terms such as art criticism, literary criticism, architecture criticism and film criticism are so familiar that they require little explanation, whether we are interested in reading their products or not. They are all activities with obvious, readily identifiable roles and job descriptions attached: "art critic," "film critic" and so on. They bring to mind the names of writers who specialize in the subject, achieve a continuous critical presence through their publications and are identified with a particular sensibility, style of writing, set of ideas and point of view. Compared to art or film criticism, the term "graphic design criticism" has an unfamiliar, slightly uncomfortable ring. It is one that even the most avid reader of graphic design magazines and books will encounter rarely, if at all.

In the 1990s, the call for such a criticism has nevertheless become steadily louder, the few exponents increasingly prepared—though still fairly tentatively—to identify themselves as such. A collection of critical writings on graphic design—some drawn from *Eye*—has recently been published.[1] Ten years ago the more forward-thinking designers urged the development of such a criticism, believing that it was part and parcel of a mature profession. Now that it is happening there are murmurs of discontent and, despite the example of neighboring disciplines, the critic's motivation is in doubt. "Criticism," one internationally renowned designer declared, "usually takes the form of the negative and the overly judgmental."[2] So what exactly is graphic design criticism? Who practices it, or ought to practice it, and what are its aims? And can it, in the sense that we might talk about art or film criticism, be truly said to exist at this point?

Michael Rock

While we might not recognize it as such, design criticism is everywhere, underpinning all institutional activity—design education, history, publishing and professional associations. The selection, description and reproduction of designed artifacts in books and magazines, for instance, is the work of theory. Objects are represented to make a point—even if the point is as simple as "My, isn't Rick Valicenti a genius"—and that is a critical position.

Famous designers, complaining about over-zealous design critics, forget that their fame is created through exposure. For example, while I have rarely encountered actual work by Neville Brody, I have seen hundreds of examples published in the international design press and his own books, carefully organized and edited to give the impression of complete artistic continuity. Thus Brody has an influence and reputation through publishing that he could never have in practice.

Writing has a profound effect on Institution Design, the elaborate apparatus that surrounds design production.[3] Design work is exchanged intra-professionally, through publishing, lectures, promotional material and other written forms. Publication may lead to speaking engagements, workshops, teaching invitations and competition panels—all of which in turn further promote certain aesthetic positions. At the same time, an historical canon is perpetually generated, a canon of that will influence the next generation of designers by indicating what work is of value, what is worth saving, what is excluded.

So the relationship between practice and theory is symbiotic. The 40-year expansion of the post-war design industry has been both critiqued and promoted through writing.

RP

We are at an interesting juncture, where those with a stake in graphic design writing are starting to debate the forms such a criticism should take. The principal forums for the critical writing undertaken to date have been the professional magazines. Even in the more critically-minded publications, criticism has run side by side with ordinary journalism and other reader services. Established editorial formats and the need to engage a broad professional audience place pragmatic restrictions on what can be attempted and said. There are those who now feel that such "journalistic criticism" is lacking, that it fails to make its critical positions sufficiently explicit, and that we need, in short, a more academic form of criticism to compare with those generated by, for instance, art, literature, or cultural studies.[4] This is potentially of great educational value, but in Britain academic graphic design criticism is at such a rudimentary stage of development, with so little to show in terms of published research, that few conclusions can be drawn.

To what extent such a criticism will be able to address the working designer is a moot point, though experience suggests that the kinds of journals and books that would carry it will have limited appeal to professional readers. What we hope to achieve with *Eye* is not so much a "journalistic criticism"—the term makes it sound like something that has fallen short of the real thing—as a *critical journalism.* By this I mean the kind of writing you find on the arts pages of the Sunday papers: informed, thoughtful, skeptical, literate, prepared to take up a position and argue a case, aware of academic discourse and debates (perhaps even written by academics), but able to make these issues relevant and accessible to a wider readership—writing with a firm sense of its audience's interests and needs. That, at least, is the ideal.

and with the same variety of perspectives, it will need dedicated writers." Looking back at the trajectory of our work over that decade and a half, it seems that you have become exactly that: a dedicated writer of design criticism. And, clearly, that impressive body of work enacts a very specific cultural criticism that draws on many of the sources we discussed so long ago. I, of course, took a different path.

We ended that discussion on an optimistic note, looking forward to a flowering of criticism in the coming years. How are you feeling about that development now? Was my optimism justified? What have you surmised about the subject of design? Does it hold up? And who are you writing for now? Is there a public out there that's getting elevated? Or is it more rarefied? In "Post No Bills," Walter Benjamin wrote: "For the critic his colleagues are the higher authority. Not the public. Still less posterity." Has the institution of design criticism effectively changed the institution of design?

RP

I see scattered growth rather than a great blossoming. There has certainly been plenty of talk about design criticism since our dialogue in *Eye*. A few personal essay collections have been published and, as with other fields, these are good indicators of critical vitality, a sign that a writer has achieved a certain presence and a degree of traction. They are also the most concentrated and cogent way of finding out what a critic has to say. Blogs are clearly a notable development. Then there is the emergence in the last two years of the design writing and criticism MFA and MA courses at the School of Visual Arts, London College of Communication, and Konstfack in Stockholm. The Royal College of Art in London has also announced an MA in Critical Writing in Art & Design. These phenomena tell us something about the perceived importance of criticism within design.

I don't, however, care much for criticism as some purely abstract ideal and I don't think we need too many more vague academic "calls" for criticism. We need some action. We need a lot more criticism and places to disseminate it. Criticism is a highly motivated personal act, so the litmus test for its presence is pretty simple: can you name the critic? Are there plenty of these people at work in the field? What is their agenda? What is their particular contribution to the discussion?

My model for what the life of a design critic might be has always come from outside the academy and especially from the example of music writers and film writers. These are people whose commitment to their subject is so great that they want it to become their work and their living. They have enough outlets to support them. There have been many such individuals. Of course, the online environment is changing the terms of engagement for every kind of writer and anyone arriving on the scene now hoping to become a full-time design writer will require exceptional commitment. It's far more likely that most design writing will continue to be produced on the side, taking second place to better paying activities, such as designing or teaching. But, as the patchy state of design criticism shows, it's not possible to build a sustained writing presence, a convincing body of work and a committed readership by occasional weekend dabbling. Writers must write. Again, the yardsticks have to come from better established kinds of critical writing.

MR

The fragmentation you identify—and the effect it has in sidelining writing—is at the heart of the issue. We had a sense of that way back when but neither of us could predict how profoundly both the act of designing and writing would change. In fact, technology and media-driven fragmentation obscure the development of some institutions of design criticism (not that that is what you are calling for) and opens up certain opportunities as well.

Let me try to pick that apart. Take the demise of my old employer, *I.D.* magazine, as a case in point. *I.D.* was reorganized back in the early 1990s (as was *Eye*) as the model of new design journalism. The idea was to take writing seriously, to engage a broad range of topics and tap critics from other disciplines to look at design. *I.D.* and *Eye* succeeded in the mission for a while but ultimately *I.D.* became the victim of fragmentation. As web-based communication eclipsed print, blogs like Design Observer and dezeen and, more recently, social media forms like Facebook and Twitter, drew away readers and writers from *I.D.* The magazine format was too slow to follow the hyperactive conversation on the blogs.

This change is good in some ways: it has drawn new people into the dialogue, and some very good young writers are working on design. Two ex-Yale men come to mind, Rob Giampietro and Dmitri Siegel, as well as someone with a real projective practice, Daniel van der Velden. But because all that writing is unpaid, and because of the open nature of the blog format, I wonder if Design Observer can exercise an editorial framework the way that an *I.D.* or an *Eye* could. In addition, while a blog now may have the substance of printed writing, the ephemerality of the medium, coupled with the rather annoying smack-down response the format seems to engender—in which every idea slowly degenerates into a series of increasingly personal insults—can make it feel degraded.

This fragmentation of writing forums reflects the equally disruptive fragmentation in graphic design. As books and print are recast as luxury items, as budget cuts eliminate editorial positions, and as the general pace of projects accelerates, the nature of what a designer does and doesn't do transforms. Designers now often serve as editors, content-managers, proofreaders and caption writers. Design projects routinely involve art direction, technology development, social-media management, publicity, and any number of tangential activities. The design object itself is shattering just at the moment that the tools to dissect it are, too.

As a case in point, we recently developed a wayfinding project that functioned completely within an existing cellphone and SMS messaging network. There were no visible components, only a database, an SMS server, and a public cellphone network. If that project is now within the realm of graphic design, what critical tools are necessary to analyse it, and what is the forum for that analysis?

RP

Your SMS project is an intensified form of a critical problem that hamstrung design writing even at the time of our original dialogue. The practical criticism found in other disciplines—to use the concept introduced by literary critic I.A. Richards—begins with a publicly available object: a novel, a music CD, a painting, a building, a film. Buildings and paintings might only be accessible at a remove in photographs, but everything else can be experienced easily and immediately at first hand as pleasurable forms of culture to which we choose to give our time. While some types of design—the album cover, the movie title, the internationally distributed magazine, the imagery of global branding—occupy the wider public sphere, most of the work graphic designers do is relatively local, a matter of concern, if at all, only to the smaller number of people who see it.

Not only that: the object itself might be so slight that, unlike even a mediocre novel or film, it is simply not reviewable. There's very little to say and barely anyone would be interested to hear it. I remember you making this point once in conversation, using the example of a hairdresser's logo. If we were to examine hairdressers' logos collectively, as a category of symbol, could we begin to make such a piece of writing revealing or interesting? The object of study needs to have sufficient magnitude in our personal experience and to be complex enough in form and content to require and support critical interpretation. The writing needs an audience that regards the object as significant enough to want to know more about it. In any case, graphic design is usually a secondary component of the project it serves. People care a great deal about films and novels. They have no such conscious passion for transient commercial logos, which isn't to say that they don't respond to them. (I'm talking here about a general audience, not specifically about designers.)

Design writers have dealt with this by indulging in a lot of generalizing about graphic design while avoiding close engagement with objects—a tacit admission of doubt that design is really interesting enough to justify this degree of attention. The lack of specific critiques in the *Looking Closer* series of critical writings (1994–2006) made this all too clear. Critical methods needed to be demonstrated convincingly on some designed phenomena, but this rarely happened. Since 1999, as my own answer to this, I have written a regular "Critique" column for *Eye* about a single designed artifact. Some work. Some probably don't. But every time I begin one I face the same essential problem: will this be of any interest to international readers who will most likely never encounter the project I'm talking about?

So, yes, the fragmentation is even greater now when the outlets for design criticism are shrinking, as is the appetite for it. We can't ignore the fact that older forms of critical writing devoted to literature, art and film are regularly proclaimed to be in crisis for one reason or another, or even moribund—see, for instance, Irish literary critic Rónán McDonald's *The Death of the Critic* (2007). Even if we believe (and it's a big "if") that critical writing about graphic design can resist these broader trends and somehow hang on to its audience, a pressing question remains: what is criticism's primary task? In 1995, you were very clear about the role of the critic as someone with the job of "unmasking" and exposing the ideology at work in a design, and your own writing up to that point often reflected this. Fifteen years later, after so much experience as a designer, where do you stand now on the idea of unmasking?

MR

My idea about unmasking is still intact; actually, it has become more expansive. It's essential for the critic to reveal the inner workings of individual pieces via close reading—to reveal—but s/he must also link work into associative networks. Linking is another methodology that supports and extends this unmasking. Through linking, individual objects are contextualized.

Contextualization addresses the problem of insignificance (hereafter known as the "Hairdresser's Logo Problem"). I agree that many works of design are just too slight to stand up to real analysis, and the only way to understand them is to draw them into bigger socioeconomic and historical arcs. The design object must be seen as an index of something bigger.

I've tried to do this several times. Most recently, in "A Brief History of Screens," I argued that the evolution of display technology has fundamentally changed the relationship between the designer, the architect and the city. The aforementioned SMS project, then, can be seen as the apotheosis of a trajectory from the 19th-century urban flâneur, through the mid- and late 20th-century couch potato, to the contemporary hand-held device, which allows the reader to be both couch potato and flâneur. In this light, the work loses its small, individual qualities and becomes an inevitable product of historical development.

If the product of design becomes increasingly invisible, the critical project is less one of unmasking than of revealing. The critic must resuscitate the design object from the ether and set it into proper context. This is what I always admired about—and what seemed to be the mission of—the "Critique" column. You linked design objects to bigger narratives.

But the idea of revelation goes further: the critic, through his magic, must take what seems to be one way and show it to be another. The job of the critic is to disprove conventional wisdom, to create a revelation in the mind of the "public." Work that is generally lauded should be undermined; obscure work, slated to be forgotten or already forgotten, must be revived, shown to be sorely overlooked. Another quote from my current favorite, Benjamin's "Post No Bills: The Writer's Technique in Thirteen Theses": "The public must always be proved wrong, yet always feel represented by the critic." Would you agree with my reading of your column?

RP

I broadly agree with your outline of what design criticism should do. Its ultimate purpose is to elucidate the role design plays in social, cultural, economic and political contexts, but this inquiry still has to start with observable phenomena and experiences—with the "object" itself. If design criticism isn't capable of close reading, from which the networks of association you describe can be built, then any larger conclusions it might draw are open to doubt.

In reality, though, very few design writers seem concerned with drawing larger social or political conclusions about design. Their constitutional blindness to these issues duplicates the endemic blindness of design itself. They are "post-critical"—in the sense that architecture uses that term—without being conscious that this is their actual position. The idea of vigorously contesting anything is foreign to them. This would necessitate a firm, clearly thought-out position and they don't have one. While art can kid itself that it occupies a privileged zone of free thinking and critique within capitalism, design as we mostly practice it today understands itself as an integral service to and expression of capitalism. Hardly surprising, then, that the public perceives it in similar terms.

We can see the resulting critical quandary most clearly in the phenomenon of "design thinking" so much in vogue now in the business schools and in the pages of *Businessweek*. However well meaning the self-styled design thinkers might be, they are firmly embedded within capitalist ways of thinking and business models, and this dictates their social values and their instrumental view of design.

Their work might offer benefits to society, but at root it will remain economically and ideologically self-serving. It can never be a reliable source of critique. There is no perfect, ethically pure position for any kind of critic, especially not a design critic. Nevertheless, the critic must endeavor to maintain as much independence from the object of critique as possible. There can be no unmasking, no revelation, no setting of anything within its "proper context" without a clear sense of purpose on the critic's part in the first place. As Benjamin also said, "He who cannot take sides should keep silent."

If it is to mature, design criticism must acquire a new ideological awareness. It must move beyond soft, easy, self-comforting assertions that "sustainability is good" or "too much consumerism is bad for the planet"—as though the problem can be fixed by a few adroitly applied Band-Aids—and embrace the need for rigorous political analysis with the eventual goal of fundamental systemic change.

Design criticism's reluctance to engage with these issues reflects public failure to grasp the seriousness of the situation. Even after narrowly averted economic meltdown and public bailouts of the banks, many still want to believe that the system is basically sound and we can carry on in the old way. The lack of public anger is remarkable. We struggle to break the silken net of complacency spun around us by decades of superabundance. Design criticism, too, must find the nerve and the resolution to tear away this veil.

Notes

1. See also Steven Heller, "Criticizing Criticism: Too Little and Too Much," *AIGA Journal of Graphic Design*, 11 (4) (1993); and *Emigre* 31, "Raising Voices" issue (1994).

2. Letter from April Greiman, *AIGA Journal of Graphic Design*, 12 (3) (1994).

3. The phrase is borrowed from Michael Speaks' term "Institution Architecture." See "Writing in Architecture," *ANY*, 0 (May/June 1993).

4. See "A conversation with Andrew Blauvelt," *Emigre*, 31.

5. See "Escape from DWEMsville," *Times Literary Supplement*, May 27, 1994.

6. Neil Harris at the University of Chicago, Jackson Lears at Rutgers University, Stuart Ewen at Hunter College and Johanna Drucker at Yale have all produced substantial work on design subjects.

7. For further discussion of the adversarial nature of criticism see Michael Bierut, "Learning to Live with the Critics," *Eye*, 2 (8) (1993).

Chapter 4.2.2

Criticism and the politics of absence

Anne Bush

The irony of writing criticism is that one must ultimately challenge one's own convictions to remain critical. As a result, the critic must be both inside and outside of her discipline. The first is a natural position: the second a cultural one. To be inside a discipline is to engage in criticism from a collective position, to subscribe to its conventions and traditions. Such criticism supports cohesiveness, as it frames judgment in terms of right and wrong, good and bad. It nurtures loyalty and adherence to disciplinary rhetoric. The cultural critic, Edward Said, has described this interior criticism as "filial," a position so natural that it is akin to being born into it.[1] Yet to embrace only this natural criticism is problematic, since true self-reflection requires distance from one's habits and beliefs. Cultural criticism provides this external view. In Said's terms, cultural criticism is "affilial" and based on parameters beyond the prescriptions of a discipline. As a contextual perspective, it does not support conventions, but analyses the intersections between conventions and other disciplines and events. It places the object of its criticism "in the world." It is this cultural criticism, however, that is frequently eliminated from professional discussions of graphic design.

In a recent dialogue with Michael Rock on the merits of both natural and cultural criticism to graphic design, Rick Poynor—editor of *Eye* magazine—notes that criticism in the trade magazines needs to address a "broad professional audience." To do this, it needs to be both relevant and accessible to practitioners. Poynor suggests a "critical journalism" as the optimal approach for this writing since it has "a strong sense of the particular and uses a close, pragmatic acquaintance with the realities of production to ask more down-to-earth questions about individuals and bodies of work."[2] It is the antithesis of "academic," or cultural, criticism, an approach that he admits has value, but only for limited audiences. According to Poynor, academic criticism employs an "uncompromising form of analysis" that appeals only to designers who are "given to a particular type of reflection." His distinction is a dangerous one.

To champion an interior critique of graphic design in commercial publications is to continue the tradition of celebratory as opposed to investigatory discourse within the profession. It promotes agreement rather than analysis as celebratory discourse works to make invisible the actual affiliations between the world and the graphic design profession.[3] The benefits for this are clear. Representing the profession as a consensual body, composed of practitioners who subscribe to objective dialogue and believe in the merits of a pragmatically-centered discourse, serves industry by masking the economic agendas of production. It creates the illusion that the graphic design profession does not need to question its

First published in *Emigre*, 36 (1995): 8–15. © Anne Bush.

assumptions. Yet the extent to which this "making invisible" has depoliticized the practice of design is more than a bit disconcerting. In a telling moment, Poynor states;

Theory's conclusions will in some cases be profoundly opposed to certain forms of design activity. How meaningful or relevant is the unmasking of ideological operations going to be to the designer making a successful career in supermarket packaging, annual reports for Fortune 500 companies, or the world of glossy magazines? Not everyone shares the leftist political position that underpins the challenge these theories make to design.[4]

This is exactly the point. Professional identity depends upon the mutual acceptance of disciplinary conventions. It is a collective belief. The paradox of critical analysis, however, is that its role is to challenge this cohesiveness, to lay bare ideological bias. As a form of investigation, it is contradiction, not confirmation. Thus, it is self-serving to define the relevance of a critical approach by the extent to which its conclusions coincide with professional conventions. I would argue that promoting an exclusively interior or professional criticism in the non-academic design press works to trivialize both criticism and the profession itself. By eschewing contextual dialogue, such criticism does not promote analysis but stifles it. It creates an analytical void, an imbalance between internal assumptions and the external conditions that create and influence them. Interestingly enough, the absence of this contextual perspective is rooted in Enlightenment notions of the public sphere and the very concept of what constituted critical exchange.

Criticism as conversation

The view of criticism as a dialogue within a consensual public body can be traced back to the intersection of the critic and the public sphere during the seventeenth and eighteenth centuries. As outlined by Jürgen Habermas in *The Structural Transformation of the Public Sphere*, criticism was a reaction to aristocratic rule and emerged as a "theater of exchange" within a discursive public arena.[5] Supported by the technological possibilities of an industrialized printing trade, criticism was a kind of democratic dialogue, published in periodicals and mediated by discussion in public houses. Unlike contemporary criticism that is specific to the issues of a discipline, criticism at the beginning of the industrial revolution was based on popular consensus and addressed the cultural and social questions of the day. According to Habermas, the middle class viewed the critic as more conductor than composer, a facilitator and co-discourser in a social dialogue based on common sense and rational judgment. Seen in this way, criticism was part and parcel of an enlightened concept of society, a view that suspended class divisions in a purported attempt to keep discourse open and accessible to "every man."[6] This attempt, of course, was futile.

In as much as criticism became a utopian dialogue, it was inextricable from its own ideology and exclusions. Seeking to displace the aristocracy, the bourgeoisie was solidifying its own power base, which contained some of the same economic motivations that, originally, it had vowed to oppose. As a result, the democratic rationale of an open public dialogue was tainted by the autocratic echoes of a ruling voice, an enunciation that was white, male and privileged. By focusing on common sense as the measure by which rational argument was supported, the middle class excluded all who did not subscribe to their particular experiences and values including women, peasant groups and the working class. This meant that the public sphere conceived by Habermas was an abstraction, a hegemonic center from which the economic interests of the industrial elite were instituted under the guise of popular consent.[7] As these private interests grew, the utopian ideal of an open and democratic public exchange was superseded by an increasingly specialized and interior critique, one supported by the capitalist division of labor and the rise of the specialized professional.

Criticism as mediation

By the end of the eighteenth century, industrialization had produced a working class that would challenge the bourgeoisie through capitalist production and competition. Critical dialogue became a commodity, a product that could be imitated and sold to an increasingly diversified marketplace. With these changes came the initiation of new journals and the employment of the flamboyant literary hack, a writer whose job it was to construct criticism in a form that aspired to conceptions of good taste, a form that the public would buy. In response, the bourgeois critic retreated. Preferring to distance himself from the commodity-driven discourse of the market, the middle-class intellectual employed "thicker" language and the isolated persona of the knowing sage,[8] separating himself from public opinion in the process. The point was to associate true critical language with a particular expertise, endowing the critic with prestige and power through professional distance. Ironically, it would be precisely this aura of expertise that would serve to reunite the critic and the public, as society would turn to the specialized analysis of the critic to assuage their fears of a dehumanized future.

Paradoxically, industrial progress caused both anticipation and apprehension in the capitalist middle class. Although they were invigorated by the economic prosperity that mass production provided, they were uncertain about how to negotiate the social changes that accompanied this new wealth. Capitalist society needed guidance, someone who could clarify the relationship between technological advances and the human condition. The bourgeois critic answered this call. As a mediator between the productive and consumptive factions of society, the critic served both public and private interests. The goal was to quell the fears brought about by industrial change, to demystify production and consumption. This mediation, of course, was a myth. Criticism would always be subjective, influenced by the economic agenda of the producing elite, rendering the discoursing public sphere a mere phantom, a body constructed and manipulated by private interests.[9] As a response to this dilemma, criticism turned inward. In an effort to maintain their legitimacy, critics abandoned public/private mediation for empirical analysis, believing that facts provided the last bastion of true, objective discourse.

Criticism as explanation

Advocating factual description and logical method, critical evaluation in the nineteenth century not only mirrored empirical philosophy of the same period, but gestured toward the object-centered criticism that would dominate the first part of the twentieth century. By embracing the objectivity associated with science, it created the illusion that social and cultural changes could be rationally articulated and

Chapter 4.2.3

Quietude

Kenneth FitzGerald

It's a pretty, subdued time in design. Passions are running low—or are highly affected. Design continues to be a busy but overly placid, pleasant surface. There are few signs of what, if anything, lies below that surface. Our pond remains small and shallow. Anyone hoping for waves is waiting for someone else to make them.

There was some disturbance but the breakers seem to have settled out—and settled in. Have we arrived at a transition or a terminus? A breather or an expiration? A perpetual revolution (if that's what it was) is tough to maintain. Design might be process but there needs be a product. What have we produced?

That nonconformist forms were readily absorbed into the mainstream shouldn't have come as a surprise. It's the life cycle of style. The once-rebellious designers who have joined the establishment are not necessarily hypocrites. Often, that label was applied by the established. Cooption is natural, though humdrum.

The rhetoric—and the work—of the past decade did get overheated. But design actually ran a temperature for a time. Now, the field has resumed its disdain for passion. Due either to remnants of Modern objectivity or to professional control, ADs insist on an AC heart.

With heat came light. Design mattered, as it hadn't before. Or it mattered to me, who had previously dismissed it. What was exciting about the striking work is that it accompanied an intellectual agitation. It struck matches, not just eyes. And it's that adventure—that promise—which has gone missing.

Present and accounted for is a lot of sumptuous work that follows routes charted during the ferment. It's also everywhere: both on diverse and unexpected artifacts and wherever there's a design industry. A curious realization of the Modern dream—a cross-country, cultural language of form—continues to be fulfilled. Only in our here-and-now, that language is appropriated, not apprehended.

If æsthetically pleasing product is what design's all about, things are good. However, the call that cut across all the strata of discourse was that design needed some meaning. A content of its own. And that perpetual longing: respect as a substantive activity.

A permanent insurrection is an impossible brief. Somewhere along the line, though, victory seems to have been declared. Or the battle map was redrawn. A dialogue "daisy-cutter" hit and sucked all the oxygen out of our cave. Design was supposed to surge from this dark Platonic netherworld. It must have been too bright out there, since we've all ducked back into the studio. The illumination is evidently better from those expensive light booths. Enough talk, that was fun—back to work!

First published in *Emigre*, 64 (2003): 15–34. Co-published with Princeton Architectural Press. © Kenneth FitzGerald.

If you won't take my word for it, take Rick Poynor's. He's still prodding design to allow for a real criticism. With his insistence that design is worthy of an accessible, expansive, sustained, and discerning inquiry (articulated recently in *Print*), he may be the person who most believes in design. His provocations for a critical journalism are *Theses* nailed on design's front door.

Sadly, no one's reading them. Maybe he doesn't use enough imagery or needs to do his own typography for design to notice. I admire Poynor's optimism and persistence. I've simply given up on a critical writing ever developing in the design field. If it evolves, it will be from the outside, likely an aspect of the ongoing hybridization of media. Also, art may continue to drift into design in its slow absorption of all cultural production.

That would be unfortunate, as design writing could take what's best about art criticism—its intellectual rigor—and inject social and cultural relevance. It could also squelch its ardor for architecture's status and theory. Both art and architecture are overwrought and value megalomania, excessive capital, and grandiosity. ("Oh, Rem, it's so big!")

The demise of discourse is due to neglect. Designers vote with their eyes and look away. And there isn't much to look away from. No market exists for critical writing. The major publications know what their audience wants—and it's not criticism. The desired report is brief, written by a professional and professionally oriented. Anything of subtlety, depth, and breadth is ignored. Profiling a designer with some connection to celebrity and capital prevails over a think piece every time.

The passing of the intellectually tepid *Critique* symbolizes design's disinterest in anything approaching inquiry. Only the pretense of deeper readings exists in current magazines. The *AIGA Journal* transformed itself into the bookish *Trace* (now defunct) but its articles remained mostly trivia. The fussy, homogenizing design displayed detailed photographs of various mundane objects as if promising a similarly methodical examination of design issues. Instead, both only addressed the surface. Engagement with any serious topics were left to (surprise!) Rick Poynor or the token profiled fine artist.

Eye magazine seems to have read the lack of writing on the wall. It has faded from intellectually vital to commercially demonstrative. An aggressive marketing campaign and a busy layout attempts to fill the void left after the departure of its founding editor and his successor. Quantity reigns over quality of the contributors and the reviews. It's heartening that *Eye* is featuring lesser or unheard voices. So far, the newer writers are indistinct and the product often immaterial.

Meanwhile, many well-known design voices are now making it full-time. As in art, design's practitioners/writers prefer the former role. It's a problem for design when just a few people leave the field and a chasm opens. This intensifies the need for design to develop an independent body of critical writers. That still doesn't exist and the potential is dim. In the twilight, design continues to evade any substantive internal critique. If you're a designer with a book and haven't been overly contumelious, you're good to gold.

Design has no heritage of or belief in criticism. Design education programs continue to emphasize visual articulation, not verbal or written. The goal is to sell your idea to a client and/or a hypothetical audience. Design in relation to culture and society is rarely confronted.

There are also some all-too-human dimensions. Design is still a small, small world. Friends are often writing about friends. While design isn't alone or first in closed-circuit critiques, it's there. Even when writers I respect discuss designers I admire, I wonder what a less connected account might offer. That said, the paucity of critics means that fewer articles would be written if we limited such connections.

In addition, there's professional courtesy. You don't "dis" your peers. Sharing a dais on the next stop in the design conference round robins might get a tad uncomfortable. And since the outside world doesn't take us too seriously, we must stick together, right?

The insularity only reinforces the indifference to design outside its own borders. And even if that's true, it's not the real problem. Luminaries desire an imprimatur. Instead of enlisting critics on the order of Hal Foster or Dave Hickey, sympathetic insiders are tapped. Why not? It's bad business to cast doubt on your talents in your own book. Whatever the rhetoric, design monographs are promotions, period. Client testimonials continue to serve as substantiation. Though we've seen a shift from CEOs to progressive musicians or philosophers, critical intent is absent.

It's arguable that many of these books are undeserved. We cook a microwave history by beaming intense eminence on excellent but short-careered designers. What nuking does to your leftovers, it does to the quality of scrutiny: scorched on the surface, half-baked to partially-crystallized inside. It's ultimately irrelevant if attention is unmerited. I don't have to buy the book. Unfortunately, with design's failure to commission critical audits, the market is the only check on hype inflation.

Despite the brief and ironic "No More Heroes" movement (more twitch than movement, really), design craves celebrities. Stoking the desire is the publishing industry's need for product. Magazine pages must be filled; books must spew from the pipeline. To move them, the blurb and inside text better gush, too.

Our current Quaalude interlude has served to inflate the size of the volumes and the praise for their producers. Against a featureless background, every detail magnifies in enormity. It's not enough to be an exceptional designer; you must be a latter-day Geoffrey Tory with the contemporary sociological acumen of a Marshall McLuhan, or a virtual one-man Bauhaus complete with their self-promotional vigor.

Recent design monographs reveal what the field values. Also on view are themes endemic to design: the rationalization of personal indulgence into a societal benefit, that mimesis is comparable to creation, gesture can substitute for action, formal facility proves conceptual acuity, and popularity equals profundity.

Leo Lionni crafted an unintentional fable of design in his children's book *A Color of His Own.* In it, a chameleon despairs of ever gaining a distinct and stable identity, as he is forced to blend into his environment. Graphic designers often display similar crises and adopt the mien of their clientele. Often, they go them one worse. Corporate designers deport themselves as ultra-businessmen. Graphic roadies of pop musicians style themselves rock stars.

Bruce Mau clearly wants *Life Style* to rest comfortably amongst the high-culture works he regularly collaborates on. Mau is an outstanding designer, valuable for his exacting craft, and for being unapologetically intellectual. *Life Style* is welcome just so it can be dropped on the massed digits of design's "I think with my hands" crowd.

In comparison to other high-brow titles, Mau's designs for Zone Books leap out as vibrant, enticing artifacts. However, for all the talk of serendipitous, experimental, content-driven and contained design, Mau exhibits a formulaic approach to his productions, no matter the medium or forum. As he keeps to a narrow range of clientele, his strategies (restrained typographic pallet, appropriated imagery—usually from fine art and technology, exhaustive reproduction/documentation, abecedaria and indices) may be repeated appropriately. Mau does ask authors and editors to accept more design than they're used to. But while introducing some imaginative and expressive aspects to a staid genre, Mau hardly violates classical conventions. Rather than expanding the role of design-as-livery, his productions are like finely tailored, stylish suits.

Life Style is enlightening when it directly addresses design. Mau's conceptualizing on culture, though, is discomfiting. His writing is far less adapt than his form giving; he adopts his patrons' sweeping gener-alities and abstruse prose. The majority of concepts that Mau engages have been in play for many years amongst media theorists. His engagement with and restatement of these themes are germane. But a sense of *déjà vu* hovers over the book as similar or identical images and ideas encountered in books such as *Perverse Optimist* and *Pure Fuel* reappear.

The central notion that's unique to Mau is design's need to reclaim a substantial, empowering meaning for the term "life style." Instead of resisting the common depiction of design as a styling process, Mau embraces it. However, his "style" isn't superficial: it's a positive, life-generating operation. Mau hastens through his argument in a few brief and recondite paragraphs then dashes off to other theories. How this new life styling practically differs from the old isn't explained. We can only assume that Mau (and by extension his clients) practices the virtuous version.

Mau links his proposal with Guy Debord and the Situationists to provide it with a radical, anti-capitalist attitude. The inversion is obviously alluring for designers as it converts stigma to sheen simply by proclamation. But absent a proof, it's wishful thinking. The authority for Mau's position apparently rests with his having worked on books like *The Society of the Spectacle*. However meritorious the design—or having read or published the book—such contact doesn't inoculate the principals.

Rather than being "gutted of meaning" in Mau's estimation, the notion of "life style" was hollow from the start. The term deserves disdain because it ultimately bases fulfillment on consumption. You are what you own, not what you do. Designers are complicit in this process, as they regularly craft veneers of "status value" for products.

Mau and his clientele produce commodities uncertain in use value but high in status. Their own consumption and life styling—lusciously detailed in relentlessly name-dropping "Life Stories" sections throughout the book—is privileged and conspicuous. Redefining the term "life style" becomes imperat-ive, as their behavior is materially identical to one Mau labels "vacuous." His life style allows you to indulge in and consume surfaces (Mau acknowledges his reputation was established by his formal innovation), while asserting you're actually involved in a "philosophic project of the deepest order." You can debate which cover of *Life Style* you fancy without feeling shallow.

Rationalizing your activity as critically acute while servicing privileged interests takes an agility that may be appreciated but not encouraged. Mau is hardly alone here. That our valued practitioners inex-orably gravitate toward monied culture—fashion, architecture, high art establishments, *etc.*—shows their absolute priority: who can best bankroll my career aspirations? That Mau found a rewarding prac-tice within the jet-set intelligentsia is his good fortune. Offering it as a cultural imperative is something else entirely.

Life Style suggests a critical statement on the "global image economy" but one never materializes. Mau presents it as a spontaneously generated phenomenon which we should "exploit" with "critical engagement." No guidelines are given for what critical engagement is or which design feeds the "downside" of our cultural situation. What we do know is that *Life Style* is surfeited with repurposed imagery and lists at $75.

Life Style is another design spectacle and status asset—a fashion accouterment like the Rem Koolhaas collaboration *S, M, L, XL*. Mau unintentionally confirms this by twice including a photo of that book being used as a pillow. The image falls flat as wry irony or self-deprication. *Life Style* is for and about designers realizing their most grandiloquent contrivances without guilt. The ecological, economic and cultural impact of every similarly motivated artist, designer, or architect pursuing such dreams goes unexamined. Spending $25,000 to reprint a book cover (or having alternate ones) can be regarded either as a "heroic enlargement of work to an ethics" or flagrantly wasting resources. Yes, it happens in design every day. But what is *détournement* without a difference?

Design loves attestation of its heroes and ideology. When designers bring in celebrities to testify to design's import, both get extra credit. Preeminent people who walk into our temple on their own to kneel at the shrine receive our full attention—even when they have little to say. John Maeda puts forth his beliefs simply, pleasantly, and earnestly. Under the ægis of his position at MIT's Media Lab, they play as objective, scientific truth. In its titling, *Maeda on Media* says he is media. However, for someone touted as a seer, Maeda is a curious throwback to simplistic motifs on art, design, and technology popularized decades ago. Those themes are duplicates of Maeda's intellectual and formal mentor, Paul Rand.

Maeda on Media is the book equivalent of a Hollywood blockbuster: long on special effects, short on characterization. The special effects are somewhat tedious. Maeda utilizes the computer exclusively as a pattern-making device. When used insightfully, repetition can have a deep emotional resonance (hear Steve Reich and Philip Glass). Maeda has the instrument but not the sensibility. His design work is acceptable but undistinguished, adorned with variants of warped grids and default sans serif typography. Rather than announcing new directions, they evince nostalgia.

Maeda's achievement may be injecting sentimentality into the "neutral" grid. Neither his generic printed work nor his derivative conceptualizing offers anything for the cultural artifact that is design. His insights on technology never rise above platitudes. To illustrate the computer's emotive potential, Maeda musters sterile, programmed ornamentation. His posting at MIT speaks more to the Media Lab's inbreeding and comfort with hardware, than an ease with and perception of culture. The witty, visually delightful, and politically trenchant work of Amy Franceschini and Josh On of Futurefarmers proposes far more for digital media when it is in the hands of enthusiasts.

Graphic design loves inspirational guides. Case-study tutorials clog the bookstore shelves, most asserting (despite claims to the contrary) that design innovation is reducible to a formal recipe. Even the ostensive monograph frequently turns to delineating how its subject reaches apotheosis, so that others may follow. It is an eccentric conceit of the field that ultimately condescends to its audience. In art, such documents are either obvious parodies or of the *American Artist* ilk.

At 1,064 pages, Alan Fletcher's *The Art of Looking Sideways* is design's most massive self-help book yet. The author seems to recognize the messy, transcendent dynamic of inspiration—yet is still moved to represent it in print. To elude this conceptual paradox, he adopts a formless approach. The book is a data-dump of quotations, aphorisms, diagrams, reproductions, commentaries, and folderol. Excess is evidently success.

The patronizing aspect is Fletcher's assumption of massive illiteracy amongst designers. He obviously believes the average practitioner's ignorance could not only fill a book but necessitates one as thick as a cinderblock. The professional blinders widely sported in the field can be maddening, and a broader awareness would benefit design. However, *The Art of Looking Sideways* seems a wild overcompensation. In its enormity—a one-stop cultural supermarket—it suppresses, rather than encourages, individual exploration.

The book's underlying concept, dressed in bang-up graphics, is hoary: inspiration should result from mere exposure to great art, music, or texts. The selected stimuli in *The Art of Looking Sideways* are of the customary motivational genre, presented as one size fits all. The lack of concrete contextualization—how any of this material practically performed in Fletcher's work, or may in anyone else's—makes the choices arbitrary. They function the same as incantations.

Successful people frequently burnish their image. Some elite designers, casting off the stereotype of glorified ad men, posture as scholar-artists. They abstract their process as pursuit of an intellectual purity unaffected by mundanities like clients or careering. Creative genius is all. It is both egotistical and disingenuous to proffer such a selective construct. Though unstated, that's the premise of *The Art of Looking Sideways,* as its existence rests entirely on the author's reputation.

Erudite designers abound (though many are in hiding). A thousand books as worthy as *The Art of Looking Sideways* could be produced. Will Phaidon publish every one? Or, like Alan Fletcher, will the authors need to commission themselves?

In his recent book *Fast Food Nation*, Eric Schlosser profiles flavorists—a discreet group of chemist/artists who design the taste of most foods. Their intervention is necessary, as processing destroys inherent taste. Using "natural" and "artificial" flavorings (the definitions are slippery), the flavorists graft a taste onto the food. Schlosser points out that it's just as easy to make your burger taste like cut grass or body odor as it does beef. Graphic designers are often flavorists of print. They inject a factitious aspect of attraction to achieve the natural. Interest can be synthesized and applied indiscriminately to anything.

Stefan Sagmeister's *Made You Look* could bear the title *Every Trick In My Book*. The monograph is a fatiguing compendium of almost every optical, production and advertising-creative artifice devised since Gutenberg. By deploying nearly every special effect (he refrains from die cuts, possibly as a show of restraint), the pages are full-bleed with desperation to clutch a reader's attention. As the audience is designers, Sagmeister knows they're here for a rush. Boisterous pieces set within a hyperactive present-ation make *Made You Look* pure designer crack.

As it promises, the book is ". . .a traditional show-and-tell graphic design book. No revolutions or big theories in here." So begins a running thread of commentaries marshaled to deflect every attempt to probe beneath any of the surfaces. In its infinite regress of self-referential feints, *Made You Look* is graphic design's *A Heartbreaking Work of Staggering Genius*. Both authors wield formidable technical skills to ingratiate and distract from their meager stories.

Sagmeister is a self-proclaimed, old school "big idea" designer. If there's an analog to which he's digital, it's Bob Gill. Sagmeister prides himself on his professionalism, supposing that it's at odds with the image induced by his graphic products. His "STYLE = FART" motto alleges a position of concep-tual prepotency over formal-driven practitioners like David Carson and Neville Brody. In the role of

Exposition Man, writer Peter Hall also credits Sagmeister with initiating a ". . .turning point for the design profession, away from aspirations of digital perfection toward a higher appreciation for a designer's personal mark."

As with other claims of Sagmeister as innovator, this is creditable only if specified to the point of being meaningless. Designers' scrawls are common, and Ed Fella's have proven far more influential and individual. Art Chantry crafts completely hand-made work and has been on the scene far longer. And April Greiman flashed us in the mid-80s. There are numerous signifiers of "personal" in *Made You Look* but nothing that is unmasterly or that disturbs the membrane of professional detachment. The emotional exposure is in inverse proportion to the amount of flaunted skin.

Sagmeister is naughty by nature—never transgressive. The big ideas are frequently obvious or hackneyed metaphors tweaking mainstream taste. That their visualization delivers a jolt points up the timidity of most design. Though Sagmeister doesn't promote a signature formal style, his reliance on visual joybuzzers becomes style in its own right.

His hanging with rockers and the burgeoning back-to-business mentality in design fueled Sagmeister's notoriety. It is his disconnection that endears him to his primary clientele—and the design profession. Rather than exhibiting the demeanor of a "creative crazy person," Sagmeister's work is always controlled and separated from the raw and real. Rock stars must also affect emotion every night on stage and synthesize it piecemeal and repetitively in the studio. Musicians like the Rolling Stones and Lou Reed are consummate showmen who understand the veneer of passion and getting the job done. Sagmeister fits their bills. And he is completely deferential to his clients' wishes—no artiste tantrums here.

His AIGA Detroit poster, where the copy is etched onto his chest, is a signature work. The image is another stratagem that mocks what it purportedly honors. Sagmeister literally only scratches the surface—he'll itch for his art. The box of Band-Aids he grasps is a stagey wink to us: this is only a graphic design. It's a contrivance artificial as anything spawned through software. Supposedly, the image compels because it shows the maker's hand and provokes an "equally physical response." However, an intern was pressed into service to etch the carefully placed, calligraphed marks when Sagmeister balks at cutting himself. The cojones thrust into our face in the book *Whereishere* are for display only.

The heartbreaking aspect of *Made You Look* is the designer's plaintive quest to answer the question "Can graphic design touch someone's heart?" Curiously placed last on a "To Do" list, it's presented as another career aspiration, not a moral absolute. The structure of the question undermines its answering, stipulating medium before effect. It's the difference between having an idea expressed graphically and a graphic design idea. Sagmeister excels at the latter: his concepts grow out of established graphic design expressions. As such, those conventions will always be in the foreground, like a label stating "artificial flavoring." Shortening the question to "Can I touch someone?" may be the needed natural ingredient.

All art and design is a known construct. We may examine the most disturbing imagery because we know it's false. The most affecting work suspends or interrupts that awareness. Sagmeister's virtuosity is his greatest obstacle. He is constantly pulling his own curtains aside so we may view the machinations of illusion.

The relentless questioning of his work's affectiveness while asserting its effectiveness makes Sagmeister and *Made You Look* schizophrenic. Talking passion is hip; exhibiting it uncool. Are the works he rates as "Is" in the index examples of "touching design"? Or does having his "touching" essay be the book's coda—and going on a highly-touted sabbatical—mean he considers all his designs to this point crowd-pleasing failures? (If meant as a purge, the book makes a lot more sense.) Or, as is often the case with graphic designers, is he trying to have it both ways?

Usually, an expressed desire to do touching work means the same ol' design—but for a high-profile charity. Sagmeister's talent is such that we should hope he finds The Way rather than just a United Way.

There have also been monographs that indicate healthy routes to a criticism. Rick Poynor's study of Vaughn Oliver, *Visceral Pleasures,* is a lucid and stimulating text. It establishes Oliver as a rare designer by the quality of his work and willingness to undergo this analysis. Poynor argued for, and received, a restrained presentation from Oliver for the book. While the approach is arguable even if one doesn't require graphic fire-works—does restraint actually allow an objective, considered view or does it adhere to a convention of seriousness?—the resulting book is a powerful convincer, as it should be. At the very least, it's a refreshing respite from overstimulated—and ultimately insecure—offerings like *Made You Look.* Vaughn Oliver may be the one contemporary designer with the right to proclaim himself a fucking genius. *Visceral Pleasures* also proves he's the bravest.

Julie Lasky's *Some People Can't Surf: The Graphic Design of Art Chantry* is a "traditional show-and-tell graphic design book," only with assurance and standing. Chantry's work is original and rich enough to support deep inspection. However, considering its maker, the book's appreciative yet straightforward approach is fitting. Lasky provides illuminating background on the designer and for individual works. Chantry's book design allows that work to speak for itself, and reflects his sensibility. *Some People Can't Surf* is succinct and profound.

The appearance of the "attempted magazine" *Dot Dot Dot* is another encouraging sign that design writing can be eclectic, thoughtful and imaginative. The journal proves there's plenty of unexplored territory for design investigations and the forms they may take. What *Trace* promised, *Dot Dot Dot* provides. The question is if the magazine can find the audience it deserves.

We may be at a stage when all formal innovations have been exhausted: post-modern postscript time. There is no dominating formality or ideology to produce design. A congeries of theories and practices transcends physical borders. This leaves us with the final and central concerns of making design better, which are extra-design.

For the majority of designers, their activity is a job, a service. To change how they do design, you must change the conditions under which they work. A renovation of capitalism and consumer society is not on graphic design's agenda.

Debate briefly engaged around the "First Things First" manifesto. The turbulence provoked by the statement demonstrates that actual questions were asked. The manifesto was confined somewhat by being a "top down" action; however, it's incontestable that the signatories could exploit their talents to greater profit. And *Adbusters'* addition of a web page where anyone could sign on brought it to the trenches.

The swift passing of the topic is its most disquieting aspect. For many, to raise it at all was an annoyance. Outright dismissals of the manifesto as naive, elitist, or (at best) impracticable were unsurprising. When you're gaming the system, there's little incentive to change the rules. A startling cynicism was often exhibited under the guise of critical limpidity or pragmatic sobriety. It sadly dovetails with the broader societal conviction that idealism is for chumps.

Every assertion should undergo critical scrutiny. But responsibility accompanies dissension: the duty to advance discussion and promote increasing dialogue. Only if you've announced your support of the *status quo*—and a disinterest in the lot of the less fortunate—do you get to hit and run. Directing a discussion is seemly, squelching it isn't.

It's possible I'm expecting too much too soon of design. Or of people who make it (and make it making it). The channels of commercial determinism are deeply cut. Redirection requires either a massive exertion of force or constant erosion over years. We didn't get here overnight. A major obstacle is an acceptance that the world we have was inevitable. In fact, it was the result of numerous individual actions, from multiple motivations. Each must be traced and assessed.

The change of garde in design has been recent; folks are barely getting settled in. And there aren't many of them. Add to this the fact that you can't control how people interpret what happened. In design, the surface is all that counts.

Design could be a significant agora of discourse, more so than art or other creative disciplines. It's situated closest to the intersection of culture and commerce, the individual and society. What seems at first unwieldy—trying to forge a criticism to reconcile, let's say, the *Catfish* DVD and a bus schedule (or an annual report or a brochure or any familiar artifact) is design's potential. Sometimes it's realized, and it's a revelation to the eye's mind.

The friction between personal investigation such as *Catfish* and public practice (e.g. information graphics) alone is daunting. Positions are frequently staked in one or the other camp and pursued as ends in themselves. Rather than endpoints on an axis, they act across a field of activity that is design. A considered contemplation of how they inform, inspire, and rely on each other is required.

The ultimate disappointment today is that a campaign for critical thinking must again be mounted. We might remember an admonition of Socrates, "The unexamined life is not worth living." An unexamined design isn't worth doing, or seeing.

In the quiet, strange things happen. We think we hear endless, thunderous applause, and steadfastly congratulate ourselves. Breaking the silence could make us realize we're hearing only the roaring of blood in our ears.

Chapter 4.2.4

Critical graphic design: critical of what?

Francisco Laranjo

Critical graphic design is a vague and subjective term. The meaning of the word 'critical' in relation to graphic design remains unclear, resulting in an overuse and misuse in design magazines, books and websites. The term was popularized by the much-cited traveling exhibition *Forms of Inquiry: The Architecture of Critical Graphic Design* first shown in 2007, and by the Dutch design studio Metahaven, among others. Yet, the ambiguous criteria used by the *Forms of Inquiry* curators to support the term, and designers' struggle to match the ambitions of their political, social and cultural research with its visual output, indicate a continuing need for critical discussion of critical graphic design.

In recent years, however, there has been disenchantment and even skepticism toward graphic design work that is labeled as *critical*. If we look for critical graphic design online, the first search result is an open-submission *Critical Graphic Design* tumblr predominantly filled with humorous responses to design work, designers, publications and institutions generally associated with the term. Here, we can listen to the designer Michael Oswell's satirical electro track, *The Critical Graphic Design Song*, absurdly repeating the names of designer Zak Kyes (co-curator of *Forms of Inquiry*) and Radim Peško, whose typefaces Kyes often uses in his work. Also mentioned is the popular blog *Manystuff*, which disseminates many works commonly described as critical, though its press-release style of presentation is inherently celebratory and uncritical. The tendency to gather and repeat familiar names shapes an echoing, self-referential canon that is automatically self-validated.

An updated post-financial crisis cover created for Adrian Shaughnessy's book *How To Be a Graphic Designer Without Losing Your Soul* (2005) suggests that criticality is a luxury in the current conditions under which graphic design is produced. Other works include parody photos of Metahaven's three-dimensional representation of Sealand, and images that imitate the visual styles of some of the most celebrated critical designers and academic institutions—Yale is often mentioned. These references seem to have three different goals: (1) to provoke the "critical graphic design" clique exemplified by the participants of *Forms of Inquiry* and the exhibition *All Possible Futures* (2014); (2) to express disappointment toward traditional forums for public debate and legitimation: essays, lecture series, publications and academia; and (3) to challenge the shallow and predictable stylistic approaches used by designers to address critical issues. As the nonsensical critiques, literal illustrations and animated GIFs appear on

First published in *Design Observer* (April 16, 2014). https://designobserver.com/feature/critical-graphic-design-critical-of-what/38416.

the screen, they raise some pertinent questions about critical graphic design: What does this poster or image add to the issues at stake? Where is the critique? How does it contribute to written modes of research? What are the criteria and who makes these decisions?

This is not revealed on the *Critical Graphic Design* tumblr, nor does there seem to be any intention with most of these responses to construct a coherent argument. Despite their popularity online, these critiques of criticality also remain largely unquestioned. Are these hacks really contributing to a better understanding and questioning of these undebated trends? Or are they merely tickling the clique they intend to provoke? Are LOLz enough? Can jokes bring down (supposedly) critical design projects? Most of the submissions online reveal an ironic suspicion toward critical design and this attitude will presumably be reflected in the critics' own practice, as they try to avoid doing what they criticize. A clarification of what is meant by "critical" may provide some answers.

In the book *The Reader* (2009), the design researcher Ramia Mazé suggests three possible forms of criticality in design. The first has to do with a critical attitude toward a designer's own practice. The designer makes an effort to be self-aware or reflexive about what she or he does and why. Mazé argues that this can be understood as a kind of internal questioning and a way of designers positioning them-selves within their practice. The second form is the "building of a meta-level or disciplinary discourse." This involves what Mazé calls, "criticality within a community of practice or discipline," and trying to challenge or change traditions and paradigms. Designers are critical of their discipline while actively and consciously working toward its expansion and evolution. In the third kind of criticality, designers address pressing issues in society. The critique is not targeted at a designer's own discipline, practice or even at design in general, but at social and political phenomena. In practice, the three modes of crit-icality often overlap, intersect and influence each other.

Mazé's categorization is not new. A direct connection can be made with the Dutch designer Jan van Toorn's view on design pedagogy. As a design educator, Van Toorn tried to raise awareness of the tension between private and public interests. In *User-centred Graphic Design* (1997), he argues that the "student must learn to make choices and to act without attempting to avoid the tensions between indi-vidual freedom, disciplinary discourse and public interest." This assertion of the personal, disciplinary and public levels that a designer should always consider anticipates Mazé's three forms of criticality.

Two influential European design schools focus on the development of critical design practice. The Werkplaats Typographie (WT), founded in 1998 by the Dutch designers Karel Martens and Wigger Bierma, bases its educational model on a modernist form of reflexive practice, following the idea of the "workshop" developed by the English typographer Anthony Froshaug and designer Norman Potter. The WT normally concentrates on typography as a point of departure in assignments set either by the school, external clients, or the students; these usually take the form of publications. The WT's type of criticality falls between the first and second definitions put forward by Mazé.

The other Dutch design school with a strong critical orientation is the Sandberg Institute, which emphas-izes the third type of criticality. Its design department presents itself as a "Think Tank for Visual Strategies," with students seeking critical reflection and engagement through work that explores design's role and potential in relation to public and political issues and public discourse. Some examples of this are Femke Herregraven's *Taxodus*, Ruben Pater's *Drone Survival Guide*, Noortje van Eekelen's *The Spectade of the Tragedy*, Belle Phromchanya's *The Rise of the Moon* and Simone C. Niquille's *Realface Glamouflage*.

Despite the rejection of the label "critical graphic design," most notably by the designers Stuart Bailey (in *Dot Dot Dot*, 20 (2010) and James Goggin (in *Most Beautiful Swiss Books*, 2008), the term is still relevant. It emerged at a time when the discipline was in a generally uncritical state, providing a necessary distinction from routine practice and awarding a kind of merit badge to designers or studios who deviated from the norm. For designers who scorn the label, criticality in its many forms is intrinsic to graphic design and therefore a special term is unnecessary and redundant.

The term also highlights an important transition in graphic design practice and education: from the designer as author to the designer as researcher. This is not only a consequence of the maturation of the discipline, seeking legitimacy to be used as an investigative tool, but also the result of an increased importance of the social sciences, humanities and their multiple research methods being applied, changed and appropriated by design education and designers. On the one hand, graphic design aims to use its own processes and production methods to contribute new knowledge to the areas it works in. On the other, the absorption of ethnography and data collection methods shows an increasing reliance on other disciplines' methodologies. The widespread presence of "design research" in design's lexicon is a sign of these developments, despite recurrent confusion as to what constitutes research in graphic design.

In the age of *Behance*, of earning badges and *appreciations*, when one of the most used words in the site's *feedback circle* is "awesome" and likes and followers are easily bought, graphic design has another opportunity to reexamine its apparently incurable allergy to criticism. Within interaction design, speculative and critical design is now being openly questioned and the critical design projects' political accountability and relevance to society debated.

As a term, critical graphic design will probably be replaced in the permanent rush to coin the next soundbite. Criticality in graphic design will surely continue to be a topic for discussion, but a design work is not instantly critical just because of the intentions of the designer, or the pressing issue being researched. A talk, song, scarf, flag, web meme, website, installation or publication may all be valid ways to pose a critique. However, it's time to publicly discuss the means, effects and especially the quality of the critical design projects, not just to celebrate and retweet them. If that doesn't happen, critical graphic design runs the risk of not being as substantial and meaningful as it could be. Or worse, it will become irrelevant to society. For a discipline that aims to contribute to public debate—let alone social and political change—that would be a disastrously wasted opportunity.

Chapter 4.2.5

The march of grimes

Michèle Champagne

If any single book could act as a curious guide to design, Harry G. Frankfurt's *On Bullshit* (2005) would be that book. *On Bullshit* was published over a decade ago, yet its expression is relevant to how we view Western design today. *On Bullshit* was never created as a query on design. It was created as a musing on contemporary life and rhetoric, and when applied to design, the book offers a more frank and fascinating view of design and how it operates at the turn of the twenty-first century.

Frankfurt successfully argues that our culture is rife with bullshit, and one can easily deduce that design—an activity that shapes and is shaped by this culture—is rife with bullshit too. Frankfurt means bullshit not as a lie, but as clumsy speech that doesn't care for truth or lies, and that is so pervasive it is taken for granted. To pretend that design is above or beyond this culture is silly. Dutch designer Jan van Toorn might have been thinking of this when he said, "Designers are connected to the existing order. That's the reality and you have to deal with it" (Poynor 2018: 22).

At first, bullshit seems like an unnecessarily cruel word and *On Bullshit* comes across as a mean little text. Then, we realize Frankfurt is a well-mannered, analytical philosopher, a Professor Emeritus of Philosophy at Princeton University. Frankfurt is everyone's idea of a dowdy, corduroy-sporting professor. His questions are curious and his arguments are intelligent. *On Bullshit* is less of a nasty take-down and more of a gentle, philosophical view of our Western democratic culture, the dominance of bullshit within it, and what it means to give up on concepts like truth and falsity.

To pretend to hold an absolute truth is absurd. The point of the book is not to search for absurdities; the point is to explore the nature of bullshit, of something that doesn't even care for the search for truth, however subjective, temporary, or impossible that truth may be. Using *On Bullshit* as a guide to design is less of an absolutist activity, and more of a thoughtful, nuanced exploration.

At sixty-seven pages, with a small paper size, large type, and generous margins, Frankfurt begins his modest book with the following pertinent view:

> One of the most salient features of our culture is that there is so much bullshit. Every one knows this. Each of us contributes his share. But we tend to take the situation for granted. Most people are rather confident of their ability to recognize bullshit and to avoid being taken in by it. So the phenomenon has not aroused much deliberate concern, nor attracted much sustained inquiry (Frankfurt 2005: 1).

As designers and their chroniclers move from one biennale or trend to another, one could be forgiven for thinking that design is experiencing a renaissance of creativity and respectability. The gifted writer Rob Walker even went so far as to pen "A Golden Age of Design" (2014) in *T* magazine where he frames American design as the resurgence of a trustworthy marketplace for new ideas and inspiration. He cites new "technology, community and big business" as proof of a new, wonderful status quo: "an unprecedented belief in the power of design to not only elevate an idea, but be the idea" (Walker 2014). In other words, one could be forgiven for thinking design today is immune to bullshit.

The interesting question is not whether Walker provides ample evidence to support his conclusion, for he does that quite well. Rather, the question is, what does design do in the shadows of such a bright-eyed view? Even a cursory look at design on a more thorough and captivating scale reveals a plethora of unsubstantiated claims, vague platitudes, and hidden tradeoffs. These stances are frequent and to pretend they do not exist—to call them aberrations or anomalies—is to take a limited view of design's foray into bullshit.

Take, for example, the ridiculous stance that design is almighty. It is curious how there are few things that are weaker today than talking about "the power of design." It's like a *déjà vu* feeling: an eerily common expression that has spawned innumerable headlines, books, and conferences, including a mention in Walker's article. There is "The Power of Design," a *BusinessWeek* (2004) cover story by author and educator Bruce Nussbaum that markets IDEO as a firm "changing the way companies innovate" (Nussbaum 2004). There is *The Power of Design: A Force for Transforming Everything* (2008) a book by Richard Farson, a psychologist, author, and educator who argues "Design can transform the world" (Farson 2008: Blurb). There is also *The Power of Design: A Journey through the 11 UNESCO Cities of Design*, a book by author Karl Stocker (2013).

There is AIGA's *The Power of Design* conference (2003) in Vancouver that spoke to the "extraordinary opportunities for design in the 21st century." The annual *What Design Can Do* (2014) conference in Amsterdam intones and implies that the all-powerful designer can do anything and everything (as Canadian designer, writer, and curator Brendan Cormier (2014) reported, for a conference dedicated to promoting the real "impact" of design, too few presentations explored design's very real successes and failures).

The power of design is a popular notion in the United Kingdom too, with *The Guardian* publishing the words of sustainability guru William McDonough (2013) under the banner "Driving sustainable transformation via the power of design."[1] When Torino garnered a spot as a World Design Capital (2008), its organizers celebrated "what can be achieved when harnessing the full power of design."

"The power of design" is a spectacularly pompous phrase. It is amazing how much currency it carries, and yet, it is not alone. Chief among the collectors of grandiose design rhetoric are Agata Jaworska and Giovanni Innella, designers and guardians of the Institute of Relevant Studies, who remixed a plethora of chest-beating claims into Designtunes.org. Yes, design has a soundtrack, and it sounds like fun, happy electronic beats mixed with "samples of lame designer lingo" like "the world of design is so immense," and design offers "world change," "massive change," and "new ideas of the future."

This signals a change of identity for design. Expressions intended to illustrate the contribution and credibility of design now belong to a period where their impact is meaningless. The triumphant calls for design power now deliver nothing more than funny fodder for future farce.

The road is paved with good intentions, as philosopher Alan Watts (2013) once said, "on the basis of, kindly let me help you or you will drown, said the monkey putting a fish safely up a tree." Sometimes, speaking too highly of design can become amazingly destructive. Expressions intended to augment design's role in society can have an unintended impact: a negative return on expression. Too often, these expressions provide a vague, hollow stance—one that lacks depth and avoids the profound— robbing design of any real contribution it may very well offer. Design today, despite good intentions and heroic claims, may very well be an eager participant in the petty production of the great, communal heap.

But do these expressions really amount to the production of bullshit on the part of design? Probably, but without a better understanding of what bullshit is exactly, it's hard to account for the word's varied and shifting meanings. Could a better understanding of bullshit help us better understand design? Just what is it that makes bullshit such a rich and interesting viewpoint on design? Quite a lot, as a matter of fact, and that's where *On Bullshit* comes in.

Frankfurt's interest in bullshit lies in a beguiling paradox: in how something so pervasive could so easily escape scrutiny. Most everybody engages in bullshit or regales in calling it out—as did designer Stefan Sagmeister (2014) in the summer of 2014, at an FITC conference, where he called "bullshit" on creative professionals who claim to engage in "storytelling," a cheap, marketing *mot du jour*. Nevertheless, despite these high profile accusations, there's still no clear understanding of what bullshit is, what it is not, or why it blooms in such abundance. There may be no definitive answer to what bullshit is, but that didn't stop Frankfurt from asking questions or pursuing answers.

To begin, Frankfurt wonders if bullshit can be likened to *shit*, as in something that is crappy or poorly crafted. Frankfurt proposes a tango between the words "craft" and "bullshit" by evoking the charm and wit of philosopher Ludwig Wittgenstein who once claimed as his motto the poetry of Henry Wadsworth Longfellow:

In the elder days of art
Builders wrought with greatest care
Each minute and unseen part,
For the gods are everywhere.

Frankfurt finds meaning between Longfellow's historical lines, a time when crafts were fashioned with care. "Every part of the product was considered," wrote Frankfurt, "and each was designed and made exactly as it should be." What he meant was, "in the elder days" there was no bullshit. Shameful, shabby goods may have something in common with the word bullshit, as the word *shit* suggests. "Excrement is not designed or crafted at all," he wrote, "it is merely emitted, or dumped" (2005: 20–21)

Some say "that's bullshit" when pointing to shoddy goods or poorly executed communication campaigns, but is bullshit the same as lazy nonsensical *crap*? Perhaps not altogether. Frankfurt quickly points to public relations, an activity that has created some of the most intentional and sophisticated forms of bullshit the world has ever seen.

A quick look at the work of Edward Bernays (1947: 113–120), the public relations pioneer, under- scores this point, including his "engineering of consent" techniques and campaign to convince women to smoke cigarettes in the name of "freedom." In the early twentieth century, Bernays was inspired by the theory of unconscious desires set out by his uncle Sigmund Freud, the founder of psychoanalysis (Curtis 2002). Bernays reasoned that women had an unconscious desire to be like men—to "have their own penises" (Curtis 2002)—so he nicknamed cigarettes "torches of freedom" and encouraged a group of New York City suffragettes to regain their power by smoking in public at an Easter Day parade, at a time when this was taboo. To coincide with this controversial display of puff and power, Bernays invited news reporters and their flash bulbs to cover the suffragettes, which they readily did.

Bernays' strategic and concerted public relations made smoking cigarettes more popular with everyday women and, as a result, increased the female customers for the products of Bernays' client, George Hill, the President of the American Tobacco Company. It seems bullshit, in the end, was not akin to crap and could be carefully crafted after all.

Frankfurt then continues his inquiry by focusing on the tango between "lying" and "bullshitting." Many say "that's bullshit" when pointing to perceived lies. Lying and bullshitting are two closely related processes and they do share things in common: both a lie and bullshit misrepresent life in the public sphere. A liar, for example, knows he has two dollars in his pocket but publicly claims to have only one. A bullshitter also claims to have two dollars, but doesn't actually know how much money is in his pocket, or if there is any money there at all. These are both forms of misrepresentation.

Of course, the two terms are not fully synonymous either, and there is the key difference: liars think they know the truth and deliberately misrepresent it, whereas bullshitters have no concern for truth or falsity, they just whip up muck as they go. The bullshit could very well be true, or it could very well be untrue. At least the liar cares about the concept of truth, whereas the bullshitter doesn't give a damn about the truth.

The basic concept of bullshit in Frankfurt's book is a process of crafting a perfectly formed expression that is neither true nor false. His thoughtful concept stands in contrast to the two simplistic definitions that are popular with those who speak of bullshit as either crappy nonsense or deceitful lies.

Consider designer Michael Bierut's essay "On (Design) Bullshit" published on Designobserver.com (2005) (as well as writer Rick Poynor and designer Debbie Millman's comments following it). Bierut cites Frankfurt's concept of bullshit and adopts it in a very weird, loose way, as something akin to post-rationalizations that are needed to explain subjective design processes to clients. "It follows that every design presentation is inevitably, at least in part," writes Bierut (2005), "an exercise in bullshit." Bierut defines bullshit as necessary, crappy nonsense, and defends it on the basis that a certain amount of it is inevitable. In Bierut's view, bullshit in the boardroom is the name of the game.

However abstract Frankfurt may be at times, he considered both crappy nonsense and deceitful lies, and he felt out their similarities to bullshit, but he nevertheless rejected these definitions as incongruous. Bierut and other commentators rely on the crappy nonsense definition, which misses the mark set by Frankfurt. Sagmeister, for his part, relied on the deceitful lie definition, which also misses the mark. When Sagmeister said that creatives are not storytellers, he meant that marketing-driven creative professionals were lying about their role in society, that only authors or filmmakers could tell stories freely without the covert strategies to sell products. Frankfurt makes the convincing case that bullshit has its own meaning and that its impact is worth studying further.

Frankfurt briefly explores why there is so much bullshit and what it means for the concept of truth. He entertains the notion that in a democratic society, people are expected to know an ever-increasing litany of things on subjects they know very little about. "Bullshit is unavoidable whenever circumstances require someone to talk without knowing what he is talking about," he writes. "Thus the production of bullshit is stimulated," Frankfurt continues, "whenever a person's obligation or opportunities to speak about some topic exceed his knowledge of the facts that are relevant to the topic" (2005: 63).

Wondering what will happen to the concept of truth, Frankfurt writes, "through excessive indulgence in [bullshitting] which involves making assertions without paying attention to anything except what it suits one to say, a person's normal habit of attending to the way things are may become attenuated or lost" (2005: 60).

Are designers and their chroniclers experiencing something similar? If powerful designers can do anything and everything, are they not living in circumstances that require them to talk about too many things without knowing exactly what they are talking about? If writers attempt to summarize a grand, over-arching design *zeitgeist*, are they losing sight of some things that may not suit their summaries?

To understand why bullshit is so prominent in design culture, one can easily see how designers and their chroniclers are expected to know a growing list of things and can lose the "habit of attending to the way things are" (2005: 60), as Frankfurt put it. Many designers and writers are humble, honest creatures, in my opinion, but they rarely dominate the playbill. A more common observation is one where star chroniclers, esteemed designers, and prominent design firms attend to a rhetoric that omits "the way things are" and submits to "what it suits one to say."

For this design culture, the true meaning of what they say or write, and the rhetorical validity of their public arguments, do not matter so long as a public believes in their arguments. They may intend to be honest as a matter of general ethics, but they are not concerned enough with honesty to be rigorous with their claims or vigilant with arguments. A bullshitter's ambition is something else altogether: he or she trades in the attention market, where sales, likes, and self-promotions matter most.

In an effort to understand bullshit, a small typology could help apply Frankfurt's concept to design. This classification isn't exhaustive, but it is a good start: one kind of bullshit is "No Proof Bullshit." Many designers and chroniclers commit to claims that ring true, but cannot be easily substantiated by supporting information or by an independent third-party.

An example of "No Proof Bullshit" is Heatwave Radiator by Dutch designer Joris Laarman. He claims the decorative Baroque form of the radiator provides more surface area, therefore resulting in greater heat distribution. Laarman makes this assertion without any proof to substantiate it, nor does he seem to care about proof. In other words, his claims could very well be true but there is no apparent proof that they are, and the designer isn't vigilant enough to make them matter.

Another Frankfurt kind of bullshit is "Too Vague Bullshit," like when designers claim to "make things better" with interactive posters or claim to "save the world" by cleaning up smog. Many designers make claims that are so poorly defined that their real meanings are likely to be misunderstood by the public and the press—even other designers.

An example of "Too Vague Bullshit" is an exhibition project called *The Bureau of Doing Something About It* by the firm Bruce Mau Design. They claim their interactive exhibit is "doing something" to improve Toronto's urban domain. Inspired by the Toronto Complaints Choir, a flash mob of playful performers who sing away their urban blues, *The Bureau* attempts to seek proactive public ideas on how to solve the complaints. Bruce Mau Design makes this assertion without ever defining what they mean by "something" and they never get to the bottom of what consists of "doing" versus "not doing."

In the end, Bruce Mau Design never intended to execute the public ideas they solicited, the ideas were simply edited and published in a book for promotional purposes. What most Torontonians know, however, is that Toronto doesn't lack ideas. Rather, it lacks the ability to execute ideas, either because of convoluted public approval processes, timid business leaders, or backward municipal politics. In other words, Bruce Mau Design's claim of doing something could very well be true, but their lack of specificity allows everyone to read into the project what they want, and disables any smart evaluation on whether the exhibition was "doing" anything or not.

A third Frankfurt kind of bullshit is "Hidden Tradeoff Bullshit," which is when a phrase spotlights one aspect of a concept, but throws another into the dark. The term *invisibility design* is a great example, in which claims of seamless, intuitive, and immaterial technology overshadow the curious world of human behavior, social engineering, and material affordances. Designer, flimmaker, and researcher Timo Arnall reflected on this when he wrote,

> Intentionally hiding the phenomena and materiality of interfaces, smoothing over the natural edges, seams and transitions that constitute all technical systems, entails a loss of understanding and agency for both designers and users of computing. Lack of understanding leads to uncertainty and folk-theories that hinder our ability to use technical systems, and clouds the critique of technological developments.

(Arnall 2013)

"Hidden Tradeoff Bullshit" can hinder our ability to deliver healthy critiques of new developments in our culture, like how cloud computing—despite how cute the name sounds—can propagate tax havens, or how state authorities and security firms—despite promise of friendly connections—can mine data through social networks. "As systems increasingly record our personal activity and data," writes Arnall, "invisibility is exactly the wrong model."

In his reflection, Arnall cites a prescient quote from Dr. Matt Ratto, Assistant Professor and Director of the Critical Making Lab at the University of Toronto:

> By removing our knowledge of the glue that holds the systems that make up the infrastructure together, it becomes much more difficult, if not impossible, to begin to understand how we are constructed as subjects, what types of systems are brought into place (legal, technical, social, etc.) and where the possibilities for transformation exist.

(Rotto 2007: 25)

In addition to a culture that requires designers to talk about so many things, all at once, there are other unique situations that bring bullshit to life. At the center of this bullshit manifestation is the idea that designers and their chroniclers have not merely violated the tenets of critical thinking, they have explicitly repudiated them.

Out of a misplaced fear of negativity, some designers say they don't need criticism, as writer Rick Poynor once recorded in "The Time for Being Against is Over" (Poynor 2004). In this essay, Poynor plays the role of street crier magnificently, publicly sharing an email that landed in his inbox and that, at the top of the message, read: "The time for being against is over." Poynor explains this phrase is from the book *The World Must Change: Graphic Design and Idealism* and is a quote from a Dutch design student that reads: "I do not want to separate. I have no interest in being against. I want to include. The time for being against is over."

Poynor (2014) feels this phrase is not simply a personal expression but symptomatic of something larger, an anti-critical thinking "aspect of society and culture as we experience them today" and "a fairly general view" among designers, especially younger ones.

Alongside these designers are editors and critics who share this fear of negativity, people who behave like agents of public relations, producing a large body of affirmative design coverage and very little of anything else. Responding to the esteemed fashion editor Cathy Horyn's departure from *The New York Times* in February of 2014—and her record of open and honest reporting—writer Jason Dike (2014) reflected on the lack of honest writing when he said, "The issue isn't what Cathy Horyn's departure means for fashion, but whether the current media environment can produce another critic of Horyn's ilk."

Dike believes there is still honest opinion and independent thinking, but that there are fewer places to publish this kind of criticism, and fewer places for new critics to give their careers a good head start. He reminds us how critics like Horyn started working alongside journalists at local newspapers, but many of these publications have seen better circulation days, or have shut down altogether.

"That doesn't mean that the world is devoid of media outlets for fashion coverage. Quite the opposite," he writes, "But most fashion outlets are visually driven and depend on fashion advertising for their survival" (Dike 2014). Dike is right: it is bad for business for a critic to publish something negative about an advertiser, leaving little room for criticism that is genuinely critical.

Dike writes mostly about fashion, but this applies to design more broadly. Poynor (2010) noted this too when he said, "Design receives a consistently easy ride in the specialist press, which often seems to aspire to be nothing more than a glamorous PR platform and support service, while general media, with no other model of design discussion to go on, treat design as a lightweight consumer subject in the style and lifestyle pages."

While the compulsory affection of chroniclers is laughable, it is worth wondering why design needs to be seen in such a glaringly favorable light, and why it resorts to so much bullshit to frame its practice and public debate. Coddled like an egg by a hen, design sits surrounded by the embrace of practitioners and chroniclers who overwhelmingly cheerlead it.

It's hard to disentangle the bullshit from the meaningful because there are myriad views on design, how it's practiced, what role it plays in society, and how it will forever change into the future. Who is a trusted design guide? How will people keep up, all the while knowing they are onto something valuable and not being fooled? Understanding Frankfurt's concept of bullshit is a good start. His musings and the three types of bullshit are tools that act as those guides.

Design writer Stephen Bayley (2000: 19) may be right in claiming design is no longer the "honourable vocation" that it once was, but as a commendable practice and as applied art it still promises to consider human needs, to imagine future alternatives and to deliver designs that reflect those needs and aspirations. There are strong social, cultural, and commercial arguments for reviving this vocation.

But design must abandon bullshit and grow a thicker skin. Design must earn its keep with integrity in which serious substance, wacky ideas, and surprising appearances come together. Perhaps it is not too late for design to get unstuck and keep marching on.

Notes

1. See also McDonough's 2002 seminal book with Michael Braungart, *Cradle to Cradle: Remaking the Way We Make Things*, New York: North Point Press.

Chapter 4.2.6

Discourse this! Designers and alternative critical writing

Denise Gonzales Crisp

All that we cannot imagine will never come into being.

—hooks 1991

Scholars, critics, and journalists tend not to think of their work as stories—crafted narratives that embody alternate reality in the context of common experience and capitalize on willful suspended disbelief. These writers are given instead to rhetorical strategies that ground critical standards and maintain the terms by which they conduct their discourse. They rely upon facts, footnotes and rules that govern their respective games to examine, evaluate and elucidate practices, cultural forces and artifacts.

Add to these professionals another breed—I call them "design-wrights." These writers have surfaced here and there in the history of design discourse, and, it turns out, were often first designers. Designwrights examine, evaluate and elucidate practices, cultural forces and artifacts as well, except they do so using the rhetorical strategies of things-made-up. The characters and events they imagine into being often use unorthodox means, which is in part the power of the work. The delivery handily bellows where convention would only mumble.

Designers invent stuff, routinely reconfiguring the material world. Their best work delivers information, story, place and voice by way of creative responses to everyday experience, sometimes in hopes of helping change the tide. Designers make the familiar unfamiliar, and vice versa, determining to fuel desire and engage people to believe. Most designers have neither studied nor practiced the writing craft of critics, journalists, or historians. Those inclined to critique the design world, then, have often ventured instead into what I will refer to here as "alternative critical writing." And why not? As steeped in invention and fantasy as design is, why should its discourse be limited to the rhetoric of critical theory, journalism, biography or history?

First published in *Design and Culture*, 1 (1) (2009): 105–20. Reprinted by permission of the publisher (Taylor & Francis Ltd, http://www.tandfonline.com). © Taylor & Francis/Denise Gonzales Crisp.

The designwright's contribution is hardly new. Artist, designer and fine book producer William Morris detailed a version of the future in his novel *News from Nowhere* (1891) in which design, aesthetics and craft are integral to living a moral life (Figure 4.3). The plot, such as it is, unveils a twenty-first century utopian society through the lives of its residents, with glimpses into the grim preceding two centuries. Morris envisions his hopes for social equality and human dignity through the eyes and words of narrator William Guest. Having awoken one morning to a gloriously transformed London, Guest spends several days traveling in a Marxist-inspired dream where he encounters productive, creative, people whose labors and lifestyle mesh elegantly. Descriptions of modestly beautiful architecture, finely crafted dress, simple and aesthetic meals, rich gardens and fields underscore the political narrative:

> We passed by several fields where haymaking was going on . . . the people in the fields looked strong and handsome, both men and women, and that so far from there being any appearance of sordidness about their attire, they seemed to be dressed specially for the occasion—lightly, of course, but gaily and with plenty of adornment.
>
> (Morris 1970 [1890]: 139)

> I should like to have seen with my eyes what success the new order of things had had in getting rid of the sprawling mess with which commercialism had littered the banks of the wide stream about Reading and Caversham: certainly everything smelt too deliciously in the early night for there to be any of the old careless sordidness of so-called manufacture . . .
>
> (Morris 1970 [1890]: 141)

As a designwright, Morris paints an idyllic picture of design's social importance—equating, for instance, fulfilled haymakers with well-designed attire—and artfully sidesteps the business of working out practical historical details. The tales his characters tell read as fables, sweeping into view memories of a horrible war where many gave their lives for the new order. Exactly how the reorientation of values surfaced is less crucial to the argument than rendering them desirable, and finally inhabitable. Although the plot and characters are arguably one-dimensional, the fictional form allowed Morris scenarios and perspectives that comment by way of demonstration rather than justification.

In the end Guest awakens again to the demoralizing ugliness of 1880s industrialized London. Instead of lamenting his return to the real world, he is optimistic: "If others can see it as I have seen it, then it may be a vision rather than a dream" (Morris 1970 [1890]: 182). In short, Morris observed and critiqued What Is by proposing to his readers What If.

This tactic is reminiscent of another utopian tradition, the manifesto, a "What If" stance that imagines the means by which implicit ideals might be achieved. Assertively reasoned and often obstinate, the manifesto takes a sledgehammer to opposing forces. No conflicts, only resolution. London graphic designer Ken Garland wrote and published "First Things First," a commercial art manifesto, in 1964. He recalls the moment he scribbled it down during a Society of Industrial Arts meeting, then read it to the crowd: "I found I wasn't so much reading it as declaiming it . . . it had become . . . that totally unfashionable device, a Manifesto" (Poynor 1999: 51).[1] The document condemns the "high-pitched scream of consumer selling" which contributes "little or nothing to our national prosperity." It asks designers and photographers to apply their skills to promote trade, education, culture and global awareness:

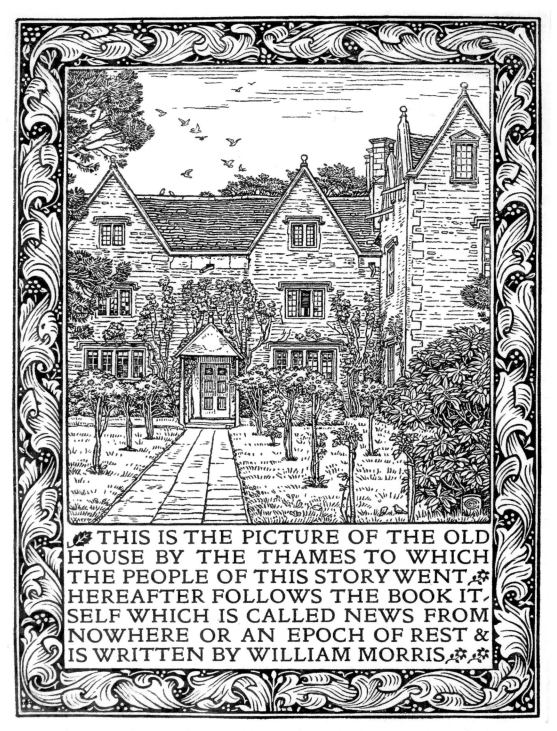

THIS IS THE PICTURE OF THE OLD HOUSE BY THE THAMES TO WHICH THE PEOPLE OF THIS STORY WENT HEREAFTER FOLLOWS THE BOOK ITSELF WHICH IS CALLED NEWS FROM NOWHERE OR AN EPOCH OF REST & IS WRITTEN BY WILLIAM MORRIS.

Figure 4.3 Frontispiece for *News from Nowhere* (1893). Author: William Morris. Publisher: Kelmscott Press. Source: archive.org. (https://archive.org/details/newsfromnowhere01morr).

> We have been bombarded with publications . . . applauding the work of those who have flogged their skill and imagination to sell such things as cat food, stomach powders, detergent, hair restorer, striped toothpaste, aftershave lotion, beforeshave lotion, slimming diets, fattening diets, deodorants, fizzy water, cigarettes, roll-ons, pull-ons and slip-ons.
>
> (Garland 1964: n.p.)

The architect of a manifesto and its signatories may not intend their earnest convictions to be read as story, or as design criticism. But any writing genre can be written as such: expository prose, interviews, speeches, reportage, biography. Similarly, non-fictional critical writing can be read as invented, or at least inventive, narrative depending upon the context, on reader expectations and of course on rhetorical style. For instance, "First Things First" grins slightly. Its light spirit encourages commercial artists to share "experience and opinions" and to pass the ideas along to "others who may be interested." The manifesto was reprinted in several design industry journals, but also in the *Guardian*. And BBC news asked Garland to read it on air. The fact that the media picked up the idea points to the document's affability in the context of a society that registered the manifesto as not so terribly real.

In 1999, Garland and design critic/historian Rick Poynor resurrected and reworked the manifesto to suit the contemporary context. As the manifesto states, this version calls for "a reversal of priorities," proclaiming that the profession is used up manufacturing demand for inessential things. "Consumerism is running uncontested; it must be challenged by other perspectives" (Garland et al. 1999: cover). Challenge consumerism? Please! The progenitors and thirty-three signatories are sophisticated designers and writers, inured to the wily ways of capitalism. Surely they noted the contradiction between the document's proclamations—stated more aggressively than the 1964 original—and what it is that graphic designers actually do. Still, they all signed it.

Reproduced simultaneously in seven industry magazines, the turn of the millennium manifesto triggered debate about social responsibility in graphic design practice, an unpopular or in many cases untenable topic rarely spotted on the professional radar. Lively exchanges via letters to editors and subsequent magazine articles kept the manifesto under debate for over a year. In a 2001 address, Poynor framed the manifesto as an attempt by the group "to test the water, to try out one or two supposedly passé ideas about design priorities, and see whether anyone agreed."[2] Post-signing accounts indicate more than a few of the thirty-three endorsed the document primarily for its symbolism.

As a work of alternative critical writing, FTF2000 was more bellwether than catalyst-that-would-refigure-practice [Eds. See *First Things First* 2000, Section 5.1.4]. The authors and signatories responded to the same forces that were at the time propelling consumer activism, an emergent social network, notions of peer production and user collaboration. They fingered a particular inertia in design practice in a form akin to a dare. Had the finger not been gloved in a manifesto, would readers have been as responsive, provoked as they were to chime in? I think not. Whether the document is viewed as misguided or grandstanding, tongue-in-cheek or pioneering, today it continues to inform the discourse focused on what graphic designers should and could be working toward.

In this light, some non-fiction critical texts can be interpreted as fictional. Canadian designer Bruce Mau is well practiced in writing soft-rant, evident in his book *Life Style* (which also includes his "Incomplete Manifesto for Growth"). Although the monograph showcases the work of his design studio, BMD, Mau commits copious space to proclamation, for instance: "At some point, as design 'professionalized,' thinking and saying were delaminated, and it became possible to say without thinking. The result? Mountains of message that mean nothing. We empty the word 'literature' and strap it to the back of 'corporate' without apology, without irony" (Mau 2000: 364). When the Bauhaus was formed in 1919, Walter Gropius wrote a Sermon, predicting how the new program would "embrace architecture and sculpture and painting in one unity . . . which will one day rise toward heaven from the hands of a million workers like the crystal symbol of a new faith" (Wingler 1986: 31).[3] Reconsidered as relative fictions, perhaps "half-fictions" written by single-minded writers, these rhetorical forms invite readers, in certain contexts, to engage in a momentary pact.

Back in the mid-1990s, amidst the buzz surrounding the digital revolution that threatened to dismantle all that is pure and humane, artists of every ilk were analyzing the implications of virtual reality, haptic illusion, fake identities in chat rooms and the World Wide Web. Editors committed plenty of ink to debates on the impact of desktop publishing and similar indignities suffered by graphic designers at the hands of programmers and users. Around that time taunting titles began to appear in *Émigré* magazine: "Route 666: Transgressing the Information Superhighway" and "Hangin' at the Zeitgeist." The stories-slash-essays fuse the ostensibly personal experiences and design speculations of one Putch Tu. We now know this work to be that of designwright Diane Gromala, also a techno-artist, recovering graphic designer and academic. In the story "Abject Subjectivities," the author Putch recounts those moments of her life in which design served as nexus between ideology and culture. We do not know whether or not Gromala, the person, was actually beaten by East Berlin police on a night train because she carried Solidarity ephemera, in the story. All we need to believe is that Putch Tu was in fact on the train. And traveling with her leads us to critical insight:

> Design is like a brick. It can be used to build a courthouse, or it can be thrown through its window . . . the concept in its unrestrained usage is a set of circumstances at a volatile juncture. [Design] is a vector, the point of application of a force moving through space at a given velocity in a given direction . . . In short, if you put your nomad glasses on, you'd re-vision design as a moving target of silly putty that makes shit happen—an act.

(Gromala [as Putch Tu] 1998: 11)

Putch Tu wrote blurring lines between fact and fiction, research and fantasy. She was explicitly political and contemptuous of anyone who would reduce computation to ones and zeros. Had Gromala attempted to promote her observations through the usual channels, she would have had to weigh each sentence on the scales of academic suitability—something she is quite capable of doing.[4] Writing fiction in a slightly dangerous persona afforded Gromala a critical sneer, and readers a tantalizing spank. Most importantly, the work introduced cultural and media theory at a time when things theoretical were held suspect among most graphic design practitioners and many educators. Through stories that tease the limits of hyperbole, Gromala alerted readers to discursive ideas impacting both practice and scholarship.[5]

Design scholars and leathered critics have employed alternative critical writing, just as a few design-ers have earned chops writing within the traditions of criticism, journalism and history. Former *Eye* magazine editor and design provocateur Max Bruinsma calls what he does "editorialism." Writings on his website are familiarly labeled essay, review, column, profile and interview. Then there are those listed as "poetic." One such work, a catalog introduction from 1993 entitled "A Dialogue between Souls," was written for *Artificial,* a computer program/art installation that generates random pictures. Bruinsma imagines a dialog between a viewer and the image-generating machine, à la Kubrick's Dave and Hal.

The computer-entity explains in Zen tones the implications of its work to the excitable viewer, who through questioning and listening learns the validity and point of the program's exercise.

> — . . . The same can be said of my drawings: they are unique moments from infinity. They are not "pictures of" it any more than they are "unlike" it.
> —So, after all: a portrayal, a reflection, a "generation of the Idea"!
> —None of those—they are.
> —Like life itself?
> —More or less like life itself—only slightly more artificial.

(Bruinsma 1993: n.p.)

The narrative attitude might be possible in a traditional introductory essay. Bruinsma's fictional approach, though, offers more. It positions the reader as participant in the story, equal to the incredulous human facing a threatening concept. Authority of the critic is replaced by a persona of authority.[6]

Peter Lunenfeld is founder and executive editor of MediaWork Pamphlets, a book series for which he commissions authors to weave life stories into "theoretical and critical praxis." He asserts that audiences are not as responsive to "disembodied theoretical and critical discourse" today as they might have been twenty-five years ago, which "opens up space for the personal, as manifested in fiction, humor, personae, and other evasions of the panoptical perspective." Not incidentally, Lunenfeld's charge required some authors to rethink their writing practice. For instance, *Writing Machines,* by media theorist Katherine Hayles (2002a), explores what the printed book can be in the digital age. Hayles explains that telling a fuller story required part of the tale be told by a made-up persona, "Kaye," to "interrogate the author . . . her background and experiences, and especially the community of writers, theorists, critics, teachers, and students in which she moves."

Playing the outsider to one's expertise and fraternity can be disorienting, but useful. Hayles' autobiographical bits become the story of a text-centric life awakening to the material realm. One moment of epiphany:

> [Kaye's] thoughts too were stimulated and changed by her interaction with the materiality of the artifacts. If books are seen only as immaterial verbal constructs, the rich potential of this interplay is lost. Literary critics have long accepted that form is content and content is form. Now Kaye wanted to shout, "Materiality is content, and content is materiality!" The artists' books had permanently changed her mental landscape, and her senses as well, including vision, tactility, smell, and proprioception.[7] She would never read books the same way again.

(Hayles 2002a: 75)

As Lunenfeld points out, when alternative critical writing turns autobiographical, the reader is asked to negotiate between "auto-myth making and the truths that can emerge from grounding theoretical discourse in lived experience."[8]

The chronicles of Kaye interlace Hayles's academic text in a work that registers neither quite as fiction nor exposition, but both at the same time. Similarly, *Shaping Things*, another in the series, maps the past, present and future of designed objects, specifically how they are determining our biological future, for better and worse. Novelist Bruce Sterling published the book under his real name but does so as a "visionary futurist" with facetious flair. Part future-think, part rant and part science fiction, the narrative is plump with neologisms. There are spime ("a set of relationships first and always, and an object now and then) (Sterling 2005: 77); wranglers ("there are no purchasers, only wranglers") (Sterling 2005: 126); and arphids (after radio frequency identification, or more descriptively, "some newfangled, infesting, autoreplicating plague") (Sterling 2005: 88). Together these terms not only render uncomfortable notions approachable, they give nameable identity to complex issues driving Sterling's critique (Figure 4.4).

Gromala, Hayles and Sterling speculate wildly, assume various voices, and materialize the abstract. They analyse the circumstances within which designed artifacts are made, they integrate with and implicate culture with tales that call out and fill in blanks; that add gristle and meat to design function in the way of all good critical writing.

I publish under pseudonyms occasionally, assume the characters of people who critique graphic design activity. There is Deborah Griffin, the New York design writer who we only hear from in fragments: a couple of pages from an ostensibly larger work, or a paragraph excerpt as needed. Cheri Newcastle, a pulp sci-fi novelist, writes about media through the character Priss, a cyber-detective with techie pals who fashion paraphernalia that transmogrify her into the media she investigates. And I am thinking about developing a fashion designer who wants to target untapped niche markets—hermaphrodites and mixed-race toddlers—but who suffers from ambiguity aphasia.[9] My most active persona is academic Denise Gonzales Crisp. She wrote the fiction-based essay "Toward A Definition of the DecoRational: In

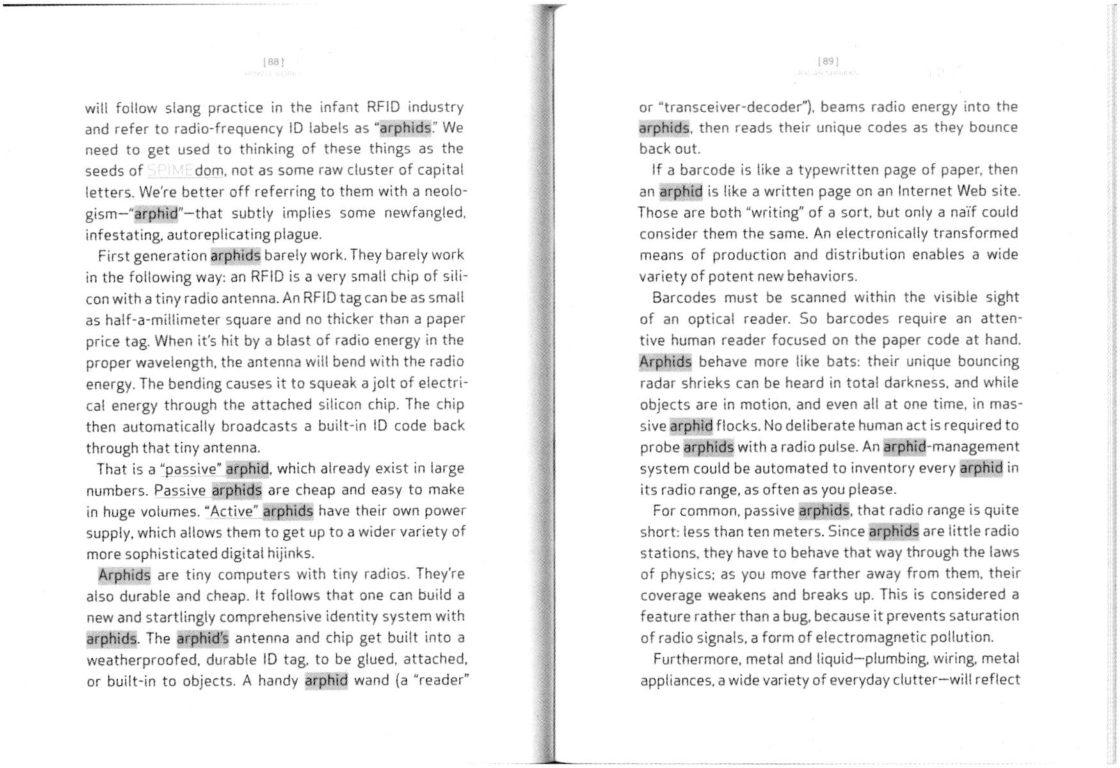

[88]

will follow slang practice in the infant RFID industry and refer to radio-frequency ID labels as "arphids." We need to get used to thinking of these things as the seeds of SPIMEdom, not as some raw cluster of capital letters. We're better off referring to them with a neologism—"arphid"—that subtly implies some newfangled, infesting, autoreplicating plague.

First generation arphids barely work. They barely work in the following way: an RFID is a very small chip of silicon with a tiny radio antenna. An RFID tag can be as small as half-a-millimeter square and no thicker than a paper price tag. When it's hit by a blast of radio energy in the proper wavelength, the antenna will bend with the radio energy. The bending causes it to squeak a jolt of electrical energy through the attached silicon chip. The chip then automatically broadcasts a built-in ID code back through that tiny antenna.

That is a "passive" arphid, which already exist in large numbers. Passive arphids are cheap and easy to make in huge volumes. "Active" arphids have their own power supply, which allows them to get up to a wider variety of more sophisticated digital hijinks.

Arphids are tiny computers with tiny radios. They're also durable and cheap. It follows that one can build a new and startlingly comprehensive identity system with arphids. The arphid's antenna and chip get built into a weatherproofed, durable ID tag, to be glued, attached, or built-in to objects. A handy arphid wand (a "reader"

[89]

or "transceiver-decoder"), beams radio energy into the arphids, then reads their unique codes as they bounce back out.

If a barcode is like a typewritten page of paper, then an arphid is like a written page on an Internet Web site. Those are both "writing" of a sort, but only a naïf could consider them the same. An electronically transformed means of production and distribution enables a wide variety of potent new behaviors.

Barcodes must be scanned within the visible sight of an optical reader. So barcodes require an attentive human reader focused on the paper code at hand. Arphids behave more like bats: their unique bouncing radar shrieks can be heard in total darkness, and while objects are in motion, and even all at one time, in massive arphid flocks. No deliberate human act is required to probe arphids with a radio pulse. An arphid-management system could be automated to inventory every arphid in its radio range, as often as you please.

For common, passive arphids, that radio range is quite short: less than ten meters. Since arphids are little radio stations, they have to behave that way through the laws of physics; as you move farther away from them, their coverage weakens and breaks up. This is considered a feature rather than a bug, because it prevents saturation of radio signals, a form of electromagnetic pollution.

Furthermore, metal and liquid—plumbing, wiring, metal appliances, a wide variety of everyday clutter—will reflect

Figure 4.4 A spread (pp. 88–9) describing "arphids" in *Shaping Things* by Bruce Sterling (2005). © 2005. Designer: Lorraine Wild. Publisher: Massachusetts Institute of Technology. By permission of The MIT Press.

Real Time" for Design Research (2003), an anthology otherwise dominated by expository, research-oriented essays. Nonetheless, the narrator tentatively embarks:

> I am at the beginning. Yes, right this moment, starting on this page I set out to understand an impulse, to investigate something I suspect to be true about graphic design. I have a hypothesis of sorts. That's something. Maybe it's not much more than a hunch, a sense. Maybe it's just a hope. But it could evolve, as pronouncements will, into a theory, a model methodology, a revolution! I have named this hypothesis the "decorational." This is where I am.
>
> I am also . . . a designer—predisposed to make something out of nothing, to connect things to other things to surprising, and if I may say not untrue, ends. My . . . means, the hypothesis and the intent convene here to spark a departure toward the unknown . . . to demonstrate that design itself can be research, or that design research is this, here. Right now . . .
>
> (Gonzales Crisp 2003: 93)

Perhaps I was unwise to allow Denise to diverge so, especially amid essays that explicate brand alignment, user requirements, ethnographic practices and other rich subjects. My instincts, it turns out, were not completely wacky. Terence Rosenberg, a design professor at Goldsmiths College in London, explores how figurative strategies serve research in his essay "The Reservoir":

> The poetic is an attempt to review and overthrow the normalizing process . . . and touch again a rawness in both thinking and experience. At the heart of poetic methodologies . . . is the "abnormal paradigm" . . . made pertinent through "points of inference," and these are configured in reference to "linguistic, contextual and general world knowledge" . . . [linking] that which has not yet been thought to that which has and is acculturated.
>
> (Rosenberg 2000: n.p.)

Rosenberg explains that literary devices—hyperbole, metaphor, ellipsis etc.—help realize research agendas because each "deviates from normal readings." Personae also offer ways to focus on the subject through alien lenses that can impact and shape the perspective of the researcher in the process of examining the subject. He names neologisms too as useful for opening up key areas. In architecture, "hyper-surfaces" or "meta-cities," for example, are in large part hypothetical topic areas, yet they engendered debate as well as possible conceptual abstracts for practice (Rosenberg 2000: n.p.).

"The Reservoir" scrutinizes how the design process examines a topic and in turn invents responses. What Rosenberg calls "poetic disruption" infuses design research with unforeseeable outcomes, in fact challenges design's long-held *modus operandi,* problem solving. Conventional research establishes a focal point in advance, whereas poetic disruption promotes enquiry that "evolves its field of focus" as it proceeds. I venture that a similar process applied to critical design writing, and added to the canon of options, has and will continue to vitalize design discourse with the promise of developing and communicating insights unique to those afforded by expository prose. It can also affect very real change.

In the first half of the twentieth century, American designer W.A. Dwiggins wrote and produced pamphlets under the pseudonym Dr. Puterschein. He also called upon the characteristics of many writing genres and voices under his given name. With his cousin Laurance Siegfried (and contributions from illustrious typographer Bruce Rogers) Dwiggins wrote *Investigation into the Physical Properties of Books (with the approval of the Society)*:

Inquirer: Mr. B_____, will you please tell the committee why you printed this book on cardboard?

Mr. B_____: To make it the right thickness. It had to be one inch.

—Why that thick, particularly?

—Because otherwise it would not sell. If a book isn't one inch thick it won't sell.

—Do you mean to say that people who buy books select them with a foot rule?

—They have to have some standard of selection.

(Dwiggins and Siegfried 1995[1919]: n.p.)

The mocking character of anonymous inquirers employed to pester the 1919 publishing industry fore-goes the niceties of reasoned critique in favor of wry confrontation. "What if," I imagine Dwiggins saying to himself, "I could put the dullards on trial?" Dwiggins' critical "review" of the publishing industry was produced by the very real Society of Calligraphers, and disseminated to practitioners and publishers alike, which significantly impacted industry practices (Figure 4.5).[10]

A gifted graphic designer (who is credited with originating the term), quintessential modern type designer, master of marionette theater, and designwright, Dwiggins called upon the same imagination

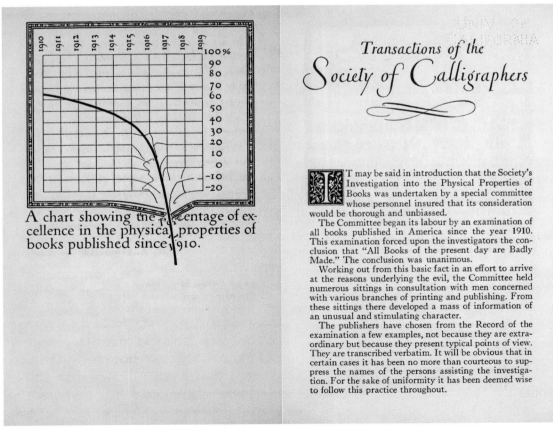

Figure 4.5 Frontispiece of *An Investigation into the Physical Properties of Books*. © 1919 Designer: W.A. Dwiggins. Publisher: W.A. Dwiggins and L.B. Siegfried. (https://archive.org/details/extractsfrominve00socirich).

and formal sensitivity in his writing as he did his design. And where his ideas would not fit traditional forms, or risked obscurity, he made something up and published it himself. On this count, Dwiggins had a distinct advantage. He was well connected with publishers and printers, had the support and means to produce chapbooks and other works in small runs.

Despite contemporary interest and writing talent that has surfaced in the last twenty years, few refereed venues exist for alternative critical writing. As in the days of Dwiggins, through to 1964 when Garland published his manifesto, up to now—in particular with the discontinuation of *Émigré* magazine—most such work is self-published. An exception is *Dot Dot Dot*, produced by designer/writers Stuart Bailey (English) and Peter Bil'ak (Czech). Their editorial position is nicely captured in the following brief "essay" compiled by Bailey, which also happens to reveal attitudes underpinning this type of critique:

> Kurt Schitters said: "Innumerable laws may be written [. . .] The most important is: never make it as someone before you did.
>
> Anthony Froshaug said: "Schwitters is, here, quite wrong. Make it AS they did, unless the constraints are changed. [. . .] 'Modern [. . .]' is not a mode: it consists of a reasoned assessment of what is needed, and of what some is done, under certain constraints. When [. . .] constraints change, the important thing is not to spray a random pattern [. . .] but to assess the new, with the old, requirements [. . .].
>
> and Mark E. Smith said: "Whenever I say anything, I often think that the opposite is true as well. Sometimes I think the truth is too fucking obvious for people to take. The possibilities are endless and people don't like that. They go for the average every time. Well, that doesn't interest me in the slightest [. . .]
>
> (Bailey 2004: 60)[11]

The introduction on the *Dot Dot Dot* website declares that since its conception in 2000, the magazine 'has immatured into a jocuserious fanzine-journal-orphanage based on true stories deeply concerned with art-design-music-language-literature-architecture . . ." (www.dot-dot-dot.us). Immatured jocuserious-ness sounds like deprecation masking under-recognized voices—frequently intelligent and insightful voices, I might add. Design needs more and new and accessible venues, specifically those that position alternative critical writing in the same discursive context as traditional genres. Publications where our "certain constraints" might be more thoroughly evaluated, and the new and old requirements challenged.

"Our genres have boundaries," writes novelist Peter Turchi, "and when they won't allow us to play the games we want to play we search for new ways to reflect our communication with the world" (Turchi 2004: 136). Traditional critical genres submit detailed and descriptive maps that serve as loci within the bigger picture. Alternative critical writing need not yield such absolute direction or explication. It is a probe, a trial, a symptom—a device through which the designwright explores and speculates in search of clarity. Alternative critical writing affords authors additional space to pose as investigators working on a viable hunch, instigators pointing up the way it is—at least for now. And these roles are as critical to our discourse as they are to design itself.

Notes

1. Ken Garland, speaking to Rick Poynor, and quoted in "First Things First Revisited" (Poynor 1999), p. 2.
2. Rick Poynor in an address entitled "The Time for Being Against," presented at the "Looking Closer: AIGA Conference on Design History and Criticism," in New York (Poynor 2001).

3. "Program of the Staatliche Bauhaus in Weimar" by Walter Gropius is reprinted in total in *The Bauhaus* (Wingler 1986).

4. See, for instance, Gromala and Bolter (2005).

5. It is no surprise that Gromala's work and that of her contemporaries were written and published during the heady 1990s, a period in which the influence of semioticians Umberto Eco and Roland Barthes, experimental writer Italo Calvino, and Jean Baudrillard, among others, figured prominently. Another essay should examine circumstances that truncated those discursive projects inspired by philosophers and cultural critics.

6. The catalog in which the article "A Dialogue between Souls" appeared was published in conjunction with *Artificial-output, Work by Remko Scha,* exhibited at Van Rijsbergen Gallery, Rotterdam, The Netherlands (October 17–November 14, 1993). See also "A Reader's Terms" (http://maxbruinsma.nl/div-jve1.htm) in which Bruinsma adapts *The Printer's Terms* (1969, written by Rudolf Hostettler and designed by Jan Tschichold) to discuss the question: What is the relation between designers and the printing process, and what implications does this have for the meaning of print? "The result," Bruinsma explains, is "a hybrid of essay, copywriting and free association . . . written-to-fit passages [placed] back into the original page lay-out, keeping the illustrations and caption lines as they were" (Bruinsma 1998: n.p.) These and other works are accessible at http://maxbruinsma.nl.

7. *Writing Machines* Lexicon Linkmap on the Web supplement http://mitpress.mit.edu/mediawork defines proprioception as "the sense of physically inhabiting one's body, produced by deep tissue sensors" (Hayles 2000b).

8. All quotes cited are from an email exchange with Peter Lunenfeld, June 28, 2008.

9. See, for instance, Denise Gonzales Crisp (as Deborah Griffin), "Everyday People Play" (Gonzales Crisp 1997a) or "Out of Context: Entrepreneurs, Designists and Other Utopians" (Gonzales Crisp 1997b) and (as Cheri Newcastle) "Speculations" (Gonzales Crisp 1998). As with the MediaWork Pamphlets, the design of these texts are integral to the telling.

10. Paul Shaw writes: "Although the Society's case was deliberately overstated, it proved effective. In the ensuing two decades American book design and production improved dramatically, despite the Depression, a fact that Dwiggins duly noted in 'Twenty Years After,' a follow-up piece to Extracts which was commissioned by *The Publishers' Weekly.* Evidence of the change can be see in the AIGA Fifty Books of the Year exhibitions, initially established in 1923 and still being held" (Shaw 1996: 37).

11. Mark E. Smith is the lead singer of post-punk band The Fall. Not all *Dot Dot Dot* issues include fiction, but much of the writing lives at the outer limits of critical writing. One notable fiction-based essay is "Life after Life and After: An Interview with George Maciunas" by Raimundas Malasauskas in which the interview takes place through David Magnus, a Medium (Malasauskas 2006/7).

Chapter 4.2.7

Acrobat reader

Anna Gerber and Teal Triggs

There are many ways to write a story, and just as many ways to show one. Typographic experimentation has long played a role in literary fiction, and last year, it resurfaced in Britain with Graham Rawle's *Woman's World*. To write his daring 437-page novel, Rawle, a collage artist and writer, clipped 40,000 text fragments from 1960s women's magazines and arranged them into a surprisingly absorbing thriller about a transvestite, Norma Fontaine, and her alter ego, Roy Little (Figures 4.6 and 4.7).

A remarkable collection of typefaces that evoke a compelling and verbose ransom note, *Woman's World* marries content and form in a unique visual language. Critics hailed the "linguistic mischief" of this "typographical rollercoaster," and its appeal, both accessible and remote, was neatly encapsulated by Rick Poynor in *Eye*: "Despite its unconventional and perhaps initially daunting appearance, Rawle's narrative grips as a reading experience from start to finish." (Figures 4.8 and 4.9).

Even as it reinvents the literary narrative, Rawle's novel delivers timeworn elements of experimental narrative to a wide audience. And he's hardly the only mainstream literary writer using such typographic devices to engage readers in a more dynamic narrative experience and to give the printed page a multi-dimensional visual surface. Rick Moody blocked out a page of text in his 2005 novel, *The Diviners,* to depict a page in a book read by a character that has itself been blocked out (leaving only the words "such" and "thirst"), resulting in a powerful visual device that peers into the character's mind while refreshing the narrative's pace. Dave Eggers embeds photographs within the text of one passage in his 2002 novel, *You Shall Know Our Velocity*: "In the parking lot, we watched a trio of milk white Broncos drive by—. . .—and we all stopped momentarily." Embedded between the dashes, at the size of the surrounding type, are photographs of three SUVs, breaking the text physically and breaking the narrative visually, making readers also stop momentarily. And Mark Danielewski's 2000 *House of Leaves* is so dependent on colored type (among many other graphic tricks) that a color-reference chart appears on the copyright page. Such playful visual devices suggest experimentalism for its own sake; it adds no depth to the narrative but it makes for a notable reading experience.

The much-discussed second novel by Jonathan Safran Foer, *Extremely Loud & Incredibly Close,* embraces a host of visual devices—proofreaders' marks, blocked-out and isolated words, phrases occupying entire pages, even a photographic flipbook of a man falling (in reverse) from the Twin Towers on September 11—to illustrate the mental landscape of Oskar Schell, Foer's 9-year-old protagonist.

First published in *Print*, July/August (2006): 62–7. © Anna Gerber and Teal Triggs.

Figure 4.6 *Woman's World* cover, by Graham Rawle. © 2005. Author and Designer: Graham Rawle Reprinted by permission of Counterpoint/Atlantic Books.

Figure 4.7 *Woman's World* page detail. © 2005 by Graham Rawle. Reprinted by permission of Counterpoint/ Atlantic Books.

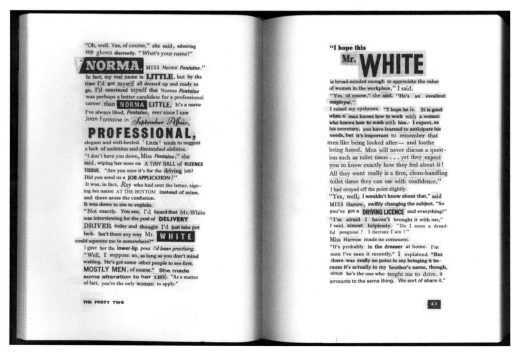

Figure 4.8 *Woman's World* page spread, pp. 42-3. © 2005. Author and Designer: Graham Rawle. Reprinted by permission of Counterpoint/Atlantic Books.

Chapter 4.2.8

How and why design matters

Debbie Millman

In November 2004 I inadvertently answered a cold call from a salesman of a brand new online radio station asking me if I'd be interested in hosting a show about anything that interests me. Immediately skeptical, my first response was to wonder what the catch was, and why anyone would be interested in anything I had to say. Surely inviting a person lacking *any* radio experience, and with negligible broad-based expertise to share, was hardly a slam-dunk. Brian, the salesman, was quick to assuage my doubts with the clarification that I was only being offered a 13-episode "try-out," and the network, Voice America, was indeed interested in niche topics from people they would be happy to train. Voice America was one of the first online radio networks to emerge in the early aughts and, after some initial success, had extended their networks to include Voice America Business and Voice America Country.

Given my branding background and my current job at Sterling Brands—a leading international brand consultancy firm—Brian was interested in having me do a show on the business of branding. But this offer coincided with a tricky phase in my career: while financially successful beyond what I could have ever imagined, I had begun to feel that I had lost my creative soul. The opportunity to create a show about branding was the last thing I was interested in doing. I countered his proposal with the concept of developing a show about graphic design, which, if absolutely necessary, could also include branding. As it happened, my counter-offer came at time when Donald Trump's reality television show *The Apprentice* was at the height of its popularity. The night before my final conversation to persuade the executives at Voice America that a show on graphic design could and would be gripping radio, the weekly exercise on *The Apprentice* featured a challenge with the Pepsi-Cola Company. The test for the young entrepreneurs included redesigning the Pepsi Edge can. I had worked on the design of the original can at Sterling Brands, and the client in the show was also my client in real life! When the execs at Voice America tried to stump me with a "what design topic would you do a show on today, if you had to come up with an idea on the spot," I said that I would want to interview the designer at Pepsi-Cola who had been featured on *The Apprentice* the previous night. When they inquired about how I would pull this off, I confidently stated that the designer was my current client, and also a friend. The allure of a Pepsi connection for them, and the design component for me, proved an amenable compromise for the decision makers at Voice America. The final negotiation came about when I was informed that in order to be on the network I would have to pay for my airtime. When I weighed the excitement I felt about this

---

new endeavor, and the notion that my current success could fund an initiative for my heart, I decided that the fee would be worth it, and on February 5, 2005, my internet radio show *Design Matters* was born.

I often say that *Design Matters* began with a dream and a telephone line. I started broadcasting the show every Friday afternoon, live from a telephone modem in my office at Sterling Brands in the Empire State Building, face to face with my guests, each of us holding a telephone handset. The sound quality that we experienced was similar to the effect that occurs when two people on a landline are on same call in the same location, on different phones: tinny and crackly. Add to this the fact that the producers were also on the line from a remote location in Arizona, and you have the makings of an episode of *Wayne's World*. As you may imagine, my early shows are quite gruesome listening. But excited by the content and the opportunity, I soldiered on, learning along the journey.

My first guests were mostly friends. As those friends began to send the links of the early shows to their friends, word spread in the design community. By the time Voice America renewed the show, and I wrote another check for the airtime, I began to invite designers beyond my circle of friends and, mercifully, most said yes. By the end of my second "season" of *Design Matters*, Milton Glaser, Paula Scher, Emily Oberman, Michael Bierut and Stefan Sagmeister had been guests on the show.

The year 2005 was a unique time on the Internet; a bit like the gold rush, new enterprises and platforms were popping up everywhere. Adam Curry (former MTV video jockey and radio broadcaster) and software developer Dave Winer created the first *ever* podcast in 2004 when they wrote a program they called iPodder. The program allowed Curry and Winer to download automatically Internet radio broadcasts to their iPods. They could then take their iPods, along with their broadcasts, anywhere. The actual term "podcasting" appeared shortly thereafter in an article by Ben Hammersley that was published in *The Guardian* (Hammersley 2004). While much of the early podcasting software wasn't user-friendly, the first commercially successful software was created by August Trometer and Ray Slakinski. First called iPodderX, Trometer and Slakinski later changed the name to Transistr, and an industry was born. In June 2005, Apple added podcasting to the iTunes 4.9 software and built a directory of podcasts in iTunes. Here, listeners could both subscribe and listen to podcasts. As soon as I read about this new technology, I decided to upload my recorded shows to iTunes, inadvertently making *Design Matters* the first-ever design podcast to be distributed in this manner.

The ultimate democratic endeavor, podcasting is (at least for now) free from government regulation. Podcasters don't need a license to broadcast programming (radio stations do) and they aren't required to conform to the United States Federal Communication Commission decency regulations. Anything and everything is allowed in podcasting, and this leniency is leveraged all over the Internet.

In the last ten years the technology has changed, as has the landscape of podcasting. Once a frantic free-for-all, podcasting is now a worldwide phenomenon. In July 2013, iTunes celebrated one billion podcast subscriptions through iTunes. The subscriptions span 250,000 unique podcasts with eight million episodes in over 100 languages. But Apple is no longer the only game in town. Upstart services including Soundcloud, Stitcher, and the Public Radio Exchange are freely available and also provide embeddable podcast files.

There are also podcasts about every aspect of design for *anyone* who has an interest: there are podcasts about graphic design, interior design, industrial design, typography design, and more. There are also myriad styles of conversations: boisterous, buoyant, revering, historical, and hysterically funny.

By 2009, as both podcasting and *Design Matters* grew in popularity, I recognized that I needed to upgrade both the sound quality and the distribution of the show. After 100 episodes on Voice America, co-founder William Drenttel invited me to publish *Design Matters* on *Design Observer*. *Design Matters* is now on *Design Observer*'s media channel, and the show is produced at the specially built podcast studio located at the Masters in Branding Program at the School of Visual Arts in New York City. I have interviewed some of the most highly renowned designers of the twentieth and twenty-first centuries, including Massimo Vignelli, Bill Moggridge, Maira Kalman, Doyald Young, and Marian Bantjes. I have also expanded my guests to include artists Lawrence Weiner, Barbara Kruger, and Shephard Fairey; writers Dave Eggers, Dani Shapiro, and Malcolm Gladwell and cultural commentators Seth Godin, Dan Pink, and John Hockenberry. I even interviewed Nobel Prize-winning scientist Eric Kandel. The show has evolved to a singular interview format, and over the course of each episode I seek to reveal the arc of a designer's life. The arc of a career is often a circuitous one; I am endlessly fascinated by how people become who they are and how the decisions in their lives impact their work. I think my audience is too: In 2011, the show was awarded the People's Choice Cooper Hewitt National Design Award.

I am often asked about *Design Matters*: "Isn't it hard to talk about something intangible that people can't actually see?" I can't help but smile at the query, as this is the *very reason* I love talking about design on the radio. *Because* the designer's work is invisible to the listening audience, it is mandatory to talk about ideas and ideology rather than process. In order to fully engage our audience, we are obligated to discuss the strategy or psychology or motivation or outcome of the work rather than how it was made or what materials were used. Consequently, it becomes mandatory to communicate well; and that is one of my favorite things about design, on or off the radio. Talking about designers on the radio in real time also provides an opportunity to hear about a designer, directly from the designer, in his or her own unique voice. Because *Design Matters* is uncensored and ad-free, each guest has an entire show to talk freely and from the heart. I laugh and cry along with my guests, commiserate with them, and debate some points, but the guest is always at the center of each show. In its most basic description, *Design Matters* is a show set up to showcase the depth and breadth of design and designers in all of their magnificent richness.

Over ten years later, I have no intention of ending *Design Matters*. I have come to realize that this little show is one of the greatest contributions I may ever be able to make to the canon of design. And with only 250 episodes under my belt, I have many, more designers I need to interview before I am done.

Chapter 4.2.9

Inquiry as a verb

Margo Halverson

DesignInquiry, which began in 2004, is an annual series of intensive open-forum, hands-on, team-based gatherings. We bring together a diverse cast of thinkers, makers, and practitioners to research design issues by collaborating on-site through presentations, discussions, workshops, and exhibitions. Participants come from graphic design, type design, industrial design, architecture, interior design, art, writing, philosophy, acting, archeology—but anyone from any field is invited to contribute ideas to each gathering. This is our story.

DesignInquiry is a non-profit organization that evolved out of the Maine Summer Institute of Graphic Design (MSIGD) at Maine College of Art (MECA) for which I was the director. These residency workshops were modeled after Yale's Brissago Summer Program in Graphic Design (1973–1996). While attending Brissago in 1991, I met Wolfgang Weingart, who was then teaching at the Basel School of Design. A year later, I invited him to teach at MSIGD, along with other influential designers and educators, including Bruno Monguzzi, Inge Druckrey, Dorthea Hofmann, Lucille Tenazas, Lorraine Wild, Michael Rock & Susan Sellers, and Elliott Earls. We wanted people who could teach without a computer—an unusual game plan in the how-to era of 1990s summer programs. Although MSIGD was successful, after ten years it was beginning to feel repetitive, and I wondered about other strategies to organize a thought-provoking group. During MSIGD, I noticed that the most inspiring "ah-ha" moments occurred during weekends at my dinner table, when two guest faculty visits happened to overlap or when a guest faculty member arrived early and joined a final critique on the spur of the moment. I realized that these were relaxed and candid situations in which everyone involved was on equal footing. It seemed to me in these relaxed moments outside of the teacher–student context that ideas and questions about design were dissected or argued more openly and "honestly" than in our more formal studio settings.

This prompted me to consider expanding these sorts of exchanges, and I asked myself what would a week-long "ah-ha" program be like? Could time together in a group be purposely constructed to inspire a non-hierarchal open dialogue? In 2000 and 2002 I invited Melle Hammer to MSIGD. Melle Hammer is a typographer from Amsterdam whose self-published chapbook *Ampersand as a Place* (2002; http://designinquiry.net/about/history) outlines his pedagogy for reaching deep into design practices. In this book Hammer describes how an individual can contribute to a holistic experimental group design process. His workshops were like no others that I had witnessed. He infused his teaching with daily on-the-spot "making." Hammer emphasized design process shifts that encouraged the participants to reframe his original prompts rather than merely working toward completing a project. Participants were eager both to experiment with process, materials, form, and content, and to work without a sure end product. At this point in the early 2000s, many designers sought opportunities to question design methodologies that maintained that the final artifact was the only answer to a design problem, so Hammer's approach was also very timely.

I shared my questions about creating a compelling, open-ended intensive program with Melle and together we outlined a new program that would become DesignInquiry. We determined that this program would focus participants' work on a specific topic and be responsive to participants' energies. This new program would also dissolve the boundaries between organizers and participants so that the character of the intensive week spent together—as well as the workshop outcomes—would be the participants' responsibility. It was Melle's insight that, in order for this new program to succeed, participants must cook together and eat every meal together. These stipulations ensured that the sense of community that can emerge around preparing and eating meals—two very basic tasks of daily life—would be an integral aspect of the inquiry.

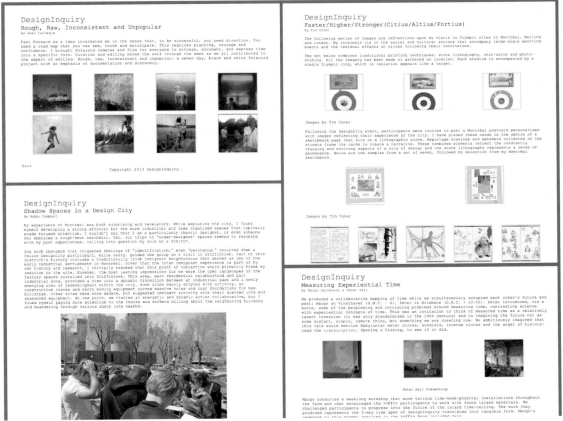

Figure 4.13 DesignInquiry.net showcases a range of work that expands our themes, topics, and research, including video snippets, longer films, ongoing collaborations, and peer-reviewed essays.

Early on, we invited Peter Hall to join us. Hall is a design writer and critic who was involved with MSIGD and was sympathetic to and enthusiastic about this experiment. Though we had no funding, we were determined to make this new program happen; we knew that DesignInquiry was like no other short-term design residency currently being offered. Melle, Peter, and I located the program to a barn on an island off the Maine coast in which we adapted the available facilities so we could cook—both literally and figuratively! DesignInquiry would not be a "how-to" continuing education program, or a conference in which the best conversations happened in the corridors or in hotel bars. DesignInquiry would be totally immersive—a 24/7 space where everyone was simultaneously teacher and student, and where we would work, live, cook, and eat together.

At DesignInquiry, the prep and cooking area is set up so that the daily flow of living and working together is always visible. Individual participant's ideas about the DI topic can simmer while washing dishes or working on a prompt in teams on the porch. These ideas may move back into the group discourse during an afternoon coastal low-tide field trip, or an impromptu performance after dinner. Each morning the previous day's work is reinterpreted by daily tag-teamed "reporters" in whatever format they choose: a group exercise, a theater play, a walk, or short film. We ensure that no ideas are left behind during the frenetically paced week of teamwork, individual projects and show-and-tell of work in progress. Our experience with the DesignInquiry format shows that living and working together in "raw" spaces and unique places—a barn in Vinalhaven, Maine; a transformed gas station in Marfa, Texas; a nunnery in Montréal, Canada; or a warehouse in Detroit, Michigan inspires "what-if" and "prove-it" conversations in the studio.

We've also found that the best topics for DesignInquiry are wide enough in scope for interpretation, yet suggestive enough to focus participants' attention. Over the years, the topics have included: JOY, Make/Do, Pass•Port, DesignCities, Being Here, DesignLess, and Access. The topic >>Fast Forward>>, for example, invited participants to rethink time, given the quickening pace of life over the last decade or two. One >>Fast Forward>> inquirer offered a "workshop of strategies" to ensure time for collaborative making and thinking. Another asked inquirers to invent a letterform to represent a sound in the English language that is not (yet) in the Latin alphabet. Peter Hall participated in >>Fast Forward>> long distance via Skype from Australia. We used the fourteen-hour time difference between Maine and Australia as a critical "from the future" >>Fast Forward>> vantage point when producing a video summary of work-in-progress.

For the STATION topic, participants were asked to consider: what are the "stations" of our work, interactions, and play? When our social networks are not only local, but also regional, global and frequently "virtual," where is activity situated? Do we yearn for both fixed place and transitory freedom? What are the tensions, if any, between these extremes? If mobility is privileged more, does place matter less? How might stations—their locations, design, histories, and potentials—benefit and/or hamper relationships and professional practices? One inquirer prompted STATION participants to explore time-based, continuous conditions, as opposed to physical places or nodes of activity, in a collaborative video workshop. In another STATION exercise an architect invited participants to create storyboards of journeys that examine the power of place as recorded by the senses and memory, and an artist and designer collaborated to investigate culinary practices from specific geographic locations. Inspired by culinary practices findings, the group then cooked for the whole week using only tools and sites

but rather is directed towards other human beings. We want to find beauty beyond all constraints. We want to look at websites, interfaces, movie titles, typefaces, TV graphics, printed matter of all kinds, logos, packaging, and magazines. We want to find the right way to acquire them—should an interface exist on its original support? Should it be interactive and should the public be able to experience it? Should it be simulated on a more current machine? Should its use be caught on video? We have a lot of work to do and many favors to call in.

Along the way, we are determined to pick and storm brains and to document the process in many ways. This written account is one, and I begin here by framing the context with a discussion of design in MoMA's collection. Museums exist to preserve selected objects that together build a consistent ensemble, and hopefully support and communicate a strong idea. In so doing, they are meant to educate and stimulate progress. Since design, both graphics and of objects, has a tremendous impact on everybody's life and a better understanding of it will work to everybody's advantage, a design museum is a meaningful and valuable construct.

At the Modern, all forms of design are introduced in strict relationship with the other forms of visual culture. Among Barr's many innovations was the establishment of six curatorial departments—Painting and Sculpture, Drawings, Prints and Illustrated Books, Film, Photography, and Architecture and Design. Interdisciplinarity facilitates the understanding of design's composite nature. The closeness to such an established discipline as architecture within one department, in particular, highlights the similarity among the design processes and gives depth to the criteria for judging the products by allowing them to go far beyond the consideration of the pure form. It so happens that many design curators at this museum, and I count myself among them, have been and are architects. On the other hand, the magnet of the fine arts has brought us to pay particular attention to aesthetics, by incorporating function in our original brand of sublime. I understand that this declaration might need further explanation.

Philip Johnson curated the Museum's second design exhibition, which also established the collection of design objects, in 1934. Machine Art, a unique display of mechanical parts, tools and objects, revealed to the world a new concept of beauty—defined in 1934 as "Platonic" because of its classical aesthetic derivation and its abstraction—based not only on form, but also on function. In 75 years, the department has produced several ideas and exhibitions, and the collection has evolved tremendously. And so has design. In February of 1994, we celebrated the exhibition's sixtieth anniversary with a renewed edition of the catalogue, for which Philip Johnson wrote a new preface. I quote from it: "How much has changed! Chaos theory has replaced classic certainties. We prefer Heraclitan flux to Platonic ideas, the principle of uncertainty to the model of perfection, complexity to simplicity." Design's appreciation still has to pass many filters, logic and aesthetics among them, but both logic and aesthetics are definitely not what they used to be. Objects carry baggage of motivations, meanings, and intentions. In order to communicate effectively with the public, today a curator has to explain the process behind every object and the program behind every architecture.

Part 4: Further reading

Anderson, S. (2015), "Critical Interfaces and Digital Making," in J. Barness and A. Papaelias (eds), Special Issue of *Visible Language: Critical Making Design and the Digital Humanities*, 49 (3): 120–39.

Banham, M. and P. Barker, S. Lyall, and C. Price (1996), *A Critic Writes: Essays by Reyner Banham*, Berkeley: University of California Press.

Bierut, M. (2013), "Graphic Design Criticism as a Spectator Sport," *Design Observer*, January 14. Available online: http://designobserver.com/feature/graphic-design-criticism-as-a-spectator-sport/37607/ (accessed January 7, 2017).

Bennett, A. (2006), *Design Studies: Theory and Research in Graphic Design*, New York: Princeton Architectural Press.

Bennett, A. (2012), "Good Design is Good Social Change: Envisioning an Age of Accountability in Communication Design Education." in Sharon Poggenpohl, ed., Special Issue of *Visible Language: Envisioning a Future of Design Education,* 46 (1–2): 67–78.

Blauvelt, A., ed. (1994–1995), *Visible Language: New Perspectives: Critical Histories of Graphic Design*, 28 (3), 28 (4), 29 (1).

Bush, A. (2016), "Double Vision: Graphic Design Criticism and the Question of Authority," in Francisco Laranjo, ed., *Modes of Criticism 2—Critique of Method*, 2: 9–24. Modes of Criticism Publication.

Camuffo, G. and M.D. Mura (2013), *Graphic Design Exhibition, Curating*, proceedings of the conference (Faculty of Design and Art of the Free University of Bolzano, June 26), Bolzano, Italy: bu,press.

Crouwel, W., ed. (2015), *The Debate: The Legendary Contest of Two Giants of Graphic Design: Wim Crouwel and Jan van Toorn*, New York: The Monacelli Press.

Crouwel, W. and J. van Toorn, (2015), *The Debate: The Legendary Contest of Two Giants of Graphic Design: Wim Crouwel and Jan van Toorn*, New York: The Monacelli Press.

Crow, D. (2015), *Visible Signs: An Introduction to Semiotics*, 3rd rev. edn, London: Fairchild Books.

de Smet, C. (2012), *Pour Une Critique Du Design Graphique*, Paris: Publisher Editions B42.

Drucker, J. (2013), "Critical Journalism in Graphic Design?" *Design and Culture: The Journal of the Design Studies Forum,* 5 (3): 395–8.

FitzGerald, K. (2015), "Fuck All," in Francisco Laranjo (ed), *Modes of Criticism 1—Critical, Uncritical, Post-critical,* 1: 87–94. Modes of Criticism Publication.

FitzGerald, K. and R. VanderLans (2010), *Writings on Graphic Design, Music, Art and Culture*, New York: Princeton Architectural Press.

Fuller, J. (n.d.), *Scratching The Surface*—A Podcast About the Intersection of Criticism and Practice for Graphic Designers. Various Podcasts, http://scratchingthesurface.fm (accessed June 4, 2017).

Heller, S. (2012), *Writing and Research for Graphic Designers*, Beverly, MA: Rockport Publishers.

Keys, Z. and M. Owens, eds (2007), *Forms of Inquiry: The Architecture of Critical Graphic Design*, London: Architectural Association.

Koskinen, I., and J. Zimmerman, T. Binder, J. Redstrom, and S. Vensween (2011), *Design Research Through Practice: From the Lab, Field, and Showroom,* Amsterdam: Elsevier.

Malpass, M. (2017), *Critical Design in Context: History, Theory and Practices*, London: Bloomsbury.

Meadows, D. (2003), "Digital Storytelling: Research-Based Practice in New Media," *Visual Communication* 2 (2): 189–93.

Schön, D. (1983), *The Reflective Practitioner*, New York: Basic Books.

Skaggs, S. (2017), *FireSigns: A Semiotic Theory for Graphic Design*, Cambridge, MA: MIT Press.

Twemlow, A. (2017), *Sifting the Trash: A History of Design Criticism*, Cambridge, MA: MIT Press.

Triggs, T. (2013), "Writing Design Criticism into History," *Design and Culture: The Journal of the Design Studies Forum,* 5 (1): 33–8.

Triggs, T. (2016), "Sites of Graphic Design Criticism New Spaces, New Critics," in R. Cunoa, and V.M. Almeida (eds), *Design, Identity and Complexity*, 102–19, Lisbon: Belas-Artes da Universiada de Lisboa.

Part 5

Political and social change

Part 5: Introduction

Political and social change is a significant issue in graphic design practice because graphic design is first and foremost about communication within and among cultures. Audiences and other stakeholders may vary widely, but a shared commitment to positive change suffuses most social design projects—a kind of design that focuses on solving social issues and promoting sustainability. The essays in this Part consider social design; they also touch on ways that designers have addressed feminism and political activism, identity politics, and global design. Several contributions present current projects and discuss contemporary ideas about social and political design.

The first Section, "Feminism and radical graphic design," concentrates on graphic design done in the service of feminism and political activism. The authors call attention to areas within the discipline in which women designers are underrepresented, and they demonstrate how designers and design can help precipitate political resistance or provoke social justice. The essays in the second Section, "Identity and world graphic design," examine the relationships among graphic design, popular culture, cultural identity, and globalism and localism. The networks linking globalism and localism are reflected in current interest in "glocal" design. The work in this Section also addresses contemporary extended design practices, in which clients, users, and designers work together to ferret out successful design solutions. While traditional "good" design was a single-designer focused operation in which the designer presented the end-product to the client, in contemporary extended practice designers become, in a sense, educational activists who encourage social and political interventions that embrace and inform all comers.

Sheila Levrant de Bretteville opens the "Feminism and radical graphic design" Section with her seminal essay, "Some aspects of design from the perspective of a woman designer" (1973). Levrant de Bretteville discusses how social activism informed her design work. She first observes that some kinds of simplification in design can undermine underrepresented groups, and then explores, in several case studies, how choice and complexity can encourage participation. Designer Sibylle Hagmann next ponders possible reasons behind, and solutions for, the lack of women type designers in "Non-existent design: women and the creation of type" (2005). Several years later, in "Pussy galore and the Buddha of the future" (2009), Catherine De Smet similarly wonders why women were mostly left out of histories of graphic design, and she seeks to revisit their importance in the history of the profession. De Smet attempts to rectify these omissions by highlighting selected work of pioneering women designers, such as MIT's Muriel Cooper, who produced provocative projects about women's causes. Despite a greater awareness of underrepresented voices in graphic design, De Smet remarks, ongoing reassessment of the skewed narratives of design history is necessary.

Political messages, and the ways that designers communicate them, are considered in the next two essays. Ken Garland published the "First Things First" manifesto in 1964 in the *Guardian* newspaper to push back against the rampant capitalist focus in graphic design. Signed by twenty-one graphic designers, and supported by 400 designers and artists, the manifesto called instead for design for the public good. The manifesto was updated and rewritten as "First Things First manifesto 2000," spearheaded by Tibor Kalman and the Canadian political magazine *Adbusters*. Jonathan Barnbrook and Anil Aykan's visual essay, "This year there is no manifesto" (2018), is a response of sorts to the "First Things First" manifestos of 1964 and 2000. Although Barnbrook and Aykan apparently agree with many of the principles in the "First Things First" manifestos, they suggest that rather than issuing manifestos, designers need to take personal responsibility for the impact their work has on society. Jan Van Toorn's visual essay, "Design and reflexivity" (1994), argues for communicative design that is produced through inclusive and reflexive practice, and that is also clear-sighted about its social ambitions. Clearly, inclusive and reflexive ways of working are not new: the ideas that are presented in the older essays in this Part are still relevant to contemporary practices.

In "Scissors and glue: punk fanzines and the creation of a DIY aesthetic" (2006), Teal Triggs discusses the graphic language of punk music fanzines. These DIY publications served as a visual medium of political resistance for both punk musicians and punk culture. Other forms of political activism have served comparable roles. Michael Dooley, for instance, discusses the street artist, graphic designer, and activist Shepard Fairey in his essay "He might be giant: Shepard Fairey" (2000). Dooley chronicles the thinking behind, and visual manifestations of, Fairey's provocative work, including *Giant* and Universal's *Man on the Moon* biopic projects. The popularization of Fairey's graphics by the mainstream press raises questions about "authenticity" and "selling-out," but this work likewise serves as a reminder of the power of images to communicate.

The second Section features essays about "Identity and world graphic design." There is an emerging discourse about decolonizing design (new work has come out as this *Reader* goes to press). Although timing prevents us from including this new work, the essays in this Section establish the foundations for discussions about design and diversity. In "From the outside in: a place for indigenous graphic traditions in contemporary South African graphic design" (2011), for instance, Piers Carey writes about indigenous South African graphic systems. He argues that effective communication happens when designers take into consideration the norms and cultures of their audiences—for example, the Zulu traditional symbols that are incorporated into the Siyazama Project AIDS symbol. Sylvia Harris similarly considers the norms and cultures of African-American designers and their audiences in "Searching for a Black aesthetic in American graphic design" (1998). Harris—whose ground-breaking work on African-American design still resonates despite her untimely death in 2011—offers a concise survey of the changing character of African-American design in America. She examines, among other periods, The New Negro Movement in art and design of the 1920s, the aesthetics of Black Power in the 1960s, and the new black media of the 1990s, including the magazine *YSB*.

In "Finding roots & taking flight: expression of identity in contemporary graphic design in India" (2018), Mohor Ray ponders the dichotomies of emerging Indian graphic design. Designers and initiatives such as Ek Type, Kulture Shop, and Anugraha, she explains, engage with Indian culture and identity. She notes that designers must be aware of stereotypes, however, when turning to Indian "roots," and they must make sure to explore new approaches to Indian design. Leong K. Chan similarly illustrates ways that ethnicity and identity are used in graphic design work in "Visualizing multi-racialism in

Singapore: graphic design as a tool for ideology and policy in nation building" (2011). The Singaporean government used both visual iconography and written language, Chan contends, to fashion a multi-racialist ideology that has shaped Singaporean culture.

Ryan Molloy defines "bling-bling" as "excessively decorated, lavish and often outsized jewelry and accessories" found within hip-hop culture. In his visual essay "'Iced up' and 'platinum plus': the development of hip-hop typographic ornaments" (2011), Molloy explains that his set of bling orna-ments, and his tongue-in-cheek essay design, glorify hip-hop excess and celebrate cultural and visual appropriation. Social and political implications are likewise relevant to Sean O'Toole, who argues that it is challenging to find a successful design approach to help mitigate the HIV/AIDS epidemic in South Africa. In "South African health campaigns dominate the political landscape" (2004), O'Toole bemoans the "clash of competing wills" that has undermined a range of efforts for South African HIV/AIDS preven-tion. Finally, in "Detachment and unification: a Chinese graphic design history in greater China since 1979" (2001), Wendy Siuyi Wong addresses previous work highlighting local design in China. She argues for the signal importance of a unified national history of Chinese graphic design rather than a series of disparate regional histories. In particular, Wong points out the increasing numbers of design practitioners, and the high quality of recent poster designs, from Mainland China. Wong elaborates the power of Chinese influences, and she points up the effect of Western design models in Chinese graphic design.

The essays in this Part present a genuine desire to engage with thorny challenges that confront graphic design. Some of the authors in this Part consider how these challenges may be addressed more effectively at local levels—they suggest that even small localized changes in how difficult issues are handled can ripple through the broader culture. Other essays contemplate how stakeholders can advance change together through democratic design processes for the social good. Social design and the role of the "citizen designer" are integral to contemporary progressive design practice. Design for the social good emerges as a conceptual thesis throughout *The Reader*, and it will continue to be a key theme in the profession.

Section 5.1

Feminism and radical graphic design

Chapter 5.1.1

Some aspects of design from the perspective of a woman designer

Sheila Levrant de Bretteville

Introduction

The design arts are public arts, and as such are major vehicles for forming our consciousness. Consciousness, in turn, is illuminated by communications, objects, buildings and environments. The design activity stands between us and our material existence, affecting not only our visual and physical environment but a sense of ourselves as well.

The process by which forms are made, and the forms themselves, embody values and standards of behaviour which affect large numbers of people and every aspect of our lives. For me, it has been this integral relationship between individual creativity and social responsibility that has drawn me to the design arts. It is possible and profitable to reinforce existing values through design. In my work, however, I try to project alternative values into society in the hope of creating a new, even utopian culture, by acting in accordance with values of my own choosing.

We can look at design and actually read its messages—thus we can locate, create and use positive modes which reject the repressive elements of dominant culture. I have been trying to use forms and processes which project and reassert aspects of society which—though of essential value—have been repressed, devalued and *restricted to women* in the private realm of the home.

As I become increasingly sensitive to those aspects of design which reinforce repressive attitudes and behaviour, I increasingly question the desirability of simplicity and clarity. The thrust to control almost inevitably operates through *simplification*. Control is undermined by ambiguity, choice and complexity, because subjective factors in the user become more effective and the user is invited to participate. *Participation undermines control.* The oversimplified, the unremittingly serious, the emphatically rational are the consistent attitudes associated with work adopted by major institutions and the men and few women who inhabit them. In the circle of cause and effect, these attitudes are reinforced and reproduced as they are visually and physically extended in our environment.

One means of simplification is to assign attributes to various groups and thereby reinforce divisions. The restriction of certain behaviour to the home and the making of women into the sole custodians of a range

---

First published in *Icographic*, 6 (1973): 4–8. © Sheila Levrant de Bretteville.

of human characteristics create a destructive imbalance. The design arts reinforce this imbalance by projecting the "male" tone only in the public realm of our large institutions: business, science, the military and even education, valuing their anonymous, authoritarian aspects and separating themselves further and further from the private realm, thus continuing to isolate women, female experience and "female" values.

Mass media and communications: a diagram of simplified separation

The mass media have a tradition of visual simplification in order to isolate their messages to attract attention. This simplification denies the complexity of life's experience. Simple statements, familiar and repeated imagery, sell the product and the idea most efficiently. They also reinforce restricting separations.

In advertising, women are described as, or permitted to be, laughing, crying, doubting, making mistakes, hesitating: women alone are seen as nurturing or as providing emotional support for children and men. When, for example, a company presents itself in a service capacity or as particularly accommodating, it uses a female figure and reinforces traditional attitudes by this symbolic imagery. The iconography for men is equally rigid. Men in work situations are shown as serious, decisive, professional, assured. No emotions, no fantasy; the few moments of relaxation or emotion permitted to men are relegated to leisure and the home. Likewise, the home becomes devalued as a place where no serious work can be done. As the woman is virtually seen only in the home, she too is devalued. By depicting women as exclusively emotional, doubting, cooperating and helping others, by only showing these activities in private, in the home, the polarities of what men and women are thought to be are reinforced and legitimized. In fact, the very characteristics which are allowed in women in the home, prevent success in the competitive public sector.

If the idea and the design are simple, complete and set, there is no opportunity to bring one's own values to the forms. If there is no ambiguity the eye is attracted once, the message understood and accepted quickly. When visual material is ambiguous the different nuances often encourage multiple and alternative reactions to the same communication. Were the mass media to include contradictions; were its images to contain suggestions rather than statements, the viewer could make an effort to bridge the gap, to interpolate, extrapolate, participate. But this is not the goal of mass media communication. Design as a problem-solving activity is assumed to involve only the acceptance by the designer of the aims of the client. If the client's goal is to sell a product or idea quickly, the problem does not include the encouragement of a thinking audience.

The modern movement in design encouraged a simplicity and clarity of form. This mode was embraced by some of the most creative and intelligent designers. It became fashionable to simplify for the clarity and power of the image, but as design becomes fashion, simplification becomes pernicious. This simplification in form and process leads to restricting and limiting separations and boundaries. By relaxing boundaries, by allowing more complexity in the image, designers could prevent this kind of visual fascism.

The reawakening of feminism has renewed the demand that the social expectations for both men and women be broadened, enabling all to participate freely in the social system according to the full range of their personalities, and allowing all individuals to create their behaviour from the whole spectrum of possibilities. Not only will we not know what immutable differences exist until expectations change, but the very values which are devalued and suppressed are consequently unavailable in viable form to both men and women. Designers could help to revalidate what have been designated as "female" values and devalued as such.

Publications: some alternative modes

People aware of design and its responsibilities are developing a design activity based on an ideology which encourages the emergence of the direct voice of the individuals who compose society.

The movements of the sixties questioned the structures and institutions that engender conformity. Alternative modes began to be developed that pointed out the limitations of hierarchical, one-directional channels of communication. For example, modern offset printing technology has begun to be used to create a model for participatory politics. By compiling a catalogue of goods and services recommended by a large number of contributors across the country, *The Whole Earth Catalog* re-established the value of individual subjectivity and designed a structure that encouraged user participation. This effort, as well as others of the youth, hippie, human-potential, counter-culture movements, helped validate some repressed "female" values, and encouraged the growth of the women's movement.

A similar attitude pervaded my design for a special publication for the International Design Conference in Aspen. Usually, six months after the conference, the participants receive a booklet containing excerpts of the speeches and comments by established and rising stars. Rather than impose my own understanding through this kind of control and simplification, I composed a newspaper of the direct voices of those participants who chose to record their experiences.

Cards were distributed on which any comments a participant might want to make could be written, drawn or typed. On the last night, these panels were glued together directly, forming pages. Then, through the use of an inexpensive, quick, rotary form of offset lithography, the newspaper was available in the morning. The distribution and assemblage of standardized panels created a non-hierarchical organization. All spreads were virtually alike, not one dominated, and all invited the readers to participate through choosing which entries to read and in what order. It is the readers who must create and combine these fragmented responses into their own personal picture of the conference. It was the participants who chose the fragments, the reader who organized them individually. As a designer, I created the structure which facilitated this process. The visual form of this newspaper was not the result of an effort to use a new form; new material, or new technological process, nor to develop a new or personal style. The forms were developed first to accord with a social context, to help achieve by their existence, the standard of behaviour they reflected. The forms are the visual expression of an effort to project information in such a way as to emphasize alternative standards of behaviour, alternative modes of design.

An increasing number of periodicals have begun to have guest editors, guest designers—*Radical Software, Design Quarterly*, *Arts in Society,* and others. As in the structure of *The Whole Earth Catalog,* special issues of publications provide alternatives to the small authoritarian establishment and expand the number of sources of information.

For example, I edited and designed a special issue of *Arts in Society* about California Institute of the Arts, a new community of the arts. The schools of this new institute were to open in one year, and I tried to create a graphic model that would reflect the formation of an alternative learning situation. These schools were being created by men who had been successful in the cultural establishment and were now creating an institution by working out some other ideas and goals, among them those of the movements of the sixties. I wanted to devise a design which would project the concepts of a horizontal, person-centred community. Every design decision was made to reinforce these concepts through the form of the publication.

I chose several types of visual and textual material and organized them in waves of information. Letters between the Provost and future faculty members were scattered throughout the magazine, as well as taped fragments of dean's meetings, memoranda, student applications. These were interspersed with photographs from television and newspapers which described the social context of the United States during the decade in which the institute was being planned. The organization of the magazine purposefully avoided the presentation of information in a simple, clearly logical, linear manner. Instead, it was diffuse and depended on repetition of similar content, similar forms, cycles, leitmotifs, in both the writing and the imagery. Many aspects of the book had to be reconceptualized and reorganized. The traditional table of contents, and its position in the book was not an appropriate form for introducing material. I substituted an alphabetical index placed after the first signature which included each type of information to be encountered in the book. Throughout the magazine, the author is listed by name only, and in the index, in alphabetical order. This was done in an effort to avoid hierarchy and authority and to guide the reader to a different way of reading.

The tentativeness of fragmented organization encouraged the reader to participate in the ultimate conceptualization of the community. Since California Institute of the Arts was yet to open, and consequently, was not clearly defined, its character could, in some sense, be shaped by the individual reader's subjective response. I felt that it was possible to establish a real and dynamic relationship between the institute and a readership. The non-hierarchical, fragmented organization, the diffusion of formal elements had become attractive to me as a visual projection of alternative modes of relationship. Certainly it is an alternative to the method of projecting set, simplistic messages that distort communications in the mass media.

Projecting data in a clear, systematized manner is most sensible in the communication of certain types of information, such as maps and catalogues, but when it is used to communicate ideas or information about people and their relationships, it distorts. Designers are taught to reduce ideas to their essence, but in fact that process too often results in the reduction of the ideas to only one of their parts. A more diffused manner of organizing material maintains enough complexity, subtlety and ambiguity to entice the readers who normally dart away with someone else's encapsulated vision, rather than remaining long enough and openly enough with the idea to make it their own.

I invited students in my class at CalArts to investigate this form and process, using content that was personally meaningful to them.

I asked them to create a whole of their own. The whole was to be greater than the sum of the parts. A woman student explained her solution:

Its cryptic presence overshadows that of its ingredients. We recognize these symbols in an understanding of their total symbology (or at the very least, in a resolution that they may be unified meaningfully) . . . Masculine hands describe, define, offer, repulse, threaten . . . the only feminine elements are solely and grotesquely sensual—bodies fulfilling a seemingly obligatory sexual role, and hair-do's delineating a faceless area, a non-existent identity . . . It seems that many of the superficial accoutrements of a culture are present, and yet little of the whole human being is seen. Despite the constant sexual innuendo, despite the care given to the tools of a communicative sort . . . despite the hands that gesticulate and promise or threaten . . . there is no real touching . . . the accoutrements, the parts have less graphic, linguistic and psychological importance than the whole.

As the community becomes used to ambiguity, complexity, subtlety in design and content, it will be more able to support the formation of individual conclusions, the expression of individual subjective opinions and will advocate the sharing of authority. For me this is a good, that Design can encourage.

The organization of material in fragments, multiple peaks rather than a single, climactic moment, has a quality and rhythm which may parallel women's ontological experience, particularly her experience of time. Although I came to use this fragmented organization in an effort to reflect a community of the arts in formation and to encourage the reader to participate, this form of visual organization corresponds more to a women's world.

There are several genres of women's work, quilts and blankets, for example, which are an assemblage of fragments generated whenever there is time, which are in both their method of creation as well as in their aesthetic form, visually organized into many centres. The quilting bee, as well as the quilt itself, is an example of the essentially non-hierarchical organization. Certainly the quality of time in a woman's life, particularly if she is not involved in the career thrust toward fame and fortune, is distinct from the quality of time experienced by men and women who are caught up in the progress of a career.

The linearity of time is foreign to the actual structure of a day as well as to the rhythm of women's monthly biological time. Thought processes released from the distortions of mechanical progress are complex, are laminated with myriad strings, are repetitive and permeated with the multiple needs of others as well as oneself. Unbounded relationships cause most women to think not only about work, but about the groceries needed, dinner, a child's dental problems, etc, in between thoughts about work. Women's tasks in the home are equally varied and open-ended—child-rearing is the classic example— while a man's work in the home has a beginning and an end, it has specific projects, like the fixing of windows, appliances or plumbing. The assemblage of fragments, the organization of forms in a complex matrix, projects this experience of time, suggests depth and intensity as an alternative to progress.

When the design arts are called upon to project aspects of the women's movements, it is particularly appropriate to challenge existent assumptions about form and process. When I was asked by a group of women artists to design a special issue of *Every woman*, a feminist newspaper, I tried to incorporate the visual projection of the egalitarian, collective form of the small group process. In weekly meetings, small groups of women throughout the country talk in turn so that those easily dissuaded from speaking by more vibrant, dominant personalities, are assured of being heard. In this *Every woman* design I avoided the associations of space and length of article with quality, and gave each woman a large photo of herself and a two-page spread, regardless of the length of her copy. I tried to link the spreads visually and to make no spread dominant. Looking alike, the articles did not visually compete with each other for the reader's attention; it was left to the reader to discern differences which might be subjectively more meaningful. In addition, I encouraged the women artists to stay within the limits of the budget and printing process used by the ongoing publication, even though they had access to special funds.

It seemed that we could provide a more viable model if we did not inflate the object and participate in the existent attitude that whatever is technologically or financially possible must be made available—at least to a few.

Designing a structure that will encourage participating, non-hierarchical, non-authoritarian relationships between the designer and the user, also results in visual and physical forms that are outside the mainstream of design as much as these ideas and attitudes are outside mainstream culture. The way these publications look is different from the way our national publications look: this difference is much less the result of creating another style of designing structures which encourage different values. Desirable as it is that these values become diffused into society, such design structures are often modest in appearance, rather than powerful, elegant, simplified, clear and dynamic forms. Perhaps the importance of dynamic visual relations should be questioned and quiet, literary forms re-evaluated.

Design appears to be a particularly ambiguous enterprise—and design for social change, even more so—in comparison with the other arts. The designer is often paid by those very institutions which would be affected by her attitudes in forming and shaping design: the contradictions for a free-lance designer who wishes to effect social change is thus apparent. Because design is attached to the world of business and industry in this way, it is difficult to know in advance if one's design will be used to reinforce values that the designer opposes.

Designers must work in two ways. We must create visual and physical designs which project social forms but simultaneously we must create the social forms which will demand new visual and physical manifestations. Those designs of mine which I have discussed are the products of situations in which I was called upon to give physical form to efforts to create new social contexts. In this case, the major thrust was to rethink assumptions—profit was not a consideration and the budget was modest, and the audience (unfortunately) was limited. In this way I was exempt from the pressures that make it difficult for a larger, money-making project. But as such situations are rare and because I could no longer separate physical and social design, I found myself needing to create an interface. I wanted to investigate the possibility of working with other women. I allowed myself to indulge the notion that this method would locate problems and design solutions free of the design system in which both commercial stars and commercial hacks were always subject to the pecuniary ethos. Further, without losing the social context implied in the activity of design, I had actively to erode the idea of design as a private activity. It has always been the public nature and responsibility of design that I have believed definitive. Accordingly, I initiated a *Women's Design Program* at California Institute of the Arts. In this program I was able to explore the relationship between design and feminism. The personal and ideological involvement offered the opportunity of finding a sphere of action that allowed these values to survive. I wanted to give attention not so much to what could be produced as to an operative ethic. That does not mean that we were not to design using concrete forms, but points to the need to protect these ideas from being buried under the subservient design process. Working with communications, rather than object-making, made it easier to infuse a design with these attitudes.

It was clear to me that women designers could only locate and solve design problems in a responsive way if they simultaneously studied their own history, tried to isolate female values and worked cooperatively. I designed procedures and projects which could reinforce the idea that design is a social in the production of metal type. Graphic designers gained easy access to designing their own fonts as type design and production moved closer together. These technological advancements led to an increased "democratization" of type production; they marked the rise of the independent type designer and the exhilaration of intensive typographic inventions. Over the last few years this type euphoria has dulled down as the deconstruction and mismatching of (existing) digital typefaces have been exhausted.

Another reason for the calming of the typeface development frenzy might be the difficulties of earning sufficient revenues from type design, which in turn put a damper on revolutionary ambitions. Despite the fact that the creation and production of type became a more woman-friendly working process and therefore opened up opportunities for female designers to practice in this field more than ever before, type design nevertheless remains predominantly a white, Western, male working field. The creation of letters is an expert profession traditionally dominated by men. By the nineteenth century, women were employed in the printing industry to polish imperfections from metal type. At the end of the century Linn Boyd Benton and RV Waldo developed the pantographic punch-cutting machine.[4]

This marked the beginning of the development of hot-metal composing machines produced by Linotype and Monotype. The development of the pantographic punch-cutting technique made it possible, for the first time, to produce punches in different sizes from a single pattern. A typeface offered, for example, by Monotype in a range of sizes involved the preparation of large numbers of character drawings. The drawings from which the patterns for punch-cutting were produced were prepared in the type drawing office. The key priority was to adhere as much as possible to the type designer's original intentions. Judging from a number of photographs demonstrating the working processes at Monotype, c. 1956, reproduced in *Type and Typography* (Baines and Haslam, 2002), these tasks were carried out by less-skilled labor (token women), while the actual design of letter forms remained a male domain (Figure 5.2, 5.3, and 5.4).

Figure 5.2 Translating the designer's idea into working drawings with the use of a set square and French curves. © 1956. Public Domain. Originally published in *The Monotype Recorder*, 40 (3) (Autumn 1956). Reprinted in *Type & Typography* (2002), p. 77. Authors: Phil Baines and Andrew Haslam. Publisher: Watson-Guptill.

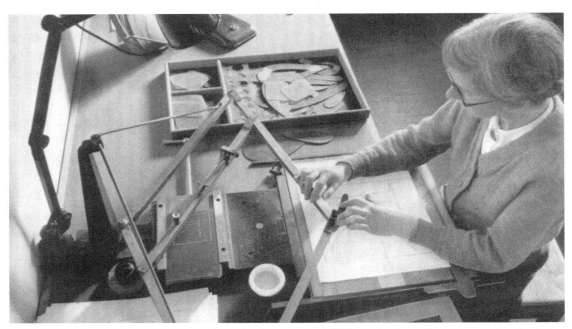

Figure 5.3 Tracing the working drawing on the table of a pantograph. While tracing the outline of the drawing, the design was cut at a reduced size into a wax-coated glass plate. © 1956. Public Domain. Originally published in *The Monotype Recorder*, 40 (3) (Autumn 1956). Reprinted in *Type & Typography* (2002), p. 77. Authors: Phil Baines and Andrew Haslam. Publisher: Watson-Guptill.

Figure 5.4 Checking for the accuracy of the outline wax pattern. © 1956. Public Domain. Originally published in *The Monotype Recorder*, 40 (3) (Autumn 1956). Reprinted in *Type & Typography* (2002), p. 77. Authors: Phil Baines and Andrew Haslam. Publisher: Watson-Guptill.

Chapter 5.1.3

Pussy Galore and the Buddha of the future: women, graphic design, etc.

Catherine de Smet
(Translated from the French by Miriam Rosen)

She felt in italics and thought in capitals.

—Henry James, *The Figure in the Carpet* (1896)

"Fun things to do in museums: invade the bookstore. Slap stickers to alter book titles." Most essays on graphic design would merit a corrective analogous to what the Guerrilla Girls recommend in their *Art Museum Activity Book,* where the proposed stickers are intended to transform the cover of a *History of Art* into a *History of Mostly Male Art.*[1] As a recent discipline, graphic design history might well have been expected to adopt more egalitarian habits from the outset, but even today, the attention paid to women who have worked in the field remains slight. The fact that they were a minority during much of the twentieth century does not explain such treatment, even from a point of view dominated by the most traditional values, exalting the heroic figure of the innovative creator. Indeed, even those women who seemingly complied in every way with the profile required for figuring in the textbooks have been excluded nonetheless. Such is the case of Muriel Cooper: despite the fact that she co-founded the Visible Language Workshop at the Massachusetts Institute of Technology (MIT) in 1973 and headed it until her death in 1994, Philip Meggs does not mention her in any of the successive editions of his pioneering work *A History of Graphic Design* (in spite of the corrections introduced over the years).[2] Initially published in 1983, this history, which runs from the Lascaux caves to the contemporary period, was the first of its kind and still remains a major reference work. As a creator, researcher and teacher at a leading institution like MIT, Cooper, a pioneer of interactive design, clearly belongs to the category of influential figures who would normally be cited by those, like Meggs, seeking to provide readers with a survey of the field concerned. She was one of the first graphic designers convinced of the importance of computer technology and immediately sought to introduce high visual standards for the layout of the information

First published in Catalogue *elles@centrepompidou: Women Artists in the Collections of the Centre Pompidou.* (2009), 309–13. © Editions du Centre Pompidou/Catherine de Smet.

presented, and animated, on the screen. In addition, she trained and inspired several generations of students.[3] Meggs' book can be reproached for its Western, English-speaking and more specifically United States orientation, but the reasons which might have motivated the omission of the American citizen Cooper must be sought elsewhere. It is also true that Meggs, who had little familiarity with the new technologies, privileged traditional graphic design media, but this second limiting factor still does not allow us to understand the exclusion of Cooper, who was also art director of the MIT Press and as such realized many memorable layouts associating the principles of a functional sobriety inherited from European modernism with elements inspired by contemporary daily life.[4] Among her notable contributions to editorial creation was the clean, airy layout of the original edition of *Learning from Las Vegas*.[5] Cooper was also responsible for a logo of exemplary visual quality and effectiveness—that of the MIT Press itself (Figure 5.6). Designed in 1963, it is still in use today: seven vertical black bars of equal width, with the two at the far right extended, one upwards, for the ascender of the T, and the other downwards, for the descender of the P. It is only at second glance that the publishing house's initials emerge from the compact geometric image—a remarkable instance of visual economy in the conception of a symbol.

Thus, nothing justifies Meggs' omission—apart from the fact that Cooper was a woman and one who, in addition, did not seek to promote her own name but on the contrary, privileged the spirit of collective work which characterizes design practice. In fact, integrating Cooper into the Pantheon of twentieth-century graphic design as a single individual, duly glorified according to the current criteria, would have betrayed the feminist cause, for which it is indispensable to call into question the tools used in the construction of history. Indeed, the term "pioneer," which I myself applied to Cooper earlier on, is also suspect: In an article reviewing the feminist positions relative to design in the professional literature, Carma R. Gorman indicates, "Describing an artist or a designer as a 'pioneer' suggests (at least to me) a desire to position that person within a eurocentric, masculinist, modernist canon of 'greats'."[6] In

Figure 5.6 MIT Press logo. © 1963. Designer: Muriel Cooper, for The MIT Press. Reproduced courtesy of The MIT Press.

support of her argument, she cites a review by Ellen Mazur Thomson denouncing the biographical approach of an essay devoted to graphic designer Cipe Pineles: "To concentrate on the life of individual designers would appear to distort graphic design history."[7] Pineles was a magazine art director trained by Mehemed Fehmy Aghi at *Vogue* and *Vanity Fair* in the 1930s and a teacher at the Parsons School of Design in New York. But she also married two famous graphic designers, William Golden and Will Burtin—information which accompanies the smallest note on her career, whereas, obviously, the reverse is rarely true. Only a radically different perspective would permit an adequate appreciation of women's activity, for it cannot be recognized without being associated with other productions which have been hidden or marginalized until now, as the fruits of the practice of individuals insufficiently esteemed within western society or coming from other cultures, and for whom the idea of the "author" is not necessarily important.[8] This is what Cheryl Buckley, for example, maintains in her article "Made in Patriarchy," which calls for a redefinition of design in order to include craft production.[9] Johanna Drucker and Emily McVarish pursue a similar vein in their *Graphic Design History. A Critical Guide,* where they include ephemera—posters and other anonymous signs usually absent from general histories of graphic design—and place the objects, more than individual creators, at the heart of their approach (but without failing to mention Muriel Cooper).[10] If the corpus studied by Drucker and McVarish attests to a desire to modify the conventional perception of graphic design, however, it still remains a prisoner of the Anglo-American, or North American, geographical sphere, especially for the contemporary period. The decentering process now underway must also lead, as Buckley, Gorman and others have suggested, to new attention brought to bear on what is happening in countries which have been less well served by historians, without forgetting that such countries may, like France, be located in the West.

The defence of women's rights and feminist demands has, like all social struggles, made use of street posters, the distribution of leaflets and other printed matter and the publication of ads in the press, and they have seized on all the media permitting the combination of text and image, from t-shirts and buttons to cyberspace. In *Suffragettes to She-Devils*, Liz McQuiston explores the women's movement through a visual compendium of its graphics.[11] Whether signed by one person or a collective, or strictly anonymous, such works most often draw on the typographic and iconographic vocabulary of their times. Apart from the plus sign surmounted by a circle which became the movement's symbol in the 1960s and underwent multiple manipulations in order to stress its activist intent (in particular, the addition of a clenched fist), no distinctive sign runs through the whole of this production. On the contrary, we often sense the desire to employ the most ordinary communication codes. Thus, the Guerrilla Girls posters, without departing from the rules of professional-quality design, do not show any particular stylistic pursuit, and the subversion of their famous ad "The Advantage of Being a Woman Artist" recently proposed by the young New York art collective LTTR ("The Advantage of Being a Lesbian Artist," signed Ridykeulous, Figure 5.7), uses the effects of hand-written correction—heavy, awkward cross-outs, irregular letters—and the raw look of the four strips of masking tape hastily tacked around the edges of the sheet. Such an improvised, do-it-yourself esthetic is present in the group's other works and often found in the most recent international graphic production.[12]

Graphic designers committed to the women's cause have made use of their skills and means in a specific way. Sheila Levrant de Bretteville, who set up the Women's Design program at the California

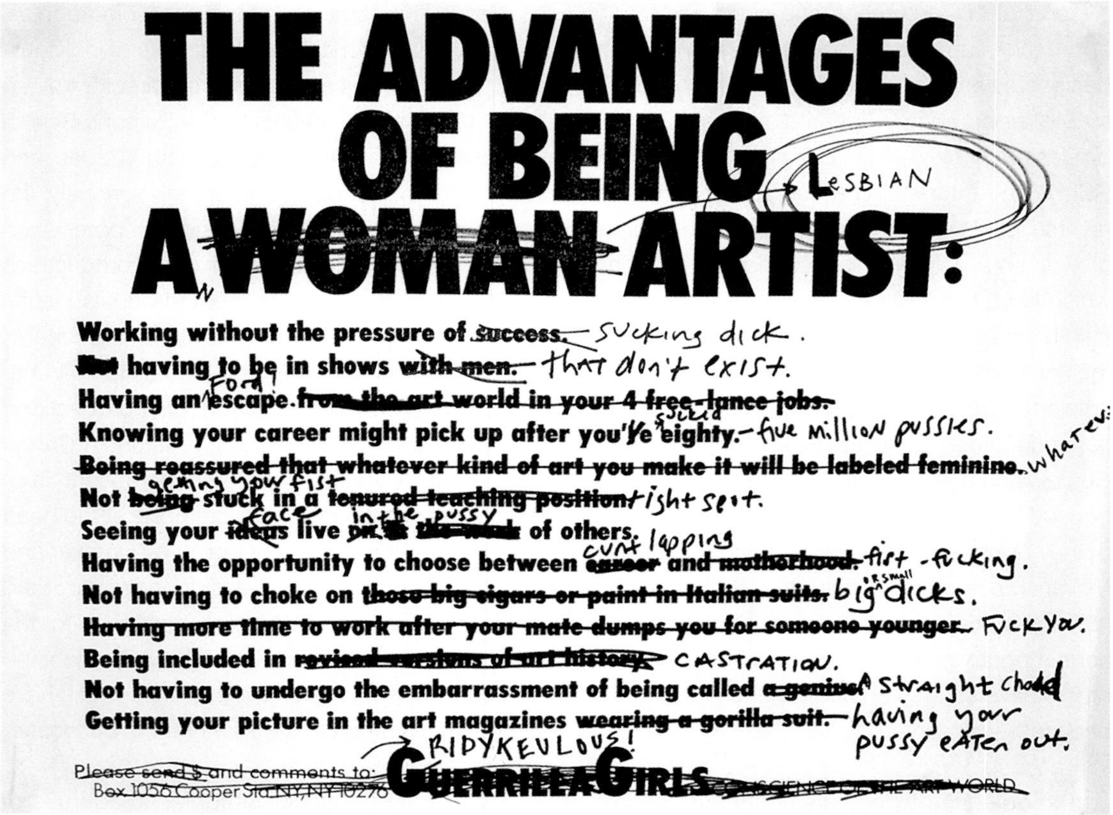

Figure 5.7 The Advantages of Being a Lesbian Artist. © 2006. Designers: A.L. Steiner and Nicole Eisenman. Courtesy of Ridykeulous.

Institute of the Arts (CalArts) in Los Angeles in 1971, has developed collective practices based on user participation and the sharing of experiences.[13] In her view, it was clear that "women designers could only locate and solve design problems in a responsive way if they simultaneously studied their own history, tried to isolate female values and worked cooperatively."[14] The poster *Pink is Childish* (1974, Figure 5.8) which she designed at the request of the American Institute of Graphic Design (AIGA) for an exhibition on the colour pink at the Whitney Museum of American Art, illustrates her positions and her concern with bringing out multiple voices. Its patchwork composition—alluding to a woman's craft—reproduces in their original state texts and/or images contributed by different women asked to comment on the significance the colour pink had for them. Two decades later, when the new possibilities of computer graphics were setting off a typographic fervor among graphic designers, Siân Cook, Liz McQuiston and Teal Triggs, associated under the banner of the Women's Design and Research Unit (WD + RU) in Great Britain, created *Pussy Galore* (Figure 5.9), a font comprised of different kinds of signs (pictograms, words or expressions, isolated or grouped together) playing on several semantic levels accessed with the computer keyboard. The name comes from the high-powered heroine of the James Bond novel *Goldfinger*, incarnated in the 1964 movie version by Honor Blackman.[15] The aim was to provide, with a

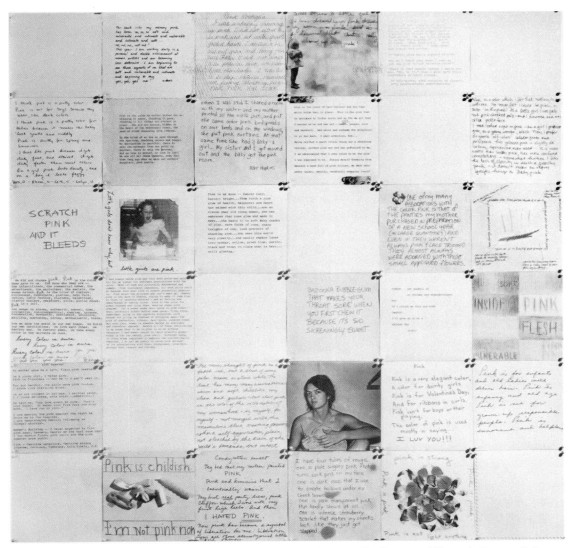

Figure 5.8 Pink is Childish poster (1974). Designer: Sheila Levrant de Bretteville. Courtesy of Women's Community Inc.

good dose of irony, an "interactive tool" which would allow anyone to compose personalised messages by delving into an activist repertory (the project was conceived for an issue of the typographic magazine *Fuse* on the theme of propaganda).[16] The considerable imbalance between the sexes which prevailed in graphic design until the past few decades seems to be declining.[17] The anecdote about the hiring of typographer and printing historian Beatrice Warde in 1926—she was approached by the Monotype foundry in London because they thought she was a man, owing to the male pseudonym she used to sign her articles in *The Fleuron*—belongs to the past. Nonetheless, as German font designer Sybille Hagmann indicated in 2005, her profession remains predominantly male.[18] And the visibility of women

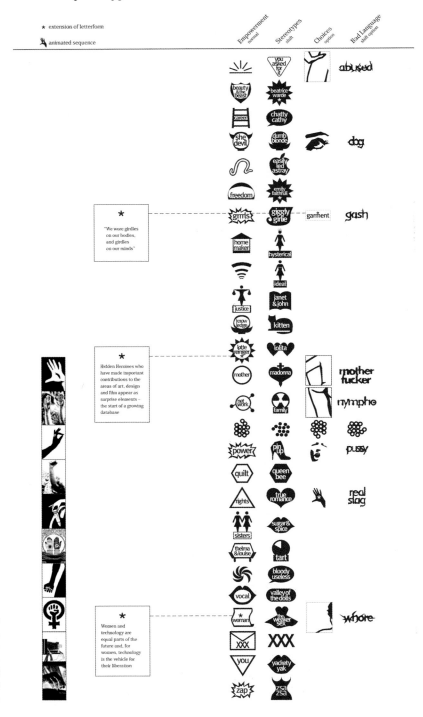

is still grossly inferior to that of men, as reflected in specialized reviews, magazines, books, conferences and exhibitions. Notwithstanding the risk that the criterion of "gender" can be used to other ends, the present situation provides a convincing argument for the interest of exhibitions or essays exclusively devoted to the creation of women graphic designers and thus liable to change a persistent discriminatory tendency.[19] Throughout *What Is Graphic Design?*, the book's author, Quentin Newark, employs the pronoun "she" to designate the graphic designer rather than the *conventional* "he"; in addition to stressing the mixed nature of the profession, this substitution (worthy of the feminist *herstory* of the 1960s) also serves to recall the machismo of lexical uses.

Some authors have attempted to repopulate the history of the book and printing with the women figures who have been unjustly excluded from it, despite the fact that they were active from the fifteenth century on, in a field supposed to be exclusively male.[20] This much-needed research effort becomes even more convincing when the foregrounding of women's work also opens unexpected doors or sheds new light on what were thought to be familiar subjects. As is the case, for example, with Swiss typography specialist and font designer François Rappo: recalling that France, "in typography as elsewhere, is modern but no longer aware of it," he cites the ("amazing") research of Jeanne Veyrin-Forrer, whose book *La Lettre et le Texte* reveals a "three-hundred-year field of graphical modernity [. . .] within the reach of your pencil."[21] Veyrin-Forrer, director of the Rare Books Collection at the Bibliothèque Nationale de France, studied the work of Auguereau, Garamond, the Fourniers and the Didots and was one of the first in France to adopt the principles of the Anglo-American analytical bibliography, which profoundly transformed the history of the book. Going back even further, to the origins of printing. Far Eastern historian T.H. Barrett has devoted a study to the woman he considers the real inventor of printing, towards the end of the seventh century: the Chinese empress Wu–who chose to be called "Iron Lady," "Wise Mother," "Emperor" (in the masculine) or "Buddha of the Future."[22] By drawing attention to this remarkable person and stressing the continuity between wooden and lead type, Barrett questions Western knowledge about the history of mechanical reproduction of text, invented seven centuries before Gutenberg, on another continent and under the impulse of a woman. In particular, he insists on the importance of the Chinese religious context of the period for understanding the reasons behind the spread of block printing during Wu's reign and thus broadens our knowledge of the development of a technology with major cultural impact.

Contemporary research on graphic design and the role played by women changes the way we look at the past of the book, writing and printing. Beyond the necessary reintegration of neglected works and creators, it imposes a continuous reappraisal of a history which is all the more open because of the newness of the discipline itself. Women's voices from the past can also help to bring out what is sometimes still difficult to express today and to recall the virtues of otherness for revitalizing our ways of seeing. In eleventh-century Japan, the woman of letters Sei Shÿnagon expressed better than anyone else the power of the visual presentation of information. The lists of objects, impressions and feelings in her *Pillow Book* include a category based on the image of words which serves to bring out the importance of such an image for our perception of the world: "Words That Look Commonplace but That Become Impressive When Written in Chinese Characters: strawberries, a dew-plant, a prickly water-lily, walnut, a Doctor of Literature, a Provisional Senior Steward in the Office of the Emperor's Household, a red myrtle."[23] An original way of thinking about graphic design.

Notes

1. Guerrilla Girls, *Art Museum Activity Book* (New York: Printed Matter, Inc., 2004), p. 12.
2. Philip B. Meggs, *A History of Graphic Design* (1983) (New York: John Wiley & Sons, 1998). I am referring here to the last edition published during the author's lifetime; a new edition, entitled *Meggs' History of Graphic Design,* revised by Alston Purvis, was published in 2005.
3. Among Cooper's students, we may cite John Maeda, who succeeded her at MIT and, through his books, lectures and exhibitions, helped to convince a growing public of the possibilities offered by the encounter of computers and graphic design. On Cooper, see David Reinfurt's extensive study of her work, "This stands as a sketch for the future. Muriel Cooper and the Visible Language Workshop," 2007: http://www.o-r-g.com/view.html? project = 117
4. For example, Herbert Muschamp's *File Under Architecture,* printed on brown wrapping paper with the text composed on an IBM typewriter, or Edward Allen's *The Responsive House,* where the sub-title "Do Your Own Thing," roughly drawn in large, irregular white capital letters on the cover, is juxtaposed with the title in Helvetica type discreetly placed in the upper portion of the page.
5. Robert Venturi, Denise Scott Brown, Steven Izenour, *Learning From Las Vegas* (Cambridge, MA: MIT Press, 1972). The authors abandoned this layout as of the first new edition, in particular because of the Bauhaus influence they detected and considered unsuited to the content of a book intended to criticize the latter's mark on architectural design. On Cooper's layout and graphic changes between the first and subsequent editions, see in particular Michael Golec, "'Doing It Dead Pan' Venturi, Scott Brown and Izenour's *Learning from Las Vegas*," *Visible Language,* 37 (1) (2004): 266–87.
6. Carma R. Gorman, "Reshaping and Rethinking: Recent Feminist Scholarship on Design and Designers," *Design Issues,* 17 (4) (Autumn 2001): 72–88.
7. Ellen Mazur Thomson, review of Martha Scottford's *Cipe Pineles: A Life of Design,* in Pat Kirkham and Ella Howard (eds), *Women Designers in the USA, 1900–2000,* special issue of *Studies in the Decorative Arts,* 8 (1) (Autumn–Winter 2000–2001). Cited by Carma R. Gorman, op. cit., p. 76.
8. David Reinfurt's booklet on Muriel Cooper, op. cit., is presented as a "work-in-progress," which seemed to the author "like the right approach to Muriel's work"—i.e., an alternative to the conventional monograph.
9. Cheryl Buckley, "Made in Patriarchy: Toward a Feminist Critique of Design," *Design Issues,* 3 (2) (Spring 1986): 3–14.
10. Johanna Drucker and Emily McVarish, *Graphic Design History. A Critical Guide* (New York: Prentice Hall, 2008).
11. Liz McQuiston, *Suffragettes to She-Devils* (London: Phaidon, 1997).
12. I would like to thank Sofia Hernandez for having brought the LTTR collective to my attention: http://www.lttr.org/journal/5/the-advantages-of-being-a-lesbian-woman-artist.
13. See the extensively documented article by Benoît Buquet, "Art, graphisme et féminisme à Los Angeles autour de Sheila Levrant de Bretteville," *Histoire de l'art,* 63 (October 2008): 123–32.
14. Sheila Levrant de Bretteville, "Some Aspects of Design from the Perspective of a Woman Designer," *Icographic,* 6 (1973): 6.
15. In the film version of *Goldfinger*, Pussy Galore, a pilot at the head of a squadron of young Amazons, declares herself immune to male seduction (which is refuted by what follows).
16. *Fuse 12: Propaganda,* Winter 1994.
17. In 1988, Liz McQuiston, citing an article which had recently appeared in *ID Magazine,* stated that the proportion of women in the field had gone from 25 percent to 52 percent between 1980 and 1985 *Women in Design* (London: Trefoil Publications, 1988), p. 6. Thirteen years later, Maud Lavin, in the introduction to her "Portfolio: Women and Design" *Clean New World* (Cambridge, MA: MIT Press, 2001), p. 108, cites a publication of the

American Institute of Graphic Design (AIGA) indicating that there are now more women entering the profession than men—but that women are still less well paid.

18. Sybille Hagmann, "Non Existent Design: Women and the Creation of Type," *Visual Communication,* 4 (2) (June 2005): 186–94.

19. Besides the works by Liz McQuiston and Maud Lavin's "Portfolio" essay already mentioned, we may cite in particular two essays by Ellen Lupton: "Graphic Design in the Urban Landscape," in Joan Rothschild (ed.), *Design and Feminism: Re-Visioning Spaces, Places, and Everyday Things* (New Brunswick, NJ: Rutgers University Press, 1999), and "Women Graphic Designers," in Pat Kirkham (ed.), *Women Designers in the USA, 1900–2000: Diversity and Difference* (catalogue of the exhibition of the same name at Bard Graduate Center for Studies in the Decorative Arts, Design and Culture [New Haven/London: Yale University Press, 2000]) (also available on the author's website: http://www.elupton.com/index), as well as Bryony Gomez-Palacio and Armin Vit's recent *Women of Design. Influence and Inspiration from the Original Trailblazers to the New Groundbreakers* (Cincinnati, OH: HOW Books, 2008). It should also be recalled that the 2007 Échirolles graphic design festival, in France, included an exhibition entitled "9 Women Graphic Designers."

20. See in particular Jef Tombeur, *Women in the Printing Trade* (Mons, Belgium: Talus d'approche/Paris: Convention typographique, 2004) and Paul W. Nash, "The Distaff Side: A Short History of Female Printer," *Ultrabold*, 1 (Autumn 2006): 12–18.

21. François Rappo, "Vieille France," *Sang Bleu,* 3–4 (December 2008), available (in English) on the site http://ianparty.com/;Jeanne Veyrin-Forrer, *La Lettre et le Texte. Trente années de recherche sur l'histoire du livre* (Paris: École nationale supérieure de jeunes filles, 1987).

22. T.H. Barrett, *The Woman Who Discovered Printing* (New Haven and London: Yale University Press, 2007).

23. *The Pillow Book of Sei Shÿnagon,* Ivan Morris (trans. and ed.) (New York: Columbia University Press, 1967), p. 159.

Not visual essays

Chapter 5.1.4

First Things First manifesto, 1964
First Things First Manifesto 2000, 1999

Ken Garland and Adbusters

Editors' note: Manifestos have long been a favored format for graphic designers whose political positions or motives are declared in statements and made public. Here we republish two versions of the *First Things First* manifesto, which clearly reflect the mood of the periods in which they were created: 1964 and 1999, respectively. The authors and signators are critical of the economic conditions underpinning the profession, which they see as complicit in promoting a specific ideology of commercialization and consumer culture.

Figure 5.10 *First Things First* manifesto. © 1964. Author: Ken Garland. Written and proclaimed at the Institute of Contemporary Arts on an evening in December 1963, the manifesto was published in January 1964. © Ken Garland.

A manifesto

We, the undersigned, are graphic designers, photographers and students who have been brought up in a world in which the techniques and apparatus of advertising have persistently been presented to us as the most lucrative, effective and desirable means of using our talents. We have been bombarded with publications devoted to this belief, applauding the work of those who have flogged their skill and imagination to sell such things as:

cat food, stomach powders, detergent, hair restorer, striped toothpaste, aftershave lotion, beforeshave lotion, slimming diets, fattening diets, deodorants, fizzy water, cigarettes, roll-ons, pull-ons and slip-ons.

By far the greatest time and effort of those working in the advertising industry are wasted on these trivial purposes, which contribute little or nothing to our national prosperity.

In common with an increasing number of the general public, we have reached a saturation point at which the high pitched scream of consumer selling is no more than sheer noise. We think that there are other things more worth using our skill and experience on. There are signs for streets and buildings, books and periodicals, catalogues, instructional manuals, industrial photography, educational aids, films, television features, scientific and industrial publications and all the other media through which we promote our trade, our education, our culture and our greater awareness of the world.

We do not advocate the abolition of high pressure consumer advertising: this is not feasible. Nor do we want to take any of the fun out of life. But we are proposing a reversal of priorities in favour of the more useful and more lasting forms of communication. We hope that our society will tire of gimmick merchants, status salesmen and hidden persuaders, and that the prior call on our skills will be for worthwhile purposes. With this in mind, we propose to share our experience and opinions, and to make them available to colleagues, students and others who may be interested.

Edward Wright
Geoffrey White
William Slack
Caroline Rawlence
Ian McLaren
Sam Lambert
Ivor Kamlish
Gerald Jones
Bernard Higton
Brian Grimbly
John Garner
Ken Garland
Anthony Froshaug
Robin Fior
Germano Facetti
Ivan Dodd
Harriet Crowder
Anthony Clift
Gerry Cinamon
Robert Chapman
Ray Carpenter
Ken Briggs

Published by Ken Garland, 13 Oakley Sq NW1
Printed by Goodwin Press Ltd. London N4

FIRST THINGS FIRST MANIFESTO 2000

We, the undersigned, are graphic designers, art directors and visual communicators who have been raised in a world in which the techniques and apparatus of advertising have persistently been presented to us as the most lucrative, effective and desirable use of our talents. Many design teachers and mentors promote this belief; the market rewards it; a tide of books and publications reinforces it.

Encouraged in this direction, designers then apply their skill and imagination to sell dog biscuits, designer coffee, diamonds, detergents, hair gel, cigarettes, credit cards, sneakers, butt toners, light beer and heavy-duty recreational vehicles. Commercial work has always paid the bills, but many graphic designers have now let it become, in large measure, *what graphic designers do*. This, in turn, is how the world perceives design. The profession's time and energy is used up manufacturing demand for things that are inessential at best.

Many of us have grown increasingly uncomfortable with this view of design. Designers who devote their efforts primarily to advertising, marketing and brand development are supporting, and implicitly endorsing, a mental environment so saturated with commercial messages that it is changing the very way citizen-consumers speak, think, feel, respond and interact. To some extent we are all helping draft a reductive and immeasurably harmful code of public discourse.

There are pursuits more worthy of our problem-solving skills. Unprecedented environmental, social and cultural crises demand our attention. Many cultural interventions, social marketing campaigns, books, magazines, exhibitions, educational tools, television programs, films, charitable causes and other information design projects urgently require our expertise and help.

We propose a reversal of priorities in favor of more useful, lasting and democratic forms of communication — a mindshift away from product marketing and toward the exploration and production of a new kind of meaning. The scope of debate is shrinking; it must expand. Consumerism is running uncontested; it must be challenged by other perspectives expressed, in part, through the visual languages and resources of design.

In 1964, 22 visual communicators signed the original call for our skills to be put to worthwhile use. With the explosive growth of global commercial culture, their message has only grown more urgent. Today, we renew their manifesto in expectation that no more decades will pass before it is taken to heart.

Jonathan Barnbrook
Nick Bell
Andrew Blauvelt
Hans Bockting
Irma Boom
Sheila Levrant de Bretteville
Max Bruinsma
Siân Cook
Linda van Deursen
Chris Dixon
William Drenttel
Gert Dumbar
Simon Esterson
Vince Frost
Ken Garland
Milton Glaser
Jessica Helfand
Steven Heller
Andrew Howard
Tibor Kalman
Jeffery Keedy
Zuzana Licko
Ellen Lupton
Katherine McCoy
Armand Mevis
J. Abbott Miller
Rick Poynor
Lucienne Roberts
Erik Spiekermann
Jan van Toorn
Teal Triggs
Rudy VanderLans
Bob Wilkinson

Figure 5.11 *First Things First Manifesto 2000*. © 1999. Author: Adbusters. This was an updated version of Ken Garland's original inspirational 1964 manifesto. Signed by some of the most prominent designers around the world, the new version was launched in *Adbusters*, *AIGA Journal*, *Blueprint*, *Emigre*, *Eye*, *Items*, and *Form* magazines.

Visual essay

Chapter 5.1.5

This year there is no manifesto

Jonathan Barnbrook and Anıl Aykan Barnbrook

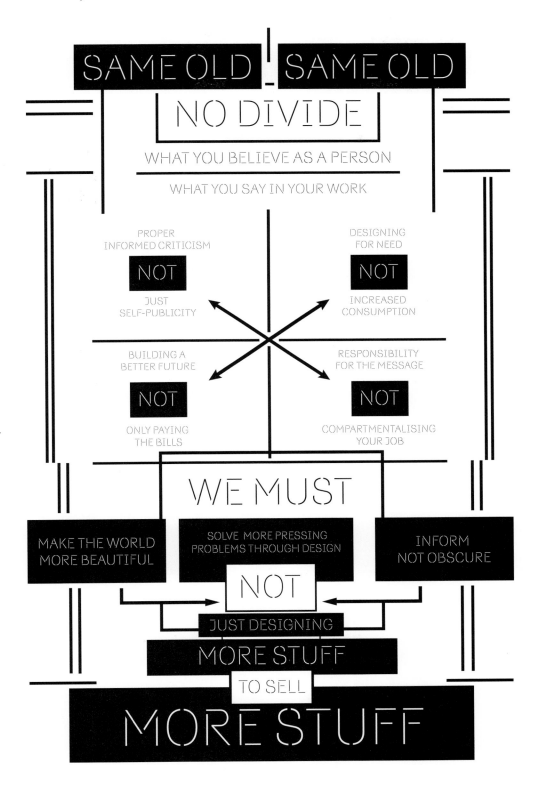

Visual essay

Chapter 5.1.6

Design and reflexivity

Jan van Toorn

First published in *Visible Language*, 28 (4) (1994): 316–25. © Jan van Toorn.

cation. This communicative dependency is particularly evident in the "solutions" that the dominant culture proposes for the social, economic, and political problems of what is defined as the "periphery"—of those who do not (yet) belong.

By definition, the confrontation between reality and symbolic representation is uncertain. This uncertainty has now become undoubtedly painful, since, as Jean Baudrillard puts it, the experience of reality has disappeared "behind the mediating hyperreality of the simulacrum." A progressive staging of everyday life that gives rise to great tension between ethics and symbolism, because of the dissonance between the moral intentions related to reality and the generalizations and distinctions of established cultural production.

For an independent and oppositional cultural production, another conceptual space must be created that lies beyond the destruction of direct experience by the simulacrum of institutional culture. The point is not to create a specific alternative in the form of a new dogma as opposed to the spiritual space of the institutions. On the contrary, the point is to arrive at a "mental ecology" that makes it possible for mediating intellectuals, like designers, to leave the beaten path, to organize their opposition, and to articulate that in the mediated display. This is only possible by adopting a radically different position with respect to the production relationships—by exposing the variety of interests and disciplinary edifices in the message, commented on and held together by the mediator's "plane of consistency."

and Mediocrity

Opportunities for renewed engagement must be sought in initiatives creating new public polarities, according to Félix Guattari, in "untying the bonds of language" and "[opening] up new social, analytical, and aesthetic practices." This will only come about within the context of a political approach that, unlike the dominant neoliberal form of capitalism, is directed at real social problems. If we are to break through the existing communicative order, this "outside thought" should also reverberate in the way in which designers interpret the theme and program of the client. In other words, the designer must take on an oppositional stance, implying a departure from the circle of common-sense cultural representation. This is an important notion, because the point is no longer to question whether the message is true, but whether it works as an argument—one that manifests itself more or less explicitly in the message, in relation to the conditions under which it was produced and under which it is disseminated.

Such activity is based on a multidimensional, complementary way of thinking with an essentially different attitude to viewers and readers. It imposes a complementary structure on the work as well, an assemblage that is expressed both in content and in form. The essence of this approach, however, is that, through the critical orientation of its products, the reflexive mentality raises questions among the public that stimulate a more active way of dealing with reality. In this manner it may contribute to a process that allows us to formulate our own needs, interest, and desires and resist the fascination with the endless fragmented and aestheticized varieties created by the corporate culture of commerce, state, media, and "attendant" disciplines.

Subversive Pleasures

Despite the symbolically indeterminable nature of culture, communicative design, as reflexive practice, must be realistic in its social ambitions. In the midst of a multiplicity of factors too numerous to take stock of, all of which influence the product, the aim is to arrive at a working method that produces commentaries rather than confirms self-referential fictions. Design will have to get used to viewing substance, program, and style as ideological constructions, as expressions of restricted choices that only show a small sliver of reality in mediation. The inevitable consequence is that the formulation of messages continues to refer to the fundamental uneasiness between symbolic infinity and the real world.

This mentality demands a major investment in practical discourse in those fields and situations where experience and insight can be acquired through work. This is important not only because it is necessary to struggle against design in the form of design, echoing Rem Koolhaas's statement about architecture, but also because partners are required with the same operational options.6 It is furthermore of public interest to acquaint a wider audience with forms of communication contributing to more independent and radical democratic shaping of opinion.

Moving from a reproductive order to a commentating one, operative criticism can make use of a long reflexive practice. All cultures have communicative forms of fiction that refer to their own fictitiousness in resistance to the established symbolic order. "To this end," Robert Stam writes, "they deploy myriad strategies—narrative discontinuities, authorial intrusions, essayistic digressions, stylistic virtuosities. They share a playful, parodic, and disruptive relation to established norms and conventions. They demystify fictions, and our naive faith in fictions, and make of this demystification a source for new fictions!" This behavior alone constitutes a continuous "ecological" process for qualitative survival in social and natural reality.

Chapter 5.1.7

Scissors and glue: punk fanzines and the creation of a DIY aesthetic

Teal Triggs

The fanzine producer Chris Wheelchair [sic] remarked in the editorial of Ruptured Ambitions *(1992) that his Plymouth-based fanzine is "all about helping promote the DIY punk/alternative/underground movement, which is, at present, extremely healthy in many areas, and certainly improving." From the early 1930s, fan magazines or "fanzines" have been integral to the creation of a thriving communication network of underground culture, disseminating information and personal views to like-minded individuals on subjects from music and football to anti-capitalism and thrift store shopping. Yet, it remains within the subculture of punk music where the homemade, A4, stapled and photocopied fanzines of the late 1970s fostered the "do-it-yourself" (DIY) production techniques of cut-n-paste letterforms, photocopied and collaged images, hand-scrawled and typewritten texts, to create a recognizable graphic design aesthetic. The employment of such techniques and technologies has had an impact on an overall idiosyncratic and distinctive visual style affiliated with punk fanzines. For fanzine producers, the DIY process critiques mass production through the very handmade quality it embraces, but also in the process of appropriating the images and words of mainstream media and popular culture. Arguably, the DIY approach reached its peak in the 1990s and still continues today, having been co-opted into the worlds of commercial mainstream lifestyle magazines and advertising which trade on its association with punk authenticity. The intent of this essay is to explore the development of a graphic language of resistance and to examine the way in which the very use of its DIY production methods reflected the promotion of politics and music of 1970s' punk and DIY underground activity. In addition, this piece will, through interviews with fanzine producers, attempt to recover from history an area of graphic design activity that has largely been ignored. This will be achieved by focusing on three punk fanzine titles that were initiated during the first wave of the punk period:* Panache *(Mick Mercer, 1976–1992),* Chainsaw *(Charlie Chainsaw, 1977–1985) and* Ripped & Torn *(Tony Drayton, 1976–1979). These examples will be measured against a discussion of* Sniffin' Glue *(Mark Perry, 1976–1977), which has been acknowledged by the punk community as the first punk DIY fanzine in Britain.*

First published in the *Journal of Design History,* 19 (1) (Spring 2006): 69–83. It is republished here with the kind permission of Oxford University Press on behalf of The Design History Society and the *Journal of Design History.* © OUP/Teal Triggs.

Introduction

What is a fanzine?[1] The American writer and academic Stephen Duncombe describes fanzines as "little publications filled with rantings of high weirdness and exploding with chaotic design" where the producers "privilege the ethic of DIY, do-it-yourself: make your own culture and stop consuming that which is made for you".[2] For Duncombe, fanzines represent not only a "shared creation" of a producer's own, often alternative, culture but also a "novel form of communication".[3] In particular it is worth noting Duncombe's reference to the "chaotic design" of the fanzine page and use of the term "chaotic" in relationship to the development of a graphic language of resistance. Later he refers to the layout of the fanzines as "unruly cut-n-paste" with barely legible type and "uneven reproduction," drawing comparisons between "professional-looking publications" and the fanzine as amateur, falling somewhere between "a personal letter and a magazine."[4]

A plethora of fanzines emerged during the first wave of punk in Britain (1976–1979). This was a period of substantial cultural, social and political change where punk reacted against the "modern world" and the absorption of "hippy culture" into the mainstream. According to the cultural historian Roger Sabin, "Although punk had no set agenda like its hippie counter-cultural predecessor it did stand for certain identifiable attitudes. Among them an emphasis on working class 'credibility.' A belief in various hues of class politics [notably anarchism] and an enthusiasm for spontaneity and doing it yourself."[5]

Punk also reacted against the mid–1970s "hit parade" rock music scene. The writer Henry Rollins reflects in his introduction to one punk musician's memoirs, *The Andy Blade Chronicles,* that at this time "rock was boring, rock was damn near dead."[6] Punk music was seen as an alternative to the mainstream music industry and provided something new and liberating through its independent and "do-it-yourself" approach. In addition, Julie Davies, writing in her 1977 book *Punk,* argues that "Punk Rock is a live experience; it has to be seen and heard live. Playing a record at home just doesn't communicate the sheer energy, excitement and enthusiasm which are the hallmarks of the music."[7] Punk fanzines attempted to recreate the same buzz visually—an ethos encapsulated by the Sex Pistols who famously remarked in the *New Musical Express* "We're not into music . . . we're into chaos."[8]

Fanzines adopted the DIY, independent approach that punk musicians had espoused. With the rise of newly formed bands came the establishment of impromptu clubs, small, independent record labels and record stores, including the London-based shop Rough Trade (which also distributed fanzines). In the same way, fanzines offered fans a "free space for developing ideas and practices," and a visual space unencumbered by formal design rules and visual expectations.[9] As one member of the community reflects "our fanzines were always clumsy, unprofessional, ungrammatical, where design was due to inadequacy rather than risk."[10] As the plethora of punk-inspired fanzines materialized, a unique visual identity emerged, with its own set of graphic rules and a "do-it yourself" approach neatly reinforcing punk's new found "political" voice. The Sex Pistols single release of "Anarchy in the UK" (1976) summed up punk's radical position where Malcolm McLaren, the self-proclaimed punk creator and Sex Pistol's manager, was quick to point out, "'Anarchy in the UK' is a statement of self-rule, or ultimate independence, of do-it-yourself."[11] As if to punctuate this point graphically, the producer of *Sideburns* (Brighton, 1976) famously provided a set of simple instructions and a diagram of how to play three chords—A, E, G—alongside the punk command "Now Form a Band." As with its music and fashion, punk advocated that everyone go out and produce fanzines. As independent self-published publications, fanzines became vehicles of subcultural communication and played a fundamental role in the construction of punk identity and a political community.

As cultural mouthpieces for punk bands, fanzines disseminated information about gig schedules, interviews with bands and reviews of new albums alongside features on current political events and personal rants. They fostered an active dialogue with a community of like-minded individuals often evidenced through the readers' pages of fanzines and also at the gigs themselves. As the American writer Greil Marcus suggests, punk was "a moment in time that took shape as a language anticipating its own destruction . . . it was a chance to create ephemeral events that would serve as judgements on whatever came next."[12] Fanzines formed part of this fleeting cultural performance. Each in their own way contributed to the development of a distinct and enduring DIY graphic language of punk.

Sniffin' Glue

The first punk fanzine to reflect the punk movement visually in Britain was Mark Perry's *Sniffin' Glue* (1976–1977). Mark P.'s *Sniffin' Glue* is credited as the first British punk fanzine amongst punk historians such as Jon Savage, who writes: "Perry's achievement was to unite for a brief time all the tensions— between art and commerce, between avant-garde aesthetics and social realist politics—that eventually tore punk apart, and write them out in a sharp mix of emotion and intention that still makes his words fresh."[13] Others writing at the time, including Charlie Chainsaw, producer of the punk fanzine *Chainsaw*, who altered the form of his production just to differentiate his fanzine from the multitude of *Sniffin' Glue* "look-a-likes" that had appeared so soon after its first issue.[14] These attributes were the way in which the typewritten text was used with mistakes in spelling as well as cross-outs, all caps, handwritten graffiti text, photographs of bands used on two-thirds of the cover, and so forth.

Tributes to Mark P.'s success were even witnessed in the way the fanzine itself was referenced graphically. *Murder by Fanzine* Nr. 2 (c.1983, Ross-Shire, Scotland) for example, pastes a flyer promoting issue 6 of *Sniffin' Glue* and overlays it on the head of a guitar player thereby rendering him anonymous (Figure 5.12). Despite this Mark P. is "clear about refusing the 'first fanzine'" tag and is careful to credit earlier rock-n-roll publications such as Greg Shaw's *Who Put the Bomp!*, *Crawdaddy* and Brian Hoggs' *Bam Balam*. He comments, "I would like to claim that the idea of doing a fanzine on this new music was my own, but I can't because it wasn't. At the time there were loads of fanzines knocking about. Mostly on country music, R&B and the like." [15] *Sniffin' Glue* soon established itself as part of the evolutionary line of fanzine publishing by taking on what would become a characteristic approach to fanzine production with its A4, stapled, photocopied pages and layouts using handwritten and typewritten texts.

The title, *Sniffin' Glue: And Other Rock'n'roll Habits* was inspired by the Ramones' London gig and song "Now I wanna sniff some glue"—a verse that is reprinted in Issue 1 (1976). Mark P. remarks that "In this issue we lean heavily towards being a Ramones fan letter" and promises in future issues to cover "other punks who make and do things we like." [16] *Sniffin' Glue* was often abbreviated to *SG* and,

Figure 5.12 *Murder by Fanzine* no. 2 cover
(c. 1983). Place of publication: Ross-Shire,
Scotland.

while drawing upon earlier formats and content of the rock'n'roll publications, it did differ from its predecessors in that it defined itself from an insider's and working-class perspective on the burgeoning punk music scene in Britain. Issue 1 defined itself as "for punks," as a mouthpiece for their music and anger. In Issue 4 he signs one review as "Mark 'angry young man' P." Also in Issue 4, collaborator Steve Mick writes ". . . punks have been telling us we've got the best mag around. Well, of course we have 'cause we're broke, on the dole and live at home in boring council flats, so obviously we know what's goin' on!" Mark P. left his job as a bank clerk and home in Deptford to start the fanzine. In true punk spirit, Mark Perry even shortened his surname to the letter "P" in order to avoid the attention of the dole officers (as did many other fanzine producers at the time, including Tony Drayton (Tony D.) of *Ripped & Torn*). Produced initially in Mark P.'s back bedroom, *Sniffin' Glue* found a gap in the "market" with an audience of like-minded punk music enthusiasts. His initial photocopier run was 50 but by the end of *Sniffin' Glue* in 1977 up to 10,000 were in circulation. Perry stopped producing *Sniffin' Glue* with number 12 (August/ September 1977) about the same time that he suggests punk had been assimilated into the music industry.[17] Like punk itself, fanzines moved from positions of independence to rapid co-option into the mainstream.

Sniffin' Glue was a true DIY production. Mark P. first put together the fanzine using a "back to basics" approach with the main text typed out on an "old children's typewriter"—a Christmas present from his parents when he was ten.[18] Texts were used as they were written with grammatical and punctuation corrections made visible in crossing outs. This stressed the immediacy of its production and of the information, but also the transparency of the design and journalistic process itself. Mark P. advertises subscriptions at "£1.40 for four issues and paid with postal orders only" (Issue 3 ½: 4), although this was not a cost effective measure when the cover price of each issue was 10p. At the time the cost of photocopying was 3 pence per sheet and most issues average 12 pages. Mark P. and other producers obtained free copies by using copiers found in their workplace or through friends' jobs. *Sniffin' Glue,* for example, was produced on Mark P.'s girlfriend's office copier.[19] Unlike publishers of some of the later fanzines, Mark P. kept production simple, using only single-sided copies, with an occasional inclusion of a pin-up page of punk band members (e.g. Chelsea or Brian Chevette of Eater), double-sided and backed by an advertisement for a Sex Pistols gig or an independent record shop.

Mark P. had developed his own brand of DIY "punk journalism" and encouraged others to participate actively in "having a go yourself." *Sniffin' Glue*'s readership was primarily other fans who purchased copies, amongst other places, in London's Compendium bookstore (Camden) and through Bizarre Books (Paddington). Mark P. was also very much aware of his new found position as punk provocateur and of the influence he had on other fanzine producers. Even in Issue 3 of *Sniffin Glue,* Mark P. comments that the back issues had already "SOLD OUT! Collectors items already?" In a special edition of *Q* magazine (April 2002), Mark P. reflects that "*Sniffin' Glue* was the best rock magazine in the world bar none, because it was so connected to what it was writing about."[20] Mark P. also speculates that his fanzine was successful because it was unlike other fanzines, in that *Sniffin' Glue* was "more discerning than the others." He felt that other fanzines said what was fashionable rather than being honest and telling readers exactly what they thought.[21]

A graphic language of resistance

But what does the DIY esthetic that emerged in fanzines such as *Sniffin' Glue* actually represent? Before turning to a more detailed discussion of other punk fanzine titles, it is worth exploring what a "graphic language of resistance" in contemporary Western culture means: is it even possible to characterize it in any systematic way? Language, according to cultural historian Mikko Lehtonen, is essentially abstract and exists only through certain material forms such as "writing, photographs, movies, newspapers and magazines, advertisements and commercials."[22] These are conduits through which meaning is conveyed and where signs which stand for "mental concepts" are arranged into languages. Just as grammars and syntax are created through written or spoken language so too might be the structures of visual language. The semioticians Gunther Kress and Theo van Leeuwen observe a shift taking place in the "era of late modernity" from a dominance of "monomodality," a singular communication mode, to "multimodality," which embraces a "variety of materials and to cross the boundaries between the various art, design and performance disciplines."[23] Language may be communicated through verbal or non-verbal means, or a combination thereof. The grammars of design operate in the same way as the grammars of semiotic modes and may be codified. The music historian Dave Laing, for example, comments that punk language drew upon discourses found in the areas of pornography, left-wing politics and obscenity. Explicit sexual words such as "cunt" and swearing such as using the word "fuck" permeated the lyrics of punk songs, performances on stage and in the pages of fanzines.[24] All these facets incorporated an explicit and violent use of language as part of a general shock tactic strategy meant to offend and draw attention to punk itself. The DIY approach to fanzine production ensured the menacing nature of the words in the use of cut-up ransom note lettering.

For punk fanzines, language is communicated graphically through a system of visual signs and specifically in the conveyance of a message of "resistance," In the essay "Retheorizing Resistance," Beverly Best examines the way in which the popular cultural text functions on "behalf of oppositional cultural and political practice." Best argues in a similar way to Michel Foucault that there "cannot be power relations *without* resistances, and that the latter are real and effective because they are formed at the point where power relations are exercised."[25] Punk fanzines are sites for oppositional practice in that they provide a forum for cultural communication as well as for political action, which should be included in any broader political discourse. George McKay observes that British punk may be considered as a "cultural moment of resistance" and part of a DIY culture that "activism means action."[26] It is the self-empowerment component of a do-it-yourself culture where direct action begins.

Yet, what of a "graphic language of resistance"? *The Oxford Modern English Dictionary* defines "resistance" as the "act of resisting"; a "refusal to comply," for example as might be defined as in resist-ing authority.[27] Duncombe, editor of the *Cultural Resistance Reader,* suggests that through the process of resistance we are freed from the "limits and constraints of the dominant culture." In turn, "cultural resistance" allows us to "experiment with new ways of seeing and being and develop tools and resources for resistance."[28] This may be represented either through content, graphically or both, where rules and prescriptions are disregarded intentionally. Michael Twyman establishes that the "language element in graphic communication" is the relationship between information content and visual present-ation, which he suggests must take into account a number of factors including the "users of language" and "the circumstances of use."[29] Twyman is also clear in his argument about the role technological developments have in relation to the "language of the messages that need to be communicated." He suggests that the three major means of production—the manuscript age, the printed age and the elec-tronic age, provide different forms, and, "we have, therefore, to ask ourselves how each of these different forms can be made to respond to our needs."[30]

Such a distinction is useful for a study of fanzines. In this case, the use of handwriting or typewritten texts maintains a similar function in terms of language while the "graphic treatment responds to the particular technology being used."[31] "Graphic language" is a visual system incorporating not only image-based symbols but also a typographic language. The way in which graphic language is depicted will add value to its intended meaning. For example, Stuart Mealing, writing in *Visible Language,* has observed that "font styles and parameters such as size and color are selected to lend additional interpretive potential to plain text message." This is formalized by using salient elements including italics, bold, underlined, capital letters, fonts, size and weight, etc., but also through the way images and texts are juxtaposed and presented in order to extend visually "the semantic potential of a message."[32] Such acts of resistance are normally "shared" and in the process provide a "focal point" and help to establish a community of like-minded individuals. Such a community is often considered as subcultural, borne out of a resistance to a dominant or parent culture, and seen as "subordinate, subaltern or subterranean."[33]

The "art" of punk

Punk arguably represented the politics of the working-class experience,[34] but also the more "artful" "aesthetics of proletarian play," and was also middle-class in that there was significant art school input.[35] Malcolm Garrett, for example, states that he was introduced to techniques of collage, stencilling, use of Letraset and the photocopier while at college. His own fanzine *Today's Length* (one issue, 1980), concocted with Joe Ewart and others, reflects this. He was also associated with punk performer and artist Linder, whose own collages were profiled on the cover of the Buzzcock's first single *Orgasm Addict* (1977), and Peter Saville whose own references were visible on *OK UK Streets,* a single for Manchester-based punk group The Smirks (1978). Garrett remarks "punk really stood out, there was a sense of hostility on the street, and you felt a sense of energy which was aggressive in expression."[36]

Out of this connection emerged a language of graphic resistance steeped in the first instance in the ideology of punk and its anarchical spirit and in the second instance, that which emerged from their position in a continuous timeline of self-conscious Dadaist and Situationist International "art" practices.[37] According to Guy Debord, Situationist International promoted the notion that contemporary society had become the "society of the spectacle," opposing this by employing strategies such as that defined by *détournement* (diversion) and of "recuperation" (recovery) including commandeered comic-strip imagery and other popular culture forms. This is exemplified by fanzine producer and Pogues' frontman Shane MacGowan, who admits in his publication *Bondage* (Issue 1, 1976), "this whole thing was put together . . . with the help of a box of safety pins. All the photos are ripped out of other mags."[38]

The Sex Pistols' art director Jamie Reid had an interest in Situationist International and its antecedents including Dada and Futurism. Along with self-proclaimed punk historian Malcolm McLaren, Reid was a member of the English Situationist group King Mob while an art student at Croydon College of Art in the late 1960s. His early affiliation with Situationist International writings was established and, in 1974, Reid and McLaren helped to publish Christopher Gray's anthology *Leaving the 20th Century.* Reid's own publication (co-produced with Jeremy Brook and Nigel Edwards) titled *Suburban Press* (Issue 1, 1970) played tribute to the agit-prop collage-style illustrations, cartoons and DIY production techniques he had been exposed to in the flyers, handbills and early Situationist works. Such techniques had become synonymous with the radical politics of student protests of 1968. Reid's approach, and those of subsequent punk fanzine producers drew upon these techniques in order to establish a specific visual immediacy to their message. Ultimately this process provided an identifiable DIY esthetic unapologetic for its raw and amateur production quality.

Many producers, whether knowingly or not, often combined a graphic language of "resistance" instigated as a result of Situationists' *King Mob Echo* (c. 1968), Jamie Reid's *Suburban Press* (1970) and Mark P.'s *Sniffin' Glue*'s seemingly fresh punk attitude. Richard Reynolds, for example, in his "post punk poetry" fanzine *Scumbag* (1980–1981, 1988) drew on *Sniffin' Glue* as well as Wyndham Lewis' *BLAST!* and the language of concrete poetry.[39] On the other hand, it would be misleading to suggest that all fanzine producers were aware of these specific traditions. *Panache* (London 1976–1991) producer Mick Mercer comments, "I started in '76. There was only *Sniffing* [sic] *Glue* and *Ripped and Torn,* and I hadn't seen either. I just kept it simple and did what I liked."[40]

Panache

Writer and fanzine producer, Mick Mercer was nineteen years old when he began *Panache* in 1976 as a 12-page, A4, stapled, photocopied fan publication whose audience comprised like-minded individuals with interests in punk bands such as Siouxsie and the Banshees and The Adverts (Figure 5.13). Copies of *Panache* sold for 20 pence. Fifty-five issues of *Panache* were produced by the time Mercer discontinued its irregular publication in 1992. This was despite its growing popularity with larger print runs numbering in the thousands. Mick Mercer worked with regular contributors Neil Sherring and Jonathan Rawlings who "helped with writing photography *and* sales."[41] From 1982–1988, Mercer produced the publication by himself with occasional contributions from Kim Igoe, bassist for the punk band Action Pact. *Panache,* according to Mercer was "Not like any other fanzine" and was also considered the "King of the Fanzine Frontier". These slogans ran on the front covers of Issue 13 and Issue 20 respectively.

In addition to its feature articles, *Panache* published interviews with band members, critiqued club gigs and reviewed the current album releases. Although *Panache* was distributed primarily in London, Mercer was acutely aware of the lack of press coverage for bands based outside main cities including Stanwellbred band Dead Man's Shadow and Action Pact from Bristol. Mercer felt these bands were on a trajectory to becoming well known nationally and that *Panache* could not "pass up a chance to document such success."[42] As a producer of an alternative press mouthpiece and as an enthusiast for punk rock music, Mercer negotiated a mutual "trust" between himself as a fan writer and the bands he featured. This, he suggests, gave him access to "better and more natural interviews." He explains, "the question of interest in particular bands that often gets called favouritism is often that. Ha ha—it is why fanzines have those first three letters as inspiration. I can write about bands but still be objective. I am an objective fan."[43]

Figure 5.13 *Panache* no. 10 cover (c. 1978). Place of publication: London.

Although this is an oxymoron, Mercer and other punk fanzine producers were often critical of a band's performance or album recordings. The cultural critic Thomas McLaughlin proposes "that in zines we can find the fans seeing through the ideological operation itself, practising a vernacular cultural criticism." In addition, he suggests that it is producers (makers) working at the local level and with local concerns who provide a valid line of questioning and critique of the dominant paradigm. Punk fanzines operated against the mainstream. They were self-regulated with complete editorial control that made "theoretical reflection" possible.[44] Ironically, it is such an approach to fanzine writing where many producers who wanted to write about music professionally could practise "fringe journalism." This often led producers such as Mercer to move into the mainstream publishing industry, where he eventually became a free-lance journalist for *Melody Maker* and *Record Mirror* and later editor of the popular UK music magazine *Zig Zag*. While this provided professional success, Mercer writes that for him *Panache* was "integrated into my personal worldview. It was what kick started my brain, which lay dormant at school."[45]

As amateur DIY publications, fanzines were produced on an irregular basis, without concerns for formal publishing conventions. This "do-it-yourself" punk ethos manifested itself visually through low-budget graphic techniques enhanced by the production qualities offered by the use of the photocopier. Mick Mercer explains his methods used in creating *Panache*: "It was exciting enough to eventually learn about reduced type on a photocopier!! I always kept it simple but tried to cram each issue full. Type it up, reduce it, loads of cut-outs (relevant to a theme) and as many photos as possible."[46] The use of the photocopier as a means of production further strengthened the visual relationship between fanzines and the flyers as did the lyrics of punk bands. The photocopier and the subversion of copyright was recognized by Adam & the Ants in their song "Zerox" (1979),

"I may look happy, healthy and clean
a dark brown voice and suit pristine
but behind the smile there is a
Zerox machine."[47]

In the process of drawing upon low-value production techniques, such as photocopying and Letraset, employing the graphic elements including ransom note cut-outs, handwritten, stencilled, scrawled or typewritten texts, or collage images, a specific graphic language began to emerge which shared similar visual characteristics from fanzine to fanzine. This approach went some way to establish a set of commonly used principles and a way of creating a distinctive graphic language, which ulti-mately mirrored the particular aesthetic of punk music.

Mercer, along with the other first wave British punk fanzine producers including Mark Perry (Mark P.) of *Sniffn' Glue* and Tony Drayton (Tony D.) of *Ripped & Torn,* was among the first to break the rules of conven-tional practices in the use of grammar and punctuation. He flaunted typographic mistakes and employed an eclectic mix of typographic styles, preferring the visual aggressiveness of the "punk attitude" created by visually overcrowded pages and grainy black and white photocopied images. For Mercer, such an approach mirrored visually the fanzine's punk content. He remarks, "The punk attitude prevailed, in so much as the editorial tone was always, if you're not enjoying this there's something wrong with you."[48]

One element of the graphic language of punk fanzines may be defined by the way it featured the co-option of popular media images and typeset texts from national newspapers and magazines. In a similar way to the Situationist's notion of "recuperation," co-option in this context means to knowingly take from one source and reposition the image and/or text in a new context. Margaret Thatcher's cut-out head, for example, was collaged on top of a buxom female body while cutout newspaper headlines were re-contextualized and ironically juxtaposed with new images. Gee Vaucher of the anarcho-punk band CRASS also used photo-collage techniques for the image of a poster insert for the single *Bloody Revolutions* (1980). She represents four band members based on a publicity shot of the Sex Pistols from their single "God Save the Queen," and the statue of Liberty. George McKay, in *Senseless Acts of Beauty,* writes that the "modes of juxtaposition and subversion are so entwined in punk; the safety pin and the Queen, the bin liner on the body . . . the *bricolage* of CRASS is a patchwork of ideas, strategies, voices, beliefs and so on."[49]

Jon Savage, writing in 1983 observed that "we are inundated by images from the past, swamped by the nostalgia that is splattered all over Thatcherite Britain." He continues to suggest that "Punk always had a retro consciousness—deliberately ignored in the cultural Stalinism that was going on at the time— which was pervasive yet controlled." Savage cites a number of key examples in fashion, including Vivienne Westwood's use of 1960s" Wemblex pin-collars to "mutate into Anarchy shirts"; The Clash wearing winklepickers; and in music the Sex Pistols cover versions of 1960s" bands, The Who and Small Faces.[50] Greil Marcus writing in *Lipstick Traces: A Secret History of the Twentieth Century* defines punk as a "load of old ideas sensationalised into new feelings almost instantly turned into new clichés. . ."[51]

Record covers were perhaps the most visible use of images taken from the past. For example, the layout and use of typography of The Clash's *London Calling* (1979) album drew directly from Elvis Presley's eponymous 1956 album. The choice of photographic image of a single artist with his guitar is mimicked, although Elvis is seen in a frontal pose and looking upward, the guitarist for The Clash is caught in motion striking the guitar on the stage floor.[52] Such intentional plagiarism demonstrated punk's disregard of established publishing traditions and in this way may be interpreted as a political act. The way in which this was achieved visually is "symbolic" but also subcultural "plundering." *Panache* for example, reproduced frames from mainstream comic books such as DC Comics" *Batman* and used still images of the puppets originating from the British children's television show, *Thunderbirds.* Issues of the fanzine were also themed including those using reproduction 1960s bubblegum cards for studio film stills.[53]

Despite these popular cultural references, however, punk fanzines remained decidedly underground and *Panache,* during its time of publication, was no exception. While *Panache* shared a similar status with punk fanzines *Sniffin' Glue* and *Ripped & Tom,* it was unique in that its sheer longevity allowed Mercer to reinvent the publication as his own musical interests shifted. By the early 1980s, *Panache* had transformed itself into a fanzine for Britain's Goths, and later established itself as a fanzine for the emerging Indie music scene. In both cases it retained the "do-it-yourself" esthetic for which the fanzine had become known.

Ripped & Torn and *Chainsaw*

Despite an emerging set of punk "conventions," which included the A4 stapled format, page layout, the production values of the photocopier and mixture of typographic elements such as cut-n-paste, ransom notes and handwritten and typewritten letterforms, each fanzine maintained its own individualized approach. The techniques of DIY encouraged this to occur. The manner in which the graphic marks, visual elements and their layout were presented not only reflected the message but also by default the individual hand of the fanzine producer. This we can see in a comparison of covers from *Sniffin' Glue, Chainsaw* and *Ripped & Torn* (see Figures 5.13, 5.14, and 5.15). Charlie Chainsaw, for example, in his first issue of *Chainsaw* (No. 1, 1977; Figure 5.14) used stencil letters for the title and a series of cutout newspaper texts collaged with photography of the Sex Pistols and reference to its namesake, an image from the poster of the film *The Texas Chainsaw Massacre*. Mark P. of *Sniffin' Glue* (No. 1, 1976) on the other hand, employed his own quickly produced handwriting scrawl where letters were all caps and visually presented in the same weight. Alternatively, Tony Drayton's *Ripped & Torn* (Issue No. 1, November 1976, Glasgow; Figure 5.15) took a more formal approach combining one photographic image of The Damned with handwritten caps and lowercase letter-forms in a hierarchical sequence from the title, the stories promised inside to the smaller, self-effacing tag lines "This is too fantastic . . . buy it now."

Ripped & Torn also enjoyed a long run—from Issue 1, November 1976 to Issue 18 September 1979, and it is important in that it covered the punk music scene in both London and Glasgow. This fanzine

Figure 5.14 *Chainsaw* no. 1 cover (c. 1977). © Charlie Harland. Publisher: Wrench Records.

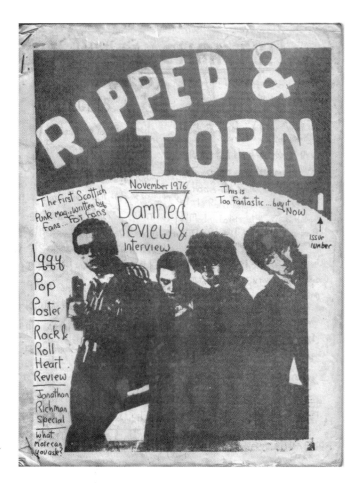

Figure 5.15 *Ripped & Torn* no. 1 cover
(November 1976). © Producer: Tony Drayton.

attempted to broaden out an understanding of punk's political agenda. As Tony D. himself explains in a
rant titled "Politics and Punk,"

> "The whole idea of politics is enough to put anyone off it, and therefore the closest most of us get to
> it is either signing on once a week, or filling in a tax return form once a year. But that's the way the
> government wants it, so they can get on with their business of running us the way they think we should
> be run."[54]

Despite its exclusion from most academic histories of punk,[55] *Ripped & Torn* was considered one of
the key publications of the period by both the underground and mainstream press. As Jon Savage
offers in a review of fanzines for the British music paper *Sounds* (1977), *Ripped & Torn* was ". . . again
one of the very first, and now important—set to take over from *SG* should the latter fold. As such, could
be more broad-minded on occasions, but ish 7 is well laid out and contains material not covered elsewhere: ants, chars and reviews of the Pistols/Clash bootlegs. Full at 25p."[56] Savage co-opts the punk
abbreviations "ants" and "chars" often found in the pages of the fanzines meaning "rants" and "charts"
respectively.

Ripped & Tom also provided an alternative model to that of *Sniffin' Glue* and one that influenced the types of production decision made by other producers. Tom Vague, for example reveals that he adopted colour for his fanzine *Vague* (1977–79, London) in order "to be like *Ripped & Tom.*"[57] In the same review as *Ripped & Tom,* Jon Savage finds fault with our other example *Chainsaw,* "New, little criticism—most things are 'bleein' beaut.' Maybe its unfair to compare this with 30 or so others but it just doesn't stand up very well. No pix (bar one collage from music press/record sleeves) and identikit articles. No fun. 20p."[58]

Despite Savage's criticism, however, *Chainsaw* is important to include in any discussion of punk fanzines. In the first instance this is because of its relative longevity and consistency of production. *Chainsaw* ran irregularly for 14 issues covering a seven-year period. In the second instance, its later issues demonstrated an innovative use of colour not found in other fanzines of the time. It was also through the efforts of *Chainsaw* that lesser-known punk bands were recognized. Charlie Chainsaw acknowledges that his fanzine began as a *"Sniffin' Glue* and *Ripped & Tom* clone, but it quickly developed its own distinctive style by concentrating on (then) totally unknown bands and featuring seriously sick cartoons, articles and newspaper cuttings."[59] Kid Charlemagne (Hugh David) as well as cartoonists Willie D. and Mike J. Weller (the latter known for his work in the School Kids issue of *OZ* and in *Cozmic Comics* in the early 1970s) occasionally produced work for *Chainsaw.* These contributors also established a visual link between 1960s' countercultural activity and 1970s' punk. Phil Smee, who did the cartoons for *Ripped & Tom* and occasionally contributed to *Sniffin' Glue* (1976), was a graphic artist and designed album covers for 1960s psychedelic bands. He was founder of the independent record label Bam Caruso and also coined the term "freakbeat" in 1980 to describe mod and R&B bands.

In the first issue of *Ripped & Tom,* 18-year-old producer Tony D. asks in the first sentence of his punk fanzine editorial "What's in it for me??" By the top of the second column he has found the answer admitting "My excuse for this self-indulgent escapade ... it's the only way to read my views on punk."[60] Fanzines are self-indulgent productions and in the view of one ex-fanzine producer, "elitist" in the way they focus on their own individual interests in bands, gigs and records. While this may be true, the auto-biographical narratives established both in the content and its visual form provided an interesting, if not useful, history of punk experience. The question of narrative in contemporary historical theory is worth considering in terms of the way in which it may be used to explain the literary and visual construction of the fanzine. *Ripped & Torn,* for example, is a historical narrative formatted as a series of accounts—editorial, interviews, gigs, reviews, charts, etc. Skid Kid, for example, acts as a foil to Tony D.'s editorship in Issue 1 and is made visually evident through the use of different handwriting to reflect the process of banter. Kid's hand rendering is measured and methodically realized; whereas Tony D.'s aggravated interjection is represented in a scrawled and hurried cursive hand. On a later page of the issue, Tony D., who even typed out Skid Kid's contribution, continues his discursive practice in his seemingly jealous complaint through the headline, "The SKID KID PAGE (HOW COME HE GETS A WHOLE PAGE?)."[61]

The typewriter text is also unique to the machine from which it was produced. In the case of *Chainsaw* the punctuation marks appear darker (as if double strikes) from the main body of text, which is uneven in weight but also in line, thereby reflecting the type of pressure that was used to hit individual keys. In addition, the typewriter he used from Issue 5 had dropped the letter "n" throughout. He writes "the missing 'N' was filled in by hand—a laborious process!," but also that he did not have the funds required at the time to repair the missing key.[62] The typographic treatment mixing a handwritten "N" with the type-written forms, establishes Chainsaw's trademark or "signature."

Chainsaw developed a house style for his fanzine which reflected his individual approach but also an awareness of standard "professional" typewriter and printing conventions. Alistair McIntosh has written of house styles that "each express the personality (and often the haphazard variations in what they were taught at school) of its originators."[63] For example, Charlie Chainsaw tabs two spaces after the punctuation marks, indenting by two spaces the first word of each paragraph opening and without line separations between paragraphs, standard use of correct quotation marks, and establishes a hier-archical structure for headlines with body text justified, ragged right. His word breaks also follow the convention of breaking words between syllables. And in keeping with convention, he uses the two columns with adequate margins, which is deemed preferable for a standard A4 page.[64] Ironically, Charlie Chainsaw is using conventional practices in an unconventional artefact.

Conclusion

Whether fanzine producers were recounting their experiences inside or outside London, the notion of resistance remains a key element in the construction of a punk identity. Fanzines are democratic in that they provide accessible forums for writing through their "anyone can do it" production strategies. They also encourage participation (e.g. readers' letters) and suggest reflexivity (or reflectivity in this case) in terms of their autobiographical manner of communication.

The art critic Michael Bracewell writes "In terms of contemporary culture, therefore, punk has become the card which cannot be trumped; and the reason for this enduring reputation must lie in punk's unri-valled ability to confront the processes of cultural commodification; or rather, to play cultural materialism at its own game, by creating a culture which was capable of pronouncing its host environment exhausted and redundant."[65] Like the music and fashion of the first wave of punk, fanzines continue today to display many of the early graphic characteristics and aggressive rhetoric associated with punk publi-cations. My analysis of fanzines emphasizes their position as "political" forums and mouthpieces for expressing the views of individuals and also punk collectively. It demonstrates how such resistance was defined by the graphic language, which had emerged not only from a punk "do-it-yourself" ethos, but also from the use of symbols, photographic images, typefaces and the way in which they were laid out. It is as much the graphic language that differentiated fanzines from the mainstream as the content of these publications.

Notes

1. Russ Chauvent in the United States first coined the term "fanzine" in 1941 to describe a mimeographed publi-cation devoted primarily to science fiction and superhero enthusiasts. The word "zine" appeared sometime in the 1970s as a shortened version of "fanzine" or fan magazine, usually used to describe an A4, photocopied, stapled, non-commercial and non-professional, small circulation publication. See P. Nicholls (ed.), *The Encyclopedia of Science Fiction: An Illustrated A-Z,* Granada, 1979, p. 215.

2. S. Duncombe, *Notes From the Underground: Zines and the Politics of Alternative Culture,* Verso, 1997, pp. 1–2.

3. Frederic Wertham coined the phrase "a special form of communication" in the title of his 1973 book, *The World of Fanzines: A Special Form of Communication.* It may be suggested that by using the term "novel," Duncombe is playing upon the form of fanzines as unique narrative forms.

4. Duncombe, *Notes From the Underground: Zines and the Politics of Alternative Culture,* 1997, p. 11. The relationship between the amateur and fanzines extended beyond punk and formalized through the range of "how to" fanzine books that were published in the 1990s including: B. Brent, *Make a Zine!: A Guide to Self-publishing Disguised as a Book on How to Produce a Zine,* Black Books, 1997; and F. Lia Block and H. Carlip, *Zine Scene: The Do It Yourself Guide to Zines,* Girl Press, 1998.

5. R. Sabin, Interview with author, London, 2005.

6. Blade *The Secret Life of a Teenage Punk Rocker: The Andy Blade Chronicles*, Cherry Red Books, 2005, p. 5.

7. J. Davis (ed.), *Punk*, Millington, Davison Publishing Limited, 1977, n. p. This publication was a compilation of articles and editorial rants from punk fanzines including *Chainsaw, Live Wire, Flicks, 48 Thrills, Ripped & Torn, Negative Reaction* and *Jolt.*

8. N. Spencer, "Don't Look Over Your Shoulder but the Sex Pistols are Coming," *New Musical Express,* 14 February 1976. Steve Jones is reportedly to have made the comment.

9. S. Duncombe *Cultural Resistance Reader,* Verso, 2002, p. 5.

10. J. Ewart, Interview with author, London, 1991.

11. M. McLaren quoted in G. Marcus, *Lipstick Traces: A Secret History of the Twentieth Century.* Secker & Warburg, 1989, p. 9.

12. G. Marcus, *Lipstick Traces: A Secret History of the Twentieth Century.* Secker & Warburg, 1989, p. 82.

13. J. Savage, "Sniffin' Glue: The Essential Punk Accessory," *Mojo*, 81 (August, 2000): 129.

14. Charlie Chainsaw, "Alio Punks," *Chainsaw* 5, London 1978, n.p.

15. E. Eichenberg and M. Perry, *And God Created Punk,* Virgin, 1996, p. 11.

16. M. Perry, *Sniffin' Glue,* No. 1, London, 1976, n.p.

17. M Perry, *Sniffin' Glue,* No. 12 August/September, London, 1977, n.p.

18. M. Perry, *Sniffin' Glue: The Essential Punk Accessory,* Sanctuary House, 2000, p. 15.

19. Ibid, p. 16.

20. P. Stokes, "Sniffin' Glue Fanzine: We Love UHU," *Q: Special Edition: Never Mind the Jubilee,* 2002, p. 105. Mark P. was not the only fanzine producer to suggest a longer-term value of their fanzines. Charlie Chainsaw predicted in *Chainsaw* (Issue 1, July/August 1977), "Anyway in years to come this mag will become a collector's piece, you'll be able to sell it for thousands of quid." Private fanzine collections do exist but it is rare for copies of British punk fanzines to come onto the collector's market. However, over the last decade, museums such as the Victoria & Albert Museum, The Women's Library, London, The British Library, and The New York Public Library, have developed substantial fanzine collections. The recent popularity for collecting such material has been borne out in the book by Julie Bartel, *From A to Zine: Building a Winning Zine Collection in Your Library,* American Library Association, 2004.

21. T. Parsons, "Glue Scribe Speaks Out," *NME* 12, February 1977. Reprinted in *NME Originals,* April 2002, p. 12. Author and fanzine producer Amy Spencer elaborates on this emphasis of the unprofessional and the notion of "truth" by equating it with punk fanzine's visual chaos. She observes, "the sloppy style seemed to be a badge of authenticity. If a zine wasn't slick in appearance or perfect in terms in presentation, and was not interested in reaching a mass audience, then the content was seen as truthful and therefore something to believe in." A. Spencer, *DIY: The Rise of Lo-Fi Culture,* Marion Boyers, 2005, pp. 195–6.

22. M. Lehtonen, *The Cultural Analysis of Texts,* Sage Publications Ltd, 2000, p. 48.

23. G. Kress and T. van Leeuwen, *Multimodal Discourse: The Modes and Media of Contemporary Communication,* Arnold, 2001, p. 2.

24. D. Laing in K. Gelder and S. Thornton (eds), *The Subcultures Reader,* Routledge, 1997, p. 413.

25. Best also asserts we should see the "everyday" as an equally significant site of confrontation between power and resistance as other more "traditionally" political spaces. For Foucault it is the way in which we define social spaces which determines "how we are able to envisage the practices that take place there." B. Best, "Over-the-counter-culture: Retheorizing Resistance in Popular Culture," in S. Redhead (ed.) with Derek Wynne and Justin O'Connor, *The Clubcultures Reader,* Blackwell Publishers, 1997, pp. 26–7. See also Ben Highmore (ed.), *The Everyday Life Reader,* Routledge, 2002, pp. 10–11.

26. G. McKay, *DIY Culture: Party & Protest in Nineties Britain,* Verso, 1998, p. 4. Duncombe has argued that American fanzines are more about cultural production than political action and bemoans the fact that there has been little radical political action through this medium. He calls this process "virtual politics" when underground culture is unable to effect "meaningful social change." Duncombe, *Notes from the Underground,* p. 192.

27. J. Swannell (ed.), *Oxford Modern English Dictionary,* Oxford University Press, 1992, p. 920.

28. Duncombe, *Cultural Resistance Reader,* 2002, p. 5.

29. M. Twyman, "The Graphic Presentation of Language," *Information Design Journal*, 3 (1) (1982): 2.

30. Ibid, p. 6.

31. Ibid, p. 5.

32. S. Mealing, "Value Added Text: Where Graphic Design Meets Paralinguistics," *Visible Language* 37 (1) (2003): 43. See also Kress and van Leeuwen, 2001 op. cit.

33. S. Thornton, "The Social Logic of Subcultural Capital" (1995) reprinted in Gelder and Thornton, *The Subcultures Reader,* 1997, p. 4. These arguments about "resistance" need to be qualified to some degree, however, in the light of Sarah Thornton's ideas on subcultural capital. This concept she defines as "conferring status on its owner in the eyes of the relevant beholder" (S. Thornton, *Club Cultures: Music, Media and Subcultural Capital* (1995) London: Polity, p. 11). It is therefore not directly connected with notions of resistance as previously understood by a previous generation of cultural studies scholars such as Hebdige and others.

34. J. Clarke, S. Hall, T. Jefferson, and B. Roberts, "Subcultures, Cultures and Class: A Theoretical Overview," in S. Hall and T. Jefferson (eds.), *Resistance Through Rituals: Youth Subcultures in Post-war Britain,* Hutchinson, 1975, pp. 9–74. See also D. Hebdige, *Subculture: The Meaning of Style,* Methuen, 1979.

35. L. Grossberg, "Another Boring Day in Paradise: Rock and Roll and the Empowerment of Everyday Life," in Gelder and Thornton, 1997, pp. 477–93.

36. M. Garrett, Interview with author, London, 1999.

37. For a detailed discussion of the art practices in relationship to punk, see T. Henry, "Punk and the Avant-Garde art," *Journal of Popular Culture* 17 (4) (1984): 30–6; M. Rau, "From APA to Zines: Towards a History of Fanzine Publishing," *Alternative Press Review,* (Spring/Summer, 1994): 10–13, and G. Marcus, *Lipstick Traces: A Secret History of the Twentieth Century,* 1989.

38. S. MacGowen, *Bondage,* Issue 1, 1976, n.p.

39. R. Reynolds, Response to author's questionnaire, 1999. Jon Savage writes that his fanzine *London's Outrage* (1976–1977) was influenced by the photocopied, A4 format of *Sniffin' Glue* and its "enthusiasm" as well as "the type of detail offered in the writing of *Bam Balam*." J. Savage, Response to author's questionnaire, 1999.

40. M. Mercer, Response to author's questionnaire, 1999.

41. M. Mercer, "Ed," *Panache,* Issue 20, London, 1981, p. 2. *Panache* also had stories on conspiracy theories as well as humanitarian and social-based issues. In the first few years of publication it had a print run ranging on average from 200–500 copies.

there have been "Giant" sightings in Singapore, Russia, and on the Paris gravesite of Doors singer Jim Morrison. Supporters consider him a courageous street activist,' a contemporary Dadaist or Situationist, or a postgraffitist who uses the print medium instead of the spray can for tagging.

Along with "Giant," Fairey himself has unwittingly become an urban legend famous for being obscure. But he finds it "totally ironic" that people think he's cool. "I'm a dork. I'm a loser. I'm not cool at all. Everybody just projects their idea of what's cool on me. I'm boring. I never go out. I don't know what's hip in music right now or anything."

The self-proclaimed loser has been the subject of a documentary short, *Andre the Giant Has a Posse*, that's screened at New York's Museum of Modem Art as well as Sundance and other festivals. His own work is now being shown at galleries around the world. And he says his obeygiant.com Web site gets 15,000 hits daily.

Frequent targeting of Los Angeles has also gained him the attention of the entertainment media. As a result, his handiwork occasionally pops up in the background on MTV and HBO shows and can also be glimpsed in movies like *Gone in Sixty Seconds, The Devil's Own,* and *8mm. He* claims the one in *Batman Forever* was digitally inserted without official approval by a fan working on the film.

Not everyone is a devotee, though. Some people find him naive and delusional about the ability of his graphics to affect change. Most critics simply consider him a vandal. And, in fact. he's willfully engaged in civil disobedience, reclaiming pockets of public space already glutted with establishment propaganda. Consequently, he's been busted five times and continues to risk imprisonment. But he remains unfazed, saying he doesn't care whether people love him or hate him, as long as they respond to what he's doing.

The roots of Fairey's style are diverse. His visual minimalism was inspired by skateboard graphics, which have to jump off the wall in stores to compete with all of the others on display. His appropriation of preprinted source material and his handcrafted production methods grew out of the do-it-yourself punk music aesthetic. His humorous use of mass-media characters is akin to the Church of the SubGenius, a satirical mock-religion that anointed a 1950s clip-art drawing of a pipe-smoking dad as their divine savior. And like Andy Warhol, Fairey has an affinity for high-contrast visuals and for elevating the mundane to the iconic. Covering large surfaces with multiple posters also evokes the pop artist's style, but the repetition motif is based on necessity rather than homage.

Fairey's strongest early influence was L.A.-based guerrilla postermaker Robbie Conal. He says when he saw Conal's 1987 yellow-and-black "Contra Diction" poster, an attack on President Reagan's public lies and obfuscations regarding covert government operations in Iran, "I thought it was so powerful. He had this really unflattering portrait that was a great painting, well executed, but with clever, bold type. I just thought it was a beautiful wav to combine art and politics. I loved it." Since then, Fairey and Conal have participated in joint exhibitions.

And like Conal, Fairey has run afoul of the law. He believes his harassment is largely based on community fear of copycat defacements, and suggests that he's being unfairly singled out. "If there's anything that's going to overrun the city, it's movie posters. They're coming down on me for my stuff when it's mostly Universal Pictures or Warner Bros. Records that are paying these snipers to go out and do it. And they're probably a lot easier to track *down* than I am." He says he's stopped canvassing his home base of San Diego because the city found him out and threatened his company with a lawsuit.

Figure 5.18 *Giant* looms large on a Chicago water tower. © 1999. Designer and Photographer: Shepard Fairey.

Figure 5.19 *Chinese Stencil*. To create the *Chinese Stencil* poster, Fairey photographed a stencil he'd done on a lamp base. © 1999. Designer: Shepard Fairey.

Figure 5.20 Shepard Fairey in action near his San Diego office. © 1999. Photographer: Monica Hoover.

That company is Black Market Inc., which he started with partners Dave Kinsey and Philip DeWolff shortly after his 1996 move from Providence to the West Coast. Hidden in a building on the outskirts of downtown San Diego, Black Market is a ten-person visual communications agency that proclaims itself an anomaly. They conduct "guerrilla marketing on a corporate scale" that operates in the gap between underground subculture and the public at large. Specializing in "the development of high-impact marketing campaigns," they number Pepsi, Hasbro, Netscape, NBC, and GTE, as well as film studios and record labels, among their clientele. They're sought out by corporations, staffed by, as Fairey puts it, "a bunch of fifty-year-old schmucks who don't know what's going on," who want to achieve credibility with the youth-culture crowd, the ones who resent and resist typical corporate sales strategies. He now finds himself in a position of designing Mountain Dew graphics during the work week, while liberating Sprite billboards in his free time.

Fairey recently created two-color illustrations of bad-boy comedian Andy Kaufman and his alter ego, Tony Clifton, for Universal's *Man on the Moon* biopic. It was a secondary, supplemental campaign that deviated from the traditional broad-based mainstream ads. Vibrant, harshly colored stickers, stencils, and posters with the words "Andy Lives" were rolled out to fifteen major cities as a way of stimulating curiosity and creating pre-release buzz. He also helped put up some of the posters.

DeeDee Gordon, co-president of Look-Look, the marketing and trend analysis firm that assigned the project, said Fairey was hired "because his style of art resonates with youth. He's created his own grassroots following. People seek out his posters and collect them." She commends Fairey for doing an effective job driving major traffic to the AndyLives.org Web site. As for the unauthorized use of public display space, she has no comment.

Fairey spent only a few hours on the Kaufman drawings. He's managed to streamline his way of creating images to the point where he's pretty fast. "There are a lot of illustrators and painters who do beautiful work that I either don't have the skill or the patience to do," he says. "But you don't have to be God's gift to art to be effective. My technique is not that noteworthy. Anybody can steal images and refine them with a little practice. But for me, it's all about impact, and an illustration that's well crafted but doesn't capture somebody's attention is not serving its purpose.

It seems to me there's more visual stuff than ever out there, more billboards, more ads, more everything. It's gnarlier than ever, and there just isn't as much room for time- consuming illustration. I look at everything commercially. Supply and demand. If people aren't willing to pay for it, how do you justify the time?

These days, 'Fairey's personal project is funded with BlackMarket profits. "I don't even think about 'Giant' as making money, ever. I only think that the more money I make from it, the more stuff I can put out there." He recently agreed to let Lisien.com, a music Web site, create 3,500 posters and 60,000 stickers with "Giant" as its centerpiece. He figures it's another way to mess with people's minds, to have them wonder if "Giant" has just been a ten-year teaser campaign. He also says he was well-compensated in the deal.

Fairey is ambivalent about his role in capitalizing on the capitalists.

I want to encourage people to do not just posters but anything creative that is contrary to being spoon-fed your culture by MTV and all the liber-hip companies. So it's kind of ironic that I'm doing work for those companies. But somebody's going to do it. There are a few different forces battling here, and I'm just to the point where I don't have a problem with the contradictions. The world is full of contradictions.

In a 1996 Wired magazine article, Fairey was quoted as saying, "I don't like advertising." He now claims his remark was taken out of context.

I was never trying to say advertising in and of itself is wrong. What I was saying was, I don't like the way advertising tries to manipulate, to make people insecure. It's very, very competitive psychological warfare with no rules of combat. It's definitely fair game for vandalizing and critiquing, especially the national campaigns. But everybody makes their own decisions. Nobody twists your arm to smoke or drink. Nobody's making you puke your lunch up to be like women in fashion magazines.

Once upon a time, "Giant" was anti-advertising, a silent spokesperson without a product. Now it's become its own brand, with Fairey negotiating licensing deals for T-shirts, hats, and backpacks. He figures it still has enough street credibility to last a while longer. When he began his project he fantasized it could be taken pretty far, but he never imagined it would be as big as it is now.

Reflecting on the trajectory of his own life, he recalls his childhood in the conservative, old- money section of Charleston, South Carolina, as being very repressed, fraught with frustrations and insecurities. His family discouraged his involvement in punk rock, skateboarding, and other rebellious behavior.

Finally in eighth grade, I had to take a stand for myself and stop fading into the woodwork, even though I risked getting persecuted by my parents and teachers and friends. But I'm glad it happened. I think a lot of people, even if they're unhappy, spend all their lives following the path of least resistance. They're just very meek and obedient.

When asked about the extent his youthful anxieties contribute to his prolonged preoccupation with "Giant," Fairey pauses, then declares, "All the stuff I criticize I'm totally guilty of. Which is why I feel I can comment on it so effectively. I have made, and am still making, the mistakes I'm ridiculing."

If you had to sum up who I am, "Giant" is like a mirror to me. It totally reflects my need to get my imprint out there, to satisfy my adrenaline craving, and my artistic craving. You can really understand me quickly just by looking at 'Giant.' There's not much more to it.

When the time comes to canvass another area of town, Fairey climbs into his Civic and drives off, continuing to obey his inner "Giant."

Section 5.2

Identity and world graphic design

The Siyazama Project began in 1999 as a series of workshops specifically addressing the need to provide HIV/AIDS information to rural female head-workers in the Valley of a Thousand Hills, the Inanda Valley, the Msinga region, and the Ndwedwe informal settlements, all in KwaZulu-Natal Province, South Africa. Thus, it was much more focused than the other campaigns mentioned. The project has demonstrated how visual communication can make a contribution in a community in which large numbers of people do not look to writing or print for their information.[22] More specifically for this essay, it demonstrates how visual symbols that resonate with the indigenous cultural history can play a part in this communication process.

The project developed a collegial and friendly workshop ethos that allowed rural women to become comfortable seeking and expressing information about previously taboo sexual subjects, including HIV/AIDS and other STDs, abuse, and violence. It has enabled them to communicate this information to their communities through the visual medium of beaded dolls and tableaux. The use of a visual medium, in turn, has allowed expression of the issues to the wider society outside the workshops, which would still be taboo to discuss verbally.

A major visual motif in the various dolls and tableaux has been a geometrical version of the AIDS red ribbon. The ribbon was first used as a symbol of awareness and support in the HIV/AIDS struggle during 1991, in the United States, by organizations such as Visual AIDS, Broadway Cares, and Equity Fights AIDS.[23] Its use spread internationally, and by the mid- to late-1990s, the ribbon was featured widely in South African AIDS campaigns and was becoming familiar in the South African context.

Because of the geometric design structure of most South African beadwork, such as that made in the Siyazama Project, the depiction of the ribbon became very stylized and geometrical, and even almost abstract (Figure 5.23). Abstracted or stylized versions of the ribbon have also become common in the various South African AIDS campaigns. The ribbon itself, or a realistic rendering of it, is not so common, which suggests that the two-dimensional graphic device is what has taken hold in the local culture. This traction might have resulted simply from the repetition of a more easily reproduced version of the symbol, but it seems likely that it results from its cultural resonance.

The cultural resonance refers to a system or group of traditional graphic symbols used by the amaZulu and other South African peoples. Credo Mutwa has described "Bantu Symbol Writing" as having once been widespread among the black peoples of sub-equatorial Africa but as having "died out fast as the people learned the European alphabet."[24] He gives approximately 250 symbols that cover a wide range of meanings, some presented in the form of short texts, others as lists of related concepts. All are linear in execution but vary in style: Some are completely abstract; some are simplified pictorial or pictographic representations; some resemble the angular geometric style of Ndebele house decorations (Figure 5.24).

How many of these symbols are widely understood today is not known, but some clearly do still have currency in isiZulu-speaking culture. They are familiar to many, particularly in the more remote rural areas, where the population remains substantially separate from Westernized South African culture.

In particular, the symbols for "man" and "woman" are still known. The conventionalized and geometricized version of the AIDS ribbon, used as a logo in many South African AIDS campaigns, shows a clear and fortuitous visual relationship with the male and female symbols (Figure 5.25). This resemblance,

Figure 5.23 Siyazama Project poster. © 2006. Accreditation: Kate Wells/The Siyazama Project.

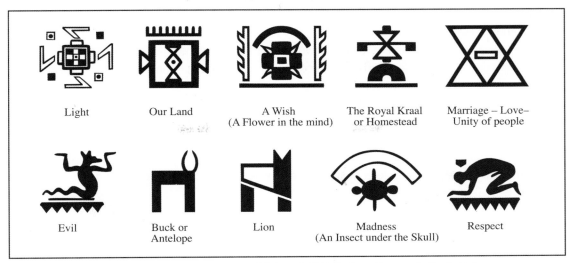

Figure 5.24 Bantu Symbol Writing. From *Indaba my Children*, © 1998. Author: Vusamzulu Credo Mutwa.

Figure 5.25 Mutwa male (left) and female (middle) signs. Compare their structure with examples of the geometric version of the AIDS "Love-Letter" ribbon as used in Zulu beadwork (right). From *Indaba my Children*. © 1998. Author: Vusamzulu Credo Mutwa. Photographer: Piers Carey.

Wells believes, is a substantial factor in the widespread acceptance of the graphic version of the AIDS ribbon and its preference over the three-dimensional version or its more realistic representation.[25]

This cultural resonance with an older but not quite forgotten visual tradition is particularly important for large numbers of rural people, such as the women of the Siyazama Project. Many of the women are illiterate and speak only isiZulu and thus are excluded from most communication by written or print means. In this society, information is typically communicated orally and in social settings, but women are further constrained by cultural traditions from seeking or expressing information about sexual matters. They are thus doubly excluded from information and counseling about AIDS.

The Siyazama Project workshops encouraged the expression of concerns initially through non-verbal, three-dimensional forms of communication: the dolls and tableaux. Awareness and use of the AIDS ribbon/logo was encouraged, but again, it was the stylized, graphic version that the women preferred, rather than trying to make, for example, three-dimensional bead versions.

According to Kate Wells, combining elements of both male and female, and thus symbolizing their union, with all its joy and pain, allowed the AIDS symbol in this context to "convey a profound message of life and death, thus effectively triggering awareness of AIDS, promoting care for the sick, and encouraging behavioral change."[26] Few of its products are considered to be traditional graphic design, but Siyazama's process has communicated the AIDS issues successfully with the bead-working women.

Virtually every product of the project incorporates the symbol, and it is broadly understood as a significant element within the overall AIDS message. The women's improved understanding of the epidemic and its associated risk factors has been shown in their three-dimensional illustrations of the various events and issues. Nevertheless, understanding unfortunately has not enabled them to protect themselves better, because of the unequal, traditional power relations surrounding issues of sexuality.[27]

Research has yet to establish the extent to which the effect of this particular symbol could be repeated and expanded across South Africa, either with other symbols or, farther afield, using other systems—or whether this was just a lucky coincidence. What has become clear is that the availability of a symbol that resonates with the audience, and that the audience is able to adapt and assimilate on its own terms, has made a huge difference in the effectiveness of the communication process developed in the project.

This case study is just one example of the use in design of symbolism and social concepts that may be unfamiliar to Western (or Westernized) designers, and it could well be repeated many times. If designers, particularly in Africa, wish to communicate with communities or peoples for whom such concepts or symbolism are not only familiar but natural, understanding and valuing the symbols and systems, as well as the cultures from which they spring, becomes vital.

Given the "Western" emphasis of most South African graphic design, only a conscious effort by both the profession and the graphic design educators, as well as intentional research of the several cultures with which they might work in South Africa, can lead to this level of communication. Designers and students do engage in research for particular projects, but this kind of research typically is not written up systematically or published. For example, no graphic communication literature has as yet been located that deals with the visual culture as a whole of either traditional or contemporary indigenous cultures in South Africa.

Such a process can only begin if both the education and experience of the designers engage with these cultures. In graphic design education, because of the complete practical domination of the discipline by Western technology, the emphasis is likely to be on history and theory. A history of graphic design or visual communication for South Africa might thus include not simply the visual traditions of the pre-colonial indigenous societies, or the development of "Westernized" graphic design in the country, but also the range of accommodations and adaptations made between the two types of tradition over time. Given the dearth of existing literature, extensive research will be required.

Conclusion

This article has discussed the case for indigenous African graphic systems as appropriate subject matter for the history of graphic design in South Africa. It has examined the relationship between certain Zulu traditional symbols, the AIDS symbol, and the social context in which the Siyazama Project has taken place. It proposes that a more culturally equal relationship between designer and audience, based on cultural respect and knowledge, actually produces a more effective form of communication than is the current norm. Such a relationship can help to promote a revaluation of indigenous cultures, including languages that are currently under threat from globalization. This relationship is likely to develop among designers only if their experience includes research and study of both historical and contemporary aspects of all South African visual traditions, including the languages and cultures in which they are embedded. This broad scope is therefore proposed as the aim of graphic design history in South Africa, using the Siyazama project to illustrate an investigation of the effectiveness of this type of graphic symbol.

Finally, it must be suggested that the relationship between designer and audience, reflecting as it does the gap in cultural power between dominant and marginalized elements in South African society, is likely to remain unequal; however, both partners may strive toward each other's position. The marginalized may adapt, subvert, or appropriate communication material or processes for their own use, but the sheer volume of output from the globalized cultural media makes it extremely difficult for them to relate equally with designers or other cultural producers. This appropriation is possibly the only way for them to gain or maintain some level of control over their cultures, but until this independent control is developed and sustainable, equal relationships between designers and marginalized audiences are likely to remain extremely rare.

Notes

1. The Siyazama Project was previously discussed in *Design Issues,* 20 (2) (Spring 2004): 73–89. That article focused on the project's history and scope, and on the effectiveness of beadwork as a mode of expression.
2. As in many African languages, "Zulu" is the root form of the word, and different prefixes specify meaning. Thus, the Zulu language is properly known as "isiZulu," and the Zulu people as "amaZulu."
3. Graphic design history and research at the Durban University of Technology has recently developed beyond an entirely eurocentric emphasis, although Phillip Meggs's *A History of Graphic Design* remains the set text. American and British sources generally remain the exemplars for the discipline, and their emphases remain the norm.
4. Crystal, D. *Language Death* (Cambridge: Cambridge University Press, 2000), 3–4.
5. Carey, P. 2004. *African Graphic Systems.* Durban: Durban Institute of Technology (unpublished MTech dissertation).
6. Mafundikwa, S. *Afrikan Alphabets: the Story of Writing in Afrika.* (New York: Mark Batty Publisher, 2004).
7. Dugast, I. and M.D.W. Jeffreys, 1950. *L'Écriture des Bamum* (Paris: Mémoires de L'Institut Francais D'Afrique Noire).
8. Duarte Lopez (1591) quoted in J.N. Pieterse, *White on Black; Images of Africa and Blacks in Western Popular Culture.* (New Haven & London: Yale University Press, 1992), 69.
9. Barthes, R. 1971. "From Work to Text." Available at: http://homepage.newschool.edu/~quigleyt/vcs/barthes-wt.html (2001) (accessed January 4, 2008).
10. R. Barthes, *Mythologies* (London: Vintage, 1991).
11. I. Noble and R. Bestley, *Visual Research—An introduction to Research Methods for Graphic Designers* (Worthing: AVA Academia, 2005), 189.
12. C. Faik-Nzuji, *Symboles Graphiques en Afrique noire* (Paris: Editions Karthala, and Louvain-la-Neuve: CILTADE).
13. J. Fiske, 1990. *Introduction to Communication Studies* (London: Routledge, 1990), 2.
14. M. Barnard, *Graphic Design as Communication* (London: Routledge, 2005), 85.
15. M. Barnard, *Graphic Design as Communication* (London: Routledge, 2005), 67.

16. UNAIDS (Joint United Nations Programme on HIV/AIDS (UNAIDS) and World Health Organisation (WHO)) 2006. *AIDS Epidemic Update: Special Report on HIV/AIDS: December 2006.* Geneva: UNAIDS. 11. Lowest estimate.

17. UNICEF. 2007. South Africa Statistics. Available from: http://www.unicef.org/infobycountry/southafrica_statistics.html 3 (accessed July 11, 2007).

18. Hartzell, Dr. J. 2006. Personal conversation, July 18.

19. Department of Health South Africa (2006). *National HIV and Syphilis Antenatal Prevalence Survey, South Africa 2005.* Pretoria, Department of Health South Africa. Quoted in UNAIDS, 2006:11.

20. "LoveLife" is South Africa's national HIV prevention programme for youth, and can be found at www.lovelife.org.za. "Soul City," a broader youth/health organization, is at www.soulcity.org.za.

21. Keeton, C. 2007. "Is the Aids message getting through?" *Sunday Times*, March 25–31. p. 6. Johannesburg: Johnnic Publishing.

22. For more information, see. Wells, K., Sienaert, E., and Corolly. J. 2004. "The Siyazama Project: a Traditional Beadwork and AIDS Intervention Programme." *Design Issues,* 20 (2): 73–89 Spring 2004, (Cambridge, MA: Massachusetts Institute of Technology Press); and Wells, K. 2006. *Manipulating Metaphors: A Study of Rural Craft as a Medium for Communicating on AIDS and Confronting Culture in KwaZulu-Natal* (Durban: University of KwaZulu-Natal. Unpublished Doctoral Thesis).

23. Avert.org. "History of AIDS from 1987 to 1992." Available from: http://www.avert. org/his87_92.htm (accessed November, 9, 2007).

24. Mutwa. C. 1998. *Indaba, My Children*, Edinburgh: Canongate Books (First published 1964), 664.

25. Wells, K. 2006. Personal conversation, August 14.

26. Wells, K., Sienaert, E., and Conolly, J. 2004. "The Siyazama Project: a Traditional Beadwork and AIDS Intervention Programme," *Design Issues*, 20 (2): 73–89, (Spring 2004. Cambridge, MA: Massachusetts Institute of Technology Press), 75.

27. Wells, K. 2006. Personal conversation, August 14.

Chapter 5.2.2

Searching for a black aesthetic in American graphic design

Sylvia Harris

What influence have African Americans had on contemporary graphic design? Is there such a thing as an African-American design aesthetic? These are questions that I have been asking designers and art historians for the last ten years. The answer I am usually given is, "I don't know." The relationship of ethnic minorities to the development of American graphic design is rarely discussed or documented by our profession because of the historic lack of racial diversity in the field. However, increasing numbers of African Americans entering the profession are calling for a fresh look at graphic design history in order to discover the aesthetic contributions of their people.

In 1971, when I entered design school, there was only one other black student in attendance. Twenty-five years later, this situation has improved slightly. Today, I teach graphic design at the university level and have one or two black students in my department each year. Those students often exhibit insecurities that negatively affect their performance. In fact, they experience a problem common to many black design professionals: the feeling that they are not completely welcome in the profession. Lack of exposure to the prevailing aesthetic traditions also puts them at a disadvantage. This outsider posture leads many black designers to compulsively imitate and assimilate mainstream aesthetic traditions in order to feel accepted and be successful. More often than not, black designers and students are trapped in a strategy of imitation rather than innovation.

The graphic design profession is driven by visual innovation. The most visible and celebrated designers are those who are continuously innovating within, or in opposition to, the prevailing schools of design thought. Black designers are working at a disadvantage when they do not feel a kinship with existing design traditions and also have no evidence of an alternative African or African-American design tradition upon which to base their work. In 1995, Claude Steele completed groundbreaking research on the links between performance and self-esteem, which indicated that self-confidence may be the single most important influence in the lives of successful African Americans. For instance, the spectacular success of black musicians demonstrates the relationship between confidence, leadership, and success. Black musicians have been successful because they feel confident and secure about their work. They are secure because they are working within intimately known traditions

First published in *The Education of a Graphic Designer*, ed. S. Helled, New York: Allworth (1998), 125–9. © Gary Singer/ Sylvia Harris.

built by others like themselves, and they are motivated by the thrill of adding to that successful body of work.

Is there a potential design tradition that can fuel black designers in the same way that black music traditions fuel black musicians? By "black tradition" I do not mean black subject matter or imagery, but the styling and expressions common to people of African descent. I believe this tradition does exist, but black contributions to America's rich graphic design history have been overlooked, so far, by design historians who have focused either on European influences or on the current phenomenon of cultural hybridity. Buried in libraries and design journals is evidence of black graphic styles and influences stretching from the New Negro movement of the 1920s through the hip-hop aesthetics of the latest generation of designers. I believe that this material, if uncovered, has the potential to nurture a new generation of designers.

How do we construct and document a black design tradition? There is already a small body of research on the lives of America's first black designers. Chronicling the work of these pioneers is an important first step, but most of these brave people were so concerned with surviving within a hostile profession that their work expresses little that is uniquely African American. I believe that the building blocks of a black design aesthetic are scattered across many disciplines and will be found in unlikely places. For instance, some of the best examples of the potential for a black design vocabulary are found in the work of white designers who have been inspired by black culture and take advantage of the market for black expressive styles.

We must also look outside the design disciplines to the performing arts and to fine arts movements, such as the Afri-Cobra, which have based visual explorations on African and jazz rhythms. We can study these disciplines for characteristic black expression (improvisation, distortion, polyrhythms, exaggeration, call and response) that can be translated into graphic form. Black design traditions must be pieced together from a variety of sources to make a complete canon of black expression.

In discussion with design educators (both black and white), many argue that to focus too much attention on black aesthetics will limit the full creative expression of black designers. They argue that black designers have spent the last twenty years working to erase race and class bias in the profession; to them a focus on blackness invites discrimination. I disagree. Black designers have access, training, and opportunity; what they lack is the drive that comes from innovation. And in order to thrive, innovation requires a tradition to either build on or oppose. It is up to us as historians and educators to research and teach in a way that addresses the unique cultural experience of all our students. Right now, black design students would benefit greatly from a study of their design traditions. Otherwise, they may be doomed to a future of bad imitations.

The notes below are excerpts from my ongoing search for black influences in American design.

Notes on African-American style in American graphic design

1920s: The New Negro movement

In his first design history book, *A History of Graphic Design*, Philip Meggs stated that "a collision between cubist painting and futurist poetry spawned twentieth-century graphic design." Early twentieth-century cubist artists were obsessed with visualizing modern technological and social freedom. The style of the non-Western people of the world, particularly those who had perfected forms of abstraction and symbolism, were quickly drawn into the stylistic vortex created by this modernist revolution. In this way, black graphic expressions made their debut in the Western world indirectly, through the works of cubist artists such as Georges Braque, Pablo Picasso, and Fernand Léger. All these artists later acknowledged the significant impact of African art on their work; however, most scholarly writing about cubism has obscured its African roots. Postmodern art scholarship, starting with William Rubin's book *"Primitivism" in Twentieth-Century Art: Affinity of the Tribal and the Modern*, has begun to record and study the role of African art in the invention of cubism and the success of the modernist movement.

By the 1920s, "jazz" became not only a musical term, but a stylistic one. European designers, who were influenced by the pioneering work of cubist painters, struggled to capture the spirit of modernism through the expression of jazz rhythms and motifs. The expression of jazz style in the design of popular communications in the 1920s represents the first appearance of what can clearly be considered a black-inspired graphic design style. The jazz-era climate of relative freedom in the North created an environment for blacks to publish and design their own publications. During this "renaissance," Alain Locke cited the emergence of the "New Negro" and declared that black culture was the appropriate source of inspiration and content for African-American artists. He argued that the art of black people was a powerful inspiration to successful white artists, so why shouldn't black artists also work with this powerful force. One of the first designers to give graphic expression to this call was a European modernist, Winold Reiss, who created African-inspired logotypes and titles for the book *The New Negro.* Young black artists, most notably Aaron Douglas, were encouraged by Reiss and Locke to expand the emerging modernist trends and lead the emerging New Negro art and design movement.

The line between artist and designer was still blurred in the 1920s. Many artists were illustrators, and illustrators were often typographers. The best examples of the African aesthetic in the designs of the 1920s are seen in black-owned journals. The designers of these publications were often black artists, influenced by European cubist painters, who were, in turn, influenced by African art. Artists such as Aaron Douglas, one of the best of these artists/designers of the time, learned to recognize and resonate with the African in cubism. Douglas and other black designers had a unique opportunity to express black style in a world that was starved for fresh, anti-Victorian imagery. Douglas's covers for the quarterly magazine *Fire!!* show the emergence of a unique graphic design expression that combines the syntax of cubism with the forms of African art.

The prolific jazz-age production of black art and design was cut short by the depression of the 1930s. However, during the thirties and early forties, a revival of black folk traditions occurred, prompted by the direct observations of anthropologists and folklorists such as Zora Neale Hurston, Southern white writers such as DuBose Heyward, and interviewers for the WPA oral history project on slavery. Artists supported by federal arts programs and socialist groups interpreted black folk and labor themes in programs, posters, fliers, and other printed materials. It is not clear how much of this material was designed by blacks; examples buried in archives await inspection, interpretation, and inclusion in the design history texts.

1940s to 1950s: commercial art

Printing and publishing before and during World War Two were significantly segregated. Unlike the fine arts professions, publishing institutions were restricted by racism and classism. Most printed publications and commercial art that circulated in black communities was generated by white-owned presses and designers. However, we do know that some black printers and photographers worked successfully in black communities; their products, including letterpress posters for popular music performances, were based on vernacular traditions and contributed directly to a continuing black graphic aesthetic.

1970s: The aesthetics of black power

It is interesting to note that the bursts of black graphic production in the twentieth century occurred during eras in which young people were preoccupied with concepts of freedom. It is no surprise that the 1960s saw a renewed interest in African-American visual expression fueled by black cultural nationalism. Some of the work of this period combined socialist protest-art forms with black in-your-face bodaciousness to create a graphic design product that was uniquely African American. This decade of black graphics reflects the aesthetics of resistance and black power.

1980s to 1990s: tribal chic

Popular designers and illustrators such as Keith Haring and David Carson benefited from the lack of black participation in the design profession during the late 1980s surge of interest in rebellious urban style. They shaped new styles and lucrative careers based on bold public vernacular expression such as graffiti and rap, class rebellions and black rhythms, and tribal symbolism. At the first Organization of Black Designers conference, filmmaker Arthur Jaffa cited David Carson's *Ray Gun* magazine as offering the best example of a visual jazz aesthetic.

1990s: The New New Negro movement

There are a handful of black designers who are designing for black audiences and, in doing so, are continuing black visual traditions into the next century. For instance, designers for new black media, including the magazine *YSB*, give graphic form to contemporary black culture. Like the artists of the original New Negro movement of the twenties, these designers use black vernacular stylings and African expression to inform their aesthetic decisions. The designers of this new generation are not isolated. They are working within a long tradition that, though they may not be aware of it, stretches across the century.

   These notes are presented as snapshots and pointers to the research waiting to be undertaken. It is my hope that American designers and scholars will contribute to this body of knowledge and support a generation of designers hungry to see their people and experience reflected in the mirror of our profession.

Chapter 5.2.3

Finding roots & taking flight: expression of identity in contemporary graphic design in India

Mohor Ray

The physical, cultural, and social contexts in which design is rooted help define the cultural identity that we recognize as belonging to a community, city, state, or country. The presence of this identity, in addition to the core functionality of the design, is what helps a design product or solution to create impact—and to be accepted and used by the people for whom it is intended. Identity emerges, naturally, from an approach that is empathetic and sensitive to cultural context. Identity may be visible in tangible form only at the culmination of a design project, but it is elicited through the manner that a design opportunity is approached.

Eliciting Indian identity in design through a range of "approaches" is in transition in response to the evolving transformation of India's social and cultural contexts. Changes that influence economy and society, varying from influx of international brands into the Indian market, growing purchasing power to gender equality and increased literacy, have rapidly altered the context of end-users as we traditionally know it. This wave of change, in a country that is extraordinarily diverse—geographically, economically, and culturally—has produced new microcosms: the *old-new* and the *new-old*, the *modern-traditional* and the *conservative-liberal*, the *big village* and the *small town*. And the already diverse Indian identity is exploding into new overlapping classifications that were hitherto unknown. As part of this complex scenario, Indian design is as rich with opportunities as it is fraught with challenges. New audiences warrant new design narratives, and new design narratives warrant a new vocabulary of design.

One of the important topics of discussion about contemporary graphic design in India is the indiscriminate appropriation of Western aesthetics or Indian kitsch, regardless of the socio-cultural context of the project. A major reason for this approach has been a lack of emphasis in design practice on the context in which the design solution is consumed; instead, the final "form" of the artifact is the main focus in design processes and for design projects. Often, customized frameworks to guide design development and to evaluate its efficacy have not been developed at the onset of a design project. This important missing aspect of design processes—immersion in the particulars of users and contexts—is finally making its way into Indian graphic design. While industrial design adopted this approach early, since the 1970s, graphic design in India has only begun to employ a user- and context-based approach in a widespread manner recently. This change has sparked the emergence of work that is both sensitive to its Indian context and that carries a contemporary representation of its Indian roots. In parallel, new investigations into symbology, indigenous scripts, and narratives have emerged. The reason that I am calling this development recent is not because socio-cultural approaches haven't ever been employed in Indian graphic design. Instead, my assertion is based on a new large-scale recognition of the value of this approach taken by students and practicing designers across a spectrum of work from brand identity to illustration and type design.

This shift has not emerged solely from discussions within the "design fraternity" in India, but it also has arisen from shifting perspectives of the clients. Realizing that India is a large and important emerging market, commercial brands have started to investigate the unique qualities of Indian consumers in order to create better engagement and to foster stronger connections with their products/services. This interest in the character of Indian consumers has spurred a greater effort to look again at forms of narrative and aesthetic. An interesting instance of this sort of query is the annual documentation that is conducted by one of India's most significant brand consultancies—Futurebrands, called the Bharat Darshan (*Bharat: India, Darshan: Viewing*). Founded in 2011, The Bharat Darshan works to understand the processes through which India embraces change. A team of researchers ranging from diverse backgrounds such as design, business, and sociology is embedded in the field among the people to observe them, talk with them, and absorb shifts in traditions and choices. The Bharat Darshan chooses locations beyond the known cosmopolitan centers of progress like Mumbai and Delhi. They investigate peri-urban and semi-urban locales in which change of any sort is typically more nuanced and rooted in local identity and culture. The rich visual documentation that emerges from this effort is a telling tale of the change in the life and ambitions of the people. The information that investigators gather feeds the commissioned consultancy projects that Futurebrands undertakes, and this data eventually informs briefs for brand design. This process ensures the consideration of a changing consumer ethos, and it translates into contextualized design approaches for emerging India. Talking about the learning from the Bharat Darshan initiative, Anirban Mukherjee, Head of Strategy and Design at Futurebrands says

> Located outside the traditional imagination of the consuming class this (Bharat Darshan 2013) unveils people and their interaction with new ideas, categories, experiences, and language. What we see is a dynamic landscape where new meanings are created, new trajectories of desire defined. These new interactions, across education, fashion, technology, food, identity, gender role, and more, allow designers to work with principles and mental models that are rooted in the behavior of people (Mukherjee 2013).

Design education & empathy

Interest in cultural contexts in design is a critical building block for Indian design education. The National Institute of Design (NID), India's first multi-disciplinary design school, was founded in response to the seminal *India Report* penned by Charles and Ray Eames at the behest of the government of India and the Ford Foundation in 1958. The report urged "a restudy of environment and skill and to think anew on detailed problems of services and objects. To restate solutions in theory and actual prototype." Purposeful sensitization to design context continues to be a leitmotif in the Institute's educational framework, and this approach is part of a foundation module for first-year entrants called Environmental Perception. The Environmental Perception module places students—who primarily come from urban backgrounds—in a new rural/semi-rural context for a short, but intensive, period of time with the objective that students observe and document their environment. Students record their observations and experiences using basic tools, including conversation, observation, and drawing (Figure 5.26). This approach marks a significant departure from the designer's workspace as an isolated, individual "desk," and encourages design students to engage actively with their environments as a way of enriching their design process.

More recently, Srishti School of Art, Design and Technology, which was founded in 1996 by privately owned Ujwal Trust in Bangalore, initiated Centres and Labs as part of its institutional framework in an effort to create a "community of learners." As part of its mission, the school states: "We believe that education is beyond instruction and skill; that knowledge is inherently integrated and complex and, hence, learning must be embedded in real-world problems and situations."[1] The Centres and Labs incubated at the school offer practice- and research-based environments, enriching the learning experience for students, through hands-on learning-by-doing approach. The various Centres and Labs nurture a range of real-time interdisciplinary projects addressing issues, across healthcare, finance,

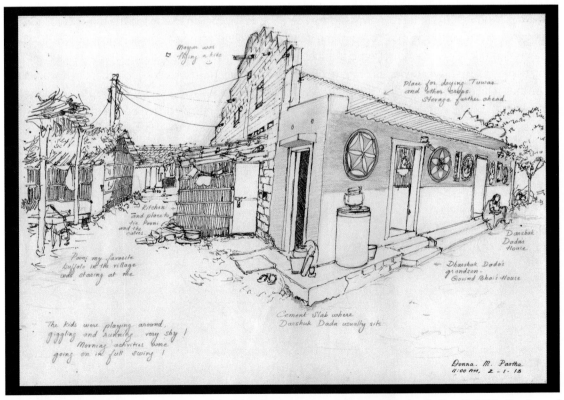

Figure 5.26 Environmental perception module field sketch by student Donna Mekerira Partha. © 2013. Courtesy of National Institute of Design.

education, employment, and democracy that give students opportunities to make meaningful choices during their education; the Centres and Labs also offer students exposure to working with design practitioners. The interdisciplinary composition of project teams helps students to understand the eco-systems of relationships within which contexts for design production reside. It gives them opportunities to participate in these interdisciplinary relationships, to learn to keep open minds and to develop deeper empathy for the end-user. The participants in the Law+Environment+Design Laboratory (LED Laboratory), for example—one of the first collaborative labs initiated by Natural Justice and the Srishti School of Art, Design and Technology—explored synergies between law, design, and environment. This group focused on how overlapping areas of these three fields could influence policy-making to consider the importance of a resilient future for the environment.

The ROOTS project that emerged out of this Lab addressed the pastoralist camel breeder community in the Kutch region of Gujarat in Western India and their effort to reclaim their rights over grazing "common-lands." The project placed students in the rural region in an effort to immerse them in the essential qualities of the people and the place. According to LEDLaboratory Director Deepta Sateesh, this immer-sion brought into play the feelings and emotions of the local people in the complex mapping of interconnected social, economic, and legal components of the problem. Student Varda Schneider explained that "Being close to these people for some days also brings to question many things that are rooted in our culture. Our idea of happiness for example, our relationship with money, our tendency to complain." The ROOTS student team used play as a mode with which to engage the rural users, and the team created the prototype of a board game that explained the complex Forest Rights Act 2006, which protects the rights of forest-dwelling communities to land and other resources. These resources had been denied to them over decades of the continuance of colonial forest laws in India that did not acknow-ledge their relationship with the forest land. The prototype enabled the community members to understand both areas of both areas of conflict and their rights using representation of stakeholders, resources, and choices in a simple board game format (Figure 5.27). (LEDLaboratory View Book 2014: 16)

Figure 5.27 Student team in the field. Photographer: Deepta Sateesh, Director, LEDLaboratory.

Purposeful sensitization to Indian contexts, and continuous dialogue about these contexts, in the Indian graphic design community is generating a new body of design that is responsive to and representative of India today. Moving beyond form and style, projects by several emerging designers and design practices explore the roots and motivation behind design intervention.

A type foundry for India

One such initiative is the collaborative type foundry—Ek Type, which includes type designers, researchers, and academicians. The word *Ek* is synonymous with the English word "one" in several Indian languages. True to its name, this type foundry brings together multi-script fonts for Indian languages, and has built a holistic environment that incorporates research, design, and technology. The core founding team represents this integrated approach: Sarang Kulkarni and Noopur Datye are calligraphers and type-designers, and Girish Dalvi is an educator with a background in computer engineering and design. Dalvi's[2] doctoral research was on the theoretical modeling of Devanagari typefaces. Until very recently there have been limited efforts to systematically develop fonts for the eleven vernacular scripts in India (Devanagari, Gujarati, Gurumukhi, Bengali-Assamese, Tamil, Telegu, Kannada, Malayalam, Odia, Urdu, and Meitei Mayek). The need for the systematization of vernacular fonts has been immense in the public communication, vernacular publishing, and media spheres. Ek Type's holistic approach to type development will bridge this gap by addressing simultaneously compatibility, standardization, and diversity (Figure 5.28).

Driven by the passion for calligraphy among the founders, one focus of the foundry is the revival of traditional Indian calligraphic styles. Recognizing the opportunity to bring traditional calligraphic styles out of dusty museum archives, Ek Type is invested in creating usable display typefaces that are inspired by this calligraphy. This is a significant initiative because it moves beyond revival to revitalization of

Ek Devanagari / Ek Latin   © 2013 Ek Type

Figure 5.28 Ek Devanagari & Ek Latin type. © 2013. Designers: Ek Type. www.ektype.in

Figure 5.29 Painter Suhail Extended type. © 2013. Designers: Ek Type. ww.ektype.in

traditional knowledge. Going beyond preservation of calligraphic styles, these fonts both enhance the usability of Indian traditional calligraphy as display typefaces and make this craft relevant to contemporary contexts. The incorporation of traditional scripts with digital font design creates a new slant on Indian calligraphic traditions.

Another uniquely "Indian" approach to letterforms involves the development of hand-painted Latin typefaces done by Ek Type in collaboration with independent type designer Hanif Kureshi. Hand-painters in India are self-trained artists who have evolved a vibrant, intuitive language of lettering by mixing styles, as well as decorative flourishes and colors. With the growth of economical "DTP" (Desktop Publishing) "shops" and digital printing, however, demand for hand-painted signs is declining. While the erstwhile sign painters have moved to more profitable Desktop Publishing opportunities, the art of the hand-painted letterform is beginning to fade from the visual landscape. The collaboration between Ek Type and Hanif Kureshi will build a body of fonts that preserve the character of Indian hand-painted type, while strengthening this visual tradition through technology. While vernacular fonts have typically been designed to complement the more widely used Latin fonts, the hand-painted type project builds on the language of the vernacular to create Latin letterforms (Figure 5.29).

New aesthetics & graphic illustration

Graphic illustration is another space that fosters graphic designers' exploration of visual storytelling. This visual form is beginning to find both critical and popular acceptance in India. Designers' personal sketchbooks can be a rich canvas for exploration and expression of very personal storytelling, unfettered by the requisites of commissioned projects. While these sorts of explorations may veer more towards "art," they are invaluable to understanding the evolution of a new graphic language in India. These pieces give graphic designers the freedom to draw from personal experience and to react instinctively to their environments, and this approach inspires innovative visual expressions of Indian identity and diversity. Recognizing the value of this kind of self-styled expression—and its significance to contemporary Indian graphic design and Indian culture—a new brand called Kulture Shop was launched in late 2013. Founded by a five-member team with a range of experience in art, design, marketing, digital media, and product development, Kulture Shop aims to curate leading Indian graphic illustrators from around the world, and to create affordable boutique lifestyle products with their art.

Curating is a critical component for initiatives like the Kulture Shop. Creative Heads Kunal Anand and Arjun Chiranjiva describe an intensive process through which they evaluated more than 200 artists before selecting the first curated set of seventeen artists. The curators balance artistic merit with cultural relevance in the work in order to offer fresh visual commentary on Indian culture and identity. The current line-up is young, and they present the viewpoints of a generation that has grown up in, and is still adapting to, recent economic and structural changes in India. Believing that there are deep and powerful Indian stories that need to be told, the Kulture Shop curators seek new perspectives in the art they curate. As a start-up enterprise that provides a financially viable platform for established and up-and-coming Indian graphic artists to monetize their work, the Kulture Shop is instrumental in bringing graphic design to the public—both for commercial consumption and as a critical assessment of the evolving visual landscape (Figures 5.30 and 5.31).

Figure 5.30 People and their Colours. Designer: Sameer Kulavoor. Featured on KultureShop Label Showcase.

Figure 5.31 Tiffin Towers. Designer: Kunal Anand. Featured on KultureShop Label Labs.

Design(ed) content

A new breed of Indian graphic designers are also embracing the role of content creators or orchestrators, and a new kind of "design product" emerges through this ownership of content. Deshna Mehta grew up and did her undergraduate studies in applied arts in India. She obtained her Masters degree in Visual Communication from the Royal College of Art, UK, and then returned to India to co-found a design and publishing platform. Called Anugraha, this platform encourages collaborative practices that derive from and contribute to elusive aspects of Indian culture and philosophy. One of Anugraha's first and most ambitious projects is "Being in it and being of it"—a textual and visual documentation of the Kumbh Mela 2013 through a handbook and documentary film. The Kumbh Mela is a mass pilgrimage of Hindus, in which devotees gather to bathe at an appointed site in the sacred river during a stipulated auspicious time. In 2013, over a hundred million people visited the Kumbh Mela in the city of Allahabad, making it one of the largest congregations of a religious group in recent history. Many people from educated and privileged segments of Indian society view the Kumbh Mela with apprehension due to media accounts of vulgar political agendas, infrastructural breakdowns, and fraudulent spiritual leaders. On her return to India after her graduate work, Mehta found a patron in her ex-client Madhoor Builders, who were familiar with her research for her master's dissertation in which she compared the cultural landscapes of the Thames River in London and the Ganga River in Varanasi. Madhoor Builders was part of the team that organized the logistical and structural infrastructure for the Kumbh Mela. They commissioned the handbook and documentary film from Mehta in order to create a deeper understanding of the spiritual and cultural significance of the Kumbh Mela for a contemporary audience that is struggling with ways to express its faith. Anugraha brought together a team of photographers, writers, filmmakers, and designers at Allahabad for more than six weeks and they worked together to first understand and then convey the essence of this massive spiritual congregation.

Talking about the book that will be one of the key outcomes of this collaborative project, Mehta says:

> Although there exists a large volume of visual as well as literary text documenting and describing the Kumbh Mela, most of it is either scholarly and inaccessible or personal, at times biased and more often than not, of the coffee table variety. The intentional or unintentional omission of context and relevance leads to an exoticism which distances the audience from the essence of the content.
>
> (interview with Deshna Mehta, October 17, 2013).

Citing "exoticism" as the cause of a rift in understanding an iconic Indian spiritual multitude is both brave and refreshing. On the surface, the Kumbh Mela, even for most urban Indians, appears exotic in a way that is alien. Most documentation of this event over the years has further cemented this image of a fantastic spectacle. Anugraha's recognition and questioning of this "exoticism" has encouraged a new inquiry into the Kumbh from within, by those who are involved, as opposed to spectators' points-of-view. Most of the content in Mehta's book comes from conversations between the design team and people who are at the Kumbh—the organizers, the saints and holy men, the pilgrims, the street vendors, and the tourists. The core content of the book comes from their narratives—their experiences, beliefs, and feelings. This core is supplemented by the field team's notes and academic readings by anthropologists, archeologists, and other researchers. The final design artifact will be a consolidation of these experiences in eight books—each book highlighting one aspect of the Mela, and each book constructed through interlinked photo stories, diary scraps, poetic extracts, interviews, and infographics. While the book is in process, the inside-out mode of query and the resultant editorial framework promises a new view of the Kumbh Mela, and a new reading of a landmark spiritual congregation. Furthermore, this kind of engagement—in which designers create the core content—will be fundamental to finding Indian perspectives on story-telling, alongside the query for photo stories, diary scraps, poetic extracts (Figure 5.32).

Looking back, and forward

The emerging face of Indian graphic design is one of fascinating dichotomies. Designers and initiatives such as Ek Type, Kulture Shop, and Anugraha have found distinctive ways to engage with their Indian roots, and to create work that is both a response to and an expression of Indian identity. A renewed interest in "roots," however, must also be tempered with an awareness of certain limitations. Traditional methods of immersion in the field or in the users' context, while valuable, can sometimes be limited by known stereotypes about people and cultures. To ward off this limitation, designers will need to seek out

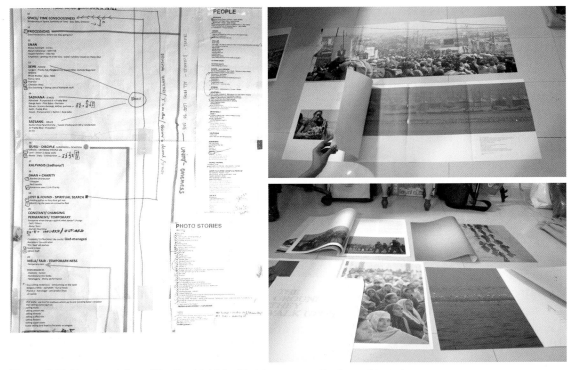

Figure 5.32 Documentation of the Kumbh Mela. Work in progress. Designer: Anugraha.

that which is not yet known. The contemporary Indian identity in design is in the making, and in the true spirit of a culture that embraces change, one hopes, Indian graphic design will continue to find newer means to respond to and reflect contemporary culture.

Notes

1. One of the "Values" on the Srishti Institute of Art, Design & Technology, Pune website: http://pune.srishti.ac.in/about-us (accessed May 5, 2018).
2. Dalvi, G. (2010), "Conceptual Model for Devanagari Typefaces. Industrial Design Centre", IIT Bombay, India.

Chapter 5.2.4

Visualizing multi-racialism in Singapore: graphic design as a tool for ideology and policy in nation building

Leong K. Chan

For Anthony D. Smith, "Imagery has always played a crucial role in politics and nowhere more so than in our understanding of nationalism." The truth of this statement, he says, is exemplified by recent and prominent "'uses of imagery'. . . in attempts to *explain* the formation of nations and the spread of nationalism."[1] From the turn of the twentieth century to the contemporary era, graphic design—in the form of banners, posters, and print advertisements—has been used in the process of nation-building to create awareness; affect behavioral change; and represent notions of everyday experience, identity, and ideology.[2] However, the design/representation matrix is not static; the practice of graphic design concerns meaning-making in the production and consumption of knowledge, and this [meaning—making bears a direct relationship to social processes and institutions—in this instance, how information about socio-cultural identity in the Republic of Singapore is commodified and mediated for consumption as public knowledge about ethnicity and national consciousness]. This case study focuses on graphic design as a tool for national ideology and policy in Singapore, particularly the visualizing of multi-racialism as a continuing reference for national identity and social harmony.

Birth of a nation

During the post-World War II era, politics in South and Southeast Asia was characterized by the rise of national consciousness in the colonies of the British in India and Malaya, and in those of the Dutch in Indonesia. The British granted Malaya and Singapore self-rule in 1957 and 1959 respectively. In 1963 Malaya and Singapore achieved full independence as part of a new nation, Malaysia, as a result of the union of the Federation of Malaya, Singapore, Sarawak, and Sabah. The relationship between Malaysia and Singapore was brief and constrained by conflicting differences in nation-building objectives, as well

First published in *Design Issues*, 27 (1) (Winter 2011): 63–9. © Massachusetts Institute of Technology/Leong K. Chan.

as by irreconcilable differences between the Federal government in Kuala Lumpur and the state government in Singapore that resulted in the expulsion of Singapore in 1965.[3]

The Republic of Singapore was created on August 8, 1965. Race is a politically sensitive issue:
Singapore is the only nation with a Chinese-dominated population within a geographical space bordered
by Indonesia, Malaysia, and Thailand. The 2000 census reported a total population of 3,263,200
Singapore residents, with a racial composition of Chinese (76.8 percent), Malay (13.9 percent), Indian
(7.9 percent), and Other (1.4 percent).[4]

A plural society: Chinese, Malay, Indian, and others

Singapore inherited from the British administration a system of social stratification based on
ethnicity and occupation, or trade specialization, which was managed by segregating a pluralistic
society of immigrants from China, India, Indonesia, and Malaya. The immigrants were characterized
by closely bonded ethnic groups, divided geographically and socially by culture, language, religion,
trade, and social class.[5] For example, the Indians were employed in colonial administration and
public works, the Hokkiens were well-regarded as merchants in view of their domination of international
trade, the Cantonese and Hakkas specialised in building and construction, and the Hainanese in food
retail.[6] This system of social stratification categorized culturally diverse immigrants into the four broad
racial groups identified—Chinese, Malay, Indian, and Other (CMIO)—and it continues in use to the
present day.[7]

Pluralistic societies are created as a result of peoples from diverse cultures, with diverse ethnicities,
languages, and religions, coming to co-exist within the same political boundaries. This coming together
might result from colonialization, economic migration, forced or voluntary relocation, political persecu-
tions, trade, and warfare. The Republic of Singapore, in 1965, was a new state and a new society
in which ethnic segregation meant that there were no foundations of a national identity and social
cohesion based on collective history and culture found in older societies, such as India or Indonesia.[8]
Central to the objectives of the People's Action Party (PAP), which formed a government in 1965, was
the imperative to control all mechanisms and policies to prioritize "economic progress and ethnic
harmony" in a society where segregation and loyalty along ethnic lines were not conducive to the
formation of a community with common interests.[9] For the Singapore government, the rationale for
nation-building has always been and continues to be the fostering of the development of a Singaporean
national identity among the population, particularly one that prevails over the demands of the Chinese,
Malay, or Indian communities in the city state.[10]

Multi-racialism and nation-building

As part of nation-building, the Singapore government espouses "multi-racialism" as "the ideology that
accords equal status to the cultures and ethnic identities of the various 'races' that are regarded as . . .
compos[ing] a plural society."[11] For Singapore, the concept of multi-racialism also concerns ethnicity

and ethnic relations because of several features set within its urban, national, and regional contexts: the ethnic and social heterogeneity of its people; the historical and social relations among ethnic groups and social interactions among ethnic individuals; and the state's management of ethnic issues and ethnic relations.[12]

Further examination of multi-racialism raises issues about "race" and "inter-race," concepts that interact in the continuous construction of community and identity for the three ethnic groups at local and national levels. "Race" is kept in check politically by the explicit recognition that Singapore is a multi-racial society, and racial tolerance is protected by the law. In making multi-racialism a national policy, the government is placed in a neutral position, where legislation prevents acting in ways that cannot advantage any particular ethnic group; hence, racial cultural matters are directed to the domain of private and voluntary, individual or collective, practices.[13] The neutral stance has preserved for the state a very high level of autonomy and insulates it from pressures that might arise from matters related to race issues. Multi-racialism has a two-pronged effect: "a high visibility of race is promoted voluntarily in the social body, and concurrently, the strategic effect is one of pushing race out of the front line of politics."[14]

Visualising multi-racialism

Multi-racialism, as a "cultural and social *institution,*" has become ingrained almost invisibly in the fabric of life in Singapore.[15] Since 1965, the implementation of multi-racialism as ideology and policy in nation-building has led to a rich history of the representation of ethnicity and multi-racialism in Singapore. The process of cultural representation raises two concepts that affect the visualization of ethnic groups: "'Cultural definition' involves being identified by oneself (and by others) as belonging to a distinctive cultural group; and 'cultural control' involves members of a specific cultural group exerting social, economic, and/or political influence over laws, issues, and representations of that group."[16] In this case, the Singapore government clearly takes on the role of "cultural control" in steering the socio-cultural construction of ethnic identity and multi-racialism in posters and other forms of graphic design produced for a specific ethnic group or the nation. The "official" graphic designs draw from contemporary, historical, and ethnographic diacritic for inclusion as cultural markers in the design. A survey of the typology of diacritics from language reform campaign poster designs for the Chinese community from 1979 to 2002 indicates two categories of diacritics: (1) ethno-specific, including costume, festival, food, mythology, calligraphy, art/craft, auspicious symbols, architecture, color, cartoon characterization, and patterns; and (2) culture-specific, including family, career, work, children, relationship, school, commerce, social situations, and social spaces.

The policy of multi-racialism is represented graphically, for domestic consumption, through the inclusion of ethnic representation from the three groups in images that portray national identity or the nation. These graphic designs are layered with meanings of ethnicity and national identity (e.g., the display of large posters and banners in August 2006 in celebration of the 41st National Day for constituents living in the East Coast district). The foreground of the poster design prominently featured five People's Action Party (PAP) representatives (three Chinese, one Malay, and one Indian) who are the Members of

Parliament for the local electorate, as well as the slogan, "Together. We Celebrate Our 41st National Day," in the four official languages. A photographic montage of women and children filled the background: to the right, an Indian woman in a dark blue sari and a Chinese woman in a red *qipao*-style dress; and to the left, a Malay woman wearing a white *hijab*. The Singapore flag as a symbol of the nation-state was emphasized by the image of children waving small flags while a large billowing flag framed the top left-hand corner of the poster.

Bilingualism and ethnic identity

The Republic of Singapore has designated four official languages: Mandarin or *huayu* for the Chinese, *bahasa* for the Malays, and Tamil for the Indians, while English, historically a "neutral" language for cross-cultural interaction during British administration, is for commerce, communication, and science and technology. *Bahasa* is also the national language and is used for the national anthem and ceremonial purposes. As part of the nation-building process, the Singapore government recognized the need for an education system that would nurture in young people the values that would ensure their loyalty and commitment to the nation. The government introduced the policy of bilingualism to promote racial harmony and integration, with the rationale that "English is seen as the language of technology and management, and the Asian languages as the carriers of cultural values."[17] The post–1966 bilingual policy in education prescribed the use of English with either Mandarin, Malay, or Tamil, depending on the "mother tongue" of the student. Through the preservation of the use of the three main ethnic languages in Singapore, the bilingual policy is seen as a bridge to the three cultural heritages in Singapore, and as such provides the "cultural ballast" for maintaining a cohesive and stable society.[18]

The policy of bilingualism is manifest in the use and display of language in official campaign graphics for communicating to the Singapore populace. From a survey of graphic designs produced in Singapore since 1979, three categories of how the official languages were presented could be identified: (1) all four languages in one graphic application for a national audience; (2) combinations of English and Chinese, English and Malay, and English and Tamil, in a series of generic or integrated graphics for a national audience; and (3) individual language in one graphic for a specific ethno-cultural group. Together, the policies of bilingualism and multi-racialism enable a flexible system of design strategies for communicating via language and images in social campaigns (e.g., National Day posters to reinforce identity and collective values, or the "Speak Mandarin" campaign posters for language reform in the Chinese community).

Speak Mandarin campaign

In 1979 Prime Minister Lee Kuan Yew inaugurated the Speak Mandarin campaign with the two-fold aim of encouraging young Chinese Singaporeans to speak in Mandarin within five years' time and of making Mandarin the language of "the coffee shop, of the hawker centre, of the shops" within a decade.[19] The rationale for the adoption of Mandarin as the *lingua franca* of the Chinese community included the following: the function of Mandarin for the retention of Chinese cultural traditions and values, Mandarin as the language for instruction and teaching, Mandarin as the language to unify all dialect-speaking Chinese in Singapore, and Mandarin as the language for trading with mainland China (although this last reason was not publicly announced in 1979 because China was still regarded with suspicion during the late 1970s).[20]

Although the bilingual policy strengthened the use of the mother tongue among the three main ethnic groups in Singapore, the continuing emphasis on the Speak Mandarin campaign caused the Malays and Indians to feel "threatened and perhaps even alienated by the repeated exhortation to speak Mandarin" and consequently heightened the racial consciousness of all Singaporeans.[21] The poster designs for the annual Speak Mandarin campaigns focus on themes that feature "traditional" cultural markers, including Chinese architecture, decorative arts, mythology, and painting, as well as contemporary images of the individual and/or family in social scenarios.

For the tenth anniversary of the Speak Mandarin campaign, in 1989, the selected theme was "More Mandarin, Less Dialect. Make it a Way of Life." Produced by the Ministry of Information and the Arts, the bilingual poster was designed to focus on two images: the first, a couple and three children in a family scenario, and the second, a workplace setting with three adults (two men and one woman). Although the dominant use of red—an auspicious color in Chinese culture—was conspicuous as a cultural marker, the first image can be interpreted in the context of a revision in socio-economic planning and policy by the government—namely, population growth and labor. The image of the Chinese "family of five" underscored the government's anxiety of a reduced labor force because of falling birth rates, and contrasted sharply with typical poster images of the "ideal" Singaporean family from 1966 to 1980, when the Singapore government introduced three five-year plans for birth control that encouraged women to adopt the national policy of a two-child family.[22]

Public housing policy

As a consequence of the poor economic conditions of migrants and the British administration's policy of racial segregation, the population of Singapore in the late 1950s was characterized by relatively homogenous enclaves based on racial and social affiliations. For the Singapore government, public housing represents one of the major priorities and instruments to promote the development of a national identity among Singaporeans through desegregation of the ethnic groups. In 1960 the Housing Development Board (HDB) was established by the government to provide low-cost public housing to alleviate a housing shortage, poor housing conditions, and rapid population growth.[23] The conditions attached to obtaining a public housing flat were citizenship, income, and family size—and not ethnic or racial affiliation. In addition to solving the housing shortage during the first two decades of independence, the government's public housing programs played a significant role in nation-building by establishing public housing estates, where desegregated communities of Singaporeans of different racial, linguistic, or religious groups could co-exist and interact with one another, and in many instances, for the first time.

Town councils were established in 1988 as part of the transfer of limited powers from the government to Members of Parliament, to grassroots leaders, and ultimately to the residents in public housing estates. The intention was to empower the residents with more responsibility for their own living environment. As part of the management process, town councils regularly produced posters that encouraged all residents to behave responsibly and to maintain good neighborly relationships with others. These posters were displayed on special notice boards to inform residents of local council regulations, housing estate regulations, news, and events.

The "Keep our estates clean for gracious living" poster, produced by the East Coast Residents Council and People's Association in 1998, typifies the message and graphics for this purpose. The composition of the illustration idealized two males, Malay and Indian, and a Chinese couple in the foreground, framed by modern apartment blocks and lush gardens in the background. Because this poster was designed for use in a multi-racial environment, the design incorporated cultural markers—skin color and clothing—to differentiate the ethnicity of individuals, as well as to symbolize the "multi-racial community" in an inclusive message for all residents.

Conclusion

This case study illustrates briefly the role of graphic design as an instrument for mass communication, particularly the representation and management of ethnicity and identity in nation-building. It demonstrates how the Singaporean government influenced the production and consumption of knowledge about multi-racialism as ideology and policy through the use of iconography and language, and it shows the socio-cultural and political effects on national consciousness. The case study calls for further research in graphic design history that examines the cognitive authority of the narrative, without which concrete design forms of past and present would seldom be noteworthy.

Notes

1. Anthony D. Smith, "The Nation: Invented, Imagined, Reconstructed?", in *Reimagining the Nation,* M. Ringrose and A.J. Lerner, eds (Buckingham and Philadelphia: Open University Press, 1993), 9.
2. Victor Margolin, "The Visual Rhetoric of Propaganda," *Information Design Journal*, 1 (1979): 107–22.
3. R.S. Milne and Diane K. Mauzy, *Singapore: The Legacy of Lee Kuan Yew* (Boulder: Westview Press, 1990), 59–61.
4. Bee Geok Leow, *Census of Population Statistical Release 1: Demographic Characteristics* (Singapore: Singapore Department of Statistics, 2000), 9. The Singapore Department of Statistics defines Singapore residents as citizens and permanent residents with local residence.
5. C.M. Turnbull, *A History of Singapore, 1819–1975* (Kuala Lumpur: Oxford University Press, 1977, 1980), 34–77.
6. Cantonese, Hainan, Hakka, and Hokkien represent some of the dialect groups in Chinese Singaporean society and reflect the diversity of immigrant cultures from southern Chinese provinces.
7. For a definition of the diverse ethnicities that fall under the CMIO classification system, refer to Glossary: Census 2000 Concepts and Definitions http://www.singstat.gov.sg/statsres/glossary/population.html#C (accessed September 26, 2010).

8. Raj Vasil, *Governing Singapore: A History of National Development and Democracy* (Sydney: Allen & Unwin, 2000), 47–8.

9. Ibid, 51.

10. Ah Heng Lai, *Meanings of Multiethnicity: A Case Study of Ethnicity and Ethnic Relations in Singapore* (Kuala Lumpur: Oxford University Press, 1995), 15.

11. Geoffrey Benjamin, "The Cultural Logic of Singapore's 'Multiracialism'," in *Singapore: Society in Transition,* R. Hassan, ed. (Kuala Lumpur: Oxford University Press, 1976), 115.

12. Ah Heng Lai, *Meanings of Multiethnicity,* 15.

13. Beng-Huat Chua, *Communitarian Ideology and Democracy in Singapore* (London and New York: Routledge, 1995), 106–7.

14. Ibid.

15. Geoffrey Benjamin, "The Cultural Logic of Singapore's 'Multiracialism'," in *Singapore: Society in Transition,* R. Hassan, ed. (Kuala Lumpur: Oxford University Press, 1976), 115.

16. Fath Davis Ruffins, "The Politics of Cultural Ownership," in *Looking Closer 2: Critical Writings on Graphic Design,* M. Beirut, W. Drenttel, S. Heller, and D. K. Holland, eds (New York: Allsworth Press, 1997), 142–4.

17. John Clammer, *Singapore: Ideology, Society, Culture* (Singapore: Chopmen Publishers, 1985), 133.

18. Ibid, 22.

19. Kuan Yew Lee, "Mandarin or Dialect?", *Straits Times* [Singapore], November 24, 1979.

20. Eddie C.Y. Kuo, "Mass Media and Language Planning: Singapore's 'Speak Mandarin' Campaign," *Journal of Communication,* 32 (2) (1984): 25–6.

21. Raj Vasil, *Asianising Singapore: The PAP's Management of Ethnicity* (Singapore: Heinemann Asia, 1995), 72.

22. Singapore Family Planning and Population Board, Fourteenth Annual Report 1979 (Singapore: Singapore Family Planning & Population Board, 1979), 3.

23. Riaz Hassan, "Public Housing," *Singapore: Society in Transition* (Kuala Lumpur: Oxford University Press, 1976), 241.

Visual essay

Chapter 5.2.5

"Iced up" and "platinum plus": the development of hip-hop typographic ornaments

Ryan Molloy

First published in *Visual Rhetoric and the Eloquence of Design*, ed. Leslie Atzmon, West Lafayette, IN: Parlor Press (2011), 373–90. © David Blakesley/Parlor Press/Ryan Molloy.

"Bling-bling" can be loosely defined as the excessively decorated, lavish and often outsized jewelry and accessories common in hip-hop circles. In my design process for the typographic ornaments that are the focus of this essay, I took inspiration from the love of excess that pervades hip-hop culture and then finds its way into hip-hop artifacts such as bling-bling. My set of ornaments—which continues to expand as I try to keep up with the latest hip-hop fashions—references embellished hip-hop-style automobile hubcaps, gold teeth, silver chains and necklaces, and other diamond-encrusted accessories. My ornaments and my visual essay glorify hip-hop excess, celebrate cultural and visual appropriation, and serve as a tongue-in-cheek satirical comment on the mainstreaming of hip-hop.

Ornament was ubiquitous in printed media until the early twentieth century. Twentieth-century modernist designers, who embraced the so-called "machine aesthetic," broke with tradition and vehemently condemned ornament. They shortsightedly defined it as frivolous form with no function. Jan Tschichold's ardent distaste for ornament became the cannon recited by designers. In 1928, Tschichold wrote in *Die neue Typographie*, "The use of ornament in whatever style or quality comes from an attitude of childish naivety. It shows a reluctance to use 'pure design,' a giving-in to a primitive instinct to decorate" (1995, 69). This disparagement of ornament spanned the twentieth century. In their 1985 book *Typographical Ornaments*, for example, graphic designers Philipp Luidl and Helmut Huber define the role of typographic ornament by claiming that, "the sole function of ornament is to decorate something" (1985, 9). They argue that ornament is devoid of meaning, and they distinguish ornament from symbols, which they believe carry a consistent message (1985, 10).[1]

My interest in developing a new set of typographic ornaments that responds to this still-prevalent anti-ornament sentiment has two facets. First, I am searching for representational forms that will call into question traditional definitions of typographic ornament, ornament created solely for the sake of decoration. I believe my bling-bling ornamental forms are not merely decorative; as I will explain in more detail in the pages that follow, they contain a visual narrative that structures information for those who create them and use them. Second, I am interested in creating forms with the rhetorical capacity to signify beyond their original context. Recently, I have noticed a resurgence of the use of ornament in graphic design work. The majority of the forms used, though, are motifs appropriated from pre-twentieth-century and early twentieth-century design that are then pasted into an alien context. Although the designs utilizing these forms are executed with great attention to craft, they seem foreign, and they are incongruous with contemporary themes. Such is the case with the work of designer Marian Bantjes, whose laborious ornamental work employs motifs based on everything from baroque ornamentation to art nouveau styling—connections that often appear unrelated to the content of Bantjes designs. Design critic Alice Twemlow notes that Bantjes does struggle with "the extent to which what she creates is superfluous stuff, and whether there is deeper meaning to be found through working with ornament" (2005, http://www.eyemagazine.com/feature.php?id=126&fid=560). I believe that arbitrarily using outdated motifs and ornaments does little to address the contemporary cultural contexts in which the work exists. If ornament is to become more than merely decoration, then it should carry meaning that relates to the cultural narratives that more immediately and pressingly surround its creation and use. In my bling-bling ornament and in my visual essay, I *purposely* appropriate typographic ornament from past centuries. Like a hip-hop DJ, I integrate these older forms with my newly designed bling-bling ornaments. I am not, however, merely borrowing indiscriminately; I am deliberately choosing these ornamental forms and assimilating them in celebration of hip-hop culture's penchant for discontinuity.

According to music journalist Danyel Smith, hip-hop is characterized by dissonances and contradictions: rappers wearing gold chains and driving luxury vehicles, for example, while rapping about living in poverty. What is more, these types of contradictions are embraced and, indeed, celebrated throughout hip-hop culture. Smith observes that in our American culture "feminists chant sexist rhymes, reformers boogie to money lust, white people sing along to songs that curse their existence on this planet. Black people memorize joints that extol self-destruction" (1999, ix). Contradictions like these are embraced and performed with the knowledge of hip-hop's participants.

It could be the very nature of hip-hop music that spawns these contradictions. The foundation of DJ-ing requires finding and then sampling a "break beat" from previously recorded music and looping it for the duration of the song. DJ Danger Mouse cleverly juxtaposes different types of content in his remixing of the Beatles *White Album* and Jay-Z's *The Black Album*. The remix album's title, *The Grey Album*, and method of combining music is by and large a clever play on words; often there's no particular logic or historical resonance at play in the selection of the break beat, only its sound. The action of the DJ creates aesthetic juxtapositions among smooth fluid beats, breaks where each sample is revealed, and instances where samples are aggressively altered by scratching the record to produce new sounds. Greg Dimitriadis notes that, "hip hop aesthetic, broadly speaking, allows for sharp and abrupt discontinuities or 'cuts' as it encourages continuity by way of the all-important mix" (1996, 183). He even extends this analysis to b-boying (break dancing) in which "the sharp fragmentation of the individual body parts gives the art a feeling of indeterminacy, evoking a postmodern aesthetic. However, fluid execution gives the dance an overriding sense of cohesion" (1996, 183). In all these ways, the creative methods of hip-hop provide fertile ground for contradictions and dissonances to take root.

My process always starts with pencil touching paper. I enjoy the tedium of draftwork, taking careful measure when drawing each line or curve. A set of compasses, French curves, oval templates, and drawing triangles are my constant companions. Most of the time, the drawing begins with a circle that is six inches in diameter. This measurement is arbitrary; it seems to fit well on the 8.5 by 11-inch page that is taped down to my drafting table. I believe the entire process should be laborious. Ornament, which until very recently was designed by craftsmen, demonstrates a deep commitment of time and effort that adds artistic value to the process and the artifact. It is this very traditional notion that forces me to construct each form as accurately as possible, first drawing it by hand to recreate the basic geometry of the original object and then studying carefully how light and reflection affect the form.

RYAN MOLLOY

The speakers in my studio thump Jay Z's *The Black Album*; music is my entry point into the cultural zeitgeist. Hip-hop culture has become a global phenomenon. More than just the music, it is a visually articulated lifestyle sold to and bought by a growing audience. Anyone can adopt the visual rhetorical trappings of hip-hop culture: the walk, the talk, and the gear. These trappings can signal one's membership in a youth movement, an outsider movement, or a political movement; hip-hop is a malleable culture capable of transforming and adapting itself to a whole host of visual and rhetorical permutations (Murray 2004, 6).

Hip-hop culture is intrinsically visual. DJ Kool Herc explains that, "people talk about the four hip-hop elements: DJ-ing, B-Boying, Mc-ing, and Graffiti. I think that there are far more than those: the way you walk, the way you talk, the way you look, and the way you communicate" (quoted in Chang 2005, xii). As Guillemette Bolens argues in her essay for this collection, bodily gestures constitute a powerful form of visual rhetoric. B-boying (breakdancing), graffiti, and fashion are central to hip-hop culture narratives—achievement of status, the quest for power, economic freedom, political might, or the desire to confront mainstream ideals (Williams 2007, 40).

Status in hip-hop culture is often awarded to the one whose displays of visual excess push beyond all precedents. This penchant for excess has been a consistent feature of hip-hop since the 1980s. However it wasn't until 1999 that rapper BG, Baby Gangsta, coined the term "bling-bling," referring to the extravagant jewelry worn by emcees. Bling-bling, which is onomatopoetic for the imaginary sound made when light is reflected off a diamond, references the excessive lifestyle ostensibly led by hip-hop emcees. Most associated with jewelry—watches, medallions, chains, earrings, and caps for teeth—"bling" has made its way into accessories such as cell phones, SUVs, televisions, cars, tire rims, and even—most recently—water bottles (Bling H20 2007). Bling-bling is perhaps hip-hop culture's most visible display of excess (Murray 2004, 18).

"Bling-bling," however, is not merely aesthetic. In his book *Ornament: A Modern Perspective*, James Trilling elaborates on the various functions of ornament. One of the earliest functions of ornament was as a rhetorical expression of wealth and social status. Trilling explains: "Considerations of status frequently affect the character and applications of ornament, as when ornament is used to transform ordinary goods into luxurious ones" (2003, 77). This is the primary function of "bling"—to embellish the wearer who subsequently becomes a living status symbol. Wearing bling imbues the wearer with instant veneration. Its visual rhetoric of excess takes on a potent, almost fetishistic value for the wearer. Hip-hop journalist Touré writes that, "in the bling-bling generation, if you've got money, you never leave home without wearing it" (2006, 367).

In front of me is a catalog for Diablo automobile rims. I prefer to draw using manufacturer's photographs; the rims are lit to perfection, accentuating the polished chrome. The photography renders the objects in three values: the mid-tone silver-grey of the metal, the white specular highlights, and a black reflection of the darkened studio space it was photographed in. The latter two values are what I am most interested in translating to page.

The goal of drawing the images is capturing the essence of bling: its flashy shine. Each object is rendered to reproduce the effect of light on a reflective surface. In my opinion, it is the detail of the reflection that creates the inherent beauty of the ornament. The form of the rim is often a basic combination of shapes and symmetry. It is drawing the reflection that adds a high level of complexity to my motifs. The forms I create are part imagined—my own fantasies about "bling" made manifest. The reflections are deliberately drawn falsely, straying from an exact reproduction of the manufacturers' photographs, yet they remain realistic by virtue of my knowledge of how objects reflect light. The drawing process seeks to create a heightened illusion of depth, an immaculate shimmer on the surface of the page. Simultaneously, it is an exaggeration of form that fuels the underlying satire. The fascination with surface glitter—as opposed to underlying substance—is so overblown that it seems to feed on itself, culminating in a frenzied desire for the most glittery glitter imaginable.

I am particularly fond of the chrome Diablo Teardrop for its flowerlike forms. I purposefully choose to draw ornaments whose forms evoke qualities of art nouveau's asymmetry and its use of curvilinear forms. Other forms found in the ornaments borrow from art deco, characterized by its repetition of rigid, rectilinear geometries. The formal characteristics of both periods stereotypically suggest a sense of opulence, gaudiness, and wealth, which can be found in hip-hop culture. I liken this part of my process to the sampling of a DJ; like a DJ, I am choosing my break beats.

RYAN MOLLOY

The documents I create while drafting, as time-consuming as they are, are only studies. I use them as means to familiarize myself with the forms before redrawing them digitally. Prior to digital type foundries, typographic ornament was disseminated in the form of cast lead type. I feel it is important that the typographic ornaments I create can be disseminated as a functioning typeface. The move to the computer isn't a time-saving measure; several hours still go by as I redraw each ornament digitally. I still pay homage to craft. At the same time, crafting the forms in such a time-consuming manner seems to sit in opposition to the artifact's intended ease of use as a simultaneously high-end and off-the-shelf application of luxury. I enjoy the parallel this has to the contradictions found in hip-hop culture.

If I imagine myself as a DJ as I design my visual essay, my ornaments become my track. I continue to borrow and sample from various periods. I make use of the tradition of pattern books, produced by manufactures of decorative goods to demonstrate suggested uses of their products. The ornaments become borders, rows, and flourishes. I continue to borrow from many historical periods of typography, from rococo, neoclassicism/academicism, and early twentieth-century design. I do this with some regard for the meaning of the original, but I also look for the patterns/structures that would best fit my ornaments. The designs, however, are not reproductions where I simply swap out traditional ornament for my own. Like the ornaments themselves, which stray from being exact representations, the page design in my visual essay is part imagined. I modify the formats to communicate over-the-top extravagance; the ultimate goal is an extension of the celebration of visual excess in hip-hop culture by melding it with vintage ornamental forms and rigorous production methods from history.

I create further tensions and contradictions in my work by also flouting historical conventions for designing typographic ornament. I ignore typographic conventions of type size, line height, and line width. In traditional printing, cast lead type dictated the foundation of all measures; in my process I ignore these measurements. Type size is slightly skewed from conventional sizes. I employ measures of 10.123 or 17.98 points, measurements unheard of when using lead type. It is executed subtly, undermining my earlier attention to craft in favor of ease of use and malleability. I purposely treat type as an easily applicable commodity, ignoring typographic convention while making these minor adjustments. In my mind, I see my ornaments as cousins of commercial objects such as Bling Ring, a set of easily applied stick-on Swarovski crystals for cell phones or the much cheaper alternative Bling Ring Too.[2]

My visual essay also spotlights my commentary on the appropriation of hip-hop visual mannerisms by mainstream culture. It is through the application of the ornaments to printed media that I intend the satire to become apparent. My intent in the visual essay is to expose the adaptability of bling by taking it beyond its role as fashion accessory. In my visual essay, I *refashion* bling into various objects: wallpapers, business cards, letterheads, and book design motifs. My commentary culminates in the final spread that ultimately offers the ornament as a commodified decoration, even for workaday objects such as business cards. The final page text reads "you've officially been pimped," which I borrowed from MTV's *Pimp My Ride*. On this show, ordinary cars are transformed into extravagant, glittering street machines, a process by which visual transformation becomes an ironic celebration of excess.

My typographic ornament gently lambastes mainstream media's exploitation of hip-hop culture's fascination with status, luxury, and wealth by transforming these values into a set of artifacts, a typeface that anyone can use with the ease of a keyboard stroke. At the same time, my ornaments interrogate the tenets of traditional typographic ornament design aesthetics, applications, and processes. My bling-bling ornaments are forms whose visual rhetoric carries two main messages: an original meaning that resonates in bona fide hip-hop culture and a satirical meaning that functions in both graphic design and mainstream cultural contexts.

RYAN MOLLOY

Notes

[1] The idea that typographic ornament is devoid of meaning is prevalent even in the publications of twentieth-century printers and designers who used ornament in their designs. One such example is Douglas McMurtrie, who in his 1930 book *Typographic Ornament* writes, "It seems to be essential to their function that they shall be of formal or conventional design—in other words, purely typographical in spirit, and not representative of other objects." Douglas McMurtrie, *Typographic Ornament* (Chicago: Privately Printed, 1930), 10.

[2] See Bling Ring Crystal Phone Cover Accessories. Bling Ring, Bling Your Ring, http://www.myblingring.com/ (accessed August 5, 2007).

you've officially been pimped

Chapter 5.2.6

Fighting Aids with pictures and words: South African health campaigns dominate the political landscape

Sean O'Toole

The words on the T-shirts are unambiguous: "HIV positive" reads the simple sans-serif legend on the white tops worn by members of the South African HIV/AIDS lobby group, the Treatment Action Campaign (TAC). Inelegant as the design is—its concept borrowed from Benetton's 1993 HIV Positive campaign— the cumulative package clearly articulates the burden confronting South Africa's emergent democracy. The burden being that 5.3 million South Africans, or nearly ten per cent of the population, are infected with HIV/AIDS. "Sort it out," the T-shirt demands.

Sadly, the graphic design interventions aimed at confronting the challenges of the country's HIV/AIDS problem have not always contributed much to the greater objective: a reduced incidence of HIV. A look at the short history of such work demonstrates the difficult, often circuitous, journey travelled by designers searching for coherent visual strategies aimed at curbing the upward march of the statistical barometer: 4.7 million infected by late last year; 5.3 million by the nation's tenth birthday on April 2004; 8 million projected by 2010.

Learning through stories

With nearly 25 per cent of South Africa's economically active individuals HIV-positive, the socio-political impact of the disease is clear. This has led to a variety of macro-level initiatives aimed at encouraging behavioural changes in sex and hygiene among a broad range of South Africans.

One of the most prominent of these initiatives is the social-change project initiated by the Soul City Institute for Health and Development Communication, which aims to "impact on society at the individual, community and socio-political levels." A non-governmental organisation established in 1992, Soul City uses an extensive multimedia strategy that combines television, radio and print, with branding focused on one core identity.

Soul City's printed HIV/AIDS Action Pack includes materials aimed at a broad range of people involved in education or training. The two comic books in the pack, for instance, talk about issues

First published in *Eye*, 52 (13) (Summer 2004). © *Eye* magazine/Sean O'Toole.

ranging from transmission, prevention, stigma and discrimination to the HIV test, care and support. There is a strong narrative content to all these materials—Soul City's credo being that "human beings have always learnt through stories."

Branded strategies

Taking its cue from the integrated branded strategies initiated by Soul City, loveLife also aims for a multi-pronged media plan. Launched in September 1999, loveLife is South Africa's largest and most visible national HIV/AIDS prevention program. It has brought together a broad-based coalition that includes international foundations working in HIV/AIDS prevention, the South African government, significant South African media organizations and private corporations, and leading South African non-government organisations. The foundation's stated goal is to "substantially reduce the HIV infection rate among young South Africans."

The target audience of loveLife's campaign are pre- and newly-sexually active adolescents aged twelve to seventeen. This age group is about to enter a dangerous period of their lives. A recent study showed HIV prevalence among 15- to 24-year-old South Africans to be 10.2 percent. Prevalence was significantly higher among women (15.5 percent) than among men (4.8 percent), and in the 20- to 24-year-old age group (16.5 percent) as compared to the 15- to 19-year-old age group (2.5 percent).

HIV has disproportionately affected young women. Among the 10.2 per cent of South African youth who are HIV positive, 77 percent are women. Nearly one in four women aged 20–24 are HIV positive, as compared to 1 in 14 men of the same age. The greater susceptibility to HIV infection among women is attributable to both biological and social factors.

Among its many media strategies, loveLife has embarked on a massive billboard campaign. There are over 1,000 billboards and signs on water towers proclaiming loveLife's message along the country's main arterial routes: these have become a familiar part of the South African visual landscape.

Since first staking their claim to the public consciousness five years ago, the creative content of these billboards has been the subject of heated debate. The mishmash graphic style of the early campaigns, such as "Foreplay" and "The future ain't what it used to be," now look naive. The early campaigns appear to have been more concerned with proclaiming that it was good to be young, black and proud than actually challenging the viewer to think about changing their sexual habits.

The Big Ad spend

It was only in 2002 that loveLife's billboard campaigns acquired coherence, with a campaign formed around a series of abrupt quotes discussing real-life scenarios. LoveLife's somewhat unruly coming of age in the public view has earnt it many detractors. In addition to outraged callers to radio talk shows, media critics have been vocal in labelling the billboard campaign as 'extravagant' (for its £1.3 million ad-spend per annum) and "subliminally racist" (because of its early focus on black subjects). Its aspirational images have also been accused of promoting "conspicuous consumption."

Yet the campaign is partially protected from criticism by a "gagging clause" that prohibits three partner newspapers from publishing "material that will harm the loveLife images." Journalist Chris Barron, writing in *The Media*, an upmarket monthly offering astute analyses of the South African media, has argued that loveLife is cynically leveraging its ad spend (roughly £2 million per annum) in a way that elevates the campaign above the vicissitudes of public criticism.

In its defence, loveLife points out that its billboards are but one element of a targeted multimedia campaign that is actively supported by grass-roots initiatives. Research has also shown a two-thirds (65 percent) awareness of at least four loveLife programmes or products among all South African youth. The same study also reported a high level of awareness across all geographic areas. More than three-quarters of young people living in rural areas reported awareness of loveLife, while in urban areas this rose to 93 percent. This begs the question as to whether awareness and visibility automatically imply success. For instance, many of us are aware of Coca-Cola's marketing campaigns without actually drinking Coke.

Tackling government and industry

If one accepts visibility as a marker of success, then the Treatment Action Campaign (TAC) certainly comes across as a huge success. Whereas loveLife and similar organizations are focused on pro-active campaigning, with success predicated on a fall in HIV statistics, the TAC is a vocal lobbying group. It consists of an association of organizations and individuals, all operating independently of both the government and the pharmaceutical industry, who have pitted themselves against the slow response of President Thabo Mbeki's government to the treatment of the virus.

Launched on December 10, 1998 (International Human Rights Day), the TAC has vociferously campaigned for the affordable treatment of people affected by HIV/AIDS. It famously challenged the pricing of AIDS drugs set by multinational pharmaceutical companies in court, and influenced a policy turnaround with regards to the national roll-out of anti-retroviral drugs such as AZT. On August 8, 2003 the South African cabinet approved the provision of anti-AIDS drugs for HIV-positive people through the public health system. (In addition to denying a causal link between HIV infection and AIDS, the government of President Mbeki had previously denounced anti-retroviral drugs as an attempt to poison black people.) For his singular efforts, Zackie Achmat, a leading activist with the TAC, has been shortlisted for the 2004 Nobel Peace Prize.

Echoes of the old struggle

The TAC's graphic activism is interesting for a number of reasons. Foremost among these is its confrontational placard-and-protest style. This has direct historical antecedents in the techniques and values espoused during the struggle against apartheid. Indeed, there is little to differentiate the grass-roots activism that has mushroomed around the "HIV Positive" banner from that which took shape around the twin slogans of "Free Nelson Mandela" and "Stop Apartheid." The message is also urgent enough to excuse the TAC's poor stock of graphic visual material.

However, the TAC's activism is more than simply throwback politics—it is of the age. During the short period of its existence, the TAC has been vocal in linking a regional health concern with the drift of the new global activism. "Through mass mobilization, civil disobedience, legal action, extraordinary personal sacrifice and visionary leadership, Zackie Achmat and the TAC have helped to galvanize a global movement to provide hope and gain access to treatment for those with HIV/AIDS," the American Friends Service Committee, a US-based Quaker organization, observed in their written statement nominating the TAC for the Nobel Prize.

The success of the TAC's activism bears out a point made by Tony Barnett and Alan Whiteside— authors of *AIDS in the Twenty-First Century: Disease and Globalisation* (Palgrave Macmillan, 2003)—that "HIV/AIDS is a problem that is not handled easily by the mechanisms and methods of the nation state." Barnett and Whiteside go on to state in their book that HIV/AIDS has "drawn out from the world community a response that depends of fluidity rather than extreme bureaucracy."

This statement acknowledges the vital role that activist groups, collectives and individuals have played in defining how the HIV/AIDS problem is visualised. This is particularly true in South Africa. Beyond the highly visible, often contested, campaigns initiated by both government and non-government organizations, there exists a vast panoply of creative resistance and graphic activism. This is shaping a new visual language that expresses the HIV/AIDS issue.

Community voices on the street

One relatively recent phenomenon is the community mural. South Africa has a long tradition of mural advertisements, particularly in the townships, executed by sign writers, graphic artists, and painters. Mural art, though, is much newer. Before the 1990s it was practiced on a small scale due to political repression and a rigidly regulated conservative bureaucracy. Art historian Sabine Marschall links its rise as a popular graphic form to the country's gradual socio-political liberation.

Usually collaborative by nature and dominated by male artists in black communities, mural art is characterized by the suppression of individual self-expression in favor of a mutual style. Remarking on the general content of these murals, Marschall says: "Murals are about asserting identity and resistance; they create a sense of place and ownership; they 'talk' in a specific language targeted at a local community audience."

Largely overlooked by the art establishment, owing to its perceived inadequacies in terms of technical and conceptual sophistication, mural art has also been criticised for confirming rather than challenging the prevailing stereotypes of race and gender identity. Nevertheless mural art offers a fascinating parallel narrative in a visual landscape where branding, not message, is regarded as the key virtue of the country's signature HIV/AIDS campaigns.

A similarly ignored narrative is discernible in the story of glass beadwork projects. Glass beadwork has a rich cultural history among the diverse ethnic groups inhabiting South Africa. The geometric precision of

Ndebele beadwork, for instance, is reminiscent of the linearity of De Stijl. Older examples of glass bead-work are highly sought-after and collectable.

In part, this accounts for the popularity of the Monkeybiz beadwork products. Made by a collective of disadvantaged women in Cape Town townships, the glass bead products, which include wall-hung murals and red-ribbon lapel badges, articulate something of the complexity of the HIV/AIDS problem in South Africa.

Disease as commodity

The point is best argued by way of an analogy. The essayist and critic Daniel Harris, also the author of *The Rise and Fall of Gay Culture* (Hyperion, 1997), attributes the proliferation of HIV/AIDS products in the US to harsh political realities. "My thesis is this," he has written, "in the early days of the epidemic, the Reagan and Bush administrations refused to allocate the money necessary to cover basic costs of research and treatment, with the result that movie stars, and not government officials, became the epidemic's states-men, its panhandlers, the ones who were forced to seek alternative sources of funding out in the open market, in charity balls, rock concerts and fashion benefits. Because of insufficient federal funds, activists were forced to turn the disease into a commodity and sell it to the public like any snack food."

Harris further argues that charitable contributions were extorted from the public by arousing pity for the victims "by packaging the epidemic in sentimental clichés that reduced potential donors to a state of maximum susceptibility. The more money that was needed for the disease, the kitschier it became." Substitute the Reagan and Bush for Mbeki and the approach described above illustrates why so much craft art flirts with becoming sentimentalized, kitsch product.

The Zimbabwean graphic designer Chaz Maviyane-Davies has made some interesting comments about the overlapping red ribbon and its emergence as a universal HIV/AIDS solidarity symbol. [Inspired by the yellow ribbons that honoured American soldiers participating in the Persian Gulf War, the design was the outcome of a collaborative project initiated by the Artists Caucus of Visual AIDS. Conceived in the spring of 1991, the Ribbon Project was officially launched at the 45th Annual Tony Awards ceremony on June 2, 1991.]

After attending the fourteenth International AIDS Conference in Spain in 2002, Maviyane-Davies offered a report to Design for the World [www.designfortheworld.org]. "Ribbons, ribbons everywhere and on everything," he observed in his review entitled "Graphic Design for AIDS: The sense of the possible." "In all shapes and sizes, like lipstick, distorted, enhanced, patterned, manipulated, given a national or ethnic slant and even sold. Tag this motif on to anything and avoid the risk and challenges of communicating about this pandemic." Maviyane-Davies concluded his report with a concise rebuke. "In effect," he writes, "I found this stylized zealousness to be a classic hallmark of graphic design's denial and laziness."

Art initiatives

Some of the aforementioned laziness and reductiveness has insinuated itself into South African art claiming to make sense of the lived experience. With the proliferation of the HIV/AIDS pandemic, South

The era of local design education began in the 1970s. Fundamental Bauhaus design principles were introduced and widely read among young designers in Hong Kong through the books of Wucius Wong, an active design educator from the mid–1960s to the early 1980s in Hong Kong. Wong was an American-trained Chinese, whose two books, *Principles of Two-Dimensional Design* and *Principles of Three-Dimensional Design,*[14] brought a strong Western influence to design theory education in the region. In turn, the new generation of emerging Hong Kong designers was heavily imbued with Western sensibilities and design values.

Among the pioneer local designers in interpreting and exploring the use of traditional Chinese folk art and high art elements in their design work is Kan Tai-keung. The retrospective of his work published in 1998[15] reveals that Kan's early 1970s works were devoid of Chinese elements, and simply followed the Western style. Starting in the mid–1970s, he began to employ Chinese symbols and images in his designs.[16] In a 1977 poster design produced for a graphic design course," a private design school, Kan explored the integration of traditional Chinese calligraphy together with the constructive lines borrowed from Western typographic design. Choi Kai-yan was a pioneer who attempted to apply Western typographic theory to Chinese writing. In his work for the Baptist Press in 1977 (Figure 5.34), Choi employed Chinese characters but used icons to replace parts of them. For example, the logotype design for the company places an icon of a book at the top right of the character. In spite of the replacement, the character's original meaning still can be read. This technique of adding icons and meaning to Chinese characters became Choi's design signature.

The late 1970s marked the beginning of cultural exchange activities between Hong Kong designers and institutions in mainland China. After the cultural revolution ended in 1976 and prior to the official announcement of China's Open Door Policy in late 1978, some art and design institutions began to interact with overseas organizations. Activities such as Kan Tai-keung's lecture on packaging and graphic design at the Guangzhou Institute of Arts in 1978,[17] and the visit of the First Institute of Art & Design Association of Hong Kong to the Central Arts and Crafts Academy in Beijing in 1979,[18] stimulated new developments in graphic design in mainland China. These two visits were followed by exhibitions. The first, the Hong Kong Designers Show, was held in 1979 at the Guangzhou Institute of Arts. The second, Design '80, was held both in Hong Kong and Beijing in 1980. These two events were some of the activities that introduced outside influence into the development of contemporary graphic design directions in mainland China.

China had been cut off from the outside world, and there were hardly any commercial art activities there for almost three decades. Under such circumstances, the modern Chinese design movement started in the 1930s by Shanghai designers was not able to keep pace with the international design trends throughout this period. With the introduction of the latest design trends through an increasing number of international exchanges, very little influence of the older generation of mainland designers was passed on to the younger generation in the 1980s and 1990s. The main direction of the design education system in mainland China, in today's context, is still based on a skill-training curriculum from the 1960s Russian model.[19] Creative and conceptual thinking have not been emphasized in design education. Thus, the influx of overseas design concepts, in which Hong Kong initially was significant, played an influential and inspirational role for young people and students such as Wang Xu and Wang Yue-fei, who later became a pioneer in graphic design in mainland China.

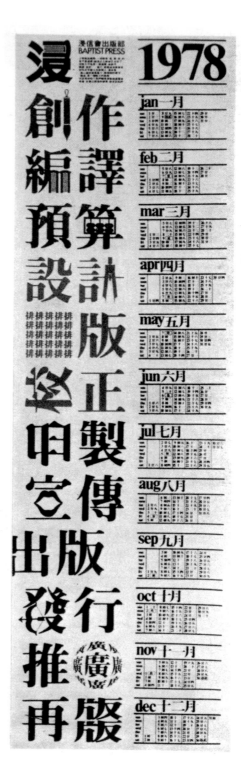

Figure 5.34 Baptist Press calendar.
© 1977. Designer: Choi Kai Yan.
Accreditation: Choi's Concept.

Spreading the seeds of communication in the 1980s

The 1980s was the era during which Hong Kong played a major role in fostering and building connections with design practitioners and institutes in mainland China and Taiwan. Hong Kong designers responded to the invitation of a Taiwanese graphic design group to participate in the Exhibition of Asia Designing Masters held in Taiwan in 1982.[20] Compared to work from Hong Kong, Taiwan graphic design was less exposed to Western design, due to the political constraints, censorship, and martial law on the island until 1987. The early 1980s also saw the rise of the awareness of Hong Kong Chinese of their identity due to the coming handover to Chinese sovereignty in 1997, which led to the development of two divergent design trends in Hong Kong. The incorporation and exploration of traditional Chinese elements, begun in the mid–1970s, was expanded and refined while, at the same time, other local design work developed in another direction toward the expression of pure Western themes.

Among the prominent Hong Kong designers to continue with the inclusion of Chinese elements in graphic design was Kan Tai-keung. As a practitioner of modern Chinese shuimo painting, Kan Tai-keung often used Chinese high art objects and brush strokes in his designs. For example, his transitional work between his Chinese style works in the mid–1970s and late–1980s is illustrated by a poster design for *Shui Mo: The New Spirit of Chinese Tradition* exhibition in 1985. Its black brush strokes, Chinese painting pallet, and red paint formed the basis for his future stylistic signature. The simplicity of the use of only red, white, and black is evidence of the continuity of his style from the late 1970s.

Another Hong Kong local trained designer to gain prominence in the 1980s was Alan Chan. As a collector of Chinese antiques, Chan benefited from his knowledge of artifacts from the past, which he often used in his designs. For example, in corporate identity work for the Canton Disco Club in Hong Kong in 1983 (Figure 5.35), Chan borrowed images of swimmers from the illustrations of 1930s Shanghai publications, and set them against brightly colored backgrounds to give the illusion of flying through space. Although Chan was best known for this modernized nostalgic style, his other works also demonstrate a sophisticated understanding of the blending of Chinese images with modern graphics. In the poster design for *Hello Hong Kong* in 1987, he created a central image of a black dragon on a red background. The traditional image of the dragon is modified in two ways, with the top half pixilated to evoke a computer image and the bottom half in a stylized brush stroke to evoke traditional calligraphy. Kan and Chan are the best known pioneers of the modern Chinese graphic design style. Other local designers, trained both in Hong Kong and overseas, who did not identify their style with Kan and Chan also found their own way without featuring a blend of Chinese and Western elements in their design work. Designers such as William Ho, Alan Zie Yongdar, Lillian Tang, Michael Miller Yu, John Au, Jennings Ku, Tony Tam, and Winnie Kwan continued their Western design approach without the incorporation of Chinese concepts and icons as part of their own characteristic styles.

By the mid–1980s, when Hong Kong designers were developing into two divergent design trends, their works began to be exhibited in mainland China on a regular basis. For example, the winning pieces from the HKDA shows of 1986 and 1988 traveled to Guangzhou.[21] Through such shows, as well as visits from Hong Kong designers, Hong Kong was able to export some influence to mainland China. Although Hong Kong played a leading role through the 1980s because of its relatively free and liberal environment for creative ideas, starting in the 1990s, the quality of graphic design work in mainland China and

Figure 5.35 Canton Disco Club corporate identity work. © 1983. Designer: Alan Chan.

Taiwan improved rapidly to reach an international standard. By the late 1980s, the more liberal political situation in Taiwan, together with continued economic development, supported international exchanges. From this period on, rapid improvements in the quality of Taiwanese design can be seen, and Taiwanese design organizations began to initiate joint ventures within Greater China.

A new era of interaction in the 1990s

In the early 1990s, the outstanding representative designers in mainland China and Taiwan noticeably followed the style of Kan Tai-keung and Alan Chan. By that time, Kan and Chan were well established as the masters of Chinese graphic design within Greater China design circles. Kan, in particular, played an active role in promoting his work in both Taiwan and China, and frequently was invited to give lectures, donate his works to institutions, judge competitions, and participate in shows and solo exhibitions on the mainland. There is no doubt that Hong Kong graphic design, especially as represented by

Kan Tai-keung, has played an important role in Chinese graphic design history. However, with more active designers in recent times, a great diversification of style has developed. The 1990s can be seen as the era of the rapid establishment of graphic design associations, expanding activities including many events centering on poster design and graphic design publications within Greater China, and the active participation of Chinese designers in major international poster design competitions. The various locales of Greater China had never been so connected and interactive, with a fully merged history of modern Chinese graphic design.

The proliferation of professional associations

Professional design organizations in Greater China always have played an important role in stimulating and promoting the local design industry, as well as establishing overseas connections, following the original example of the Hong Kong Designers Association (HKDA) in Hong Kong. Established in 1973, HKDA was one of the earliest professional design organizations in the region. Since then, HKDA has played a key role in organizing local design awards competitions and maintaining contacts with the outside world. In Taiwan as well, professional design organizations have played a central role in the development of graphic design, although not until much later.

The Amoeba group was formed in Taiwan by professional graphic designers in the early 1980s, but never generated much local or regional attention. Not until 1991, with the establishment of the Association of Taiwan Image Poster Designers (renamed the Chinese Poster Association in 1997) was a stable and influential professional association formed.[22] The primary objective of this association was promoting the quality of Taiwanese graphic design through creative poster design. Taiwanese graphic design was still searching for its own developmental direction at this stage. With the awareness of the needs of internationalization, new professional graphic designer groups such as the Taiwan Graphic Design Association, formed in 1994, and the Kaoshiong Graphic Design Association were established in Taiwan.

The development of graphic design associations in mainland China first began in Shenzhen. Due to the geographic proximity of Shenzhen to Hong Kong, Shenzhen design work for many years was the most advanced in mainland China. Before the establishment of the first graphic design association on the mainland, the Shenzhen Graphic Design Association in 1996, many future members of the Association already were active in organizing shows such as the Graphic Design in China Show in Shenzhen in 1992.[23] The event was a design competition accepting entries from Taiwan and mainland China, co-organized with the Taiwanese magazine *Taiwan Graphics Communications Monthly.* Soon after 1994, the quantity and quality of activities in inland cities in mainland China also increased rapidly. By the late 1990s, Shenzhen was no longer the dominant city in graphic design in mainland China.

Some other inland cities have quickly gained ground, and have been organizing their own activities including corporate identity conferences, nationwide design competitions, and international design exhibitions. The Shanghai Graphic Designers Association, established in 1998, was the second professional group to be formed on mainland China.[24]

Within Greater China, Macau is a relatively small city compared to Hong Kong both in terms of area and population. It was under Portuguese colonial rule until 1999, when it returned to Chinese sovereignty. The Department of Design at Macau University was not established until 1994. Since that time,

Macau designers have had the option of obtaining local training and education. The Association of Macau Designers also was established in 1994, and included members from various design disciplines. Although the membership is small compared to comparable associations in Taiwan, Hong Kong, and mainland China, the members remain active in intra-regional design competitions and other events.

The intra-regional poster design frenzy

The idea of thematic poster design invitational exhibitions is influenced by the Japanese and Europeans, but it is fair to say that the Chinese Poster Association of Taiwan started the thematic poster design frenzy, which later spread to Hong Kong and mainland China. Its main yearly event is a thematic poster design exhibition. The theme of the first invitational exhibition, held in 1991, was "The Beauty of Taiwan," and participation from 1991 to 1994 was restricted to its members.[25] Starting in 1995, the Chinese Poster Association Exhibition began to invite other Chinese participants from outside Taiwan to participate. In 1995, two designers from China and two from Hong Kong were invited.[26] The design theme for that year was "Written Chinese Characters." Designers could create freely within this theme, using written Chinese characters in the design.

The thematic poster exhibitions organized by associations within Greater China often centered on themes related to Chinese identity, and when the stated theme was not clearly related to Chinese-ness, participants often would include Chinese elements or interpretations in their works. The nature of this type of poster design exhibition primarily is to display the personal creative expression of the invited designers. However, the early exhibition on written Chinese characters also opened up new possibilities for Chinese typographic design. The theme of Chinese characters was used by many participants to explore explicitly Chinese subject matter, and to interrogate the cultural meanings of written characters. In Freeman Lau's work, the symbolic character for "good luck," normally used at the start of the Chinese New Year, is altered and thus reinterpreted to make a personal statement about the love of nature (Figure 5.36). Mainland Chinese designer Wang Xu reinterpreted the ideogram elements of Chinese characters, replacing them with pictures of the objects they represent, such as chicken feet for "claw" and vertical stones for "valley."

Compared to the development of Hong Kong graphic design, the mainland graphic designers have taken only a very short time to reach an international standard, especially in the area of poster design. The key figure in mainland China graphic design is Wang Xu, who had been working in Hong Kong since 1986 and returned to Guangzhou in 1995 to open his own design and publication business. Designers such as Wang Yue-fei, Zhang Da-li, Zhou Peng, Xia Yi-bo, Chen Shao-hua, and Han Jia-ying were key figures on the Shenzhen design scene in the mid–1990s. Chen Shao-hua was invited to the thematic poster invitational exhibition held by the Chinese Poster Association in 1996 under the theme of the "Colors of Taiwan." The following year, a thematic poster invitational exhibition was held for the first time on the mainland, in Shenzhen. The exhibition was co-organized by graphic design associations from Shenzhen, Hong Kong, Taiwan, and Macau under the theme of "Communication."

Again, many of the participants interpreted the theme in specific relationship to Chinese identity and culture, or in relation to cross-cultural themes. For example, mainland designer Zhou Peng utilized a Chinese paper cut of the character for "double happiness" along with black, superimposed icons for

Figure 5.36 Written Chinese Characters: The Love of Nature, thematic poster. © 1996. Designer: Freeman Lau.

"male" and "female" to convey the idea of male-female communication within marriage. Chen Shao-hua's work depicts a sleeping Chinese man dreaming a garbled mass of Romanized alphabet letters. A third example, Wang Xu's Coca-Cola bottle, is a porcelain version with a Chinese dragon in blue and green tones. These latter two examples represent cross-cultural communications with some humor and criticism. Together with mainland China, Hong Kong and Taiwan have become the three major players in most of the intra-regional events, but there are a few outstanding works from Macau. Ung Wai-meng, one of Macau's outstanding graphic designers, was born on the island and received his education in Portugal. His unique artistic drawing style shows a European influence, and his work has won many awards within Greater China.

Hong Kong has a tradition of concentrating on commercial works rather than on noncommercial creative poster design works. To respond to the intra-regional poster design frenzy, the HKDA adopted the thematic design idea for their biannual member shows. In 1997, their member show was organized under the theme of "Harmony." One of the major intra-regional poster design competitions held by Hong Kong organizations was the Asia-Pacific Poster Exhibition in 1997.[27] This exhibition called for entries from Asian countries including those of the Greater China region as well as Japan, Korea, Malaysia, and Singapore. The show reflected the quality and standard of work in Greater China compared to other Asian countries. The quality of Japanese work always has been considered the highest in the Asia-Pacific region, so the competition provided an opportunity for the designers of Greater China to have their work judged against this standard.

Since the first event of the intra-regional poster design invitational exhibition in 1997, different groups have organized various thematic poster exhibitions such as *Celebration of Reunification of Hong Kong With China* in 1997, *Establishment of the Shanghai Graphic Design Association* in 1998, *Celebration of Reunification of Macau With China* and *Opening of Design Museum in Beijing* in 1999. These intra-regional design competitions and invitational shows enabled the region to produce a large number of posters within a short time. However, because some of the invitational events did not include a referee system, the quality of the work produced varied considerably.

Another important recent trend in invitational poster exhibitions is their expansion beyond Greater China into the international sphere. For example, one of the latest invitational exhibitions, *Shanghai International Poster Invitational Exhibition '99,* invited not only Greater China designers, but also solicited the participation of designers from Japan, Korea, the Netherlands, Germany, England, the Czech Republic, France, Finland, Poland, Switzerland, and the United States.[28] The creative theme for the Greater China participants was "Interaction," while the overseas participants were invited to submit any of their poster works. Like the Asia-Pacific Poster Exhibition held in Hong Kong in 1997, events of this type provide an opportunity for Greater China designers to gain insight into how the standard of local works compared with the international standard. This trend of creating a theme and inviting overseas designers to also submit their works also has been adopted in Hong Kong. The biannual member show of the HKDA under the theme "Designers' Eyes on Hong Kong 2000" also invited prestigious overseas designers to submit their work without necessarily following the given theme. Subsequently, the same exhibition strategy also has been used by the Hong Kong Poster League, newly founded in 1998 by Kan Tai-keung, Alan Chan, Stanley Wong, Tommy Li, and Freeman Lau. The primary purpose of the group is to identify themes and to organize corresponding exhibitions on a regular basis. In their first show in 2000, under the theme of "People," they displayed their own thematic works and invited international designers[29] to submit works on any subject matter.

Publishing the sources of inspiration

An active intra-regional design scene and the flow of information have played a very important role in elevating the standard of work in mainland China. Together, these elements provide designers with creative opportunities as well as chances to display their work. Very often, works from intra-regional poster design shows have generated media exposure and publication opportunities. Before the 1990s, the flow of information was so limited that mainland designers had to purchase magazines and other publications imported from Hong Kong in order keep up with recent developments in the field. Due to the loosening of the political environment in mainland China, leading to a more liberal attitude toward commerce and advertising, the publication business for international graphic design books and local graphic design magazines has experienced a boom since the mid–1990s. The mainland printing industry also has developed rapidly through Hong Kong investment and experience, particularly in Shenzhen and southern coastal areas.

With the expanding of the local market as well as the demand of local designers to have access to knowledge about international developments and trends, magazines such as the Beijing-based monthly *Art and Design,* and the Guangzhou-based *Design Exchange* and *Packaging Design,* often report major overseas design competitions and exhibitions. *Hi-Graphic* is a magazine published since January 1998 by the Shanghai Graphic Design Association, and is another trendy graphic design periodical. This publication plays a role in introducing outstanding work from overseas, as well as providing a venue for members to display their work and report on their activities. Magazines have become an important means for mainland designers to learn from established international designers. Major book series of collections of individual designer's works such as *Graphic Designer's Design Life,* edited by Wang Xu, invite international designers such as Niklaus Troxler (Switzerland), James Victore (USA), Kari Piippo (Finland), Art Chantry (USA), Koichi Sato (Japan), Tanaka Ikko (Japan), Louise Fili (USA), and Henry Steiner (Hong Kong), to allow their work to be published and circulated in Chinese for a mainland audience. Other Hong Kong designers also have published their own individual portfolio books. Examples include Kan Tai-keung's book of his poster works, and the Freeman Lau and Tommy Li retrospective collections.[30] This type of design portfolio collection book often simply displays the design work by category or theme, seldom adding any analytical perspective or much informational text.

International poster graphic design events

In the year 2000, Hong Kong no longer enjoys a leadership role on the intra-regional design scene. Rather, new trends and developments now are being established in many of the cities within Greater China, and the common ground on which Greater China designers compare their work is the realm of overseas international competitions. Mainland designers have played a particularly active role in participating in these overseas competitions since the mid–1990s, and designers from other parts of Greater China have taken up the practice as well. For example, starting from the mid–1990s, mainland designers were represented at the International Poster Biennale in Warsaw, Poland, the Lahti Poster Biennale at the Lahti Art Museum in Finland, the International Computer Art Biennale in Rzeszow, Poland, the Colorado International Invitational Poster Exhibition in the U.S., the International Biennale of Graphic Design in the Czech Republic, the International Poster Trienniale in Toyama, Japan, and the Seoul Triennale Exhibition of Asian Graphic Posters in Korea. Many of the mainland entries won awards in these international competitions. For example, a series of posters designed by Zhang Da-li and Tang Di on the theme of "Human and Nature" won major awards at the International Computer Art Biennale in Rzeszow, Poland in 1999. Chen Fang also was one of the three highest award winners at the Colorado International Invitational Poster Exhibition in the U.S. with his poster *Victory* depicting a hand gesturing the "peace sign," with the two peace-sign fingers intact and the other three apparently violently blown away (Figure 5.37).

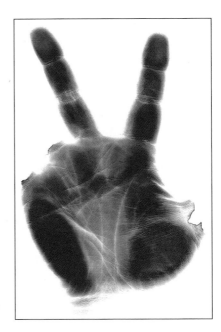

Figure 5.37 Victory, experimental poster.
© 1998. Designer: Chen Fang.

Compared to mainland designers, Hong Kong and Taiwan designers have not received many international awards. However, Hong Kong and Taiwanese work continues to receive international recognition on a regular basis. For example, in 1999, posters of four Hong Kong artists, as well as three from the mainland and seven from Taiwan, were selected for the 12th International Poster Salon in Paris. In 2000, John Au was awarded the Savignac Grand Prize at the 13th International Poster Salon in Paris. This can be considered the most prestigious international award ever received by a Hong Kong designer. It represents a new stylistic direction in the territory, without the incorporation of Chinese elements in the design. The international recognition of a wide range of designers from the Greater China region also symbolizes a new era characterized by a lack of dominance any individual or group of designers or particular style. The scene at the beginning of the new millennium is full of potential for diversification. The next stage of Chinese graphic design history within the region will likely continue the search for international visual languages with the subtle expression of Chinese stylistic and aesthetic characteristics.

Conclusion

In this article, I have provided a brief survey of Chinese graphic design in Greater China. I have taken an historical view of the pioneering role of Hong Kong designers within the region, and have established the importance of treating the whole region as having one, unified history. The article has demonstrated the leadership role of early Hong Kong designers such as Henry Steiner, Kan Tai-keung, and Alan Chan, whose styles were influential throughout Greater China in the 1970s and 1980s. Their use of Chinese elements in design works is now thoroughly established as one means of expressing Chinese identity and culture in design works, although expressions of regional identity today certainly are not limited to the use of Chinese elements in design. The current direction of stylistic expression is more towards a universal language that can be understood internationally in any culture.

The developments in the various locales of Greater China are so intertwined that a separate history of any one area necessarily would leave out key influences and developments involving the others, and thus would create a distorted and inaccurate view of Chinese graphic design history. In addition to the regional influence of the styles of early Hong Kong designers, regional history has been linked through the regular organization of intra-regional design competitions, exhibitions, and publications. Although many developments such as the establishment of professional design organizations have been at the local level, other important events have taken place among the various cities within Greater China. In order to maintain their competitiveness within the region and beyond, local designers have found it necessary to organize and participate in intra-regional events and international competitions.

Graphic design in Greater China definitely is entering into a stable environment, with the economy and politics of the region in a relatively secure state. Hong Kong once enjoyed a leading position but, with the developments of recent years, it seems unlikely that this former dominance will return. While Hong Kong and Taiwan are likely to continue their high-quality work, their sheer volume of output will never equal that of the mainland designers, who recently have been outstripping their Hong Kong and Taiwanese counterparts in sheer numbers of awards won. This is largely due to the fact that there are many more active designers in mainland China than elsewhere throughout the Greater China region. The future definitely will see an increasing visibility of mainland designers on the international scene. Thus, although mainland design had a slow start, its present and future importance and potential influence cannot be underestimated. Today, the high quality of mainland graphic design in poster works cannot be questioned. Quality design works in other commercial application areas of graphic design should improve rapidly in the near future.

Acknowledgment

The author would like to express sincere thanks to all the designers who offered assistance to this article, especially Henry Steiner and Freeman Lau. This article also owes an earnest indebtedness to the generous support of the Labalin Curatorial Fellowship granted by the Cooper Union School of Art.

Notes

1. Matthew Turner, "Early Modern Design in Hong Kong," in Dennis P. Doordan, ed., *Design History: An Anthology* (Cambridge: MIT Press, 1995), 212. This article was first published in *Design Issues,* 6 (1) (Fall 1989): 79–91; also Matthew Turner, "Development and Transformations in the Discourse of Design in Hong Kong," in Rajeshwari Ghose, ed., *Design and Development in South and Southeast Asia* (Hong Kong: Centre of Asian Studies, University of Hong Kong, 1990), 123–36.

2. The translation of the Chinese names used in this paper is based on the Chinese system in which the family name is first and the given name last. English names are used if they have been established by individual designers. The system of translation of Chinese names to English used in this article is based on the Romanization of

Cantonese for Hong Kong and Macau designers, or the Romanization of Mandarin for mainland China and Taiwanese designers, and the Romanized names already established by individuals.

3. Shou Zhi Wang, "Chinese Modern Design: A Retrospective," in Dennis P. Doordan, ed., *Design History. An Anthology* (Cambridge: MIT Press, 1995), 213–41. This article was first published in *Design Issues,* 6 (1) (Fall 1989): 49–78; also Shou Zhi Wang, "The Internationalization of Design Education: A Chinese Experience" in Rajeshwari Ghose, ed., *Design and Development in South and Southeast Asia* (Hong Kong: Centre of Asian Studies, University of Hong Kong, 1990), 267–76.

4. Scott Minick and Jiao Ping, *Chinese Graphic Design in the Twentieth Century* (London: Thames and Hudson, 1990), 38.

5. Minick and Jiao, *Chinese Graphic Design in the Twentieth Century,* 38.

6. Wang, "Chinese Modern Design: A Retrospective," 230.

7. Matthew Turner, *Ersatz Design: Interactions Between Chinese and Western Design in Hong Kong, 1950s–1960s* (Unpublished Ph.D. dissertation. Royal College of Art, London, 1993). His dissertation provides a detailed account of the interactions of modern Hong Kong design with Chinese, British, and United States traditions in the 1950s through 1960s.

8. Turner, "Early Modern Design in Hong Kong," 209.

9. Henry Steiner graduated from the Art and Architecture School at Yale University with an MFA in Graphic Design in 1957. Before starting his career in Hong Kong, he worked in Paris and New York in various graphic design positions. He arrived in Hong Kong in 1961, and established his own company, Graphic Communication Limited, in 1964. He is the first designer based in Hong Kong to receive international attention and recognition. See Wang Xu, ed., *Henry Steiner: A Graphic Designer's Design Life* (Beijing: Chinese Youth Publishing, 1999). [In Chinese.]

10. Henry Steiner and Ken Haas, *Cross-Cultural Design: Communicating in the Global Marketplace,* (London: Thames and Hudson, 1995), 2.

11. The elements of cross-cultural design that Steiner generated in the book are "iconography," "typography," "symbolism," "split imagery," and "ideography." The book provided directions for designers to achieve a harmonious juxtaposition and interaction with their own culture and new surroundings. See Henry Steiner and Ken Haas, *Cross-Cultural Design.*

12. A Beijing-based magazine, *Art and Design,* published a special feature for Chinese readers entitled "100 Years Retrospective on Graphic Design in China." Contributors, including professors from major art institutes in China, give a brief account of graphic design on the mainland in the past hundred years. A study of articles in this special feature indicates that the major graphic design categories are publication design, old Shanghai advertising calendar posters, propagand a posters, and logo type design since the Open Door Policy in 1979. See *Art and Design* (Beijing: Art and Design Publishing House, 2000–2, issue 94), 3–20. [In Chinese.]

13. Wang, "Chinese Modern Design: A Retrospective."

14. Wucius Wong, *Principles of Two Dimensional Design* (New York: Van Nostrand Rhinehold, 1974) and *Principles of Three-Dimensional Design* (New York Van Nostrand Rhinehold, 1974).

15. Kan Tai-keung, *Selected Posters by Kan Tai-keung: Sentiments and Harmony* (Hong Kong: Kan and Lau Design Consultants, 1998).

16. See Wang Xu, ed., *Kan Ta-keung, Graphic Designer's Design Life.*

17. Ibid.

18. See First Institute of Art & Design Association, *Design '80* (Hong Kong: First Institute of Art & Design Association, 1980).

19. Lin Jiayang, "On Design Education," in *Art and Design* (Beijing: Art and Design Publishing House, June 2000), 29–34. [In Chinese.]

20. Amoeba Group, *Leaflet of Asian Designers' Invitational Exhibition & Amoeba Annual Show* (Taiwan: Amoeba Group, 1982). [In Chinese.]

21. Hong Kong Designers Association, *HKDA Members Profile* (Hong Kong: Hong Kong Designers Association, 1998).

22. Chinese Poster Association, *2000 Exhibition of Chinese Poster Design Association* (Taiwan: Chinese Poster Association, 2000). [In Chinese.]

23. Wei Yew, "Graphic Design in China Show," in *Communication Arts* (Communication Arts, September/October, 1992): 48–57.

24. Shanghai Graphic Designers' Association, *Hi-Graphic* (Shanghai: Shanghai Graphic Designers' Association, Issue 1, 1998).

25. Chinese Poster Association, *2000 Exhibition of Chinese Poster Design Association.*

26. Two designers from China were Yu Bingnan and Wang Xu, and from Hong Kong, Kan Tai-keung and Freeman Lau.

27. The Asia-Pacific Poster Exhibition was organized by the Provisional Regional Council and the Hong Kong Designers Association from November 22, 1997 to December 12, 1997.

28. Shanghai Graphic Designers' Association, *Shangh ai International Poster Invitational Exhibition '99* (Shanghai: Joint Publishing House, 1999).

29. The international designers invited included Michel Bouvet from France, Alan Fletcher from England, Helfried Hagenberg from Germany, Pekka Piippo from Finland, and Ralph Schraivogel from Switzerland. Freeman Lau's book of his own poster design works, *Looking Back: Freeman Lau's Poster Design,* was published by Kan and Lau Design Consultants in March 1999. The Kan and Lau books both were funded by the Hong Kong Arts Development Council. Tommy Li self-funded a book on his retrospective works, *Tommy Li: My Work My Words,* published in May 1999.

30. Kan Tai-keung's book of his poster works, *Selected Posters by Kan Tai-keung: Sentiments and Harmony,* was published by his own company, Kan and Lau Design Consultants in 1998.

Part 5: Further reading

Balaguer, L. (2016), "Tropico Vernacular," *Triple Canopy*, May 3. Available online: https://www.
canopycanopycanopy.com/contents/tropico-vernacular/#title-page (accessed August 4, 2017).

Barnbrook, J., and K. Lasn (2007), *Barnbrook Bible: The Graphic Design of Jonathan* Barnbrook, London:
Booth-Clibborn Editions.

Berman, D. (2009), *Do Good Design: How Designers Can Change the World*, Berkeley: New Riders.

Bichler, K. and S. Beir (2016), "Graphic Design for the Real World? Visual Communication's Potential in Design
Activism and Design for Social Change," *Artifact* 3 (4): 11.1–11.10. Available online: https://scholarworks.
iu.edu/journals/index.php/artifact/article/view/12974/28417 (accessed August 10, 2017).

Flood, C. (2012), *British Posters Advertising, Art & Activism*, London: V&A Publishing.

Frascara, J., B. Meurer, J. van Toorn, and D. Winkler (1997), *User-Centred Graphic Design: Mass Communication
and Social Change*, London: Taylor & Francis.

Fry, T. (2008), *Design Futuring: Sustainability, Ethics and New Practice*, London: Berg.

Glaser, M., M. Ilic, and T. Kushner (2005), *The Design of Dissent*, Gloucester, MA: Rockport Publishers.

Gunn, W. (2013), *Design Anthropology: Theory and Practice*, London: Bloomsbury.

Heller, S. (2004), "Graphic Intervention," *Typotheque,* November 29. Available online: https://www.typotheque.
com/articles/graphic_intervention (accessed August 10, 2017).

Heller, S. and V. Vienne (2003), *Citizen Designer: Perspectives on Design Responsibility*, New York: Allworth
Press.

Hosey, L. (2012), *The Shape of Green: Aesthetics, Ecology, and Design*, Washington, DC: Island Press.

Klein, N. (2003), *No Logo,* New York: Picador.

Lavin, M. (2002), *Clean New World: Culture, Politics and Graphic Design*, Cambridge, MA: The MIT Press.

Manzini, E. (2015), *Design, When Everybody Designs: An Introduction to Design for Social Innovation,* trans by
R. Coad, Cambridge: The MIT Press.

Markussen, T. (2013), "The Disruptive Aesthetics of Design Activism: Enacting Design Between Art and Politics,"
Design Issues, 29 (1): 38–50.

McQuiston, L. (2016), *Visual Impact: Creative Dissent in the 21st Century*, London: Phaidon.

Metahaven (2015), *Black Transparency. The Right to Know in the Age of Mass Surveillance*, Berlin: Sternberg Press.

Morley, M. (2017), "Why Self-publishing is a 'Decolonizing' Act in the Philippines: Hardworking Goodlooking on
Refusing to Conform," *AIGA Eye on Design*, February 13. Available online: eyeondesign.aiga.org/
why-self-publishing-is-a-decolonizing-act-in-the-philippines/ (accessed June 17, 2017).

Pajaczkowska, C. (2001), "Issues in Feminist Design," in F. Carson and C. Pajaczkowska (eds), *Feminist Visual
Culture*, 123–8, London: Routledge.

Resnick, E. (2016), *Developing Citizen Designers,* London: Bloomsbury.

Scalin, N. and M. Taute (2012), *The Design Activist's Handbook: How to Change the World (or at Least Your Part of
It) with Socially Conscious Design*, New York: How Design Books.

Shea, A. (2012), *Designing for Social Change: Strategies for Community-Based Graphic Design*, New York:
Princeton Architectural Press.

Papenek, V. (1985), *Design for the Real World: Human Ecology and Social Change* (revised edition), London:
Thames & Hudson.

Poynor, R. (2005), *Jan van Toorn: Critical Practice (Graphic Design in the Netherlands),* Rotterdam: nai010.

Stevenson, P.S. Mackie, A. Robinson, and J. Baines (2017). *See Red Women's Workshop: Feminist Posters 1974–1990,* London: Four Corners Books.

Triggs, T. (2001), "Graphic Design," in F. Carson and C. Pajaczkowska (eds), *Feminist Visual Culture*, 147–70, London: Routledge.

Van Toorn, J., ed. (1998), *Design Beyond Design: Critical Reflection and the Practice of Visual Communication,* Maastricht: Jan van Eyck Akademie.

Part 6

Changing visual landscapes

Part 6: Introduction

Contemporary graphic design frequently functions in complex political, economic, and cultural contexts. Designers have considerable amounts of information at their fingertips, and current political and technological environments have enabled a "post-truth," "fake-news" media culture. The "democratization" of information has made all information suspect. Social media offers yet another kind of democratization—as a catalyst for collective action. These new sorts of information dissemination and kinds of human relationships inform the ways that we understand ourselves and our identities.

Many of these matters are discussed in the previous Section in Part 5, "Identity and world graphic design." In Part 6, however, we explore how historical and contemporary representations—in logos, branding, and data visualizations—shape our visual and social landscapes. Current debates about the function of visual representations raise questions about graphic design's relationship to the complex, and often contradictory, challenges of transnational identity, transnational contexts, and "intercultural collaboration and intersections."

Branding and graphic design play a significant role in this conversation. The articles included in the first Section, "Branding and the image makers," suggest possible frameworks for these contemporary debates through branding practices. In "My country is not a brand" (2004) William Drenttel argues against commercializing branding wars for the cultural identities of countries. Commercialization, Drenttel asserts, utilizes incongruous approaches and inappropriate vocabularies for political and diplomatic concerns. Drenttel's strategy has unfortunately been more or less abandoned in contemporary political discourse.

In his 1991 essay "Logos, flags, and escutcheons," Paul Rand argues that, although good logo design is important, logos take on the character of the company or group they represent. This is also the case, Rand points out, for logos that have nothing intrinsic to do with the product they represent—for example, the Lacoste alligator. Rand's argument seems self-evident, but it attests to the power that political and corporate identities have to shape people's experiences. "A certain commitment: art and design at the Royal PTT" (1991), which also considers the impact of political identity, presents the pioneering work of Jean François van Royen at the Netherlands Postal and Telecommunications Service (PTT). Author Paul H. Hefting writes that Van Royen—a printer and typographer who became General Secretary of the PTT in 1919—insisted that design produced by the PTT present a clear, well-considered identity for Dutch government agencies. Elizabeth Glickfield next discusses the vexed redesign of the 2009 logo for the Australian city of Melbourne in "On logophobia" (2010). The press and public controversy surrounding the new logo revealed a lack of awareness of both the creation and function of design within culture. Margaret Andersen, on the other hand, describes effective image making in "How the first typeface designed for the Māori community is changing the way New Zealand understands its own cultural identity," (2018) which is about Johnson Witehira's New Zealand Māori typography. Witehira considers his type design—which comes from Maori imagery and oral tradition, with a bit of Western influence thrown in—to be a kind of "cultural resistance." This essay demonstrates how identity can be both shaped and reflected by design.

In past decades, designers presented information that was compiled and curated by others. Contemporary information designers still present prepared information, but they also compile, curate, and convey raw data as well. This phenomenon is explored in the next Section on "Information Visualization."

The variable ways that information may be visualized has stimulated debate at different periods in the history of the subject. In "Making sense of Making Sense" (2018), Louise Sandhaus discusses the impact that designer April Greiman's piece *Does It Make Sense* had on design in 1986. At the time, Sandhaus explains, graphic designers' roles were well-defined, and designers were perplexed by the recent introduction of computer technology. Graphic design in America, Sandhaus concludes, was somewhat uninspiring. Greiman's piece shook things up; she used digitizers and computer technology to produce a radical edition of the journal *Design Quarterly* (1953–1993; previously titled *Everyday Art Quarterly*, 1946–1953). Greiman's visual narrative reflected both the Zen Buddhist notion that everything is part of the same entity, and physicist Benoît Mandelbrot's concept of fractals in which each part contains *within it* a whole. Greiman's lushly layered piece—a collective narrative which played with ideas of shallowness and depth—depicted interplay among scientific, mathematical and spiritual symbols.

In the next piece in this Section, we turn to the relevance of infographics. Beginning with one of Abraham Lincoln's maps showing the slave states of the southern US, Gareth Cook discusses the history and popularity of data visualization in "Why Abraham Lincoln Loved Infographics" (2013). Late eighteenth-century Scottish engineer William Playfair made use of the human brain's ability to recognize patterns by presenting data as bar charts, line graphs, and pie charts. Since then, and especially in recent decades, Cook shows how infographics has come to play a critical role in the communication of information.

The design of the London Underground diagram is one of the most widely recognized information visualization projects. John A. Walker opens "The London Underground Diagram: a semiotic analysis" (1995) by discussing how the London Underground Diagram functions as a diagram rather than a map. The Diagram is an abstract schematic representation of the underground system: when enlarged to actual size, the Diagram wouldn't match London geography as a map would. Walker next analyses the components of the Diagram to understand its pictorial and coding mechanisms; he considers this diagram's network, background, border, grid, color, river, stations, language, and miscellaneous symbols. The London Underground Diagram is a design with great social utility that is used daily, but also evolves as needed.

In "Bubbles, lines, and string: how information shapes society" (2011), Peter Hall argues that visualizations of data move science forward and, also reshape society. Data, however, is specific to a time and situation and therefore must be interpreted and presented with a lot of forethought. He divides visualization of data into three categories—scientific practice, journalistic practice, and artistic practice—arguing that artistic practice adds more to information than just visual styling. Artistic visualization, Hall points out, needs to challenge the transparency of data visualizations, and to point out the situatedness of those who interpret these pieces.

The authors of the 2011 essay "Tell them anything but the truth: they will find their own. How we visualized the *Map of the Future* with respect to the audience of our story," likewise envision a situated, collective narrative. Michele Graffieti, Gaia Scagnetti, Donato Ricci, Luca Masud, and Mario Porpora produced a narrative piece that depicts 7,000 different scenarios of the future over ten years for *Wired* magazine. They compare creating their narrative piece, entitled the *Map of the Future*, to producing and directing a film. They also determine from their working process that information can be organized into many possible "truths" that can be arranged to let the audience decide what the future will bring.

Finally, Karin von Ompteda writes about data manifestation, which uses designed objects, installations and environments to communicate quantitative information. In "Data manifestation: a case study" (2018), von Ompteda introduces four MA student group projects from data manifestation workshops that she ran at the Royal College of Art in London beginning in 2012. These projects used collapsing glass bottles filled with varied amounts of water to illustrate global water shortages in 2025 (*Bottled Stress*); twenty-two quarter-circle wooden pieces representing countries, which tilted precariously when presenting high percentages of people who are not willing to pay taxes to reduce pollution (*Balance*); a swing set that allowed participants to experience, through swinging, "satisfaction" levels in five different countries (*My Life Don't Mean A Thing If It Ain't Got That Swing*); and, columns of various widths representing the top-ten arms importing countries, which the students set on fire to communicate the belief that the arms trade is collaborative (*Ashes to Ashes*).

In this Part, we have argued that graphic designers are in a unique position to create brands and images borne out of cultural, social, political identity. Contemporary graphic designers will have opportunities to filter, and then curate, data sets by creating infographic systems or information experiences that make knowledge accessible to others. Ethics must play an essential role in this process. The consequences of the ways that we first consider and then design information permeate our visual landscape, and this information plays a crucial role in shaping the character of the cultures in which we live.

Section 6.1

Branding and the image makers

Chapter 6.1.5

How the first typeface designed for the Māori community is changing the way New Zealand understands its own cultural identity

Margaret Andersen

The most compelling typefaces are the ones that serve a purpose beyond the functionality or esthetics of the letterforms themselves. For New Zealand-based graphic designer Johnson Witehira, that purpose was to create the first typeface designed specifically for the Māori community.

Witehira is of Tamahaki (Ngāti Hinekura), Ngā Puhi (Ngai-tū-te-auru), Ngāti Haua, and New Zealand European descent, and his undergraduate education in graphic design was taught from a predominantly Western perspective. During grad school, he researched augmented reality at exchange programs at the University of Nottingham and at Austria's University of Upper Applied Sciences, in the futuristic-sounding Office of Tomorrow.

The idea for developing a Māori typeface came about after he returned to New Zealand to pursue his doctorate in Māori design at Massey University. In an essay co-written by Witehira and colleague Paola Trapani on the development of the typeface, he explains that Māori typography is "a means of cultural resistance through engagement with postcolonial discourse." Witehira is particularly interested in typography because it concerns both design *and* the written language.

The *wero* (challenge) was to create the first by Māori-for-Māori typeface, a typeface that reaffirms Māori ideas about the world and stakes a claim to the printed page.

Adding to the challenge is the fact that Māori culture is based on an oral tradition, and therefore has no native writing system from which to base new letterforms on. Missionaries originally brought the Latin-Roman alphabet to New Zealand in the 1800s and linguist Samuel Lee of Cambridge University worked with the chief Hongi Hika to develop a systematized Māori written language using the Roman letterforms.

Trapani and Witehira write that, "Following the rapid urbanization of Māori from 1945 [to] 1985, Māori found themselves living in towns and cities whose architecture and language mirrored that of Britain rather than their own culture. With the introduction of the Roman alphabet and the written word, Māori oral methods of storing knowledge also quickly began to fade."

First published in *AIGA Eye on Design*, June 7, 2017. © Margaret Andersen.

Figure 6.10 Whakarare typeface display poster. Designer: Johnson Witehira. © AIGA.

Because of the legacy of colonialism attached to the Roman alphabet, Witehira says, "A few other designers have looked at developing completely new forms. But for me, I felt that's probably not the best way to work. Considering that many Māori are still struggling to learn and engage with our own cultural language, it's best that we try and create some typefaces that can be ours, but that can't be totally unfamiliar, either." He instead restricted the character set to letters that only appear in the Māori alphabet, making sure to include macrons to indicate long vowels, a feature that's often missing from Roman alphabets.

Using a design-based model of analysis, Witehira was able to articulate the visual systems found in traditional Māori art, particularly carving, and then applied them to the letterforms that would become his typeface titled Whakarare. Witehira says, "At the heart of Whakarare is an attempt to create some-thing based on Māori design principles, rather than Māori esthetics, and because of that I think it created something new."

This distinction between design principles and esthetics is in response to prior attempts by other designers trying to create typefaces that borrow bits and pieces of traditional Māori art, removing the forms from their original cultural contexts (Joseph Churchward's typeface, Churchward Māori, is a prime example).

"What bothers me with some of the typefaces that have been created is they're essentially taking sans serif fonts and attaching little items from Māori art onto parts of it. I found that to be not just ad hoc, but kind of culturally inappropriate. You know, taking significant cultural forms and thinking, 'I'm gonna use these to create a letter.' When in reality, our phonetic letters and sounds have nothing to do with those design elements."

Though his Whakarare typeface is intended for a Māori audience, much of Witehira's work seeks to combine traditional Māori forms and patterns with ideas from graphic design and a contemporary Western art practice. But does bringing a traditional vernacular into a globalized design system homo-genize those cultural traditions? Witehira says, "The majority of Māori New Zealanders are of mixed heritage, myself included. So a lot of my projects, even though they have a Māori face, are deliberately created from a bicultural perspective. That's a huge part of my practice, combining Western design and Western design theory with Māori esthetics and Māori design theories."

Beyond trying to push Māori design forward, it's trying to evolve New Zealand design.

Witehira balances a career as an educator with a multidisciplinary practice that includes editorial design, product design, and packaging, as well as large-scale interactive installations, murals, and environmental graphics. He's recently been commissioned to design for Auckland International Airport, one of his biggest projects to date. He says, "For the most part, there's been a continued push in New Zealand to really bring Māori design into a lot of practices, particularly government agencies and their use of Māori cultural advisors. They really see the value in expressing New Zealand's biculturalism. But also because New Zealand was founded on a bicultural treaty."

He says that the next step forward is for companies and government agencies to hire cultural advisors that are not just of Māori heritage, but to hire Māori designers, "those who are familiar with the forms and esthetics and the rules that go along with that." Assuming that a Māori cultural expert is going to help you with graphic design is like me assuming that any white person of European descent is going to know something about grid systems or the Bauhaus.

Whakarare Display

Figure 6.11 Whakarare display font. Designer: Johnson Witehira. © AIGA

Despite the continued progress made by Māori designers, New Zealand design culture is still largely homogeneous. Witehira recalls a symposium he attended a few years ago in which a discussion arose around New Zealand's unique design identity. Taken aback by the conversation's failure to acknowledge Māori design, Witehira commented, "You've talked about culture all day, and I haven't heard anyone mention the indigenous people in New Zealand. You're trying to figure out what's unique about New Zealand design? Maybe look around you. Because right now you're looking to North America and to Europe for answers." Witehira is motivated to use his design practice to "actually change the visual landscape of New Zealand, and to create one that's bicultural, rather than monocultural."

Section 6.2

Information visualization

Not a visual essay

Chapter 6.2.1

Making sense of *Making Sense*

Louise Sandhaus

It was 1986. Two years earlier Apple had released that iconic first mass-market computer with the user-friendly face. Beatings of breast and tearing of hair ensued within the graphic design community; designers were fearful that the craft of graphic design as we knew it was about to implode. Few embraced this electronic invader with optimism, and even fewer welcomed it with artistic vision and imagination.

In 1986, the visual landscape of graphic design in America was a bit uninspiring. Not that the design wasn't well crafted, competent, and perhaps even beautiful. Not that there weren't exquisitely rendered illustrations, dignified photography, and lots of (once again) serifed typography. We'd overcome the sure conviction that a graphic designer could prevail by tendering the one-note aesthetic wonder of Swiss Modernism. It was a visual language able to transform any message into the steady, cool gloss of refined corporate dignity—no matter what the content (petrochemical multi-national or the local grocery chain). Who needed diversity when one "look" fit all?

Gone was the graphic risk of the sixties and early seventies—those works often produced by folks with an expansive artistic but limited means of production: the pop graphics of Corita Kent, punk productions by Jamie Reid, or Art Nouveau-inspired typographic wizardry offered by Victor Moscoso. We professional graphic designers, on the other hand, had not yet learned from Las Vegas—exemplar of the vernacular language of populism to which Robert Venturi, Denise Scott Brown, and Steven Izenour had lovingly drawn attention in their classic volume of 1972, *Learning from Las Vegas*. For us the land-scape looked steady and even. Solid. Colorful and warm. Flat and two-dimensional. And, more than anything else, professionalism prevailed. Refinement ruled. Business blossomed. Experimentation was nowhere to be found.

In 1986, roles for professional graphic designers were clearly demarcated. The perimeters and para-meters of our specialized field did not include typesetting, photography, illustration, or copywriting. We worked *with* these folks, and even though there were exceptions, these tasks weren't our domain. We were yet to adopt the methods and modes—the computer and design software—that would integrate these disparate occupations.

It was at this moment, too, that the clarion call for women's rights was sounding with one of the largest protest marches in US history taking place in Washington D.C., followed by marches in other cities across the nation. It was "boots on the ground," participating in the seemingly endless war on women in order to acknowledge both our place and our part in the world. It was at this moment, like a gift from the goddesses, that an issue of the periodical *Design Quarterly* (Walker Art Center, Minneapolis) arrived at my desk. And here it was. The publication—entitled *Does It Make Sense?*—was not the usual thirty-two-page format, but rather folded and unbound, unwrapping into a giant poster (Figure 6.12) that embodied everything that 1986 design was about to become. Nothing would be the same again.

The subject of this poster/publication was, in essence, the parts representing the whole. This was an idea that author and designer April Greiman appeared to draw from the Zen Buddhist notion that nothing is separate and distinct, but rather everything in the universe is part of the same entity no matter how seemingly disparate. At the same time, Greiman's piece also reflected Benoît Mandelbrot's mathematical concept of fractals in which each part contains *within it* a whole—"completeness" infinitely reflected—a model that was momentously introduced to the design community at the 1982 International Design Conference in Aspen by Mandelbrot himself. These concepts, which suggest other ways of comprehending the nature of the universe including the universe of design, confronted viewers/readers/users as they navigated an unfamiliar realm that departed from the conventional design Flatland into the vistas of "space." A sense of depth and dimension is achieved in Greiman's piece through graphic scale shifts and through layering—a formal device that was not yet part of the mid-1980s graphic design vocabulary. Texts appear at once both closer and further away rather than seeming to lie on the same plane, and the pixelated details of images are as intriguing as the complete image. Greiman reveals minor notions, such as her struggle to use the limited technology, that become, in Mandelbrot-like fashion, as compelling and significant as grand schemes and philosophies. Everything connects. Everything mirrors. The default mid-1980s "rational," "linear," and "reasoned" operating principles are gone. Instead of the conventional trajectory of coherence, Greiman sets up play and interplay between signs and symbols that come from various systems, such as science, math, and spiritual beliefs, along with a system of ambiguous hand gestures of her own invention.

These devices, which are both formal and conceptual maneuvers, were not intended to reflect the philosopher Jacques Derrida's deconstructionist theories that were soon to have wide impact in the "hothouses" of graphic design (which had begun with students at the Cranbrook Academy of Art). The connections between Greiman's maneuvers and Derrida's deconstructionist theories nonetheless seem to emerge coincidentally. In both instances, text operates with and through design to provide and perform meaning, thus suggesting an expanded cosmos in which design might operate.

In Greiman's pixels, we found strange beauty: a first-ever life-size scan of the author/designer's body rendered in blue fragments juxtaposed with a particle diagram and layered with cave drawings; plus, luridly colored ambiguous images that are accompanied by texts that leap from metaphysics to mundane technical descriptions. In these details—these small bits that comprise parts of a whole and yet each comprise a whole of their own—we saw a design world that changed from flat and simple to complex, layered, and dynamic, and from a more "masculine" straightforward response to a more "feminine," less directed, poetic, and unfolding one. In these small details we found a designer who authored her own work, made herself the subject and determined that an unfamiliar esthetic was worthy of investigation. It was at this moment that Greiman's hybrid poster/publication inscribed a line in the sand and marked new territory for what design could say, who could say it, what it looked like, and where and how it would appear. Design never looked or acted the same again. It did make sense to answer the question posed by the poster's title, but not for those who were looking for it on the same old well-trodden path.

Editors' note: April Greiman is a designer/artist whose trans-disciplinary ideas and multi-media projects have been influential worldwide. Explorations of image, word, and color, as objects in time and space, are grounded in the singular fusion of art and technology. This is the basis for a multi-media, multi-scaled body of work. Greiman is recognized for revolutionary digital imaging work and has been instrumental the acceptance and use of advanced technology in the creative process since the early 1980s. In 2014 she was featured in the Apple documentary *Mac @ 30* recognizing the contributions of 30 diverse creative individuals. Greiman is an educator, the former director of Visual Communications Program at California Institute of the Arts; former faculty of Southern California Institute of Architecture; and current faculty member at Woodbury University School of Architecture. Greiman has been published extensively, including four monographs, and she has lectured and exhibited worldwide with works in collections of many major museums, among them the Pompidou Center, Paris and MOMA, New York. Greiman has four honorary doctorates, and currently lives in Los Angeles.

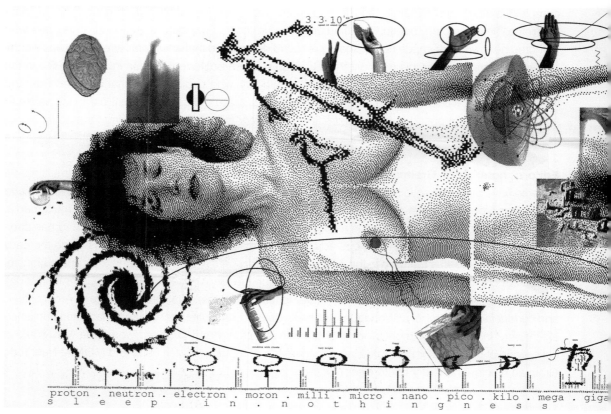

Figure 6.12 *Does It Make Sense?* Special issue of the journal *Design Quarterly*. © 1986. Designer: April Greiman.

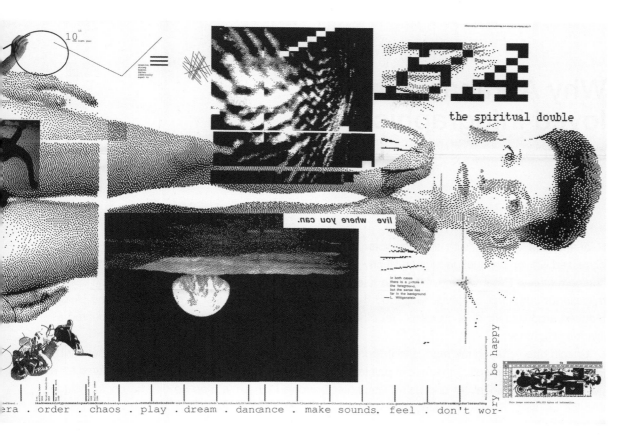

the spiritual double

live where you can.

In both cases
there is a picture in
the foreground,
but the sense lies
far in the background
— L. Wittgenstein

. be happy

era . order . chaos . play . dream . dancance . make sounds. feel . don't wor-

Chapter 6.2.2

Why Abraham Lincoln loved infographics

Gareth Cook

Near the end of 1861, with the American Union crumbling, President Abraham Lincoln became obsessed with an unusual document. Nearly three feet in length, it appeared at first to be a map of the southern states. But it was covered with finely rendered shading, with the darkness of each county reflecting the number of slaves who lived there. South Carolina, the first to secede from the Union, featured a particularly dark coastline. Yet other parts of the South (like western Virginia) appeared as islands of lightness.

Lincoln often studied the map, and it "bore the marks of much service," according to a memoir by Francis Bicknell Carpenter, an eminent painter who was at the White House conducting research for a portrait of the President. At one point, Carpenter borrowed Lincoln's map so that he could include it in the painting. Some time later, the President visited him in his studio and, spotting his precious map, declared, "Ah! . . . *you* have appropriated my map, have you? I have been looking all around for it." Then Lincoln slipped on his glasses, sat on a trunk by a window, and "began to pore over it very earnestly."

In the map, Lincoln saw testimony that the American south was not a uniform bloc. Areas of heavy slavery—the darkened banks along the Mississippi River, for example—tended to be secessionist, but the areas in between held the hope of pro-Union sympathy. Unlike traditional cartography, the map was designed to portray political terrain and, in Lincoln's mind, moral terrain. The President called it his "slave map." Today we would call it an infographic.

Infographics are clearly having a cultural moment. They have become pervasive in newspapers, magazines, blog posts, and viral tweets; they appear on television and in advertising, in political campaigns and at art openings. As a Google search term, "infographic" has increased nearly twenty-fold in the last five years. Yet infographics have been popular, in one form or another, for centuries. The source of their power isn't computers or the Internet, but the brain's natural visual intelligence.

Credit for the world's first infographics should probably go to William Playfair, a Scottish engineer, economist, and failed silversmith. In 1786, Playfair published the "Commercial and Political Atlas,"

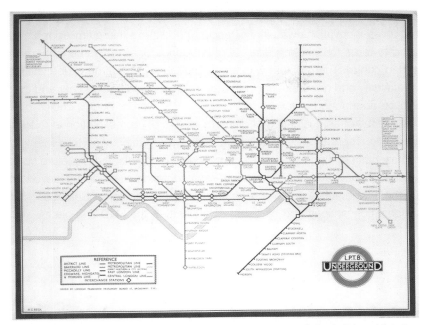

Figure 6.16 London Underground Diagram (1933). Designer: H.C. Beck. Printer: Waterlow & Sons Ltd. © TfL. From the London Transport Museum collection.

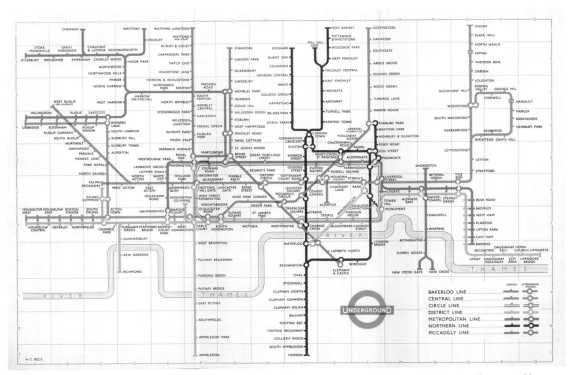

Figure 6.17 Underground Diagram of Lines (1959). Designer: H.C. Beck. © TfL. From the London Transport Museum collection.

(horizontal, vertical and diagonal); and (3) enlargement of the central area. The design problem which prompted these innovations was that of accommodating within a limited rectangular space all the lines radiating towards the outlying districts of London and, at the same time, maintaining clarity in the overcrowded centre. The problem was aggravated every time a new tube line was introduced. Beck realised that clarity and geographical truth were antithetical to one another and that geographical accuracy had to be abandoned in favour of clarity. In other words, Beck's choice of diagram rather than map was the result of an evaluation of different modes of representation in relation to the needs of the traveling public. There is a general lesson here: no representation tells the whole truth about reality, every representation is partial and selective in what it depicts; every picture conceals as much as it reveals. Consequently, an artist's choice of representation must be based on what he or she considers are in the best interests of those he or she has chosen to serve. Before consideration can be given to the pictorial conventions and coding mechanisms of the LUD it is necessary to tabulate its components:

Network

The diagram consists of a number of lines converging towards a central core delimited by the Circle line. The lines intersect at various points to form a network structure. To ensure clarity this network is inscribed on a uniformly white ground.

Background

The rectangular poster is displayed vertically like a painting but, unlike a picture, its four dimensions have directional properties, that is, top/bottom and left/ right are implicitly understood by the viewer to represent North/South and East/West. In one version of the diagram a north-pointing arrow was introduced but it was quickly realised that this symbol was redundant.

Border

Most large posters of the diagram have borders consisting of a thick blue line while diagrams printed as pocket-sized folders have borders consisting of a narrow black, or blue, line.

Grid

The ground of the current diagram is divided into squares by a co-ordinate grid which, when used in association with a list of station names, enables strangers to London to pinpoint the location of stations on the diagram.

in the PowerPoint age: that the persuasiveness of a presentation is due not entirely to its logical strength, but also to its emotional appeal and the character of the speaker—in classical terms, not only its logos but its pathos and ethos.[28] If Cognitive Media's informative and visually rich graphics do convey a rich and situated representation of the information as delivered by a particular speaker, then are they not a better paradigm than, say, a flow chart, geometric mind map, rectilinear graph, or table versions of the same information?

Situatedness and contingency are certainly not alien to the language of visualization. Arguably, the sheer fecundity of the field is beginning to shift the ground away from the fixed, objective, atemporal, and totalized visual rhetoric. In visualizing the extensive changes made to Darwin's *Origin of Species* during the course of its publication through six editions, for example, Ben Fry unsettles the idea that scientific notions appear as fixed ideas.[29] In visualizing the changes to specific entries in *Wikipedia,* Wattenberg and Fernanda Viégas zoom in on the disputes and controversies that surround topics that might otherwise seem long since settled. An encyclopedia page becomes a contested territory.[30]

The unaddressed question so far in this discussion is the role of graphic designers in this vast, flourishing field. Clearly designers are at work in all three categories of visualization outlined above, but in increasingly collaborative environments. Traditionally, the designer might produce static graphics, or come in to clean up dynamic visualizations once the hard-core statistical, analytical work and programming were complete. But increasingly, there are designers with programming skills and mathematicians with design skills making inroads into each other's professions. The web-enabled availability of data sources, notably from governments and nongovernmental organizations aspiring to transparency, and the proliferation of free visualization tools and forums—from Many Eyes (visualization platform spawned at IBM) to Gephi (a Paris-based open source consortium)—has brought host of practitioners to the field, designers among them.[31]

Visualization depends increasingly on a cadre of interdisciplinary skills. Fry, codeveloper of the ubiquitous Processing open source programming environment, recently argued at a conference that the typical process of scientists throwing the parsed, filtered, mined data "over the wall" to the graphic and interaction designers is "a terrible way of doing things." As a designer capable of building dynamic visualizations and participating at the data-mining and parsing stage, Fry finds that "the way the interaction works is going to affect how you do the data-mining portion. You can't really separate these things."[32]

At MIT's Humanities + Digital Visual Interpretations conference in 2010, Wattenberg, a trained mathematician who codeveloped the Many Eyes visualization platform at IBM, argued that the visualization explosion has had a curious effect on visual literacy. It now takes two forms, he argued: reading and creating. Reading is "not in bad shape," he claimed, but knowing whether a line chart, pie chart, or a bar chart is the suitable form for the visualization you are trying to make requires a certain amount of expertise. "One of the things I'm hoping is that people can teach each other, that was one of the hopes for Many Eyes."

Visual literacy, however, is not the only skill required for navigating the deluge of data. The list of facets underemphasized or ignored in the dominant language of visualization is long enough to present a worthy challenge to any research group. The perplexing part is that while the art and critical design world has been riffing off the yawning gaps in the infoviz view of existence, the mainstream practice continues to deploy a visual rhetoric that treats data as pure and judges questions of visual form only in terms of a universalist idea of usability. This seems all the more curious when one considers that the art of typography has long since passed through the perceived crisis that clarity of communication would be lost with the loss of the appearance of objectivity.

For visualization to fully mature requires a better cross-fertilization between the three contexts of visualization practice. The journalistic practice of making data accessible and legible has much to teach the sciences; the forms and critiques of artistic practices can inform, question, and reinvigorate the scientific and journalistic ends of the spectrum; and scientific visualization can provide the journalistic and artistic practices some fundamental lessons in rigor.

Notes

1. Hans Rosling, "Hans Rosling Shows the Best Stats You've Ever Seen" (presentation at the TED Conference, February 2006), accessed July 8, 2011, http://www.ted.com/talks/hans_rosling_shows_the_best_stats_you_ve_ever_seen.html.
2. *TED* blog, June 27, 2011, http://blog.ted.com/2011/06/27/the-20-most-watched-tedtalks-so-far/.
3. Hans Rosling, "Hans Rosling's New Insights on Poverty" (presentation at the TED Conference, March 2007), accessed July 13, 2011, http://www.ted.com/talks/hans_rosling_reveals_new_insights_on_poverty.html.
4. Johanna Drucker, *SpecLab: Digital Aesthetics and Projects in Speculative Computing* (Chicago: University of Chicago Press, 2009), 73.
5. Linton Freeman, "Visualizing Social Networks," *Journal of Social Structure* 1 (2000), http://www.cmu.edu/joss/content/articles/volume1/Freeman.html.
6. Toby Segaran and Jeff Hammerbacher, *Beautiful Data: The Stories Behind Elegant Data Solutions* (Sebastopol, CA: O'Reilly Media, 2009), 348.
7. See, for example, feature stories of projects developed at the Texas Advanced Computer Center, University of Texas at Austin, accessed July 15, 2011, http://www.tacc.utexas.edu/news/feature-stories/.
8. Benjamin B. Bederson and Ben Shneiderman, *The Craft of Information Visualization: Readings and Reflections* (Burlington. MA: Elsevier, 2003), xix.
9. See, for example, the work of Jarke Van Wijk, Colin Ware, Ben Shneiderman, and Stuart Card.
10. Gestalten.tv, *All the News That's Fit to Post* (documentary video podcast about the New York Times Graphics Department), accessed July 18, 2011, http://www.gestalten.com/motion/new-york-times and http://infosthetics.com/archives/2010/08/how_the_new_york_times_creates_its_infographics.html#extended.
11. Hans Rosling, "Visual Technology Unveils the Beauty of Statistics and Swaps Policy from Dissemination to Access," *Statistical Journal of the IAOS* 24 (2007):103–104.
12. Martin Wattenberg. "Numbers, Words and Colors" (presentation at the MIT HyperStudio Humanities + Digital Visual Interpretation conference, Cambridge, MA. May 20, 2010), accessed July 4, 2011, http://flowingdata.com/2010/08/11/martin-wattenberg-talks-data-and-visualization/.
13. Ben Shneiderman, *Designing the User Interface: Strategies for Effective Human-Computer Interaction* (Boston: Addison-Wesley, 2010). See also Shneiderman's "Eight Golden Rules of Interface Design," accessed July 13, 2011, http://faculty.washington.edu/jtenenbg/courses/360/f04/sessions/schneidermanGoldenRules.html.
14. Quoted in Warren Sack, "The Aesthetics of Information Visualization," in *Context Providers: Conditions of Meaning in Media Arts,* ed. Margo Lovejoy, Christiane Paul, and Victoria Vesna (Bristol, UK: Intellect Ltd., 2011). Distributed by University of Chicago Press.
15. Johanna Drucker, "Humanistic Approaches to the Graphical Expression of Interpretation" (presentation at the MIT HyperStudio Humanities + Digital Visual Interpretation conference, Cambridge, MA, May 20, 2010), accessed July 8, 2011, http://mitworld.mit.edu/video/796.

16. Peter Barber and Tom Harper, eds., *Magnificent Maps: Power, Propaganda and Art* (London: British Library, 2010). See also BBC Four, "The Beauty of Maps: Seeing the Art in Cartography" (2010), http://www.bbc.co.uk/bbcfour/beautyofmaps/.

17. Jeremy Crampton, *Mapping: A Critical Introduction to Cartography and GIS* (New York: John Wiley & Son, 2010), 9.

18. Ibid.

19. J. B. Harley, "Maps, Knowledge and Power," in *The New Nature of Maps: Essays in the History of Cartography,* ed. Paul Laxton (Baltimore: John Hopkins University Press, 2001), 67.

20. See, for example, Barrett Lyon, "Opte Project Map of the Internet" (2003), in *Else/Where: Mapping—New Cartographies of Networks and Territories,* ed. Janet Abrams and Peter Hall (Minneapolis: University of Minnesota Design Institute, 2006).

21. Valdis Krebs, "Finding Go-To People and Subject Matter Experts [SME]" (2008), accessed July 11, 2011, http://www.orgnet.com/experts.html.

22. Freeman, "Visualizing Social Networks."

23. Daniel Rosenberg and Anthony Grafton, *Cartographies of Time: A History of the Timeline* (New York: Princeton Architectural Press, 2010).

24. James Moody, Daniel A. McFarland, and Skye Bender-DeMoll, "Dynamic Network Visualization: Methods for Meaning with Longitudinal Network Movies," *American Journal of Sociology* 110 (2005): 1206–1241.

25. Drucker, "Humanistic Approaches to the Graphical Expression of Interpretation."

26. Nicholas Felton, *Feltron Annual Report* (2005), accessed August 22, 2011, http://feltron.com/ar05_01.html.

27. Bruno Latour, "A Cautious Prometheus? A Few Steps Toward a Philosophy of Design (with Special Attention to Peter Sloterdijk)" (presentation at the Networks of Design meeting of the Design History Society, Falmouth, Cornwall, UK, September 3, 2008), http://bruno-latour.fr/articles/article/112-DESIGN-CORNWALL.pdf.

28. Cognitive Media, "RSA Animate—Philip Zimbard: The Secret Powers of Time and Other Things" (June 2, 2010), accessed July 18, 2011, http://www.cognitive media.co.uk/wp/?p=272. For a discussion of rhetoric in design, see Richard Buchanan, "Declaration by Design: Rhetoric, Argument, and Demonstration in Design Practice," in *Design Discourse: History, Theory, Criticism,* ed. Victor Margolin (Chicago: University of Chicago Press, 1989), 91–109.

29. Ben Fry, *On the Origin of Species: The Preservation of Favoured Traces* (2009), accessed July 18, 2011, http://benfry.com/traces/.

30. Martin Wattenberg and Fernanda Viégas, *IBM Communication Lab, History Flow* (2003), http://www.bewitched.com/historyflow.html. See also Wattenberg and Viégas, "The Hive Mind Ain't What It Used to Be" (reply to post by Janon Lanier, "Digital Maoism"), http://www.edge.org/discourse/digital_maoism.html#viegas.

31. Gephi Consortium (founded October 2010), accessed August 22, 2011, http://consortium.gephi.org.

32. Ben Fry, "Computational Information Design" (presentation at Adaptive Path UX Week Conference, August 24–27, 2010), http://www.youtube.com/watch?v=z-g-cWDnUdU.

Chapter 6.2.5

Tell them anything but the truth: they will find their own. How we visualized the *Map of the Future* with respect to the audience of our story

Michele Graffieti, Gaia Scagnetti, Donato Ricci, Luca Masud, and Mario Porpora

What is it all about?

Let's start from the origins of the title.

In 2003, filmmakers Spike Jonze and Lance Bangs began to shoot *Tell them anything you want*,[1] a short documentary feature about American writer and illustrator Maurice Sendak, author of the classic children's picture book *Where the Wild Things Are.* The title of this article makes reference to that short documentary in which Sendak himself pronounces the title sentence referring to what parents were supposed to tell children in order to bring them up in the best way. According to Sendak, people should consider children not as little specimens of organism who are not able to understand what adults usually are: to him, children are simply humans and, as with all humans, one should behave honestly. "In the discussion of children and the lives of children and the fantasies of children and the language of children," he asserts, "I said anything I wanted, because I don't believe in children. I don't believe in childhood. I don't believe there's this demarcation."

In this paper, the target subjects are not specifically children nor a particular category of adults: "them," in the title, refers to the general audience of any visualization "we," the designers, produce. And the purpose of this paper is to point out a method for telling visual stories taken from complex systems of information, and not to dig into kids' experiences.

However, revising Sendak's statement, we can easily share his conclusions: the designer must not underestimate the viewers of his/her work, especially when he acts as a narrator for them. As a matter

First published in *Leonardo,* 44 (3) (June 2011): 250–1. This paper was presented as a contributed talk at Arts/Humanities/Complex Networks—a Leonardo satellite symposium at NetSci2010. See http://artshumanities.netsci2010.net. © The International Society for the Arts, Sciences, and Technology.

Figure 6.21 A detail of the *Map of the Future*. © 2009. Designers: DensityDesign Research Lab—Politecnico di Milano.

of fact, when any kind of narrator (a movie or theater director, an illustrator of children's books, an author of comics, a song-writer) tells a story, he/she has to rely on a public's imaginary in some degree. Stories convey information, cultural values, and experiences:[2] everything is evoked by the narrator but, eventually, interpretation is the observer's duty.

In fact, interpretation is an instinct for the observer, more than a duty. If a story is visually well-told, the viewer finds it compelling, deserving of wonder: the more qualitative the narrator evocation is, the more the observer is favorably disposed towards its meaning and the connections of its elements.

Sometimes the observer feels so deeply related to the story that he/she becomes co-author of the story itself through the personal or collective imagery that he/she offers to the interpretation: those are the times in which the amount of information held in the images might be grasped more quickly by the audience.

So what?

Information visualization is a process that transforms data, information, and knowledge into a form that relies on the human visual system to perceive its embedded information. Its goal is to enable the viewer to observe, understand, and make sense of the information.[3] Guaranteeing this goal is the designer's duty.

By nature, in the visualization of complex systems, we tend to obtain a truthful synthesis out of data, to implement a process of transcription from concrete words or numbers to visual signs; but what do we do when we are facing abstract notions that remind us of qualities more than quantities? Narration, considered as a tool with the paramount function of myths to find a shape, a form, in the turmoil of human experience,[4] is a great assistant for this kind of job.

Modern research in cognitive psychology states people have two different modes of thought: the paradigmatic and the narrative. Unlike the paradigmatic mode of thought, which is used to persuade somebody of the truth of a *sound argument,* narrative thought uses a *good story* to persuade of plausibility.[5]

Designing for narrative means adopting methods that come from disciplines built on narrative purposes. Take cinema: As the movie director, the designer aims to choose the visualization that best preserves the complexity of the environment. He directs actors (the elements of a system), judges light design (the choice of elements to visualize) and set designs (the imagery to evoke), and chooses different optical lenses (the power of focusing) and, most importantly, the critical point of view of the camera (intentionality).

That's it! But . . . example please

A case study we're glad to present consists in the *Map of the Future* that we designed for the Italian edition of *Wired* magazine.[6]

In 2009 during a long session of brainstorming and simulation games, 7,000 visionary players all around the world elaborated different scenarios for the future. This research was carried out by *The Institute for the Future* that transformed the data in a very complex network of tendencies and previsions in the form of a table full of words.

As designers, our work consisted in representing visually all the scenarios and giving the viewers a look at what they might expect over the next 10 years. To do that, we followed an initial two-step analysis that, persisting in our cinematic metaphor, we can call "pre-production":

1. *Create a logic structure,* find patterns and correlations between the different scenarios and semantic areas of the single predictions (the predictions were classified in 5 areas—politics, infrastructure, environment, economy, society—and then clusters of the classified predictions were made inside any of the 5 chosen fields—for example, in the Economy area, predictions of "micro-philanthropy networks" and "seed networking" were clustered under "solidarity networks");

2. *Arrange* the discovered structure to achieve one macro reading orientation (the 5 areas had different degrees of abstraction, i.e., the predictions in one area were more abstract than the predictions in another, so we have ordered them from the more abstract—politics—to the less—society).

These first two interventions set the stage. The actors (the elements of the system—the predictions) were cast; the light design was ready (lights pinpoint the network's most important clusters). At the same time, as the casting and pre-production were going on, everything led to the narrative idea, the third step:

3. *Think about the story*; write down the "script" evoking a precise imagery (the idea came from the retro-futurism of the 1950s when everything seemed possible and the consequences of the smallest transformation were exaggerated on purpose to open people's minds in wonder).

This is the step in which set design is conceived in detail (deciding how to represent and to style characters and environment plays a fundamental role in capturing the attention and emotions of the audience) and the lenses for shooting are chosen (the power of focusing on some elements is very important to enhance narration and capture the cognitive thread of the audience[7]—here the optical lens zooms in from abstract to tangible and figurative level of scale).

Then there's the set-up of "direction." The designer, as a director, takes political stances which cannot go unheeded:

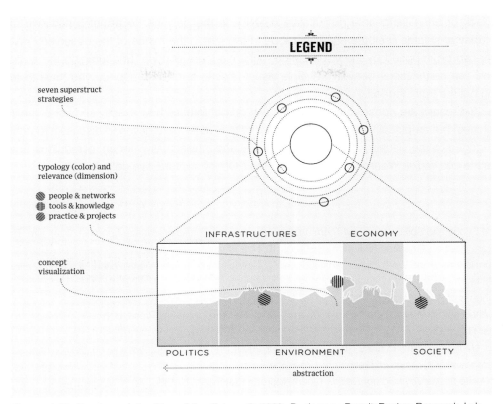

Figure 6.22 Structure of the *Map of the Future*. © 2009. Designers: DensityDesign Research Lab—Politecnico di Milano.

4. *Be aware of the intentionality*; you are the designer, you're interpreting with your own point of view, but use it to tell a story made up of multiple tales and not to convey one privileged solution to the audience, in any way (the faraway viewpoint of the *Map of the Future* communicates our distance from the future and gives the observers a panorama).

Now, we were ready for the final step:

5. *Shoot.*

"Oh joy, rapture, I've got a brain!" said the Scarecrow

In designing a map of the future, based on some semi-scientific cooperative predictions, there's no such thing as truth, or better, there are lots of very likely truths, all different from one another, depending on which combination of "evolution-factors" is taken into consideration. Therefore, the designer can choose either to visualize every possible future (truth) or to tell the story of a possible world in which many futures could coexist (plausibility), leaving the audience the chance and the charge of deciding which future is more likely to them.

The lack of unchallengeable quantitative data leads the designer to adopt a narrative mode of thought that stimulates itself the narrative mode of thought in the minds of the observers: no truth or certainty can be imposed by the visualization, because there is none. Encouraging the audience to think and see connections between multiple visual tales is a form of respect: you have to tell them anything but the truth, indeed.

Expected results are not scientific of course (we do not foresee how exactly someone can interpret visual stories) but empirical: Observers of the *Map of the Future* were driven to discuss it together; they were engaged to the visualized system, emotionally and intellectually, like an incredulous Scarecrow towards the end of *The Wizard of Oz*[8] who exclaims: "Oh joy, rapture, I've got a brain!"

Notes

1. Lance Bangs and Spike Jonze, *Tell Them Anything You Want: A Portrait of Maurice Sendak* (2009), film. The documentary aired on American television (HBO) on 10/14/2009 for the first time.
2. Nahum Gershon and Ward Page, "What storytelling can do for Information Visualization," *Communications of the ACM*, 44 (8) (August 2001): 31.
3. Gershon and Page [3], pp. 32–3.
4. Umberto Eco, *Six Walks in the Fictional Woods* (1994), Harvard University Press, p. 87.
5. Bruner [1], p. 15.
6. *Wired Magazine* Italian Edition, No. 7 (September 2009) pp. 25–31, http://www.wired.it/extra/mappadelfuturo, http://www.densitydesign.org/research/map-of-the-future/.
7. Colin Ware, *Visual Thinking: for Design* (2008), Morgan Kaufmann, p. 138.
8. Victor Fleming, *The Wizard of Oz* (1939), film.

Chapter 6.2.6

Data manifestation: a case study

Karin von Ompteda

Introduction

Data manifestation is a design practice involving the communication of quantitative information through objects, installations, and other sensory experiences with the purpose of stimulating dialogue on import-ant and timely topics. I have developed this practice by teaching workshops in the United Kingdom, China, and Canada to students, professionals, and the public. In this essay I will discuss the opportun-ities afforded by data manifestation through four projects that were produced by MA students at the Royal College of Art (RCA) in London. These projects illustrate the potential for cross-disciplinary collaboration, design authorship, and exploring the ways in which we communicate complex information.

I began teaching data manifestation workshops in 2010 as a response to two important shifts within the design world. First, the explosion of data visualization as a creative practice was being fueled by unprecedented access to information via the Internet, and by easier access to visualization software. Second, designers from across disciplines were engaging in the visual representation of abstract data—traditionally a communication design practice—while communication designers were increasingly working across a wide variety of media beyond the page and screen (e.g., Klanten *et al.* 2012). Thus, while there was a plethora of print- and screen-based visualizations, there was also a proliferation of unexpected forms of information representation. Yavuz and Kurbak's (2008) *News Knitter* project, for example, conver-ted information gathered from online political news into unique visual patterns for knitted sweaters.

My data manifestation workshops were first run at the RCA, where I was a doctoral student in Visual Communication. Having a background in biology, I was particularly receptive to the burgeoning world of data visualization in design, which combined my training in both graphic design and statistics. At the time, data visualization was not part of the curriculum at RCA; I believed that this practice should not be taught in one program, but across a range of disciplines on offer at the university. Fortuitously, there was a new initiative, entitled "AcrossRCA," in which students from every program came together for a week of cross-college workshops. Another biologist-turned-graphic-designer, Peter Crnokrak, and I ran the first workshop as part of this program. Over the next six years, I continued to run data manifestation workshops annually as a part of AcrossRCA.

The workshop immerses participants in the communication of data as a design practice, and encourages them to work collaboratively as they explore online open-access global statistics. The set brief asks students to translate these statistics into an object, installation, or experience that stimulates dialogue and has the potential to change an audience's view on an important or timely topic. Over the years I have come to call this practice "data manifestation" in order to describe a process that is visual (i.e., data visualisation), as well as physical and experiential (von Ompteda 2013).

Workshop participants initially drew their datasets from the World Values Survey (e.g., Figures 6.24 and 6.25 below), an online repository of global statistics compiled by an international network of social scientists spanning fifty-seven countries. This is a fascinating survey of changing global values and their impact on social and political life, based on questions such as: "How important is God in your life?" (World Values Survey Association 2015). In recent years the students have been using the World DataBank (e.g., Figure 6.26 below), a compilation of statistics on over two hundred countries from international sources including the World Bank, World Health Organization, and the United Nations. The World DataBank contains a diverse collection of statistics including countries' annual CO_2 emissions and number of Internet users, and the proportion of seats held by women in national parliaments (World Bank Group 2015). While the vast majority of workshop participants focus on these data sources, others have discovered their own.

In 2012, three RCA students who were passionate about global water shortages created a project entitled *Bottled Stress* (Figure 6.23) that was based on data they found in a United Nations report (UN-Water/FAO 2007). Iban Benzal (Service Design), Tom Price (Architecture), and Peter Spence (Innovation Design Engineering) were interested in communicating the number of people globally who were predicted to live under conditions of water stress and scarcity in 2025. The students manifested this data by lining glass bottles up along a shelf—each bottle representing one billion people. They filled the bottles with differing amounts of water and deformed them to various degrees—as if the bottles were collapsing into themselves—in order to represent those people predicted to be living in countries or regions with water shortages. Through the use of analogy, these students were able to create a

Figure 6.23 *Bottled Stress.* Communicating global water shortages through deformed bottles, based on United Nations' data. © 2015. Designers: Iban Benzal, Tom Price, and Peter Spence. Photographer: Iris Xinru Long.

connection between abstract quantitative data and the relatable experience of having available drinking water. In a "poetic" statement of sorts, the severely distressed bottle in the foreground of Figure 6.23 leaked. While this aspect of the project was not planned, the leaking bottle provided a tangible representation of loss to be experienced by the audience in real time.

In order to create *Bottled Stress*, the students had to use RCA's Glass Furnace Room for the first time. In so doing, they had to rely on fabrication methods and materials with which they were unfamiliar. Staying true to the content, these students—like all workshop participants—chose the materials and methods best suited to the communication of their data. As such, no one group member entered into the cross-disciplinary collaboration as the "expert," facilitating a context of equal exchange. In the workshops, the students integrated their diverse perspectives and approaches, and worked together toward their collective goal to tell the stories that are found within the data.

Data manifestation as authorship

Data visualization is traditionally viewed as a scientific tool for analysis that is neutral, dispassionate, and objective (Vande Moere and Patel 2010). Designers however employ a subjective approach (von Ompteda and Walker 2015) when engaging in data visualization as a creative practice. Using the techniques of emphasis and omission, designers highlight particular aspects of a dataset (Dörk *et al.* 2013), creating projects that embody a distinct point of view (Viégas and Wattenberg 2007). While some have voiced concern over the responsibility that designers assume when choosing to emphasize or omit information (Klanten *et al.* 2010), others see it as a strength (Viégas and Wattenberg 2007) that is in step with the inherent non-neutrality of data that is collected, processed, and presented for specific purposes (Hall 2008).

The data manifestation workshops were specifically designed to celebrate the power of subjectivity, involving a highly diverse participant group that was given freedom in their choices of topic. The open-ended nature of the brief—which asks students to explore statistics that they find interesting and worthy of dissemination—has resulted in outcomes that reflect the varied passions of the workshop participants. Projects have focused on a wide range of subjects including the environment, gender equality, religion, the media, and education, and students often care deeply about the particular issues on which they have chosen to focus.

Art and Design, a leading magazine in China, wrote about the RCA data manifestation workshops, framing the students as "data activists" (Changzheng 2013). Illustrating their article, they featured a workshop outcome entitled *Balance* (Figure 6.24) created by Marcel Helmer (Design Interactions), Jessica Morgan (Visual Communication), and Paul Stawenow (Innovation Design Engineering). These students worked with World Values Survey data, and focused their attention on the percentage of people who agreed with the following statements: "The Government should reduce environmental pollution, but it should not cost me any money" and "I would agree to an increase in taxes if the extra money were used to prevent environmental pollution" (World Values Survey Association 2015). The students created twenty-two circular wooden objects—each one representing a country—that were placed in a row along a wooden platform. For every country, the percentage of people who agreed with each of the

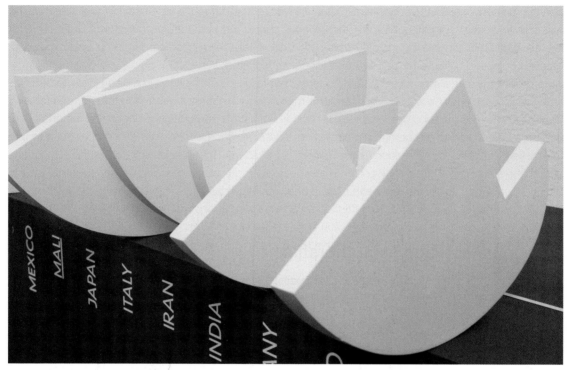

Figure 6.24 *Balance*. Visualizing diverse perspectives on pollution reduction within different countries, based on the World Values Survey. © 2015. Designers: Marcel Helmer, Jessica Morgan, and Paul Stawenow. Photographer: Dominic Tschudin/ Royal College of Art Archive.

two statements was translated into two radii, resulting in objects comprised of quarter circles of different sizes. If a higher percentage of people believed that pollution reduction should not cost them any money, a country's object tilted dangerously toward the edge of the platform. Conversely, if a higher percentage of people supported an increase in taxes, the country's object tilted toward the "safety" of the wall.

This piece elegantly communicates the "balance" (or lack thereof) between two divergent perspectives on the costs of reducing pollution through simple wooden objects on a platform. In order to enhance the richness of the narrative, and to facilitate its reading by an audience, the students made noteworthy decisions both about the countries they chose and the placement of the associated wooden objects. They purposely chose the country Mali, for example, which had almost equal percentages of people who agreed with the two statements, resulting in two equal radii, and thus a perfectly "balanced" object (i.e., a half circle). The students drew attention to the half-circle object by underlining the label for Mali, as well as placing it centrally among the other objects on the platform. The object representing Mali facilitated audience readings of the data manifestation: it provided a baseline for comparison with the other objects, which tilted one way or the other. The students also chose to include numerous top GDP (Gross Domestic Product) nations including Japan, Italy, and India, with the intention of garnering audience interest, as these are globally influential countries about which people are familiar. Countries were also selected on purpose if they displayed extreme differences in the two perspectives. This decision showcased off-kilter objects that contrasted with countries with more moderate differences. The country with the most extreme difference in perspectives (toward no cost to reduce pollution) was placed directly on the edge of the platform, threatening to fall at any moment and further intensifying the sense of drama.

Balance addressed a contradiction between what people demand and their willingness to sacrifice (Helmer 2015). In the students' view, it was contradictory to support pollution reduction without accepting personal financial sacrifice. Conversely, accepting an increase in taxes was considered a non-contradictory position. As such, the objects that tilted toward the edge of the platform revealed the degree of this contradiction within different countries. *Balance* is a non-neutral manifestation of data, as the students are not simply communicating information but also their perspective on it. Through these objects, some of which appear to be at risk of falling off the platform, the project conveys the danger of not taking personal responsibility for pollution within one's own country. In so doing, the piece attempts to place responsibility for pollution reduction onto the public instead of on governments. As a representation of citizens' beliefs on an important and timely topic, the final outcome offers a metaphor for the precariousness of our collective future.

Data manifestation can also be used to facilitate intimate discussions about social and political issues among workshop participants themselves. At CAFA Art Museum in Beijing (2013), for example, I ran a workshop with thirty people, ranging from students enrolled at China Central Academy of Fine Arts (CAFA) to members of the public without a background in art or design. Participants were given a selection of data from which they could choose, which was sourced from the World DataBank (World Bank Group 2015), and they were tasked to manifest this data physically using string and paper. Not surprisingly, they were interested in information that was relevant to life in China. Two groups focused on global net migration data, which led to an emotionally charged dialogue about how many people leave China every year to live in other countries. Thus, instead of communicating world statistics to an outside audience, these were students and members of the public who manifested statistics in physical form to create a tangible context for their own conversations.

Data as object, installation, and experience

While most people are familiar with data visualized on the page and screen, physical visualizations (e.g. data sculptures) have become increasingly common (Jansen *et al*. 2013). The most obvious method by which data can be communicated physically involves giving "depth" to a two-dimensional chart or graph (Vande Moere and Patel 2010). The project *Balance* (Figure 6.24) is an example of a graph-like physical visualization, which further offers a metaphor for our precarious future through its unbalanced forms. The use (and modification) of everyday objects to represent data is another method of physical visualization, which is exemplified by the previously discussed project *Bottled Stress* (Figure 6.23). By communicating predictions of global water shortages through bottles and water, an audience is able to engage with abstract data through familiar objects and materials that directly relate to the subject. Still other physical manifestations of data go one step further, offering an opportunity to "experience" information through the human body.

The project *My Life Don't Mean A Thing If It Ain't Got That Swing* (Figure 6.25), which was created by Polly O'Flynn (Visual Communication), James Pockson (Architecture), and Peter Shenai (Information Experience Design), is an example of "data experience." The students were intrigued by the World Values Survey question "All things considered, how satisfied are you with your life as a whole these days?" (World Values Survey Association 2015). They challenged the idea of visualizing the associated data since satisfaction is an experience that people "feel" rather than see. The students decided to build a swing set, which gave people the opportunity to experience physically the "satisfaction" level in five different countries through the act of swinging. They accomplished this by adjusting the height of the swing's seat with a rope that was attached to a country's flag that was painted alongside the swing set's frame (see Figure 6.25). A higher percentage of "satisfied" people within a country translated into a higher placed flag, a longer rope, a larger swing arc, and theoretically a more satisfying swing experience. This project was a highlight at the *Data Manifestation* exhibition at RCA (von Ompteda 2013), and many gallery visitors engaged with the statistics through the act of swinging.

Figure 6.25 *My Life Don't Mean a Thing if it Ain't Got that Swing*. Experiencing data; the percentage of people "satisfied" with their lives in different countries, based on the World Values Survey. © 2015. Designers: Polly O'Flynn, James Pockson, and Peter Shenai. Photographer: James Pockson.

While the creators of *Swing* explored the possibilities of experiencing information, what is more interesting is their approach to data manifestation as a critical practice (Hall 2011). The students juxtaposed the American flag with the Ethiopian flag placed directly below it; both countries have lower percentages of people who are "satisfied." By putting these two statistics in close proximity, they subtly posed the question: can one really compare survey results across countries? Thus, the students are communicating the data, but they are also encouraging people to question the data. It has become crucial for the design community to address the uncertainty associated with data (von Ompteda 2015). When data is made physical or is beautiful, audiences are more apt to accept it as truth (e.g., Spiegelhalter *et al*. 2011). This context has led to the *Data Provocation* workshops that I currently run, which pose the essential question: how can the communication of data reflect its inherent uncertainty?

There are numerous ways to communicate the uncertainty associated with data, and the project *Ashes to Ashes* offers some insight into these possibilities (Figure 6.26). This project focused on global arms trade data from the World DataBank (World Bank Group 2015) and the Stockholm International

Figure 6.26 *Ashes to Ashes*. A performance of global-arms-trade data sourced from the World DataBank and the Stockholm International Peace Research Institute. © 2015. Designers: Corina Angheloiu, Maria Izquierdo, Andrea Tam, Mireia Gordi Vila, and Iddo Wald. Photographer: Mireia Gordi Vila.

Peace Research Institute (SIPRI) (2015), and was created by Corina Angheloiu (Architecture), Mireia Gordi Vila (Design Products), Maria Izquierdo (Design Products), Iddo Wald (Innovation Design Engineering), and Andrea Tam (History of Design). The students used a large rectangular board as their foundation, upon which they affixed columns of matches of various widths. The matches represented the top ten countries that import arms. The students created a long demarcated striking surface, divided into various widths, which represented the top ten arms-exporting countries. Finally, they ran the striking surface along the matches to set the project on fire, revealing their perspective that the arms trade is a fundamentally collaborative effort.

The intentions behind *Ashes to Ashes* were not focused on the uncertainty associated with data, and yet this performance offers insight into ways that this aspect of presenting data can be communicated. The audience experiences this work as dynamic as the flames leap, transformative as matches become ashes, and as a moment in time as the fire is ignited and dies. Statistics change, algorithms are updated, and data does not represent a whole truth. Also of interest here is the mark of the hand; a robot did not create this data manifestation, humans did. Data is, after all, created by people (e.g. Gitelman and Jackson 2013).

The human touch is inherent in all of the pieces that are produced in the data manifestation work-shops, both honoring the nature of data (as human artifact) and reflecting a wide interest in low-tech sculptural creations (e.g. Klanten *et al.* 2012). While the students use digital means to develop the projects—exploring statistics through software and working with digital production processes (e.g., CNC milling)—the outputs themselves are consistently analogue. The mark of the hand is implied through the tangible methods employed in the fabrication of these works (e.g., shaping glass, painting, building, performing). It has been suggested that such time-intensive labor asks for a reciprocal slow reading by an audience (Klanten *et al.* 2012), an interesting proposition in the context of contemporary interactions with digital information that often lack focus and time investment. Through the physical manifestation of data, these workshop projects strive to create a meaningful connection between abstract information and people.

Summary

The communication of data has become an established creative practice involving designers from across disciplines. The data manifestation workshops have been a part of this shift within the design community, offering cross-disciplinary collaborative opportunities for over 150 students from more than 20 programs at the Royal College of Art. These students have engaged passionately in data manifest-ation as authorship—sourcing, analyzing, and communicating information on issues they believe deserve an audience. While this area of design represents an exploration into forms for creative prac-tice, it is also an exploration into forms for data. Data can be transformed into deformed bottles, precarious objects, critical swings, a performance of fire—and data may be more than just visualized, when translated into physical, tangible, and experiential forms. Ultimately, the data manifestation projects seek to create a context for people to engage with important social and political issues, and the nature of information itself.

Acknowledgements

I gratefully acknowledge AcrossRCA, Royal College of Art for the funding and support of my workshops since 2010. Thank you also to Peter Crnokrak for his contribution to early workshop development and teaching in 2010. I am appreciative of funding and support for the CAFA Art Museum workshop by the British Council and ADPP (Asian Design Publication Project) and thank Kevin Walker for help with the CAFA workshop and *Data Manifestation* exhibition. I am grateful to the editors, whose insights have been extremely valuable to the essay's development. Finally, I am indebted to my students whose passion and boundless capacity remain my core source of inspiration.

Part 6: Further reading

Ashworth, G. and M. Kavaratzis (2014), "Cities of Culture and Culture in Cities: The Emerging Uses of Culture in City Branding," in T. Haas and K. Olsson (eds), *Emergent Urbanism Urban Planning & Design in Times of Structural and Systemic Change*, London: Routledge.

Baur, R. M. Roskowska, and S. Thiery, eds (2013), *Don't Brand My Public Space!* Zurich: Lars Müller Publishers.

Black, A., P. Luna, O. Lund, and S. Walker, eds (2017), *Information Design: Research and Practice*, London: Routledge.

Carson, D. (2012), *The End of Print: The Grafik Design of David Carson*, 2nd edn, London: Lewis Blackwell.

Christianson, S. (2012), *100 Diagrams That Changed the World: From the Earliest Cave Paintings to the Innovation of the iPod,* New York: Plume.

Dinnie, K. (2016), *Nation Branding: Concepts, Issues, Practice*, 2nd edn, London: Routledge.

Drucker, J. (2014), *Graphesis: Visual Forms of Knowledge Production*, Cambridge, MA: Harvard University Press.

Halpern, O. (2015), *Beautiful Data: A History of Vision and Reason Since 1945*, Raleigh, NC: Duke University Press.

Harland, R. (2016), *Graphic Design in Urban Environments*, London: Bloomsbury.

Holt, D. B. (2004), *How Brands Become Icons: The Principles of Cultural Branding*, Cambridge, MA: Harvard Business Review Press.

Ind, N. (2006), *Beyond Branding: How the New Values of Transparency and Integrity Are Changing the World of Brands,* London: Kogan Page.

Johnson, M. (2016), *Branding in Five and a Half Steps*, London: Thames & Hudson.

Kane, C. L. (2016), "Gifs that Glitch: Eyeball Aesthetics for the Attention Economy," *Communication Design,* 4 (1–2): 41–62.

Kirk, A. (2016), *Data Visualisation: A Handbook for Data Driven Design*, London: Sage.

Lima, M. (2013) *Visual Complexity: Mapping Patterns of Information*, New York: Princeton Architectural Press.

McCandless, D. (2012), *Information is Beautiful,* New York: Collins.

Meirelles, I. (2013), *Design for Information: An Introduction to the Histories, Theories, and Best Practices Behind Effective Information Visualizations,* London: Rockport.

Millman, D. (2013), *Brand Thinking and Other Noble Pursuits*, New York: Allworth.

Müller, J. and R. R. Remington (2015), *Logo Modernism (Design)*, Cologne: Taschen.

Olins, W. (2014), *Brand New: The Shape of Brands to Come*, London: Thames & Hudson.

Paradis, L. with R. Früh and F. Rappo, eds (2017), *30 Years of Swiss Typographic Discourse in the Typografische Monatsblätter:1960–1990*, Lars Müller Publishers.

Pike, A. (2013), *Brands and Branding Geographies*, Cheltenham: Edward Elgar Publishers.

Reas, C. and B. Fry (2015), *Processing: A Programming Handbook for Visual Designers and Artists,* 2nd rev. edn, Cambridge, MA: MIT Press.

Sandhaus, L. (2014), *Earthquakes, Mudslides, Fires & Riots: California & Graphic Design 1936–1986*, London: Thames & Hudson.

Tufte, E. R. (1990), *Envisioning Information*. Cheshire, CT: Graphics Press USA.

Tufte, E. R. (2001), *The Visual Display of Quantitative Information*, 2nd edn, Cheshire, CT: Graphics Press USA.

Ware, C. (2012), *Information Visualization: Perception for Design*, 3rd edn, Burlington, MA: Morgan Kaufmann.

Wozencroft, J. (1988), *The Graphic Language of Neville Brody 1,* London: Thames & Hudson.

Wozencroft, J. (1994), *The Graphic Language of Neville Brody 2*, London: Thames & Hudson.

Yikun, L. and D. Zhao, (2016), *Visual Storytelling: Infographic Design in News,* Melbourne: The Images Publishing Group.

Part 7

Graphic design futures

Part 7: Introduction

Graphic design is no longer circumscribed by print media. In the twentieth century, the broadened scope of graphic design prompted a change in what we call ourselves from "graphic design" to "visual communication." Today, the field is often referred to by the umbrella term "communication design," a reflection of how the scope of graphic design has expanded once again. The new roles for designers typically include non-traditional purviews, such as design of sound, the moving image, and digital and immersive experiences. These disparate media oblige graphic designers to work across disciplinary boundaries, which means that graphic design is co-produced with other disciplines, such as geography, biology, or physics. This work can be cross-disciplinary—people viewing one discipline from the perspective of another—or multidisciplinary—people from different disciplines bringing together their disciplinary knowledge—or interdisciplinary—people synthesizing knowledge and methods from different disciplines. These projects sometimes produce new hybrid spaces. The essays in Part 7 offer an expedition into how we integrate media from other disciplines into design. The authors also explore how both old and new technologies affect the ways that we access and absorb information. In this last Part of the *Reader*, we hint at possible future graphic design practices, but we also present comprehensive themes: these include the necessity of implementing social and political contexts of design, and of framing historical contexts for contemporary and future design practices.

The first Section, "The future of print media/the book," begins with an exploration of the topic of publishing and reading visual and textual information; both are activities that have long been the domain of graphic design practice. Johanna Drucker opens with "What is the cult future of the book?" (2010). Drucker discusses the future of the book in the context of contemporary digital media, and she presents a history of books in their cultural milieu. She reveals that the invention of print media and the codex form of the book—our common form of bound book with multiple pages—generated struggles for control over communication. Drucker next asks how digital reading formats are similar in character to traditional books, concluding that both kinds of formats shape communication, community, and collective memory. Nanette Hoogslag similarly explores how digital media shapes the communication of editorial illustration in "The signifier of incompleteness: editorial illustration in the new media age" (2012). She argues that there is no guarantee of interplay between text and image in digital media—sometimes editorial illustration will, therefore, be read independently of related text. Hoogslag concludes that this disconnect may be resolved by tablet readers, which are able to echo the design and production cycle of print, while offering the material and technological qualities of digital media. David Small also considers navigating physical and information spaces in "Rethinking the book" (2002). Information spaces, unlike those in the physical world, require the negotiation of fluid information environments. Small suggests ways to control both the focus and the transparency of multiple, simultaneous bits of information through his case study of MIT Media Lab's "The Talmud" project. Stéphanie Vilayphiou and Alexandre Leray navigate the visual information spaces produced by programming in "Writing design: towards a culture of code" (2011). Beginning with the ideas of 1960s Swiss graphic designer Karl Gerstner, the authors provide several case studies in which designers use programming to create print and digital design and designed environments. They argue that graphic designers should embrace the "language of code" as a design tool, and they make clear how code is a language—one that can be used to shape physical and digital graphic design work.

Graphic design practice inevitably embraces social issues: the so-called wicked problems that are associated with big societal challenges, with attention paid specifically to localized solutions. The next Section features essays that reflect upon society and "The forefront of graphic design practice." In "Social design: the context of post-conflict Lebanon" (2018), Joanna Choukeir defines social design as an interdisciplinary investigative process that produces solutions for a better society rather than as an artifact-creation process. She then introduces a case study—a design for a social integration project that is focused on barriers to social integration in Lebanon—and her evaluations of its outcomes.

Exploring old and new methodologies and technologies often presents graphic designers with opportunities to experiment and to re-evaluate contemporary practices. In "Emil Ruder: A future for design principles in screen typography" (2011) Hilary Kenna shows how twentieth-century designer Emil Ruder's typographic principles, such as contrast, form, and counterform, and shades of grey, rhythm, and kinetics, are relevant to the design of screen-based typography. Ruder's systematic methodology, which according to Kenna encompasses experimentation on various forms of the same material, is also relevant to screen-based typography. Engaging with novel digital technologies often demands unorthodox ways of working, such as the open-ended collaborative and interdisciplinary teams discussed in "Everything to come is designed by you" (2018). In this essay, Tea Uglow considers Google Creative Lab, Australia, which, she explains, comprises an international group of programmers, filmmakers, producers, philosophers, and business people who work on a range of individual, collective, and collaborative projects. Uglow explains how the group works together, describing several projects carried out by the Lab including "YouTube Symphony Orchestra" (2009), the film project *Life in a Day* (2012), and googlehangouts "Hangouts in History." We wrap up this Section with a reminder of how the past informs the future of graphic design education and the profession. In the visual essay "RCA graphic design: 1960s–2010s" (2018) Rosy Penston investigates the relationships between the social backgrounds of graphic design tutors (faculty) and students who attended the RCA prior to 2013. An alumna of the College, Penston follows design work that students produced—some of which is presented here—to see if there is a link among social class, privilege, and talent.

The authors in this Part reflect the ways in which graphic designers critically investigate the history of their profession, but also how they speculate about what lies ahead. Big challenges or "wicked problems" call for designers to rethink their practices, focusing on how critical thinking and making, and new tools and processes, can take into consideration complex global contexts and shifting social, political, cultural, economic circumstances. Along with this complexity comes new interdisciplinary incarnations (e.g. bio- and sensorial-design), and new hybrid spaces such as those that incorporate generative typography, information experiences, and digital direction. At the heart of our discussion of these complex practices is graphic design, which provides a unique lens through which we engage and interact with others—and helps shape the world around us.

Section 7.1

The future of print media/the book

its readers. Its entire constructed content, the style and layout, the use of metaphor and imagery, connect the reader beyond the story to the underlying values of the newspaper. With its aim to bind all expression within one editorial context, and with illustration expressing the editorial voice that lies behind the accompanying articles, editorial illustration is an instrument par excellence of a newspaper's ideology.

Roland Barthes (1977) describes the principles of the relationship between image and text within a newspaper setting and presents them as two independent yet co-operative structures, one visual and one textual. The image is placed in direct relation to captions, headlines, introduction, body-text, etc., and the development of meaning comes from the physical closeness of the structures. The understanding of the article emerges through this co-operation of image and text. Where in the first instance the image engages and directs the initial reading, it is the text that in turn shapes the interpretation of the image. This process of understanding can come through a conscious analysis of both independent structures as well as the meaning built between them, but importantly, it equally comes through a continuous but semi-conscious awareness of the image, which directs the interpretation.

Because of the visual dominance of the image over text, it is the image that first engages and directs the decision to read, thus affecting the way the story will be read (Berger 1972; Barthes 1977; Hillis Miller 1992). It presents a hierarchical, symbiotic and fluid shaping of meaning, where in reading, the image loads the text, followed by continuous mutual influence of one on the other. Meaning hovers somewhere between the headline and the image and is continuously present throughout the reading of the story.

Barthes points to the presence of the caption next to the editorial image as having an important first role in verifying this image. This might well be true for a photograph or info-graphic, but in contemporary editorial contexts, an illustration does not have a caption[6]. Illustration does not verify or explain, rather it reflects and suggests. As a coded handmade image it cannot offer explicit answers or clear solutions, no facts are given. It is suggestive and ambiguous, it demands interpretation by the reader and proudly so.

In order for the illustration to be able to give meaning to a news story, a core quality of the illustration, the story needs to be reflective and contained, the illustration and story should be directed at a homogeneous public and set within the distinctive ideology of the newspaper. I call these the conditions of incompleteness and I would like to propose that these are essential for editorial illustration to flourish. I propose that the incompleteness of text, the overt ambiguity of the handmade image and the incomplete intertextual relation between them, to be filled in by the reader, are essential for an editorial illustration.

> Something's deliberately left unanswered, other than through the vagueness of the notion of belief, and trust in an ideology, present in the condition of the printed form.
>
> (Žižek 1997)

The online information setting

When it comes to servicing our need to remain permanently informed (Newton 2000), online editorial news media seem to be the logical extension of the printed newspaper. Online a multitude of information streams, sources and media types are available and online news media follow these ways of information distribution. They offer a wide range of sources and media types woven into a single website, into a single interface. Digital technologies brought together the network capabilities of the internet, the archiving and the computational capacities of computers and multi media techniques for collating text, (moving) image, sound and interaction (Kittler 1999). All this can be updated and distributed through an automated content management system which allows for the continuous flow of information. Where the aim of news media is to keep the readers informed, paradoxically, this superfluity of information has only heightened the sense of 'unknowing' (Žižek 1997; Dean 2010). On the one hand it highlights a failure of the message to reach its audience, and on the other a loss of the ability to create meaning. The message can no longer be trusted or accepted as finite and therefore definitive. On the web, browsing or surfing can bring all kinds of unexpected information, which can be surprising and enhancing, but without first understanding its intertextual and coded cultural contexts, it can equally lead to false understanding (Dean 2010). Jodi Dean calls this a failure of transmission—when the designated message fails to reach the designated audience. Stuart Hall (1972: 128) described this as breaking the essential chain of communication. A chain of communication demands that all the signs contained in one particular message are presented within one specific ideology, in order for the signs to be continuously coded and decoded in the intended way—the symbolic efficiency. It depends on the sender and receiver sharing the same codes (Dean 2010). Online the direct linkage between the sender and receiver is no longer contained. It has become unclear where the information comes from, whether it is "complete" and whether we have all the information and background to decode it sufficiently. It leads us to ask whether we can create a stable understanding, and whether meaning can be trusted. Online the possibility for acquiring information is a broad, continuous and open offer. The web might give us more information but doesn't help support the formation of meaning. Whereas in a contained environment the trust is founded on a shared ideology, online trust seems to be in the information itself.

> The contemporary setting of electronic mediated subjectivity is one of infinite doubt, ultimate reflexivization. There's always another option, link, opinion, nuance or contingency that we haven't taken into account. Some particular experience of some other who could be potentially damaged or disenfranchised, a better deal even a cure. The very conditions of possibility for adequation (for determining the criteria by which to assess whether a decision or answer is, if not good, then at least adequate) have been foreclosed. It's just your opinion. Additionally, as the efficiency of the symbolic declines, images and affective intensities may appear all the more powerful, relevant, and effective. A picture is worth a thousand words.
>
> (Dean 2010: 6)

Dean points to the power of the image, but images, too, suffer in this context, where their connotative relations are undermined by the same mechanisms. This is particularly true for editorial illustration, which is commissioned to be linked to a specific text and context. In editorial illustration the loss of symbolic efficiency reduces the meaning that comes from both its close link to the story and its ideological setting and with this meaning no longer fixed, the illustration is lost for words.

Online news media

With the following example of a typically illustrated article in the *Guardian* online I can show how these ideas from Žižek and Dean appear within the context of a news webpage and further how the editorial web conditions impact on the illustration (Figure 7.1).

Figure 7.1 Matt Kenyon illustration for *The Guardian* web page, April 18, 2012: "On fracking and wind we are having the wrong debates." © 2012. Guardian News & Media Ltd.

The first thing you notice when you arrive at the primary window of the web page—the part of the page which is visible when you first open it—is the diversity and quantity of potential information. In this particular window there are almost one hundred links to information elsewhere. The links all lead to other locations, some within the same section, but many bring you to different web environments either within the *Guardian* or elsewhere.

Continuing down the page, the amount of visible page elements can fluctuate with every visit. This depends on personal and screen settings, as well as the size of the advertising which frequently changes. But in all cases it follows the format where the top six to eight horizontal rows of information are menu bars, including those of the browser window and advertising. From the three vertical columns, two present more selection options and advertising; only one column is dedicated to the story.

The story column presents the headline, a short introduction text, the author and the illustration. But because the layout of the page is not set, it is quite possible that the illustration is only partially visible and can even be pushed below the primary window; it can only be seen when you scroll further down. Scrolling down brings the reader to the news story and comments; once reading begins all previous text and image elements are soon out of sight. Most news media websites are based on a strict design format implemented through a Content Management System which allows for the automation of various editorial, visual design, navigation and storage processes, such as the formatting of text, embedding multi-media, hyperlinking, metadata and archiving. Furthermore it also controls readability on the diverse range of screen standards and screen settings of the readers. This system is hugely beneficial for the linking and distribution of all kinds of content and media, and brings with it a system of reading based on the individual's preferences and selection from the multitude of sources. This in favor over the intertextual relationships, where the particular positioning of the elements is believed to be important and meaningful.

For the image this means there are limited options for positioning, scaling and subtle interplay with the text and context. In print the placement of the image is an important design decision and the particular alliance of text and image are part of the creation of meaning (Barthes 1972; Kraus 2009: 88, 172). The present Content Management System cannot provide these kind of relationships. There is no longer the guarantee of a continuous intertextual relationship, neither with the title nor with the text, since on the crucial first online page it might be altogether absent or randomly cropped.

While there is no longer a guarantee that an illustration can function as an element of first attraction, it has also lost the ability to create meaning through the co-operation of image and text. The physical closeness and the fluid interplay between text and image are no longer guaranteed. To view an illustration within this editorial space will have to be a deliberate act and it forces the illustration into a more independent position, more likely to be read as a piece of associated information.

This subtle shift in position presents two particular negative effects for the traditional form of editorial illustration. When meaning coming from the intended subliminal reading is lost, editorial illustration is in danger of becoming a predominantly decorative experience. Secondly, placed in a more isolated position, its meaning needs to be self contained within the image, and so loses its ability to relate to the gaps in the text. Online, traditional editorial illustration as an aid to reflection and engagement is severely disabled. Where the approach to content and the way it is enabled through design run counter to the necessary conditions for effective editorial illustration, it is unsurprising that in its present form it is rarely commissioned. As long as editorial media websites value the fullness of information above incompleteness[7] as the way to create meaning and understanding, editorial illustration will struggle to function.

The reflective role

Should we conclude that editorial illustration is inseparable from the printed editorial environment and unsuitable for the fast paced environment of online editorials? With the ongoing development of new media, this conclusion would be premature, especially where the entire publishing industry is undergoing an existential crisis and is searching for a more satisfactory publishing mode!, not only in business terms but also for the consumer's reading experience. Within the current arrangements and structures of web based platforms, editorial illustration can still play an important reflective role. Exploring the position of the illustration as an independent editorial option could bring a much needed reflective alternative to text and evidential image. Beyond the political cartoon and with the developing interest in authorial illustration (Braund et al. 2012) the illustrator's potential for critical and expressive image making can give alternative insight into complex current issues as well as putting forward the newspaper's point of view.

Online there are examples such as the experimental platforms like OOG[8]—a visual commentary platform in a Dutch online Newspaper "de Volkskrant," the independent Illustration Daily[9] or individual illustrators like Christophe Niemann who tweeted a real time visual reportage of his attempt to run the New York Marathon in the online edition of the *New York Times* (Niemann 2011).

But other than in the web editions of editorials, at the moment the only real opportunity to extend the relational qualities of editorial illustration is most likely to be found in the development of newspaper and magazine editions for the slate—iPad or tablet readers—made available through a mobile app. Though still in its infancy, it is hailed by the magazine industry as a possible way forward (Pogue 2012) and offers a more reflective experience as Alan Rusbridger, editor of the *Guardian*, stated at the launch of the tablet edition (*Guardian*, Anon 2011). It follows the so-called walled garden model, a publishing model in which the users access to internet content and services is controlled. This move, however, is also not without controversy, given the extended control held by the publisher over access, content, media and platform (Arthur 2012).

The tablet echoes the content, design and production cycle of print, but allied with the material and technological qualities particular to this medium including multimedia, interactivity and haptic navigation, it holds the potential for a fluid relationship between text and image, extending that of print. With this model based on the deliberate setting of limits and boundaries and setting the richness of the reading experience as a primary concern, it can offer a solution for the intrinsic need for reflective space to be filled in by the reader, and I suggest that illustration might be its guide.

Notes

1. In earlier research I found that the shift in printing technologies of the late 19th century periodicals was crucial to the moment editorial illustration became distinct. The change from wood engraving to halftone printing brought not only the reproduction of photography but also a direct copy of the illustrators drawing into the papers. This brought an end to the tradition of translating the illustrator's sketch onto a wood engraving and led to the birth of the illustrator as the individual expressive visual contributor (Beegan 2008; Benjamin 1936; Carrington 1905; Hutt 1973; Reed 1997; Ruskin 1872; Sinnema 1998).

2. Based on a sample study of the *Guardian* in April/May 2011 and 2012. Further from dialogue and observation presented in the workshop Think Editorial Illustration November 2011. To fully confirm these details a more thorough research will be needed

3. Though very much part of the editorial tradition and sometimes overlapping in form, content and qualities, I wish to make a distinction for the political cartoon as a separate category with its own distinguished history and use of visual language (Male 2007). Where the editorial illustration is related to a specific text, the cartoon is seen as a independent contribution of the illustrator as author.

4. This use of the term ideal and ideology perhaps needs some further definition, where it is not referring to a political idea, but to a psycho-analytical concept comes from the term Ideology defined by the French psychoanalyst Jacques Lacan (Lacan 1949; Žižek n.d.). It refers to an instilled desire to become the perfectly imagined—ideal—self, which Lacan calls the Other. This sets our values, ambitions and boundaries. Outside ourselves this Other is present in the culture we inhabit, and the values to which we relate. This in turn determines our actions, builds our

ideas, judgments and (visual) language. It is language that allows us to connect with the Ideal and we use this index of subconscious references, codes and signs to create meaning, to verify and understand what we see. It's through the media we choose, including newspaper and its images, that this Ideology is continually reaffirmed and updated.

5. No matter how controversial the image might seem, ultimately the illustrator commissioned and the illustration approved are consented by the editors and therefor representing what the paper stands for (Kraus 2009; Holland 2000). The amount of control by the art director and the artistic freedom are much debated issues amongst illustrators and often referred to in terms of quality of the newspaper and art director.

6. In Victorian newspapers where illustration held an evidencing task and still in some contemporary (children's) literature, where illustration refer to a precise phrase or event described in the text, captions are used. In present editorial context captions can be present, but are part of the illustration and have a deliberate connotation function (Hillis Miller 1992: 66).

7. The issue of *too much information, 'information overload'*, and the problems of the loss of control with the internet and computer as operative tools is widely recognized and discussed. In the *Plague of Fantasies*, Slavoj Žižek (1997) disseminates these issues and presents the risks of the internet and the computer as all consuming information systems. He pleads for the importance of a mental space left open, not filled with (virtual) experiences and information, but something that is deliberately left unanswered, *other than through the vagueness of the notion of belief, and trust in an ideology*; he makes a plea for the importance of incompleteness.

8. http://www.hoogslag.nl/curatorial-practice/oog

9. http://www.illustrationdaily.nl/

Chapter 7.1.3

Rethinking the book

David Small

Navigation and wayfinding

The use of three-dimensional typography has fundamentally changed the way we think about the use of space in graphic design and how the surface of the computer screen is understood by the designer. When the design of three-dimensional typography is cast as a landscape design problem, we understand that it has more to do with creating compelling views than with the strict arrangement of elements. As a garden design will lead one through a series of vantage points that hide, reveal, and accentuate a series of features,[1] a journey through an information landscape should provide a meaningful context for the information elements.

Just as one reads the physical landscape in order to navigate the world, so too must people be able to find their way about information spaces. The designer should be careful, however, not to confuse the abstract spaces of typographic information with the roads, subways, and buildings of our built environment. In the visual design of information spaces it is much more important to understand relative and ultimately fluid relationships between shifting and mutating information chunks than the fixed elements of the real world.

For example, in navigating the urban environment, we make use of fixed signs and landmarks, transportation systems, and place-based addressing schemes such as street addresses in the United States or *chome* (postal neighborhoods) in Japan. In information systems, the data itself can have an inherent address (e.g., Exodus 4:12 or *Romeo and Juliet,* act 3, scene 1). Since we can move instantaneously from one location to another, getting the "lay of the land" may be less important than having a clear view of your current location and meaningful jump points from there.

The tools for getting from one location to another are unclear, but we can understand what is required for a usable interface. It is always easier to find your way to something that you can already see. Through use of scalable text that can be layered, we can keep much more information simultaneously visible than was previously possible. Nonetheless, we still require clear indications of where we are within a space and what lies just out of our view.

We must also consider that any journey through space is also one through time. No movement is ever truly instantaneous, and the way in which we move and how the journey unfolds through time can be of great help in revealing the underlying structure of a landscape.

First published in *Graphic Design & Reading: Explorations of an Uneasy Relationship,* ed. Gunnar Swanson, New York: Allworth Press (2000), 188–200. © David Small.

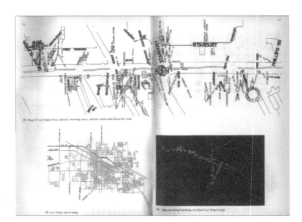

Figure 7.2 The Forgotten Symbolism of Architectural Form, page spread from *Learning from Las Vegas*, pp. 30–31. © 1977. Designer: Robert Venturi. By permission of The MIT Press.

The correspondence between narrative space and architectural space or the landscape is a natural one. There are many examples, from the friezes in which the story is organized along the lines of the architectural structure[2] to the songlines of the Australian aboriginal people.[3] In his book *Learning from Las Vegas,* Robert Venturi describes the strip as a textual event.[4] In her design of the book, Muriel Cooper visually demonstrated the sign map of the strip (Figure 7.2).

Layering, juxtaposition, and scale

The primary problem designers encounter when moving to the digital medium is that the resolution they are accustomed to in print is completely lacking on the computer screen. Often, it is desirable to show more information at one time than can reasonably fit onto the display. We can take advantage of the computer's ability to create multiple dynamic layers of information and to rapidly change the scale of information elements to overcome that constraint and to go beyond anything that was possible in the realm of ink on paper.

The context within which we find information often tells us as much as the information itself. Although markup languages, such as HTML, allow designers to link many pieces of information together, the information elements are still viewed as isolated, fragmentary bits. It is now possible to control the focus and transparency of information objects—as well as color, typeface, and other variables—dynamically. This gives us the opportunity to concurrently display multiple threads of information and dynamically shift visual focus from one to another.

Through the use of transparency and focus we can effectively layer multiple threads of text. One layer can recede into a blurry cloud while another will suddenly "pop" into focus and float above the other layers. If the computer can deduce which layer is of current interest, this focus shifting can be, at least partially, automatic. Scale has always been implicit in design because one designed real, physical objects that had a certain size and relationship to the human form. Objects are designed to fit the body, such as a book that one can hold in one's lap. Architectural design is likewise intimately connected with the human form. This extends even to the more abstract realm of graphic design. Typefaces are made to be read from a certain distance and occupy a certain size on the retina. In the virtual space of the computer screen, we are free to explore a vast range of scales. In particular, I am interested in how to design for both the reading scale, where a display can hold five hundred or a thousand words, and a contextual scale, where a million or more words can be in some way visible. While we understand a great deal about how people read characters that occupy a hundred or so pixels, it is unclear how to abstract text for display at single-pixel or subpixel resolutions.

The Talmud project

The Talmud project, one of a series of electronic book experiments I conducted at MIT's Media Lab, directly addresses the issue of working with multiple texts simultaneously. Because it was necessary to show several texts and the relationships between them in the same space, the Talmud, in its complexity, helped clarify the visual and interaction problems involved.

The Talmud is a collection of sacred writings on the Torah, or Old Testament. This project was built around an essay by the philosopher Emmanuel Levinas,[5,6] whose commentary on a tract of the Talmud, which itself is a complex, nested series of references to the Torah, forms an intricate web of text and references. This style of writing is called "hermeneutics," the reference of scripture to support an argument.

The primary goal of the Talmud project was to create a workspace in which the relevant texts could coexist and interact. The fact that these texts are themselves complex and carry a long history of study brings the issues into a sharp relief. The system should be fast and responsive—after all, it only takes a moment to flip through a book and find a particular passage. It should give the sense that all of the material is close by and accessible. It should also reward further study, meaning that even though a novice should be able to quickly orient himself in the texts, an expert should be able to "perform" with a degree of precision that is evidence of his or her knowledge and experience.

The chosen texts deal with the subject of the Cities of Refuge. When one has caused the accidental death of another, the law recognizes that this is not the same as murder. For example, if a man is chopping wood in his yard, and the axe head flies loose and strikes dead a person walking down the street, the law recognizes that there was no intent and the manslaughterer is "subjectively innocent." Nonetheless, the family of the slain man has the right of blood vengeance. This paradox, of existing in a state of both guilt and innocence, forms the basis for the reading. Levinas, in his approach to the Talmud, brings this paradox into the context of twentieth-century life and tries to give the text the widest possible reading.

A visual representation of these interconnected texts should construct a space for discussion and argument in which scholars can pull and push the words as they dissect the intellectual issues posed by the text. Some of the initial designs for this project used graphic controls for navigating and controlling the three layers of text (the Levinas text, the Talmud, and the Torah). This proved to be unsatisfactory for a variety of reasons. First, the controls existed in the same visual space as the data being manipulated, and it was often difficult to keep one from visually conflicting with the other. Also, because graphic widgets rely on the computer mouse for control, it was difficult for more than one person to have control at any one time. Finally, there simply wasn't a good feel to the controls—they lacked the tactile quality of leafing through an actual book.

From *Learn Talmud* by Judith Abrams: ". . . Get used to having many volumes of books out at one time. By the end of a study session you could have several books spread out on the table: the volume you are studying, a Bible to look up the verses that are cited in the Talmud, the Reference Guide for this set of Talmud, volumes of the *Encyclopaedia Judaica* to provide additional historical background information, various Hebrew or Aramaic dictionaries, and other volumes of rabbinic literature. This isn't messiness. This is the traditional mode of study and it really feels great. . . ."[7] The Talmud is studied in a particular manner, which although not unlike the method in which most would approach a scholarly work, has been made explicit over many centuries of study. The Talmud should be studied with another person (hevruta) and one of the two should be more experienced than the other. The act of reading should be punctuated with argument and discussion of the issues raised by the text. In a typically Talmudic expression, this is described with the prescription—there should be crumbs that fall into the binding of the Talmud because the scholars will be so engrossed in discussion that their lunch will find its way into the book.

The solution to these problems was to create physical controls that exist in the space immediately surrounding the display. I concentrated on the visual problems posed by the requirement that the various texts, under the immediate physical control of one or more readers, can visually coexist in a smooth and natural manner.

The primary problem faced by the designer in electronic media is the lack of resolution and space afforded by paper. The average computer display has about one million pixels and can display perhaps one thousand words. The resolution of paper allows for a larger number of words in the same space, and, because the resolution and contrast of ink on paper is much higher, the type itself is of higher quality. And, because paper is thin and inexpensive, many sheets can be bound into a book, which can easily contain more than one million words.

Despite these limitations, electronic media have some distinct advantages over paper, which we can exploit. The electronic display is a dynamic surface, which can change and adapt over time. More important, however, is the fact that the computer processor can manipulate and understand the underlying model of the information. Unlike paper, which knows not what is printed on it, the computer can be programmed to intelligently react to changing inputs and models of both information and the user.

Layering with focus control

"Layering" is defined as the simultaneous display of two or more information objects within the same two-dimensional space of the projected display surface. This can occur when two objects are in fact occupying the same space or when a particular view into a three-dimensional landscape of information causes one layer to occlude, or pass in front of, another.

Even though you may want to display several information objects at the same time and in the same space, the reader's attention will only be focused on one at a time. If we know which layer is of interest at the moment, we can adjust the display so that the various layers appear to either "pop" out to the front or recede into the background. This is accomplished through a combination of focus and

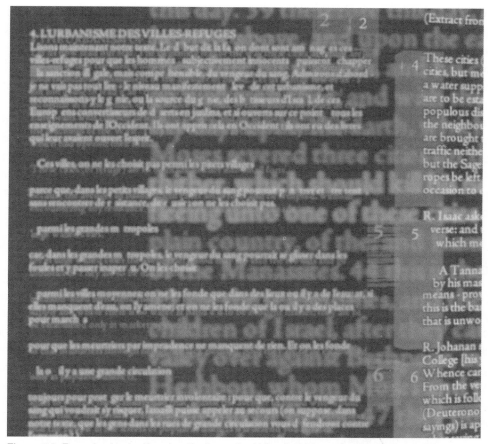

Figure 7.3 Example of textual layering. Designer: David Small. © Massachusetts Institute of Technology.

transparency controls. Different colors can also be used in this way, although it may not be desirable to constantly shift the color of an object. The goal is to make the minimum amount of change to allow the selected layer to be easily read, without giving the impression that any of the layers have really changed.

We can see this in the treatment of the three basic information layers of Levinas, Talmud, and Torah. Although all three reside in the same space, only one is ever fully in focus at any moment. So, for example, you might be reading a passage from the Torah while the referring page from the Talmud appears to hang behind the Torah and just enough out of focus so as to maximize the legibility of the Torah. This goal of "just enough" is quite difficult to achieve. The optical size of the two texts, their orientation to each other, and their color and transparency all have an effect on legibility.

Although a fully rigorous study was not done, a couple of general observations can be made: First, the smaller the text, the less of an effect blurring will have. Once text gets below a few pixels in width, it is too small to see the blur. In general, the smaller the text, the more you want to increase the transparency to give the same overall density to blurred text. Second, the more that the texts align with each other, the greater the blur needed to keep them separated. So, if two texts are at the same point size and the lines appear to be nearly on top of each other, the background text will tend to impair the legibility of the foreground text. If they are at different angles or significantly different point sizes, there will be less interference, and, consequently, less blur may be needed to keep the foreground text legible.

By using changes in both blur and transparency, it was possible to create dynamic shifts between the three information layers, which provided clear, legible text in the foreground layer. Because this could be done without otherwise changing the position or scale of any of the layers, there was far less chance of confusion about where specific areas of text were on the screen, even those that were temporarily illegible. Before going on to discuss juxtaposition, let's talk in more detail about the method used to create smooth transitions of focus.

A method for real-time focus control

To blur an image such as the letter A, you multiply it against a filter. This process, known as convolution, requires a multiply and add for each element of the filter at each pixel. The greater the blur, the larger the kernel, and the number of computations increase by the square of the filter width. Early experiments by Laura Scholl and Grace Colby with Media Lab's Connection Machine supercomputer took advantage of parallel processing for these computations, but each image took minutes to blur and display.[8] Even with today's fast processors, it is not possible to filter images in real time. So, to create text that could smoothly change from perfectly sharp to bleary-eyed blurry, a new technique had to be developed.

Of course, we are not dealing with an infinite number of images. We only need to consider the hundred or so characters commonly used in each typeface. So, the idea of precomputing the required blurry characters and caching the results is compelling. Still, there is a limit to the amount of memory that can be allocated for all of the copies of each typeface, especially when you consider that the most efficient rendering can only occur when the images are cached in the graphics pipeline.

Even if you cache ten or more images per character, the reader will be able to see discrete changes in focus. In order to provide truly smooth gradations and to limit the number of images to be cached, a weighted average of just two images is used. This is done by drawing two versions of the character directly atop each other and varying the transparency of each. You can think of this as a process of compression, where the image of the letter is broken into discrete spatial frequencies and then reassembled. The sharp image corresponds to the highest spatial frequencies, and the blurred image has only lower spatial frequencies. Surprisingly, this method produced results indistinguishable from individually filtered text. It was decided to use just three master images—the original, a 3×3 Gaussian filtered image, and a 9×9 Gaussian. If an even blurrier image was needed, a 27×27 filter would be used. To display an image corresponding to any filter in between, the two neighboring filters are weighted and combined.

Dynamic juxtaposition

In traditional graphic design, the space of the paper is used as a kind of map to the underlying inform-ation. Elements that are related are located on the page in proximity to each other. These spatial relationships are fixed once the page is printed. In the dynamic context of the computer, the elements are in a continuous state of change. In order to maintain a specific relationship between two typo-graphic elements, they have to constantly adjust to changing conditions.

Let's look at two examples from the Talmud project. Each devises a solution to the problem of keeping related texts next to each other. In the first, two versions of the same text must be compared line by line. In the second, blocks of text maintain proximity despite changes in size, position, and orientation.

Levinas's writing only reveals itself after long and careful study. Even after several readings, a passage may not be entirely clear. As with any translated work, the next step is to reread the text in its original language. This can be difficult when using printed books: The two versions are often in separate books, and it is difficult to go back and forth without losing the essence of the passage. The pages do not corres-pond to each other, and as the books usually will have different publishers, the type design is different. To combat this problem, an approach in which different languages run in different columns through the pages of the book can be used. Otl Aicher's *Typographie* is a good example of this technique.[9]

A recently published Dutch monograph by designer Harry Ruhé takes a different approach. The Dutch and English texts are directly superimposed in transparent inks—red for Dutch and green for English. A pair of colored gels provided with the book selectively reveals each layer. This has the advantage of putting the control directly into the hands of the reader as well as conserving space. Still, it is difficult to go back and forth between the languages, and colored text is not nearly as easy on the eye as black text.

The goal in providing both English and French versions of the Levinas text was to allow the reader direct control over which language was primary and to show both languages when needed. A simple dial moves the display from one language to the other and various levels in between. At first the texts were superimposed, and transparency was varied to fade one language into another. One could read the English, turn the dial, and then read the corresponding French. This proved unsatisfactory when you wanted to see both texts at the same time—it wasn't enough to hold the image of one in the mind and switch quickly between them. The image of the one text tended to obliterate the memory of the other. (This effect is called masking.)

To address this, I tried to put the French text in the spaces between the English lines (leading). It wasn't legible unless the leading was increased dramatically, which was undesirable. Finally, I tried increasing the leading dynamically as one text faded into the other. In this way, each text seen solo was set nice and tight, but when the dial was halfway between, the French text sat just above each line of English with some leading in between each pair of lines. The two languages were different colors, so it was easy to track either one from line to line or to glance at both simultaneously. Since the French text contained accents above characters, it was placed above the English. This increased the legibility of the French without compromising the English. This dynamic juxtaposition of the two texts gives partic-ular affordances to the task of reading Levinas in the original and in translation (Figure 7.4).

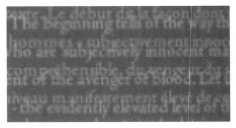

Figure 7.4 Example of textual dynamic juxtaposition. Designer: David Small. © Massachusetts Institute of Technology.

The second example has to do with the relationship between the Levinas essay and the tractate of the Talmud, to which his essay refers. The goal is to be able to jump back and forth between the two texts easily as well as scale each larger or smaller. Each chapter of the Levinas text corresponds to a group of lines from the Talmud. To keep them separated, the Levinas text hugs the left edge of the display and the Talmud tends to the right. A control shifts the boundary between the two texts. In the original design, this was seen as a dynamic margin—it could move so that one text had the majority of the screen space and the other shrank to fit into the remaining margin. By adjusting the scale of each text to fit the available space, it ensured that each text was always visible, even if it shrank to minuscule proportions.

As the prototype developed, this simple scheme became difficult to maintain. The Talmudic text could rotate to reveal either the *mishnah* (oral text circa 200 BC) or the *gemara* (commentaries circa AD 150). Also, the overall scale of the Talmud (several volumes) dwarfed the scale of the Levinas essay. And it became clear that each chapter of the Levinas essay should be in proximity to those few lines of the Talmud to which it referred. This juxtaposition is accomplished by connecting the texts with springs that maintain the spatial relationships despite any rotation or scaling of either text and keep the Levinas text always to the immediate left of the Talmud. Although the texts exist in three-dimensional space, the visual relationship refers to the two-dimensional projection of the texts. This was accomplished by creating special spring anchors that were outside of the normal object hierarchy, at the intersection of a plane parallel to the view plane and a ray from the viewpoint to the anchor point of the text. So, as the Talmud was scaled larger or smaller, or rotated or scrolled up and down, each Levinas chapter would dynamically adjust to maintain a specific juxtaposition—aligned to the top of the referring section, its right edge to the right of the Talmud, and its left edge to the left edge of the display. Using a spring model for the constraint added a slight dynamic to the adjustment—following any user input that changed an element, the other elements would "catch up."

In each of the two preceding examples, we see how a dynamic constraint can maintain a useful juxtaposition between multiple texts. The visual relationships that are clearly apparent to the reader must match the structural relationships of the information. Moreover, we must be aware of the ways in which a reader's eyes weave about the display and design accordingly.

Scale

I would like to concentrate on problems associated with presenting several texts of different scales simultaneously. One of my early design goals was to keep all of the elements visible at all times, in keeping with one of the great advantages that books have over electronic displays: their persistence. If I have three books laid out on my desk, and I start reading one of them, the other two do not "disappear" off the desktop or behind an opaque window. They remain in the background but available.

Although computer window systems allow you to keep several views open at a time, only the information in the topmost window is visible. This places the burden on the user to remember what was on the various other windows. Furthermore, there is no smooth transition from one view to the next. So, it is difficult for the user to maintain a consistent mental model of the relationships between the different information objects. By allowing the various texts to scale between reading size and down to postage-stamp size, it is possible to keep everything in the current visual space and still have enough room to work. As well, the smooth transitions allow readers to track where they are going within a text and what the relationships are between texts.

One difficulty encountered in the smooth scaling of columns of text is that a reader would often move close to a specific passage only to find that the neighboring columns would be equally strong typographically, despite the fact that they may be inconsequential. It is analogous to reading a story in a newspaper and accidentally jumping over a column into an unrelated story. When seen at a small scale, columns of text form a meaningful image that can "read" as the underlying information structure. You can tell at a glance how the stories on the front page of a newspaper are constructed and plan a path through them.[10] You may pick up a paper, read its structure, and then bring it closer to a comfortable reading distance as you work your way through and around the page. You adjust the scale simply by moving the paper relative to your body.

In the case of the Talmud project, it was possible to scale the text to many more orders of magnitude than our newspaper example. Different elements had to respond differently at different sizes in order to maintain a legible focus on the section in question. In order to clearly indicate which was the column of interest, the neighboring columns would be rendered in a kind of sketchy way to show that they were there but were not the primary focus. At a far distance, all the columns would still look like quite the same. There are many other ways in which different elements of a text could respond to scaling: In the case of the Talmud, it might be sensible to scale the *gemara,* which comprises a smaller fraction of the total text, at a different rate than the *mishnah,* with which it is interwoven.

In addition to the problem of showing texts at the same scale in different ways in order to guide the reader's attention, the Talmud project, with its multiple texts, had to allow the reader to work between texts that may be at different scales. For example, a notation sketched by the user over the Levinas text may also direct the reader to a particular phrase in the Talmud or the Torah. As the three texts vary in scale, the notation may lose any visual sense. Future work in this area could examine what types of structure add distinctiveness to scaled text so that small images of large works could present a more complete picture from a distance.

While this project primarily focused on the disposition of space in the information display, the sequential presentation of typography over time is, in a sense, another method of layering.

Almost all the animation in the Talmud project was under the direct control of the user. This sort of motion is very easy for the user to read, as long as the interaction loop between the controls and the graphics are fast and responsive. The user would turn a dial, for example, and an element would rotate in response. Because the feedback is immediate and the user can always return the dial, and therefore the information, back to its original position, there is little training required. Moreover, the user feels in control of the interaction because he can effect change in the display when and how he wants. Unfortunately, if you make a control for every possible movement of each and every object, you soon will have a control system that overwhelms the information itself. By building dynamic constraints between information objects and limiting controls to those dimensions that are meaningful, we can keep the interaction manageable without overly restricting the user.

Simple constraints were easy to implement because of the message-passing system used in the software. Each object can both send and receive messages. So, for example, if an object receives a message from a control to change scale, it can, on the receipt of that message, send a message to another object to change its position. Any of the messages can also include a duration, which will direct the recipient to smoothly animate from its current state to a new state in a specific amount of time. Because these animations were built into the system at such a low level and were very easy to use, it meant that the designer could choose to animate any change (e.g., color, focus, position, etc.) without any extra work. While these simple animations meant that transitions were smooth and continuous, there was need for more complex motion.

The Talmud project used a physical spring model for maintaining spatial relationships during interaction. The goal was to keep certain texts next to each other, even as they changed in scale and position. As the user interacted, they would introduce energy into the system, and the springs, acting in a damping field, would move to reduce the energy. The user could, through the motion, literally see the underlying constraints and how they were solved. Initial designs damped the springs only slightly, so it would take a considerable amount of time (ten or more seconds) for the system to reach equilibrium. This motion was felt to be far too distracting, so the damping was increased to nearly cancel out the stiffness of the springs. The system would now reach equilibrium in about a second. This brief motion was still enough to reveal to the reader the underlying constraints (Figure 7.5).

Animation was also used when the reader followed a link in the text to a particular verse of the Torah. If you think about how links work in most Web applications, clicking a link wipes the current Web page from the screen and then (slowly) paints the new Web page. The starting location is gone, and there is no indication of how it might be related to the end result. To find a verse in the Torah, the text would

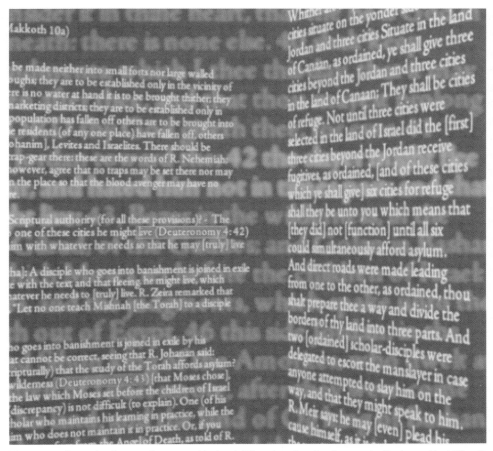

Figure 7.5 Example of presenting several texts of different scales simultaneously. Designer: David Small.
© Massachusetts Institute of Technology.

smoothly slide from the current verse to the new book, chapter, and verse. This worked best when the view allowed both the start and end points to be visible so that the path from one to the other could be easily traced. If the camera was close in and the verses far apart, the animation blurred into a meaningless smear, like the view out a window of a speeding car. In his thesis, Tinsley Galyean proposed a method for planning a path through virtual spaces, such as a museum.[11] While some of these techniques are applicable to a more abstract and purely typographic space, future work might examine how to plan paths through information spaces that are most meaningful and keyed to the legibility of typography.

In making information accessible to people, we need to go beyond historical models. The computer screen is not a piece of paper and should not be treated as one. By taking advantage of the ability of the computer to display dynamic, flexible, and adaptive typography, we can invent new ways for people to read, interact with, and assimilate the written word. Like a well-designed landscape, information should be legible, inviting, and comfortable, and its exploration can and should be a true delight.

Notes

1. Charles W. Moore, William J. Mitchell, and William Turnbull, Jr., *The Poetics of Gardens* (Cambridge, MA: MIT Press, 1988).
2. Richard Brilliant, *Visual Narratives: Story-telling in Etruscan and Roman Art* (Ithaca, NY: Cornell University Press, 1984).
3. Bruce Chatwin, *The Songlines* (New York: Penguin Books, 1987).
4. Robert Venturi, *Learning from Las Vegas* (Cambridge, MA: MIT Press, 1972).
5. Emmanuel Levinas, *Beyond the Verse: Talmudic Readings and Lectures* (Bloomington, IN: Indiana University Press, 1994).
6. Emmanuel Levinas, *L'Au-Dela Du Verset: Lectures et Discours Talmudiques* (Paris: Les Éditions de Minuit, 1982).
7. Judith Abrams, *Learn Talmud: How to Use the Talmud, The Steinsaltz Edition* (Northvale, NJ: Jason Aronson, Inc., 1995).
8. Laura Scholl, "The Transitional Image" (master's thesis, Massachusetts Institute of Technology, 1991).
9. Otl Aicher, *Typographie* (Berlin: Ernst and Sohn, 1988).
10. Louis Silverstein, *Newspaper Design for the Times* (New York: Van Nostrand Reinhold, 1990).
11. Tinsley Galyean, "Narrative Guidance of Interactivity" (PhD thesis, Massachusetts Institute of Technology, 1995).

Chapter 7.1.4

Writing design: towards a culture of code

Stéphanie Vilayphiou and Alexandre Leray
(Translated from the French by John Lee)

Created, edited and stored on a computer, printed matter is above all digital. Mainstream software still conceals this fact through the emulation of traditional creative methods. The use of programming, a preferred method for creating and editing digital objects, seems however to be gaining interest among graphic designers. The projects presented here,[1] revealing different trends, look into the articulation between graphic design and programming. Does code serve only to eliminate redundancies? How do we move on from the purely aesthetic attraction of the machine and build up a critical view of the code and its effects?

The program as efficiency

Problem solving, workflow, reduction, time, control, machinist-designer

Karl Gerstner[2] was one of the first designers to experiment with a computer, way back in the early sixties, at a time when computing was mostly restricted to the military and scientists. Close to the Ulm School, where he actually taught, Gerstner's method followed a functionalist, rationalist logic. For him, the computer's main feature was its computing capacity from which he derived—conceptually or practically[3]—all the solutions to a design. The main idea was then to **discretize** the design in order for it to be computable (Figure 7.6).

While the computer enabled him to calculate all the solutions to a given equation, Gerstner however was aiming at getting only one. Therefore he sought to use an iterative process, to eliminate possibilities that were deemed no good. To do this, he used a scientific approach based on the astronomer Fritz Zwicky's **morphological analysis**, involving the elimination of results not by subtracting variables but by excluding illogical combinations.

This approach today remains unusual regarding this relationship between design and programming. A similar process is claimed by Petr van Blokland,[4] a figure of contemporary Dutch design. For him, "All

21

a   Basis

1. Components	11. Word	12. Abbreviation	13. Word group	14. Combined	
2. Typeface	21. Sans serif	22. Roman	23. German	24. Some other	25. Combined
3. Technique	31. Written	32. Drawn	33. Composed	34. Some other	35. Combined

b   Colour

I. Shade	11. Light	12. Medium	13. Dark	14. Combined	
2. Value	21. Chromatic	22. Achromatic	23. Mixed	24. Combined	

c   Appearance

1. Size	11. Small	12. Medium	13. Large	14. Combined	
2. Proportion	21. Narrow	22. Usual	23. Broad	24. Combined	
3. Boldness	31. Lean	32. Normal	33. Fat	34. Combined	
4. Inclination	41. Upright	42. Oblique	43. Combined		

d   Expression

1. Reading direction	11. From left to right	12. From top to bottom	13. From bottom to top	14. Otherwise	15. Combined
2. Spacing	21. Narrow	22. Normal	23. Wide	24. Combined	
3. Form	31. Unmodified	32. Mutilated	33. Projected	34. Something else	35. Combined
4. Design	41. Unmodified	42. Something omitted	43. Something replaced	44. Something added	45. Combined

12.13

Figure 7.6 An example of discretization of the elements of a design from *Designing Programmes*.
© 2007. Designer: Karl Gerstner. Publisher: Lars Müller Publishers.

the possibilities are there, it's just that there are too many options."[5] His workflow involves the constant reassessment of a design with the aim of refining it—a method comparable to Gerstner's through its recursive aspect. If the loop is infinite (since, according to him, a design can always be improved), the end is determined by time. So the computer is a way for Blokland of accelerating these cycles and hence of perfecting a design as much as possible within the allotted time.

Blokland works chiefly for large companies such as Rabobank or the Dutch Post Office, which need frequently to update a large number of documents. He is not satisfied with the software currently on the market, which can be separated into two distinct categories: those placing the emphasis on graphic quality,[6] and those aimed at automated page layout.[7] So he has designed the Xierpa software[8] to produce printed or online publications, from content embedded by the customer via a web interface. The page layout is then generated automatically through an algorithm that handles text, images, tables, etc. In this way Blokland encodes the graphic design, the page layout in the algorithm, in the same way as a house style guide sets out rules and constraints. But unlike such a guide, an algorithm executed by a machine cannot omit any of the possibilities. Blokland in fact calls this field of action "systematic design" (Figure 7.7).

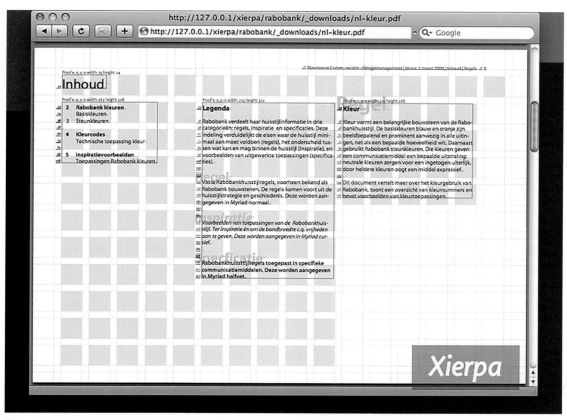

Figure 7.7 An example of a Python code, which composes pages with elements to make sure they do not overlap and will exhibit 'good' relations when placed on the page. In the back of the programme are AI (Artificial Intelligence) decision parameters, simulating the decisions the designer would take in layout composition. This works for print-documents, with a fixed pages size, eventually generating PDF as output. © circa 2009?. Designer: Petr van Blokland. From presentation at Print/Pixel.

The delegation of certain designer gestures and knowhow to a program raises the question of losses and gains in quality notably in design terms. Blokland here abandons the precision of handcrafted work (micro-typography, management of exceptions, etc.) in favour of extra productivity and reactivity. He says he is satisfied with average graphic quality, provided there are no "major mistakes."[9] The quality of such a design is to be seen from the perspective of a system and not in its individual documents.

Blokland's rhetoric and work focus on the notion of time and the rationalization of time: he talks readily of the "branch factor" or the "tool horizon." For him, time is "always what counts."[10] While the time factor is also present with Gerstner, it is not for reasons to do with economics and productivism, but rather for conceptual reasons. Gerstner's aim is to run systematically and exhaustively through all the solutions to a given problem. Blokland has a much more pragmatic approach; he is quite capable of putting the computer to one side in favour of manual tools such as pencil and paper if a sketch is going to save time. The machine is seen as one of the means to achieve an end, and the chief concern is choosing the *right tool* to do the job at hand. While this tool analogy places value on the designer by suggesting that he controls a technology used to serve him, it nonetheless fails to take into account the social, cultural or contextual dimensions of technology.

The program as fascination

Magic, expansion, autonomy, discovery, spectator-designer

The Dutch group Conditional Design[11] has a still more sensitive approach. The code/design relationship that it upholds indeed seems to arise chiefly from a fascination with forms emerging from code. The group separates the design from the execution of a project through prior notation of instructions. As with Blokland, the control designers usually perform on final productions is thus moved upstream. However while, to quote Paul Gredinger's analogy,[12] both design the "bulb," Conditional Design does so without knowing if it is going to turn out as an onion or as a tulip; it is looking for the emergence of unexpected designs.

While the members of Conditional Design distinguish their workshops from their professional work, the two often bear certain similarities. The "Graphic Design in the White Cube" poster series, the fruit of a workshop headed by Luna Maurer and Jonathan Puckey in 2006, is one of their earliest works showing the premises of Conditional Design. A tool kit including instructions and stickers is handed out to the "student-machines." The work environment is materialized by white stripes. The posters come off the work line formed by the students. They are all different and are thus the fruit of a collective (but not collaborative) effort where the exact outcome is not foreseeable, and the different performers are not identifiable.

These rules take the form of a pseudo-code (a mixture of formal notation and natural language) sometimes borrowing from computer programming terminology: conditional if/then structures, monospace typography, indentation . . . Contrary to Blokland's algorithms which require a high level of expertise, these instructions are generally executed by humans. Certain parameters are deliberately left to the performer's appreciation, like cloze deletion texts (texts with missing words), hence the machine cannot execute the program. This seems to be one of the key elements in Conditional Design's work: human computation as an escape from mathematical logic in favour of other forms of logic (associations of ideas, *détournements* . . .). It is also a way of increasing the probability of "errors"[13] and stimulating the imagination, the way Oulipo does, in order to discover novel forms.

Conditional Design has formalized its principles and intentions in a manifesto.[14] While this text is meant overall to be rational, we surprisingly find among their sources of inspiration "mystics" alongside "philosophers," "engineers" and "inventors." And when the group talks about Logic, it is to "accentuat[e] the ungraspable." The manifesto was originally supposed to include a paragraph devoted to magic but in the end it was left out.[15]

Since the summer of 2008, the members of the group have been meeting on a regular basis for plastic experimentation sessions, taking turns to set the rules of the game. These meetings are held on Tuesdays around Luna Maurer's kitchen table. The scene is carefully set: sophisticated video capture installation (ceiling-mounted camera, play of mirrors for monitoring), meticulous framing and lighting. From the furniture to the color of the felt-tip pens used, and taking in the paper type and format, the scene is always the same. These meetings have become a well-oiled ritual. It is a kind of laboratory cut off from the outside world, almost like a sanctuary.

2008" posters are evidence of this. They chiefly involve multiple vector illustrations arranged on a grid. They have one or more "connection points" enabling them to be connected to each other. These drawings were done by hand with the Inkscape graphic software.[22] The files were named following a nomenclature describing their connection points (for instance, the drawing called "FILENAME_1_0_1_0_. svg" has a connection at the top and at the bottom). **Command line** programs, usually used by systems administrators, were used to calculate multiple arrangements of drawings in function of these points. The results, saved in the form of lists containing the filenames, were imported into the Processing software[23] to create multiple posters, all different. Each of the programs used was chosen for its intrinsic qualities: *visual design* with Inkscape, *design by text* with the command line and *design by numbers*[24] with Processing. Lafkon takes over and utilizes the materiality of the code—or rather codes—but also the materiality of what may be termed the "paracode" (filenames, tree structures, comments, error logs . . .). This approach is a radical break with the idea of a unified design environment as offered in applications suites.

If through its expansive combinatory nature this work can be likened to the work of Conditional Design or Lust, it shows a rather different understanding of the design/code relation, seen notably in the way the process is explained and documented. While the work of the abovementioned designers generally comes with an explanation of the method and a commentary on the forms produced, with Lafkon we get to see the source itself. The creation code, available on its site, is commented on in order to explain how the program works. Distributed as *free* software, it is also an invitation to the reader to make the design his own and use it to construct things upon. By disclosing the technique like this, Lafkon is adopting a stance at once against the idea of the **transparent** tool and the romantic creative genius, and also against the machine as an autonomous entity.

The designers presented here share a certain enthusiasm for digital design, which is a change from the mistrust of new media we usually find in graphic design circles. There are many reasons for using programming, each approach presented has its own specific qualities and to separate them seems impossible. Moreover, whether consciously or not and to varying degrees, the aforementioned graphic designers borrow something from each of them.

This great interest must however be tempered by a critical view, above and beyond the visual aspects and the implications of the technology, so as to avoid being no more than the pure fascination of a technophile. While the visual outputs do not necessarily reveal the creative process, "[programs] condition our practice in terms of division of labour, vocabulary and the physical relationship with the digital medium."[25] We need to understand the software as being design products that carry values, give impulse to uses and social dynamics. So they are not *transparent*. While code as a control structure always implies limitations, programming offers the opportunity to design one's own limitations instead of accepting those defined by a software company. All the same, it is not a matter of designers learning programming languages, as recommended by Blokland, but rather of learning the "language of code". Designers must position themselves as players and not just as users of off-the-shelf technology. In this, the hackers' approach is exemplary: understand and make it your own, take over, invent the technology and adapt it to your needs. Technology must not be just for engineers, but something that you can do yourself at home.

Glossary

Algorithm

A set of formal, i.e., mathematically logical, instructions, executable therefore by a computer.

ASCII art

A process using the characters of a fixed-width (non-proportional) font arranged according to their optical gray to create images. Emblematic of the hacker culture, it was invented in order to get round the limited graphics available on hardware in those days, which could display nothing but text.

Command line

Interface through which the user interacts with the computer via written instructions.

Discretize, to

To break down a continuous element into quantifiable parts. Digital data are discrete by nature, and the binary system is the most extreme form of this. By contrast, analog is termed continuous.

Free/libre and/or Open Source software

Free and open source software (F/OSS, FOSS) or free/libre/open source software (FLOSS) is software that is liberally licensed to grant the right of users to use. study, share, change, and improve its design through the availability of its source code.—Not to be confused with freeware, which is software free of charge: FLOSS software may not be gratis, and freeware is often not libre, i.e., modifiable, reusable and distributable. http://en.wikipedia.org/wiki/FLOSS

Morphological analysis

"A method developed by Fritz Zwicky (1967, 1969) for exploring all the possible solutions to a multi-dimensional, non-quantified problem complex." http://en.wikipedia.org/wiki/Morphological_analysis_ %28problem-solving%29

Problem solving

Problem solving is a mental process and is part of the larger problem process that includes problem finding and problem shaping. http://en.wikipedia.org/wiki/Problem_solving

Transparency

In computer programming, "transparency" is a word to describe software that you can forget about.

UNIX philosophy

"This is the Unix philosophy: Write programs that do one thing and do it well. Write programs to work together. Write programs to handle text streams, because that is a universal interface."
http://en.wikipedia.org/wiki/Unix_philosophy

Notes

1. For the sake of clarity, and to dissociate the **computation** from the output medium, we will not cover any "on-screen" productions, but only printed productions, which is the traditional graphic design medium. Notice that the designers we have catalogued mostly come from the Netherlands, Switzerland . . . Is this due to their being historically deeply anchored in modernism, rationality? This observation would be worth analysing more closely.
2. His work is examined in an article by Richard Hollis: "Karl Gerstner: principles not recipes", *Dot Dot Dot,* 4 (Winter 2001/2002). A French translation has been published in *Back Cover,* 1 (Summer/Autumn 2008).
3. Most of Gerstner's productions seem to have been done by hand, maybe owing to unavailability of machines. However, what is interesting here is not *de facto* use of a computer, but the conceptual model that it inspired in him.
4. Bureau Petr van Blokland + Claudia Mens http://petr.net/
5. Petr van Blokland at the "Print/Pixel" conference organized by the Piet Zwart Institute, Rotterdam, 2009.
6. Adobe Indesign, Quark XPress, etc.
7. Adobe Framemaker.
8. Xierpa is still under development. During his "Print/Pixel" presentation in May 2009, Petr van Blokland announced that he would be publishing it under Open Source licence by December 2009. http://xierpa.com/
9. Blokland at "Print/Pixel": "The liking of a page is not the criterion. The criterion is 'are there major mistakes in it?'"
10. "Print/Pixel," *ibid.*
11. Luna Maurer, Roel Wouters, Jonathan Puckey and Edo Paulus http://conditionaldesign.org/
12. "Creative pleasure lies in design of the formula (image: a tulip bulb) and not in the design of the form (image: the tulip)." Paul Gredinger, Introduction to *Designing Programmes,* Lars Müller Publishers, 2007.
13. Notice that these errors are indeed being looked for, according to manifesto (see following note). So we should really be talking of a "surprise" rather than an "error."
14. http://conditionaldesign.org/manifesto
15. Taken from a forthcoming interview with Conditional Design and Femke Snelting at http://else-if.net/
16. Jeroen Barendse, Thomas Castro, Dimitri Nieuwenhuizen and Daniel Powers http://lust.nl/
17. The day's posters can also be seen on the web at http://lust.nl/posterwall/. The project is not a printed production, but the fact that they use the term "posters" allows us to consider it as such.
18. Excerpt from http://lust.nl/posterwall/
19. OSP is a Brussels-based cross-disciplinary group making designs with *free/libre* software only. http://ospublish.constantvzw.org/

20. The term "personal computer" first came into use in 1975 with the Altair 8800, when cost $297 on the mass market. www.computerhistory.org/timeline/?year=1975
21. Christoph Haag, Daniel Scheibel, and Benjamin Stephan http://lafkon.net/
22. Inkscape is a vector graphics *free* software program.
23. Processing is a programming language and environment intended for designers and visual artists.
24. Term referring to the book by John Maeda and to the eponymous programming environment on which Processing is based.
25. Open Source Publishing, "Awkward Gestures," in *The Mag.net reader 3: Processual Publishing. Actual Gestures,* page 91, 2008. http://live.labforculture.org/2008/10/mag.net/MagNetReader3.pdf

Section 7.2

The forefront of graphic design practice

Chapter 7.2.1

Social design: the context of post-conflict Lebanon

Joanna Choukeir

1. Defining social design

Social design involves tackling social challenges through designing solutions for a better society. Examples of twenty-first-century social challenges are violent or non-violent conflict, poverty, life-threatening health conditions, and high-risk health behaviors. Other contemporary challenges include poor mental health care, poor access to basic amenities, limited education, and unemployment. Yet other challenges involve anti-social behavior, crime, domestic violence, child abuse, human rights violations, climate change, and its impact on the quality of life and biodiversity, on emigration and immigration, and their impact on both the countries of origin and destination. Social designers identify these sorts of social challenges and they make themselves aware of the contexts and communities surrounding the challenges. These designers produce tailored interventions to social challenges that first disrupt them, and then reframe them in positive and productive ways. Productive interventions may include newly conceived spaces and services, policies and strategies, or frameworks and systems. Social design repositions design as a social investigative process rather than a process that is focused on a final artifact. A social design process yields a designed intervention, but social design is not the designed intervention in itself.

For this essay, I draw upon my social design experience as a design director at Uscreates—a London-based design agency working to improve health and wellbeing—as an an associate lecturer at the London College of Communication, and as a PhD researcher who has developed design interventions for social integration that will convey the scope of social design.

2. The changing paradigms of [social] design

Design paradigms evolve in response to both advancements in science and technology and to shifts in social needs. The Industrial Revolution led directly to the early twentieth-century Bauhaus notion of design as a discipline that should embrace advances in technology. The late-Bauhaus design faculty members and students created products that were both modernist and functional—that simultaneously met people's needs, were aesthetically pleasing in their simplicity, and could be mass produced. Visual Culture theorist Malcolm Barnard observes that "where modernity stressed production . . . the post-modern world is one of consumption" (Barnard 2005: 139). When mass production and consumption became more conspicuous between the 1960s and the 1990s, design paradigms emphasized visual form or style in order to achieve differentiation among the competing aesthetics in industry (Barnard 2005: 138–9). In contrast, other, more socially conscious design paradigms arose during this same period: these approaches were initiated by Buckminster Fuller, Vance Packard, Victor Papaneck, Jorge Frascara, and Ken Garland, notably through the *First Things First* manifesto (1964). These paradigms advocated that socially and morally involved designers must address the needs of the world (Papanek 1971: xxvi). The belief was that the role of design should be "to make life possible, to make life easier and to make life better" (Frascara 2002: 39). These propositions led to the current social design movement. Over the last decade, industrial, product, interaction, and graphic designers have become interested in human-centered design, co-design—which encourages users to develop solutions for themselves—participatory design—which actively involves all stakeholders—and open design—which uses publicly shared design information. All of these approaches are methods that help designers refocus the design process onto human needs. Designers and design writers such as Jorge Frascara (1997), Bruce Mau (Mau and Leonard 2004), John Thackara (2006), Elizabeth Sanders (Sanders and Stappers 2008), Tim Brown (2009), Dan Lockton (Lockton, Harrison, and Stanton 2010), Ellen Lupton (Lupton and Phillips 2011), Andrew Shea (2012), and Jeremy Myerson (2013) have further reframed design paradigms as processes that address "social" agendas by providing supporting theoretical frameworks, case studies, and design tools and methodologies for designers. John Thackara, for example, argues for an approach in which "people are designed back into situations" (2006: 4), Andrew Shea makes clear that community engagement in design "requires designers to work with a

The changing paradigms of [social] design
- ● Designer
- ● Audience/beneficiary/user

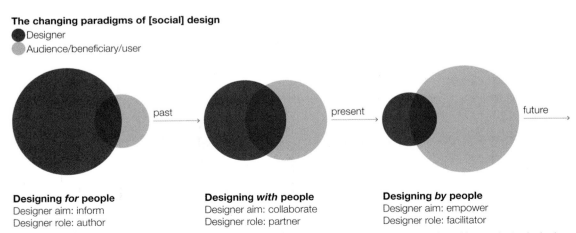

past   present   future

Designing *for* people
Designer aim: inform
Designer role: author

Designing *with* people
Designer aim: collaborate
Designer role: partner

Designing *by* people
Designer aim: empower
Designer role: facilitator

Figure 7.12 The changing paradigms of [social] design from designing for people, to designing with people, to designing by people, 2010. Designer: Joanna Choukeir.

range of people who have strong opinions and a lot of emotions and pride invested in their community" (2012: 9), and Tim Brown calls for the need to design products, ideas, and strategies that meet the needs of society and tackle global challenges (2009: 3).

Many designers are increasingly interested in design processes that are less centered on the designer and the designed artifact, and more centered around users and their needs and preferences (Yee, Jefferies, and Tan 2013: 8). The social designer is stepping back as the author of a design artifact and stepping forward as facilitator of a design intervention. Art historian and scholar Desmond Rochfort points out that "design is moving from being simply designing *for* users to being one of designing *with* users (Rochfort 2002: 160). In the last few years, the paradigm is shifting yet again from designing *with* people—in which designer and stakeholders are partners in collaboration—to designing *by* people—in which a designer facilitates an information transfer in order to empower stakeholders to design in response to their own needs (Brown 2009: 59) (Figure 7.12).

3. An interdisciplinary and collaborative field

Social design tackles issues beyond those that are common in design; doing social design, therefore, requires designers to understand methods, theories, and contexts outside of design. This interdisciplinary approach can be defined as:

> A mode of research by teams or individuals that integrates information, data, techniques, tools, perspectives, concepts, and/or theories from two or more disciplines or bodies of specialised knowledge to advance fundamental understanding or to solve problems whose solutions are beyond the scope of a single discipline or area of research practice.
>
> (National Academies 2005: 2)

Designing an intervention to encourage people to stop smoking, for example, would require those involved, including the designers, to understand smoking behaviors such as barriers to quitting and drivers of smoking addiction. All stakeholders would have to be aware of the health and economic effects of smoking, as well as the policies about and regulations against smoking. Stakeholders should also have a grasp of past interventions for smoking cessation and statistics about their impact. A rigorous social design process, therefore, requires primary and secondary research into both the interdisciplinary literature the practices that surround the issue. As I discuss above, social design commonly pertains to social issues and behaviors. Primary social design research (on smokers and smoking behaviors, for example), therefore, typically adopts and adapts social science methods in order to design a well-aligned intervention. Figure 7.13 maps the range of subjects— sociology, political science theory, conflict resolution, urban studies, social structures, and design activism, for example—that I researched while developing communication design methods to prompt social integration in post-conflict communities in Lebanon. The communities I studied suffered from war, strife, and violence, which led to the segregation of the social groups in conflict and to the decline in community collaboration and cohesion. A number of design critics, including Frascara (1997), Poggenpohl (2002), Svensson (2003), Laurel (2003), Plowman (2003), and Sanders (2008)

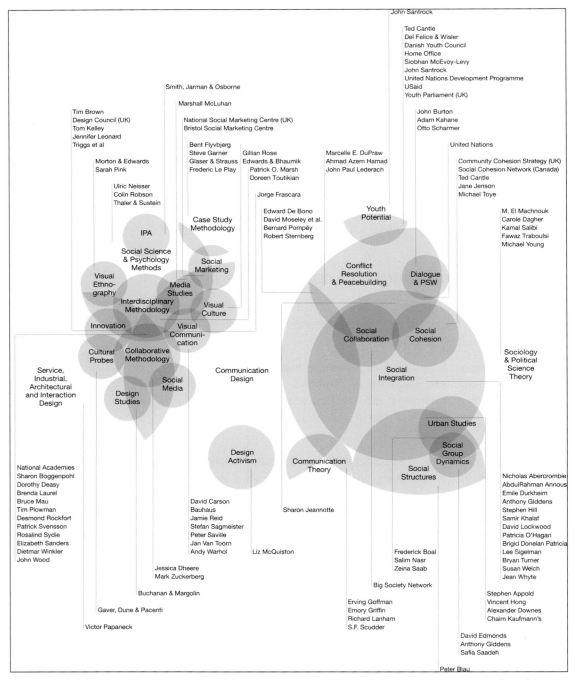

Figure 7.13 Mapping the literature review disciplines around communication for social integration (2010). Part of Joanna Choukeir's PhD research at the University of the Arts London. Designer: Joanna Choukeir.

advocate for interdisciplinary design research to produce a robust, theoretically informed, and critical practice.

Time, budget, and capability constraints sometimes hinder social designers from fully researching the contexts that are critical to a particular social issue. Fortunately, social designers typically collaborate with experts from relevant disciplines to devise problem-solving, solution-making processes. For example, I collaborated with a broad range of stakeholders and experts to research and develop social integration interventions that were targeted at young people in Lebanon. Academic researchers contributed their theoretical expertise on social integration methods, activists provided enthusiasm for making change happen, and community volunteers shared familiarity with local contexts. I collaborated with social and political experts who contributed expertise on local social structures and legislation, entrepreneurs who shared a capacity to actualize ideas quickly, and other designers who offered innovative suggestions. Last, but not least, I worked with the young people at whom these interventions were targeted; no expert or stakeholder better understands the lifestyles and thinking of Lebanese youth, or the hurdles and motivations that were needed to engage them with a new intervention. All of these stakeholders contributed to a collective understanding that aided the development of solutions that encouraged young people to meet, interact, and collaborate with others outside of their social group (such as those with different religious beliefs or political ideologies). Bruce Mau calls this process "distributing problem solving" (Mau and Leonard 2004: 95), and others have used terms such as *participatory design* and *co-design* to describe this process (Triggs, McAndrew, Choukeir, and Akama 2011: 3). Ten years ago, Elizabeth Sanders, one of the pioneers of collaborative design, rightly described this process as the future of design:

> Post design is co-design, i.e. people designing together. It can harness the collective and infinitely expanding set of ideas and opportunities that emerge when all the people who have a stake in the process are invited to *play the game*.

(Sanders 2002: 6)

It is clear that Sanders' prediction has materialized as a growing community of social design practitioners[1] situate co-design at the core of their processes.

4. Problem to process, input to impact

I often utilise the "7D design process"[2] in my own social design practice and my teaching pedagogy. This process exploits seven phases of research and experimentation: (a) *discover*, (b) *delve*, (c) *define*, (d) *develop*, (e) *deliver*, (f) *determine impact*, and (g) *diverge* (Figure 7.14). The stages of this process are developed from an amalgamation of the UK's Design Council *Double Diamond Design Process Model* (Design Council 2010) and the National Social Marketing Centre's *Total Process Planning Model* (NSMC 2010), both of which incorporate research rigor and focus on the evaluation of social impact.

The following discussion introduces the aims of each phase:

(a) *Discover*: identify social issues that could benefit from a design intervention, outline the multitude of questions that the research needs to answer, and draft a suitable research methodology.

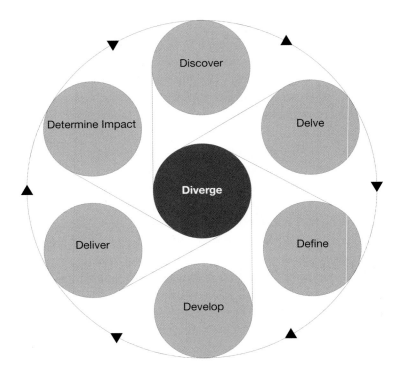

Figure 7.14 7D design process developed by Darren Raven and Joanna Choukeir in 2009. Part of Joanna Choukeir's PhD research at the University of the Arts London. Designer: Joanna Choukeir.

Example research methods at this stage include literature and practice review, stakeholder and issue mapping, explorations and observations.

(b) *Delve*: plug information gaps identified in the *discover* stage mainly through undertaking primary research. Research methods may involve ethnographic analysis (Plowman 2003), research with users and stakeholders, interviews, surveys, shadowing, cultural probes (Gaver, Dunne and Pacenti 1999), peer-to-peer conversations (Payne and Bell 2011), video diaries, or other custom-made and interdisciplinary methods that suit the research aim, audience, and setting.

(c) *Define*: analyze and synthesize research data from *discover* and *delve*, and define the design brief. This will often involve a reframing of the challenge based on the new insights uncovered in *Discover* and *Delve*. Research methods may include quantitative and qualitative analysis, segmentation of target audience (National Social Marketing Centre 2010), user journey mapping, personas, defining barriers, drivers, gaps and opportunities, and visual analysis.

(d) *Develop*: generate ideas in response to the *defined* design brief and test and refine with users and stakeholders. *Develop* methods could include lateral thinking activities (De Bono 2009), scenario setting, co-design workshops (Uscreates 2013), prototyping (Nesta & Innovation Unit 2011), user testing, role-play, experience blueprinting (Hamilton 2011), etc.

(e) *Deliver*: produce and implement the design interventions. Deliver methods may involve piloting, monitoring, iterating, managing resources, and exploring scalability and sustainability.

(f) *Determine Impact*: evaluate the impact of the intervention on the social issue it is designed to tackle. An *Impact Framework* we developed at Uscreates to assist social designers involves

(c) *Regions and mobility*: the perception that each region "belongs" to a social group majority, which reduces mobility to regions that are dominated by different social groups.

(d) *Media and influence*: the majority of mainstream media portals are funded, supported, or directed by political parties, which limits the choice of unbiased content, and normalizes people's acceptance of extremist political views.

(e) *Language and prejudice*: the young people's choice of language and language combination (Arabic, English, or French) is perceived as indicative of their social group, status, and literacy level, and this clouds and distorts first impressions.

Imagination Studio was set up as a series of five workshops, using briefs defined by the *target segments* and *barriers* described above, as a co-creation space that brought youth from various regions together with social experts, activists, entrepreneurs, and designers (Figure 7.19). The workshops were designed to *develop* initiatives that encouraged young people to engage with those outside of their social group at school, university, work, home, and in the community.

With over thirty active *Imaginers* contributing to the process, we first developed and then piloted five ideas during a weekend in July 2012 at a pop-up *Imagination Market* (Figure 7.20). The market

Figure 7.19 Interdisciplinary teams generating ideas at the first Imagination Studio workshop in September 2011. Part of Joanna Choukeir's PhD research at the University of the Arts London. Photographer: Joanna Choukeir.

Figure 7.20 "Imaginers" getting ready to test their social integration interventions at Imagination Market in Byblos Town Square in July 2012. Part of Joanna Choukeir's PhD research at the University of the Arts London. Photographer: Joanna Choukeir.

introduced each idea in its own market booth setting in order to engage with and gather feedback from young visitors. The ideas were:

(a) *Love*: a card game that allows young people to choose the gender, age, and religious sect of each person in a relationship, and to receive information about the marriage, divorce, custody, and inheritance legislation that applies for that particular relationship in Lebanon. The game empowers young people with information; and it presents possibilities for and barriers to mixed marriages. Information about mixed marriage, divorce, custody, and inheritance legislation is often distorted or inaccessible due to social stigmas about mixed marriages.

(b) *Friendship*: a theater-based peer education flash mob in which performers who represent friends supporting two unnamed political parties act out a conflict scenario that quickly escalates. The performers stop the scenario during the performance just before it becomes violent, and young people in the audience are invited to reflect on what they have seen, and to participate in re-creating the scenario to avoid seemingly inevitable clashes and conflicts. This process helps young people to reflect on the ways that changes in political polarities might affect their current friendships, and how these tensions might be avoided in the future.

(c) *Road Trip*: an online platform that matches hosts in various regions of Lebanon with guests from other regions. The hosts offer a menu of activities around their own and their guests' shared interests. This process reduces stigmas that are associated with specific geographic regions, it helps young people focus on similarities rather than differences, and it drives geographic mobility and internal tourism.

(d) *Story*: a crowd-sourced social media channel consisting of a blog with links to YouTube, Facebook, and Twitter. The channel invites Lebanese youth to contribute their own audio/visual/textual content. The channel also provides training in peace journalism to active contributors. This channel offers young people a medium through which to disseminate an inclusive voice that counters politicized and extremist media portals in Lebanon.

(e) *Chit Chat:* a series of games and activities that encourages Lebanese youth to collaborate in order to leverage their shared languages (Arabic, English, and French) by solving game challenges. The process addresses prejudices that are associated with the use of Arablic, English, or French, and encourages collective learning among young people with different language preferences.

To *determine the impact* of the five piloted ideas, visitors to *Imagination Market* were invited to leave feedback on blackboards at the end of their visits (Figure 7.21). This feedback was accompanied by exit interviews and a simple form for visitors to complete about the *before* and *after* shifts in their attitudes toward social integration.

Evaluation of these research processes revealed the following effects on social integration in Lebanon:

(a) *Outputs*: five pilot ideas were tested, thirty *Imaginers* participated in the development process, 100 young people visited *Imagination Market*, a TEDxBeirut event shared the co-creation approach of *Imagination Studio*, and a research blog (Imagination Studio 2012) disseminated the project to a global audience.

(b) *Outcomes*: 150 young people visited *Imagination Market* and were receptive and supportive of the five ideas that were piloted. Following their experience at the market, participants offered construct-ive suggestions and 70% of them expressed a positive shift in their attitudes about their willingness to integrate with those from other social, political, or religious backgrounds. Additionally, mainstream Lebanese television channels and newspapers[3] covered *Imagination Studio* and *Market*, promoting social integration to a national audience beyond the *Imaginers* and market visitors.

(c) Impact: *Imaginers* gained confidence and learned skills throughout their *Imagination Studio* exper-ience. *Imaginers* also positively influenced at least five people each from their social networks; i.e. a total of 100 young people were exposed to the positive outcomes of this project.[4] The five ideas were tested and are ready for implementation on a wider and longer-term scale, and ten of the *Imaginers* are interested in being involved in this process in the future. Finally, transferable guidelines that are based on the research methodology are in development. These guidelines will help to support organizations worldwide that intend to use a social design approach to reduce social segregation.

Figure 7.21 Blackboard and feedback forms were used by visitors of Imagination Market following their visit to measure the impact of the market on their attitudes towards social integration in Lebanon (2012). Part of Joanna Choukeir's PhD research at the University of the Arts London. Photographer: Joanna Choukeir.

6. Social design and education, business and government

Social issues are urgent and complex, so it is crucial that designers recognize that the basic disciplinary tools and methods in graphic design may not be sufficient to tackle these sorts of issues. In this essay, I am arguing that innovative and creative thinking, in addition to collaborative and interdisciplinary methods, are necessary to address challenging problems that cannot be resolved by replicating or adapting existing best practices. These creative and collaborative social-design processes, however, call for a triangulation of agendas among education, business, and government. College and university design programs should equip future designers to be socially conscious and conscientious, and at the same time teach designers to develop new processes and to work with others outside of design (LCC 2012). Businesses are beginning to realize the need to invest in social issues in order to sustain business activity in the future (Uscreates 2013), and this new outlook should create more opportunities for social designers. Government and volunteer organizations, whose work is concerned with improving society, have begun embracing design and innovation (Nesta & Innovation Unit 2011). This triangulation among education, business, and government will ensure that social design has the opportunity to expand and evolve. My hope is that the valuable approaches that I have presented in this essay will help plug the gaps in the emerging field of social design and, by doing so, will empower readers with an interest in design to make a positive contribution to society.

Notes

1. Such as IDEO.ORG, Uscreates, STBY, Innovation Unit, The Helen Hamlyn Centre for Design, Think Public, Policy Connect, Future Gov, etc.
2. I initiated the "7D design process" in 2009 with Darren Raven as part of the teaching curriculum for the BA Design for Graphic Communication at the London College of Communication. I am currently working on developing the process further in my PhD research at the University of the Arts London.

3. Media portals included a report on LBC News, an interview on OTV, and articles in *The Daily Star*, Shabab al Safir, L'Orient Le Jour, Tayyar.org, and Beirut.com. Please visit this link for a full list of press coverage: http://imaginationstudio.org/press.

4. This was revealed during in-depth interviews with *Imaginers* three months following *Imagination Market*, and was based on the number of friends and family members *Imaginers* said were positively inspired by their stories of *Imagination Studio* and *Market*.

Chapter 7.2.2

Emil Ruder: a future for design principles in screen typography

Hilary Kenna

Introduction

This paper sets out to explore the way in which the renowned Swiss typographer, Emil Ruder, has influenced a practice-led PhD study focusing on the need for creating new design principles for screen-based typography. Specifically, the paper examines Ruder's seminal book *Typographie: A Manual for Design* (1967), wherein historical knowledge created for a print-based context has made a sustainable contribution to the future development of typography within the context of the screen. In addition, this study has led to a re-examination of the relevance of Emil Ruder's teaching at the Basel School of Design, and his work as positioned within a contemporary context.

Emil Ruder (1914–1970) is distinguishable in the field of typography for developing a holistic approach to designing and teaching that encompasses philosophy, theory, and a systematic practical methodology. After 25 years of teaching, Ruder published the heavily illustrated book, capturing his ideas, methods, and approach. The book represents a critical reflection on Ruder's teaching and practice and a lifetime of accumulated knowledge. It has been published in nine languages and is now in its seventh edition. Today, more than 40 years after the book was first published, it is still widely used and referenced by education and industry practitioners alike.[1]

Background to the research

This paper is drawn from PhD research that centers on the need for a clearer understanding of the nature and practice of typography in a screen environment and on trying to define the current and emerging design principles and methodologies that govern that practice.

The research question arose from the day-to-day experience and practice of the researcher, who works both as a designer and as a lecturer in design for digital media. As a teacher and a practitioner, I have found that traditional knowledge and experience fall short of the challenges of designing and

First published in *Design Issues,* 27 (1) (Winter 2011): 35–54. © Massachusetts Institute of Technology/Hilary Kenna.

teaching typography for screen. Through experience, I have found that there are many differences between print and screen typography at both macro and micro levels, and that traditional practical methods require revision and extension to address nontraditional aspects, such as motion, sound, and interactivity presented by screen-based design contexts.

Ongoing critical reflection on these issues in the course of my daily design and teaching practice and my own educational experience have greatly influenced the motivation and point of view from which this research has developed. Through the course of trying to solve typographic design problems for screen in my own practice and through the development of teaching material for my students, I have been practically exploring this territory for some time. The requirements of PhD research presented an academically rigorous context, and a systematic methodology to further examine this territory.

This paper sets out a critical discussion about how the direction of this research has been influenced by the work of Emil Ruder.

Emil Ruder and his method

The broad nature of this PhD research subject (design principles for typography) and the emergent nature of the field (screen typography) required a contextual examination that encompassed a critical review of both relevant literature and contemporary practice. During the analysis of findings, Emil Ruder's practical methodology for designing typography emerged, proving to be particularly relevant to this research. Four main reasons for Ruder's significance became apparent and form the basis of discussion in this paper:

- The location of Ruder's book within the broader canon of literature on typography and design principles, and how it is referenced by and linked to the literature as a whole;

- The distinctive nature of Ruder's book and practice methodology among those in the field;

- The renewed interest in modernism, and how Ruder represents a paradigm of modernist aesthetics and methodology;

- The relevance of Ruder's approach to screen media.

Ruder's location and links with the literature on typography and graphic design

In selecting from among the broad spectrum of literature related to the design practice of typography, careful analysis of relevance resulted in a process of conceptual and visual mapping techniques that became a key research methodology for editing, classifying, ordering, and analysing the seemingly broad range of typographic literature. After several iterations, the result of this methodology was a "literature map" visualization (see Figure 7.23). The map provides a chronological and contextual overview of all the relevant literature in the field from the beginning of the twentieth century. Criteria for inclusion are based on:

- Relevance to category;
- Established use in education and course curricula;
- Referral and recommendation on reading lists from educational and professional design organizations, and from online resources;
- Reputation of author(s) (as practitioner/educator/critic) and bibliographic references;
- Consumer popularity and contemporaneity; and
- Frequency of occurrence in one or more of the above.

The literature map illustrates the material split into two groups: *for practice* and *about practice,* with an additional five categories in each group (see the key in Figure 7.23, below). The visual display of these thematic groupings made it easier to identify critical patterns in the literature that would have been more difficult to uncover using written methods alone. One such pattern identified was the dominant influence of Swiss typography in the literature.

Note that while the literature map was very useful, it was not the only research methodology used in the literature review; its limitations required the use of other methods as well. For example, the literature map displays only book publications and not journal papers or articles (traditional or online versions), with the exception of the legibility category. This focus was mainly a result of the diverse nature of periodical materials and the difficulty of gauging their use in mainstream practice. As a result, other methods, including the use of RSS information feeds and content aggregators and the authoring of a research blog, were used to track and analyse this type of literature.

The overall findings from the literature map, combined with the findings from these other research methods, revealed a number of critical directions for investigation, which led to the focus on Emil Ruder.

Findings revealed that the bulk of titles published about practical design principles for typography have occurred since 2000, and that the majority of these publications make reference to Ruder either within the text itself or in the selected bibliography.

This finding prompted the realization that a modernist legacy continues to underpin many of the contemporary publications on typographic design practice (e.g., by Robin Kinross, David Jury, Phil Baines, Ellen Lupton, etc.), as well as exerting influence on the different and reactionary approaches (e.g., deconstruction, grunge graphics, postmodernism, etc.) that emerged in the latter part of the twentieth century.

Visualizing the literature has also helped to reveal significant connections between publications including the dominant influence of Swiss typography in the literature and connections between authors and subject matter (Figure 7.22). A number of key publications chart the path of development of Swiss typography and the International style. First was Max Bill's publication, *Über Typographie* (1946), which established a number of principles for the new typography; a number of designers then started to follow these principles. The magazine, *Neue Grafik* (1958–65), and the book, *Die neue Grafik* (1959), by Karl Gerstner and Markus Kutter also spread awareness of Swiss typography to an international readership. Emil Ruder was a regular contributor to *Neue Grafik,* as well as to another magazine, *Typographische Mönasblatter.* Between 1959 and 1965, he published a series of articles about the underlying principles of his teaching and this new movement, which he called "the typography of order" (Schmid 1981).

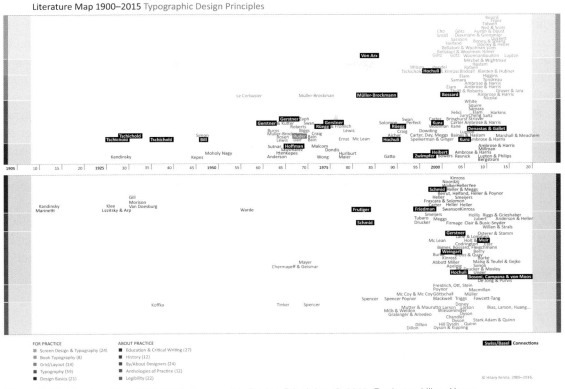

Figure 7.22 Literature Map 1900-2015. Typographic Design Principles. © 2015. Designer: Hilary Kenna.

In 1961 Josef Müller-Brockman published a book, *The Graphic Artist and his Design Problems,* which became a primary publication in the international dissemination of Swiss typography and its methods. Müller-Brockman detailed at length the core principles of this new "graphic art," including:

- A striving for objective presentation through the elimination of decorative and expressive effects;

- An unadorned typography that clearly conveys the message to be communicated;

- The use of a grid for ordering the information and graphic elements;

- The restriction of type sizes and typefaces (san serif, because it was an "expression of our age");

- Unjustified text setting; and

- The use of photography instead of illustration.

In his 2006 book, *Swiss Graphic Design: The Origins and Growth of an International Style 1920–1965,* Richard Hollis credits Müller-Brockman and Theo Balmer as having the primary influence on the development of Swiss graphic design. However, Kenneth Heibert (an ex-Yale design professor and colleague of Hollis), who was a student at Basel during the 1950s, strongly argues that Emil Ruder and Armin Hofman's influence was of much greater significance and points to a number of inaccuracies in Hollis's chronology of development (Heibert 2007). For example, he claims that Müller-Brockman's own practice changed significantly toward the "modernist" style, for which he remains famous, only after his company hired graduates of the Basel School of Design who had studied under Armin Hofmann in 1955. According to Heibert, this chronology means that Hofmann and Ruder predate Müller-Brockman's mature style, and their influence should not have been placed by Hollis as a separate and later development.[2]

Ruder's book, *Typographie,* is centrally located on the timeline of the literature map, and although his book was not published until 1967, his influence begins much earlier, back to 1942 when he began teaching at the Basel School of Design. As mentioned, Ruder had been publishing shorter essays about his ideas and methodologies in *Typographische Monatsblätter* (TM), a Swiss journal of typography, as early as 1944. His contributions to TM throughout the 1940s, 1950s, and 1960s were testing ground for much of the material that would later appear in his book. In TM, Ruder's academic rebuttal of contemporaries, such as Jan Tschichold, who favored classical typography, and the passion of his arguments for all things modern, including his promotion of Fruitger's typeface Univers, soon established him as an opinion leader in Swiss typography. Armin Hofman, director of the Basel School of Design during this time, said of Ruder:

> . . . he saw the return to classical form as a disastrous interruption of progress. . . . one could say that the efforts of the Basel School . . . laid the foundation for a new typographic consciousness . . .[3]

By the time Ruder had published *Typographie* in 1967, his philosophy and methodologies were already internationally renowned in the field of typography.[4]

Highlighting titles on the literature map that are linked to modernist or Swiss typography (Figure 7.23) demonstrates a significant and widespread representation across the literature. The number of highlighted titles after Ruder increases significantly. He can be linked to many authors and titles directly or indirectly, from a number of perspectives, including through geographic location (Bill, Gerstner), through his teaching at Basel (Heibert, Kunz, Schmid, Weingart), as a work colleague (Hoffman, Von Arx, Frutiger), as a peer rival (Tschichold), or through use of his work in books (Hollis, Meggs, Schmid). This web of connections presents a sketch of the broad sphere of influence of Swiss typography and the location of Ruder within it. Although Ruder's lineage warrants more detailed study, it is beyond the scope of this particular research. Nevertheless, the widespread influence of the Basel School of Design and Swiss typography on the development of international typographic practice has been documented by other contemporary research, notably McCoy (2005), Hollis (2006), Heibert (2007), and Jobling and Crowley (1996).

The position of Ruder within the literature and the extensive links forward and backward from him to other authors, as well as the prevalent use of Ruder's book today, provided the initial prompt to investigate his work and methodologies in more detail.

The difference with Ruder

Another aspect of reviewing the selected literature focused on a critical comparison of the books' structure (including their contents pages) and their approach to explaining the practical principles for

modernist graphic design images. Numerous design blogs, including www.swissmiss.com, www.swisslegacy.com, and www.aisleone.com, and Flickr sites insect 54 (www.flickr.com/photos/insect54) and outofprint (www.flickr.com/photos/22309082@N07/) are dedicated to modernist graphic design and typography, and they provide an instant visual reference for free to any interested party.

Even though the widespread adoption of a minimalist design style (e.g., see www.smashingmagazine.com online showcase of minimalist design examples and resources) might have started superficially, it has coincided with a resurgence of interest in the historical and theoretical work of modernist designers. The literature review findings reveal a significant increase in publications about modernist design principles revisited (Kunz, 1998; Bossard, 2000; Lupton and Philips, 2008; Schmid, 2009; Burrough and Mandiberg, 2009); monographs about renowned modernist designers (e.g., Otl Aicher, Josef Müller-Brockman, Max Bill, Karl Gerstner, and Max Huber); and reprinted editions of classic modernist texts (Gerstner, 2008; Hoffman, 1988; Ruder 2001).

In this contemporary environment, Ruder's modernist methodology and aesthetics are not only valid and relevant, but valuable.

Ruder applied to screen media

As discussed, Ruder's methodology is not specific to any technology, nor is it led by technique. Rather, it is driven by conceptual critical design principles grouped under themes such as contrast, form and counterform, shades of grey, rhythm, and kinetics (Figure 7.25).

At first glance, these themes seem transferrable to a screen context, capable of being adapted to the new properties of screen typography (e.g., 3D space, motion, sound, and interactivity). For example, kinetics and rhythm can be applied to the design of typography on screen that incorporates motion and sound. While Ruder discusses kinetics from the perspective of inferring motion on a page, his ideas can be translated to actual movement on screen. In fact, a colleague of Ruder at Basel, Peter Von Arx, integrated Ruder's design basics course into his course in Film Design, the results of which are demonstrated in his book.[14] The images of student work (Figure 7.26) in Von Arx's book are remarkably contemporary, as they represent neither traditional live action nor classical animation, but suggest the beginning of what we know today as motion graphics.

Some of Ruder's other themes also seem to suit the medium of the screen. The problem of composition in the virtual three dimensions of screen space necessitates the use of underlying grids to ensure not only consistency from screen to screen but also an overall impression of rhythm in the sequence or layout. Ruder is renowned for his typography of *order* and of *rhythm*. He used grids to create a system of order when arranging elements on a page and rhythm to humanize the composition by varying type sizes, leading, and line lengths. Ruder's mix of technical precision and poetic expression are fundamental to his philosophy. For him, excellent craft provides a license and basis for experimental interpretation. Other concepts that Ruder extols, such as *integral design,* recognize the need for formal unity in typography. When applied to screen typography, this concept easily translates into visual consistency, a key factor in designing user interfaces on screen. Equally, *shades of grey* presents a fundamental principle for setting any body of text, whether on page or screen. It is especially relevant

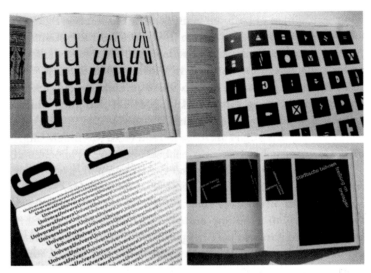

Figure 7.25 Images from *Typographie: A Manual of Design* (pp. 135, 53, 154–5, and 240–1). © 1967. Designer: Emil Ruder. Publisher: Verlag Niggli.

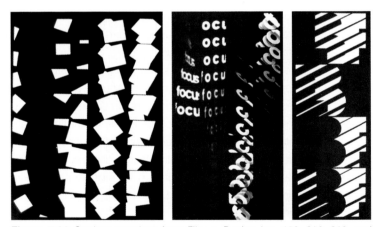

Figure 7.26 Student exercises from *Film + Design* (pp. 152, 216, 218, and 223). © 1983. Courtesy of Haupt Verlag. Designers: Peter Von Arx, Walter Bohatsch, and Suzanne Morch.

for screen typography because it creates a depth effect, which is an important consideration in legibility on screen, in motion graphics composition, and in the usability of dynamic interfaces. In web typography, where there is generally a limitation of two typeface weights (regular and bold), achieving typographic texture or "shades of grey" can be difficult and time consuming. However, the benefits to the form and function of the typography as explained by Ruder are worth pursuing, despite technical limitations in production methods.

Also central to Ruder's methodology is critical reflection through comparison of multiple *variations* and iterations of the same elements. This reflection ensures that a design principle is fully understood and not applied as a once-off success. Again, this process maps appropriately to screen typography, where digital tools can be easily manipulated to change a single parameter to render multiple variations of a single design idea. At the same time the quick efficiencies offered by digital media can be detrimental to design because of the little effort required to manipulate type. Employing Ruder's method of critical and comparative analysis presents a qualitative intervention to evaluate the design.

The iterative nature of Ruder's methods are similar to recognized contemporary design methods in the field of human–computer interaction (HCI), such as rapid prototyping (Moggridge 2007) for user interface design, and the agile process (Agile Manifesto 2001) used in software engineering. Some of the contemporary screen typographers discussed earlier, many of whom come from a computer science background, use similar methods.

When considered in their entirety, Ruder's philosophy, conceptual design principles, and systematic methodology, which incorporate experimentation, present a unique model for practice in the field of typography. This research has identified Ruder's work as a worthwhile platform upon which to build a new practice methodology for screen typography. It remains the continuing practical endeavor of this research to critically analyse and practically explore how Ruder's methodology can be applied, adapted, extended, and transformed into a new practice model for designing screen typography.

Notes

1. Association Typographique Internationale (ATypI), (March 2004), *Type and Typography Textbooks Required by Educators on ATypI Educators List,* Educators Discussion Summary, ATypI Publication.
2. R. Hollis, *Swiss Graphic Design: The Origins and Growth of an International Style, 1920–1965* (Yale University Press, 2006), 214.
3. H. Schmid, "Emil Ruder: Typography from the Inside," *Baseline* 36 (1): 5–12.
4. H. Schmid (ed), (March 2009), Ruder Typography, Ruder Philosophy, IDEA 333, Toyko.
5. R. Poynor, *No More Rules: Graphic Design and Post Modernism* (Laurence King Publishers, 2003).
6. V. Malsy, P. Teufel, and F. Gejko (ed.), *Helmut Schmid: Design is Attitude* (Birkhäuser, Switzerland, 2007), 281.
7. S. Wurman, *Information Anxiety 2,* Que; 2nd rev. edn, 2000.
8. W. Kunz, *Typography: Macro and Microaesthetics,* Verlag Niggli AG, 1998.
9. L. Manovich (2002a), Generation Flash, essay in exhibition catalogue for Whitney Biennial 2002 exhibition.
10. J. Helfand, *Screen: Essays on Graphic Design, New Media and Visual Culture* (Princeton Architectural Press, 2001), 62.
11. E. Ruder, (1967), *Typographie:A Manual for Design,* Arthur Niggli Ltd, Switzerland.
12. L. Manovich, (2002a), Generation Flash, essay in exhibition catalogue for Whitney Biennial 2002 exhibition.
13. J. Helfand, *Screen: Essays on Graphic Design, New Media and Visual Culture, Minimalism/Maximalism: The New Screen Aesthetic* (Princeton Architectural Press, 2000).
14. Von Arx, P. (1983), *Film Design,* P. Haupt.

Chapter 7.2.3

Everything to come is designed by you

Tea Uglow

Welcome to a new age of design—a time when anyone, anywhere can instantly iterate, model, prototype, publish, and promote. This is a fascinating by-product of the almost overnight democratization of production (making) and distribution (sharing) that has occurred via free web-based software and near ubiquitous hardware in pocket or laptop or tablet computers. These tools are accessible to billions of users. The world is full of creative, brilliant, curious, passionate people who could do almost anything. Isn't that exciting? We could, for example, with some coordination, direction, and aptitude, rewrite all of *Wikipedia each day*, or perhaps do something even more productive.

But there's a downside to this instantaneous digital production and distribution. The world's problems are monumental, yet we respond primarily to the minutiae of daily existence. We have apps for this, apps for that—a "digital" rhetoric that is mainly self-interested. We design for ourselves. My hope is that Google's in-house Creative Lab can push against this self-interest to produce experimental work that showcases what digital technology can do for productivity, creativity, entertainment, or simply for day-to-day living.

Google Creative Lab is a small division at Google, there are four groups—two in America, one in Europe, and my group in Australia that "looks after" Asia. It was founded in 2007 by Andy Berndt, an advertising giant who was lured to Google to build a design and creativity laboratory that would enchant and delight, and remind Google's users what it is they love about the search giant. After more than seven years Andy is still deciding what this ambition means, but it includes between 100 to 150 people across the world who "develop interactive games, visualize big data fly-throughs of the galaxy, or enable crowd-sourced animation projects that get exhibited in London's Tate Modern" (McMillan 2013). Creative Lab has designers all over, but we also have programmers, filmmakers, producers, philosophers, operations, and business folks. We explore collectively the new digital tools of our generation, but with a variety of focuses.

I came very late to design. I didn't like design at school; I still don't consider myself a designer. I am frequently asked "What do you design?" and until this very moment I have always answered "websites" (even though I might as well say tanks, or fishing rods). I have realized, however, that I design ideas. I use the "websites" line for the immigration officers when I visit New York, but as part of Google's in-house Creative Lab, my role is to have ideas and then iterate those ideas, much like any designer. I use words to work through the structure of an idea or a concept, and eventually I share those words with my team. I guess it is fair to say they are frequently quite unusual ideas.

I worked first in London, joining Google in 2006, and building a big team for the European market. I moved to Australia several years ago, though, specifically so I could work with a very small team (five to eight people) and with even smaller budgets than I had in London. I feel that both of these factors—small size and budget—elicit especially creative work.

Creative teams

This essay is a "pen-portrait" of how I construct and manage my creative teams; I will explore briefly what I expect from our "design practice." We don't really have a strict way of doing things. In the work world, small, innovative groups eventually become so big that they need to bring in people who know how to run projects "professionally," but that is not the organizational set-up that our Creative Lab team wants. We believe that it is better to be frustrated by too little prescribed process than to be stifled by too much established process. We have learned almost everything by doing. Ours is a speculative and exploratory set of processes. Speculative design is often most appropriate to internal, funded teams since it is a form of creative Research & Development that relies on solid relationships, and on an in-depth knowledge of an organization's strategies and strengths.

Think about the information world for a moment. We are moving out of an era of printed words solidified in books, and cinema solidified in physical media, and we are moving into a time of fluid information. This fluid information can be about anything and everything—sometimes it is raw data about your weather or location or your health. Sometimes this information is incredibly well organized data about the world, such as the material found on Wikipedia or Google or Facebook. How you access this information, and the information itself, change constantly; information access will be different for you who are reading this essay than it is now for me. One thing is certain, though: contemporary information organization and access is more fluid than were earlier information structures and processes.

Moving from an era of static information to an era of fluid information means that curious and passionate people will need to figure out how make the most of the new information structures, such as finding information from multiple sources and discovering ways to "crash it together" in order to make sense of the world in new ways. To be able to do this, people need to be fluid-minded, passionate, curious, and creative. I know what designers typically do. I hire people whose interests excite me, and I hire them for their fascination with novelty, and their ability to play with ideas. And then I try to let these people do what they enjoy the most—as long as this activity also explores one of the team's ideas.

This approach has been described as an artistic practice combined with a variant of design thinking. At the Creative Lab, one of our fundamental goals is to focus on empathy with everyday people (i.e. you and me, and people all around the world): how we can make technology feel more human, more natural, and more obvious. The Creative Lab team members also explore the convergence of technology and culture. Often our convergence statements begin: "I think that x (technology) would allow z (people) to explore y (subject) in a new way"—which is often paraphrased as "wouldn't it be cool if z was able to use x to do y?" One time, for example, we created a pop video that began with: "wouldn't it be great if we could do a pop video in a web browser."

This kind of question—wouldn't it be cool if z was able to use x to do y?—pushes the Creative Lab team to look for and find opportunities to explore unexpected ramifications for each project. What might that process look like? In our team we get to influence the future of scientific development by creating technological narratives that help to blur the boundaries between art and science—what my Creative Lab colleague Robert Wong calls "writing the fiction of the science" (McMillan 2013).

At the beginning of our projects, the creative team joins legal meetings, deals with contracts and venue issues, and oversees logo designs and web banner advertisements. If there is a set brief, then we consciously work to push the narrative parameters of the brief. We remain wary of predefined outputs. During a project, different teams come together to develop posters and mock-ups that sell ideas, or to start working on the website or experimental side projects. Wong also points out that "We lead by comping" (McMillan 2013). Our comps include posters, videos, short films, mock-ups, and prototypes, all of which also help us to imagine unexpected narratives. This way of working helped to turn a project about speaking to computers, for example, into a year-long exploration of whether we could use the process of speaking to computers to help people who are learning English with their pronunciation. Creative teams also come together to program school outreach, or to start planning filming. Ultimately, hundreds of people typically touch each project in which one Creative Lab team member is involved.

Creative Lab projects

One of our earliest, and most recognizable, projects is the "YouTube Symphony Orchestra" (2009) during which we worked with the London Symphony Orchestra. For this project, the LSO used YouTube to audition classical musicians. Musicians auditioned by posting a video to YouTube of themselves playing the Internet Symphony No. 1 (Eroica) by Tan Dun, plus another performance video. The musicians that the LSO chose were brought together for a one-off performance at Carnegie Hall in 2009, and in 2011 they performed at the Sydney Opera House in Australia. The project ran for over five years from the very first meeting (when a young Google marketer suggested the idea) to the final night in Sydney when 35 million people watched live on YouTube.

For our film project *Life in a Day* we invited everyone in the world to send us footage on YouTube from July 24, 2010 in what has been described as a "historic cinematic experiment to create a documentary film about a single day on earth" (*Life in a Day* 2012). *Life in a Day* began as a video comp; a team member made a video to "encapsulate the big systematic idea" (McMillan 2013). Writing about *Life in a Day* for *Communication Arts* (*CA*) magazine, Sam McMillan explains "When people saw the trailer that read, '*Life in a Day*, a film produced by Ridley Scott. Shot by you', it made the idea tangible, so people could react to it" (McMillan 2013). Our team received over 5,000 hours of footage from 80,000 people, and we worked with producer Ridley Scott and director Kevin McDonald to turn 5,000 hours of YouTube video from that one day into a 90-minute documentary film. We also worked on lots of related digital sub-projects both for the site and for cinemas. *Life in a Day* was screened at the Sundance Film Festival in addition to its theatrical release.

Sometimes projects may at first seem positively outrageous, but end up being riveting. In the summer of 2013, the Royal Shakespeare Company presented *Midsummer Night's Dreaming* in which they performed Shakespeare's *A Midsummer Night's Dream* in real time in Stratford, England over three days. The RSC wanted to adapt the methods that social media uses to report news to a Shakespeare play, and they chose *A Midsummer Night's Dream* because its "alternative reality in the forest seemed a particularly rich space for the internet" (Collinge and Ellis 2013). "The RSC focused on the commissioning and development of the creative content, while Google in Australia looked at how we could share the work online and invite people to participate" (Collinge and Ellis 2013). The RSC and our team established rules together, for example, primary characters from the play couldn't share material on the Internet. Our Creative Lab team created a simultaneous extended online universe on Google+ that was comprised of characters who would witness the action, but did not have lines in the play, and we let these characters offer contemporary commentary on the action during the performance.

Most recently, we have been exploring the potential of "Google Hangouts"—our online instant messaging and video chat platform—as an interactive educational tool. "Hangouts in History" uses video conferencing to bring history to life for students. This tool can be accessed at any school that has an Internet connection, and it lets children interact with actors who perform historical roles, such as well-known or infamous scientists, explorers, nuns, or Nazis. To bring medieval England to life, for example, we took over one of Google's conference rooms in Sydney, Australia, and placed actors playing a monk, a doctor, and a widow in front of three separate webcams. A small team of actors led by our "doctor," Jack Yabsley, worked with educators to research and script an interactive fifteen-minute hangout, which depicted plague victims and their lives as accurately as possible. The live Hangout on Air lasted 40 minutes during which the cast improvised responses to the students' questions about the Black Plague that were based on known facts. "Hangouts in History" is a very simple way of bringing history to life for students, and it allows them to ask questions and to challenge historical information in a fun, fluid way.

How do projects like these come to life?

We have some simple ideas that we employ, such as "firewalling" the team; in other words, we cloister the team, and let them articulate, discuss, and make. We try to give our team members a very clear sense of significance and direction—a mission—that allows all of us to understand the value of the project. At the same time, we try not to be concerned at the lack of a clear roadmap, and we enjoy the process "journey." We try to minimize time spent presenting the work-in-process or attending meetings. Too many presentations tend to fix a project and limit creative outcomes. When a parameter becomes fixed, or a scope shifts, then the team engages in a series of "sprints"—which are highly focused periods of intense output focused toward defined goals. These sprints help fixed parameters to become structural and essential rather than letting them impair the project. Most important, we try and fail, and share, and try again. This process does not make for the most polished outputs, but it creates "collisions of creativity."

Collisions of creativity can be intellectual or visual or technical. They can be as simple as putting images up on walls, playing videos next to each other, having two people speak with each other, or having one person present his or her ideas. Personally, I like collisions in which I explain ideas over and over again in a constant cycle of showing and telling, iterating, listening, and refining. Collisions are great—they cause energy and motion within the group, and they very often produce fragments of ideas that can be used later in different ways. And generating creative collisions produces happy teams. The most productive teams we have are the happiest ones—and that is because happy teams are productive, not the other way around.

Enable everyone

On any given project, Creative Lab team members parlay three to eight roles, such as developer, graphic designer, filmmaker, UX designer, producer (technical or theatrical), writer, creative strategist, or project manager. Team members often stretch in order to carry out a kind of work that is not usual for them. Sometimes one person takes on all of the roles for a project—doing everything, though, almost certainly will not lead to a satisfying process or outcomes for this one person. We try to be mindful of such situations; if dissatisfaction begins to occur, we make a conscious effort to open the door to collaborators. Whatever role people play in our teams, they should feel that they have agency—and not just over their own actions. They should have some authority within the group that will allow them to define and shape aspects of the project output. If they don't feel this way, we change it up. For managers, the challenge is to be conscious of the motivations and psychology of each individual, and to be aware that everyone is different and that motivations fluctuate.

Flexible work situations

We expect people to work from wherever they are, and we expect to be able to assimilate the skill sets that we need by sharing access to documents, designs, and presentation decks online. We frequently work with small agencies and freelancers worldwide, and we expect these participants to dial in to a Google hangout when we need to chat, wherever they happen to be. Collaboration means letting everyone contribute to everything, informing people what everyone else is doing, and letting everyone do what they do really well. This kind of collaboration stresses fluidity in individual and group skill sets, and encourages a capacity to "dive in" and contribute. There is a strong emphasis on finding time to pause, to talk, share, show, and make as a group. Very little lasts long in our work process—either offline or online—and bringing a sense of impermanence into our practice is hugely beneficial. After all, it is not worth spending time in a meeting room fighting about something that may only exist for a matter of weeks. Working online is like building snowmen—soon the snowman just melts away, or is submerged beneath a fresh snowfall that forms the foundation of a new effort.

Learn by doing

Successful, high-profile work for my Creative Lab team may end up being large-scale or global, but this work normally begins with small, scrappy models or prototypes on a workbench. We rarely start with a big idea; more typically we start with investigations or explorations of a particular technology. All of our Hangouts in History work, for example, started with an open experimental project called "Extreme Hangouts." Extreme Hangouts was a two-month-long research and development workshop. The outputs were never published, but the group did a number of live demos using hangouts as suggestions for more effective emergency services, interactive gaming, speed eating, and teaching history using actors. The group documented the Extreme Hangouts sessions and produced short videos detailing the experience. Even now I am not sure what the point of those videos is except to demonstrate some really absurd uses of Google Hangouts. The Extreme Hangouts video prototype in which an eleven-year-old boy tried to help Guy Fawkes and two other Catholic terrorists as they plotted to blow up the Houses of Parliament (over Hangouts), however, felt gripping. The idea of teaching history by immersing children in a particular historical period evolved into the Hangouts in History project described above. In the Creative Lab, big things typically start small, then we change direction, find uses, reimagine, or discard.

Sometimes our projects get to a certain point and then we shelve them and pick them up at a future time. Our current projects with video cubes, which started with a cube experiment a few years ago, was idle until the mobile technology caught up with what we hoped to do with the cubes. These new cubes play video on all six sides, and they work on phones. Or so we thought. A week after launching the first pop-video cube in 2014, the Chrome browser updated itself and upended the whole project (on Android). There is a six-week release cycle for Chrome updates, so we had to wait another six weeks before our video cubes worked again. Described as a "crazy, non-linear video player: Instead of putting clips in a rectangular frame, it stretches a single narrative across all six faces of an interactive cube," these cubes had to wait for the right time and circumstances to come into being (VanHemert 2014).

The outcome of our approach is that our design is speculative, which is an indulgence because most design teams or creative groups work as part of a directed process with expected outcomes that are set up front. It takes a lot of courage for a company to allow small groups to explore without boundaries or expectations. The Creative Lab team creates aims for a synthesis of knowledge, creativity, and output; we believe in prototyping by design, by video, by modeling. We believe in beginning with the minimum viable products, and the ephemeral nature of our tools. Our work is as much a matter of creative strategy as it is design—and that feels like the best way to create.

Epilogue

Notes from the forefront of graphic design: adaptive communication, complex networks, and local and global design

Teal Triggs and Leslie Atzmon

The conditions under which graphic design is practiced today are wildly varied. Emergent digital technologies and resurgent old technologies together shape aspects of the design landscape. Design projects commingle digital and physical iterations to investigate what digital and physical media together have to offer design challenges. Designers adapt graphic design methods to complex social issues, such as climate change, migration, and global health. The processes and resulting solutions engage networks of people, things, and environments around these kinds of social concerns. Graphic designers sometimes function as curators, presiding over intricate data sets in information visualization projects, multi-layered broadcasting platforms for participatory design, structured languages of coding and computation in adaptive design, and entangled experiences in immersive design spaces. In this Epilogue, we will consider various practices that require expansive design thinking and iterative making processes, and we will introduce how entangled networks are fundamental to contemporary graphic design.

Considering artifacts and design thinking

Contemporary design practices draw attention to the relationships between design thinking and designed artifacts. Object Oriented Ontology (Bogost 2009, 2012), a school of thought that emerged from philosophy, suggests that graphic design artifacts have their own qualities and networked "social lives." According to Object Oriented Ontology, artifacts—and their frameworks for design thinking—change those who make, use, or experience them, and those who make and use artifacts are likewise changed by them. Critical design practice, in which provocations are used to create ideas as well

---

as things, likewise foregrounds objects by considering how the thinking behind the design of artifacts can unearth new theoretical directions for design. Other strategies for exploring "what might be" include speculative, critical, or discursive design, as well as design fiction. While design fiction challenges assumptions about everyday objects by opening up imagination and generating "new ideas" about design "through prototyping and storytelling" (Malpass 2017: 54), speculative design reconsiders the roles of objects in light of predicted socio-scientific and socio-technical concerns (Malpass 2017: 56).[1] The Dutch design group Metahaven, for example, takes a speculative approach to "nation branding" by exploring how "space is punctuated, divided up and shaped by power and politics through buildings, fonts, logos, laws and institutions." They interrogate the complexity of these propositions through both the verbal content and material form of their dystopian-age book *Uncorporate Identity* (O'Reilly 2010).

Other approaches challenge design thinking as a process that only leads to final artifacts. Service design doesn't necessarily center on the design of artifacts; instead it focuses on ways of thinking about and addressing unresolved situations. Inclusive practices, like service design, however, often incorporate traditional design artifacts into solutions that take into consideration, for example, how diversity and accessibility can improve people's lives. Embracing both traditional artifact-oriented outcomes and new inclusive processes expands the purview of design.[2] Taken together, these approaches can liberate the "design process from designers in a way that should be taken not as a challenge to the hegemony of designers," according to Tim Marshall, Provost at The New School in New York. Rather they should be viewed as "crucial to the transformation of design practice from a closed guild practice to a fully implicated social and material practice" (Marshall 2014: 244). Marshall surmises that recognizing how design shapes our interactions with things, environments, organizations, and other people is so essential that design thinking processes are being embraced by disciplines outside of design (2014: 245).[3]

In "Design in Tech Report, 2017," John Maeda describes "Design Thinking" as a "consensus" among "multiple stakeholders" (Maeda 2017: 7). In the report, Maeda also proposes that many "classic" designers will eventually become "computational" designers, who "deal mostly in code and build constantly evolving products that impact millions of people's lives" (Stinson 2017). Computational designers, according to Liz Stinson of *Wired* magazine, utilize iterative, digitally situated processes both to "understand their users" and to "bang out" design solutions as "lines of Javascript" (Stinson 2017). Computational design is also used to explore the aesthetic qualities of digital artifacts and experiences. In the late 1990s, Dutch designers Erik van Blokland and Just van Rossum, as part of the design group Letterror, integrated programming into their experimental and applied typographic work. Van Blokland's animated breathing 'PEACE' GIF, for example, tests how "expressive typography customized in accordance with the aesthetics intentions of the typeface itself" might be visualized (Vinh 2017). Such integrated practices are also found in the work of Korean graphic designer Kyuha Shim, who works at the nexus of computational art, design and technology. He uses computational thinking as a methodology for design, "creating generative systems informed and driven by data."[4] Designers have also built upon simple digital displays to produce sensorial, transmedia storytelling in immersive environments, such as virtual reality and augmented reality.

Bibliography

2000 Exhibition of Chinese Poster Design Association (2000), Taiwan: Chinese Poster Association.

"2020 Forecast: Creating the Future of Learning," *KnowledgeWorks.org*. Available online: http://knowledgeworks. org/future-of-learning (accessed July 29, 2016).

Abdulla, D., E. Canli, M. Keshavarz, L. Martins, and P. de Oliveria (2016), "A Statement on the Design Research Society Conference 2016." Available online: http://www.decolonisingdesign.com/statements/2016/ drs2016statement/ (accessed August 16, 2017).

Abrams, J. (1994), "Muriel Cooper's Visible Wisdom," *I.D.,* 4 (5): 48–55.

Abrams, J. (1995), *Learn Talmud: How to Use the Talmud, The Steinsaltz Edition*, Northvale: Jason Aronson, Inc.

Adam and the Ants (1979), "Zerox," *Dirk Wears White SOX* [music song/album].

Aesthetics + Computation, MIT. Available online: http://acg.media.mit.edu/people/fry/zipdecode/

"Afternoons in Studios: A Chat with Mr. G.H. Boughton, ARA" (1894), *The Studio,* 3 (17): 130–6.

"Afternoons in Studios: A Chat with Mr. Whistler" (1894), *The Studio*, 4 (1): 116–21.

Aicher, O. (1988), *Typographie*, Berlin: Ernst and Sohn.

AIGA (2003), *The Power of Design: AIGA National Design Conference*, 23–26 October. Available online: http:// powerofdesign.aiga.org (accessed September 20, 2014).

AIGA (2009), "Designer of 2015 Trends," *American Institute of Graphic Arts*. Available online: http://www.aiga.org/ designer-of–2015-trends/ (accessed September 19, 2010).

Akama, Y. (2012), "A 'Way of Being': Zen and the Art of Being a Human-centred Practitioner," *Design Philosophy Papers*, (1): 1–10.

Akama, Y. (2014), "Passing On, Handing Over, Letting Go—The Passage of Embodied Design Methods for Disaster Preparedness," *Service Design and Innovation Conference 2013*.

Akama, Y., R. Cooper, L. Vaughan, S. Viller, M. Simpson, and J. Yuille (2007), "Show and Tell: Accessing and Communicating Implicit Knowledge through Artefacts," *Artifact* (1): 172–81.

Alberti, L. (1991), "On the Art of Building in Ten Books," in Book 9: *Ornament to Private Building*, trans. J. Rykwert, N. Leach, and R. Tavernor, Cambridge: MIT Press.

Aldersey-Williams, H. (1990), *Cranbrook Design: The New Discourse*, New York: Steelcase Design Partnership.

Alexander, C. (2002), *The Nature of Order. Book One: The Phenomena of Life,* Berkeley: Center for Environmental Structure.

Alimenti, M.G. and M.V. Christiansen (1987), "La Comunicación Visual en la Universidad Nacional de La Plata," in R. Rollie (ed.), *tipoGráfica*, 2 (September).

All the News That's Fit to Post (2010), [Documentary video podcast] Gestalten.tv, August 4. Available online: http://www.gestalten.com/motion/new-york-times and http://infosthetics.com/archives/2010/08/ how_the_new_york_times_creates_its_infographics.html#extended (accessed July 18, 2011).

Allen, E. (1974), *The Responsive House,* Cambridge: The MIT Press.

Ambrose, G. and P. Harris (2006), *The Fundamentals of Typography*, London: AVA Publishing.

Amoeba Group (1982), *Leaflet of Asian Designers' Invitational Exhibition & Amoeba Annual Show*, Taiwan: Amoeba Group.

Anand, K. and A. Charanjiva (2013), Email Communication, November 18.

Andersen, M. (2017), "Op-ed: Why Can't the US Decolonize Its Design Education?," *AIGA Eye on Design,* January 2, 2017. Available online: http://eyeondesign.aiga.org/why-cant-the-u-s-decolonize-its-design-education/ (accessed July 24, 2017).

Anderson, P. (1976), *Considerations on Western Marxism,* New York: New Left Books.

Anderson, P. (1984), "Modernity and Revolution", in *New Left Review*, 144, March to April.

"An Interview with Charles F. Annesley Voysey, Architect and Designer" (1893), *The Studio*, 1 (6): 231–7.

Annual of Advertising and Editorial Art, New York, 1922–. This first was published as a catalogue "for the first Annual exhibition of Advertising Paintings and Drawings held by the Art Directors Club of New York," The twelfth annual was advertised *Gebrauchsgraphik,* 11 (2) February 1934.

Antonelli, P. (2010), "Design Takes Over," *The Economist,* November 22. Available online: http://www.economist.com/node/17509367 (accessed August 1, 2017).

Antonelli, P. (2012), "Foreword: Vital Design," in W. Myers, *Biodesign: Nature, Science, Creativity*, 6–7, New York: Museum of Modern Art.

Aranguren, J.L. (1967), *Human Communication*, New York and Toronto: McGraw-Hill, World University Library.

Archer, B. (1995), "The Nature of Research," *Co-Design, Interdiscliplinary Journal of Design* (January): 6–13.

Aristotle (1941), "Metaphysics," *The Basic Works of Aristotle*, trans. W.D. Ross and R. McKeon (eds), New York: Random House.

Armstrong, H., ed. (2009), *Graphic Design Theory: Readings from the Field*, New York: Princeton Architectural Press.

Arnall, T. (2013), "No to NoUI," Elastic Space, March 13. Available online: http://www.elasticspace.com/2013/03/no-to-no-ui (accessed September 22, 2014).

Arnell, A. (1989), *The Telephone Book,* Lincoln: University of Nebraska.

Arpke, O. (1929), *Gebrauchsgraphik,* 7 (12).

Arpke, O. (1934), *Gebrauchsgraphik,* 12 (1).

Arpke, O. (1938), "International Handicraft Exhibition," *Gebrauchsgraphik,* 15 (7): 49–57.

Art and Design (2000–2) 94: 3–20.

Arthur, C. (2012), "Walled Gardens Look Rosy for Facebook, Apple—and Would-be Censors," *Guardian online*, April 17. Available online: http://www.guardian.co.uk/technology/2012/apr/17/walled-gardens-facebook-apple-censors.

"Artists as Craftsmen No. 1 Sir Frederick Leighton, Bart, P.R.A., as a Modeller in Clay" (1893), *The Studio*, 1 (1): 27.

Ashwin, C. (1976), "*The Studio* and Modernism," *Studio International*, 193: 103–12.

Ashwin, C. (1981), *Drawing and Education in German-speaking Europe, 1800–1900*, Ann Arbor: UMI Research Press.

Ashwin, C. (1993), "The Founding of *The Studio* in High Life and Low Life: The Studio and the Fin de Siècle," *Studio International,* Special Centenary Number 201.1022/1023: 5–10.

Association Typographique Internationale (ATypI) (March 2004), "Educators Discussion Summary," *Type and Typography Textbooks Required by Educators on ATypI Educators List,* ATypi Publication.

Atkinson, P. (2010), "Boundaries? What Boundaries? The Crisis of Design in a Post-Professional Era," *The Design Journal: An International Journal for All Aspects of Design*, 13 (2): 137–55.

Atzmon, L. (2009), "Visual Rhetoric. What We Mean When We Talk about Form," August 5, *Eye, The International Review of Graphic Design*. Available online: http://www.eyemagazine.com/blog/post/visual-rhetoric (accessed July 27, 2017).

Atzmon, L., ed (2011), *Visual Rhetoric and the Eloquence of Design*, Anderson, SC: Parlor Press.

Atzmon, L. and R. Molloy (2014), *The Open Book Project*, Ypsilanti: Eastern Michigan University.

Australian Graphic Design Association (2009). July. Available online: http://blogs.agda.com.au/suite7/view/year/2009/month/7/post/an-open-letter-to-the-lord-mayor-of-melbourne.

Avert.org. History of AIDS from 1987 to 1992 (1992). Available from: http://www.avert.org/his87_92.htm. (accessed November 9, 2007).

Aynsley, J. (1989), *Gebrauchsgraphik: Style and Ideology in German Graphic Design 1910–1939*, London: Royal College of Art.

Baas, J. (1987), "Reconsidering Walter Benjamin: The Age of Mechanical Reproduction in Retrospect," in G.P. Weisberg, *The Documented Image: Visions in Art History*, 339–40, New York: Syracuse University Press.

Baddeley, A.D. (1990), *Human Memory. Theory and Practice,* Boston: Allyn and Bacon.

Bahro, R. (1982), *From Red to Green*, London: New Left Books.

Bailey, S. (2004), "2: Doublethought," *Dot Dot Dot,* 8 (Summer): 60–1.

Bailey, S. (2010), "TITLE," *Dot Dot Dot*, 20.

Bailey, S. and Bilak, P. (2000–2008), *Dot Dot Dot*, Amsterdam: DOT DOT DOT.

Baines, P. and A. Haslam (2002), *Type and Typography,* New York: Watson Guptill.

Bal, M. (1985), *Narratology: Introduction to the Theory of Narrative,* trans. C. van Boheemen, Toronto: University of Toronto Press.

Balaguer, L. (2016), "Tropico Vernacular," *Triple Canopy*, May 3. Available online: https://www.canopycanopycanopy.com/contents/tropico-vernacular/#title-page (accessed August 4, 2017).

Baldry, A.L. (1898), "The Future of Wood Engraving," *International Studio*, 5: 10.

Baldwin, J. (2005), "Abandoning History," New Views: Repositioning Graphic Design History conference, October 27–29.

Banham, R. (1980), *Theory and Design in the First Machine Age*, Cambridge, MA: MIT Press.

Barber, P. and T. Harper, eds (2010), *Magnificent Maps: Power, Propaganda and Art*, London: British Library.

Barendse, J., T. Castro, D. Nieuwenhuizen, and D. Powers. Available online: http://lust.nl/

Barnard, M. (1998), *Art, Design and Visual Culture: An Introduction*, Basingstoke: Macmillan Press.

Barnard, M. (2001), *Approaches to Understanding Visual Culture*, Basingstoke: Palgrave.

Barnard, M. (2005), *Graphic Design as Communication*, London and New York: Routledge.

Barney, D., et al. (2016), "The Participatory Age: An Introduction," in Barney et al. (eds), *The Participatory Condition in the Digital Age,* Minneapolis: University of Minnesota Press.

Barney, D., G. Coleman, C. Ross, J. Sterne, and T. Tembeck, eds (2016), *The Participatory Condition in the Digital Age*, Minneapolis: University of Minnesota Press.

Barnhurst, K.G. (1993), *Seeing the Newspaper,* New York: St. Martin's Press.

Barnhurst, K.G. (2009), "The Internet and News: Changes in Content on Newspaper Websites," Political Communication, Chicago: International Communication Association.

Barnhurst, K.G. and J. Nerone (2002), *The Form of News: A History*, 1st edn, New York: Guilford Press.

Barrett, T.H. (2007), *The Woman Who Discovered Printing*, New Haven: Yale University Press, 2007.

Bartel, J. (2004), *From A to Zine: Building a Winning Zine Collection in Your Library*, Chicago: American Library Association, 2004.

Barthes, R. (1971), "From Work to Text." Available online: http://homepage.newschool.edu/~quigleyt/vcs/barthes-wt.html (accessed January 4, 2008).

Barthes, R. (1971), "The Rhetoric of the Image," *Working Papers in Cultural Studies*, Spring: 37–50.

Barthes, R. (1977), "Change the Object Itself," in S. Heath (ed.), *Image-Music-Text*, Harmondsworth: Penguin.

Barthes, R. (1977), *The Pleasure of the Text*, London: Jonathan Cape.

Barthes, R. (1978), *Image-Music-Text*, New York: Hill and Wang.

Barthes, R. (1985), "Rhetoric of the Image," in R.E. Innis (ed.), *Semiotics: An Introductory Anthology,* 192–205, Bloomington: Indiana University Press.

Barthes, R. (1988), *The Semiotic Challenge*, trans. R. Howard, New York: Hill and Wang.

Barthes, R. (1991), *Mythologies,* London: Vintage.

Baudelaire, C. (1964), "The Painter of Modern Life," in J. Mayne (ed.), *The Painter of Modern Life and Other Assays*, London: Phaidon Press.

Baudrillard, J. (1981), *For a Critique of the Political Economy of the Sign*, Kent: Telos.

Baudrillard, J. (1983), "The Precession of Simulacra," *Art and Text*, 11 (Spring): 32–3.

Baudrillard, J. (1984), *In the Shadow of the Silent Majorities*, New York: Semiotext(e).

Baudrillard, J. (1984), *The Mirror of Production*, Kent: Telos.

Baudrillard, J. (1985), "The Ecstasy of Communication," in H. Foster (ed.), *Post-modern Culture,* London: Pluto Press.

Bayley, S. (2000), 'Taste: The Story of An Idea,' *General Knowledge*, London: Booth-Clibborn Editions.

Beck, H.C., Typewritten Statement.

Bederson, B.B. and B. Shneiderman (2003), *The Craft of Information Visualization: Readings and Reflections*, Burlington: Elsevier.

Beegan, G. (2001), "The Up-to-Date Periodical: Subjectivity, Technology, and Time in the Late-Victorian Press," *Time and Society*, 10: 113–34.

Behrmann, H. (1925), "Amerikanische Reklamemethoden in Europa," *Gebrauchsgraphik,* 2 (3): 73.

Bell, D. (1973), *The Coming Post Industrial Society*, New York: Basic Books.

Bell, N. (2004), "Brand Madness, Part 1," *Eye*, 53.

Beng-Huat, C. (1995), *Communitarian Ideology and Democracy in Singapore*, London and New York: Routledge.

Benjamin, G. (1976), "The Cultural Logic of Singapore's 'Multiracialism,'" in R. Hassan (ed.), *Singapore: Society in Transition*, 115, Kuala Lumpur: Oxford University Press.

Bennett, T. (2003), "Stored Virtue: Memory, the Body, and the Evolutionary Museum," in S. Radstone and K. Hodgkin (eds), *Regimes of Memory*, 41/42/52, New York: Routledge.

Berg, S. (1924), *Offset Buch und Werbekunst Das Blatt für Drucker, Werbefachleute und Verleger* (3), J. Aynsley translator.

Berger, A. (1975), "London's Underground as a Work of Art," *San Francisco Chronicle,* June 12: 21.

Berger, J. (1972), *Ways of Seeing,* London: Penguin Classics.

Berger, J. (1979), *Pig Earth,* New York: Pantheon Books.

Berger, J. (1982), *Another Way of Telling*, New York: Pantheon Books.

Berger, J. (1984), *And Our Faces, My Heart, Brief as Photos*, New York: Pantheon Books

Berger, J. (1992), *About Looking*, New York: Vintage.

Berger, J. and J. Mohr (1975), *A Seventh Man,* London: Writers and Readers Publishing Cooperative.

Berlow, D. (1993), "The Shape of Things to Come," *Publish*, January: 34–8.

Berman, M. ([1867] 1982), *All That Is Solid Melts into Air*, New York: Verso.

Berman, M. (1983), *All That's Solid Melts into Air*, New York: Simon and Schuster.

Berman, M. (1984), "The Signs in the Street: A Response to Perry Anderson," *New Left Review*, March/April: 144.

Bernays, E.L. (1947), "The Engineering of Consent," *The Annals of the American Academy of Political and Social Sciences*, 250: 113–20.

Corbin, J.M. and Strauss, A.L. (2008), *Basics of Qualitative Research—Techniques and Procedures for Developing Grounded Theory,* Los Angeles: Sage.

Cormier, B. (2014), "Confronting Impact," *Domus*, June 5. Available online: http://www.domusweb.it/content/domusweb/en/design/2013/06/5/confronting_impact.html (accessed October 1, 2014).

Craig, J. (1990), *Basic Typography: A Design Manual,* New York: Watson Guptill.

Craig, J. and B. Barton (1987), *Thirty Centuries of Graphic Design*, New York: Watson-Guptill Publications.

Crampton, J. (2010), *Mapping: A Critical Introduction to Cartography and GIS*, New York: John Wiley & Son.

Cramsie, P. (2010), *The Story of Graphic Design*, New York: Abrams.

Crawford, W. (1925), "Das Plakat," *Gebrauchsgraphik,* 2 (5): 3–50.

Crawford, W. (1930), "Crawfords Reklame Agentur," *Gebrauchsgraphik,* 7 (8).

Crnokrak, P. (2015), "The Luxury of Protest." Available online: http://theluxuryofprotest.com/ (accessed July 19, 2015).

Crow, T. (1996), "Visual Culture Questionnaire," October (77): 25–70.

Crowley, D. (2006), "The Modern World," *Creative Review* (April): 53–6.

Crowley, D. and P. Jobling (1996), *Graphic Design—Reproduction & Representation: A Critical Introduction—Reproduction and Representation Since 1800 (Studies in Design & Material Culture)*, Manchester: Manchester University Press.

Crystal, D. (2000), *Language Death,* Cambridge: Cambridge University Press.

Cullen, M. (1995), "The Space Between the Letters," *Eye*, 19 (5): 70–7.

Curtis, A. (2002) [Director] "Happiness Machines," *The Century of The Self*, BBC, April 29.

Dahl, F. (1928), "Max Bittrof," *Gebrauchsgraphik,* 5 (12): 3–18.

Dalton, B., T. Simmons, and T. Triggs (2017), "Chapter 7 Knowledge Exchange Through the Design PhD," in L. Vaughan (ed.), *Practice-Based Design Research*, 65–76, London: Bloomsbury.

Dalvi, G. (2010), "Conceptual Model for Devanagari Typefaces. Industrial Design Centre," India: IIT Bombay.

Darnton, R. (1986), "Pop Foucaultism," *The New York Review of Books* (October): 15.

David Ross, S., ed. (1985), *Art and Its Significance: An Anthology of Aesthetic Theory*, New York: State University of New York Press.

David-West, H., ed. (1983), *Dialogue on Graphic Design Problems in Africa,* London: ICOGRADA.

Davis, J., ed. (1977), *Punk*, London: Millington.

Davis, J.W. (1972), "Unified Drawing Through the Use of Hybrid Pictorial Elements and Grids," *Leonardo*, 5 (1): 1–9.

Davis, M. (2008), "Toto, I've Got a Feeling We're Not in Kansas Anymore," *Interactions*, 15 (5): 28–34.

Davis, N.Z. (1981), "The Sacred and the Political in Sixteenth Century Lyon," *Past and Present*, 90 (February): 40–70.

De Bono, E. (2009), *Lateral Thinking: A Textbook of Creativity*, London: Penguin Books.

de Man, P. (1979), *Allegories of Reading: Figural Language in Rousseau, Nietzsche, Rilke, and Proust*, New Haven: Yale University Press.

Dean, J. (2010), *Blog Theory: Feedback and Capture in the Circuits of Drive,* Cambridge: Polity Press.

Deepta, S. (2013), Email Communication, December 11.

Delgado, M. and J. Tompkins (2015), "Editing Matters: An Editorial," *Contemporary Theatre Review*, 12 February: 11–16, Available online: http://www.tandfonline.com/doi/full/10.1080/10486801.2015.1007759 (accessed August 16, 2017).

Delwiche, A. and J. Jacobs Henderson (2013), *The Participatory Cultures Handbook,* London: Routledge.

Department of Economic Development, Jobs, Transport and Resources, *State of Design*. Available online: http://www.stateofdesign.com.au (accessed November 2009).

Department of Health South Africa (2006), *National HIV and Syphilis Antenatal Prevalence Survey, South Africa 2005.* Pretoria, Department of Health South Africa. Quoted in UNAIDS, 2006: 11.

Department of Labor, *The Occupational Outlook Handbook* (1996), Lanham: Bernan Reprints.

Department of Statistics, Ministry of Trade & Industry, Republic of Singapore (2000), *Census of Population Statistical Release 1: Demographic Characteristics*, Singapore: Singapore Department of Statistics. Available online: https://www.singstat.gov.sg/docs/default-source/default-document-library/publications/publications_and_papers/cop2000/census_2000_admin_report/cop2000admin.pdf (accessed September 3, 2017).

Derrida, J. (1976), *Of Grammatology*, Baltimore: The Johns Hopkins University Press.

Derrida, J. (1978), *The Truth in Painting*, Chicago: University of Chicago Press.

Derrida, J. (1978), *Writing and Difference*, Chicago: University of Chicago Press.

Derrida, J. (1983), *Dissemination*, Chicago: University of Chicago Press.

Des Hist, J. (1992), *Journal of Design History*, 5 (1).

Design Council (2010), "The, double diamond, design process model," Design Council. Available online: http://www.designcouncil.org.uk/about-design/How-designers-work/The-design-process/ (accessed February 6, 2011).

Design Industry Advisory Committee (2004), DIAC Design Industry Study, Toronto. Available online: www.dx.org/diac.html.

Designophy Homepage. Available online: http://www.designophy.com (accessed June 1, 2007).

"Design Thinking Comes of Age" (2015), *Harvard Business Review*, September. Available online: https://hbr.org/2015/09/design-thinking-comes-of-age (accessed August 9, 2017).

De Vinne, T.L. (1900), *Practice of Typography: Vol. 1. Plain Printing Types*, New York: The Century Co.

De Vinne, T.L. (1902), *Practice of Typography: Vol. 3. A Treatise on Title Pages*, New York: The Century Co.

Dewey, J. (1958), *Art as Experience*, New York: Capricorn Books.

Die Form: Zeitschrift für Gestaltende Arbeit (1925–34), Berlin: Organ des Deutschen Werkbundes.

Diggins, J.P. (1995), *The Promise of Pragmatism: Modernism and the Crisis of Knowledge and Authority*, Chicago: University of Chicago Press.

Dike, J. (2014), "Can the Current Media Environment Produce an Honest Critic?," Business of Fashion, February 24. Available online: http://www.businessoffashion.com/2014/02/op-ed-can-current-media-environment-produce-honest-critic.html (accessed September 24, 2014).

Dikovitskaya, M. (2005), *Visual Culture: The Study of the Visual after the Cultural Turn*, Cambridge, MA, and London: MIT Press.

Dilnot, C. (1984), "The State of Design History, Part II: Problem and Possibilities," *Design Issues,* 1 (2).

Dimitriadis, G. (1996), "Hip Hop: From Live Performance to Mediated Narrative," *Popular Music*, 15 (2): 179–94.

Dimson, T. (1979), *Great Canadian Posters*, Toronto: Oxford University Press.

DiSalvo, C., et al. (2012), "Toward a Public Rhetoric Through Participatory Design: Critical Engagements and Creative Expression in the Neighborhood Networks Project," *Design Issues* (Special Issue on Participatory Design), 28 (3): 48–61.

Dixon, C. (1991), "Why We Need to Reclassify Type," *Eye*, 19 (5): 86–7.

Donnelly, B. (2001), "Reading Kurschenska: On the Centres and Boundaries of Design History," unpublished paper delivered at the Universities Art Association of Canada annual conference, Montreal, October.

Donnelly, B. (2005), "Memory and History," panel discussion including A. Bush, J. Williamson, V. Williams, and K. William-Purcell, October 29.

Dörk, M., P. Feng, C. Collins, and S. Carpendale (2013), "Critical InfoVis: Exploring the Politics of Visualization," in *Extended Abstracts of the 2013 Annual Conference on Human Factors in Computing Systems (CHI 2013),* ACM: 2189–98.

Dourish, P. and M. Mazmanian (2013), "Media as Material: Information Representations as Material Foundations for Organizational Practice," in P.R. Carlisle, et al. (eds), *How Matter Matters: Objects, Artifacts, and* Materiality, 58–91, Oxford: Oxford University Press.

Downe, L. (2016) "What We Mean by Service Design," *Blog: Government Digital Service*, April 18. Available online: https://gds.blog.gov.uk/2016/04/18/what-we-mean-by-service-design/ (accessed April 24, 2017).

Downs, R.B. (1978), *Friedrich Froebel*, Boston: G.K. Hall.

Doyle, R., quoted in Gilchrist, I. (2009), "Hip to be Square: Melbourne's modern new logo a chunky move," *MX*, July 22: 1.

Drayton, T. (1976), "The Skid Kid Page," *Ripped & Torn*, 1: 9.

Drayton, T. (1976), "What's in it for me?," *Ripped & Torn*, 1: 3.

Drayton, T. (1977), *Dayglow, Ripped & Torn*, 5.

Drayton, T. (1999), letter to Teal Triggs.

Drenttel, W. and J. Helfand (2010), "An Introduction to Graphic Design," *Design Observer,* November 10. Available online: http://designobserver.com/feature/an-introduction-to-graphic-design/8727) (accessed August 7, 2017).

Droste, M. (1982), *Herbert Bayer: das künstlerische Werk 1919–1938*, Berlin: Bauhaus-Archiv/Gebr. Mann Verlag.

Drucker, J. (1999), "Who's Afraid of Visual Culture," *Art Journal*, 58 (4): 36–47.

Drucker, J. (2009), *SpecLab: Digital Aesthetics and Projects in Speculative Computing*, Chicago: University of Chicago Press.

Drucker, J. (2010), "Humanistic Approaches to the Graphical Expression of Interpretation." Available online: http://mitworld.mit.edu/video/796 (accessed July 8, 2011).

Drucker, J. and E. McVarish (2008), *Graphic Design History: A Critical Guide*, Upper Saddle River: Pearson Prentice Hall.

Dugast, I. and M.D.W. Jeffreys (1950), *L'Écriture des Bamum.* Paris: Mémoires de L'Institut Francais D'Afrique Noire.

Duncombe, S. (1997), *Notes from the Underground: Zines and the Politics of Alternative Culture,* New York: Verso.

Duncombe, S. (2002), *Cultural Resistance Reader,* New York: Verso.

Dunne, A and F. Raby (2013), *Speculative Everything: Design, Fiction, and Social Dreaming*, Cambridge, MA: MIT Press.

Dwiggins, W.A. and L. Siegfried ([1919] 1995), "Extracts from an Investigation into the Physical Properties of Books as They Are at Present Published," in R. McLean (ed.), *Typographers on Type*, New York: Norton & Company.

E. B. S. (1895), "A Chat with Mr. And Mrs. Nelson Dawson on Enamelling," *The Studio*, 6 (33): 173–8.

E. B. S. (1898), "Eleanor F. Brickdale, Designer and Illustrator," *The Studio,* 13 (60): 103–8

E. B. S. (1895), "The Paintings and Etchings of Elizabeth Stanhope Forbes," *The Studio,* 4 (249): 186–92.

Eagleton, T. (1983), *Literary Theory: An Introduction*, Minneapolis and London: University of Minnesota Press.

Eagleton, T. (1990), *The Ideology of the Aesthetic*, Oxford: Basil Blackwell.

Eagleton, T. (1991), *The Function of Criticism: From the Spectator to Post Structuralism*, London: Verso.

Eames, C. and R. Eames (1958), "The India Report," *National Institute of Design*, India: Ford Foundation.

Eco, U. (1976), *A Theory of Semiotics*, Bloomington: Indiana University Press.

Eco, U. (1994), *Six Walks in the Fictional Woods*, Cambridge, MA: Harvard University Press.

Ehrenfeld, J. (2008), *Sustainability by Design: A Subversive Strategy for Transforming Our Consumer Culture*, New Haven: Yale University Press.

Ehrenfeld, J. and A. Hoffman (2013), *Flourishing: A Frank Conversation About Sustainability*, Sheffield: Greenleaf Publishing.

Ehses, H. (1984), "Representing Macbeth. A Case Study in Visual Rhetoric," *Design Issues*, 1: 53–63.

Ehses, H. H. J. (1984), "Rhetoric and Design," *Icographic*, 2 (4): 4–6.

Eichenberg, E. and M. Perry (1996), *And God Created Punk,* London: Virgin.

Eisler, H. (1978), *A Rebel in Music,* Berlin: Seven Seas.

Elam, K. (1990), *Expressive Typography: The Word as Image*, New York: Van Nostrand Reinhold.

Eliot, G. ([1876] 1967), *Daniel Deronda*, London: Penguin Books.

Elkins, J. (2003), *Visual Studies: A Skeptical Introduction*, New York and London: Routledge.

Elliman, P. (2005), *Recollected Work: Mevis and Van Deursen*, Amsterdam: Artimo.

Emerson, R.W. (1860), *The Conduct of Life*, Boston: Houghton, Mifflin and Co.

Eng, L.A. (1995), *Meanings of Multiethnicity: A Case Study of Ethnicity and Ethnic Relations in Singapore*, Kuala Lumpur: Oxford University Press.

Engeström, Y. (1987), *Learning by Expanding. An Activity-theoretical Approach to Developmental Research,* Helsinki: Orienta-Konsultit Oy.

Eskildsen, U. (1979), *Film und Foto der zwanziger Jahre,* Stuttgart: Württemberg. Kunstverein.

Eskilson, S.J. (2007), *Graphic Design: A New History*, New Haven: Yale University Press.

Ewart, J. (1991), Interview with Teal Triggs, London.

Fabricius, J. (2006), "Some questions, some answers. Interview with Barnaby Drabble," *A*DESK: Critical Thinking* N003, April 10. Available online: http://www.a-desk.org/spip/spip.php?article735 (accessed August 24, 2017).

Faik-Nzuji, C. (1992), *Symboles graphiques en Afrique noire,* Paris/Ciltade: Editions Karthala/Louvain-la-Neuve.

Farson, R. (2008), *The Power of Design: A Force for Transforming Everything*, Belmond: Greenway Communications.

Fathers, J. (2003), "Peripheral Vision: An Interview with Gui Bonsiepe Charting a Lifetime of Commitment to Design Empowerment," *Design Issues*, 19 (4): 44–56.

Fawcett, T. and C. Phillpot (1976), *The Art Press: Two Centuries of Art Magazines*, London: The Art Book Company.

Featherstone, J. (2009), Interview with Leslie Atzmon.

Felton, N. (2005), *Feltron Annual Report.* Available online: http://feltron.com/ar05_01.html (accessed August 22, 2011).

Fern, A. and M. Constantine, *Word and Image*, New York: Museum of Modern Art, 1968.

Fernández, S. (1987), La Comunicación Visual en la Universidad Nacional de La Plata, in R. Rollie (ed.), *tipoGráfica*, 2 (September).

Fernández, S. (2006), "The Origins of Design Education in Latin America: From the hfg in Ulm to Globalization," *Design Issues*, 22 (1): 3–19.

Findeli, A. (2001), "Rethinking Design Education for the 21st Century: Theoretical, Methodological, and Ethical Discussion," *Design Issues*, 17 (1): 5–17.

First Institute of Art & Design Association (1980), *Design '80*, Hong Kong: First Institute of Art & Design Association.

Fischenden, R.B., ed. (1938), *Penrose Annual,* 40.

Fischer, G. (2002), "Beyond couch potatoes: from consumers to designers and active participants," *First Monday* 7. Available online: http://firstmonday.org/htbin/cgiwrap/bin/ojs/index.php/fm/rt/printerFriendly/1010/931 (accessed July 29, 2016).

Fischer-Defoy, C. (1986), "Artists and Art Institutions in Germany 1933–45," *Oxford Art Journal,* 9 (2).

Fishel, C. (2001) *Paper Graphics: The Power of Paper in Graphic Design*, Beverley, MA: Rockport Publishers, Inc.

Fiske, J. (1990), *Introduction to Communication Studies*, London: Routledge.

Fleischer, A. and F. Kämpfer (1990), "The Political Poster in the Third Reich," in B. Taylor and W. van der Will (eds), *The Nazification of Art,* Berlin: Winchester Press.

Fleishman, G. (2017), "How Letterpress Printing Came Back from the Dead," *Wired*, June 21. Available online: https://www.wired.com/story/how-letterpress-printing-came-back-from-the-dead (accessed July 22, 2017).

Flew, T. (2012), *The Creative Industries: Culture and Policy*, Thousand Oak: SAGE Publications.

Florida, R. (2005), "The World is Spiky," *Atlantic Monthly,* October: 48–51. Available online: http://www.theatlantic.com/past/docs/images/issues/200510/world-is-spiky.pdf.

Foer, J.S. (2005), *Extremely Loud & Incredibly Close*, New York and London: Penguin Books.

Forceville, C. (1996), *Pictorial Metaphor in Advertising*, London and New York: Routledge.

Ford, H. (1900), "The Work of Mrs. Adrian Stokes," *The Studio,* 19 (85): 149–56.

Ford, P. (2003), "Processing Processing," *FTrain,* September 2. Available online: http://www.ftrain.com/ProcessingProcessing.html.

Forlizzi, J., E. Stolterman, and J. Zimmerman (2009), "From Design Research to Theory: Evidence of a Maturing Field," 2889—98, Human-Computer Interaction Institute, School of Computer Design, Carnegie Mellon University. Available online: https://www.academia.edu/2830166/From_design_research_to_theory_Evidence_of_a_maturing_field (accessed August 7, 2017).

Forty, A. (1993), "A Reply to Victor Margolin," *Journal of Design History*, 6 (2), 131–2.

Foster, H. (2002), *Design and Crime (and Other Diatribes)*, New York: Verso.

Foster, H. (ed.) (1983), *The Anti-Aesthetic: Essays on Postmodern Culture*, Port Townsend: Bay Press.

Franciscono, M. (1971), *Walter Gropius and the Creation of the Bauhaus in Weimar: The Ideals and Artistic Theories of its Founding Years,* Chicago: University of Illinois Press.

Frankfurt, H.G. (2005), *On Bullshit*, Princeton, NJ: Princeton University Press.

Frankovits, A. (1984), *Seduced and Abandoned: The Baudrillard Scene*, Glebe, NSW: Stonemoss Services.

Frascara, J. (1988), "Graphic Design: Fine Art or Social Science?," *Design Issues,* 5 (1): 18–29.

Frascara, J. (1995), "Graphic Design: Fine Art or Social Science?," in V. Margolin and R. Buchanan (eds), 44–55, *The Idea of Design: A Design Issues Reader*. Cambridge, MA: MIT Press.

Frascara, J. (1997), *User-centered Graphic Design: Mass Communication and Social Change,* London: Taylor & Francis.

Frascara, J. (2004), *Communication Design: Principles, Methods, and Practice*, New York: Allworth Press.

Frascara, J. (2014), "Graphic Design: Fine Art or Social Science?," *Design Issues,* 5 (1): 18–29.

Frascara, J. (ed.) (2002), *Design and the Social Sciences: Making Connections*, London and New York: Taylor & Francis.

Frascara, J., B. Meurer, J. van Toorn, and D. Winkler (1997), *User-Centred Graphic Design: Mass Communication and Social Change*, London: Taylor & Francis Ltd.

Fraser, N. (1993), "Rethinking the Public Sphere: A Contribution to the Critique of Actually Existing Democracy," in B. Robbins (ed.), *The Phantom Public Sphere*, 1–9, Minneapolis: University of Minnesota Press.

Frayling, C. (1993/4), "Research in Art and Design," *Royal College of Art Research Papers,* 1 (1).

Freeman, L. (2000), "Visualizing Social Networks," *Journal of Social Structure*, 1. Available online: http://www.cmu.edu/joss/content/articles/volume1/Freeman.html.

"Fregio Mecano (Carattere scomponibile)" (1991), in J. Rothenstein and M. Gooding (eds), *Alphabets and Other Signs,* London: Redstone Press.

Frenzel, H.K., ed. (1925), *Gebrauchsgraphik*, 2 (5).

Frenzel, H.K., ed. (1924), *Ludwig Hohlwein, Sein Leben und Werk,* Berlin: Phönix Verlag.

Frenzel, H.K., ed. (1925), "Betrachtungen zur Reichsreklamemesse," *Gebrauchsgraphik,* 1 (9): 1–5.

Frenzel, H.K., ed. (1925), "Vorwort," *Gebrauchsgraphik,* 2 (1).

Frenzel, H.K., ed. (1925), *Gebrauchsgraphik*, 2 (1)

Frenzel, H.K., ed. (1925), *Gebrauchsgraphik*, 2 (3).

Frenzel, H.K., ed. (1925), *Gebrauchsgraphik*, 2 (4).

Frenzel, H.K., ed. (1925), *Gebrauchsgraphik*, 2 (6).

Frenzel, H.K., ed. (1926), "Vorwort," *Gebrauchsgraphik,* 3 (10).

Frenzel, H.K., ed. (1926), *Gebrauchsgraphik*, 3 (12).

Frenzel, H.K., ed. (1926), *Gebrauchsgraphik*, 3 (5).

Frenzel, H.K., ed. (1926), *Gebrauchsgraphik*, 3 (8).

Frenzel, H.K., ed. (1926), *Gebrauchsgraphik*, 3 (9).

Frenzel, H.K., ed. (1927), *Gebrauchsgraphik*, 4 (1).

Frenzel, H.K., ed. (1927), *Gebrauchsgraphik*, 4 (4).

Frenzel, H.K., ed. (1928), "New York After Two Years', *Gebrauchsgraphik,* 5 (9): 63–9.

Frenzel, H.K., ed. (1928), *Gebrauchsgraphik,* 5 (10).

Frenzel, H.K., ed. (1928), *Gebrauchsgraphik,* 5 (7).

Frenzel, H.K., ed. (1930), "How American Advertising Agencies Advertise Themselves," *Gebrauchsgraphik,* 7 (5): 33–45.

Frenzel, H.K., ed. (1930), "Where is Advertising Going?," *Gebrauchsgraphik,* 7 (1).

Frenzel, H.K., ed. (1930), *Gebrauchsgraphik*, 7 (7).

Frenzel, H.K., ed. (1933), *Gebrauchsgraphik*, 10 (1).

Frenzel, H.K., ed. (1933), *Gebrauchsgraphik*, 10 (12).

Frenzel, H.K., ed. (1933), *Gebrauchsgraphik*, 10 (8).

Frenzel, H.K., ed. (1934), "Wrappings and Boxes of the Wards Company, Chicago," *Gebrauchsgraphik,* 11 (3): 12–13.

Frenzel, H.K., ed. (1936), "The Influence of Market Fluctuations on the Demand for Advertising," *Penrose Annual,* 38: 23–6.

Frenzel, H.K., ed. (1936), *Gebrauchsgraphik*, 13 (7).

Frenzel, H.K., ed. (1937), *Gebrauchsgraphik*, 14 (10).

Frenzel, H.K., ed. (1937), *Gebrauchsgraphik*, 14 (11).

Frenzel, H.K., ed. (1938), *Gebrauchsgraphik*, 15 (6).

Frenzel, H.K. (1936), "Ausstellung 'Die Deutsche Werbung,' Essen 1936," *Gebrauchsgraphik,* 13 (10): 16–32.

Friedman, D. (1994), *Dan Friedman: Radical Modernism*, New Haven, CT, and London: Yale University Press.

Friedman, T. (2007), *The World is Flat: A Brief History of the Twenty-first Century*, New York: Farrar, Straus and Giroux.

Friedman, T. (2016), *Thank You for Being Late: An Optimist's Guide to Thriving in the Age of Accelerations,* New York: Farrar, Straus and Giroux.

Fry, B. (2010), "Computational Information Design," *Adaptive Path* UX *Week Conference*, August 24–27. Available online: http://www.youtube.com/watch?v=z-g-cWDnUdU.

Fry, B., Isometricblocks, *BenFry.* Available online: http://benfry.com/isometricblocks/

Fry, F. (2009), *On the Origin of Species: The Preservation of Favoured Traces.* Available online: http://benfry.com/traces/ (accessed July 18, 2011).

Frye, N. (1981), *The Great Code: The Bible and Literature*, New York: Harcourt Brace Jovanovich.

Galyean, T. (1995), "Narrative Guidance of Interactivity," PhD thesis, Massachusetts Institute of Technology.

Gamble, W., R.B. Fishenden, A. Delafons, and H. Spencer, eds (1982), *Penrose Annual*, London: Percy Lund, Humphries & Co.

Garfinkel, H. (1967), *Studies in Ethnomethodology,* Upper Saddle River: Prentice-Hall.

Garland, K. (1964), "First Things First." Available online: http://www.kengarland.co.uk/KG-published-writing/first-things-first/ (accessed December 9, 2013).

Garland, K. (1964), *First Things First Manifesto*, London: Self-published. Available online: http://www.xs4all.nl/~maxb/ftf1964.htm (accessed August 14, 2008).

Garland, K. (1969), "The Design of the London Underground Diagram," *Penrose Annual*, 62 (issue): 68–82.

Garland, K. (1974), "Obituary: Henry C Beck," *Design,* 312 (December): 86.

Garland, K. and R. Poynor (2000), "First Things First Manifesto 2000," *Adbusters, AIGA Journal*; *Blueprint*; *Emigre*; *Eye*; *Form*; *Items. Emigre* (51): cover, http://www.emigre.com/EMag.php?issue=5 (accessed September 3, 2017).

Garrett, M. (1999), Interview with Teal Triggs, London.

Gass, W. (1997), *Habitations of the Word*, New York: Simon & Schuster.

Gaver, W., A. Dunne, and E. Pacenti (1999), "Cultural Probes," *Interactions*, 6: 21–9.

Gayatri Spivak quoted by Rogoff (2001), in I. Rogoff, "Studying Visual Culture," *The Visual Culture Reader*, Nicholas Mirzoeff, ed., 14–26, London: Routledge.

Geiger, M. (1921), "Ästhetik," in P. Hinneberg (ed.), *Systematische Philosophie (Die Kultur der Gegenwart)*, Part 1, Section 6, trans. O. Neumaier in *'What is the Subject of Aesthetics?* 3rd rev. edn. Available online: sowi.iwp.unilinz.ac.at/DIALOG/MITARBEITER/Sub_Aesth.html (accessed August 2004)

George, R.A. (2004), "Conscientious Objector: Why I Can't Vote for Bush," *The New Republic*, October 14.

Gephi Consortium (2010). Available online: http://consortium.gephi.org (accessed August 22, 2011).

Gershon, N. and W. Page (2001), "What Storytelling Can Do for Information Visualization," *Communications of the ACM,* 44 (8): 31–3

Gerstner, K. ([1964] 2007), *Designing Programmes*, Switzerland: Lars Müller Publishers.

Gerstner, K. (2007), *Designing Programmes*, Baden: Lars Müller Publishers.

Gerstner, K. and M. Kutter (1959), *die Neue Graphik,* Teufen: Arthur Niggli.

Gezri, V. (2007), "Helvetica: 50 and Still Faulous," *St. Petersburg Times*, September 20. Available online: http://articles.chicagotribune.com/2007–09–20/features/0709190680_1_typeface-sans-serif-swiss-design.

Gilchrist, I. (2009), "Hip to be Square: Melbourne's modern new logo a chunky move," *MX*, July 22: 1.

Gill, R. (2009), "Our City Must Go for a Song," *Age*, August 8: A2, 7.

Gitelman, L. and V. Jackson (2013), "Introduction," in L. Gitelman (ed.), *"Raw Data" Is an Oxymoron,* Cambridge: MIT Press.

Glossary: Census 2000 Concepts and Definitions. Available online: http://www.singstat.gov.sg/statsres/glossary/population.html#C (accessed September 26, 2010).

Goffman, E. (1966), *Behavior in Public Places: Notes on the Social Organization of Gatherings,* Glencoe: The Free Press.

Goggin, J. (2008), *Most Beautiful Swiss Books,* Bern: Swiss Federal Office Of Cultur.

Goldschmidt, G. (2003), "The Backtalk of Self-Generated Sketches," *Design Issues*, 19 (1): 72–88.

Golec, M. (2000), "A Typography of Impoverishment: D.C. McMurtrie's Reception of European Modernist Typography and an American Depression," *Visible Language*, 34 (3): 264–2.

Golec, M. (2004), "'Doing It Dead Pan' Venturi, Scott Brown and Izenour's *Learning from Las Vegas*," *Visible Language*, 37 (1): 266–87.

Gombrich, E.H. (1960), *Art and Illusion. A Study in the Psychology of Pictorial Representation,* Princeton: Princeton University Press.

Gomez-Palacio, B. and A. Vit (2011), *Graphic Design Referenced: A Visual Guide to the Language, Applications, and History of Graphic Design*, London: Rockport.

Gonzales Crisp, D. (2003), "Toward a Definition of the Decorational," in B. Laurel (ed.), *Real Time. Design Research,* 92–8, Cambridge, MA: MIT Press.

Gonzales Crisp, D. (2009), "Discourse This! Designers and Alternative Critical Writing," *Design and Culture,* 1 (1): 105–20.

Gonzales Crisp, D. (as Cheri Newcastle) (1998), "Speculations," *Émigré* (47): 41–50.

Gonzales Crisp, D. (as Deborah Griffin) (1997a), "Everyday People Play," *Émigré* (41): 12–21.

Gonzales Crisp, D. (as Deborah Griffin) (1997b), "Out of Context: Entrepreneurs, Designists and Other Utopians," *Émigré* (43): 50–63.

Gonzales Crisp, D. and R. Poynor (2008), "A Critical View of Graphic Design History," *Design Observer*, June 2. Available online: http://designobserver.com/feature/a-critical-view-of-graphic-design-history/6827.

Gorman, C.R. (2001), "Reshaping and Rethinking: Recent Feminist Scholarship on Design and Designers," *Design Issues,* 17 (4): 72–88.

Gorz, A. (1982), *Farewell to the Working Class*, trans. M. Sonenscher, London: Pluto Press.

Gorz, A. (1985), *Paths to Paradise*, London: Pluto Press.

Goudy, F. (1977), *Typologia: Studies in Type Design and Type Making*, Berkeley: University of California Press.

Gräff, W. (1929), *Es Kommt der neue Fotograf!*, Berlin: H. Reckendorf.

Graffieti, M., D. Ricci, L. Masud, and M. Porpora, DensityDesign Research Lab (2010), "Tell Them Anything but the Truth: They Will Find Their Own. How We Visualized the Map of the Future with Respect to the Audience of Our Story," *Wired Magazine* (7): 25–31. Available online: http://www.wired.it/extra/mappadelfuturo and http://www.densitydesign.org/research/map-of-the-future/.

Grafton, A. and M. Williams (2009), *Christianity and the Transformation of the Book: Origen, Eusebius, and the Library of Caesarea*, Cambridge: Belknap.

Gray, N. (1986), *A History of Lettering: Creative Experiment and Letter Identity*, Boston: David R. Godine.

Gredinger, P. (2007), "Introduction," in *Designing Programmes*, Zurich: Lars Müller Publishers.

Greenfield, A. (2006), *Everyware: The Dawning Sge of Ubiquitous Computing*, Berkeley: New Riders.

Greenhalgh, P., ed. (1997), *Modernism in Design,* London: Reaktion Books.

Greenhalgh, P. (2000), *Art Nouveau 1890–1914*, London: V&A Publications.

Greenhalgh, P. (2005), *The Modern Ideal: The Rise and Collapse of Idealism in the Visual Arts from the Enlightenment to Postmodernism*, London: Victoria and Albert Museum.

Greiman, A., ed (1994), *AIGA Journal of Graphic Design,* 12 (3).

Gretton, T. (2005), "Signs for Labour-Value in Printed Pictures after the Photomechanical Revolution: Mainstream Changes and Extreme Cases Around 1900," *Oxford Art Journal*, 28 (3): 371–90.

Gromala, D. (as Putch Tu) (1998), "Abject Subjectivities," in *American Center for Design Journal: Remaking History*, 6–11, Chicago: American Center for Design.

Gromala, D. and J.D. Bolter (2005), *Windows and Mirrors: Interaction Design, Digital Art, and the Myth of Transparency*, Cambridge, MA: MIT Press.

Gropius, W. ([1969] 2003), *Program of the Staatliche Bauhaus in Weimar. Bauhaus*, Cambridge, MA: MIT Press.

Grossberg, L. (1997), "Another Boring Day in Paradise: Rock and Roll and the Empowerment of Everyday Life," in K. Gelder and S. Thorton (eds), *The Subcultures Reader*, 477–93, London: Psychology Press.

Grove, J. (2009), "Towards Illustration Theory: Robert Weaver, Harold Rosenberg, and the Action Illustrator?," *Journal of Art Criticism,* 24 (1). Available online: http://sbsuny.academia.edu/JaleenGrove/Papers/453409/Towards_Illustration_Theory_Robert_Weaver_Harold_Rosenberg_and_the_Action_Illustrator.

Guattari, F. (1984), *Molecular Revolution, Psychiatry and Politics*, Harmondsworth: Penguin.

Guattari, F. and G. Deleuze (1983), *Anti-Oepdipus: Capitalism and Schizophrenia*, Minneapolis: University of Minnesota Press.

Guégan, B. (ed.) (1927–39), *Arts et Métiers Graphiques*.

Guégan, B. (ed.) (1930), *Arts et Métiers Graphiques*, 15: 909–13.

Guégan, B. (ed.) (1930), *Arts et Métiers Graphiques*, 16.

Guégan, B. (ed.) (1930), *Arts et Métiers Graphiques*, 19: 46–54.

Guégan, B. (ed.) (1930), *Arts et Métiers Graphiques*, 21: 135–9.

Guégan, B. (ed.) (1930), *Arts et Métiers Graphiques*, 25: 357–64.

Guerrilla Girls (2004), *Art Museum Activity Book,* New York: Printed Matter, Inc.

Haag, C., D. Scheibel, and B. Stephan. Available online: http://lafkon.net/

Habermas, J. (1989), *The Structural Transformation of the Public Sphere: An Inquiry into a Category of Bourgeois Society*, trans. T. Burger and F. Lawrence, Cambridge, MA: MIT Press.

Hacker, A. and C. Dreifus (2010), *Higher Education?: How Colleges Are Wasting Our Money and Failing Our Kids—And What We Can Do About It*, New York: Times Books.

Hadank, O.H.W., ed. (1939), *Gebrauchsgraphik,* 16 (7).

Hagen, L. (1898), "Lady Artists in Germany," *The Studio* 13 (60): 91–9.

Hagmann, S. (2005), "Non Existent Design: Women and the Creation of Type," *Visual Communication,* 4 (2): 186–94.

Hagmann, S., Email Communication with AIGA National Office, New York.

Hall, M. (1986), *Harvard University Press: A History,* Cambridge: Harvard University Press.

Hall, P. (1993), "A Fucked Up World Deserves Fucked Up Type," *Graphics International*, September: 29.

Hall, P. (2008), "Critical Visualization," in P. Antonelli (ed.), *Design and the Elastic Mind,* New York: Museum of Modern Art.

Hall, P. (2011), "Bubbles, Lines, and String: How Information Visualization Shapes Society," in A. Blauvelt and E. Lupton (eds), *Graphic Design: Now in Production,* Minneapolis: Walker Art Center.

Hall, S. (1992), *Culture, Media, Language: Working Papers in Cultural Studies, 1972–79,* London: Routledge.

Hamilton, R. (2011), "Experience Prototyping Methods," *Everything I Know*. Available online: http://everythingiknow.squarespace.com/blog/2011/6/3/experience-prototyping-methods-whats-it-like-to-be-the-servi.html (accessed December 15, 2013).

Hammer, M. (2002), *Ampersand as a Place,* Portland, Maine: DesignInquiry.

Hammersley, B. (2004), "Audible Revolution," *Guardian*, February 11. Available online: https://www.theguardian.com/media/2004/feb/12/broadcasting.digitalmedia (accessed August 5, 2016).

Hansard, T.C. (1825), *Typographia*, London: Baldwin & Co.

Hara, K. (2015), *Ex-Formation*, Zurich: Lars Müller Publishers.

Hardison, O.B. (1967), "The Rhetoric of Hitchcock's Thrillers," in W.R. Robinson (eds), *Man and the Movies*, 137–52, Baton Rouge: Louisiana State University Press.

Harley, J.B. (2001), "Maps, Knowledge and Power," in P. Laxton (ed.), *The New Nature of Maps: Essays in the History of Cartography*, 67, Baltimore: Johns Hopkins University Press.

Harling, R. (ed.) with James Shand and Ellic Howe (1936), *Typography 1*. London: The Shenval Press.

Harling, R. (1939), *Typography,* London: James Shand at The Shenval Press.

Harper, C. (1893), "Drawing for Reproduction by Process: Lithographic Chalk on Various Papers," *The Studio*, 2 (9): 99–100.

Harper, C. (1894), *A Practical Handbook of Drawing for Modern Methods of Reproduction*, London: Chapman and Hall.

Harris, D. (1997), *The Rise and Fall of Gay Culture*, New York: Hyperion,

Harris, J. (2001), *The New Art History: A Critical Introduction*, London and New York: Routledge.

Hartzell, J. (2006), Personal conversation with Piers Carey, July 18.

Harvey, D. (1980), *The Condition of Postmodernity,* Oxford: Blackwell.

Hassan, R. (1976), "Public Housing," *Singapore: Society in Transition*, Kuala Lumpur: Oxford University Press.

Haycock Makela, L. (1991), "Three Days at Cranbrook," *Émigré* (19): 18–19.

Hayles, K. (2002a), *Writing Machines*, Cambridge, MA: MIT Press Mediawork Pamphlet Series.

Hayles, K. (2002b), *Writing Machines*, Cambridge, MA: MIT Press Mediawork Pamphlets Series, Lexicon Linkmap. Available online: http://mitpress.mit.edu/mediawork (link, defunct, accessed August 14, 2008) and https://archive.org/stream/writing_machines/Hayles_N_Katherine_Writing_Machines_djvu.txt (accessed September 3, 2017).

Hayles, N.K. (2005), *My Mother Was a Computer: Digital Subjects and Literary Texts*, 1st edn, Chicago: University of Chicago Press.

Heafford, M. (1967), *Pestalozzi*, London: Methuen.

Hebdige, D. (1979), *Subculture: The Meaning of Style*, London: Methuen.

Hebdige, D. (1988), "The Bottom Line on Planet One: Squaring Up to *The Face*," in *Hiding in the Light*, London: Comedia/ Routledge.

Hébert, M-N. (2014), "Re-envisioning Graphic Design as a Dialogic Practice: An Investigation into the Constructive Potential of Disruption within Aesthetic Practices," MA Thesis, York University, Toronto, Canada.

Heidegger, M. (1927), *Sein und Zeit*, Tuebingen: Max Niemeyer.

Heinen, U. (2008), "Bildrhetorik der Frühen Neuzeit—Gestaltungstheorie der Antike. Paradigmen zur Vermittlung von Theorie und Praxis im Design," in G. Joost and A. Scheuermann (eds), *Design als Rhetorik*, 143–89, Basel: Birkhäuser.

Helfand, J. (2001), *Minimalism/Maximalism: The New Screen Aesthetic*, New York: Princeton Architectural Press.

Helfand, J. (2001), *Screen: Essays on Graphic Design, New Media and Visual Culture*, New York: Princeton Architectural Press.

Heller, S. (1984), "Towards an Historical Perspective." *AIGA Journal of Graphic Design*, 2 (4): 5.

Heller, S., ed. (1985), "The History of Graphic Design: Charting a Course," *AIGA Journal of Graphic Design*, 3 (4).

Heller, S. (1992), "Yes, Virginia, There is a Graphic Design History," *AIGA Journal of Graphic Design*, 10 (1): 4.

Heller, S. (1993), "Criticizing Criticism: Too Little and Too Much," *AIGA Journal of Graphic Design,* 11 (4).

Heller, S. (1993), "The Cult of the Ugly," *Eye*, 3 (9): 52–9.

Heller, S. (1994), "Raising Voices," *Émigré* (31).

Heller, S. (1995), "Design (Or Is It War?) Is Hell," *Émigré* (33): 48.

Heller, S., ed. (2002), *Graphic Design Reader*, New York: Allworth Press.

Heller, S. (2005), *Wolfgang Weingart: Making the Young Generation Nuts,* Voice: AIGA Journal of Design.

Heller, S. (2008), *Iron Fists: Branding the 20th-Century Totalitarian State*, London and New York: Phaidon Press.

Heller, S. and M. Arisman (2000), *The Education of an Illustrator,* New York: Allworth Press.

Heller, S. and G. Ballance (2001), "A Danziger Syllabus" in S. Heller (ed.), *The Education of a Graphic Designer*, 333, New York: Allworth Press.

Heller, S. and G. Ballance, eds (2001), "The Case for Critical History," in *Graphic Design History*, 2nd edn, 94, New York: Allworth Press.

Heller, S. and G. Ballance, eds (2001), *Graphic Design History*, New York: Allworth Press.

Heller, S. and S. Chwast (1988), *Graphic Style: From Victorian to Postmodern*, New York: Harry N. Abrams.

Heller, S. and P.B. Meggs, eds (2001), *Texts on Type: Critical Writings on Typography*, New York: Allworth Press.

Heller, S., and V. Vienne, eds (2003), *Citizen Designer: Perspectives on Design Responsibility*, New York: Allworth Press.

Helmer, M. (2015), "Balance," *Marcel Helmer*. Available online: http://www.marcelhelmer.de/ (accessed August 3, 2015).

Helvetica (2007), [Film] Dir. Gary Hustwit, USA: Swiss Dots

Henry, T. (1984), "Punk and the Avant-Garde Art," *Journal of Popular Culture*, 17 (4): 30–6.

Herdeg, W. (1944), *Graphis*, 1 (1).

Herf, J. (1984), *Reactionary Modernism, Technology, Culture and Politics in Weimar and the Third Reich*, Cambridge: Cambridge University Press.

"Heritage," (1990), *Émigré* (14).

Herman, A., J. Hadlaw and T. Swiss (2015), "Introduction," in *Theories of the Mobile Internet: Materialities and Imaginaries*, 1–14, London: Routledge.

Hernández, V. (2011), "Argentina Marks 'Night of the Pencils'," *BBC World*. Available online: http://www.bbc.co.uk/news/world-latin-america–14910859 (accessed on November 23, 2015).

Heskett, J. (1978), "Art and Design in Nazi Germany," *History Workshop Journal*, 6: 139–53.

Heskett, J. (1980), "Modernism and Archaism in Design in the Third Reich," *Block*, 3: 13–24.

Hiatt, C. (1893), "The Collecting of Posters: A New Field for Connoisseurs," *The Studio*, 1 (1): 61–4.

Hiatt, C. (1895), *Picture Posters; A Short History of the Illustrated Placard*, London: Bell.

Highmore, B. ed (2002), *The Everyday Life Reader,* London: Routledge.

Hill, C.A. and M. Helmers, ed. (2004), *Defining Visual Rhetorics*, New Jersey and London: Lawrence Erlbaum Associates.

Hinz, B. (1979), *Art in the Third Reich,* Blackwell, Oxford.

Hobsbawm, E. and T. Ranger, eds (1983), *The Invention of Tradition*, Cambridge: Cambridge University Press.

Hocks, M.E. and M.R. Kendrick (2005), *Eloquent Images: Word and Image in the Age of New Media,* 1st edn, Cambridge, MA: MIT Press.

Holland, D.K., ed. (2001), *Design Issues: How Graphic Design Informs Society*, New York: Allworth Press.

Hollis, R. (1994), *Graphic Design: A Concise History*, London and New York: Thames and Hudson.

Hollis, R. (2001), "Karl Gerstner: Principles Not Recipes," *Dot Dot Dot*, 4.

Hollis, R. (2006), *Swiss Graphic Design: The Origins and Growth of an International Style, 1920–1965*, New Haven: Yale University Press.

Hollis, R. (2008), "Karl Gerstner: Principles Not Recipes," *Back Cover*, 1.

Hölscher, E. (1938), "Container Corporation of America," *Gebrauchsgraphik*, 15 (7): 19–28.

Hölscher, E. (1938), "Herbert Bayer," *Gebrauchsgraphik*, 15 (6): 2–16.

Hong Kong Designers Association (1998), *HKDA Members Profile*, Hong Kong: Hong Kong Designers Association.

Hoogslag, N. (2011), "The Significance of a Modest Medium," *Varoom*, 17: 56–8.

Hoogslag, N. (2012), "Think Editorial Illustration: Workshop." Available online: http://www.hoogslag.nl/research/think-editorial-illustration-2 (accessed January 2, 2017).

Hooks, B. (1991), "Narratives of Struggle," in P. Mariani (ed.), *Critical Fictions: The Politics of Imaginative Writing*, 53–61, Seattle: Bay Press.

Horsham, M. (1999), "The Value of Confusion," *Stealing Beauty* exhibition catalogue, London: ICA.

Hostettler, R. (1969), *Technical Terms of the Printing Industry*, St. Gallen: Rudolf Hostettler.

Houfe, S. (1997), *Fin de Siècle*, London: Barrie and Jenkins.

Houghton, H.A. and D.M. Willows (1987), *The Psychology of Illustration: Basic Research,* New York: Springer-Verlag.

Hughes, A., K. Moore, and N. Kataria (2011), "Innovation in Public Sector Organisations," Nesta. Available online: http://www.nesta.org.uk/publications/innovation-public-sector-organisations (accessed March 28, 2013).

Hume, D. ([1757] 1965), "Of the Standard of Taste," *Aesthetics*, New York: Jerome Stolnitz McMillan.

Hurlburt, A. (1978), *Grid: A Modular System for the Production of Newspapers, Magazines, and Books*, New York: Van Nostrand Reinholt Co.

Hustwitt, G. (2007), *Helvetica*, London: Swiss Dots Ltd.

Hutcheon, L. (1989), *The Politics of Postmodernism*, London and New York: Routledge.

Hutchings, R.S. (ed.) (1964), *Alphabet: International Annual of Letterforms,* England: The Kynoch Press.

Illustration Daily. Available online: http://www.illustrationdaily.nl/.

Innis, H.A. (1950), *Empire and Communications*, Oxford: Clarendon Press

Innis, H.A. (1951), *The Bias of Communication*, Toronto: University of Toronto Press.

Innis, H.A. (2000), "The Communication Thought of Harold Adams Innis (1894–1952)," in R.E. Babe, *Canadian Communication Thought: Ten Foundational Writers*, Ch. 3, Toronto: University of Toronto Press.

International Free Magazine 2 (1985), Swatch magazine advertising supplement to *The Face*.

"Introducing the *Guardian* iPad edition—video" (2011). Available online: http://www.guardian.co.uk/technology/video/2011/oct/10/guardian-ipad-edition-video.

Irwin, T. (2015), "Transition Design: A Proposal for a New Area of Design Practice, Study and Research," *Design and Culture,* 7 (2): 229–46.

Ischia, T. (2012), "The Rise of the Riso," March 4. Available online: desktopmag.com.au/features/the-rise-of-the-riso/#.WSx318kpCYU (accessed May 29, 2017).

Isin, E. (2015), "Framing the Future Citizen," *The Future Citizen Guide*, 12–21, London: Tate.

Is That All There Is? (1980), [Song] Cristina, ZE Records.

Jameson, F. (1984), "Foreword," in J-F. Lyotard, *The Postmodern Condition: A Report on Knowledge*, vii–xxii, Manchester: Manchester University Press.

Jameson, F. (1984), "Post Modernism, or, the Cultural Logic of Late Capitalism," *New Left Review*, 146: 59–92.

Jansen, Y., P. Dragicevic, and J-D. Fekete (2013), "Evaluating the Efficiency of Physical Visualizations," in *Proceedings of the 2013 Annual Conference on Human Factors in Computing Systems (CHI 2013),* ACM: 2593–602.

Janser, A. (2004), *Frische Schriften/Fresh Type,* Zürich: Museum Für Gestaltung.

Jay, M. (2005), "Introduction to Show and Tell," *Journal of Visual Culture*, 4 (2): 139–43.

Jay, M. (2005), [Interview], in M. Dikovitskaya (ed.), *Visual Culture: The Study of the Visual After the Cultural Turn*, Cambridge, MA: MIT Press.

Jay, M. (2007), "That Visual Turn: The Advent of Visual Culture," *Journal of Visual Culture*, 1 (1): 87–92.

Jencks, C. (1992), "The Post-modern Agenda," in C. Jencks (ed.), *The Post-Modern Reader,* London: Academy Editions.

Jenkins, H., et al. (2009), *Confronting the Challenges of Participatory Culture: Media Education for the 21st Century,* Cambridge, MA: MIT Press.

Jerry, G.H. (2000), *The Tacit Mode, Michael Polanyi's Postmodern Philosophy,* New York: State University of New York Press.

Jiayang, L. (2000), "On Design Education," in *Art and Design*, 29–34, Beijing: Art and Design Publishing House.

John, T. (2006), *In the Bubble: Designing in a Complex World*, Cambridge, MA: MIT Press.

Johnson, C. (1955), *Harold and the Purple Crayon*, New York: Harper & Brothers.

Johnson, J. (1824), *Typographia or the Printers' Instructor*, London: Longman, Hunt, Rees, Orme, Brown & Green.

Johnston, M. (2009), [No title available]. *Herald Sun,* July 24: 3.

Johnston, M. (2009), "Madness . . . and they haven't finished spending yet," *Herald Sun,* July 23: 7.

Jonas, W. (2012), "Exploring the Swampy Ground," in W. Jonas and S. Grand (eds), *Mapping Design Research*, 11–41, Basel: Birkhäuser.

Jones, J.C. (1970), *Design Methods*, New York: Wiley.

Jones, P. (2017), *The Bones of the Book: Schematic Structure and Meaning Made from Books*, PhD Thesis, London: London College of Communication, University of the Arts.

Joost, G. and A. Scheuermann (2006), "Design as Rhetoric. Basic Principles for Design Research," in Swiss Design Network (eds), *Drawing New Territories*, 153–66, Zurich: SDN.

Joost, G. and A. Scheuermann, eds (2008), *Design als Rhetorik. Grundlagen, Positionen, Fallstudien*, Basel: Birkhäuser.

Jubert, R. (2006), *Typography and Graphic Design: From Antiquity to the Present*, English edn, Paris: Flammarion.

Julier, G. (2006), "From Visual Culture to Design Culture," *Design Issues*, 22 (1): 76.

Julier, G. (2014), *The Culture of Design*, London: Sage.

Julier, G. and V. Narotzky (1998), "The Redundancy of Design History," *Leeds Metropolitan University*.

Julier, O. (1994), "The Thames and Hudson Encyclopedia of 20th Century Design and Designers," *The Art Book*, 1 (3): 17.

Jürgen Kleindienst (1977), *Wem Gehört die Welt? Kunst und Gesellschaft in der Weimarer Republik,* Berlin: Neue Gesellschaft für Bildende Kunst.

Jury, D. (2004), *About Face—Reviving the Rules of Typography*, Brighton: Rotovision.

Kalman, T. (1990), "Modernism & Eclecticism" symposium, *School of Visual Arts in New York City*.

Kalman, T. (1991), "I Don't Think of You as Black," *International Design*, 18 (2): 56–9.

Kämpfer, F. (1985), *Der Rote Keil: das politische Plakat Theorie und Ideologie,* Berlin: Gebr. Mann Verlag.

Kandinsky, W. (1979), *Point and Line to Plane*, New York: Dover.

Kane, J. (2002), *A Type Primer,* London: Laurence King Publishing.

Kant, I. ([1781] 1952), *The Critique of Judgement*, trans. J.C. Meredith, Oxford: Oxford University Press.

Kaplan, G. (2009), Interview with Leslie Atzmon.

Kapr, A. (1983), *The Art of Lettering*, Munich: K.G. Saur.

Kaptelinin, V. and B.A. Nardi (2006), *Acting with Technology. Activity Theory and Interaction Design*, Cambridge, MA: MIT Press.

Keats, J. (1819), "Ode on a Grecian Urn," Anonymous.

Keedy, J. (1995), "An Interview with Rick Poynor," *Emigre*, 33: 35.

Keeton, C. (2007), "Is the Aids Message Getting Through?," *Sunday Times,* March 25–31: 6.

Kelley, R.R. (1977), *American Wood Type, 1828–1900*, New York: Da Capo Press.

Kemp, S. (2001), "BHP spills the goods on new logo and its profits," *Age*, August 21: 1.

Kenney, K. and Scott, L.M. (2003), "A Review on the Visual Rhetoric Literature," in L.M. Scott and R. Batra, *Persuasive Imagery*, 17–56, Mahwah, NJ and London: Lawrence Erlbaum Associates.

Kimbell, L. (2013), "The Object Strikes Back: An Interview with Graham Harman," *Design and Culture,* 5 (1), 103–17.

King, E. (2006), "Illustrated Guardian," *Varoom,* 8.

Kinross, R. (1986), "Semiotics and Designing," *Information Design Journal*, 4: 192.

Kinross, R. (1990), "*Émigré* Graphic Designers in Britain: Around the Second World War and Afterwards," *Journal of Design History,* 3 (1): 35–59.

Kinross, R. (1992), "Conversation with Richard Hollis on Graphic Design History," *Journal of Design History,* 5 (1): 73–90.

Kinross, R. (1992), *Modern Typography: An Essay in Critical History,* London: Hyphen Press.

Kinross, R. (1993), "Design History: No Critical Dimension," *AIGA Journal of Graphic Design*, 11 (1): 7.

Kinross, R. (1994), *Fellow Readers: Notes on Multiplied Language*, London: Hyphen Press.

Kirkham, P. (2000), "Women Designers in the USA, 1900–2000: Diversity and Difference," *Studies in the Decorative Arts*, 9 (1): special issue.

Kirkham, P., ed. (2000), *Women Designers in the USA, 1900–2000*, New Haven: Yale University Press.

Kirsh, D. (1995), "The Intelligent Use of Space," *Artificial Intelligence*, 73 (1–2): 31–68.

Kittler, F. ([1986] 1999), *Gramophone, Film, Typewriter*, trans. G. Winthrop-Young and M. Wutz, Stanford: Stanford University Press.

Klanten, R., S. Ehmann, N. Bourquin, and T. Tissot, eds (2010), *Data Flow 2: Visualizing Information in Graphic Design,* Berlin: Gestalten.

Klanten, R., S. Ehmann, and M. Hubner, eds (2008), *Tactile: High Touch Visuals*, Berlin: Gestalten.

Klanten, R., S. Ehmann, M. Hübner, and A. Sinofzik, eds (2012), *High Touch: Tactile Design and Visual Explorations,* Berlin: Gestalten.

Kolko, J. (2015), "Design Thinking Comes of Age," *Harvard Business Review,* 93 (3): 66–71.

Kostelnick, C. (1989), "Visual Rhetoric. A Reader-Oriented Approach to Graphics and Designs," *The Technical Writing Teacher*, 16: 77–88.

Kraus, J. (2009), *All the Art That's Fit to Print (and Some That Wasn't): Inside the New York Times Op-Ed Page*, Reprint edn, Columbia: Columbia University Press.

Krauss. R. (1987), "1967/1987: Genealogies of Art and Theory," in H. Foster, ed. *Dia Art Foundation: Discussions in Contemporary Culture*, Seattle: Bay Press.

Krebs, V. (2008), "Finding Go-To People and Subject Matter Experts [SME]," *Orgnet*. Available online: http://www.orgnet.com/experts.html (accessed July 11, 2011).

Kress, G. and T. van Leeuwen (2001), *Multimodal Discourse: The Modes and Media of Contemporary Communication,* London: Hodder Arnold.

Kress, G. and T. van Leeuwen (2006), *Reading Images: The Grammar of Visual Design*, 2nd edn, New York: Routledge.

Kulkarni, S. (2013), Email Communication with Mohor Ray, December 13.

Kulture Shop (2013), Press Release.

Kundera, M. (1984), *The Unbearable Lightness of Being,* New York: Harper & Row.

Kunst im Exil in Großbritannien 1933–1945 (1986), catalogue, Neue Gesellschaft für Bildende Kunst, Berlin.

Kunz, W. (1998), *Typography: Macro and Micro Aesthetics,* Switzerland: Verlag Niggli AG.

Kuo, E.C.Y. (1984), "Mass Media and Language Planning: Singapore's 'Speak Mandarin' Campaign," *Journal of Communication*, 32 (2): 25–6.

L., K. (1934), "Jean Carlu," *Gebrauchsgraphik*, 12 (1): 42–9.

Lab. Available online: http://mlab.uiah.fi/www/research/doctoral_studies/<ill/>_journals/ (accessed June 1, 2007).

Lacan, J. (2004), *Ecrits: A Selection,* New York: W.W. Norton & Co.

Lacan, J. and D. Porter (1997), *The Ethics of Psychoanalysis, 1959–1960*, New York: W.W. Norton & Co.

Ladefoged, J. (2010), "How a Soccer Star is Made," *The New York Times,* June 6. Available online: http://www.nytimes.com/201%6/06/magazine/06Soccer-t.html?pagewanted=all.

Lahey, K. (2009), "Shades of the Yellow Peril as Melbourne gets logo makeover," *Age*, July 23: 3.

Laing, D. (1997), "Listening to Punk," in K. Gelder and S. Thornton (eds), 406–19, *The Subcultures Reader*, London and New York: Routledge.

Lambert, C. (1999), "The Stirring of Sleeping Beauty," *Harvard Magazine,* 101 (1). Available online: http://www.harvardmag.com/issues/so99/beauty/html (accessed April 2015).

Landor (1996), Available online: http://www.landor.com (accessed November 2009).

Landow, G. (1971), *The Aesthetic and Critical Theories of John Ruskin*, Princeton: Princeton University Press.

Lanier, J. (2006), "Digital Maoism: The Hazards of the New Online Collectivism," *The Edge*, May 29. Available online: https://www.edge.org/conversation/jaron_lanier-digital-maoism-the-hazards-of-the-new-online-collectivism.

Lanier, J. (2011), *You Are Not a Gadget: A Manifesto,* London: Penguin.

Laplanche, J. and J.B. Pontalis (1973), *The Language of Psychoanalysis,* trans. D. Nicholson-Smith, New York: W.W. Norton.

Laranjo, F. (2017), "Opinion: Delusion and Data-Driven Design," *Creative Review.* Available online: https://www.creativereview.co.uk/delusion-data-driven-design/ (accessed April 24, 2017).

Latimer, D. (1984), "Jameson and Post Modernism," *New Left Review*, November to December.

Latour, B. (1992), "Where are the Missing Masses," in W.E. Bijker and J. Law (eds), *Shaping Technology/Building Society: Studies in Sociotechnical change*, 225–58, Cambridge, MA: MIT Press.

Latour, B. (2008), "A Cautious Prometheus? A Few Steps Toward a Philosophy of Design (with Special Attention to Peter Sloterdijk)," Networks of Design meeting of the Design History Society, Cornwall, UK, September 3). Available online: http://bruno-latour.fr/articles/article/112-DESIGN-CORNWALL.pdf.

Lau, F. (1999), *Looking Back: Freeman Lau's Poster Design,* Kan and Lau Design Consultants, Hong Kong: Hong Kong Arts Development Council.

Laurel, B. (2003), *Design Research: Methods and Perspectives*, Cambridge, MA: MIT Press.

Lave, J. and E. Wenger (1991), *Situated Learning: Legitimate Peripheral Participation*, Cambridge: Cambridge University Press.

Lavin, M. (2001), "Portfolio: Women and Design," *Clean New World*, Cambridge, MA: MIT Press.

"Leading Lights on Design" (2004), Institute of Design, *National, Institute of Design*, India.

LCC (London College of Communication) (2012), "Join the conscientious communicators community at LCC (Lightgeist Media)," University of the Arts London. Available online: http://blogs.arts.ac.uk/london-college-of-communication/2012/10/19/join-the-conscientious-communicators-community-at-lcc/ (accessed January 5, 2013).

LEDLaboratory (2014), "View Book." Law + Environment + Design Laboratory. Available online: http://srishti.ac.in/ledlab/wp-content/uploads/2014/04/LED_Viewbook_finalx.pdf

Lee, K.Y. (1979), "Mandarin or Dialect?," *Straits Times* [Singapore], November 24.

Lees-Maffei, G. and D. Huppatz (2017), "A Gathering of Flowers: On Design Anthologies," *The Design Journal,* 20 (4): 477–91.

Lehtonen, M. (2000), *The Cultural Analysis of Texts,* Thousand Oaks: Sage.

Leishman, D. (2010), *Cross-Media Communications: An Introduction to the Art of Creating Integrated Media Experiences; Will Internet Narrative Art Ever Grow Up?,* Pittsburgh: ETC Press.

Leontiev, A.N. (1978), *Activity, Consciousness, and Personality,* Hillsdale: Prentice-Hall.

Leontiev, A.N. (1981), *Problems of the Development of the Mind,* Moscow: Progress.

Lethalin, H. (1993), "The Archeology of the Art Director? Some Examples of Art Direction in
    Mid-Nineteenth-Century British Publishing," *Journal of Design History*, 6 (4): 229–46.

Levinas, E. (1982), *L'Au-Dela Du Verset: Lectures et Discours Talmudiques*, Paris: Les Éditions de Minuit.

Levinas, E. (1994), *Beyond the Verse: Talmudic Readings and Lectures*, Bloomington: Indiana University Press.

Levine, S. (2008), *Lacan Reframed: Interpreting Key Thinkers for the Arts (Contemporary Thinkers Reframed): A
    Guide for the Arts Student,* London: I.B. Tauris.

Levrant de Bretteville, S. (1973), "Some Aspects of Design from the Perspective of a Woman Designer,"
    Icographic, 6: 6.

Lewis, F. (2001), *Touch: Graphic Design with Tactile Appeal,* Gloucester: Rockport Publishers.

Lewis, J. (1963), *Typography: Basic Principles,* London: Studio Books.

Li, T. (1999), *Tommy Li: My Work My Words,* Hong Kong.

Lia Block, F. and H. Carlip (1998), *Zine Scene: The Do It Yourself Guide to Zines,* Los Angeles: Girl Press.

Linotype Library. Available online: http://www.linotype.com/fontdesigners.html (accessed January 4, 2005).

Lipps, A. and E. Lupton (2015), *Beauty—Cooper Hewitt Design Triennial*, New York: Cooper Hewitt Publications.

Lissitzky-Kuppers, S. (1968), *El Lissitzky: Life Letters Texts,* London: Thames & Hudson.

Lockton, D., D. Harrison and N.A. Stanton (2010), "Design with intent toolkit: 101 patterns for influencing
    behaviour through design," *Requisite Variety*. Available online: http://requisitevariety.co.uk/
    design-with-intent-toolkit/ (accessed December 9, 2013).

Loftus, E. (1994), "Tricked by Memory," in J. Jeffrey and G. Edwall (eds), *Memory and History: Essays on Recalling
    and Interpreting Experience*, 17–32, Lanham: University Press of America.

Logan, F. (1950), "Kindergarten and Bauhaus," *College Art Journal*, 10 (1): 36–43.

Logan, N. (1985), Interview in the *The Observer Colour Supplement*, January.

"Logo not a-go-go," (2008), *Australian*, August 21: 26.

Loi, D. (2005), *The Book of Probes. Lavoretti Per Bimbi: Playful Triggers as key to foster collaborative practices and
    workspaces where people learn, Wonder and play,* PhD diss., RMIT University, School of Business, Melbourne.

Lotz, W. (1929), "Werkbundausstellung Film und Foto 1929," *Die Form,* 9.

Luckombe, P. ([1771] 1965), *Concise History of the Origin and Progress of Printing*, London: Gregg Press Ltd.

Luckombe, P. (1771), *Concise History of the Origin and Progress of Printing*, London: W. Adlard and J. Browne.

Luidl, P. and H. Helmut (1985), *Typographical Ornaments,* New York: Blanford Press.

Lukas, B. (2009), "Madness . . . And They Haven't Finished Spending Yet," *Herald Sun,* July 24: 37.

Lunenfeld, P. (2003), "Preface: The Design Cluster," in B. Laurel (ed.), *Design Research: Methods and
    Perspectives*, 10–15, Cambridge, MA: MIT Press.

Lupton, E. (1999), "Graphic Design in the Urban Landscape," in J. Rothschild (ed.), *Design and Feminism:
    Re-Visioning Spaces, Places, and Everyday Things*, New Brunswick: Rutgers University Press.

Lupton, E. (2000), "Women Graphic Designers," in P. Kirkham (ed.), *Women Designers in the USA, 1900–2000:
    Diversity and Difference*, New Haven: Yale University Press. Available online: http://www.elupton.com/index.

Lupton, E. (2004), *Thinking with Type: A Critical Guide for Designers, Writers, Editors and Students*, New York:
    Princeton Architectural Press.

Lupton, E. (2008), "Women Graphic Designers," in B. Gomez-Palacio and A. Vit, *Women of Design. Influence and
    Inspiration from the Original Trailblazers to the New Groundbreakers*, Cincinnati: HOW Books.

Lupton, E. and J.C. Phillips (2011), *Graphic Design Thinking: Beyond Brainstorming,* New York: Architectural Press.

Lyon, B. (2006), "Opte Project Map of the Internet," in J. Abrams and P. Hall, *Else/Where: Mapping—New
    Cartographies of Networks and Territories,* Minneapolis: University of Minnesota Design Institute.

Lyotard, J-F. (1984), "The Sublime and the Avant Garde," *Art Forum*, 22 (8): 36–43.

Lyotard, J-F. (1984), *The Postmodern Condition: A Report on Knowledge*, vii–xxii, Manchester: Manchester University Press.

MacDonald, K. (2012), The "Life in a Day" Trailer, *Life in a Day*. Available online: https://www.youtube.com/user/lifeinaday (accessed June 3, 2014).

MacDonald, S. (1970), *The History and Philosophy of Art Education*, London: University of London Press.

Macfall, H. (1928), *Aubrey Beardsley: The Man and His Work*, London: John Lane.

MacGowen, S. (1976), *Bondage*, 1.

Maeda, J. (2017), "Design in Tech Report 2017." Available online: https://designintechreport.files.wordpress.com/2017/03/dit–2017–1–0–6-smallest.pdf (accessed May 1, 2017).

Mafundikwa, S. (2004), *Afrikan Alphabets: The Story of Writing in Afrika,* New York: Mark Batty Publisher.

Mainberger, G. (1989), "Transformation der Rhetorik ins Design," in H. Holzhey and J-P. Leyvraz (eds), *Studia Philosophica*, 48: 147–61.

Malasauskas, R. (2006/7), "Life After Life and After: An Interview with George Maciunas," *Dot Dot Dot* 13: 93–102.

Maldonado, T. (1958), "New Developments in Industry and the Training of the Designer," *Ulm,* 2 (October): 25–40.

Maldonado, T. (1970), *La Speranza Progettuale. Ambiente e società*, Turin: Einaudi.

Maldonado, T. (1977), "Vanguardia y Racionalidad. Artículos, ensayos y otros escritos: 1946–1974," *Colección Comunicación Visual*, Barcelona: Editorial Gustavo Gili.

Maldonado, T. (1963), *Ist das Bauhaus aktuell?*, Ulm School for Design, Ulm, Germany. *Ulm*, 8/9.

Male, A. (2007), *Illustration: A Theoretical & Contextual Perspective*, 1st edn, Lausanne: Ava Publishing.

Malone, T.W. (1983), "How do People Organize their Desks?," *ACM Trans. Inf. Syst.*, 1: 99–112.

Malpass, M. (2017), *Critical Design in Context: History, Theory, and Practices,* London: Bloomsbury.

Malsy V., P. Teufel, and F. Gejko, eds (2007), *Helmut Schmid: Design is Attitude,* Switzerland: Birkhäuser.

Manfra, L. (2005), "Research—Its Role in North American Design Education," *Metropolis Magazine*, 10: 132–6. Available online: http://www.metropolismag.com/August-2005/School-Survey-2005/ (accessed April 20, 2008).

Manovich, L. (2002a), "Generation Flash." Available online: manovich.net/index.php/projects/generation-flash (accessed July 22, 2017).

Manovich, L. (2002b), *The Language of New Media,* Cambridge, MA: MIT Press.

Manzini, E. (1999), "Strategic Design for Sustainability: Towards a New Mix of Products and Services," *Proceedings First International Symposium on Environmentally Conscious Design and Inverse Manufacturing*, IEEE, 434–7.

Manzini, E. (2015), *Design, When Everybody Designs: An Introduction to Design for Social Innovation*, Cambridge, MA, MIT Press.

Marcus, G. (1989), *Lipstick Traces: A Secret History of the Twentieth Century*, London: Secker & Warburg.

Marcuse, H. (1966), *One Dimensional Man*, Boston: Beacon Press.

Marggraff, G. (1938), *Gebrauchsgraphik,* 15 (10).

Margolin, V. (1979), "The Visual Rhetoric of Propaganda," *Information Design Journal*, 1: 107–22.

Margolin, V. (1992), "Design History or Design Studies: Subject Matter and Methods," *Design Studies*, 13 (2): 104–16.

Margolin, V. (1994), "Narrative Problems of Graphic Design History," *Visible Language*, 28 (3): 233–43.

Margolin, V. (1997), *The Struggle for Utopia: Rodchenko, Lissitzky, Moholy-Nagy 1917–1946*, Chicago and London: University of Chicago Press.

Margolin, V. (2002), *The Politics of the Artificial: Essays on Design and Design Studies*, Chicago and London: University of Chicago Press.

Margolis, J. and A. Fisher (2002), *Unlocking the Clubhouse: Women in Computing*, Cambridge, MA: MIT Press.

Marien, M.W. (1997), *Photography and its Critics: A Cultural History 1839–1900*, Cambridge: Cambridge University Press.

Marsh, E.E. and M.D. White (2003), "A Taxonomy of Relationships between Images and Text," *Journal of Documentation,* 59 (6): 647–72.

Marshall, T. (2014), "Afterword: The Designer and the Designed," in S. Yelavich and B. Adams (eds), *Design as Future Making*, London: Bloomsbury.

Mau, B. (2000), *Life Style*, London: Phaidon.

Mau, B. and J. Leonard (2004), *Massive Change/Institute Without Boundaries*, London: Phaidon Press.

Maurer, L., R. Wouters, J. Puckey, and E. Paulus (2008), *Conditional Design*. Available online: http://conditionaldesign.org/

Maviyane-Davies, C., *Design for the World*. Available online: www.designfortheworld.org.

May, M.G. (1909), "Appendix," *Special Reports on Educational Subjects*, 22: 137–251.

May, M.G. (1909), "The Provision Made in Germany and Switzerland for the Care of Children Under the Compulsory School Age," *Special Reports on Educational Subjects*, 22: 137–251.

Mazé, R. (2009), "Critical of What?/Kritiska mot vad?," in M. Ericson, M. Frostner, Z. Kyes, S. Teleman, and J. Williamsson (eds), *Iaspis Forum on Design and Critical Practice—The Reader*, 378–98, Berlin: Sternberg Press/Iaspis.

McCarthy, S. (2013), *The Designer As . . .*, Netherlands: BIS Publishers.

McCarthy, T. (1978), *The Critical Theory of Jürgen Habermas*, Cambridge, MA: MIT Press.

McCauley, E. (1994), *Industrial Madness: Commercial Photography in Paris 1848–1871*, New Haven: Yale University Press.

McCoy, K. (1993), "Shedding Paradigms (a Letter to the Editor)," *Eye,* 3 (10): 3.

McCoy, K. (2005), *Another 60s Revolution: Rob Roy Kelly brings Swiss design education to the U.S. at the Kansas City Art Institute 1964–1974*, AIGA Conference, Schools of Thought 2.

McDonough, W. (2002), *Cradle to Cradle: Renaming the Way We Make Things*, New York: Farrar, Straus and Giroux.

McDonough, W. (2013), "Driving sustainable transformation via the power of design," *Guardian*, August 19. Available online: http://www.theguardian.com/sustainable-business/sustainable-transformation-power-design (accessed October 1, 2014).

McGuire, E. (2009), "Focus," *Herald Sun*, July 26: 70.

McIntosh, A. (1965), "Typewriter Composition and Standardization in Information Printing," *Printing Technology,* 9 (1): 68.

McKay, G. (1996), *Senseless Acts of Beauty: Cultures of Resistance,* New York: Verso.

McKay, G. (1998), *DIY Culture: Party & Protest in Nineties Britain,* New York: Verso.

McKeon, R., (1979), *Objective Knowledge: An Evolutionary Approach*, Oxford: Oxford University Press.

McLaughlin, T. (1996), *Street Smarts and Critical Theory: Listening to the Vernacular*, Madison: The University of Wisconsin Press.

McLean, R. (1980), *The Thames and Hudson Manual of Typography,* London: Thames and Hudson.

McLuhan, M. (1962), *The Gutenberg Galaxy: The Making of Typographic Man*, Toronto: University of Toronto Press.

McLuhan, M. (1964), *Understanding Media: The Extensions of Man,* Cambridge, MA: MIT Press.

McMahan, E.M. (1989), *Elite Oral History Discourse: A Study of Cooperation and Coherence*, Tuscaloosa: University of Alabama Press.

McManus, E. (2011), "The 20 Most-Watched TEDTalks (so far)," *TEDTalks Blog*, June 27, Available online: http://blog.ted.com/2011/06/27/the-20-most-watched-tedtalks-so-far/.

McMillan, S. (2013), "Life in a Day," *CA Communication Arts*. Available online: Glebehttp://www.commarts.com/Columns.aspx?pub=9542&pageid=2122 (accessed June 4, 2014).

McMurtrie, D. (1930), *Typographic Ornament*, Chicago: Privately Printed.

McQuiston, L. (1988), *Women in Design*, London: Trefoil Publications.

McQuiston, L. (1997), *Suffragettes to She-Devils*, London: Phaidon.

Mealing, S. (2003), "Value Added Text: Where Graphic Design Meets Paralinguistics," *Visible Language*, 37 (1): 43.

Meggs, P. (1983), *A History of Graphic Design*, New York: Van Nostrand Reinhold.

Meggs, P. (1992), *A History of Graphic Design*, 2nd edn, New York: Van Nostrand Reinhold.

Meggs, P. (2005), *Meggs' History of Graphic Design*, 4th edn, Toronto: John Wiley & Sons.

Meggs, P. B. (1985), "Design History: Discipline or Anarchy?" *AIGA Journal of Graphic Design,* 3 (4): 2.

Meggs, P. B. (1998), *A History of Graphic Design*, New York: John Wiley & Sons.

Mehta, D. (2010), "The Indian Frame of Reference: Contextualising the current state of graphic design in India in order to situate it in the past for it to appropriately fit the Indian context," *Visual Communication*.

Mehta, D. (2013), Interview with Mohor Ray, October 17.

Melles G. (2007), PhD Design International Overview. PhD@JISCMAIL.AC.UK (accessed June 15, 2007).

Menand, L. (1995), "The Trashing of Professionalism," *New York Times Magazine*, March 5: 43.

Mercer, M. (1981), "Ed," *Panache*, 20: 2.

Mercer, M. (1997), Letter to Teal Triggs.

Mercer, M. (1999), Letter to Teal Triggs.

Meroni, A., and D. Sangiorgi (2011), *Design for Services*, Farnham: Gower.

Messaris, P. (1997), *Visual Persuasion. The Role of Images in Advertising,* London: Sage Publications.

Metahaven (2016), "Captives of the Cloud, Part III: All Tomorrow's Clouds," in J. Aranda, B. Kuan Wood, and A. Vidokle (eds), *The Internet Does Not Exist*, 245–78, Berlin: e-Flux, Inc. and Sternberg Press.

Metahaven (2007), "Secret Practices: Markus Miessen in conversation with Metahaven, Vinca Kruk and Daniel Van Der Velden," in Z. Kyes and M. Owens (eds), *Forms of Inquiry: The Architecture of Critical Graphic Design*, 164, London: Architectural Association, London.

Miller, J. A. (1996), *Dimensional Typography*, Princeton: Princeton Architectural Press.

Miller, P. N. (2015), "Is 'Design Thinking' the New Liberal Arts?" *Chronicle of Higher Education*, March 26. http://www.chronicle.com/article/Is-Design-Thinking-the-New/228779 (accessed August 5, 2017).

Miller-Lane, B. (1985) *Architecture and Politics in Germany 1918–1945*, Cambridge: Harvard University Press.

Mills, M. (1992), "The (Layered) Vision Thing," *Eye,* 2 (8): 8–9.

Milne, R.S. and K. Diane (1990), *Mauzy, Singapore: The Legacy of Lee Kuan Yew*, Boulder: Westview Press.

Minick, S. and J. Ping (1990), *Chinese Graphic Design in the Twentieth Century,* New York: Thames & Hudson, Ltd.

Mirzoeff, N., ed. (1998), *The Visual Culture Reader*, London: Routledge.

Mirzoeff, N., ed. (2002), *The Visual Culture Reader*, 2nd edn, London and New York: Routledge.

Mirzoeff, N. (2005) (interview) in *Visual Culture: The Study of the Visual after the Cultural Turn*, M. Dikovitskaya, Cambridge, MA: MIT Press, 232.

Mirzoeff, N. ([1999] 2009), *An Introduction to Visual Culture*, 1st edn, London and New York: Routledge.

Mitchell, W.J.T. (1998) (interview) in *Visual Culture: The Study of the Visual after the Cultural Turn*, M. Dikovitskaya, Cambridge, MA: MIT Press, 256.

Mitchell, W.J.T. (2002), "Showing Seeing: A Critique of Visual Culture," in N. Mirzoeff, *The Visual Culture Reader*, 86–101, New York: Routledge.

Moggridge, B. (2007), *Designing Interactions,* Cambridge, MA: MIT Press.

Moholy-Nagy, L. (1925), *Malerei, Fotographie, Film,* Munich: Albert Langen.

Moholy-Nagy, L. (1969), *Painting–Photography–Film,* London: Lund Humphries.

Moholy-Nagy, L. (1929), "Fotogramm und Grenzgebiete," *Die Form*, 4 (10): 256–9.

Moholy-Nagy, S. (1960), "The Bauhaus and Modern Typography: The 'Masters' Liberate the Typographic Image," *Print*, 14 (1): 45–8.

Moles, A. (1989), "The Legibility of the World: A Project of Graphic Design," in V. Margolin (eds), *Design Discourse: History, Theory, Criticism,* 119–29, Chicago: University of Chicago Press.

Molloy, R. (2009), Interview with Leslie Atzmon.

Moody, J., D.A. McFarland, and S. Bender-DeMoll (2005), "Dynamic Network Visualization: Methods for Meaning with Longitudinal Network Movies," *American Journal of Sociology,* 110: 1206–41.

Moody, R. (2005), *The Diviners*, New York and London: Little, Brown and Co/Faber and Faber.

Moore, C.W., W.J. Mitchell, and W. Turnbull, Jr. (1988), *The Poetics of Gardens*, Cambridge, MA: MIT Press.

Morison, S. (1924), *Four Centuries of Fine Printing—Two Hundred and Seventy-Two Examples of the Work of Presses Established Between 1465 and 1924*. London: Ernest Benn.

Morison, S. (1973), *A Tally of Types*, Cambridge: Cambridge University Press.

Morris, B. (1993), "*The Studio* Prize Competitions: The Early Years 1893–1900," in "High Life and Low Life: The Studio and the Fin de Siècle," *Studio International*, 201 (1022/1023): 80–4.

Morris, C. (1955), *Signs, Language and Behaviour,* New York: Braziller.

Morris, I., ed. (1967), *The Pillow Book of Sei Shÿnagon,* trans. I. Morris, New York: Columbia University Press.

Morris, M. (1983), "des Epaves/Jetsam", *On the Beach* 1 (Autumn).

Morris, M. (1984), "Room 101 or a Few Worst Things in the World," in A. Frankovits (ed.), *Seduced and Abandoned: the Baudrillard Scene,* Glebe, NSW: Stonemoss Services.

Morris, W. ([1890] 1970), *News from Nowhere or an Epoch of Rest*, J. Redmond (ed.), London: Routledge & Kegan Paul.

Mourey, G. (1897), "Auguste Lepère, A French Wood Engraver," *The Studio,* 12 (57): 143–55.

Moxon, J. ([1683] 1962), *Mechanick Exercises on the Whole Art of Printing*, London: Oxford University Press.

Moyano, M.J. (1995), *Argentina's Lost Patrol: Armed Struggle, 1969–1979*, New Haven: Yale University Press.

Mühlmann, H. (1996), *Die Natur der Kulturen*, Vienna and New York: Springer.

Mukherjee, A. (2013), Head of Strategy and Design at Futurebrands, Email conversation with Mohor Ray on Bharat Darshan, December 24.

Müller-Brockmann, J. (1971), *A History of Visual Communication*, Teufen: Verlag Niggli.

Müller-Brockmann, J. (1971), *A History of Visual Commuunication,* Teufen: Arthur Niggli,

Müller-Brockmann, J. (1981), "Grid and Design Philosophy," in *Grid Systems*, New York: Hastings House.

Müller-Brockmann, J. (1996), *Grid Systems in Graphic Design*, Sulgen: Verlag Niggli.

Müller-Brockmann, J. and S. Müller-Brockmann (1971), *History of the Poster,* Zürich: ABC Verlag.

Murgatroyd, K. (1969), *Modern Graphics*, London and New York: Vista/Dutton.

Murray, D.C. (2004), "Hip-Hop vs. High Art: Notes on Race as Spectacle," *Art Journal,* 63 (2): 4–19.

Murthy, L., A. Kagal, and A. Chatterjee (2000), "Learning from the Field: Experiences in Communication," India: National Institute of Design.

Muschamp, H. (1974), *File Under Architecture*, Cambridge, MA: MIT Press.

Mutwa. C. ([1964] 1998), *Indaba, My Children,* Edinburgh: Canongate Books.

Myerson, J. (2013), "Design with People," *Designing with People*. Available online: http://designingwithpeople.rca.ac.uk (accessed December 9, 2013).

"My Note Book" (1890), *The Art Amateur,* 23 (3): 109.

Naiman, L. (n.d.), "Design Thinking as a Strategy for Innovation," *Creativity at Work*. Available online: creativityatwork.com/design-thinking-strategy-for-innovation (accessed June 30, 2017).

Nash, P.W. (2006), "The Distaff Side: A Short History of Female Printer," *Ultrabold*, 1: 12–18.

"Reviews of Recent Publications" (1898), *The Studio,* 14 (63): 10–16.

Reynolds, R. (1999), Response to Teal Triggs.

Ridykeulous (2006), "Positively Nasty," *LTTR Collective*, 5. Available online: http://www.lttr.org/journal/5/
the-advantages-of-being-a-lesbian-woman-artist.

Riordan, M. (2004), *An Unauthorized Biography of the World: Oral History on the Front Lines*, Ontario: Between the
Lines Press.

Rittel, H.W.J. and M.M. Webber (1973), "Dilemmas in a General Theory of Planning," *Policy Sciences*,
2 (June 4): 155–69. Available online: https://link.springer.com/article/10.1007%2FBF01405730 (accessed
July 10, 2017).

Robert Doyle quoted in Lahey, K. (2009), "Shades of the Yellow Peril as Melbourne gets logo makeover," *Age*,
July 23: 3.

Rochfort, D. (2002), "Making Connections: Design and the Social Sciences," in J. Frascara (ed.), *Design and the
Social Sciences: Making Connections*, 158–66, London and New York: Taylor & Francis.

Rock, M. (1992), "Responsibility: Buzzword of the Nineties," *AIGA Journal,* 10 (1).

Rock, M. (1994), "Beyond Typography," *Eye,* 15 (4): 31.

Rogers, W.S. (1901), *A Book of the Poster*, London: Greening and Co.

Rogoff, I. ([1998] 2001), "Studying Visual Culture," in N. Mirzoeff (ed.), *The Visual Culture Reader*, 14–26, New
York: Routledge

Rogoff, I. ([1999] 2009), "Studying Visual Culture," in N. Mirzoeff (ed.), *The Visual Culture Reader*, 27, London/New
York: Routledge.

Rollie, R. (1987), "La Comunicación Visual en la Universidad Nacional de La Plata," *tipoGráfica*, 2 (September).

Romero-Tejedor, F. and W. Jonas, eds (2010), *Positionen zur Designwissenschaft*, Kassel: Kassel University Press.

Rosenberg, D. and A. Grafton (2010), *Cartographies of Time: A History of the Timeline*, New York: Princeton
Architectural Press.

Rosenberg, T. (2000), "The Reservoir: Toward a Poetic Model of Research in Design," *Working Papers in Art and
Design*. Available online: http://www.herts.ac.uk/artdes/research/papers/wpades/vol1/rosenberg2.html (see
also the most recent version at http://eprints.goldsmiths.ac.uk/266).

Rosling, H. (2006), "Hans Rosling Shows the Best Stats You've Ever Seen," TED Conference presentation,
February. Available online: http://www.ted.com/talks/hans_rosling_shows_the_best_stats_you_ve_ever_seen.
html (accessed July 8, 2011).

Rosling, H. (2007), "Hans Rosling's New Insights on Poverty" (presentation at the TED Conference, March.
Available online: http://www.ted.com/talks/hans_rosling_reveals_new_insights_on_poverty.html (accessed
July 13, 2011).

Rosling, H. (2007), "Visual Technology Unveils the Beauty of Statistics and Swaps Policy from Dissemination to
Access," *Statistical Journal of the* IAOS*,* 24:103–4.

Rothschild, D., E. Lupton, and D. Goldstein (1998), *Graphic Design in the Mechanical Age: Selections from the
Merrill C. Berman Collection*, New Haven and London: Yale University Press.

Royal College of Art (2017), "CX^2 Workshop on Living Networks: Designing for Adaptive Communication: Call for
Participation," Unpublished paper.

Ruben, P. (1913), *Die Reklame: Ihre Kunst und Wissenschaft,* Berlin: Verlag für Sozial Politik.

Ruder, E. (1967), *Typographie: A Manual for Design,* Teufen: Arthur Niggli.

Rüegg R. and G. Frohlich (1972), *Basic Typography: Handbook of Technique and Design*, London: ABC Verlag.

Ruffins, F.D. (1997), "The Politics of Cultural Ownership," in M. Bierut, W. Drenttel, S. Heller, and D.K. Holland
(eds), *Looking Closer 2: Critical Writings on Graphic Design*, 142–4, New York: Allsworth Press.

Rugg, J. and M. Sedgwick, eds (2007), *Issues in Curating Contemporary Art and Performance,* London: Intellect Press.

Sabin, R. ed. (1999), *Punk Rock: So What?: The Cultural Legacy of Punk,* New York: Routledge.

Sabin, R. (2003), 'Quote and Be Damned . . .?' in V. Cassel (ed.), *Splat Boom Pow! The Influence of Cartoons in Contemporary Art,* 12, Houston Contemporary Art Museum.

Sabin, R. (2005), Interview with Teal Triggs, London.

Sabin, R. and T. Triggs (2000), "'Below Critical Radar': Fanzines and Alternative Comics From 1976 to Now," *Slabo-O-Concrete.*

Sack, W. (2011), "The Aesthetics of Information Visualization," in M. Lovejoy, C. Paul, and V. Vesna (eds), *Context Providers: Conditions of Meaning in Media Arts,* Bristol: Intellect Ltd.

Sadokierski, Z. (2017), "From Paratexts to Primary Texts: Shifting from a Commercial to a Research-Focused Design Practice," in L. Vaughan (ed.), *Practice-Based Design Research*, 175–88, London: Bloomsbury.

Sagmeister, S. (June 16, 2014), "You Are Not a Storyteller—Stefan Sagmeister @ FITC," FITC, June 16. Available online: http://vimeo.com/98368484 (September 29, 2014).

Said, E. (1983), "Opponents, Audiences. Constituencies and Community," in H. Foster (ed.), *The Anti-Aesthetic,* 128, Post Townsend: Bay Press.

Said, E. (1983), *The Text, The World, The Critic,* Cambridge, MA: Harvard University Press.

Said, E.W. (1981), "Opponents, Audiences, Constiuencies, and Community," in H. Foster (ed.), *The Anti-Aesthetic: Essays on Postmodern Culture*, Port Townsend: Bay Press.

Sanders, E. (2000), "Generative Tools for CoDesigning," *Collaborative Design: Proceedings of CoDesigning 2000.*

Sanders, E. (2002), "From User-centered to Participatory Design Approaches," in J. Frascara (ed.), *Design and the Social Sciences: Making Connections*, 1–8, London and New York: Taylor & Francis.

Sanders, E. (2006), "Scaffolds for Building Everyday Creativity," *Design for Effective Communications: Creating Contexts for Clarity and Meaning*, New York: Allworth Press.

Sanders, E. and J.P. Stappers (2008), "Co-creation and the Landscapes of Design," *CoDesign: International Journal of CoCreation in Design and the Arts*, 4: 5–18.

Sartre. J-P. (1943), *L'Être et le néant*, Paris: Librairie Gallimard.

Satué, E. (1988), *El Diseño Gráfico: Desde los Orígenes hasta Nuestros Días,* Madrid: Alianza Editorial.

Savage, J. (1977), "Fanzines: Every Home Should Print One," *Sounds*, 10: 29.

Savage, J. (1996), *Time Travel: From the Sex Pistols to Nirvana: Pop, Media and Sexuality 1977–1996,* London: Chatto & Windus.

Savage, J. (2000), "Sniffin' Glue: The Essential Punk Accessory," *Mojo*, 81: 129.

Savage, W. (1841), *A Dictionary of the Art of Printing*, London: Longman, Brown, Green & Longman.

Savage, W. (1965), *A Dictionary of the Art of Printing*, London: Gregg Press Ltd.

Scarry, E. (1999), *On Beauty and Being Just*, Princeton: Princeton University Press.

Scheuermann, A. (2009), *Zur Theorie des Filmemachens. Flugzeugabstürze, Affekttechniken*, München: *Film* als rhetorisches Design.

Scheuermann, A. (2013), "Medienrhetorik, Wirkungsintentionalität, Affekttechniken. Zur Konzeption von, Design als Rhetorik' als notwendige Ergänzung der Kunstgeschichte," in G. Ueding and G. Kalivoda (eds), *Wege moderner Rhetorikforschung. Klassische Fundamente und interdisziplinäre Entwicklung,* 807–20, Berlin and Boston: Waher de Gruyter GmbH.

Schiller, H. (1978), *Communication and Cultural Domination*, New York: Pantheon.

Schiller, H. (1981), *Who Knows: Information in the Age of the Fortune 400*, New York: Ablex.

Von Ompteda, K. and Walker, K. (2015), "Translating the Quantum World to Human Scale: An Art-Science Collaboration," *IEEE Computer Graphics and Applications*, 35 (3): 74–81.

Vyas, H.K. (2000), "Design: The Indian Context," India: National Institute of Design.

Walker Art Center (2017), announcement for talk on March 21, 2017, "Insights: Clara Balaguer & Kristian Henson, Office of Culture and Design/Hardworking Goodlooking." Available online: https://walkerart.org/calendar/2017/insights-clara-balaguer-kristian-henson-offic (accessed August 4, 2017).

Walker, J.A. (1983), *Art in the Age of Mass Media*, London: Pluto Press.

Walker, J.A. and S. Chaplin (1997), *Visual Culture: An Introduction*, Manchester: Manchester University Press.

Walker, L. (1995), "The Arts and Crafts Alternative," in J. Attfield and P. Kirkham, *A View from the Interior Women and Design,* 165–73, London: The Women's Press.

Walker, R. (2014), "A Golden Age of Design," *T Magazine—The New York Times*, September 22. Available online: http://tmagazine.blogs.nytimes.com/2014/09/22/design-golden-age/ (accessed September 24, 2014).

Walker, S. (2001), *Typography and Language in Everyday Life: Prescriptions and Practices,* Harlow: Longman.

Walker, S. (2017), "Research in Graphic Design," 549–59, *The Design Journal,* 20 (5). Available online: www.tandfonline.com/doi/abs/10.1080/14606925.2017.1347416 (accessed August 16, 2017).

Wallis, L. (1988), *A Concise Chronology of Typesetting Developments, 1886–1986,* London: Antique Collectors Club Ltd.

Wallis, L. (1991), *Modern Encyclopedia of Typefaces, 1960–90*, Chichester: John Wiley & Sons Inc.

Wang, S.Z. (1989), "Chinese Modern Design: A Retrospective," *Design Issues,* 6 (1): 49–78

Wang, S.Z. (1990), "The Internationalization of Design Education: A Chinese Experience," in R. Ghose (ed.), *Design and Development in South and Southeast Asia,* 267–76, Hong Kong: Centre of Asian Studies, University of Hong Kong.

Wang, S.Z. (1995), "Chinese Modern Design: A Retrospective," in D.P. Doordan (ed.), *Design History. An Anthology*, 213–41, Cambridge, MA: MIT Press.

Warde, B. ([1930] 1937), "The Crystal Goblet, or Printing Should Be Invisible," New York: Marchbanks Press. Available online: www.stbride.org/conference2002/beatricewarde.html.

Warde, B. (1955), *The Crystal Goblet: Sixteen Essays on Typography*, London: World Pub. Co.

Ware, C. (2008), *Visual Thinking: for Design*, Burlington: Morgan Kaufmann.

Watson, J. (1713), *The History of the Art of Printing*, Edinburgh: James Watson.

Watson, J. (1965), *The History of the Art of Printing*, London: Gregg Press Ltd.

Wattenberg, M. and F. Viégas (2003), "History Flow," *Bewitched*. Available online: http://www.bewitched.com/historyflow.html.

Wattenberg, M. and F. Viégas (2006), "The Hive Mind Ain't What It Used to Be," *Edge*. Available online: http://www.edge.org/discourse/digital_maoism.html#viegas.

Wattenberg. M. (2010), "Numbers, Words and Colors," MIT HyperStudio Humanities + Digital Visual Interpretation conference, Cambridge, MA, May 20. Available online: http://flowingdata.com/2010/08/11/martin-wattenberg-talks-data-and-visualization/ (accessed July 4, 2011).

Watts, A. (2013), "Alan Watts—Mind over Mind," March 24. Available online: https://www.youtube.com/watch?v=9bB5X5vzbSY (link defunct, accessed September 29, 2014).

Weingart, W. ([1972] 1987), "How Does One Make Swiss Typography?," *Octavo,* 87 (4).

Weingart, W. (2000), *My Way to Typography,* Baden: Lars Müller Publishers.

Weingart, W. (2000), *Typography*, Baden: Lars Müller Publishers.

Weitz, M. (1964), *Hamlet and the Philosophy of Literary Criticism,* Chicago: University of Chicago Press.

Wells, K. (2006), *Manipulating Metaphors: A Study of Rural Craft as a Medium for Communicating on AIDS and Confronting Culture in KwaZulu-Natal,* Durban: University of KwaZulu-Natal. Unpublished Doctoral Thesis.

Wells, K. (2006), Personal conversation, August 14.

Wells, K., E. Sienaert, and J. Corolly (2004), "The Siyazama Project: a Traditional Beadwork and AIDS Intervention Programme," *Design Issues,* 20 (2): 73–89.

Wells, L. (2007), "Curatorial Strategy as Critical Intervention: The Genesis of Facing East," in J. Rugg and M. Sedgwick (eds), *Issues in Curating Contemporary Art and Performance,* 29–44, London: Intellect Press.

Wertham, F. (1973), *The World of Fanzines: A Special Form of Communication*, Carbondale: Southern Illinois University Press.

Wertsch, J.V. (1998), *Mind as Action,* New York: Oxford University Press.

"We Smile" (1891), *British Printer*, 4 (24): 7.

What Design Can Do (2014), available online: http://www.whatdesigncando.nl (accessed September 20, 2014).

White, G. (1893), "Drawing for Reproduction: Outline Work and Tint Boards," *The Studio*, 1 (2): 65–72.

White, G. (1895), "The National Competition South Kensington, 1895," *The Studio,* 6 (31): 42–50.

White, H. (1980), "The Value of Narrativity in the Representation of Reality," *Critical Inquiry,* 7 (1): 8.

White, J.G. (1893), "Photographic Portraiture: An Interview with Mr. H.H. Hay Cameron," *The Studio*, 2 (8): 84–9.

White, J.G. (1894), "Decorative Illustration, with Especial Reference to the Work of Mr. Paton Wilson," *The Studio,* 3 (18): 182–4.

White, J.G. (1896), "The National Competition: South Kensington," *The Studio*, 8 (42): 224–37.

White, J.G. (1897), "The Coloured Prints of Mr. W.P. Nicholson," *The Studio*, 12 (57): 177–83.

Whiteley, N. (1993), *Design for Society*, London: Reaktion Books.

"White Man in Hammersmith Palais/The Prisoner" (1978), [song] The Clash, Sandy Pearlman and The Clash.

Wieynck, H. (1928), "Neue Typographie," *Gebrauchsgraphik*, 5 (7): 28–9.

Wieynck, H. (1931), "Leitsätze zum Problem zeitgemässer Druckschriftgestaltung," *Gebrauchsgraphik*, 8 (2).

Wild, L. (1990), "Transgression and Delight: Graphic Design at Cranbrook," in *Cranbrook Design: the New Discourse*, New York: Rizzoli.

Wildhagen, E. (1927), "Reklame in Japanische," *Gebrauchsgraphik,* 4 (5): 46–60.

Williams, L. (2007), "Heavy Metal: Decoding Hip-Hop Jewelry," *Metalsmith,* 27 (1): 36–41.

Williams, Z. (2012), "On Fracking and Wind We Are Having the Wrong Debates," *Guardian*, April 18. Available online: http://www.guardian.co.uk/commentisfree/2012/apr/18/fracking-and-wind-wrong-debates.

Williamson, J. (1982), *The Meaning of the Merode Altarpiece,* Master's thesis, Ann Arbor: University Microfilms.

Williamson, J. (1983), *Decoding Advertisements: Ideology and Meaning in Advertising,* 4th edn, New York: Marion Boyars Publishers Inc.

Willis, A-M. (2006), "Ontological Designing," *Design Philosophy Papers*, 2: 1–11.

Wingler, H.M. (ed) (1978), *The Bauhaus: Weimar, Dessau. Berlin, Chicago*, Cambridge, MA: MIT Press.

Winkler, D.R. (1990), "Morality and Myth: The Bauhaus Reassessed," *AIGA Journal*, 7 (4).

Winkler, D.R. (2009), Helvetica, the Film and The Face in Context," *Visible Language,* 44 (3): 367–78.

Witham, S. (2005), *Touch This: Graphic Design That Feels Good*, Beverly: Rockport Publishers Inc.

Witham, S. (2006), *Touch This: Graphic Design That Feels Good,* Gloucester: Rockport Publishers.

Wittkower, R. (1973), *Architectural Principles in the Age of Humanism*, London: Academy Editions.

Wlassikoff, M. (2005), *The Story of Graphic Design in France*, Corte Madera: Gingko Press.

Wolff, L. (2007), *Massin*, London and New York: Phaidon Press.